Mastering

Virtual Machine
Manager 2008 R2

Mastering
Virtual Machine
Manager 2008 R2

Michael Michael

Hector Linares

WILEY

Wiley Publishing, Inc.

Acquisitions Editor: Agatha Kim
Development Editor: Denise Santoro Lincoln
Technical Editor: Rakesh Malhotra
Production Editor: Christine O'Connor
Copy Editor: Judy Flynn
Editorial Manager: Pete Gaughan
Production Manager: Tim Tate
Vice President and Executive Group Publisher: Richard Swadley
Vice President and Publisher: Neil Edde
Book Designer: Maureen Forys, Happenstance Type-O-Rama and Judy Fung
Proofreader: Corina Copp, Word One New York
Indexer: Nancy Guenther
Project Coordinator, Cover: Lynsey Stanford
Cover Designer: Ryan Sneed
Cover Image: © Pete Gardner/DigitalVision/Getty Images

For general information on our other products and services or to obtain technical support, please contact our Customer Care Department within the U.S. at (877) 762-2974, outside the U.S. at (317) 572-3993 or fax (317) 572-4002.

Wiley also publishes its books in a variety of electronic formats. Some content that appears in print may not be available in electronic books.

Library of Congress Cataloging-in-Publication Data

Michael, Michael, 1977-
 Mastering Virtual Machine Manager 2008 R2 / Michael Michael, Hector Linares.
   p. cm.
 ISBN 978-0-470-46332-1 (paper/website)
 1. Virtual machine manager. 2. Virtual computer systems. I. Linares, Hector, 1980- II. Title.
 QA76.9.V5M53 2010
 005.4'3–dc22
                  2010038769

10 9 8 7 6 5 4 3 2 1

Dear Reader,

Thank you for choosing *Mastering Virtual Machine Manager 2008 R2*. This book is part of a family of premium-quality Sybex books, all of which are written by outstanding authors who combine practical experience with a gift for teaching.

Sybex was founded in 1976. More than 30 years later, we're still committed to producing consistently exceptional books. With each of our titles, we're working hard to set a new standard for the industry. From the paper we print on, to the authors we work with, our goal is to bring you the best books available.

I hope you see all that reflected in these pages. I'd be very interested to hear your comments and get your feedback on how we're doing. Feel free to let me know what you think about this or any other Sybex book by sending me an email at nedde@wiley.com. If you think you've found a technical error in this book, please visit http://sybex.custhelp.com. Customer feedback is critical to our efforts at Sybex.

Best regards,

Neil Edde
Vice President and Publisher
Sybex, an Imprint of Wiley

To my wife, Liberty, and daughter, Aliki, my precious
family. I love you.
– Michael

Cristina mi dulce amor, con tus manos sobre me
corazón me haces tan feliz, te adoro con todo mi ser
– Hector

Acknowledgments

This book would not have been possible without the endless support and love of our families. Hector would like to thank his wife, Anna, for being so understanding, for the constant encouragement, and for the late-night coffee runs. He would also like to thank his parents, Mario and Aida Linares, for their support and encouragement throughout the years. Michael would like to thank his wife, Liberty, for letting him hijack their weekends and for supporting him throughout the book. This book would not have been possible without her and he thanks her for always being there for him. Michael would also like to thank his parents, Leonidas and Toulla, "You are my inspiration and made me who I am today."

Writing this book is easy in comparison to the amazing effort put forward by the Virtual Machine Manager team. It all started in 2005 with an idea to build a virtualization management product. With an excellent group of engineers, four years, and three releases later, Virtual Machine Manager 2008 R2 was released. Paired with a flagship virtualization platform in Hyper-V and a best-of-breed service management solution in Operations Manager 2007, Virtual Machine Manager 2008 R2 provides the end-to-end virtualization management that customers have long been waiting for.

We would like to thank the Virtual Machine Manager team for building a complete and easy-to-use solution. You have listened to your customers throughout the releases and delivered a product that meets their high demands. Virtual Machine Manager 2008 R2 is a game-changing release. Congratulations, and we are looking forward to more excellent releases.

Many people helped in various ways with this book. We want to especially thank Cheng Wei, our contributing author, and Rakesh Malhotra, who served as our technical editor and wrote the foreword. Credit goes to Operations Manager expert Vlad Joanovic for his technical review of Chapter 9.

We would also like to thank the Sybex team. Even though we never met most of you in person, we feel like we know you. Agatha Kim, our acquisitions editor, thank you for the opportunity to write this book and putting up with our crazy schedules. Even though we squirmed when we received your status emails telling us of our missed deadlines, you were the motivation that helped us keep pushing. Denise Santoro Lincoln, our developmental editor, the book would not have been as polished and well written without your excellent feedback. Christine O'Connor, Pete Gaughan, Judy Flynn, Corina Copp, and Nancy Guenther, thank you for your valuable contributions.

About the Authors

Michael Michael is a software architect on the Virtualization & Data Center Management team at Microsoft, working on the development and future direction of System Center Virtual Machine Manager. Michael is primarily focused on partner interactions and ensuring that a healthy ecosystem exists for virtualization products. He joined Microsoft Corporation in August 2002 as a software design engineer and has since worked on management products in the Windows Server division. Such products include previous releases of Virtual Machine Manager, Virtual Server 2005 R2, Windows Storage Server, and Data Protection Manager. During this time, he held various roles from senior software design engineer to senior development lead and focused on the research, design, and development of new features and functionality. For the past three years, Michael has been telecommuting from Houston, Texas.

Michael holds a master's degree in computer science from Stanford University, a technology MBA from the University of Phoenix, and a bachelor of science degree in computer science from the University of Texas at Austin. He moved to the United States from the beautiful island of Cyprus in 1997 to study computer science with the goal to go back upon completing his academic studies. Twelve years later, he is still in the United States working with the best engineering team on some of the most exciting and innovative products. Michael lives in Houston with his wife, Liberty, his 20-month-old daughter, Aliki, and his English Staffordshire bull terrier, Yogi. In his spare time, Michael enjoys spending time with his friends and family, watching TV, playing a competitive game of basketball, and watching mixed martial arts fights.

Hector Linares is a senior program manager on the Virtualization and Data Center Management team in the Management and Solution Division at Microsoft. Primarily, Hector is focused on the feature sets that enable the provisioning of virtual machines in Virtual Machine Manager. Hector has also developed strong relationships with several key Microsoft partner teams that rely on Virtual Machine Manager, including Visual Studio Lab Manager, Customer Support Services, and Global Foundation Services.

Hector is a "born-and-raised" New Yorker, originally from Brooklyn. He studied with several top jazz and classical musicians and was honored with several opportunities to perform at Carnegie Hall and several other famous New York venues. In 1998, Hector moved to Boston and attended Boston University. After earning his bachelor's degree in mathematics in 2002, Hector moved back to New York City and started working full time on Wall Street. Three large financial institutions later, Hector joined the Virtual Machine Manager team in 2007 and moved to Bellevue, Washington. He married another native New Yorker, Anna Cristina Cardenas, in May 2008. He loves to travel, play video games, and spend time with his wife and two dogs.

About the Contributing Author

Cheng Wei is a senior program manager on the Virtualization and Data Center Management team in the Management and Solution Division at Microsoft. Cheng joined Microsoft in 2004 in the Developer Division, where he helped ship Visual Studio 2005, .NET Framework 2.0, and .NET Framework 3.0. After that, Cheng moved to the System Center Configuration Manager team, where he directed Software Distribution and Server Infrastructure feature teams for System Center Configuration Manager 2007 release (previously known as SMS). Two years later, Cheng joined the Virtual Machine Manager team where he helped build and release System Center Virtual Machine Manager 2008 and 2008 R2. In VMM projects, Cheng led a team of engineers that owned the agent deployment and host configuration feature areas.

Prior to Microsoft, Cheng worked at Hewlett-Packard for five years as project manager and system engineer in Cupertino, California. Before that, he wrote management software for one of the largest commercial banks in China. System management has always been the center and focus of Cheng's career. Cheng holds dual master's degrees in computer science and telecommunications from the University of Louisiana and a bachelor of science degree in applied mathematics from Qingdao University in China. He also studied in the MBA programs at Santa Clara University and Seattle University. Cheng lives with his wife, Lin, and two kids, Vincent and Adeline, in Issaquah, Washington. He loves to travel, watch movies, and spend time with his family.

Contents at a Glance

Contents

Foreword

Virtualization promises to fundamentally change the way customers think about datacenter and IT management. What was previously science fiction is now operational reality. With the help of virtualization, customers are able to migrate running desktops and servers between physical hardware, dynamically add resources on demand in response to real-time business demands, and achieve unprecedented levels of operational agility, all while saving money. These are the promises of virtualization. Yet in order to realize these benefits, customers need the right technologies, tools, and most importantly, the right guidance. If you're reading this book, you likely already have many of the right tools and technologies but want the best possible guidance.

Michael Michael and Hector Linares are very uniquely positioned to ensure that you are armed with the right knowledge to make the most effective use of your datacenter assets and realize the software's full potential. Aside from being experts in virtualization management, they are key members of the System Center Virtual Machine Manager (SCVMM) engineering team at Microsoft. Michael and Hector know how to get the best from SCVMM. Not only does their in-depth technical understanding make them experts, but their work in the trenches with real IT professionals — people like you who have deployed and used SCVMM — gives them essential hands-on experience.

In fact, Hector's previous work at a large IT organization before working on SCVMM put him in your shoes. Prior to working on SCVMM, Michael spent a good deal of time working with customer support teams and the System Center user community, so he has an excellent understanding of how product design decisions impact your daily operational life. This book lets you take advantage of the combined experiences of Michael, Hector, and the countless IT organizations that they have engaged with and learned from. This is critical because as any software engineer will tell you, customers inevitably use software in ways that were never intended. This is why real-world deployment knowledge plus a deep technical understanding are both equally important.

While it's exciting to think about new features and dynamic, agile datacenters, the reality is that most organizations need to support multiple generations of technology. Having virtualization snap alongside the infrastructure that you've had in place for years is an important concern that is directly addressed throughout the book. And while it's also important to understand how SCVMM works, simply describing all of the capabilities in detail might be more overwhelming than helpful in planning your deployment. After all, there are lots of features in SCVMM, and you might read hundreds of pages simply describing them. This book is different because it describes not only how the product works, but also how the product will work in *your* organization. It puts the features and capabilities into context, and it describes how they work together so that you can map them to your specific needs and requirements. It's written in plain English so if you're new to SCVMM and virtualization, you can quickly get started and begin realizing the benefits. As your knowledge and needs become more sophisticated, Michael and Hector don't shy away from detailed technical drilldowns so you can learn at your own pace. You'll be walked through various use cases and scenarios to help create a customized deployment experience. Every customer is different, so providing a spectrum of options along with advice allows you to make the best possible design decisions. With Michael and Hector's expert guidance, you'll also be sure to avoid unintended consequences, limitations, or surprises down the line.

During the writing of this book, Microsoft was on the third and most exciting release of SCVMM. When this project was started more than four years ago, we really had no idea how big the virtualization and management revolution was going to be. Michael and Hector have been instrumental in taking SCVMM from its rather humble beginnings as a primarily development/test and consolidation tool to the mission-critical datacenter management application that it has become. When I was first asked to contribute to this effort, I was enthusiastic and delighted. We come to work every day with a single goal — to try to make our customers' lives easier and more productive. This book is an excellent complement to the software and helps achieve that goal. I couldn't think of two better or more knowledgeable people to write it.

— *Rakesh Malhotra*
Principal Group Program Manager
System Center Virtual Machine Manager

Introduction

We believe that hardware virtualization is the disruptive technology of our generation and one of the hottest technology topics being discussed today. Even though hardware virtualization has been around since the mainframe days, widespread adoption in the enterprise did not start until later this decade. The benefits of adopting virtualization focus primarily on savings from power, cooling, and rack space. However, management is the only way to reap the benefits of virtualization at a large scale. System Center products like Virtual Machine Manager and Operations Manager help deliver better management at scale.

This book provides the scenarios to get you started with VMM as a beginner as well as the in-depth knowledge necessary to implement advanced virtualization solutions. The biggest value of the book comes in the form of documented best practices, real-world examples, and in-depth explanations of advanced features of VMM. With virtualization being such a hot topic today, there aren't many books on the Microsoft virtualization technologies. We hope this book will fill in the gap and become a valuable aid in creating the best virtualization architecture for your company.

A Short History of Virtualization

Enterprises that initially evaluated and deployed virtualization in its early forms (Virtual Server, VMware GSX, VMware ESX, and so on) used virtualization primarily in dev/test scenarios. Users enjoyed the advantages of virtualization: fast self-provisioning, computer isolation, hardware independence, and ease of configuration changes to the virtual hardware like adjusting memory and adding disks. The success of those scenarios, coupled with the widespread availability of virtualization solutions, leads to virtualization being considered for production workload consolidation. Enterprises started to identify workloads that were underutilized in their datacenter or near hardware end of life. These workloads were ideal candidates for being consolidated to virtual machines in the datacenter.

Hardware consolidation gave the administrators a first taste into the benefits of reducing datacenter costs through lower power and cooling consumption and space optimizations. This was the key initial driver for virtualization adoption. As hypervisors matured by improving overall density, performance and reliability, there was a shift of focus to management solutions. Administrators started to look for virtualization management products that enable them to increase the scale of their virtual environments while continuing to take advantage of the cost benefits and maintaining high availability.

With increased pressure to continue cutting costs, deliver better infrastructure solutions, and "do more with less," administrators started making virtualization a priority. The shift in priority lead to a new trend: New workloads were first evaluated for feasibility as virtual workloads instead of being deployed to physical hardware. The initial concerns that end users typically voiced regarding the performance delta between physical and virtual machines and resource sharing diminished over time as experience with virtualization increased. Hardware vendors helped improve performance by introducing the missing piece of the virtualization stack: improvements in hardware through extensions to support virtualization.

Building on the success of virtualization, the industry is now realizing the long-sought potential of the dynamic datacenter scenarios. Virtualization management, advanced monitoring and reporting, and service management are coming together to form a solution that administrators can deploy in their datacenters.

VMM is an important piece of the dynamic datacenter as the virtualization management product in the following ways:

- A comprehensive, cross-platform management solution for the virtualized datacenter, facilitating the decoupling of guest operating systems and applications from physical hardware
- Virtual machine mobility
- Increased server utilization
- Rapid provisioning of workloads
- Template management
- Physical and virtual server management
- High availability through failover clusters
- Self-service provisioning
- Automation through scripts, allowing administrators to utilize VMM and its Windows PowerShell interface to build advanced custom solutions tailored to their needs

VMM and Operations Manager

The Virtual Machine Manager and Operations Manager (OpsMgr) products team together to provide administrators with the dynamic resource optimization of IT infrastructure and to ensure that their virtualization environment is functioning with optimal performance. Health issues can be automatically resolved, maintaining a balanced and reliable environment without user intervention and providing the highly coveted end-to-end services management of the dynamic datacenter. Customers today have a lot of choices for hypervisors and virtualization products. However, the combination of Hyper-V, VMM, and OpsMgr is the only comprehensive solution that manages the entire stack, starting from the hardware all the way to the applications running inside virtual machines.

Who Should Read This Book

As the title implies, this book is intended for people who want to learn and master Virtual Machine Manager. Such people probably fall into these basic groups:

- IT administrators who are starting to think about virtualization and want to gather more knowledge about the existing management software
- Seasoned IT administrators who have used Virtual Machine Manager and want to get a more detailed view of the product
- IT architects who want to better understand the Microsoft virtualization products and create the virtualization architecture for their company
- VMware administrators who are evaluating the Microsoft virtualization products and want to compare VMM with Virtual Infrastructure
- Third-party vendors who would like to develop a PRO management pack for Virtual Machine Manager and Operations Manager

For all of these people, there will be a learning curve. At the time of this writing, there are no published books on Virtual Machine Manager. Use this book in conjunction with a deployment of Virtual Machine Manager to try the concepts as you read about them. For complimentary resources on Virtual Machine Manager, visit the product website at http://www.microsoft.com/SCVMM. In the book, we are also making an effort to document and point you to other helpful resources.

There are several ways you can use this book. The most straightforward way is to start at the beginning and read all the chapters in order. Alternately, you can skip around to the chapters that contain your topic of choice and read any referenced material as needed.

What You Will Learn

This book is the technical foundation you will need to help you manage your virtualized environment at scale. Going beyond the basics, this book brings together the technical know-how, best practices, and actual code required to tailor your VMM deployment to the needs of your organization. The details and insight collected in these chapters will serve you on an ongoing basis as you explore new capabilities of the product. The heart of this book is around the management of a virtualized environment. The goal is to make you more productive in your day-to-day activities of managing hypervisor hosts and the virtual machines that reside on these hosts.

The exciting technologies available with Windows Server 2008 R2 and Hyper-V allow you to host multiple virtual machines on a single storage location and migrate them between hosts with no perceived downtime. If you have VMware ESX in your environment in addition to Microsoft Hyper-V, this book also covers VMM's in-box capabilities to manage multiple hypervisors. Managing the life cycle of a virtual machine with VMM is really about how you as an administrator add value to your organization through standardization of practices and procedures, building rich automation through Windows PowerShell and proper delegation of your environment. This is especially true when you decide to integrate VMM with System Center Operations Manager and enable Performance and Resource Optimization (PRO). As of the writing of this book, no other resource details how to write a PRO pack.

All examples and code samples in this book are provided as is, with no warranties, and confer no rights.

Appendixes

There are two appendixes available in the book and one online. Be sure to take a look, as we think you'll find them all relevant and helpful.

Appendix A: Bottom Line   This appendix gathers together all the "Master It" problems from the chapters and provides a solution for each.

Appendix B: VMM Windows PowerShell Object Properties and VMM Cmdlet Descriptions This appendix includes material that is directly related to the content in Chapter 8 and covers the Virtual Machine Manager Windows PowerShell cmdlets. The appendix also lists tables of the VMMServer, VM, and VMHost Windows PowerShell objects and their properties.

Appendix C: Useful Links   This appendix is available on the book's website, located at www.sybex.com/masteringvmm2008r2. It provides a catalog of the many URLs listed throughout the book, organized by chapter. We have provided an online version of these URLs so you can directly link to the various website links listed in the book.

What You Need

To get started with Virtual Machine Manager, you need some familiarity with hypervisor technologies and the concept of hardware virtualization. Once you have that knowledge, this book will provide you with the additional know-how that is required to have a successful virtualization infrastructure. For sizeable virtualization deployments, SQL Server administration skills are required to tune the database for optimal performance.

The TechNet Evaluation Center website (`http://technet.microsoft.com/en-us/evalcenter/default.aspx`) on Microsoft TechNet provides an evaluation virtual hard disk (VHD) of Virtual Machine Manager. Download the VHD to get started with VMM and explore the rich functionality and easy-to-use user interface.

The Mastering Series

The Mastering series from Sybex provides outstanding instruction for readers with intermediate and advanced skills in the form of top-notch training and development for those already working in their field and clear, serious education for those aspiring to become pros. Every Mastering book includes the following features:

◆ The Sybex "by professionals for professionals" commitment. The authors of the Mastering books are themselves practitioners, with plenty of credentials in their areas of specialty.

◆ A practical perspective for a reader who already knows the basics — someone who needs solutions, not a primer.

◆ Real-World Scenarios, ranging from case studies to interviews, that show how the tool, technique, or knowledge presented is applied in actual practice.

◆ Skill-based instruction, with chapters organized around real tasks rather than abstract concepts or subjects.

◆ Self-review test "Master It" problems and questions, so you can be certain you're equipped to do the job right.

What Is Covered in This Book

Mastering Virtual Machine Manager 2008 R2 is organized to provide you with all the necessary information to use VMM to deploy and manage virtual machines across Hyper-V, Virtual Server, and ESX.

Chapter 1, "Introduction to System Center Virtual Machine Manager 2008 R2," builds the necessary context regarding the features, architecture, and capabilities of the product.

Chapter 2, "Planning a VMM Deployment," discusses the architecture, features, and infrastructure components you need to understand and successfully plan your deployment strategy.

Chapter 3, "Installation and Configuration," details how the various VMM components get deployed into your environment.

Chapter 4, "Managing VMware ESX Using VMM," details how VMM and VMware vCenter interact to manage ESX hosts and the core building blocks available to you for deploying virtual machines to ESX hosts.

Chapter 5, "Managing Hyper-V Using VMM," details how VMM manages Hyper-V hosts and the core building blocks available to you for deploying virtual machines to Hyper-V hosts.

Chapter 6, "Managing Virtual Server Using VMM," details how VMM manages Virtual Server hosts and the core building blocks available to you for deploying virtual machines to Virtual Server hosts.

Chapter 7, "Virtual Machine Management," discusses how VMM can help maximize the positive impact of virtualization while reducing the negative, through improved management capabilities that center on the life cycle of a virtual machine.

Chapter 8, "Automation Using PowerShell," delves into the details of the extensibility of VMM through automation. The VMM Administrator Console and Self-Service portal are built on top of the same Windows PowerShell interface already available to you. Through PowerShell, you have even greater control and flexibility to build the necessary custom solutions tailored to your environment.

Chapter 9, "Writing a PRO Pack," discusses in great detail how VMM integrates with System Center Operations Manager for end-to-end service management and how to use the Performance and Resource Optimization (PRO) infrastructure to create a new PRO pack. PRO is the enabler for dynamic IT.

Chapter 10, "Planning for Backup and Recovery," explains how to protect the VMM server, including the VMM database, and how to back up and recover Hyper-V hosts using the Hyper-V VSS Writer.

Chapter 11, "Troubleshooting," covers VMM from a troubleshooting perspective, including troubleshooting tools you should be familiar with and common issues with VMM components.

Appendix A gathers together all the Master It problems from the chapters and provides a solution for each.

Appendix B includes listings that are directly related to the content in Chapter 8: "Automation Using Powershell," the Virtual Machine Manager Cmdlet descriptions, a listing of the VMM-Server object and its properties, a listing of the VM object and its properties, and a listing of the VMHost object and its properties.

Appendix C provides a hyperlinked catalog of the many URLs listed throughout the book. We have provided an online version of this chapter at `www.sybex.com/masteringvmm2008r2` so you can directly link to the various references listed.

How to Contact the Authors

We welcome feedback from you about this book or about books and chapters you'd like to see from us in the future. You can reach us by writing to `Michael.Michael@Microsoft.com` or `Hector.Linares@Microsoft.com`. We both maintain active blogs at `http://blogs.technet.com/m2` and at `http://blogs.technet.com/hectorl`. You can subscribe to our blogs for updates on Virtual Machine Manager and to get troubleshooting tips and advice on complex scenarios.

Sybex strives to keep you supplied with the latest tools and information you need for your work. Please check the website at `www.sybex.com`, where we'll post additional content, PRO management packs, PowerShell scripts, and updates that supplement this book. Enter **Virtual Machine Manager** in the Search box (or type the book's ISBN: **978-0-470-46332-1**), and click Go to get to the book's update page.

Chapter 1

Introduction to System Center Virtual Machine Manager 2008 R2

In IT environments today, virtualization is becoming the new hot technology. With the increased emphasis on power, cooling, and space savings due to cost, virtualization has made its entry into both the enterprise and the datacenter. It was initially used as a technology to consolidate legacy hardware, but administrators are now seeing the full range of benefits offered by virtualization. Products like Virtual Machine Manager (VMM) provide end-to-end management of the entire virtualized infrastructure, from the physical hosts to the guest operating systems. VMM is one of the first products on the market today to offer heterogeneous management; you can use it to manage Microsoft's Windows Hyper-V and Virtual Server as well as VMware's ESX infrastructure through VMware VirtualCenter. The ease of use of a central console for managing the entire infrastructure is one of the key benefits of VMM.

Planning for a virtualized environment is not easy, but with the proper knowledge of the key architecture pieces and how they interact with each other, it becomes an easier process. This book will provide you with what you need to know to plan, design, and manage your virtualized environment. Most IT administrators would argue that setting up a virtualized environment and calculating growth are some of the hardest steps to take for an IT department. Once the virtualized environment is configured and you have virtualization hosts with available capacity, however, deployment of a new server as a virtual machine becomes a 1-hour process. This is compared to the number of weeks it takes today to provision a new physical server, including purchasing the new hardware.

Before we get into the details of VMM, we need to ensure that you understand all the moving pieces and how they are used. Having a common language is also essential in understanding the material in this book. You need to have this knowledge early on to maximize the benefit of reading this book. Once you have read this chapter, you will have an overall high-level knowledge of VMM and how it can be tailored to your needs. Once we lay the foundation here, further chapters will go over different scenarios and what an administrator needs to know when implementing and managing a virtualized environment. By the time you finish this book, you'll have in-depth knowledge of Virtual Machine Manager and related virtualization technologies. Armed with this knowledge, you will be ready to plan, deploy, and manage a virtualized environment.

In this chapter, you will learn to how to:

◆ Identify and explain the components in the VMM architecture

◆ Determine the ports and protocols required for communication between the various VMM components

◆ Determine the various roles and privileges of VMM

◆ Explain the differences between the migration options offered in VMM

◆ Describe the authentication methods between VMM and hosts

A Quick Overview of Virtual Machine Manager

System Center Virtual Machine Manager (VMM) is a multivendor heterogeneous virtualization management solution tailored for enterprises and virtualized datacenters. It enables the centralized and unified administration of both physical and virtual servers, increases server utilization, and provides rapid provisioning. Through its integration with System Center Operations Manager (OpsMgr), VMM provides real-time health monitoring for the virtualized infrastructure and the ability to monitor and optimize application performance. The latter is achieved through a feature of VMM called Performance and Resource Optimization (PRO). PRO is covered extensively in Chapter 9 of this book.

The following list includes some of the key benefits of VMM:

◆ Support for managing heterogeneous virtualization platforms, including Microsoft Hyper-V, Microsoft Virtual Server, and VMware ESX. (VMware ESX is managed through the VirtualCenter web interface.)

◆ A powerful and easy-to-use console that enables the management of the virtualized infrastructure.

◆ A fully scriptable environment through Windows PowerShell.

◆ PRO, a feature of VMM and OpsMgr for the dynamic datacenter.

◆ Virtual machine conversions, either Physical to Virtual (P2V) or Virtual to Virtual (V2V) are reduced to a simple wizard with VMM.

◆ Quick template-based provisioning of virtual machines. Virtual machines can be deployed at a fraction of the time it would require to provision a new physical server.

◆ Intelligent Placement, which offers an administrator the ability to ensure that virtual machines are placed on the most appropriate physical host. Behind the scenes, VMM does all the work to produce the host ratings using data gathered through performance counters from the hosts and virtual machines and capacity planning algorithms from Microsoft Research.

◆ The VMM library, which offers a centrally managed way to keep all the building blocks needed to keep virtual machines organized.

◆ The Self-Service Portal, which offers the ability to delegate the provisioning and management of virtual machines to end users through a set of permissions and privileges.

◆ Some features of VMM and OpsMgr offer health monitoring and smart reports to get a high-level view of the virtualized environment. For example, one valuable report is the Virtualization Candidates report, which helps identify physical computers that are good candidates for conversion to virtual machines.

The availability of VMM 2008 R2 was announced in August 2009, and it introduces several enhancements over VMM 2008. The most important ones are as follows:

◆ Storage migration (also known as Quick Storage Migration) for running virtual machines with minimal downtime for Windows Server 2008 R2 Hyper-V hosts and support for VMware Storage VMotion

◆ Template-based rapid provisioning for new virtual machines

◆ Maintenance mode for hosts to facilitate rapid evacuation of hosts

◆ Support for Windows Server 2008 R2

◆ Support for Live Migration of virtual machines

◆ Support for Cluster Shared Volumes (CSV) that enables many virtual machines to reside on the same LUN

◆ Support for SAN migration in and out of failover clusters

◆ Support for hot add of virtual hard disks

◆ Support for virtual machine network optimizations like Virtual Machine Queue (VMQ) and TCP Chimney

◆ Support for third-party cluster file systems like the Melio FS from Sanbolic

◆ Support for VMware vSphere (VI4) features that existed in VMware Virtual Infrastructure 3

◆ Support for processor flexibility during virtual machine migrations

We will explain these features in more detail throughout this book. You can download the 180-day evaluation version of System Center Virtual Machine Manager 2008 R2 from the Microsoft Download Center at `http://www.microsoft.com/downloads/details.aspx?FamilyID=292de23c-845c-4d08-8d65-b4b8cbc8397b&displaylang=en`.

Exploring Virtual Machine Manager Components

VMM has a distributed-system architecture comprising several components. Figure 1.1 illustrates the high-level architecture of VMM and the various components that are part of VMM.

A VMM implementation is made of various core components that are required for every VMM installation. Various other components, like the Self-Service Portal, are not required but are very useful for specific scenarios like creating a development and test virtualization environment. PRO and the integration with OpsMgr is another optional feature of VMM, and together they offer a complete end-to-end service management solution for a dynamic virtualized environment.

FIGURE 1.1
Virtual Machine
Manager high-level
architecture

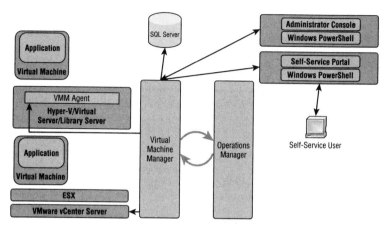

The following components are central to each VMM installation:

◆ VMM server

◆ VMM database

◆ VMM Windows PowerShell cmdlet interface

◆ VMM Administrator Console

◆ VMM library

◆ Managed virtualization hosts (VMM agents are installed on these virtualization hosts)

◆ VMM Self-Service Portal

◆ Managed virtualization managers (i.e., managed VMware VirtualCenter servers)

◆ OpsMgr management packs for monitoring, reporting, and PRO

Managed virtualization managers and the OpsMgr integration are optional components. Each VMM component fulfills a specific purpose and adds core virtualization management functionality. In the following sections, we will go through the various VMM components, introducing them to you and giving you a brief overview of their role and responsibilities. Installation and configuration of the various VMM components is covered in detail in Chapter 3. The integration of VMM with OpsMgr and the PRO functionality is covered in detail in both Chapter 3 and Chapter 9.

VMM Server and VMM Database

The VMM server component is the central component of any VMM deployment and the first VMM component that should be installed. The VMM server contains the core Windows service that includes the VMM engine. Through this service, VMM connects to the VMM database that stores all the configuration, management, and short-term performance information that VMM requires. At a high level, the VMM engine has three main purposes:

◆ It acts as the broker of information stored in the database. Any time a VMM client, such as the Administrator Console or a Windows PowerShell cmdlet, asks for information, that information is retrieved from the database by the VMM engine.

◆ It acts as the broker for communicating and executing commands with the VMM agents and for communicating and executing commands on the VMware VirtualCenter server.

◆ It coordinates the execution of VMM jobs. Every operation in VMM that has the potential to modify or modifies data either in the database or on any other VMM component (e.g., modifies a setting of a virtual machine on a virtualization host) becomes a VMM job. The engine coordinates the execution of jobs, monitors and reports on their progress, and lets clients know of any success or failures.

The VMM database can reside either locally on the VMM server or on a remote database server. Because of its importance to any VMM environment, it is recommended that you employ a highly available solution through failover clustering for the database server that hosts the VMM database. Figure 1.2 shows the connection information for the VMM database from the Administrator Console. Later in this chapter we will go through the network ports that are necessary for VMM to communicate with a remote SQL server.

FIGURE 1.2
Database connection information

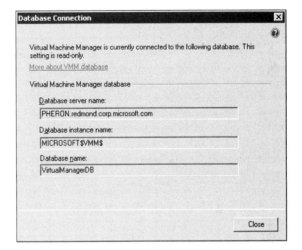

VMM clients like the Administrator Console, Self-Service Portal, and Windows PowerShell communicate with the VMM server component through a Windows Communication Foundation (WCF) private interface. The VMM server, which is the only component of VMM that communicates directly with VMM agents, uses the Windows Remote Management (WinRM) protocol to call into private interfaces on the VMM agent computer. The VMM server also uses WinRM to remotely invoke public Windows Management Instrumentation (WMI) interfaces on host and library server computers.

VMM Administrator Console

The VMM Administrator Console is the main user interface for managing a virtualized infrastructure using VMM. You can install the VMM Administrator Console either on the same computer as the VMM server component or on a separate computer and connect to the VMM server remotely. The VMM Administrator Console is built entirely on top of the VMM Windows PowerShell interface, utilizing the many cmdlets that VMM offers. This approach made VMM very extensible and partner friendly while also allowing customers to accomplish anything that VMM offers in the Administrator Console GUI via scripts and automation.

The Administrator Console has five main views and an optional view:

Hosts view facilitates the management of virtualized hosts.

Virtual machines view facilitates the management of virtual machines.

Jobs view lists the currently running jobs as well as a history of past jobs. By default, VMM will include a job history for 90 days and prune older jobs every 20 hours.

Library view lists all the building blocks for creating virtual machines.

Administration view includes the various administrative components for VMM.

Reporting view includes a list of reports and the ability to execute them against the OpsMgr reporting server. The reporting view is optional and can be enabled by integrating VMM with an OpsMgr reporting server after importing the VMM reports within the OpsMgr infrastructure.

Figure 1.3 shows the Administrator Console when the virtual machines view is selected. In this figure, you can see the various areas of the Administrator Console when virtual machines are being managed.

FIGURE 1.3
Virtual Machine
Manager Administrator
Console

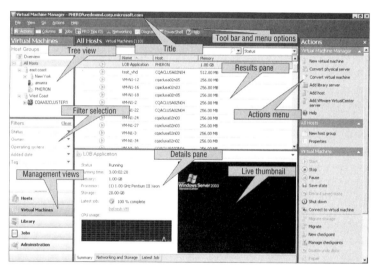

The areas shown in Figure 1.3 are as follows (similar areas exist for the other views of the Administrator Console as well):

The tree view section includes host groups, Hyper-V failover clusters, and VMware ESX hosts organized hierarchically.

The filter selection section includes owner, status, operating system, date, and user-specified tag filters.

The main management view selection section includes the five main views of the Administrator Console.

The results pane with the list of virtual machines includes a search box, a group-by selection box, and the ability to add or remove columns from the view to make it easier for administrators to find the data they need.

The details pane for the selected virtual machine includes a live thumbnail of the virtual machine console, a CPU usage graph, and other details about the virtual machine. The details include networking and storage information, latest job status, and the current running time for a virtual machine that is in a running state.

The actions menu is divided into three areas:

◆ The global actions for the Virtual Machine Manager Administrator Console

◆ The specific actions depending on the selection in the tree view (for example, host-group-specific actions)

◆ The context-sensitive actions that are specific to the virtual machine selected in the results pane

The title lists the name of the VMM server to which the Administrator Console is connected. If the VMM installation is an evaluation version, it will also list the number of days remaining in the evaluation period.

The toolbar and menu options make it easy to navigate to the different areas of the Administrator Console and to open separate windows. Separate windows are available for the following:

◆ The most recent jobs launched by the current user (Figure 1.4).

FIGURE 1.4
Jobs window

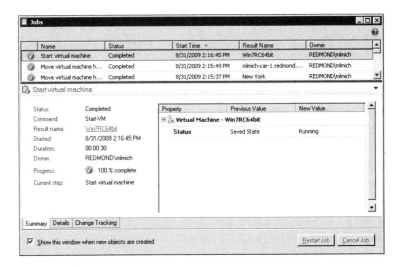

◆ The PRO tips that are currently active and waiting to be implemented (Figure 1.5).

◆ The networking view, scoped to a host group (Figure 1.6).

◆ The diagram view (Figure 1.7). When the diagram view is selected, it will launch the System Center Operations Manager Operations console and display the diagram view for this VMM server.

◆ The Windows PowerShell window with the VMM PowerShell cmdlets loaded.

FIGURE 1.5
PRO Tips window

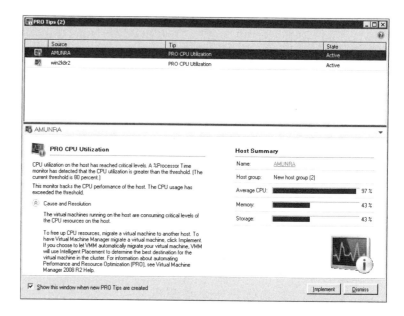

FIGURE 1.6
Networking window

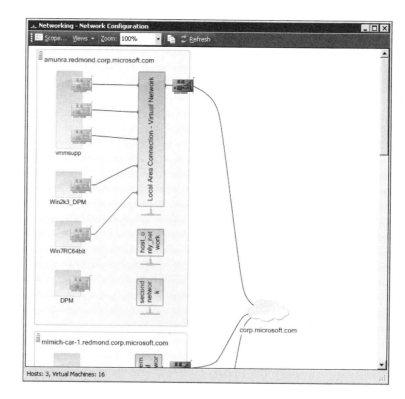

FIGURE 1.7
Diagram window

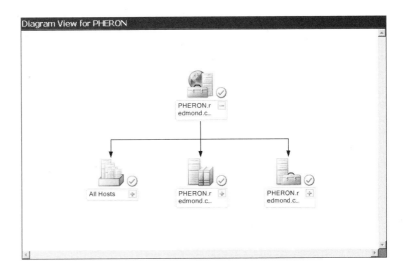

There are multiple other views of the Administrator Console, including the overview view. The views are listed here:

◆ Figure 1.8 shows the hosts view. In the details pane, all the VMs that reside on that host are listed in addition to the host details.

FIGURE 1.8
Hosts view

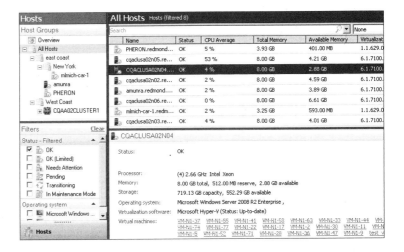

◆ Figure 1.9 shows the library view. The details pane will list the details of the selected library item.

◆ Figure 1.10 shows the jobs view. The details pane will list the details of the selected job, including change tracking information.

FIGURE 1.9
Library view

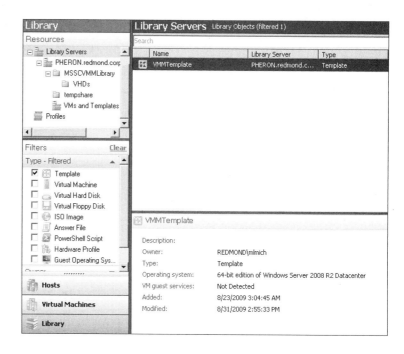

FIGURE 1.10
Jobs view

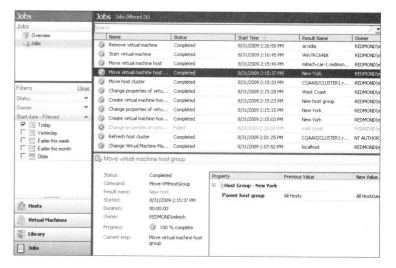

◆ Figure 1.11 shows the administration view. The results pane will list the different configuration options for each selection option in this view.

◆ Figure 1.12 shows the overview page. This page includes diagrams that provide an instant snapshot of the managed virtualized environment. This includes host information, recent job information, virtual machine status information, and a bar graph of library resources.

FIGURE 1.11
Administration view

FIGURE 1.12
Virtual Machine
Manager Overview
window

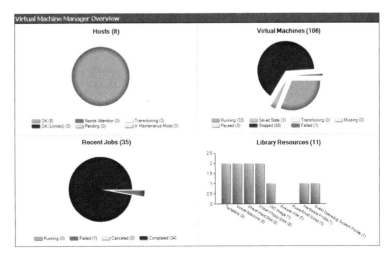

The overview view link is present in the tree view pane for all Administrator Console views. In the overview view, an administrator gets a high-level snapshot of the VMM environment for hosts, virtual machines, jobs, and library resources. Hosts, virtual machines, and jobs are organized by status. Library resources are organized by quantity per resource.

In the VMM jobs view, jobs are audited with information on which user executed a job, when it was executed, and what information or properties were changed. The change information is displayed in the Change Tracking tab of the details pane for a selected job, as seen in Figure 1.13.

FIGURE 1.13
Change tracking for a VMM job

The administration view of the Administrator Console further consists of six tree view options:

◆ General settings for Virtual Machine Manager

◆ Managed computers view

◆ Networking options

◆ User roles management

◆ System Center configuration options for Operations Manager

◆ Virtualization managers view

Windows PowerShell Interface

Virtual Machine Manager is one of the first Microsoft software products to fully adopt Windows PowerShell and give users a complete VMM management interface tailored for scripting. Windows PowerShell offers a rich scripting environment for administrators. Its full integration of cmdlets from various products and the native cmdlets of the operating system give an administrator the opportunity to write powerful PowerShell scripts and eliminate many manual daily operations.

Figure 1.14 shows the PowerShell button, which you can use to launch Windows PowerShell from the Administrator Console. Figure 1.15 shows Windows PowerShell in action, getting a list of running virtual machines and their current host.

Chapter 8 has a detailed description of the VMM Windows PowerShell interface and examples on how to automate VMM using Windows PowerShell.

FIGURE 1.14
Windows PowerShell button in the Administrator Console

FIGURE 1.15
PowerShell window with list of running virtual machines

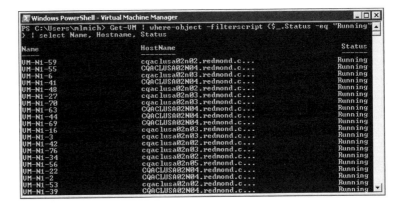

Virtual Machine Manager Agents

Virtual Machine Manager agents are installed on all Windows-based virtualization hosts and on all library servers. The Managed Computers page of the administration view in the Administrator Console lists all agents, their current version and status, and the VMM roles that the agent performs (i.e., host or library or both). Figure 1.16 shows an example view of the Managed Computers page.

FIGURE 1.16
VMM Managed Computers page

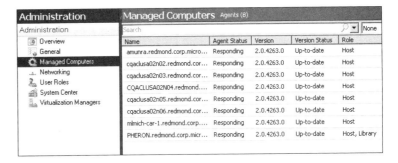

There are two ways that the VMM agent is installed:

◆ Automatically as part of adding a library server or adding a Windows-based virtualization host (e.g., Virtual Server or Hyper-V host). In this case, the VMM agent is pushed from the VMM server to the managed computer.

◆ Manually through the Virtual Machine Manager Setup. You can launch Setup and choose the Local Agent option to locally install the agent on a computer.

Local agent installation is necessary when deploying a perimeter network host. An administrator might also chose to install an agent locally on a host if the host is behind a firewall and cannot accept Distributed COM or WMI traffic across remote computers. Once the agent is installed, the VMM server will communicate with the agent through the WinRM and BITS protocols, which require only two ports to be opened on the firewall. WinRM provides the control channel and BITS provides the data channel of communication.

For Virtual Server hosts, the VMM agent also installs a set of private WMI interfaces that the VMM server invokes remotely through WinRM to get and set virtualization data. Hyper-V already has defined a public WMI interface that the VMM server invokes remotely using

WinRM. The VMM agent additionally installs and enables the BITS components that are necessary for transferring files to and from hosts and library servers. BITS file transfers are covered later in this chapter and in various other parts of this book.

Virtual Machine Manager Library

The VMM server can also act as the default library server after VMM is initially installed. The VMM library is the central repository for all the building blocks necessary for creating virtual machines. The library can be used to store all file-based resources, such as virtual hard disks and ISO images, templates, PowerShell scripts, sysprep answer files, operating system and hardware profiles, and offline (i.e., stored) virtual machines. After installation, you can use the Administrator Console to install additional library servers and add library shares to VMM. This is a recommended practice if you will be managing a large number of hosts or if your hosts are geographically dispersed. In the case of geographically dispersed hosts, file transfer times from the library to the host will be minimized if the library server is close in proximity and has high network bandwidth to the host.

The Virtual Machine Manager library provides an inventory of resources that are used to provision various types of virtual machines. The library server can be installed on any Windows Server computer acting as a file server that is capable of running the VMM agent. Physical file resources are managed through Windows shares on the library server. Each library server can have one or more shares. The library can store the following types of physical resources (listed here with their associated filename extensions):

- Virtual hard disk files (.vhd, .vmdk)

- PowerShell script files (.ps1)

- Sysprep answer files (.inf, .xml)

- ISO image files (.iso)

- Virtual floppy disk files (.vfd, .flp)

In addition, the library can store entire virtual machines in the form of templates or offline virtual machines:

- VMware templates can be imported in the VMM library through the Import Templates action when a VirtualCenter server is selected.

- Offline virtual machines stored in the VMM library need to be in an exported state for the Hyper-V virtualization platform.

The library also contains the following types of resources in the VMM database:

- Templates

- Hardware profiles

- Guest operating system profiles

These files do not have a physical representation in any library share. However, even though templates do not have a physical representation in a library share, they are linked to virtual hard disk files that do have a physical representation.

Figure 1.17 shows the VMM library with a variety of physical files and templates and their associated status organized by type. Figure 1.18 shows the details pane for a stored virtual machine. Figure 1.19 shows the profiles view of the VMM Library.

FIGURE 1.17
VMM library

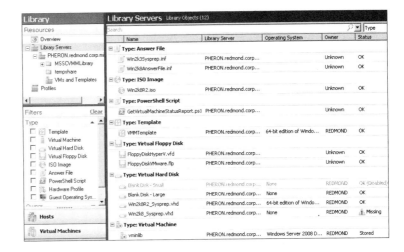

FIGURE 1.18
Details pane for a stored virtual machine in the VMM library

FIGURE 1.19
VMM library profiles

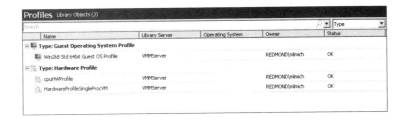

By default, the VMM library looks for new files or updates to existing files every hour. Physical files that can't be detected are flagged using the Missing status in the library view of the Administrator Console. This operation is performed as part of the library refresher that executes based on a user-customizable schedule. To configure the library refresh interval as seen in Figure 1.20, follow these steps:

1. Choose the administration view in the Administrator Console.

2. Click the General page.

3. Select the Library Settings option.

4. Change the library refresh interval to the desired value or disable the library refresher.

FIGURE 1.20
Configuring the library
refresh interval

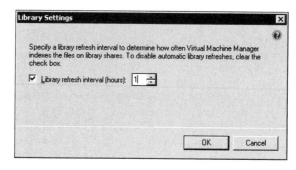

For library servers that are in remote or branch offices, it might be desirable to either disable the library refresher or configure it to execute only once a day. A library server or an individual library share can be refreshed manually by clicking on the share or the server name in the library view and selecting the Refresh action.

Virtual Machine Manager Self-Service Portal

The VMM Self-Service Portal is an optional, web-based component that a VMM administrator can install and configure to allow users to create and manage their own virtual machines within a controlled environment on a limited group of virtual machine hosts. This avoids the need to install and grant access to the VMM Administrator Console for a set of users who need to accomplish a smaller set of targeted operations. The VMM administrator can create Self-Service User Roles using the Administrator Console. These user roles will determine the following:

◆ The domain users or domain groups that are members of the user role.

◆ The scope of the user role, defined at the host group level.

◆ The permissions of the Self-Service Users' actions for virtual machines, defined through a set of predefined privileges, as seen in Figure 1.21.

◆ The ability to enable the creation of new virtual machines through a set of templates chosen by the VMM administrator. A quota system can also be enforced to restrict the unlimited use of valuable resources by Self-Service Users. A VMM administrator can set quota points to the Self-Service User Role and assign quota points to virtual machine templates to limit the number of virtual machines that a user or group can deploy.

◆ The ability to store virtual machines in the VMM library and the library share location where the virtual machines will be put.

To create, operate, and manage virtual machines, Self-Service Users use the Virtual Machine Manager Self-Service Portal (SSP). The portal can be installed on the same computer as the VMM server or on a separate remote computer. The web portal utilizes the Web Server (Internet Information Services or IIS) Windows Server role and Windows PowerShell cmdlets to execute actions within the VMM infrastructure. In essence, the SSP is another client of the VMM server that utilizes WCF to communicate with the VMM server.

After the administrator determines which host groups Self-Service Users can create virtual machines on and what templates to use, a new virtual machine is automatically placed on the most suitable host in the host group based on host ratings and the Intelligent Placement feature of VMM. Figure 1.22 shows the New Virtual Machine Wizard for Self-Service Users.

FIGURE 1.21
Self-Service User Role
privileges

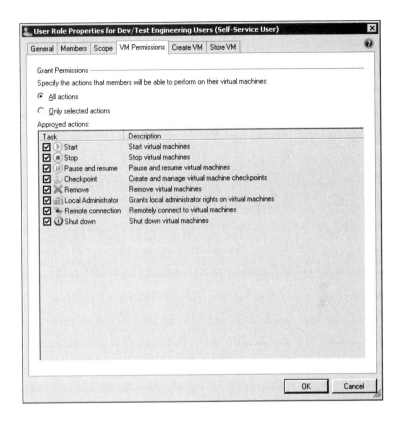

FIGURE 1.22
Self-Service Portal New
Virtual Machine Wizard

The Self-Service Portal is often leveraged in development and test scenarios and lab management scenarios as well as by help desk personnel that are responsible for fulfilling production virtual machine requests. In these scenarios, a set of common templates to provision virtual machines can be assigned ownership to a domain group in Active Directory that represents the Self-Service Users.

After a virtual machine is created, Self-Service Users can log in to the SSP and manage their virtual machines. The SSP supports two modes of authentication with the option to cache the user credentials:

◆ Anonymous forms-based authentication, where the SSP will ask users to log in first using a username and a password

◆ Windows integrated authentication

These are covered in more detail later on in this chapter.

INSTALLING THE SELF-SERVICE PORTAL ON A SEPARATE COMPUTER

If you have installed the VMM SSP on a computer other than the VMM server computer, there are two additional considerations:

◆ You need to enable Kerberos Constrained Delegation in Active Directory for the SSP computer. This is necessary because of the double-hop of Self-Service User credentials from the client computer (e.g., a computer running Internet Explorer that is used to view the portal) to the web server (i.e., the Self-Service Portal server) to the VMM server. To configure constrained delegation, follow the instructions outlined in the How to Configure Integrated Windows Authentication for the VMM Self-Service Portal section of the System Center Virtual Machine Manager TechCenter at `http://technet.microsoft.com/en-us/library/cc956040.aspx`.

◆ If you need to connect to a different VMM server or if the VMM server has changed its computer name, you can edit the VmmServerName Registry key value of `HKEY_LOCAL_MACHINE\ SOFTWARE\Microsoft\Microsoft System Center Virtual Machine Manager Self-Service Portal\Settings` to modify the fully qualified domain name of the VMM server to the new computer name. After the computer name is changed, restart the IIS services for the VMM web components to establish connections to the new VMM server.

Virtual machines that were created through the SSP will automatically show up in the web interface. If they are created through other means and then assigned to Self-Service Users, three prerequisites have to be met before they can be managed through the SSP:

◆ The owner of the virtual machine has to be set to the user or group that is trying to manage this virtual machine through the SSP.

◆ The user or group that is trying to manage the virtual machine has to be a member of a Self-Service User Role that is scoped to include a host group that manages this virtual machine.

◆ The Self-Service User Role has to define enough privileges for its users to be able to manage this virtual machine.

Figure 1.23 shows you the main page of the SSP. Users can manage their virtual machines, view virtual machine properties, start or stop virtual machines, store virtual machines in the library, view live thumbnails of virtual machines, or view the console connection to a virtual machine.

FIGURE 1.23
VMM Self-Service Portal

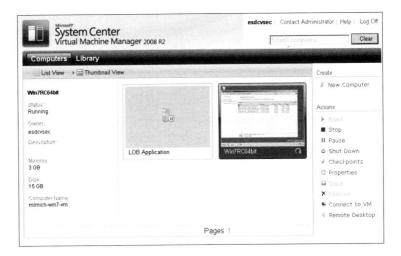

Console connections to virtual machines are offered through three different mechanisms depending on the virtualization platform of the virtual machine:

◆ For virtual machines residing on a Hyper-V host, console connections are offered through the Virtual Machine Manager Self-Service Client. The Self-Service Client is an ActiveX control that utilizes the Remote Desktop Protocol (RDP) and the Hyper-V Single Port Listener feature to provide console connections to virtual machines through the Hyper-V host.

◆ For virtual machines residing on a Virtual Server host, console connections are offered through the Virtual Machine Remote Control (VMRC) ActiveX control that ships with Virtual Server and is redistributed by VMM.

◆ For virtual machines residing on a VMware ESX host, console connections are offered through the VMware MKS ActiveX control. This control is downloaded through a secure SSL channel when you try to view a live VMware virtual machine.

Figure 1.24 shows a live console connection to a virtual machine from the SSP. A user can send a Ctrl+Alt+Del or Reconnect to the virtual machine from this window.

There are situations in which a user connecting to the SSP is a member of more than one Self-Service User Role that is scoped over the same set of virtual machines and each user role provides a different set of privileges and permissions. To apply a certain user role to a virtual machine and manage it using that user role, follow these steps:

1. Select the virtual machine in the SSP.

2. Click the Properties action.

3. Ensure that you are in the Summary tab.

4. Change the Role selection box to the user role you want to use to manage this virtual machine, as seen in Figure 1.25.

Self-Service Users can also use the VMM Windows PowerShell interface directly and invoke cmdlets as a way to interact with the VMM infrastructure.

FIGURE 1.24
Console connection to a
virtual machine

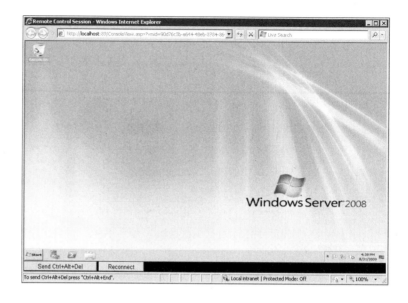

FIGURE 1.25
Changing the user role
applied to a virtual
machine

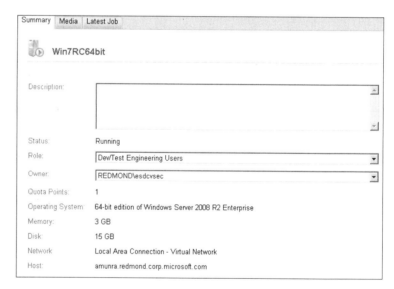

Microsoft Virtualization Management

Virtual Machine Manager manages both server virtualization technologies from Microsoft,
Windows Hyper-V, and Microsoft Virtual Server. VMM 2007 supported only Microsoft Virtual
Server, but with the release of VMM 2008, Hyper-V is supported as well.

MORE ABOUT HYPER-V

Hyper-V, formerly known as Viridian or Windows Server Virtualization, is a hypervisor-based virtualization system that is available both as a role of Windows Server 2008 and as a stand-alone product called Hyper-V Server. Hyper-V is Microsoft's first hypervisor, developed entirely out of a new code base, different than what Microsoft used for Virtual Server. Hyper-V is available on only 64-bit hardware and requires the hardware virtualization option, specifically Intel-VT and AMD-V.

VMM can manage the following:

◆ Stand-alone hosts

◆ Hosts that are part of a failover cluster (Hyper-V hosts only)

◆ Hosts that are in a perimeter network

◆ Hosts that are part of a domain that has no established trust with the domain of the VMM server

Virtual Server host clustering is managed by VMM in a cluster-agnostic way. Chapter 5 goes into more detail on managing Windows Hyper-V, and Chapter 6 is about managing Virtual Server with VMM.

HOST GROUPS

All hosts in VMM are organized into host groups, a logical grouping hierarchy that is visible in the VMM Administrator Console. Host groups are completely defined by the administrator based on the most convenient management grouping. Administrators can choose to organize hosts into host groups that represent physical geographical locations, or they can choose to organize hosts into host groups that represent product units or even staging areas in the production cycle (e.g., Testing, Staging, and Production) as seen in Figure 1.26.

FIGURE 1.26
Host groups in VMM

Multiple sub host groups can also be created to combine different types of schemes. Hosts can be moved from one host group to another through drag-and-drop operations in the Administrator Console in the tree view pane. New host groups can also be created from the same pane. VMM ships with a built-in root host group called All Hosts that cannot be modified. In addition to organizing hosts into a logical hierarchy, host groups offer a few more pieces of functionality:

◆ Delegated Administrator and Self-Service User Roles are scoped to host groups.

◆ Host reserves that are used in Intelligent Placement can be assigned at the host group level, as seen in Figure 1.27.

◆ BITS transfers offer the option of unencrypted transfers, and this option can be enabled at the host group level.

◆ PRO settings can be modified per host group.

FIGURE 1.27
Host reserves in host groups

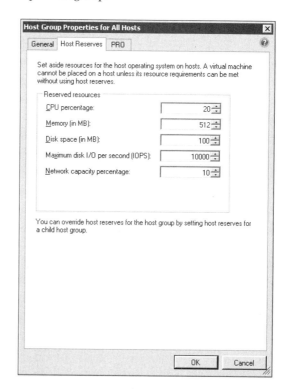

VMware VirtualCenter Management

With VMM 2008, VMM added heterogeneous virtualization support by managing VMware Virtual Infrastructure. VMM can manage stand-alone ESX hosts as well as clustered ESX nodes through the VMware VirtualCenter public web interfaces. VMM does not manage ESX nodes directly. By using this approach, any changes made to the VMware environment through VMM are automatically reflected in VirtualCenter and vice versa, so the two can coexist side by side. VirtualCenter, however, does not provide the ability to manage Hyper-V or Virtual

Server environments. Even though VMM uses VirtualCenter as a proxy to manage ESX, you can add a stand-alone ESX host to an already managed VirtualCenter server through the Add Host global action in VMM. To add a VirtualCenter server, use the Add VMware VirtualCenter Server global action. VMM does not require an agent on the VirtualCenter server in order to manage it.

Figure 1.28 shows the Administrator Console managing an ESX host using the same host group hierarchy seen in the VirtualCenter user interface. Figure 1.29 shows the Virtualization Managers page of the administration view of the VMM Administrator Console, where you can see all the VirtualCenter servers that VMM is managing and their current status.

FIGURE 1.28
Managing ESX hosts

FIGURE 1.29
Virtualization managers being managed by VMM

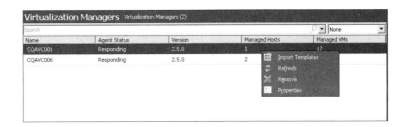

Chapter 4 goes into more detail about the support and management of VMware Virtual Infrastructure by VMM.

CASE STUDIES

The Virtual Machine Manager team has published a set of case studies on the VMM website at www.microsoft.com/systemcenter/virtualmachinemanager/en/us/case-studies.aspx. These case studies show how Virtual Machine Manager provides a comprehensive management solution for the virtualized datacenter. You can also use the Microsoft Case Study finder at www.microsoft.com/casestudies to find case studies related to Virtual Machine Manager or Hyper-V.

VMM Architecture

Figure 1.1 earlier in this chapter illustrated the high-level architecture of VMM and all its distributed components. Figure 1.30 shows the communication protocols used through the various system components.

FIGURE 1.30
The communication protocols used with the components of Virtual Machine Manager

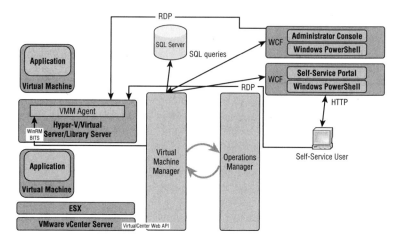

In the following sections, we will dive into the technical details and architecture of VMM and its components. We will discuss the protocols and ports used for communication among the various VMM components, time-outs that can result from communication protocols, the communication method used for interacting with OpsMgr, the different transfer methods that VMM utilizes, and the way that VMM refreshes information in the environment. In addition, we will discuss the authentication and authorization model of the various VMM components. Role-based administration of VMM is also covered.

Protocols

VMM uses a variety of protocols for connecting to its components. The central hub of communication is the VMM server. The information in this section will aid the coordination with network administrators in opening all the required network ports and adding firewall exceptions for VMM to operate properly. During setup, VMM will properly configure Windows Firewall and create the necessary exceptions for the ports mentioned, which are detailed here:

- The VMM server communicates with the VMM agents on the Hyper-V host servers, the Virtual Server host servers, and the VMM library servers via Windows Remote Management (WinRM). WinRM is also often referred to as the control channel of communication since VMM does not transfer virtual machine images through WinRM. This communication is always initiated by the VMM server, which polls for data or initiates commands with the other server roles. A default VMM agent is always installed on the VMM server during setup so that the default VMM library role can be created.

- VMM users the Background Intelligent Transfer Service (BITS) as the data channel for transferring data from one server role to another.

- Windows Communication Foundation (WCF) is used for communication between the VMM server and the Administrator Console or PowerShell cmdlets. WCF allows both the Administrator Console and the cmdlets to reside on a server other than the server on which the VMM server role is installed.

- The VMM server can connect to either a local or a remote SQL server. VMM also offers the option to install SQL Server Express on the same machine where the VMM server setup is being executed.

◆ VMM uses the Remote Desktop Protocol (RDP) in two ways to connect to virtual machines and provide a console session to the user:

   ◆ If the client machine running the Administrator Console or the Self-Service Portal web session is not executing on top of Windows Server 2008 or on top of Windows Vista Service Pack 1 (SP1), then VMM will use standard RDP to connect to the guest operating system inside the virtual machine. In order for this to be feasible, the Virtual Guest Services need to be installed inside the virtual machine and the computer name of the guest operating system needs to be surfaced in VMM.

   ◆ If the client machine uses either Windows Server 2008 or Windows Vista SP1 or later, then VMM will take advantage of the enhancements in RDP and the Credential Security Service Provider (CredSSP) to connect to the virtual machine via the host operating system. This feature is also known as the RDP Single Port Listener, and it allows VMM to connect to any virtual machine through a host connection without imposing any networking requirements on the VM.

◆ For Virtual Server hosts, VMM utilizes VMRC and the ActiveX control for VMRC to give users console access to a VM.

◆ When communicating with VMware VirtualCenter, VMM utilizes the public Web Services API for VMware Virtual Infrastructure. Transfer of files from an ESX server to a Windows-based host utilizes HTTPS or SFTP.

CONSOLE CONNECTIONS TO A HYPER-V VIRTUAL MACHINE

Hyper-V will allow only one connection at a time to a virtual machine. If a second connection is attempted, the first connection will be terminated. Virtual Server behaved a little bit differently, giving the administrator the option to enable or disable multiple concurrent VMRC connections to a virtual machine.

Hyper-V and Virtual Server will also create the necessary exceptions for the ports utilized for virtual machine console access. Table 1.1 shows the comprehensive list of ports needed by VMM to function properly.

TABLE 1.1:   Default network ports utilized by VMM

VMM COMPONENT	NETWORK PORT	PROTOCOL
VMM server	80	HTTP, WinRM
VMM server	443	BITS
VMM server	8100	WCF
SQL Server	1433	Remote SQL instance
SQL Server	1434	SQL Server Browser service
Windows host or library server	80	HTTP, WinRM

TABLE 1.1:   Default network ports utilized by VMM *(CONTINUED)*

VMM COMPONENT	NETWORK PORT	PROTOCOL
Windows host or library server	443	BITS
Windows host	3389	RDP
Hyper-V host	2179	RDP Single Port Listener for Hyper-V or Hyper-V remote connection port
Virtual Server host	5900	VMRC
VMware VirtualCenter Server	443	HTTPS for VI Web Services
VMware ESX host (all versions)	443	HTTPS for VI Web Services
VMware ESX 3.0, 3.5 host	22	SSH for SFTP
Self-Service Portal	80	HTTP (without SSL)
Self-Service Portal	443	HTTPS (with SSL)

It is a recommended practice that during VMM setup you change the default ports for WinRM, BITS, and WCF to something that is unique to your enterprise. Figure 1.31 and Figure 1.32 show the wizard pages you'll use to configure the ports for VMM server setup and for the local agent setup, respectively.

FIGURE 1.31
VMM server port assignment installation settings

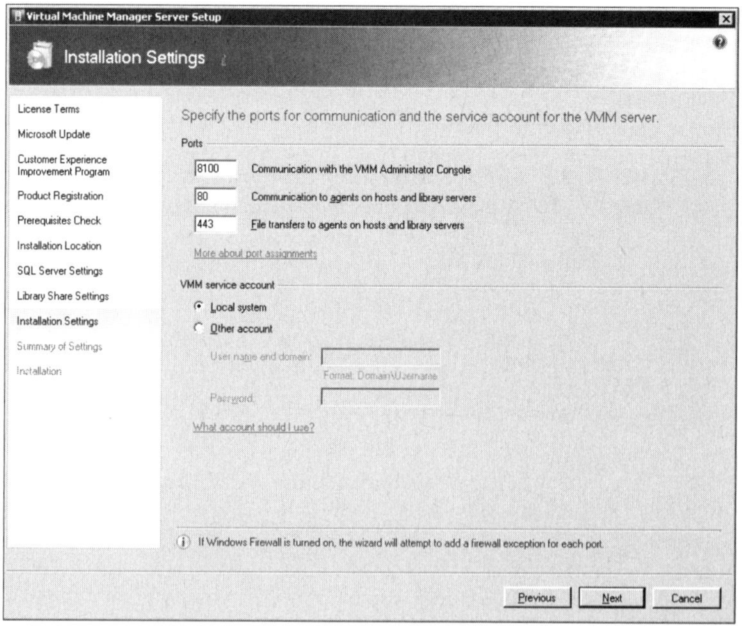

FIGURE 1.32
Port settings for local
agent installation

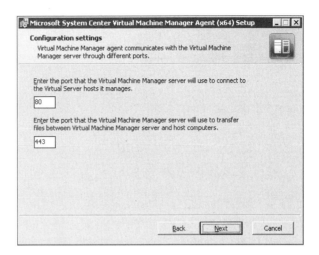

Real World Scenario

CONNECTING TO VIRTUAL MACHINES IN A PRIVATE NETWORK

The administrator for SupServers, a fictional company, has set up a private Active Directory domain environment inside a virtual machine. This domain environment is connected via an internal virtual network to three other virtual machines on the same host server. All four virtual machines comprise a test workload that the company's security officer will use to validate new software that will be introduced to the company. It is important that this workload and the four virtual machines are isolated from the main network and that any potential issues are contained within the virtual environment. The security officer, Daphne, is a VMM Self-Service User and can connect to her virtual machines through the Self-Service Portal user interface.

In order for Daphne to connect to this isolated environment, she has to utilize the Self-Service Portal UI. However, because her virtual machines are not on the corporate network, standard RDP cannot be used for connections. For standard RDP to work, a network connection between the client machine and the virtual machine is necessary. Daphne needs to connect to the portal from a computer running Windows Vista SP1 to utilize the RDP Single Port Listener. This would enable her to connect to the Hyper-V host server, which is on the corporate network, and Hyper-V would redirect the connection to the virtual machine, which is in a private network.

The Self-Service Portal of VMM allows an end user to connect to the portal from a client computer using a browser like Internet Explorer. The end user can then choose to connect to a virtual machine and view the console session.

Now, there are some requirements and advantages of each type of console connection. Here are the requirements for using standard RDP to connect to a virtual machine:

◆ The virtual machine has to be connected to an accessible network.

◆ The client computer has to be able to resolve the virtual machine's computer name through DNS.

◆ The client should have a clear firewall path for the RDP port to each virtual machine.

However, if the Single Port Listener is used, these requirements are not applicable. This is because instead of the RDP connection being routed from the client computer to the virtual machine's guest operating system, the RDP connection is routed from the client computer to the host operating system. This means that only the host computer needs to be in the network and accessible from the client computer (this is already a requirement because VMM has to be able to manage the host computer). This approach includes the following added advantages:

◆ You can view the virtual machine boot process, boot into safe mode, or change BIOS settings.

◆ You can view the console session of non-Windows operating systems.

◆ You can view the console session of virtual machines that don't have the Virtual Guest Services installed.

◆ The virtual machine does not need to be connected to any network (this works well for fenced or network-isolated computers).

◆ The client needs a clear firewall path for only the Hyper-V remote connection port to each Hyper-V server.

The many advantages of using the Single Port Listener make for a compelling reason to upgrade client computers to the Vista SP1 or Windows Server 2008 or later operating systems.

One way to change the VMM ports is during VMM server setup as per Figure 1.31 (shown earlier). If you are installing the VMM agent locally, make sure the WinRM and BITS ports match with what you specified during the VMM server setup. If your environment requirements change after deployment, the only way to alter the ports used by VMM is by manually modifying a set of Windows Registry entries.

The process for changing the ports through the Windows Registry for WinRM, BITS, and WCF is as follows:

1. Stop the Virtual Machine Manager Windows Service.

2. Open Windows Registry.

3. Navigate to `HKEY_LOCAL_MACHINE\SOFTWARE\Microsoft\Microsoft System Center Virtual Machine Manager Server\Settings`.

4. Change the value of `IndigoTcpPort` (for WCF), `WSManTcpPort` (for WinRM), or `BITSTcpPort` (for BITS).

5. Ensure that the proper firewall rules exist for communication on the changed ports. If both a hardware and a software firewall are in place in your environment, consult with the system administrator to enable these firewall rules on both types of firewall.

6. Start the Virtual Machine Manager Windows Service.

The preceding process will only change the ports on the VMM server. The Administrator Console and Windows PowerShell cmdlets will not be able to connect to the VMM server until you change the port number to the appropriate value in the connection settings.

For BITS and WinRM, you need to manually edit the same values under `HKEY_LOCAL _MACHINE\SOFTWARE\Microsoft\Microsoft System Center Virtual Machine Manager Agent\Setup` on every single host and library server that is managed by VMM. The Windows service to restart for that procedure is Virtual Machine Manager Agent. VMM will stop communicating with the hosts and library servers if the ports are changed on only the VMM server. To ensure that no interruption of management service occurs, it is recommended that all steps are followed at the same time across the entire environment before restarting all the VMM services.

Windows Remote Management

VMM utilizes WinRM to communicate with the VMM agent on the host and library servers. During the remote agent deployment, VMM will create a WinRM listener on the HTTP port specified during setup.

CHECKING THE STATUS OF THE WINRM LISTENER

From an administrator command prompt, run `winrm enumerate winrm/config/listener` to check the status of the listener created by VMM. To check the rest of the configuration settings for WinRM, run `winrm get winrm/config`.

WinRM was chosen as the communication protocol because of its ability to communicate via HTTP and limit firewall changes, its ability to run without the need for .NET, and for its native support for Windows Management Instrumentation (WMI). When VMM manages Virtual Server, which exposes only a COM interface for management, the local VMM agent implements a set of WMI providers that wrap the functionality of the COM interface. These WMI providers can be invoked remotely from the VMM server via WinRM. In supporting Hyper-V, since the native management interface is WMI, the functionality implemented by the local agent is greatly reduced since all Hyper-V–specific functions are invoked remotely from the VMM server using WMI over WinRM.

Because the P2V process in VMM does not utilize WinRM for the control channel, the appropriate ports need to be opened so that the VMM server can communicate with the source machine using WMI over DCOM. One of the reasons for not requiring WinRM in this scenario is so that the source computer does not have to be altered as a requirement for the P2V process.

Windows Communication Foundation

Windows Communication Foundation (WCF) is the protocol that VMM uses for communicating between all clients and the VMM server. The clients are the VMM Administrator Console, the Windows PowerShell cmdlets for VMM, and the Self-Service Portal web server. Communication is established over a single port via a duplex channel. The clients establish a connection to the VMM server and will keep this connection open for the duration of their session. If at any point in time the connection to the VMM server is lost, the affected client will be disconnected and a new connection will need to be made. In the case of the Administrator Console, it will prompt the user with an error and will have to be reopened.

After the initial connection to the VMM server is made, the clients query for data and execute commands via the private WCF interfaces that VMM exposes on the VMM server. However, VMM also leverages WCF callbacks to push data out to clients. Through WCF callbacks, VMM implements its own internal eventing mechanism that allows it to update all subscribed clients simultaneously with the current state of the system. For example, if a virtual machine changes its state outside VMM from running to stopped, the VMM server will detect that change on the host system using a refresher and through an event will update all clients with the new state of the virtual machine. The VMM eventing infrastructure ensures that if multiple VMM administrators have the Administrator Console open and are working on

VMM simultaneously, they are all viewing an always up-to-date view (i.e., live view) of the virtualized environment (i.e., no VMM administrator will be working with stale data because another administrator has made a change in VMM a few minutes earlier).

Background Intelligent Transfer Service

Background Intelligent Transfer Service (BITS) is the technology that VMM utilizes for transferring data from one server to another. To transfer a virtual machine or any other file from one server to another, VMM has to create a BITS job and initiate a BITS session. The VMM server is always the one to start the BITS job, and all BITS jobs created by VMM have the Foreground priority. VMM has its own implementation of a BITS server residing inside the VMM agent.

In most cases, the VMM server initiates a download of data through BITS (versus an upload). VMM initiates an upload in the following cases:

♦ When transferring data to a perimeter network host or a non-trusted domain host

♦ When transferring data from a source server during a P2V process

In the case of an upload transfer, the client of the job is the sender of the data and the server of the job is the destination host for the data. For download transfers, the roles are reversed.

In environments where IPSec is already deployed, it might be beneficial to disable the encryption that BITS offers to speed up transfers. VMM enables an administrator to allow unencrypted BITS network transfers in VMM. This property can be changed at the host group level and for each library server.

Operations Manager Connector

VMM 2008 and VMM 2008 R2 have a deeper connection with System Center Operations Manager (OpsMgr) through a connector. A connector is a standard communication method that allows OpsMgr to communicate with external software like VMM. Using this connector, VMM can share data with OpsMgr and provide the full layout of the virtualized environment managed by VMM. For scalability reasons, VMM opens 32 connectors to provide discovery information about the hosts and virtual machines under management.

For the entire environment to be fully managed in OpsMgr and take advantage of all the features and functionality, OpsMgr agents need to be installed on all the hosts and all the virtual machines.

When VMM gets configured to use a specific OpsMgr root management server, a snapshot discovery is initiated, and this will provide all the required information to OpsMgr so that it can start monitoring the environment. VMM will continue to keep the data in OpsMgr in sync and will communicate any changes that result with the addition or removal of hosts.

A snapshot discovery is issued when the Virtual Machine Manager service starts and every 6 hours thereafter. One way to trigger immediate discovery is to reconfigure the OpsMgr connection in VMM through the PowerShell interface.

VMM also uses the connector to retrieve the alerts necessary to generate and surface PRO tips in the VMM Administrator Console. These alerts are retrieved and updated every 60 seconds. When an administrator chooses to implement a PRO tip, VMM will ask OpsMgr to invoke the Recovery action of the PRO tip monitor through the connector.

Role-Based Administration

One of the main new features of VMM 2008 and VMM 2008 R2 over VMM 2007 is the introduction of role-based administration through the use of VMM roles. This feature is also called delegated administration. In VMM 2007, there were only two types of users for VMM, the administrators and the end users. End users had access only to the Self-Service Portal of VMM, while administrators had access to the Administrator Console. Starting with VMM 2008, with the introduction of roles, VMM provides the capability to designate a user in one of three categories:

◆ Administrator

◆ Delegated Administrator

◆ Self-Service User

Administrator   An administrator has full functionality privileges over the entire VMM environment and can access any virtual machine on any host server. More importantly, an administrator has direct console access to all virtual machines in the system.

Delegated Administrator   A delegated administrator can perform all the functions of an administrator; however, access is scoped down to a set of host groups and library servers. Using this role, an administrator can enable a user to fully administer a subset of the VMM environment.

Self-Service User   Through the use of the Self-Service User Role, an administrator can enable a set of users to create and manage their own virtual machines within a controlled environment. This controlled environment includes a scoped set of templates and library servers these users can use, a quota point system for creating virtual machines, a set of host groups that these users can use, and a configurable list of privileges for executing virtual machine actions. Figure 1.33 shows the list of privileges that an administrator can grant users.

FIGURE 1.33
End user role virtual machine permissions

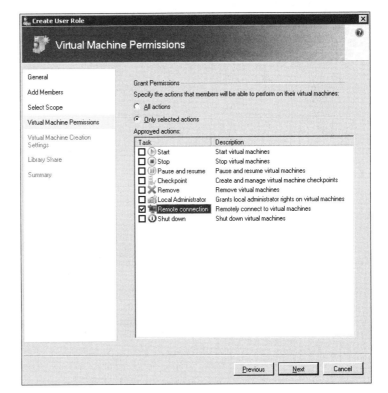

In VMM 2008 and VMM 2008 R2, Self-Service Users have access not only to the Self-Service Portal, but also to the Windows PowerShell cmdlets for VMM. When using cmdlets, Self-Service Users will be able to see only the VMM objects they have access to, and they would be able to execute only the cmdlets that the administrator specifically allowed for them in the configuration of the user role.

For Hyper-V, VMM will translate the user roles into data that can be consumed by Authorization Manager on the Hyper-V host. VMM will use a local XML file for representing the authorization store for each Hyper-V server. It is highly recommended that no application or user modifies this XML file directly. If any changes are needed to provide access to users, these users need to become a member of a user role in VMM so that the appropriate permissions can be set. A typical customer scenario is to give individual users access to connect to the console of a virtual machine. For this scenario, the recommendation is to create a user role for these virtual machines and enable only the remote connection permission. Access can then be controlled through the Owner property of a virtual machine.

Third-party applications that interface with Hyper-V directly and need access to the Hyper-V environment can create roles and tasks in the root scope of the Authorization Manager store. Properly configured roles and tasks should not interfere with VMM's operations, and VMM will be able to coexist with the third-party application while managing the same Hyper-V server.

Types of Virtual Machine Migration in VMM

Virtual Machine Manager at its core level supports four types of migrations of virtual machines from one server to another. The transfer type that will be used is displayed in the placement wizard page of VMM when you attempt to migrate a virtual machine, as shown in Figure 1.34. The Transfer Type column includes both an icon and text that describes the type of transfer method that VMM will use when migrating the virtual machine to this host. In addition, the Network Optimization column will indicate if this host has support for the new Windows Server 2008 R2 network optimization features (i.e., Virtual Machine Queue and TCP Chimney).

FIGURE 1.34
Placement star ratings and migration transfer types

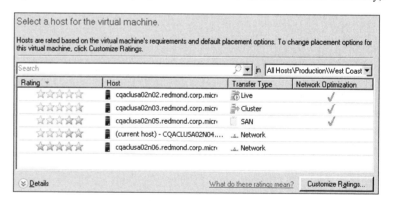

The four types of virtual machine migration (or transfer types) that VMM supports are as follows:

Quick Migration (also known as cluster transfer) This is the type of migration that is available when you have a highly available virtual machine in a Windows Server failover cluster and you move or fail over the virtual machine from one node of the cluster to another. In the VMM Administrator Console, this is also called a Cluster Migration or Cluster transfer.

SAN migration   This type of migration is available when both the source and the destination hosts have access to the same storage infrastructure (i.e., the LUN) and you can transfer the storage from one host to another. This is where NPIV, iSCSI, and VDS are introduced, and we will discuss them in depth in this section. Typically this does not require copying the actual files around, and the SAN infrastructure is used to mask/unmask LUNs, depending upon the direction of the transfer.

Live Migration and VMware VMotion   VMotion is available only for VMware ESX hosts when they are properly configured for VMotion. The VMotion technology enables the migration of a virtual machine from one ESX host to another without any user-perceivable downtime. Live Migration is available only for Hyper-V servers that are part of a failover cluster of Windows Server 2008 R2 computers. Just like VMware VMotion, Live Migration enables the migration of a virtual machine from one Hyper-V cluster node to another without any user-perceivable downtime.

Network migration   This is the slowest of the migration types since it involves a network copy of the data using BITS from one server to another. The amount of downtime introduced is directly proportional to the size of the data being transferred. With VMM 2008 R2, the Quick Storage Migration (QSM) significantly reduces the downtime for a network migration for Windows Server 2008 R2 host computers. QSM takes a snapshot of the virtual machine and begins the transfer of data to the destination host without requiring the virtual machine to be turned off during the initial and bulky transfer of data.

For SAN migration, the files associated with a virtual machine are not copied from one server to another, thus minimizing the downtime during the VM migration. VMM supports the following SAN infrastructures for SAN-based migration:

◆   Fibre Channel

◆   iSCSI SANs using the Microsoft Software Initiator

◆   N_Port ID Virtualization (NPIV)

SAN transfers are available for only the following scenarios: moving a virtual machine from one host to another, moving a virtual machine from the library to a host, and moving a virtual machine from a host to the library. In all three cases, the servers need to be properly configured and the VM has to reside on SAN storage for the SAN migration option to be available in the Administrator Console. VMM enforces the additional requirement that each SAN LUN only contains one virtual machine. In addition, the LUN has to be configured as a basic disk. Since the unit of migration is a LUN, having two virtual machines on the same LUN would introduce unexpected downtime to the second virtual machine once you start migrating the first one.

VMM requires that automount is disabled on all servers that will be hosts to virtual machines you wish to migrate via SAN. VMM does not provision or manage the SAN infrastructure. LUNs need to be created outside VMM and surfaced to the host servers before VMM can start using them.

To properly configure the environment for SAN transfers, you need to make sure the following components are installed on the various VMM servers:

◆   Fibre Channel SAN migrations require each host/library that is part of the SAN to have Virtual Disk Service (VDS) 1.1 or later installed. Windows Server 2008 comes with VDS 2.1 preinstalled and does not need any configuration. The VMM server needs to have the vendor-specific VDS hardware provider installed. Once the proper software is installed on all the nodes, you should be able to see all the providers and subsystems the VMM server has access to from either the Storage Management user interface or the diskraid utility.

◆ N_Port Identification Virtualization (NPIV) migrations require each host/library that is part of the SAN to have VDS 1.1 or later installed. Windows Server 2008 comes with VDS 2.1 preinstalled and does not need any configuration. The VMM server needs to have the vendor-specific VDS hardware provider installed.

◆ iSCSI SAN migrations require each host/library that is part of the SAN to have VDS 1.1 or later installed. Windows Server 2008 comes with VDS 2.1 preinstalled and does not need any configuration. Each host should also have the latest Microsoft iSCSI Initiator installed in it. The VMM server needs to have Microsoft VDS hardware provider installed.

If your environment utilizes Multipath I/O (MPIO), you must install the MPIO drivers provided by your storage vendor on all the host/library servers that are part of the SAN.

After the software requirements are installed, it is a best practice to create one or two test LUNs and try migrating them from one server to a different server to ensure that they are visible in the Disk Management user interface. Once you create a virtual machine on one of these test LUNs, open the Virtual Machine Manager migration wizard to ensure that the placement page of VMM correctly shows a SAN transfer as being available. If for some reason a SAN transfer is not available, VMM will have details in the SAN Explanation tab to explain the rationale behind the unavailability of SAN migration, as shown in Figure 1.35.

FIGURE 1.35
SAN transfer explanation

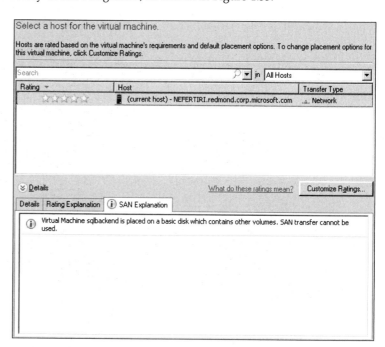

SAN migration plays a big role in a Desktop Virtualization (or VDI) environment because of its ability to do rapid migrations of virtual machines from one server to another. In a typical customer scenario, hundreds of users could be associated with a VDI solution. However, the hosts might not have enough capacity to keep all the virtual machines running at all times for all users. To load balance resources dynamically based on load, SAN migration can play a big part in migrating the resources in the smallest amount of time possible, thus keeping the downtime introduced by the migration under customer SLA requirements. With Windows Server 2008 R2 and failover clustering, Live Migration makes this scenario even more potent, allowing you to dynamically load balance resources without impacting the services of your users.

When you're using VMM to provision or migrate virtual machines, it automatically detects which types of migration are available based on the capabilities and connectivity between the host and target servers. By default, VMM uses the most efficient form of transfer, but this can be overridden by the administrator.

Authentication and Authorization Model

When talking about authentication and authorization, the main questions that administrators have are related to how VMM authenticates and authorizes hosts and how users are authorized to use the VMM interfaces. Protecting the hosts and the VMs is tantamount to having a successful virtualization deployment. In addition to properly authorizing the control channel and the APIs, VMM ensures that the data channel is protected. The data channel is utilized during the migration of virtual machines from one computer to another.

In the following sections, we will cover the authentication and authorization that is used for the different types of hosts that can be managed in VMM. Self-Service Portal authentication and authorization is also covered.

HOST SERVER AUTHENTICATION AND AUTHORIZATION

VMM manages Windows-based hosts in three different ways based on the environment requirements. Authentication and authorization of VMware ESX hosts is covered in Chapter 4.

Trusted domain hosts   If hosts are part of the same domain as the VMM server, or are part of a domain that has a full two-way trust with the domain of the VMM server, VMM manages them as trusted domain hosts. In the case of trusted domain hosts, VMM relies on WinRM and Kerberos to do both the authentication and the authorization when communicating with the hosts. The Virtual Machine Manager service account (either a domain user account or local system) is also an administrator on all host servers, ensuring that all WinRM commands are properly authorized at the host level. Transfers of files over BITS are encrypted by default because files are transferred via the HTTP protocol over SSL.

If you have deployed IPSec in your environment, there will be a double encryption of the data transferred over BITS, potentially slowing down the transfer operation because of the amount of CPU spent on encrypting and decrypting data. VMM 2008 R2 includes a new feature that gives the administrator the option to disable BITS encryption for host groups and for library servers.

Non-trusted domain hosts   If hosts are part of a domain that is not trusted by the domain of the VMM server, VMM manages them as non-trusted domain hosts. In the case of non-trusted domain hosts, authorization and authentication is done using NTLM and the random username/password that VMM creates as part of deploying the agent to these types of hosts. You can find this local account that VMM creates on your host by looking for a username that is prefixed with *VMM*, followed by an alphanumeric random number. This account will have a secure strong password assigned to it that is not user visible and only VMM would know it. BITS transfers in this environment are secured through a certificate that VMM creates and adds in the trusted root of the VMM server and the managed host.

VMM does not currently support a public key infrastructure. VMM will create the certificates and add them to the trusted root of the host and to the trusted root of the VMM server. VMM also will not support managing a Windows failover cluster for a non-trusted domain host or for a perimeter network host.

Perimeter network hosts   If hosts are in a workgroup mode or part of a perimeter network (e.g., DMZ), VMM manages them as perimeter network hosts. Authentication and authorization in this case is the same as for non-trusted domain hosts. VMM can manage such a host either by IP address or by the local computer name. Managing by the local computer name will require the name to be resolvable by DNS when the VMM server tries to access the host. VMM does not allow the management of a host that is not part of the domain unless that host is managed as a perimeter network host.

SELF-SERVICE PORTAL AUTHENTICATION AND AUTHORIZATION

The Self-Service Portal and its users have their own authentication and authorization model. End users can connect to the portal and get authenticated in two different ways.

Anonymous forms-based authentication   In this case, the administrator has not set up any authentication in IIS and the VMM Self-Service Portal site will ask end users for their credentials before they log in. Users can select the option for VMM to store their credentials for the duration of the session. This functionality has a couple of benefits: In environments where the Self-Service Portal client is running on a machine with no domain connectivity, VMM is able to propagate the credentials stored to the RDP protocol for displaying the virtual machine console. Without stored credentials, the end user would be challenged for credentials every time a new connection to a VM is necessary. This form of authentication is particularly useful when the client machines are not members of the domain or when the currently logged-on user is not the same user that owns the virtual machines in VMM.

Windows Integrated Authentication   An IIS administrator can set up Windows Integrated Authentication such that when a domain user visits the Self-Service Portal, IIS is able to utilize single sign-on and pass the credentials to your site. This is the recommended way of setting up the Self-Service Portal. RDP connections to virtual machines from the SSP will utilize the currently logged-on user's credentials. If these credentials are not authorized for the console connection to the virtual machine, the user will be challenged for authentication by RDP.

If the Self-Service Portal web server is not residing on the same computer as the VMM server, a domain administrator needs to ensure that constrained delegation is set up in Active Directory for this computer. This means that the IIS web server needs to be trusted for delegation via Kerberos only to the host service type on the VMM server. If the VMM server is not running as a local system, you would need to create an SPN for the domain user under which the Virtual Machine Manager service runs and then use that same domain user account when setting up the trust for delegation from the IIS server to the VMM server. The requirements around constrained delegation and the SSP was covered in more detail earlier in this chapter in the section "Virtual Machine Manager Self-Service Portal."

In both authentication cases, when the VMM cmdlets on the web server get to execute, they execute under the credentials of the user who logged into the portal. Once VMM authenticates this user as a valid user role user, VMM will create a connection to the VMM server for this user and properly authorize them for the objects and commands they have access to.

Refreshers

Virtual Machine Manager periodically collects information from the virtualization hosts and the library servers and compares them with knowledge that already exists in the VMM database. Any changes that are detected from the hosts or the library servers are updated in the VMM database. For every change that is updated in the VMM database through a refresh, VMM will create an audit log in the jobs view of the Administrator Console. These operations are executed through a set of system jobs called refreshers. The following sections describe all the refreshers in VMM, their intervals, and the data they refresh. In general, even though host-based refreshers say they execute every 30 minutes, not all the refreshers execute at once for all hosts. VMM uses a staggered approach of refreshing hosts to evenly spread the consumption of VMM Server resources.

Refresher times are customizable, but the VMM team has not made that information public as it can have deep performance and operational impact to the virtualized environment. Generally speaking, users should not notice the refreshers when navigating the user interface, and in all cases, users can manually refresh the status of an object if information seems to be reported inaccurately.

VIRTUAL MACHINE PROPERTIES REFRESHER

This is also called the Virtual Machine Light Refresher. It runs every 2 minutes on every host and it performs the following operations:

◆ Checks the host for successful connections through WinRM

◆ Checks the status of all the virtual machines residing on that host

◆ Marks a virtual machine as missing if it no longer exists on the host

◆ Imports newly discovered virtual machines from the host if they don't exist in VMM

Figure 1.36 shows an update to a virtual machine that was detected and audited through the Virtual Machine Properties Refresher.

FIGURE 1.36
Virtual Machine
Properties Refresher

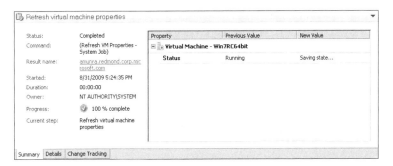

VIRTUAL MACHINE REFRESHER

This is also called the Virtual Machine Heavy Refresher because it does a more extensive refresh than the previous refresher. It runs every 30 minutes on every host and it performs the following operations:

◆ Refreshes all the virtualization information for all virtual machines on the host. This includes but is not limited to virtual machine settings, virtual disk drives, storage information, DVD information, floppy drives, networking information, and clustering information for highly available virtual machines.

◆ Refreshes all the Fibre Channel, iSCSI, or NPIV storage information for each virtual machine.

◆ Refreshes all snapshot information and differencing disk information for each virtual machine.

The Virtual Machine Refresher can also be invoked for a specific virtual machine two more ways:

◆ Using the Refresh-VM Windows PowerShell cmdlet

◆ Selecting a virtual machine in the virtual machines view of the Administrator Console

The Virtual Machine Refresher status can be checked for a virtual machine through the virtual machine properties in the Administrator Console. As seen in Figure 1.37, you can check the last refresh time and the last refresh error.

FIGURE 1.37
Virtual Machine
Refresher properties

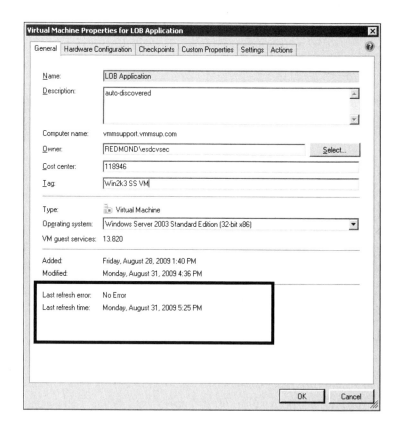

HOST REFRESHER

The Host Refresher runs every 30 minutes on every host and it performs the following operations:

- Updates virtualization host properties and status
- Updates physical disks and SAN information
- Updates networking information like physical NICs and virtual switches

The Host Refresher will not update any state information for hosts that are in maintenance mode in VMM. The Host Refresher can also be invoked for a specific host two more ways:

- Using the `Refresh-VMHost` Windows PowerShell cmdlet
- Selecting a host in the tree view pane and choosing the Refresh action in the Administrator Console

LIBRARY REFRESHER

The Library Refresher runs on a user-configurable schedule (the default is 1 hour and the maximum is 336 hours) that can be customized from the administration view of the Administrator Console. This refresher can be turned off completely. It performs the following operations for all library servers:

- It updates the library shares that are under management in VMM.
- For each library share, it finds new library objects, detects changes in existing objects, and marks objects as missing if they can no longer be found on a library share.
- It finds and imports any offline or stored virtual machines in the library that were not already under management.
- For each library object, it marks it with a VMM-specific globally unique identifier (GUID). This VMM GUID is specified in an alternate data stream of the physical file.

The Library Refresher can also be invoked for a specific library server two more ways:

- Using the `Refresh-LibraryShare` Windows PowerShell cmdlet to refresh a specific library share
- Selecting a library server or a library share in the tree view pane and choosing the Refresh action in the Administrator Console.

CLUSTER REFRESHER

The Cluster Refresher runs every 30 minutes and it performs the following operations for all clusters:

- Refreshes all cluster-related properties that are displayed in Virtual Machine Manager, including available storage for creating new highly available virtual machines
- Flags newly added cluster nodes that have not been associated with VMM
- Flags removed cluster nodes

The Cluster Refresher can also be invoked for a specific cluster two more ways:

♦ Using the `Refresh-VMHostCluster` Windows PowerShell cmdlet

♦ Selecting a cluster in the tree view pane and choosing the Refresh action in the Administrator Console

PERFORMANCE REFRESHER

The Performance Refresher runs every 9 minutes on every host or whenever there is any state changing operation on the VM (e.g., start/stop/save/etc.). It collects performance counter information for both the virtualized hosts and all the virtual machines that reside on them.

VIRTUALCENTER REFRESHER

The VirtualCenter Refresher runs every 30 minutes and it performs the following operations for all VirtualCenter servers:

♦ Refreshes VirtualCenter properties

♦ Refreshes the VMware ESX hosts that are managed by this VirtualCenter

♦ Refreshes resource pool information

♦ Refreshes the hierarchical structure of folders and datacenter objects from VirtualCenter

The VirtualCenter Refresher can also be invoked for a specific VirtualCenter server two more ways:

♦ Using the `Refresh-VirtualizationManager` Windows PowerShell cmdlet

♦ Selecting a VirtualCenter server in the Virtualization Managers page of the Administrator Console and choosing the Refresh action.

USER ROLE REFRESHER

The User Role Refresher runs every 30 minutes and updates user role properties for each host. If, for example, new domain users are added to a Self-Service User Role and the Remote Connection privilege is enabled, the User Role Refresher will ensure that these domain users have the appropriate access in the Authorization Manager store of Hyper-V to be able to remotely connect to the virtual machines through the RDP Single Port Listener.

PRO TIPS REFRESHER

The PRO Tips Refresher runs every minute and it looks for PRO-enabled alerts in OpsMgr that need to be surfaced in VMM as PRO tips. It also reconciles the PRO tips in the VMM database against the data that is brought back from OpsMgr.

TROUBLESHOOTING ISSUES WITH REFRESHERS

If any product issue is caused by the refreshers (information is not properly updated, refreshers are running for a long time, refreshers are consuming too many resources, etc.), contact Microsoft Customer Service and Support (CSS). CSS will collect additional data from your environment and will work with you to troubleshoot and fine-tune the refreshers and their intervals as needed. They will then closely monitor your environment to prevent any side effects from modifying the refreshers and to ensure that VMM is functioning as expected.

Time-Outs

Virtual Machine Manager has two main time-outs that could possibly surface in customer environments:

WinRM operation time-out   When a WinRM time-out occurs, there is a generic error code that is associated with the failed VMM job that indicates that the operation took too long to complete on the server. The default time-out is 5.5 minutes for VMM 2008 R2 (the default time-out was 2 minutes for VMM 2008); when this time-out triggers, it is a good indication that the host machine is overloaded with operations and could not complete the request in time. The recommendation to the user is to retry the operation after the host machine is in a better condition in terms of resources (e.g., CPU).

WCF operation time-out   When a WCF time-out occurs, the VMM Administrator Console or the PowerShell cmdlets will lose their connection to the VMM server. The only way to identify that this loss of connectivity was due to the WCF time-out being exceeded is to check the VMM trace logs and look for a time-out exception from WCF. WCF might exceed the default 5.5-minute time-out because of memory or CPU pressure either on the VMM server or on the machine running the Administrator Console or the VMM cmdlets. (The 5.5-minute time-out is a new VMM 2008 R2 feature. In VMM 2008, the time-out was set at 2 minutes.) Such errors could also occur if the environment scales beyond the published guidelines of 400 hosts and 8,000 virtual machines or if the hardware being used does not conform to the minimum hardware requirements for running VMM.

To change either of these two time-outs, follow these steps as necessary:

1. Go to the VMM server computer.

2. Open the Registry key HKLM\Software\Microsoft\Microsoft System Center Virtual Machine Manager Server\Settings.

3. Modify the value of IndigoSendTimeout to 500. This value is in seconds and the default in VMM 2008 R2 is 330 seconds. The default value for the time-out was lower in previous versions of VMM.

4. Restart the Virtual Machine Manager Windows Service on this computer.

5. Go to the client computer running the VMM Administrator Console that is exhibiting WCF time-out issues.

6. Open the Registry key HKLM\Software\Microsoft\Microsoft System Center Virtual Machine Manager Server\Settings and modify the value of IndigoSendTimeout to 500.

7. Close the Administrator Console and launch it again.

8. Go to the VMM agent computer(s) that is exhibiting WinRM time-out issues.

9. Open the Registry key HKLM\Software\Microsoft\Microsoft System Center Virtual Machine Manager Server\Settings and modify the value of IndigoSendTimeout to 500.

10. Restart the Virtual Machine Manager Agent Windows Service on this computer.

The Bottom Line

Identify and explain the components in the VMM architecture. Virtual Machine Manager has a distributed system architecture that administrators need to understand well before deploying VMM in their virtualized environment. Knowing the architecture of VMM gives you the opportunity to make educated choices during deployment of the various VMM components.

Master It Name the different components of Virtual Machine Manager.

Which VMM components can reside on a separate computer from the VMM server?

Name four new features of VMM 2008 R2.

Determine the ports and protocols required for communication between the various VMM components. Being able to identify the different ports and communication protocols used by VMM makes it easier to talk to the network administrator and plan for a secure network.

Master It Name the differences between regular RDP and the RDP Single Port Listener for Hyper-V.

What is the protocol that VMM uses for transferring virtual machine images from one server to another?

Describe the differences between the console access for Hyper-V and the console access for Virtual Server.

Determine the various roles and privileges of VMM. VMM allows an administrator to define a variety of roles and privileges for delegated administrators and end users. Choosing the correct user roles and delegating access to these users will ease the burden on the administrator and allow users to be self-sufficient.

Master It Name the different user roles that VMM allows you to create.

What are the differences between a delegated administrator and a regular VMM administrator?

Can end users get console access to a virtual machine?

What are the interfaces that end users can utilize to access VMM?

Explain the differences of the migration options offered in VMM. Understanding the different migration options offered in VMM allows an administrator to properly configure their environment (from a hardware and software perspective). Such a configuration will take advantage of faster migration methods and minimize downtime of a VM.

Master It What are the different transfer types that VMM utilizes?

Which is the fastest transfer type?

If you receive a zero-star rating for a host, how would you find out what is causing this result?

Describe the authentication methods between VMM and hosts.   Virtual machines are running the same type of critical workloads as physical machines. The need to secure the data in these VMs is even more important because everything is contained in a collection of a couple of files. When virtual machines move from one host to another, it is important to understand the authentication methods used to secure your data.

>   **Master It**   What encryption method does VMM use when transferring data across hosts in a trusted domain?
>
>   Are transfers of data from a trusted domain to a perimeter network host secure?
>
>   Under what circumstances is constrained delegation required for the Self-Service Portal?

Chapter 2

Planning a VMM Deployment

The key to a successful deployment of VMM is proper design. Understanding VMM's architecture, features, and infrastructure components set the stage for tackling the deployment design phase.

All of the content in this chapter applies to your datacenter regardless of its size or the intended scope of the deployment. VMM is designed for environments of all sizes and configurations. This chapter will cover all the important design decisions you will need to make as you put together a deployment plan.

In this chapter, you will learn to:

◆ Identify the different components in VMM

◆ Optimize VMM

◆ Understand important design considerations required for VMM

The Need for Virtualization

IBM first introduced virtualization into its mainframe platform in the 1970s. The mainframe used a combination of hardware components and software to create partitions, making the system act like multiple independent systems. Considering the cost of a mainframe, virtualization was an important technology, allowing its users to get more value for the investment. Over time, the dominant technology in the datacenter transitioned from large "Big Iron" systems to smaller, more affordable servers. The cheaper and smaller rack mount servers proliferated throughout the datacenter, encouraged by developers who used the server as the unit of isolation for their applications. When developers assumed full control of a server, interoperability between applications was not part of their design. It was more acceptable for poorly written applications with memory leaks, inefficient CPU usage, application instability, and OS crashes to find their way into the datacenter.

As companies deployed more servers into the datacenter, their overall usage remained low, since each server handled only one workload at any given time. For this reason, in the past five years more and more companies have found it difficult to accommodate an increasing number of servers being deployed to their datacenters. Efforts to consolidate applications on fewer servers tend to be very difficult due to interoperability issues. Realizing the inevitable shortage of power, cooling, and/or space, some companies adopted virtualization, which allowed them to partition one server into multiple virtual instances. Virtualization technology has caught the interest of CTOs and IT managers confronted with shortages in power, cooling, and rack space. By running one workload per server, most enterprises utilize an average of only

10 to 20 percent of the computational power in their datacenters. The gross underutilization of the datacenter coupled with exploding demand for more servers and tougher economic times makes virtualization very attractive.

Microsoft offers several products in the virtualization space that can help improve overall datacenter efficiency, reduce costs, and help IT personnel easily adapt to the new environment. Hyper-V, introduced with Windows Server 2008, is Microsoft's hypervisor-based solution for the enterprise. System Center offers Virtual Machine Manager as the focal point for any size virtualization environment. With VMM, you can manage Hyper-V, Virtual Server, and VMware ESX from the same UI and CLI interface.

Preplanning

Companies deploying virtualization or investigating its use do so with a specific project in mind. The project itself might vary in scope, but what the company hopes to accomplish falls into several buckets:

♦ Reducing power and cooling requirements in the datacenter by consolidating physical servers

♦ Avoiding the cost of deploying new servers into the datacenter

♦ Leveraging new capabilities around migration of workloads

Any specific project can fall into one or more of these buckets depending on the budget and time allotted.

Shifting from Physical to Virtual

One potential hurdle you must overcome with a virtualization project involves shifting from thinking about servers as physical entities in the datacenter to thinking about them as virtual instances on a hypervisor. With a virtual environment, you need to reconsider your architecture planning, infrastructure, design, deployment strategy, management toolsets, chargeback, and operational procedures. In some cases, an environment can be flexible enough to accommodate virtualization with little to no disruption in daily activities. In other cases, dedicated staff is required to handle planning, deployment, and management of virtualization.

From the perspective of an application, there is really no difference whether it executes in a virtual machine or on a physical server. Network connectivity is still required, records still need to be stored on physical media, users still need to be authenticated and authorized, and service-level agreements (SLAs) must still be honored. The impact of a virtualized environment is felt in the infrastructure serving up the applications.

In a standard application deployment, the amount of network bandwidth required and the number of ports per server depend on the workload. For most applications, a single-gigabit uplink provides sufficient bandwidth. With virtualization, any given server can host multiple applications concurrently. Each virtual machine might think it has a dedicated uplink, but in reality, the physical uplink is shared with other workloads.

The same is not true, however, for a shared environment. A shared virtual environment also has very different storage requirements compared to a stand-alone application. The same capacity and throughput that meet the need of a single workload will not meet the needs of a shared environment with multiple virtual machines executing concurrently. For both network and storage, you will need to plan accordingly to make sure bottlenecks are not introduced.

Security

Virtualization also introduces security concerns. Without a hypervisor, a physical machine can execute only one operating system instance at any given time. A malicious attempt to load another operating system would require interrupting the running instance, which is easily detectable by monitoring systems. However, with a hypervisor, since multiple operating systems can execute independently on the same machine, a rogue operating system instance can appear without interrupting the others. Typical infrastructure management tools will not easily pick up on the existence of a rogue operating system on the network. To help mitigate some of the risks, you will need to consider stringent requirements for accessing your network, such as disabling DHCP on server subnets, introducing Internet Protocol Security (IPsec), or implementing systems to properly quarantine unauthenticated systems.

Server Sprawl

Creating a virtual machine is fairly simple. With a few scripts, an administrator can create many virtual machines without requiring new hardware in the datacenter. Since virtualization makes it so easy to instantiate new operating systems in your environment, you will need to have the proper management toolsets to manage the influx of new systems in the environment. This includes controlling how virtual machines are created, choosing which operating systems get deployed, and ensuring that agents and applications that allow proper management are installed in the operating system.

Shared Environments

Virtual machine concurrency also introduces new challenges in resource sharing. Application developers, alongside IT groups, need to work together to define acceptable thresholds of a "healthy" application. Since multiple virtual machines contend for the same physical resources, it is important to deploy throughout the environment monitoring agents that understand how the applications should be performing, compare that to their actual performance, and raise alerts when performance drops below the threshold.

This book covers in detail the management of a virtual machine environment using System Center Virtual Machine Manager. The guidance provided in this book takes into account that each virtualization deployment will vary in scope, size, and complexity, depending on how you plan to use the technology.

Virtualization Types

Before we get ahead of ourselves, we need to dig deeper into the various types of virtualization in use today. This is fully explored in Table 2.1.

Each virtualization type listed in Table 2.1 addresses specific user scenarios and use cases that do not necessarily overlap. At each level, you are guaranteed a different level of isolation between operating systems, users, and processes. The level of isolation is important when considering failures and your tolerance for risk. On the one extreme, hardware virtualization multiplexes physical hardware, requiring a new operating system instance for every virtual machine. This is the coarsest granularity of virtualization and offers the highest level of isolation. Any virtual machine on the physical hardware can fail without affecting others. At the other extreme, presentation virtualization leverages the operating system's ability to execute multiple applications concurrently.

TABLE 2.1:   Types of virtualization

TYPE	DESCRIPTION	PROS/CONS	EXAMPLES
Hardware	One physical machine can run multiple independent machines (virtual machines) in its memory space. Each virtual machine can run a different operating system.	**Pros:** Full operating system isolation, including memory space. This is great for applications that do not interoperate well with other applications due to DLL conflicts, for example. **Cons:** Each virtual machine requires a full instantiation of the operating system, consuming more resources, which decreases overall density.	Citrix XenServer Microsoft Hyper-V VMware ESX
Operating system	An operating system on a machine can act like multiple independent instances of the same operating system.	**Pros:** Each virtual operating system acts like an independent instance but in fact shares the same binaries, reducing CPU and memory overhead on increasing density. **Cons:** To apply a patch to the operating system, you must shut down all virtual instances.	Virtuozzo, Sun
Application	Applications are delivered to a running operating system. The application state is decoupled from the operating system state.	**Pros:** The application executes in a sandboxed environment with its own virtual Registry and file system. **Cons:**- To reboot the operating system, you must interrupt all running applications.	Microsoft Application Virtualization (App-V) VMware Thinstall
Presentation	Decouples the execution of an application and the graphic user interface presented to the user. The application can execute in a remote location from which the application user interface is rendered for the user.	**Pros:** The application executes in a remote location, potentially hundreds of miles from where the user resides. Applications share the same operating system instance, allowing for very dense environments. **Cons:**- To reboot the operating system, you must interrupt all running applications.	Microsoft Remote Desktop Services Citrix

This is the most granular level of virtualization considering that only one operating system is required to execute multiple applications and servicing requests from multiple users. For that same reason, however, this virtualization type offers the least amount of isolation. If the operating system fails, all applications stop servicing user requests. However, they all share two common themes: resource sharing and failure domain isolation.

Resource sharing   Virtualization requires that users think of their server resources in the context of other resources running on the same physical machine. Here are the four virtualization types and how each shares resources.

Machine virtualization   Allows multiple virtual machines to run on a single physical machine.

Operating system virtualization   Makes one instance of an operating system act like many individual instances.

Application virtualization   Allows multiple versions of the same application to exist on the same box without conflict.

Presentation virtualization   Allows users to have a dedicated "virtual" desktop with applications executing from a single OS instance.

Failure domain isolation   End users working in a virtualized environment seldom know that they are sharing resources. However, when something fails in a system — a process, operating system, or physical VMM server — the impact is felt by many. With machine virtualization, any given virtual machine can fail (e.g., guest OS boot failure) without affecting other running virtual machines. However, if a processor or memory chip fails in the server, there is a good chance the physical server will fail, affecting all virtual machines. Users with a virtual desktop might cause a particular process to fail due to some error or bug. Typically the user can restart the application and continue working, but if the failed application causes the operating system to fail, then all users with virtual desktops on that server will be affected.

Differentiating between virtualization types in terms of resource sharing and failure domain isolation is an important first step to understanding and scoping your virtualization project. This book only covers management of machine virtualization, but many of the concepts discussed in this chapter will come up when you're deploying other forms of virtualization: scalability, reliability, availability, performance bottlenecks, and storage/network considerations.

Machine virtualization initially gained popularity in test and development environments. Resource sharing at the machine level has a couple of key benefits. It allows users with too few physical machines to host many virtual machines on the same hardware, enabling more testing and concurrent application development. Users with large test and development environments running on old hardware also benefit from resource sharing by using virtualization to consolidate multiple servers onto a few large servers. In both cases, users want to reduce datacenter charges by reducing the physical server footprint in the rack and power consumption.

Test and development environments do not receive as much funding as production environments and so the physical hardware handed down varies widely in configuration. Hardware "homogeneity" is another advantage of using virtualization in test and development. Since the hypervisor presents virtual hardware to the guest operating system, there was no need to worry about incompatibility or stability problems with drivers or hardware-vendor-specific applications and agents. If the virtual machine is migrated, the underlying hardware does not change. The same benefit applies to preproduction and production environments. With the virtualization of test, development, preproduction, and production, applications now live their life cycle within a virtual environment.

Deploying a new technology into production, however, requires a thorough understanding of the technology and a solid deployment plan. Unlike test and development, production is less tolerant of instability. The operating system and the application running in the virtual machine must be properly monitored and backed up. The network and storage infrastructure most provide sufficient performance to meet the workload demand. The entire system must not have any single points of failure. Confidence in the technology is a key component to success, but this builds over time and is dependent on your deployment success rate. A bad deployment plan can lead to inefficiencies and irrecoverable failures, leaving behind a bad impression of the technology.

To get the most out of your deployment of VMM, you will need to consider the design of the management layer and the underlying platform, the hypervisor (i.e., ESX, Hyper-V, or Virtual Server). We will therefore concentrate on these in the remainder of this chapter.

Designing a VMM Infrastructure

VMM architecture breaks down into three categories: the VMM server, the VMM infrastructure, and the VMM client. Each category accounts for multiple components that should be taken into account as part of your VMM deployment plan. Although this section will not cover the actual installation of the components, it will provide guidance for deployment.

VMM server   This is the core engine that handles all jobs, controls object permissions, orchestrates Operations Manager bidirectional event flow, abstracts multiple hypervisor APIs, and hosts user connects through Administrator Console or Self-Service Web Portal.

VMM infrastructure   Includes the VMM datastore on a SQL server, library server(s), and Operations Manager SDK Connector

VMM client   Includes Self-Service Web Portal, Administrator Console, PowerShell CLI

Designing the VMM Server

The VMM server is the core of your VMM design. All the heavy lifting involved within creating, deploying, migrating, storing, and deleting virtual machines across the three supported hypervisors is orchestrated by the VMM server. This includes all user action initiated from the Administration Console, Self-Service Portal, or PowerShell CLI. The VMM server performs several key functions, which are described in Table 2.2. If the server cannot perform these functions optimally, the overall management of your virtualized environment will be affected. Keep this in mind when designing the environment into which you will deploy the VMM server. Try to avoid performance bottlenecks caused by slow storage, insufficient RAM, or underpowered CPU. In addition, ensure the maximum uptime for the physical machine running the VMM server by providing two power supplies, two network connections, and two Fibre Channel connections to storage.

The sections following Table 2.2 will cover how to scale VMM, decide on a host group structure, and design a delegation model that fits the needs of your organization. These topics will help prepare for the VMM design discussion focused on optimizing your deployment.

TABLE 2.2:   VMM server functions

TYPE	DESCRIPTION
Permissions store	VMM implements its own role-based entitlements engine for all users who use the UI and CLI. The profiles are offered out of the box: Administrator, Delegated Administrator, and Self-Service User. Based on the profile associated with a user, the UI and CLI will filter certain objects and views and restrict specific actions.
Job execution engine	Jobs created in the workflow engine are executed by the job engine. The engine controls the flow and status of the job, audits changes, and controls logic for restarting and canceling jobs.
Creation, deployment, and management of virtualization objects	Users interact with VMM objects in the UI and CLI: hosts, virtual machines, templates, etc. VMM server uses the workflow and job execution engine to orchestrate the creation, deployment, and management of these objects throughout their life cycle.
Workflow engine	All tasks in VMM have a corresponding Windows Communication Foundation (WCF) workflow that is executed by the workflow engine in VMM. The workflows are not public to the user.
Job audit logging	All changes to VMM initiated by the system or by a user are audited in a job trail retrievable using the Get-Job cmdlet.
Integration point with Operations Manager	Using System Center Operations Manager's Connection SDK, VMM has a bidirectional connector from which to get events and kick off tasks in Operations Manager. This integration is referred to a performance and resource optimization.

SCALING VMM

Scaling VMM requires understanding how the different components that interact with it can affect overall performance. External components in particular introduce additional complexity into the system. Network and storage bottlenecks also impact scale. Let's now discuss the requirements needed to scale VMM.

Hosts and Virtual Machines

The maximum supported hosts and virtual machines that each VMM server instance can manage is 400 hosts and 8,000 virtual machines. VMM's tested scale maximum is much greater than VMware vCenter 2.5 scale limit of 200 hosts and 2,000 virtual machines. There is no hard limit imposed, so you can scale beyond this guideline, but that's not recommended because the configuration has never been tested by the VMM product team. The maximum supported host count is an aggregate across all three hypervisors: Microsoft Hyper-V, Virtual Server, and VMware ESX. You can have any mix of these three as long as you do not exceed the supported maximum.

Using VMware vCenter

An important fact to keep in mind is that management of VMware ESX is enabled through VMware's vCenter server management product. VMM integrates with vCenter's web service APIs to manage ESX hosts and virtual machines. VMM calls VMware's APIs remotely from the VMM server. By calling the APIs remotely, VMM avoids installing an agent on any of the VMware ESX hosts or the VMware vCenter server, leaving no footprint on the vCenter server itself. Each host managed by vCenter counts as a host managed by VMM and the same applies for virtual machines. For example, you have one Virtual Center instance with 300 hosts and 5,000 virtual machines. Managing this virtual environment through VMM means you can manage only an additional 100 hosts and 3,000 virtual machines before reaching the supported maximum.

MULTIPLE vCENTER INSTANCES PER VMM SERVER

VMM does support managing up to two Virtual Center instances at the same time with one VMM server instance. There is no restriction on managing more than two, but that configuration is not supported and not recommended because the configuration has never been tested by the VMM product team. The same limit applies with regard to host and virtual machine maximums when connected to two Virtual Center instances.

Installing VMM on Hardware

The hardware on which you install VMM is a big factor in how well the engine will scale. These are the largest load contributors in VMM:

♦ Enabling PRO functionality using Operations Manager SDK Connector

♦ Calculating effective rights

♦ Tracking status on jobs

If you choose to cohost specific components on the same server (e.g., VMM server and database), please keep in mind that each has its own performance characteristics and resource requirements. A server capable of handling either the VMM server or the SQL store may not be sufficient to handle both, especially in large-scale environments.

Storage and Network Requirements

You should consider building performance and redundancy into your storage and networking layer. For storage, you need to account for storage space requirements for the OS and VMM server software. In addition, the database will require storage as well. To achieve maximum storage performance, you should install the OS on a separate disk from the VMM server software. The database will also need to reside on its own set of disks. Follow Microsoft SQL best practice guidelines with regard to proper isolation of data and log volumes. Make sure to use Redundant Array of Independent Disks 1 (RAID-1) for your OS and software volume and RAID-5 or RAID-1+0 for the database volumes. Using a SAN will help you achieve the highest performance and availability for your database.

Protecting against network failures is possible using NIC teaming on the VMM server machine to group multiple network adapter ports for a connection to a single physical segment (http://support.microsoft.com/kb/254101). NIC teaming is supported by the manufacturer of the network adapters in the machine. Please consult the hardware documentation for more information and a location to download the required drivers.

Refreshers

VMM uses refreshers to process all host and virtual machine configuration and performance updates. Refreshers run on each virtual machine host and library server, and remotely against vCenter server, collecting updates to configuration and state. Refreshers that run locally on hosts send data back to the VMM server for processing. With a few servers and under a hundred virtual machines, the network bandwidth required at the VMM server is not high; a 100 Mbs link should suffice. If you plan to scale the environment up to hundreds of hosts and thousands of virtual machines, additional network bandwidth will be required. Refer to Table 2.3 for aggregate bandwidth averages. For a full listing of VMM refreshers and associated refresh intervals, refer to Chapter 1, "Introduction to System Center Virtual Machine Manager."

TABLE 2.3: Aggregate bandwidth

HOSTS	CONSOLIDATION RATIO (VMs PER HOST)	TOTAL VMs MANAGED	AVG. BANDWIDTH PER HOST (KBPS)	AGGREGATE BANDWIDTH (KBPS)
5	1	5	0.05	0.25
5	5	25	0.15	0.75
5	10	50	0.23	1.15
5	20	100	0.45	2.25
25	1	25	0.05	1.25
25	5	125	0.15	3.75
25	10	250	0.23	5.75
25	20	500	0.45	11.25
150	1	150	0.05	7.50
150	5	750	0.15	22.50
150	10	1,500	0.23	34.50
150	20	3,000	0.45	67.50
400	1	400	0.05	20.00
400	5	2,000	0.15	60.00
400	10	4,000	0.23	92.00
400	20	8,000	0.45	180.00

If you plan to deploy System Center Operations Manager (OpsMgr) at some point in the future, or if you already have an Operations Manager environment setup, then VMM's

Performance and Resource Optimization (PRO) feature will be of interest. PRO is a powerful and valuable feature that is the result of integration between OpsMgr and VMM. PRO leverages OpsMgr's Management Pack Framework to deliver PRO Packs that tie specific OpsMgr alerts to actionable remediation actions in VMM. To achieve this level of integration, VMM uses a dedicated bidirectional communication channel to OpsMgr to help pass information between the systems. For more information on OpsMgr and PRO, refer to Chapter 1.

PRO will require additional CPU and memory resources on the VMM Server to process alert and remediation information. This includes additional CPU, memory, and disk I/O load on the VMM database. How much load really depends on the number of hosts and virtual machines monitored by OpsMgr, including the number of applications monitored within each virtual machine. At a minimum, you should expect 2 to 3 percent CPU and 50 MB RAM overhead for every 500 virtual machine hosts that VMM manages and OpsMgr monitors. If the virtual machines on each host are monitored, then overhead will increase on the VMM server and database.

HOST GROUP STRUCTURE

VMM uses host groups to organize virtual machine hosts into logical hierarchical containers. Host groups can contain nested host groups, virtual machine hosts, or virtual machine host clusters. By default, VMM creates the first immutable host group, All Hosts. There is no limit on how many nested host groups you can create under All Hosts. Deeply nested host groups have no negative performance impact on VMM server. Aside from containing virtual machine hosts, host groups can be used for delegating administration, calculating star rating for virtual machine hosts, defaulting host reserves, and enabling PRO.

Delegation Delegation is allowed to a specific host group hierarchy for a specific user role (explained later in this chapter). Users in this user role will have access only to hosts and host clusters under the host group you specify.

Intelligent placement Placement details for a virtual machine workload can be calculated for an individual host or a set of hosts in a host group.

Host-level reserves The host group object stores the default settings for reserved resources per host in the host group.

PRO Monitoring can be enabled or disabled per host group.

The most important design decision for host groups is which delegation model you plan to use. You can create host groups based on regional or business unit requirements, for example. Each host group may have different support personnel managing the environment contained within, and your delegation model will have to reflect that.

Within the top host groups, you can further divide the environment and further delegate authority. For example, as shown in Figure 2.1, you may have top-level host groups for your major datacenters in North America and the Europe Union (NA and EU, respectively). Within each region you can have several business units, and then within each business unit, you can have different environments such as production and development.

If your environment does not require separation of authority at the host group level, then host groups simply serve as an organization container for your hosts and host clusters.

Managing a VMware environment through VMM also affects your host group design. VMware Virtual Center uses datacenters and folders to manage hosts and clusters. VMM imports VMware's tree structure and merges it with the existing host group structure. As part of the import, VMM maps datacenters and folders to host groups as indicated in Table 2.4. Figure 2.2 is an example of this mapping.

FIGURE 2.1
Nested host groups

TABLE 2.4:   VMware-to-VMM host group mapping

VMWARE	VMM
Hosts & Clusters	All Hosts
Datacenter	Host Group
Folder	Host Group

FIGURE 2.2
VMware-to-VMM
host group mapping

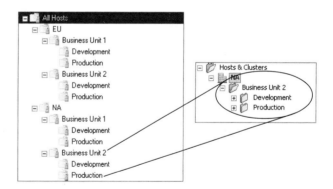

DELEGATION MODEL

VMM uses role-based administration for its delegation model. As Figure 2.3 illustrates, a role is composed of users, permitted actions, and a scope containing host groups and libraries.

VMM ships with three default profiles: Administrator, Delegated Administrator, and Self-Service User, as shown in Figure 2.4.

Administrator   By default, VMM creates the Administrator role and adds the account that installed the VMM server as the first user in the role. You will need to log in as that account and start the VMM Administrator Console to add other users. At this point you should refer to your host group design and decide on how users will administer their virtual environments. In some cases, the Administrator role is more than enough to manage your environment.

FIGURE 2.3
User roles

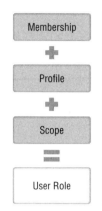

Membership:
- Determines which users are part of a particular user role
- Members may be individual user or groups
- Members may be in multiple user roles including user roles based on different profiles

Profile:
- Determines which actions are permitted
- Determines which user interface is accessible
- Determines how the scope is defined

Scope:
- Determines which objects a user may take actions on

FIGURE 2.4
Built-in profiles

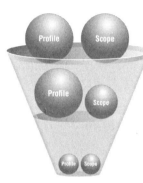

Administrators
- Full access to all actions
- Full access to all objects
- Can use the Admin console or PowerShell interface

Delegated Administrators
- Full access to most actions on hosts and VMs
- Scope can be limited by host groups and library servers
- Can use the Admin console or PowerShell interface

Self-Service Users
- Limited access to a subset of actions on VMs
- Scope can be limited by host groups and library share
- Can use the Self-Service Portal or PowerShell interface

Delegated Administrator   In other cases, each region or business unit may have its own dedicated IT staff that requires complete administrative autonomy over the objects in the host group. In this case, you would create a new user role for delegated administrators.

Self-Service User   If your users simply need to create, store, and deploy virtual machines and do not require access to the Administrator Console, then you can create a Self-Service User role. The Self-Service User profile does not guarantee administrative isolation. The user can see only virtual machines and library shares from the Self-Service Portal. The user is not aware of the underlying host group structure, hosts, or host clusters where virtual machines are running.

ADMINISTRATIVE ISOLATION VS. AUTONOMY

Role-based administration in VMM guarantees that an administrator has complete control over a portion of the environment based on the host group structure. The administrator is not guaranteed exclusive control over that environment; there is always an administrator with more privileges.

Administrative autonomy means that you, as the administrator of VMM, can grant another user access to a particular host group (scope) by adding her or him to the Delegated Administrator user role. This level of access guarantees that the Delegated Administrator can perform almost all actions a full administrator can perform, except for adding users to the Administrator user role and changing some VMM global settings within the assigned scope.

> Administrative autonomy does not mean that a Delegated Administrator has exclusive control over the scope.
>
> **Administrative isolation**, on the other hand, requires that a Delegated Administrator have exclusive control over a host group (scope). This model is not supported by VMM. Users in the Administrator user role always have ultimate control.

Designing VMM Infrastructure

The VMM server orchestrates and tracks virtual machine tasks; the infrastructure components the server relies on to perform its job include the database server, library server, and Operations Manager SDK Connector. Without the database, the server component would have no local location to get or store data. Since the database needs to handle both read and write requests, it is important to properly design this component, allowing it to scale over time. The library server serves as a repository for files not stored in the database. As a virtualized environment grows, there will be additional pressure on the library server to keep up with the I/O demand. The SDK Connector is necessary for enabling the PRO-based monitoring and alerting. With a large enough environment, PRO will impact the performance of the server and database.

DATABASE SERVER

Each install of the VMM server is autonomous and requires a dedicated Microsoft SQL database hosted on SQL Express or SQL Server 2005/2008. It is important to note that the VMM server is not cluster-aware. This means you cannot use Microsoft Clustering Service (MSCS) to make the VMM server highly available. In your design, you will need to mitigate this single point of failure by providing a standby machine with the VMM server software installed.

CREATING A STANDBY VMM SERVER

Since VMM is not cluster-aware, there is no way of making the VMM server highly available. In the event that the machine hosting VMM server fails, no tasks can be executed in the environment managed by VMM. To help mitigate this, you can take additional steps to provide a quick recovery of the VMM server:

1. Avoid cohosting the VMM server and the database server on the same machine.

2. Dedicate a separate machine in your datacenter to serve as the cold standby VMM server. This cold standby requires that you manually install VMM server software and keep it updated with the latest fixes.

3. If you want to avoid maintaining the operating system and software on a cold standby server, you can perform a bare-metal recovery of the primary VMM server to the standby. If the VMM server boots from SAN, in the event of a failure, you can reassign the LUN from the primary server to the standby host.

If the VMM Server fails on one machine, you can modify the Registry of the standby machine to point to the database and start the VMM server. Any jobs that were in-flight will be marked as failed. Please note that only some jobs can be restarted. For complete details on how to perform manual failover of the VMM server, please refer to Chapter 10, "Planning for Backup and Recovery."

You can help mitigate the single point of failure by clustering the database. The VMM server relies on Microsoft SQL Express or Server 2005/2008 as the backend database server. By design, SQL Express is not cluster-aware. Instead, you can use SQL Server 2005/2008 and MSCS to achieve high availability at the database level. Please refer to Microsoft documentation on how to set up SQL Server Failover clustering. For SQL Server 2005, see http://msdn.microsoft.com/en-us/library/ms189134.aspx.

Since the VMM server assumes complete ownership of the database, concurrent read/write operations from multiple servers is not supported. You will need to keep this in mind as you plan out your scalability goals.

LIBRARY SERVER

VMM stores virtual disk files (VHD, VMDK), virtual floppy files (VFD), ISO files, answer files (INF, XML), and PowerShell scripts (PS1) in its library. The library server is also used as a deployment point for creating and storing virtual machines and templates. Hardware and OS profiles appear under a library server but have no on-disk representation because they are stored in the database. Templates contain hardware and OS properties stored in the database with pointers to files (virtual disks, ISOs, and so on) stored on the local filesystem of the library server. A default install of VMM will install the library server on the same machine running the VMM server. The default share path is C:\Program Files\Microsoft System Center Virtual Machine Manager\VMMLibrary.

You can add additional machines as library servers to VMM. VMM supports the library server on machines with or without the hypervisor role enabled. If you need to create virtual machines with new blank virtual disks (i.e., not using an existing virtual disk stored in the library) directly to the library, the library server will need to be installed on a machine with the hypervisor installed.

Depending on the size of your environment, you may need only one machine running the library server. For larger deployments, additional instances of the library server can be installed in the same datacenter as the VMM server or in a different geographical location. VMM does not offer any native replication capabilities to populate files from one library server to another. You will need to do this manually using Robocopy or DFSN/DFSR.

REPLICATING LIBRARY FILES

DFS Replication (DFSR) and DFS Namespaces (DFSN) are supported technologies, but there are some issues that you need to be aware of.

If you decide to use DFSR to replicate files to multiple library servers, here are some of the facts about how VMM behaves with respect to DFS:

◆ Actions that require browsing a DFS path are not supported because VMM is not DFS-aware.

◆ From VMM's perspective, every share that it manages is considered a separate location, and so even if a file that appears in multiple shares is the same across all of them, VMM recognizes each file as a unique file. . VMM assigns a unique GUID to the file and stores that information.

- ◆ VMM users can use DFSR with the following caveats:

  - ◆ You will need to create and manage a virtual machine template on each library share where you want to deploy new virtual machines. The template must reference a VHD file on the local library share as well.

  - ◆ If file or folders change within a DFSR share, the file paths on that share are updated in VMM. However, the library shares where the files get replicated too show up as new files in VMM. All the original objects are marked as missing by the Library Refresher. You will have to manually remove the missing objects from VMM library shares.

The library server is nothing more than a file server, and so the design should incorporate best practice guidelines for file servers to achieve maximum performance and availability. For redundancy, store the virtual disk and ISO files on a volume using RAID-5 or RAID-1+0. For performance, assign as many physical disks to the RAID group as possible to avoid potential I/O bottlenecks when deploying or storing virtual machines. For availability, use an MSCS clustered file share.

OPERATIONS MANAGER SDK CONNECTOR

VMM's Performance and Resource Optimization (PRO) feature leverages Operation Manager's SDK framework to process requests for data and access specific features in Operations Manager relevant to VMM.

Operations Manager uses the VMM Management Pack to understand objects under management — hosts, virtual machines, host groups. Using extended management packs called PRO Packs, monitors are set up to look for specific conditions in a virtual machine or host. If a threshold is triggered, an alert is generated within Operations Manager and PRO will forward that alert to VMM along with contextual knowledge (e.g., a Hyper-V host is maxed out on CPU resources) about the alert and recommended actions (e.g., migrate virtual machines off host). In VMM, the administrator can implement the recommended action or dismiss it. VMM provides the connector to enable this bidirectional communication channel provided by the Operations Manager SDK Connector framework.

PRO places an additional resource load on the VMM server and database (in addition to your Operations Manager environment). The load increases as your environment scales up and depending on how much data each PRO Pack generates.

Designing VMM Clients

The VMM server and infrastructure components make up the backend systems that perform all the heavy lifting as part of managing your virtual environment. The VMM clients are the user-facing interfaces into that environment. The Administrator Console offers the full management experience. The Self-Service Portal offers a subset of actions focused on simple VM creation. The PowerShell CLI is the advanced scripting interface useful for automation.

ADMINISTRATOR CONSOLE

VMM's Administrator Console component offers the complete VMM user experience with full access to the managed virtual environment. The console allows users to perform all actions on all managed objects. You have the option to install the console on any machine, including the machine hosting the VMM server.

The console can handle up to 10 users executing actions concurrently. There is no restriction on allowing more than 10 users, but that configuration is not supported and not recommended because it has never been tested by the VMM product team. You can choose to deploy the console to more than one machine, but keep in mind that the performance bottleneck is actually the VMM server. Deploying additional consoles into your environment will increase the load on the VMM server.

Deploying multiple console components does have its advantages. With more than one console component in the environment, administrators can access the environment from their office machine or business laptop. You can choose to deploy the console to key administrators so they do not have to share the same console session, but since the VMM server is still centralized, network latencies might introduce unwanted delays in the user experience.

DESIGNING THE SELF-SERVICE PORTAL

VMM's Self-Service Portal is web based and offers a subset of functionality compared to the Administrator Console. Users that have access to this portal can perform very specific actions on a subset of virtual machines and templates defined in the user role and by individual virtual machine ownership. You have the option to install the web portal on any machine with IIS installed, including the machine hosting the VMM server.

The Self-Service Portal can handle up to 50 users executing actions concurrently. There is no restriction on allowing more than 50 users, but that configuration is not supported and not recommended because it has never been tested by the VMM product team. You can choose to deploy the portal to more than one web server, but keep in mind that the performance bottleneck is actually the VMM server. Deploying additional portals into your environment will not help distribute the load on the VMM server. Deploying multiple portals does have its advantages, however. With more than one portal in the environment, you have high availability and can distribute the load across multiple IIS instances hosting the portal. You can choose to deploy portals in key remote locations to improve responsiveness, but since the VMM server is still centralized, network latencies might introduce unwanted delays in the user experience. If you need to provide high availability for the Self-Service Portal, you can deploy several instances and use Microsoft Network Load Balancing (NLB) to direct traffic in the event of a machine failure.

POWERSHELL CLI

The VMM Administrator Console and Self-Service Portal build on the PowerShell interface developed for VMM. VMM ships with 160 cmdlets, so any action you take in the UI can be accomplished through the CLI. In fact, since you can use loops and conditional statements in PowerShell, you have more control over the environment. You can also access VMM's PowerShell cmdlets through managed code using runspaces.

WHAT IS A RUNSPACE

A *runspace* provides an environment in which to execute commands. Command execution is driven by the user through the command line. The user executing commands is aware of the session but not the runspace executing the commands. A hosting application can also create a runspace to invoke commands programmatically.

A single user executing commands in a PowerShell window should have no impact on the performance of the VMM engine. However, the types of actions executed might affect other components of VMM. One example of this is if the user kicks off more than 10 to hundreds of asynchronous jobs to create new virtual machines using the same VHD from the same library server to the same Hyper-V host. In this example, you can imagine the storage and network I/O impact on the library host and Hyper-V host. VMM will do a good job of managing all the jobs, but there is a good chance some or all may not complete due to limited resources on the Hyper-V host and potential time-outs of specific tasks waiting for completion.

Deployment Models

So far, we have covered the main components of VMM that will influence your deployment plan. With this information in hand, let's jump into understanding three very common deployment models: single datacenter, multiple datacenter, and branch office. The following sections also cover common optimizations to your VMM environment that can help improve performance.

Independent of the deployment model you choose, VMM has some fixed requirements:

◆ The VMM server only installs on Windows Server 2008 64-bit and must be joined to an Active Directory domain.

◆ All hosts under management must be in a trusted forest or authenticated using a certificate (DMZ hosts).

◆ All users of VMM must be valid users in Active Directory.

◆ VMM uses Background Intelligence Transfer Service (BITS) to transfer files to and from the library and Hyper-V hosts, Secure FTP for ESX 3.0 and 3.5, and HTTPS for ESXi 3.5.

Common Optimizations

In addition to the preceding requirements, you will need to consider how to best optimize VMM for your deployment. The best way to optimize VMM is to remove any potential bottlenecks in the network, storage, or server. VMM main components tend to have very predictable bottlenecks, depending on the configuration you choose to deploy. For example, as you scale, the database will be one component that needs to scale well (based on Microsoft SQL guidelines) to keep up with demand as new hosts, virtual machines, and users access VMM. Before discussing typical deployment models, first we will take a look at optimizations that will help you scale VMM as your environment grows. Chapter 3, "Installation and Configuration," covers the actual installation and configuration of the various VMM components.

ALL IN ONE

A simple deployment of VMM places the VMM server, library server, Self-Service Portal, and database on the same machine. This deployment is typical for smaller production environments or test and development. Figure 2.5 illustrates the deployment. VMM is fully supported in this configuration.

The advantage of deploying all VMM components on one server is the reduced complexity. If you need to keep complexity to a minimum in your environment, the all-in-one approach may be appropriate. There are a few benefits to doing this. Troubleshooting is very simple with no firewalls or network to account for. Response time between the database and the VMM engine is minimal. Users working on the Administrator Console or Self-Service Portal directly off the server will see fast load times.

The all-in-one approach also has some disadvantages, however. Increasing the number of hosts and virtual machines will impact overall system performance in this configuration. This is especially true if you plan to deploy large virtual disks from the library. Increasing the number of concurrent copies/migrations of virtual disks to and from the library will impact disk and network performance, which in turn impacts VMM's database and engine performance. In the event of a hardware failure, your entire VMM environment is affected and will not be available for your users until the server is restored.

FIGURE 2.5
All in one

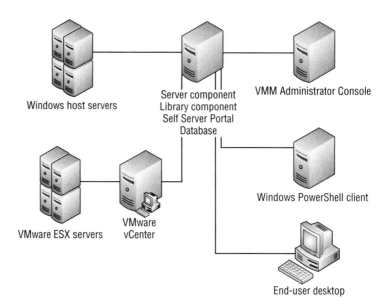

To enable PRO in your VMM environment, you will need System Center Operations Manager. You can install Operations Manager along with VMM. Note that you will see some performance degradation as you start to scale your environment with PRO enabled. In addition, you may choose to manage an existing VMware virtual environment using VMM. Doing so may introduce some performance degradation if the vCenter server is under load. In this case, tasks simply take longer to execute through vCenter. Keep in mind potential issues with performance, network port conflicts, and database I/O contention, especially if you plan on deploying VMware vCenter and System Center Operations Manager on the same host as VMM. If your environment has limited server resources, you can choose to deploy all VMM components into a virtual machine running on Hyper-V. This approach is great for testing VMM, but in production you could see limitations in scale. If the virtual machine is clustered using Windows Server 2008 failover clustering, you get high availability. Keep in mind that if you use Quick Migration to move the virtual machine hosting VMM from one host to another, the in-flight jobs will be interrupted and some may not complete.

DATABASE OPTIMIZED

As you add more virtual machine hosts and virtual machines to your environment, VMM will need to handle more jobs (creation, migration, deletion tasks, etc.). With more objects to manage, performance reporting and security data will need to be processed at larger scales in the VMM database. Finally, with larger environments, multiple users will need to access the environment. The first bottleneck you will encounter is database throughput. As you scale VMM, the all-in-one approach will simply not give the database the CPU, memory, and disk resources necessary to process all the information in VMM. To avoid this bottleneck as you scale the environment, consider separating out the database and hosting it on a dedicated Microsoft SQL Server machine. If you plan to use PRO, you should highly consider deploying a dedicated SQL server.

With the database server installed on its own machine, VMM will perform better because it is not contending for resources. In addition, as you scale your environment up, VMM has sufficient headroom to scale as well.

With the database server separate from VMM, you can choose to deploy a SQL cluster for high availability. Figure 2.6 illustrates the deployment. As you scale VMM and depend on the services provided, clustering will help reduce unplanned downtime.

FIGURE 2.6
Database optimized

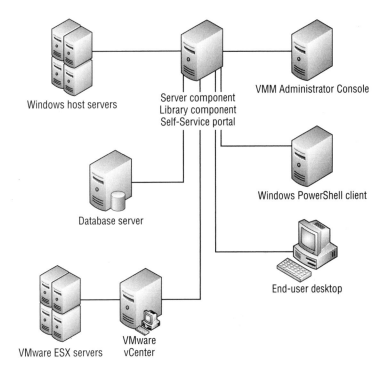

Windows host servers

Server component
Library component
Self-Service portal

VMM Administrator Console

Database server

Windows PowerShell client

End-user desktop

VMware ESX servers

VMware vCenter

I/O OPTIMIZED

As you scale your environment, more virtual machine hosts will increase the number of virtual machines deployed. With more deployments in your environment, there is more pressure on the library server to perform optimally. You and your administrators will depend on the library more and more to help streamline the deployment of virtual machines using templates. You may need to account for supporting 32-bit and 64-bit operating systems, all supported flavors of Windows client and server, and potentially non-Windows operating systems like Linux and Sun x86. If you choose to manage more than one hypervisor, then you can potentially double or even triple the number of templates in the library. Also, you will need to account for storing ISO.

As your environment grows in host and virtual machine count, the library may actually be a bottleneck as the network and disk I/O workload increases, keeping up with the demand for virtual disks, virtual machines, and templates. In the all-in-one model, increased utilization of the library server would obviously affect the database server and VMM server. In the database-optimized model, you removed the database, which is one cause of I/O contention. The next obvious optimization is to remove the library server.

VMM uses the library server like a file server for ISOs and virtual disks, so you can easily separate the library server from VMM onto a dedicated server or existing Windows file server. The library server will impose a heavy I/O burden as the number of concurrent read/write operations increases, so make sure to size the file server accordingly. Figure 2.7 illustrates the deployment.

FIGURE 2.7
I/O optimized

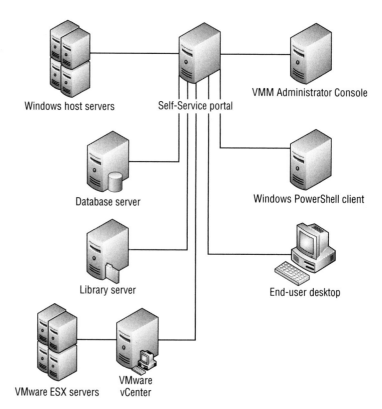

Windows host servers

Self-Service portal

VMM Administrator Console

Database server

Windows PowerShell client

Library server

End-user desktop

VMware ESX servers

VMware vCenter

FULLY OPTIMIZED

Separating the VMM server, database server, and library server will take you a long way to reducing potential bottlenecks in your environment. The few remaining VMM components that impose a small but measurable load include the Administrator Console, Self-Service Portal, and PowerShell CLI. These three components do not run as services and so consume resources only when the user is using them interactively. Each interface requires memory and CPU resources to process user-initiated tasks. The Administrator Console and Self-Service Portal require bulk data from the database to display objects in the UI. When data is pulled in from the database, each request requires disk I/O resources and network bandwidth to transfer it. Over fast network connections, this is not an issue, but over slow WAN links, it can make the UI feel "slow."

If possible, you should avoid executing the Administrator Console, Self-Service Portal, and/or PowerShell CLI on the same machine running the VMM server to avoid contending for resources. The VMM server should have access to as much of the resources available on the machine as possible. For this reason, all of these interfaces can be installed and executed on separate machines. Figure 2.8 illustrates the deployment.

FIGURE 2.8
Fully Optimized

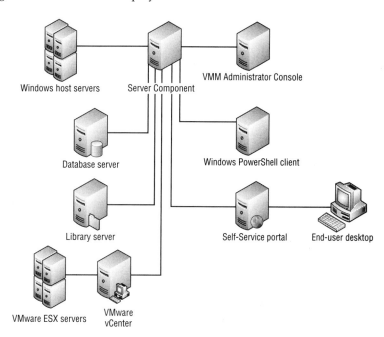

TUNING REFRESHERS

VMM relies on agent technology to get information from the environment and perform actions. The bulk of data retrieved from hosts and library servers comes from refreshers. A *refresher* is a block of code that runs periodically to collect specific information and send it to the VMM server for processing. If the incoming data from a refresher is different from what VMM has stored in the database, then the values are updated. This way, if you decide to increase the memory of a particular VM directly using Hyper-V's MMC console or VMware Virtual Center, VMM will pick up that new value and reflect it in the database.

For the purposes of optimizing VMM, Table 2.5 lists eight important refreshers you should be aware of.

With an increased number of hosts and virtual machines, the amount of data that VMM needs to process grows significantly. In very large-scale environments, the VMM may encounter some delays in processing incoming refresher information and executing jobs concurrently. Please contact product support before tuning the refreshers. Reducing the refresher frequency can reduce the load on the VMM server, but the disadvantage is that changes made to your virtualized infrastructure outside of VMM are not updated as frequently. With that said, when you click a virtual machine or host in the VMM Administrator Console, the refresher immediately runs, so you don't risk seeing stale information directly in the console in either case. Optimizing VMM for peak performance will allow it to scale as your environment grows. There is no cookie-cutter approach to some of these optimizations, however. Each environment is different and will need to be tuned accordingly. With this in mind, we can discuss the most common deployment models for VMM.

TABLE 2.5:   VMM refreshers

REFRESHER	PURPOSE	FREQUENCY
(Light) virtual machine	Retrieves specific virtual machine configuration information that tends to change very often	120 seconds
(Heavy) virtual machine	Retrieves all virtual machine configuration information	10 seconds
Host	Retrieves stand-alone host configuration information (includes Hyper-V, Virtual Server, and ESX through vCenter server)	10 minutes
Cluster	Retrieves cluster configuration information	30 minutes
Library	Retrieves library server configuration information	60 minutes
Performance	Retrieves virtual machine performance information	9 minutes
Security	Retrieves Hyper-V AzMan Security Configuration information	10 minutes
Virtual Center	Retrieves Virtual Center configuration information	10 minutes

Using the Single-Datacenter Model

Deploying VMM into a single datacenter simplifies the server, infrastructure, and client topologies since all IP, Fibre Channel (FC), and iSCSI connectivity is localized to one physical location. There are no special considerations for stretched VLANs, asynchronous storage replication, Metropolitan area network (MAN), Wide area network (WAN) topologies, high latency, or unreliable networks. This simplified deployment model still requires that you make some very important decisions regarding how you will optimize VMM:

◆ Should you install all VMM components on the same machine or do you need to separate them?

◆ If you need to separate some components, should the VMM server and database reside on the same machine?

◆ Do you need to cluster the database?

◆ Do you need more than one library server?

◆ Do you need to replicate files between library servers?

- Do you need more than one Self-Service Portal?

- Do you need to delegate administrative tasks to other users?

- What host group structure best represents your environment?

- How many hosts do you expect to manage 30 days, 3 months, 9 months, and 18 months after deploying VMM?

- Do you need to manage VMware environments with VMM?

VMM COMPONENTS

With one datacenter, your VMM deployment inherits many optimizations by default. One benefit is that IP, FC, and iSCSI connectivity tends to be plentiful and reliable within a datacenter. There is also no need to worry about saturating WAN network links when deploying virtual disks from the library. VMM will additionally experience minimal latency when processing incoming refresher data since the server and database will be deployed on the same server or within a few network hops. Depending on your scalability requirements, you have the flexibility of choosing the best deployment optimizations for VMM.

HOST GROUP LAYOUT AND DELEGATION MODEL

In a single datacenter, organizing your hosts and clusters into host groups should be straightforward. First, take some time to decide what your top-level host groups will be. If the business units in your organization like to have control over their assets, give them their own host group and nest it underneath one or two levels of generic host groups — maybe region and then the name of the datacenter. This way the business unit is neatly contained within a host group and you can model other host group structures in parallel without interfering. Figure 2.9 illustrates the deployment.

FIGURE 2.9
Host group
regional structure

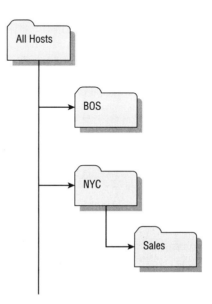

Some companies are deploying virtual machines in a utility model. In this case, IT is providing a service where business units purchase virtual machines from a centralized and managed infrastructure instead of purchasing individual physical servers. To model this with host groups, you can consider consolidating broad environment categories — production, test, and development. For accounting purposes, nested host groups can represent different classifications of virtual machine hosts — high-end clusters with storage area network (SAN) versus low-end stand-alone servers with local storage. Figure 2.10 illustrates the host group structure. Again, nest the broad categories under one or two generic levels so you are free to model other environments in parallel.

FIGURE 2.10
Host group
category structure

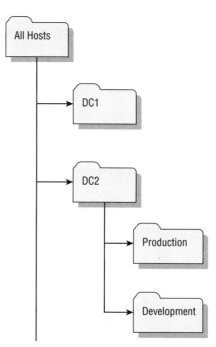

With properly nested host groups, you can easily create Delegated Administrator roles scoped at a very specific host group. These administrators do not have access to more than they really need. The same applies for self-service user roles. Depending on the size of your IT staff, this might seem like additional overhead, but having the flexibility upfront pays off over time as your environment grows.

Deploying a Multiple-Datacenter Model

Deploying VMM into an environment with multiple datacenters presents several challenges regarding the topology and desired scale. With more than one datacenter, network bandwidth and connectivity reliability will affect the stability of your virtualized environment overall. If your datacenters have very good connectivity where bandwidth and latency are not a concern, then you might consider hosting all VMM components in just one datacenter with Hyper-V hosts in all datacenters. In this configuration, the library server will serve virtual disks to multiple locations. If bandwidth is a concern, you can simply add library servers to VMM. Placing at least one library server in each datacenter localizes network traffic and avoids potentially saturating WAN links and interrupting higher-priority user/application data streams.

In fact, in a multi-datacenter model, consider deploying additional library servers and Self-Service Portals to each datacenter from the start. If you plan to use SAN, consider localizing SAN traffic as well. iSCSI, for example, performs best with minimal latency and network hop counts. It's generally not a good idea to put the VMM server and the SQL database in different datacenters. The VMM server and the SQL database communicate extremely frequently. Separating these components over geographical boundaries with increased latency is sure to decrease performance.

There is a greater potential in this model to require multiple instances of VMM to address scale limitations or internal business policies that require administrative isolation if autonomy is not good enough. VMM is not designed to scale horizontally, meaning that multiple instances of the VMM server are completely independent of each other. The agent installed locally on virtual machine hosts and library servers is designed to communicate with one VMM server instance at any given time. You can manually change the VMM server instance an agent communicates with, however, by reassociating it to a different VMM server. Additional design point questions still remain:

◆ Based on the size of the virtual environment, how much should you invest in optimizing the performance of VMM?

◆ Do you need to cluster the database?

◆ Do you need more than one library server per datacenter?

◆ Do you need to replicate files between library servers?

◆ Do you need more than one Self-Service Portal per datacenter?

◆ Will you need to deploy more than one VMM instance?

◆ How can you design your delegation model to ensure consistency across multiple VMM instances?

◆ What host group structure best represents your environment?

◆ Can you use the same host group structure across all instances of VMM?

◆ How many hosts do you expect to manage 30 days, 3 months, 9 months, and 18 months after deploying VMM?

◆ Do you need to manage one or more VMware environments with VMM?

VMM COMPONENTS

In very large virtualization deployments, if you have a large number of hosts, you might want to consider deploying additional instances of VMM. A single VMM server supports up to 400 hosts and 8,000 virtual machines. Scaling one instance of VMM to the supported maximum requires that you fully optimize VMM and tune refreshers. Another approach is to deploy an additional instance of VMM. Multiple VMMs can coexist in your environment with no issues. Figure 2.11 illustrates the deployment. However, VMM is not aware of other instances; none of the data in one VMM can be shared or synced to another instance. This means all your templates, custom properties, global settings, delegated administrators, self-service users, and performance data are exclusive to one VMM instance.

This approach will impose management overhead on your IT staff since their tasks might be split between two or more VMM instances. The amount of overhead really depends on how much you want to standardize between the two environments. Mirroring host group structure, for example, is trivial since host groups do not change very often, and so this can be accomplished manually. Replicating templates or security configuration between instances is much more complicated and tedious. You can automate the synchronization using PowerShell scripts, but there is no way to guarantee that you captured all the necessary information from one VMM to the other.

FIGURE 2.11
Fully optimized in a
Multiple-Datacenter
Deployment Model

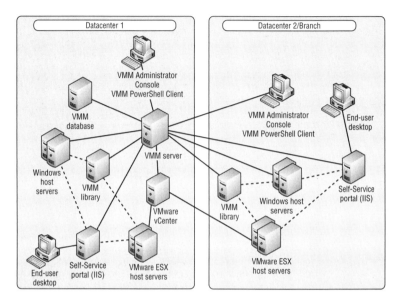

With multiple datacenters, you should avoid deploying the VMM server and the database in separate datacenters, even in a MAN topology. The closer these two components are, the faster the VMM server can read and write data to and from the database. Administrators accessing VMM should do so from a console closest to the VMM server (ideally not on the same server as VMM or the database). The console retrieves a large amount of data when it is first executed to populate the UI. The bulk load may take some time, depending on your network bandwidth and size of your environment. After the bulk load, only updates received or generated by the console need to be processed. In high-latency or limited-bandwidth datacenters, the console will seem to perform slowly.

LIBRARY PLACEMENT

Library servers are used as the source for file transfers and hosts are used as targets. To improve deployment times and file copies, co-location of the library server and the physical hosts that it is designed to serve will improve performance. VMM supports multiple library servers, but file replication is not provided natively. If all your datacenters exist within city limits and share a MAN, then connectivity should be very good. In this environment, you can get away with deploying one library server and sharing it across your datacenters. Most companies these days, however, have datacenters that are sometimes hundreds of miles apart. Even with well-connected datacenters over a WAN, bandwidth is not abundant and latency is high. Therefore, file copies from a central library server will take a very long time and consume precious bandwidth. With datacenters connected over WAN links, you should plan on deploying library severs in each datacenter to help isolate the bulk of file transfer traffic.

🌐 Real World Scenario

REPLICATING VMM TEMPLATES FROM ONE LIBRARY SERVER TO ANOTHER PROGRAMMATICALLY

A retail company with over 1,000 retail locations plans to deploy two Hyper-V hosts per retail store. It already has a local file server for the retail store, which will act as a library server. Deploying a new virtual machine over the WAN to a retail location is not very efficient and so the company needs a way of replicating existing templates to all the library servers residing locally in each retail location.

With multiple library servers in the environment, the retail company considered replicating templates from one library to another (within a single VMM instance) since a template is really only a collection of properties stored in the database and pointers to virtual disks stored on the library server (exposed through a share path).

Natively, VMM allows cloning of an existing template. By default, the new template will remain on the same library server. You can change the location of the template by manually changing the virtual hard disk attached to the template through the UI. However, for very large environments this manual effort is very error prone. So the question now is, How can a user replicate virtual disks and VMM templates to secondary library servers programmatically?

Note: The following information applies only to library servers managed by a single VMM instance.

You need to use some replication technology — for example, Robocopy or DFSR — to populate the disk in the target location. Once that is complete, you need to clone and modify templates using VMM's PowerShell CLI.

For this example, you should assume you have a library server in NY as the primary and a library server in SEA as secondary.

WindowsServer2003SP2withIIS.vhd is the virtual hard disk for the template. Follow these steps to clone a template to a different library server:

1. Copy the VHD to the secondary library server and refresh the library share so it can index the file and bring it under management.

2. Start by creating your template on the New York primary library server. Provide all the necessary hardware and guest OS profile information, including the virtual disk (i.e., WindowsServer2003SP2withIIS.vhd) stored in the library. Name the template W2K3SourceTemplate01.

3. Create a copy/clone of W2K3SourceTemplate01, leaving all settings at the default, and name it W2K3SeattleTemplate02. This step is really fast; keep in mind that the clone is simply creating a new database record for the template with pointers to the virtual disk.

4. Get the template object W2K3SeattleTemplate02.

5. Get the virtual disk drive for the template.

6. Remove the virtual disk drive. At this point, if you go to the VMM UI and open the properties for the template, the disk should no longer be present.

7. Back in PowerShell, get the virtual hard disk object, `WindowsServer2003SP2withIIS.vhd`, from the Seattle library server.

8. Create a new virtual disk drive using this virtual disk and attach it to the template `W2K3SeattleTemplate02`.

9. After the library servers refresh, the presence of `W2K3SeattleTemplate02` will switch from the primary library server to the secondary.

Here is the associated PowerShell script:

```
PS C:\> $spath = "\\Library.contoso.com\VHDs\WindowsServer2003SP2withIIS.vhd"
PS C:\> $os = Get-OperatingSystem | where {$_.Name -eq "Windows Server 2003
Standard Edition (32-bit x86)"}
PS C:\> $vhdprimary = Get-VirtualHardDisk | where {$_.Name -eq
"WindowsServer2003SP2withIIS.vhd" -and $_.SharePath -eq
"\\NYCVMMLibrary.contoso.com\MSSCVMMLibrary\WindowsServer2003SP2withIIS.vhd"}
PS C:\> $templateprimary = New-Template -Name "W2K3SourceTemplate01"
-NoCustomization -OperatingSystem $os -VirtualHardDisk $vhdprimary
PS C:\> $templatesecondary = New-Template -Template $templateprimary
-NameW2K3SeattleTemplate02
PS C:\> $vddsecondary = @($templatesecondary.VirtualDiskDrives)
PS C:\> Remove-VirtualDiskDrive -VirtualDiskDrive $vddsecondary[0]
PS C:\> $vhdsecondary = Get-VirtualHardDisk | where {$_.Name -eq
"WindowsServer2003SP2withIIS.vhd" -and $_.SharePath -eq $spath }
PS C:\> New-VirtualDiskDrive -VirtualHardDisk $vhdsecondary -Template
$templatesecondary -IDE -BUS 0 -LUN 0
```

HOST GROUP LAYOUT AND DELEGATION MODEL

With multiple datacenters, there is a good chance your support staff is regional and so your top-level host groups will mirror the same structure. If you have multiple datacenters within each region then you might nest host groups that represent subregions (e.g., NorthAmerica/ NewYork, EuropeanUnion/France). This example is only one of many possible options. Regardless of the structure you decide to use, make sure you create a few generic top-level host groups and nest your structure within those. As with the single-datacenter model, this recommendation provides some flexibility with your host groups as new datacenters come online and new virtualization projects roll out.

When designing your delegation model, keep in mind your host group structure and how that maps to your regional support staff. For host groups that represent geographically dispersed datacenters, administrators in one region would have no visibility into a different region. The level of administrative autonomy will likely depend on internal business politics more than technology. Users of the Self-Service Portal should also form part of your delegation model design.

Deploying a Branch Office Model

A branch office environment presents an interesting deployment scenario for VMM. On the one hand, a company with well-connected branch offices (i.e., a reliable network with sufficient bandwidth) will consolidate all servers into a main datacenter. This approach avoids the need to deploy servers to the branch and pay for IT personnel to support the branch. On the other hand, a company with poorly connected branch offices (i.e., an unreliable network with insufficient bandwidth) will concentrate as much activity at the branch to avoid saturating the network link (e.g., local file server, Active Directory server).

VMM depends heavily on the network to transfer virtual disk and ISO files as part of the new virtual machine creation process. So you have the option of deploying virtual machine hosts and library servers in your main datacenter, giving branch office users remote access to the virtual machines, or you can depend on the WAN connection to copy files every time. The latter option can take a very long time, and the copy itself may saturate the network link or may never complete if the connection is not reliable. For this reason, a third option is to deploy at least one library server to every branch office and a Self Service Portal.

Depending on the number of branch offices and the expected number of virtual machine hosts and virtual machines per branch, you may hit the scalability limits of VMM. If this is the case, multiple independent VMM instances might be your solution, although additional design point questions still remain:

◆ Based on the size of the virtual environment, how much should you invest in optimizing the performance of VMM?

◆ Do you need to cluster the database?

◆ Do you need more than one library server per branch office?

◆ Do you need to replicate files between library servers?

◆ Do you need more than one Self-Service Portal per branch office?

◆ Will you need to deploy more than one VMM instance?

◆ How can you design your delegation model to ensure consistency in branch offices and across multiple VMM instances?

◆ What host group structure best represents your environment?

◆ Can you use the same host group structure across all instances of VMM?

◆ How many hosts do you expect to manage 30 days, 3 months, 9 months, and 18 months after deploying VMM?

◆ Do you need to manage one or more VMware environments with VMM?

VMM COMPONENTS

Similar to the other two deployment models, separating the VMM and library server, Self-Service Portal, and database will allow for the best scale. In the typical branch office, hardware and rack space is limited, so you only need to deploy the necessary components. You can optimize the VMM server and database in your main datacenter, but at the branch, the library server and Self-Service Portal may be optional. Figure 2.11 also applies to the branch deployment with the key difference being that the number of branch offices may be in the hundreds or thousands.

Users in the branch office may need to access the Administration Console from time to time. Opening the console from a remote location, however, imposes a significant network tax as object and job data is bulked cached to the console and cached into memory. If branch office users need access, the console should not be opened remotely.

Additional Infrastructure Considerations

VMM also has a few other considerations to keep in mind as part of deployment. Migration involves moving a virtual machine from one location to another. VMM accomplishes this by using hypervisor-based migration (e.g., live migration) or by moving the storage location a virtual disk resides on. Backing up your VMM environment is also important in terms of quick recovery from failure, ensuring minimal downtime.

Migration

Deploying virtualization into a single datacenter should present few obstacles if you plan to use Hyper-V Quick Migration and/or VMware VMotion because both technologies depend on access to shared storage and a reliable network. To enable Hyper-V Quick Migration, you deploy virtual machines in a highly available configuration on top of Microsoft failover clustering. In the event that a node goes down, the virtual machines are guaranteed to restart on the remaining nodes. Microsoft failover clustering is one way of making applications that run in the virtual machines "highly available" without having to make any code changes to make them cluster-aware. Virtual machines configured as highly available require a shared LUN across the cluster for live migration. Using VMM, you cannot create a virtual machine on local storage that is not visible to all nodes in the cluster. If you do not use shared LUNs in a cluster, VMM can create and manage only one virtual machine per LUN. Deploying multiple virtual machines on a single LUN requires Windows Server 2008 R2 with failover clustering enabled using a Cluster Shared Volume (CSV) and Hyper-V.

If you do not want to use failover clustering to enable migration, VMM supports efficient SAN-based migration using N_Port Identification Virtualization (NPIV) and Microsoft Virtual Disk Service (VDS) to migrate virtual machines using the SAN instead of a network copy. Your SAN and FC or iSCSI host bus adapter hardware will need to provide support for this technology.

N_PORT ID VIRTUALIZATION

N_Port ID Virtualization, or NPIV, is a Fibre Channel facility that allows multiple N_Port IDs to share a single physical N_Port. N_Port sharing allows multiple Fibre Channel initiators to utilize a single physical port, easing hardware requirements in SAN design, especially where virtual SANs are used. NPIV is defined by the Technical Committee T11 within the INCITS standards body.

NPIV allows end users to effectively virtualize the Fibre Channel HBA functionality such that each virtual machine (VM) running on a server can share a pool of HBAs yet have independent access to its own protected storage. This sharing enables administrators to leverage standard SAN management tools and best practices, such as fabric zoning and LUN mapping/masking, and enables the full use of fabric-based quality-of-service and accounting capabilities. It also provides the most efficient utilization of the HBAs in the server while ensuring the highest level of data protection available in the industry.

Backup

Essential to any deployment is proper backup of your VMM environment. Each component within VMM requires a different level of backup to ensure that you can recover the environment in the event of a failure or catastrophic disaster.

VMM server   The server is a stateless engine that relies completely on the database for all configuration, host, and virtual machine data. For secure information that gets stored in the database (like passwords), VMM uses the machine account to encrypt the data. A full backup of the operating system and data of the host is required if you need to make sure the same computer account is used after restore. In addition, any certificates used for communication are restored and so any existing agents can continue to work as expected.

If you do not need to restore access to encrypted information in the database, then you simply need to back up the database. You can use any server running Windows Server 2008 64-bit to install VMM. After installing, you would only need to point the service to the VMM database. Without a full system backup, make sure to back up on the server the Registry key that controls time-outs and refresher intervals. These values would need to be applied to the new host after recovery and before starting the VMM service. After recovery, all virtual machine hosts will not be able to communicate with the VMM server. The hosts need to be "reassociated" so the new certificate is propogated.

The VMM Registry key is as follows:

```
HKEY_LOCAL_MACHINE\SOFTWARE\
Microsoft\Microsoft System Center Virtual Machine Manager Server\Settings
```

VMM database   The default install of VMM will install Microsoft SQL Express on the same host running the VMM server. The database is labeled MICROSOFTVMM\VirtualManagerDB. VMM ships with an executable to recover the database from a backup file, VMMRecover.exe. Microsoft SQL Standard or Enterprise is also an option as the backend database server. Backing up the database is highly recommended to ensure that you can quickly recover your environment. You should follow MS SQL database backup/recovery guidelines for the VMM database.

VMM library   The library is essentially a file server. It indexes specific file types used by VMM (Table 2.6). When backing up the library server, make sure these filename extensions are included. In addition, make sure to capture managed library shares.

TABLE 2.6:   Files indexed by Library

FILE TYPE	RELEVANT FILENAME EXTENSIONS
Virtual Disk	.vhd, .vmdk
CD/DVD Image	.iso
Virtual Machine	Hyper-V: .exp, .bin, .vsv (associated .vhd) VMware: .vmx (associated .vmdk)
Virtual Floppy Disk	.vfd, .flp
PowerShell Script	.ps1
Sysprep Answer File	.inf, .xml

The Bottom Line

Identify the different components in VMM. VMM breaks down into three areas of interest with one or more components in each. The first step in deploying VMM is to understand each component.

Master It For one instance of VMM, what is the supported maximum number of hosts and virtual machines?

Master It Name at least three functions performed by the VMM server.

Master It What component links VMM to System Center Operations Manager to enable PRO functionality?

Learn about optimizing VMM. VMM can scale to meet the demands of your virtualized environment, but you need to make sure each component is optimized to perform well. Peak-performing components minimize bottlenecks in the system.

Master It Name three refreshers VMM uses to collect information from your virtualized environment.

Master It Compared to the all-in-one configuration, what components have you placed onto a separate server in the I/O-optimized configuration?

Master It Using VMM's delegation model, how would you model your host group structure to ensure that your New York administrators do not have access to Boston resources?

Understand important design considerations required for VMM. VMM architecture breaks down into three categories: VMM server, VMM infrastructure, and VMM client. Each category accounts for multiple components that should be taken into account as part of your VMM deployment plan.

Master It Aside from serving as a container for virtual machine hosts and clusters, what other uses do host groups have?

Master It Name the three major categories of components for VMM.

Master It Explain the difference between administrative autonomy and isolation.

Chapter 3

Installation and Configuration

In Chapters 1 and 2, we've talked about System Center Virtual Machine Manager's system components, how it is architected, and some common deployment models. From a deployment point of view, the VMM product contains the following six modules: the VMM server, which consists of a set of core backend services; the SQL database; library server(s), which store all your virtualization environment "building blocks" (VHDs, ISO images, PowerShell scripts, etc.); the Self-Service Portal, which is a web-based user interface and allows end users to provision, monitor, and access virtual machines from a web browser, such as Internet Explorer; the Administrator Console, which is a desktop-based console that the VMM administrator uses as the primary user interface; the PowerShell CLI interface, which is bundled with the Administrator Console; and the VMM agent, which is the agent software running on the managed virtual machine host computer. The VMM agent can be deployed either remotely through a VMM server push install or locally by selecting the local agent install option from the media or simply launching the agent MSI package.

In this chapter, we'll guide you through the steps to evaluate your preinstall environment and setup, and you'll also see how to configure your VMM server along with other core infrastructure components, deploy VMM agents to managed host computers, and set up a fully functional VMM environment.

In this chapter, you will learn to:

◆ Identify VMM configuration prerequisites and requirements

◆ Install and configure the VMM server

◆ Install and configure the VMM Administrator Console

◆ Install and configure VMM and Operations Manager Integration Components

◆ Install and configure the VMM Self-Service Portal

Prerequisites and Requirements for Installing and Configuring VMM Hosts and Libraries

If you look at virtualization management technologies, there are two things that are key to the performance and reliability of the underlying system infrastructure: the control channel robustness and the data transfer channel bandwidth and throughput. System Center Virtual Machine Manager is no exception.

Since its inception in 2007, System Center Virtual Machine Manager builds its command communication framework based on a set of well-known industry-standard protocols (primarily WS-Management, or WS-MAN, and there are also cases where Windows Management Instrumentation, or WMI, and others are used); and it takes advantage of a proven Windows technology, Background Intelligent Transfer Service (BITS), for most of its data transfer needs (when managing VMware ESX hosts, VMM uses SFTP for content transfer).

Before we start looking at the VMM system requirements, it's important to briefly review the overall VMM system architecture, illustrated in Figure 3.1.

FIGURE 3.1
VMM architecture overview

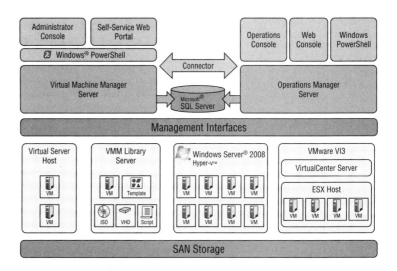

The following sections describe the minimum system requirements for each system component. To ensure that your VMM server is performing at an acceptable level against your planned environment, you may need to tweak it or use the recommended configurations according to the size and needs of your environment.

Requirements for All-in-One Configuration

You can install all VMM components (VMM server, VMM database server, VMM Self-Service Portal, VMM library server, VMM Administrator Console, VMM reporting server, and even a virtual machine host) onto a single Windows computer. We have seen consultants or customers often use this model for proof of concept, or just to "kick the tire" and give it a try.

When you install all the components on one computer, all the requirements from each VMM component apply to this computer.

HARDWARE REQUIREMENTS

Table 3.1 presents the minimum and recommended hardware requirements for the target computer to be deployed and used for all VMM system components. Please note that in practice, the more hosts you have, and more importantly the more virtual machines you have in your environment, the more capable your management server should be.

TABLE 3.1:   Hardware requirements for all-in-one configuration

HARDWARE	MINIMUM	RECOMMENDED
Processor speed	Pentium 4 @ 2.8 GHz (x64)	Dual-Core Pentium 4 @ 2.8 GHz (x64) or greater
RAM size	2 GB	4 GB or greater
Hard disk free space	14 GB	50 GB or greater

Source: http://technet.microsoft.com/en-us/library/cc764289.aspx

SOFTWARE REQUIREMENTS

As with the hardware requirements, when you decide to put all the VMM components onto a single Windows computer, all the software requirements for each VMM component will need to apply.

Table 3.2 lists the software requirements for the target computer to host all VMM system components.

TABLE 3.2:   Software requirements for all-in-one configuration

SOFTWARE COMPONENTS	REQUIREMENTS
Operating system	Microsoft Windows Server 2008 (x64) and later.
Microsoft .NET Framework	.NET Framework 3.0 is included with Windows Server 2008 by default. If the software is accidentally removed, VMM server Setup will install it.
Windows Remote Management (WinRM)	As long as the WinRM service is not disabled, VMM server Setup will start the service and set it to start automatically. Otherwise, the setup will fail.
Windows Automated Installation Kit (WAIK)	WAIK version 1.1 or later is required. VMM server Setup will install the WAIK package if it's not installed.
Windows Server Internet Information Services (IIS)	IIS version 7.0 is shipped with Windows Server 2008. VMM Self-Service Portal requires users to enable the IIS role on the target computer and install the following services before the Setup program can install the VMM Self-Service Web Portal component onto the server: IIS 6 Metabase Compatibility IIS 6 WMI Compatibility Static Content Default Document Directory Browsing HTTP Errors ASP.NET .NET Extensibility ISAPI Extensions ISAPI Filters Request Filtering To host more than one site on the same IIS server, you will need to use a different port for each site.
Database server	VMM works with SQL Server 2008 and 2005 editions (Express Edition, Standard Edition and Enterprise Edition).

Source: http://technet.microsoft.com/en-us/library/cc764289.aspx

---

LIMITATIONS FOR SQL SERVER EXPRESS EDITION

There are three limitations when you are using SQL Server Express Edition (these apply to both 2005 and 2008 SQL Server releases):

◆ SQL Server Express Edition supports up to 4 GB for the size of the database. So, if you intend to use VMM in a large environment (more than 150 hosts), a full version of SQL Server is recommended.

◆ SQL Server Express Edition does not support the reporting functionalities in VMM. If you need reporting features in VMM, a full version of SQL Server is required.

◆ By default, SQL Server Express Edition cannot be managed remotely. If you must manage it remotely, check Chapter 11 for how to enable it manually. But in general, you should be using a full version of SQL Server for VMM.

Requirements for the VMM Server

After you've experimented with and tested VMM, you are ready to deploy it to your production environment. Again, depending on the size of your virtualization environment, you may decide to install the VMM server on a dedicated Windows computer or install the VMM server, library, database server, and Self-Service Portal all in one server. Or you may choose to install the VMM server on a shared Windows server that also runs other System Center management software, for example. Installing the VMM server on a dedicated Windows server is the most commonly seen production deployment method.

HARDWARE REQUIREMENTS

As mentioned in the previous section, the more hosts you have, and more importantly, the more virtual machines you plan to manage in your environment, the more server power you will need. The hardware requirements are divided into two sets based on the host size (assuming the average host to VM ratio is around 1:20):

◆ One set of requirements for the VMM server to manage up to 150 hosts

◆ Another set for the VMM server to manage more than 150 hosts

Table 3.3 shows the minimum and recommended hardware requirements for the target computer to be deployed and used for the VMM server that is planned to manage up to 150 hosts.

Table 3.4 shows the minimum and recommended hardware requirements for the target computer to be deployed and used for a VMM server that will manage more than 150 hosts.

DISK SPACE REQUIREMENTS

Here is some additional information on the disk space requirements for the VMM server:

◆ In a small business environment, if you choose to install SQL Server Express Edition on your VMM server, the additional disk space required for the database is 4 GB.

◆ When you plan to manage a mid-size to large environment (say, more than 150 hosts), the recommendation is to use a full version of SQL Server and dedicated and distributed VMM library servers. Hence, the disk space requirement here reflects only the needs for theVMM server component.

◆ If you plan to also use the VMM server as a library server (you can specify as such in VMM server Setup), plan for additional disk space according to your intended library capacity. The minimum disk space requirement for the VMM server does not take into account any library server space.

TABLE 3.3: Hardware requirements for a VMM server managing up to 150 hosts

HARDWARE	MINIMUM	RECOMMENDED
Processor architecture	x64	x64 (Note: the VMM server requires a server with x64 CPU.)
Processor speed	Pentium 4 @ 2 GHz	Dual-Processor, Dual-Core, Pentium 4 @ 2 GHz or greater
RAM size	2 GB	4 GB or greater
Hard disk free space (with remote SQL database)	2 GB	40 GB or greater
Hard disk free space (with the default local SQL Server Express Edition)	14 GB	50 GB or greater

Source: http://technet.microsoft.com/en-us/library/cc764224.aspx

TABLE 3.4: Hardware requirements for a VMM server managing more than 150 hosts

HARDWARE	MINIMUM	RECOMMENDED
Processor architecture	x64	x64 (Note: VMM server requires a server with x64 CPU.)
Processor speed	Pentium 4 @ 2.8 GHz	Dual-Processor, Dual-Core, Pentium 4 @ 3.6 GHz or greater
RAM size	4 GB	8 GB or greater
Hard disk free space (remote SQL database)	10 GB	50 GB or greater

Source: http://technet.microsoft.com/en-us/library/cc764224.aspx

SOFTWARE REQUIREMENTS

As the central job execution unit, the VMM server needs to connect to the database for storing and retrieving information, and it needs to have WinRM to communicate with the managed VM hosts and VMM libraries. Because some of the system components are managed code, the VMM server has also a dependency on .NET Framework 3.0 or above. Last, the VMM server also installs Windows Automated Installation Kit (WAIK), which is used for physical-to-virtual conversion and other functionalities.

Table 3.5 lists the software requirements for the VMM server.

Please note that the same limitations for SQL Server Express editions apply here.

TABLE 3.5: Software requirements for a VMM server

SOFTWARE COMPONENTS	REQUIREMENTS
Operating system	Microsoft Windows Server 2008 (x64) and later.
Windows Remote Management (WinRM)	As long as the WinRM service is not disabled, VMM server Setup will start the service and set it to start automatically. Otherwise, the setup will fail.
Microsoft .NET Framework	.NET 3.0 is included with Windows Server 2008 by default. If the software is accidentally removed, the VMM server Setup will install it.
Windows Automated Installation Kit (WAIK)	WAIK version 1.1 or later is required. The VMM server Setup will install the WAIK package if it's not installed.
Database server	VMM works with SQL Server 2008 and 2005 editions (Express Edition, Standard Edition, and Enterprise Edition).

Source: http://technet.microsoft.com/en-us/library/cc764224.aspx

Requirements for the VMM Database Server

When installing the VMM server, you have two options as to where you want your data stored and what database server you want to use: one is to use the default in-the-box SQL Server 2008 Express Edition; another is to use an external SQL Server instance to host the data.

You need to consider the following key factors when making the selection:

◆ What is the size of your virtualization environment and its projected growth? The recommendation is as follows:

 ◆ When the number of to-be-managed hosts is smaller than 150 and your VM operations are not performance sensitive, you may get by with the SQL Express Edition with the 4 GB database size limit.

 ◆ When you intend to host a larger and growing host environment or you're designing for best performance, you should consider using a full version of SQL Server.

◆ Do you need the reporting feature in VMM? If so, there are a couple of things you need to be aware of:

 ◆ SQL Server Express Edition does not support reporting.

 ◆ If you need to use the reporting feature in VMM, a full version of SQL Server is required.

HARDWARE REQUIREMENTS

If you are going to install SQL Server Express Edition locally on the VMM server, please refer to the section "Requirements for the VMM Server" earlier in this chapter for hardware and software requirements.

If you are going to use an external SQL Server instance, the hardware requirements call for the minimum requirements for the SQL Server instance if the server is dedicated for the VMM database only. The requirements are very similar to the ones for the VMM server except for the disk space requirements.

You can also share an existing SQL database server or instance of a SQL database server for VMM. In this case, you need to consult with your SQL Server administrators to confirm and determine if your existing SQL server has enough system resources to support the new VMM database.

Table 3.6 lists the hardware requirements for a VMM database server that is planned to manage up to 150 hosts.

TABLE 3.6:   Hardware requirements for a VMM database server managing up to 150 hosts

HARDWARE	MINIMUM	RECOMMENDED
Processor speed	Pentium 4 @ 2 GHz	Dual-Processor, Dual-Core, Pentium 4 @ 2 GHz or greater
RAM size	2 GB	4 GB or greater
Hard disk free space (remote SQL database)	80 GB	150 GB or greater

Source: http://technet.microsoft.com/en-us/library/cc764220.aspx

Table 3.7 lists the hardware requirements for a VMM database server that is planned to manage more than 150 hosts.

TABLE 3.7:   Hardware requirements for a VMM database server managing more than 150 hosts

HARDWARE	MINIMUM	RECOMMENDED
Processor speed	Pentium 4 @ 2.8 GHz	Dual-Processor, Dual-Core, Pentium 4 @ 3.6 GHz or greater
RAM size	4 GB	8 GB or greater
Hard disk free space (remote SQL database)	150 GB	200 GB or greater

Source: http://technet.microsoft.com/en-us/library/cc764220.aspx

---

REFERENCE DB SIZES FOR DISK SPACE PLANNING

Based on some statistics, and for your reference, here are some database (DB) sizes with corresponding host/VM/velocity in your VMM environment:

◆ For 100 hosts, 1,000 VMs, and 2,000 average daily jobs: DB about 1,500 MB.

◆ For 200 hosts, 2,000 VMs, and 4,000 average daily jobs: DB about 2,900 MB.

◆ For 300 hosts, 6,000 VMs, and 6,000 average daily jobs: DB about 4,500 MB.

◆ For 400 hosts, 8,000 VMs, and 10,000 average daily jobs: DB about 7,400 MB.

SOFTWARE REQUIREMENTS

The software requirement for a VMM database server is simply the supported versions of SQL Server products. Also note that to support copying a large amount of data (for example, during P2V process), the VMM server Setup will also install SQL Server management tools on the VMM server.

Table 3.8 lists the software requirements for a VMM database server.

TABLE 3.8:   Software requirements for a VMM database server

SQL SERVER VERSIONS	SUPPORTS REPORTING IN VMM
SQL Server 2008 (32-bit and 64-bit) Enterprise Edition	Yes
SQL Server 2008 (32-bit and 64-bit) Standard Edition	Yes
SQL Server 2008 Express Edition	No
SQL Server 2005 (32-bit and 64-bit) Enterprise Edition	Yes
SQL Server 2005 (32-bit and 64-bit) Standard Edition	Yes
SQL Server 2005 Express Edition	No

Source: http://technet.microsoft.com/en-us/library/cc764220.aspx

Requirements for a VMM Library Server

The VMM library server hosts all the building blocks for all your VM management needs. It not only stores the shipped in-the-box VHD, templates, and profiles, but more importantly, it is the repository for all contents generated by users for managing their virtualized environment. For example, the VM templates, PowerShell scripts, sysprepped VHDs, and saved VMs are all saved in the library for users to automate/streamline their daily operations through VMM.

As discussed in Chapter 2, depending on the size and geographical distribution of your environment, you may have one or more library servers. And the hardware requirements can also vary drastically, based on the number and size of the resources you need to manage in your library (for example, size of VHDs can range from a couple MB to a few GBs).

HARDWARE REQUIREMENTS

Functionally speaking, there are mainly two types of operations involving a VMM library server: storing data and retrieving data. Naturally, the storage capacity and I/O throughput become the key requirements for library server.

In theory, we could provide various requirements based on the size of your hosts and VMs. However, in reality, the requirements for library server really depend on the following:

◆ The type of operations you commonly perform

◆ The frequency and the level of velocity with which you make changes to your virtual environment

◆ The number and location of your library servers

Table 3.9 is provided for your reference. As you build up your operational process around VMM, necessary adjustment to your library servers (number of library servers and individual library server hardware) may be required over time.

TABLE 3.9: Hardware requirements for a VMM library server

HARDWARE	MINIMUM	RECOMMENDED
Processor speed	Pentium 4 @ 2.8 GHz	Dual-Core 64-bit Pentium 4 @ 3.2 GHz or greater
RAM size	2 GB	2 GB or greater
Hard disk free space	2 GB	Depending on the number and size of the library resources stored

Source: http://technet.microsoft.com/en-us/library/cc764302.aspx

SOFTWARE REQUIREMENTS

Table 3.10 shows the software requirements for a VMM library server.

TABLE 3.10: Software requirements for a VMM library server

SOFTWARE COMPONENTS	REQUIREMENTS
Operating system	Microsoft Windows Server 2003 SP2 and later server platforms (excluding Windows Web Server).
Windows Remote Management (WinRM)	As long as WinRM service is not disabled, VMM server Setup will start the service and set it to start automatically. Otherwise, the setup will fail.

Source: http://technet.microsoft.com/en-us/library/cc764302.aspx

---

WHY YOU NEED WINRM ON A VMM LIBRARY SERVER

To set up a VMM database server, all you need is an open database connectivity (ODBC) connection string to the SQL server. There is no need for installing an agent or any other software component on the database server. However, you need to install a full VMM agent on a library server, the same agent you install on a VM host. And the WS-MAN/WinRM channel is the main command channel through which the VMM server sends almost all jobs to the agent to be executed. Because the communication between hosts and the library server is bidirectional (when creating a new VM, a VHD needs to be pushed to the host, and when saving a VM to the library, a VHD needs to be pushed to the library), the WinRM listener needs to be configured on all the hosts as well as on the library servers.

Requirements for the VMM Administrator Console

Now you understand the requirements for a VMM server, database server, and library server, which are the backbone of the VMM server infrastructure. Let's look at the client requirements next. The VMM Administrator Console, Self-Service Portal and PowerShell command-line interface (CLI) are the three VMM clients. Let's start with the Administrator Console. First, we'll look at the requirements.

HARDWARE REQUIREMENTS

The Administrator Console is built with the capability of intelligently caching thousands of internal objects to ensure a fast and data-rich experience for server administrators. Also, as mentioned in previous chapters, all jobs are submitted from the client (Administrator Console or PowerShell CLI or Self-Service Portal) to the VMM server and executed on the server. As such, the hardware requirements for the Administrator Console are much more relaxed than the requirements of the server-side components.

As we did with the VMM server hardware requirements, we'll divide the requirements based on the size of your intended deployment (see Table 3.11 and Table 3.12).

TABLE 3.11: Hardware requirements for a VMM Administrator Console managing up to 150 hosts

HARDWARE	MINIMUM	RECOMMENDED
Processor speed	Pentium 4 @ 550 MHz	Pentium 4 @ 1 GHz or greater
RAM size	512 MB	1 GB or greater
Hard disk free space	512 MB	2 GB or greater

TABLE 3.12: Hardware requirements for a VMM Administrator Console managing more than 150 hosts

HARDWARE	MINIMUM	RECOMMENDED
Processor speed	Pentium 4 @ 1 GHz	Pentium 4 @ 2 GHz or greater
RAM size	1 GB	2 GB or greater
Hard disk free space	512 MB	4 GB or greater

Source: http://technet.microsoft.com/en-us/library/cc764321.aspx

SOFTWARE REQUIREMENTS

The VMM Administrator Console is built, from the ground up, on top of the VMM Power-Shell CLI layer. Hence, it has dependency on Windows PowerShell. It works with Windows PowerShell 1.0 release as well as version 2.0, which was shipped with Windows 7. Because the console was built by using managed code, Microsoft .NET Framework 2.0 is also required.

Table 3.13 shows the software requirements for VMM Administrator Console.

TABLE 3.13:   Software requirements for the VMM Administrator Console

SOFTWARE COMPONENTS	REQUIREMENTS
Operating system	Microsoft Windows XP SP2 and later client platforms and Windows Server 2003 SP2 and later server platforms (excluding Windows Server Core and Windows Web Server).
Windows PowerShell	Windows PowerShell 1.0 and later. PowerShell 1.0 is included by default in Windows Server 2008 and 2.0 is included by default in Windows Server 2008 R2.
Microsoft .NET Framework	.NET Framework 2.0 or later is required.

Source: http://technet.microsoft.com/en-us/library/cc764321.aspx

Requirements for the VMM Self-Service Portal

The VMM Self-Service Portal is an IIS-based web portal that offers a subset of the functionalities available on the Administrator Console. Users have access to a set of basic VM operations from the web portal based on their granted rights (set by the VMM administrator).

In a distributed VMM deployment architecture, the Self-Service Portal can be installed on a shared or dedicated IIS server.

HARDWARE REQUIREMENTS

As with any other web-based application, the hardware requirements of the Self-Service Portal are tied to the number of concurrent requests (connections) it needs to support. Table 3.14 and Table 3.15 break down the requirements based on the number of concurrent connections that the VMM Self-Service Portal needs to support.

TABLE 3.14:   Hardware requirements for the VMM Self-Service Portal managing up to 10 concurrent connections

HARDWARE	MINIMUM	RECOMMENDED
Processor	Pentium 4 @ 2.8 MHz	Pentium 4 @ 2.8 GHz or greater
RAM size	2 GB	2 GB or greater
Hard disk free space	512 MB	20 GB or greater

TABLE 3.15:   Hardware requirements for the VMM Self-Service Portal managing more than 10 (and less than 50) concurrent connections

HARDWARE	MINIMUM	RECOMMENDED
Processor speed	Pentium 4 @ 2.8 GHz	Dual Core 64-bit, Pentium 4 @ 3.2 GHz or greater
RAM size	2 GB	8 GB or greater
Hard disk free space	10 GB	40 GB or greater

Source: http://technet.microsoft.com/en-us/library/cc764309.aspx

Depending on the size of your organization and the intended number of users for the web portal, you should consider the appropriate hardware configuration suggestions.

SOFTWARE REQUIREMENTS

Similar to the Administrator Console, the VMM Self-Service Portal is also built on top of the VMM PowerShell CLI layer. Hence, it too has dependency on Windows PowerShell. It works with Windows PowerShell 1.0 release as well as version 2.0, which was shipped with Windows 7. The web portal also has dependency on Microsoft .NET Framework.

Table 3.16 shows the software requirements for a VMM Self-Service Portal server.

TABLE 3.16:   Software requirements for a VMM Self-Service Portal server

SOFTWARE COMPONENTS	REQUIREMENTS
Operating system	Microsoft Windows Server 2003 SP2 and later server platforms (excluding Windows Server Core).
Windows Server Internet Information Services (IIS)	IIS version 6.0 or later is required. VMM Self-Service Portal requires users to enable the IIS role (built-in operating system component) on the target computer and install the following list of services before the Setup program can install the VMM Self-Service Web Portal component onto the server: IIS 6 Metabase Compatibility IIS 6 WMI Compatibility Static Content Default Document Directory Browsing HTTP Errors ASP.NET .NET Extensibility ISAPI Extensions ISAPI Filters Request Filtering
Windows PowerShell	Windows PowerShell 1.0 and later. PowerShell 1.0 is included by default in Windows Server 2008 and 2.0 is included by default in Windows Server 2008 R2.
Microsoft .NET Framework	.NET Framework 2.0 or later is required for Windows Server 2003 platforms. .NET Framework 3.0 is included in Windows Server 2008 by default.

Source: http://technet.microsoft.com/en-us/library/cc764309.aspx

---

REUSING AN EXISTING IIS SERVER TO HOST THE VMM SELF-SERVICE PORTAL

When you decide to put the VMM Self-Service Portal on an existing IIS server, please be sure to work with the IIS administrator to understand the current IIS server load and available server bandwidth/resources and make sure the configuration of the Self-Service Portal is not in conflict with the existing web applications that the IIS server is hosting.

Requirements for VMM PowerShell CLI

As shown on the upper-left corner in Figure 3.1, VMM's PowerShell layer is technically implemented as a completely modular infrastructure component, and the Administrator Console and Self-Service Portal are both built on top of it. However, it is not a separately installable module.

The core to VMM's PowerShell CLI is the PowerShell snap-in Microsoft.SystemCenter. VirtualMachineManager, which consists of two files (one DLL and one help XML file). You can get the PowerShell snap-in by installing the Administrator Console or the Self-Service Portal client component.

Hence, there is no specific requirement for the VMM PowerShell CLI component. One thing to note is that the VMM PowerShell layer is a very thin layer, which effectively translates the PowerShell calls into Windows Communication Foundation (WCF) calls and sends the request to the VMM server for execution. So the overhead and system requirements for this layer are relatively small.

Requirements for VMM Operations Manager Integration

The Performance and Resource Optimization (PRO) feature in VMM relies on a deep integration with the System Center Operations Manager product. You may see that component being referred to as OpsMgr Connector, or just Connector, as shown on the upper-right corner of Figure 3.1.

The OpsMgr Connector needs to be installed on the Operations Manager server. The supported Operations Manager versions are System Center Operations Manager 2007 SP1 and System Center Operations Manager 2007 R2.

The following management packs must be installed on the Operations Manager server before the VMM OpsMgr Connector can be installed:

♦ Microsoft Windows Server 2000/2003/2008 Management Pack (version 6.0.6321.5 or later):

   ♦ Microsoft.Windows.Server.Library

   ♦ Microsoft.Windows.Server.2008.Discovery

♦ Microsoft SQL Server 2000/2005/2008 Management Pack (version 6.0.6648.0 or later):

   ♦ Microsoft.SQLServer.Library

   ♦ Microsoft.SQLServer.2005.Monitoring (recommended)

   ♦ Microsoft.SQLServer.2005.Discovery (recommended)

♦ Microsoft Windows Server 2000/2003/2008 Internet Information Services (IIS) Management Pack (version 6.0.6539.0 or later):

   ♦ Microsoft.Windows.InternetInformationServices.CommonLibrary

   ♦ Microsoft.Windows.InternetInformationServices.2003

   ♦ Microsoft.Windows.InternetInformationServices.2008

If your Operations Manager server does not have these MPs, look up the Operations Manager management pack catalog and download the management packs from Microsoft TechNet. Refer to Chapter 9 for more information.

Requirements for VMM VM Hosts

Up to now, all the requirements we have talked about are for the VMM infrastructure. To get to a fully functional virtualized datacenter, however, you need to have virtual machine (VM) hosts. Although VMM manages (not implements) a hypervisor software stack, it wouldn't be complete without talking about the supported hypervisors and their respective requirements.

In VMM, one of the key features is that it provides a single pane of glass into your heterogeneous virtualization environment. You don't have to look far to find customers hosting Virtual Server, VMware and Hyper-V virtual machines in their environment and who are in need of having a tool that can manage across virtualization platforms and provide ways to allow migrating VMs from one platform to another. Since its v2 release, VMM has provided users with support for Virtual Server hosts, VMware ESX hosts and Hyper-V hosts through the same easy-to-use Administrator Console user interface and the PowerShell CLI.

MICROSOFT HYPER-V HOST

Hyper-V Beta shipped in Windows Server 2008. Its v1 was released in June 2008 and its v2 was released as part of Windows Server 2008 R2. Hyper-V is a Type 1 (or native) hypervisor-based virtualization technology for x64 systems from Microsoft. It is a server role that can be enabled for Microsoft Windows Server 2008 or later 64-bit server platforms.

The hardware requirements for Hyper-V are listed in Table 3.17.

TABLE 3.17:   Hardware requirements for Microsoft Hyper-V Server

HARDWARE	MINIMUM	RECOMMENDED
Processor	An x64 processor with hardware-assisted virtualization. Hardware Data Execution Protection (DEP) must be available and be enabled. It is important that you enable the Intel XD bit (execute disable bit) or AMD NX bit (no execute bit).	2 GHz or faster
RAM size	1 GB	2 GB or greater
Hard disk free space	10 GB	40 GB or greater
Network adapters	1	2 or more

Source: http://www.microsoft.com/hyper-v-server/en/us/system-requirements.aspx

VMWARE ESX HOST

VMware ESX host is VMware's Type 1 (or native) hypervisor-based virtualization technology for both x86 and x64 systems. Check this website for an architecture diagram of ESX Server:

http://www.vmware.com/support/esx21/doc/esx21_admin_system_architecture.html

According to VMware's website, the minimum hardware requirements for ESX 3.0 are as shown in Table 3.18. For the latest information, check the VMware website at www.vmware.com.

TABLE 3.18:   Hardware requirements for VMware ESX 3.0

HARDWARE	MINIMUM
Processor	At least two processors: 1500 MHz Intel® Xeon and above or AMD Opteron (32-bit mode) for ESX Server 1500 MHz Intel Xeon and above, or AMD Opteron (32-bit mode) for Virtual SMP 1500 MHz Intel Viiv or AMD A64 x2 dual-core processors
RAM size	1 GB
Network adapters	One or more Ethernet controllers. The following controllers are supported: Broadcom NetXtreme 570x Gigabit controllers. Intel PRO/100 adapters. For best performance and security, use separate Ethernet controllers for the service console and the virtual machines. Note: The 3Com 3c990 driver does not support all revisions of the 3c990.

Source: http://kb.vmware.com/selfservice/microsites/search.do?language=en_US&cmd=displayKC& externalId=1003661

WHAT VERSIONS OF VMWARE ESX DOES VMM SUPPORT?

Please note that VMM manages VMware ESX hosts through VMware vCenter Server. Hence, without vCenter Server, stand-alone VMware ESX hosts cannot be managed by VMM.

Chapter 4 will explore how to manage VMware by using VMM. For now, however, let's take a look at the supported VMware product versions. To use VMware's terminology, VMM supports its Virtualization Infrastructure (VI) 3, which consists of VMware vCenter 2.x and VMware ESX Server 3x. Specifically, the following are the supported versions of VMware vCenter and ESX hosts:

◆ VMware vCenter 2.5

◆ VMware ESX Server 3.5, 3.0.2 and 3i

With VMM 2008 R2 release, VMware vSphere 4 is also supported to the same level of VMware VI3.

MICROSOFT VIRTUAL SERVER

First released in 2004, Virtual Server is a Type 2 (or hosted) hypervisor-based virtualization technology from Microsoft. It runs on Microsoft Windows Server 2003 and Windows Server 2008 server platforms.

The hardware requirements for Virtual Server 2005 R2 SP1 are listed in Table 3.19.

TABLE 3.19:   Hardware requirements for Microsoft Virtual Server

HARDWARE	MINIMUM	RECOMMENDED
Processor	x86 550 MHz with L2 cache.	1 GHz or faster
RAM size	Depending on the hosting server OS, 256 MB	N/A
Hard disk free space	Depending on the hosting server OS, 2 GB	N/A

Source: http://technet.microsoft.com/en-us/library/cc720353(WS.10).aspx

Installing and Configuring a VMM Server

Let's assume that you are performing a brand-new installation and starting from the media. Please note that for the upgrade process, you should read and follow the upgrade guide published by Microsoft carefully because each upgrade path may have different recommended steps. To get access to the VMM media, you can either order it and get it through traditional mail or go online and download the evaluation/beta version and burn it onto a DVD by using your favorite tool. The evaluation version for VMM 2008 R2 release can be downloaded from `http://www.microsoft.com/downloads/details.aspx?FamilyID=292de23c-845c-4d08-8d65-b4b8cbc8397b&displaylang=en`.

Before you start, make sure the target computer has all the required hardware and software.

VMM Configuration Analyzer

After you pop in the VMM DVD, open the media in your Explorer window, and launch the `setup.exe` as Administrator. A splash screen will appear.

Regardless of whether this is your first time installing a VMM server or you've done this before on different machines, we recommend running the VMM Configuration Analyzer (VMMCA) prior to running the actual server setup. Why? The analyzer contains the following types of information:

◆ External dependencies that are collected from partners across all feature areas. For example, suppose you discovered an issue with Hyper-V and requested a hotfix, without which a certain operation on VMM would cause your server service to abort. This is the kind of information that's important to know before you install VMM server.

◆ Aggregated knowledge on commonly seen environmental configurations that lead to VMM failures.

WHAT ELSE DO YOU NEED TO KNOW ABOUT VMM CONFIGURATION ANALYZER?

The following are some of the facts that you should know about VMM Configuration Analyzer (VMMCA):

◆ Before you install VMMCA, you must download and install the 64-bit version of Microsoft Baseline Configuration Analyzer (MBCA). You can download the MBCASetup64.msi file at `http://go.microsoft.com/fwlink/?LinkID=97952`.

◆ VMMCA must be installed on a Windows Server 2008 (64-bit) machine, which is or will be the VMM server.

♦ VMMCA does not duplicate or replace the prerequisite checks performed during the setup of VMM 2008 components.

♦ VMMCA does not check against individual ESX hosts. VMware checks are run by selecting the Other Computers check box and then selecting VMware vCenter from the drop-down menu. Add the vCenter name and run the scan. VMMCA 2008 will access the managed ESX hosts by using information in VMM 2008.

INSTALLING MICROSOFT BASELINE CONFIGURATION ANALYZER

If you have not installed Microsoft Baseline Configuration Analyzer (MBCA), here is the installation process (the whole install process takes about 30 seconds after the download is complete):

1. First, make sure you install the 64-bit version of MBCA, which can be downloaded from `http://www.microsoft.com/downloads/details.aspx?familyid=DB70824D-ABAE-4A92-9AA2-1F43C0FA49B3&displaylang=en` (Figure 3.2).

FIGURE 3.2
Download Microsoft Baseline Configuration Analyzer (MBCA)

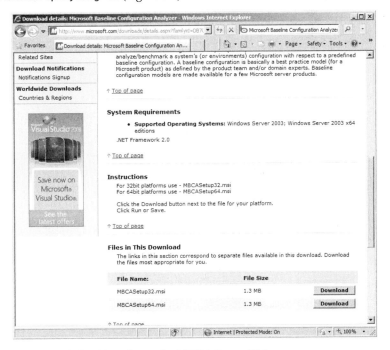

2. Upon running the downloaded MSI package, the MBCA Setup Welcome screen appears. Click Next to move on to the next screen.

3. Read the EULA and accept the license agreement to enable the Next button.

4. On the next page, you can specify the path to the location where you want to install the MBCA.

5. You are ready to start the installation of MBCA. In a few seconds, the MBCA setup should complete.

INSTALLING THE VMM CONFIGURATION ANALYZER

To install the VMM Configuration Analyzer, follow these steps (the total install time is roughly 30 seconds after the MSI package is downloaded):

1. When you click the VMM Configuration Analyzer option from the Setup splash screen, a browser window opens and you are taken to this link to download the latest VMM Configuration Analyzer package: http://www.microsoft.com/downloads/details.aspx? FamilyID=02d83950-c03d-454e-803b-96d1c1d5be24&DisplayLang=en.

2. Download the "VMMCA.msi" package from the download page and run it. The first page is the Welcome page (Figure 3.3). Click Next to proceed.

FIGURE 3.3
The Welcome page of the VMMCA Setup Wizard

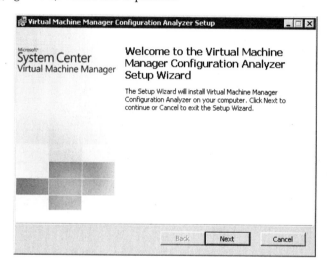

3. On the next page, accept the EULA and click Next to proceed.

4. Specify the path to the location where you want the VMMCA to be installed.

5. To start the installation of the VMMCA, click the Install button. In a few seconds, the VMMCA setup should complete.

LAUNCHING VMM CONFIGURATION ANALYZER

Upon installation, you can locate the VMM Configuration Analyzer in a program group Virtual Machine Manager Configuration Analyzer. The following describes how to run the configuration analyzer on a computer that is to be used to install VMM server:

1. Click the Configuration Analyzer option inside of the program group to bring up the VMMCA main user interface (Figure 3.4).

2. Since in this example we want to run the Configuration Analyzer for the VMM server installation, check VMM Server and uncheck the other options. Click the Scan button at the bottom of the dialog to begin the scanning process.

3. When the scan completes, VMMCA automatically generates and brings up a report in HTML format with the scan results. Figure 3.5 is a sample report run against a VMM server.

FIGURE 3.4
The VMMCA user
interface

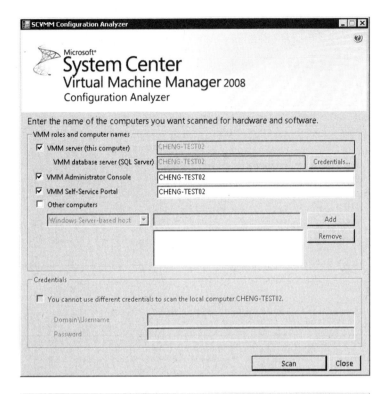

FIGURE 3.5
Scan result report

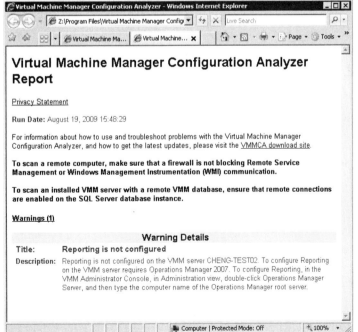

After confirming that there is no major issue with the target computer, you can proceed to the VMM server deployment.

VMM Server Deployment

As stated earlier, before you start your VMM server deployment, please be sure to check the hardware and software prerequisites of the target computer and run the VMM Configuration Analyzer. Doing so will save a lot of trouble later on, and it will ensure a quick and smooth installation experience.

Once you've made sure the prerequisites are met for the VMM server, there are three things you need to consider during the server deployment process:

◆ Where do you plan to host the data? The following questions need to be taken into account when planning for your VMM server deployment:

   ◆ Remote SQL database or local on the VMM server?

   ◆ Use SQL Server Express Edition or a full version of SQL Server?

These decisions depend on the size of your environment and the performance requirements. For basic proof-of-concept all-in-one-box testing purposes, using SQL Server Express on the VMM server can work. If you plan to use this deployment in a production environment, a full version of SQL Server on a separate computer is recommended.

You may need to consult with your DBA on the SQL Server name, instance name, and database names if you don't own the SQL servers.

◆ Do you want a default library on the VMM server? You need to be aware of the following facts about setting up a library on your VMM server:

   ◆ VMM server installation requires the existence of one library. You'd need to either use a share you preconfigured or let Setup create one on the VMM server.

   ◆ For better performance and future storage capacity flexibility, it's recommended that you use a different volume, even if you plan to let Setup to create a library share.

◆ What level of security control does your environment have? Depending on your environment's security policy and the level of security control, you should consult with your security team first on port selection as well as what account you should use to run the VMM Service.

Now, let's walk through the VMM server installation process:

1. Locate Setup.exe in the root directory of the media and launch the program in elevated privilege. The VMM Setup splash screen appears.

2. Click the VMM Server link to initiate the Virtual Machine Manager Server Setup Wizard (Figure 3.6).

3. On the first page of the wizard, accept the EULA to proceed to the next page.

4. Next, select whether you'd like to participate in the customer experience improvement program, which anonymously collects and sends data about the usage of the product to Microsoft for usability study and improvement (Figure 3.7).

5. Fill in your username and company name and click Next (Figure 3.8).

FIGURE 3.6
Launching the Virtual
Machine Manager Server
Setup Wizard

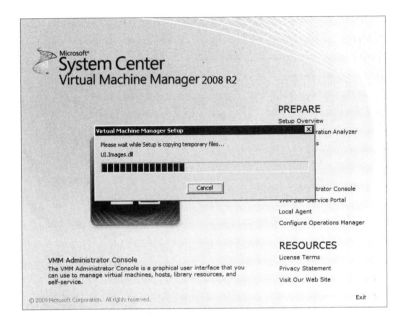

FIGURE 3.7
The CEIP page of
the VMM Server
Setup Wizard

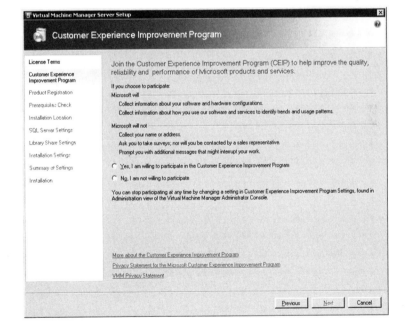

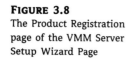

FIGURE 3.8
The Product Registration page of the VMM Server Setup Wizard Page

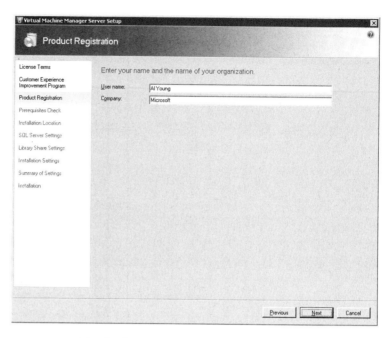

6. Next, the server setup prerequisite checker runs and checks for hardware and software prerequisites. If you've followed our recommendations in previous prerequisite sections before running the setup, you should see green checkmarks on both requirements.

   You can continue the installation if you receive warnings, but you must resolve all alerts before you can proceed with the installation. If there is any failure, the missing prerequisite will be shown and the Next button will be blocked. You can simply click Check Again after fixing the failure.

7. Next, specify the folder where you want the Setup to install the files for the MM server, and click Next (Figure 3.9).

8. This is where you need to enter information about the first decision we asked you to consider for the server deployment: Where do you want to host the data?

   If you decide to use the SQL Server Express Edition, simply click the first radio button and click Next to move on to the next page (Figure 3.10). If you decide to use a full version of SQL Server, you need to provide the following information:

   ◆ SQL server name

   ◆ Credentials to connect to the SQL server if the current user credentials do not have proper rights to create the VMM database

   ◆ SQL instance name

   ◆ Database name for VMM (name limit is 128 bytes)

   Enter the SQL Server information and click Next.

FIGURE 3.9

The Installation Location page of the VMM Server Setup Wizard

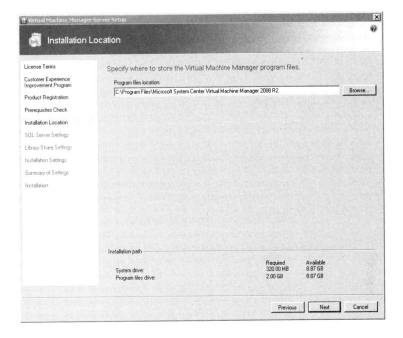

FIGURE 3.10

The SQL Server Settings page of the VMM Server Setup Wizard

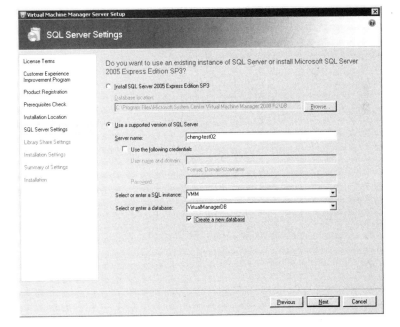

USING A SQL CLUSTER

To make the VMM database highly available, you can deploy it onto an existing clustered SQL Server instance that is running on a Windows Server 2008 or Windows Server 2003 failover cluster.

To support a SQL Server cluster, the following requirements must be met:

◆ You are using a version of SQL Server that supports failover clustering, such as version 2005 or later.

◆ The SQL Server instance must run on a Windows Server 2003 or later failover cluster.

◆ The database server must be in an Active Directory domain that has a two-way trust relationship with the domain that the VMM server is in.

◆ Since VMM requires Kerberos mutual authentication with SQL Server, the clustered SQL Server instance must associate a service principal name (SPN) with the account on which SQL Server will be running.

In addition, to allow VMM to tolerate the temporary downtime when a database fails over to a different node, you might need to change the default retry settings for the VMM database. The default settings are five retries with a 2-second retry interval. If, for example, you want to change the retry settings to six retries with a 4-second interval, you can do so by creating the following Registry keys on the VMM server.

```
HKEY_LOCAL_MACHINE\SOFTWARE\Microsoft\Microsoft System Center Virtual Machine
Manager Server\Settings\SQLValue Name=DBRetryIntervalValueType=REG_DWORDSample
value=00000004
HKEY_LOCAL_MACHINE\SOFTWARE\Microsoft\Microsoft System Center Virtual Machine
Manager Server\Settings\SQLValue Name=DBRetryCountValueType=REG_DWORDSample
value=00000006
```

CONSIDERATIONS FOR SQL DISK LAYOUT

For large-scale VMM deployment, we recommend that customers use the performance and scale guidance for databases from System Center Operations Manager 2007. As is described in the white paper (http://www.microsoft.com/downloads/details.aspx?FamilyID=a1b7610d-3dbe-4e51-bcb3-446d50dadf14&DisplayLang=en), the best practices you should apply to your VMM database server are as follows:

◆ Choose RAID-0 or RAID-1 for the database disk volumes to ensure that the disk I/O is optimized.

◆ Place your SQL database data and transaction logs on separate volumes.

◆ Use 64-bit hardware and a 64-bit operating system for larger memory support.

◆ Use a battery-backed write-caching disk controller to offload the I/O operations from database to hardware.

9. On the Library Share Settings page, you'll need to enter information on the second decision we asked at the beginning of this section. Again, you have two options here: create a new share or use an existing library share. Enter the library share information and click Next, as shown in Figure 3.11.

FIGURE 3.11
The Library Share
Settings page

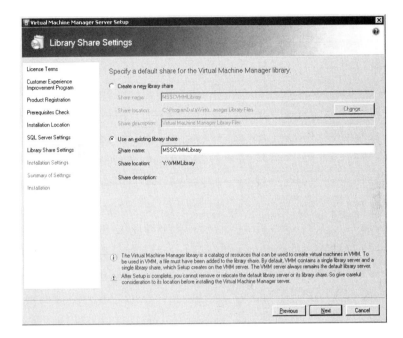

10. Last set of configuration settings are global settings that will be applied to all the VM host computers in this VMM environment, which means that you'd need to uninstall and reinstall the VMM server if you want to make a change to any of these settings. More important, since these settings actually are used for the VMM agent installation, they will be used for every VM host computer you intend to manage with this VMM server. The settings are as follows:

Ports The settings in this group define the ports through which the VMM server should communicate with the agent in the VM host computers.

VMM Service Account These settings define what account the VMM server uses to send down job requests for VM hosts to execute. The account who runs VMM service will also be configured to have administrator privilege on every managed VM host computer.

In an environment with relaxed security policies, default settings could work. But if your security team has specific requirements on what ports can be open on host computers or has restrictive policies, this is where you must customize those settings. And when you deploy an agent to target VM host computers, the matching settings must be used. Figure 3.12 shows how this page looks.

FIGURE 3.12
The Installation Settings
page

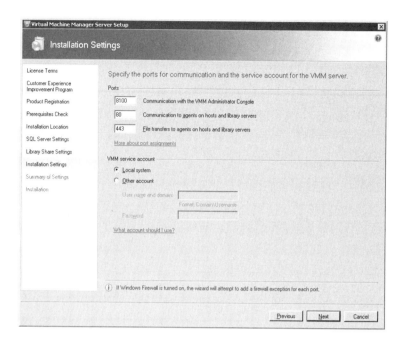

USING A DOMAIN ACCOUNT IN INSTALLATION SETTINGS

There are quite a few scenarios in which you might want to use a domain user account instead of the default VMM server machine account to run VMM service. Here they are:

◆ If you have a more restrictive AD environment (specifically, when the Restricted Groups group policy is enabled), VMMService should be run with a domain account. Since Restricted Groups policy disallows machine accounts to be part of the local administrators group, when the group policy is in effect, the machine account will be removed by it automatically. If this happens to the VM host computer, it will lead the host into a needs attention state and agent status will turn into Not Responding.

◆ If your environment is a disjointed namespace environment, which essentially describes an environment in which the computer's fully qualified domain name does not match the FQDN from the Active Directory, you must use a domain account to run VMMService. Check out the published TechNet doc for more information on disjointed namespace:

  `http://technet.microsoft.com/en-us/library/cc773264(WS.10).aspx`

◆ When you plan to share ISO files on your remote library (file share) among your VMs, you will need to enable constrained delegation on every Hyper-V server on which you plan to attach a shared ISO to the VMs running on it. You will also need to make sure the VMMService account is specified to use a domain account instead of the default machine account.

♦ If you decide to use a domain account (instead of the VMM server's local system account) to run the VMM service (VMMService), it's highly recommended that the account be designated for VMM only purposes. Here's why. When the agent is removed from the VM host, the account under which VMMService is running will be removed from the VM host's local Administrators group. And if the account is shared and used by other apps on the VM host, this can break other apps when you remove the host.

♦ Last but not least, if you use a domain account to run VMMService on the VMM server, and even if this account has administrator privilege on the VM host computer, this account cannot be used to add VM host computers.

11. After you configure the Installation Settings page and click Next, you are presented with the summary page. Review it carefully for all the settings before clicking the Install button to begin the installation process (Figure 3.13).

FIGURE 3.13
The Summary of Settings page

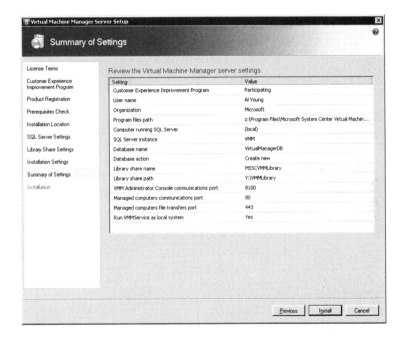

Once the actual installation process starts, a progress page shows the software component breakdown for the server installation and detailed status information for each component. Figure 3.14 shows what you should see when the installation is complete.

It's recommended that immediately after the server install, you ensure that your VMM server has the latest software updates.

FIGURE 3.14
VMM Server Install
Wizard - Complete Page

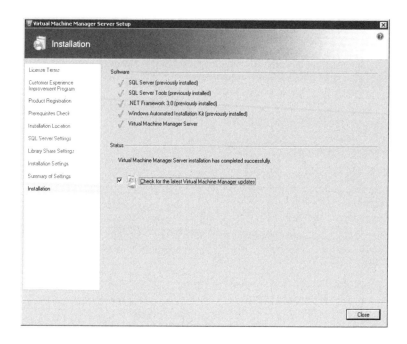

DEFAULT VMM ADMINISTRATORS

By default, when installing a VMM Server, VMM Setup automatically populates the database and adds all domain accounts in the local administrator security group on the VMM server as the VMM Administrator user role. What this means is that all the users in the VMM Server Administrator group automatically become a VMM Administrator.

If you need to add additional new users to VMM Administrator or remove ones from the list, you'll need to log on to the VMM Administrator Console as a VMM Administrator and make the desired changes to the Administrator user role properties from the User Roles node in administration view.

Installing and Configuring the VMM Administrator Console

Now that the VMM server, along with the database and at least one library, have been deployed, the next thing you need to do is to install a client.

Since the VMM PowerShell layer is an inseparable built-in component for the console and the Self-Service Portal, whether you are GUI user or a command-line user, you need to install the VMM Administrator Console.

WHAT YOU NEED TO KNOW BEFORE INSTALLING THE CONSOLE

To enable the integration between Systems Center Operations Manager and Virtual Machine Manager, you must install the VMM Administrator Console on the Operations Manager 2007 Server and install the Operations Manager 2007 Operations Console on the VMM server.

The integration will enable PRO reporting and give the OpsMgr administrators the ability to perform tasks on virtual machine hosts and virtual machines from within the System Center Virtual Machine Manager 2008 Management Pack.

So, if you are trying to set up an all-in-one-box setup (including an Operations Manager server) and you plan to enable PRO and the reporting features for your VMM deployment, do not install the VMM Administrator Console. Skip to the next section and select the Configure Operations Manager setup option on the main splash screen instead because that will install both the Administrator Console and the necessary management packs to enable PRO and reporting.

Now, let's walk through the steps to install the VMM Administrator Console:

1. Pick a target computer on which to install the console. Note that the console can be installed on Windows server operating systems as well as Windows client operating systems, and it has a wider OS support matrix (comparing with the server).

2. Make sure the prerequisites for the Administrator Console described earlier in this chapter are met.

3. Open the media in your Explorer window, launch `setup.exe` as Administrator, and select VMM Administrator Console on the Setup splash screen.

4. Read and accept the EULA and click Next.

5. Choose whether or not to participate in the Customer Experience Initiative Program and click Next.

6. If there are failures from prerequisite checks, you need to resolve the required dependencies before you can move on. If you pass the prerequisite checks, as shown in Figure 3.15, click Next.

FIGURE 3.15
The Prerequisites Check page of the VMM Administrator Console Setup Wizard

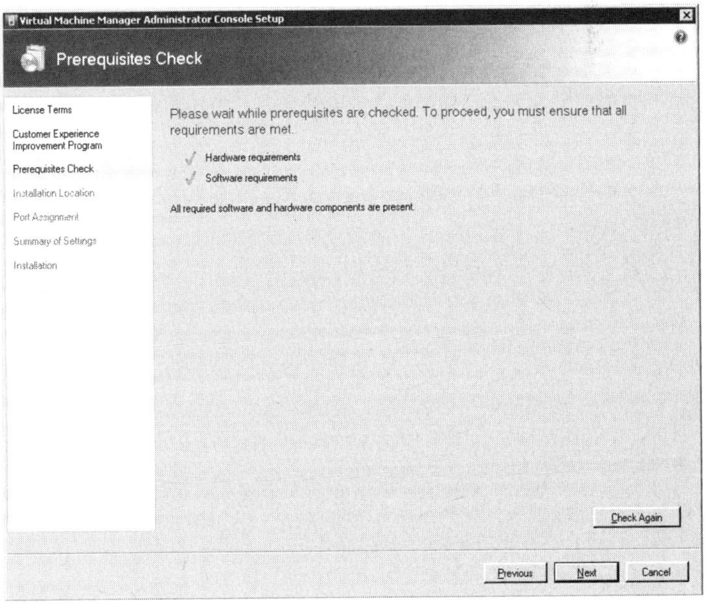

7. Select the program installation location and click Next.

8. Fill in the server port settings and click Next (Figure 3.16).

FIGURE 3.16
The Port Assignment
page

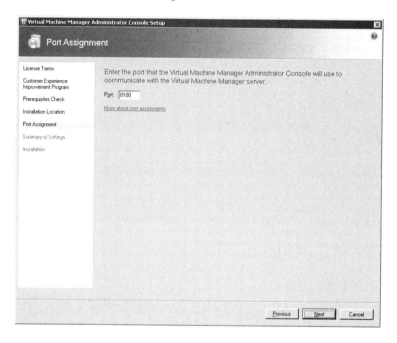

ABOUT PORT SETTINGS

In VMM, all port configurations that are used for server-agent communications are set on the VMM server when it is installed. The settings are global, which applies to all agents that are to be managed by this VMM server. Hence, when the Administrator Console is installed, the port settings must match with what was specified when the VMM server was installed.

If you need to install multiple Administrator Consoles connecting to the same VMM server, all consoles must be configured to connect to the port the VMM server listens to.

We don't recommend changing the port once the VMM server is deployed. But if you must change the port, the process is to uninstall the VMM server first and then reinstall it with the new desired port settings. During the reinstall, you will have the option of reusing your existing database so no data will be lost in the process.

---

9. After reviewing the settings for the Administrator Console, click Next (Figure 3.17).

If you've taken care of the prerequisites, the setup should complete within a couple minutes. This concludes the installation of the Administrator Console. We do recommend that you check Windows Update immediately after installation to check for the latest updates.

If this is your first Administrator Console and this is a new VMM environment, your console will look like Figure 3.18.

FIGURE 3.17
The Summary page of
the VMM Administrator
Console Setup Wizard

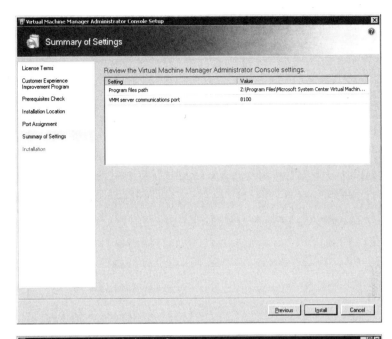

FIGURE 3.18
Newly installed VMM
environment

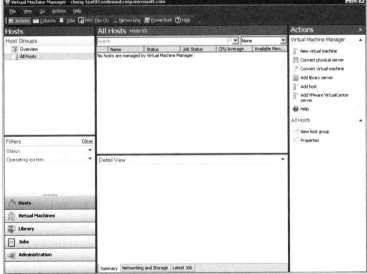

Installing and Configuring VMM and Operations Manager Integration Components

PRO stands for Performance and Resource Optimization. It's built on top of the powerful and extensible monitoring capabilities of System Center Operations Manager. To enable PRO, you need to install the deep integration component, which is also referred to as OpsMgr Connector.

Installing Prerequisite Management Packs on Operations Manager Server

As described earlier in this chapter, there are a few management packs (MPs) that you must import into the Operations Manager server before you can proceed with the configuration steps on the VMM server:

◆ Windows Server BaseOS Management Pack

◆ Windows Server IIS Management Pack

◆ SQL Server Management Pack

These steps need to be done only once at your Operations Manager's root management server (RMS). Let's walk through the steps of installing the prerequisite management packs:

1. If you don't have the required Windows Server BaseOS management packs, you need to download and import them.

2. To import the management packs, click on the Administration wunder bar menu in Operations Manager's console, select Management Packs from the administration tree view in the upper left. From the actions menu, click Actions, click Import Management Packs, and then select the MPs that you just downloaded to open the Import Management Packs dialog, shown in Figure 3.19.

FIGURE 3.19
Importing Windows
Server MPs

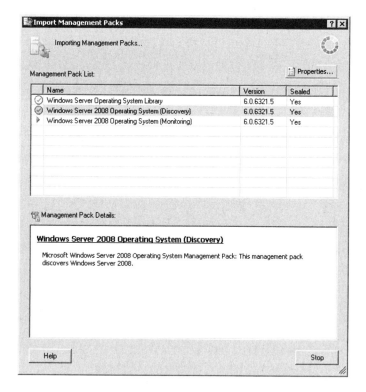

3. Next, if you don't have the required IIS management packs, you need to download them from Operations Manager's online catalog.

4. The next step is to import the downloaded IIS management packs via the Operations Manager Administrator Console. As you did in step 2, select the downloaded MPs to import (Figure 3.20).

FIGURE 3.20
Importing IIS MPs

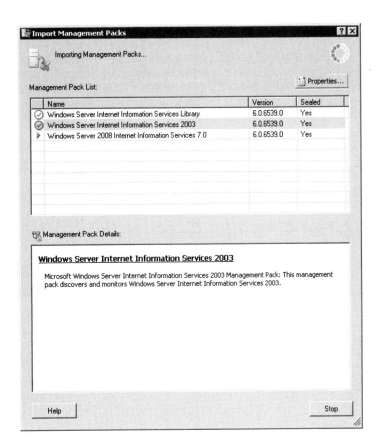

5. Last, if you don't have the required SQL Server management pack, you need to download it from Operations Manager's online catalog and import it via the Operations Manager Administrator Console, as shown in Figure 3.21.

FIGURE 3.21
Importing SQL Server
MPs

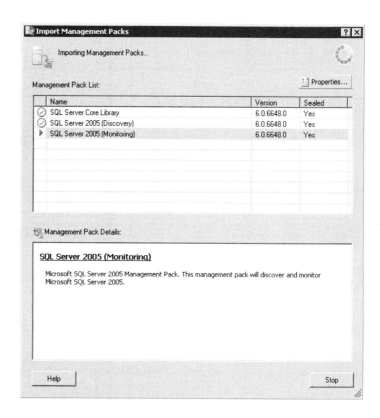

Installing the VMM OPSMGR Connector

As stated earlier, you now need to install the VMM Administrator Console on the Operations Manager 2007 server and install the Operations Manager 2007 Operations Console on the VMM server.

PREPARING OPERATIONS MANAGER SERVER

If there are any leftover prerelease version VMM 2008 management packs, they must be deleted before proceeding with configuring Operations Manager. Here is the list of possible VMM management packs that need to be removed if present, as shown in the Figure 3.22:

- System Center Virtual Machine Manager 2008 R2

- System Center Virtual Machine Manager 2008 R2 Diagram Views

- System Center Virtual Machine Manager 2008 R2 PRO Host Performance

- System Center Virtual Machine Manager 2008 R2 PRO Library

- System Center Virtual Machine Manager 2008 R2 PRO Virtual Machine Right-Sizing

◆ System Center Virtual Machine Manager 2008 R2 PRO VMware Host Performance

◆ System Center Virtualization Reports 2008 R2

FIGURE 3.22
VMM management
packs view in Operations
Manager console

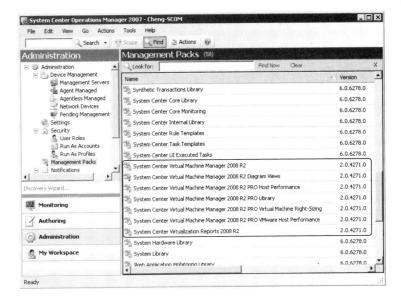

To delete a management pack, right-click it and choose Delete.

RUNNING CONFIGURE OPERATIONS MANAGER ON OPERATIONS MANAGER RMS SERVER

Even if your Operations Manager environment has multiple management servers, you only need to run the Configure Operations Manager setup step once on the root management server. To do this, follow these steps:

1. Launch `setup.exe` from your VMM 2008 R2 installation media, and select the Configure Operations Manager option.

When you install the VMM Administrator Console, the console Setup installs the Windows PowerShell — Virtual Machine Manager command shell, which is required for Operations Manager administrators to perform VM- or VM-host-related tasks.

THE OPERATIONS MANAGER INTEGRATION COMPONENT INCLUDES A VMM ADMINISTRATOR CONSOLE

If you are running an all-in-one setup (including the Operations Manager product), you will need to select the Configure Operations Manager setup option on the main splash screen before you install Administrator Console. If you accidentally installed the Administrator Console first, when you click on the option Configure Operations Manager, you would get the warning message and prompt for console uninstall, as seen here.

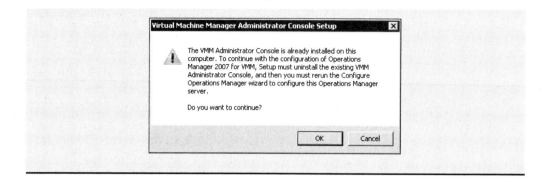

The setup experience appears very similar to the UI experience for installing Administrator Console. Besides installing the VMM Administrator Console on the Operations Manager's RMS, it also imports the VMM 2008 R2 management packs and grants the service account of the VMM server necessary access to Operations Manager.

2. Read and accept the EULA and then click Next.

3. On the Customer Experience Improvement Program page, note that you no longer have options to participate the program because the choice was made when the VMM server was installed. Click Next to continue.

4. On the Prerequisites Check page, if there are failures, you'll need to resolve the required dependencies before you can move on. If you pass prerequisite checks, click Next.

5. Select the program installation location and click Next.

6. Similar to the Administrator Console install, fill in the matching server port settings and click Next.

7. After reviewing the settings for the Administrator Console, as shown in Figure 3.23, click Next.

8. During the installation of the Administrator Console, the process of importing MPs can take a while. Depending on your machine's resource, you may have to wait for a couple minutes before seeing the results.

9. If one or more of the required MPs is not imported to the Operations Manager server, the install will fail with the error message shown in Figure 3.24.

If you've taken care of the prerequisites before the setup, the setup should complete in a couple minutes.

INSTALLING THE VMM ADMINISTRATOR CONSOLE ON ALL NON-RMS MANAGEMENT SERVERS

If your Operations Manager management group has multiple management servers, after running the Configure Operations Manager setup on the root management server, you need to install a VMM Administrator Console on all other management servers in the management group.

FIGURE 3.23
The summary page

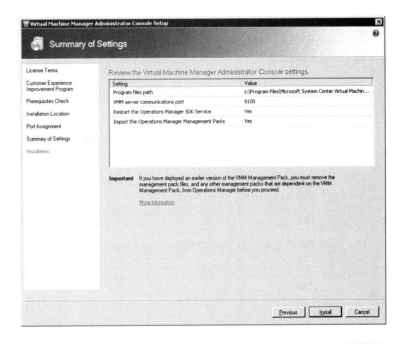

FIGURE 3.24
Missing required MP
error message

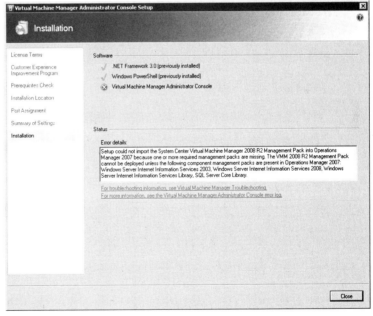

Launch `setup.exe` from your VMM 2008 R2 installation media, and select the VMM Administrator Console option. The process here for each VMM Administrator Console install on each Operations Manager management server is identical to the process described in "Installing and Configuring the VMM Administrator Console" earlier in this chapter.

Configuring the VMM Server and Management Servers

After the OpsMgr Connector is installed, you need to continue the configuration steps on the VMM server and on Operations Manager's management servers.

CONFIGURING THE VMM ADMINISTRATOR ROLE

Before you proceed any further, note all the default agent action accounts for all the management servers. Here is how to get that information:

1. Open Operations Manager's Administrator Console and choose the administration view from the wonder bar menu.

2. Expand the Security node in the administration tree view in the upper-left corner of the console. Click Run As Profiles.

3. From the list view in the middle of the console, double-click Default Action Account to bring up the Run As Profile Properties – Default Action Account dialog.

4. Click the Run As Accounts tab on the dialog.

5. The Run As Accounts list includes the information that you need to note. The options for these steps are shown in Figure 3.25.

FIGURE 3.25
Finding the default agent action accounts

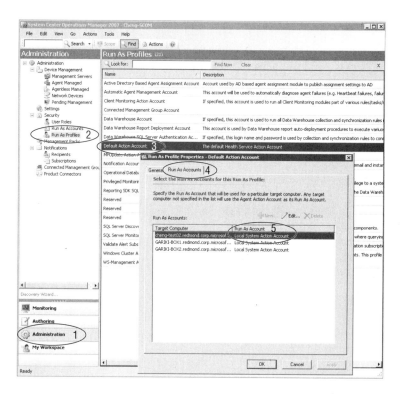

Next, switch to a VMM Administrator Console, log in as a VMM administrator, and add all the default action accounts for each of the Operations Manager management servers to the Administrator role in VMM. Here is how to do this:

1. Open VMM's Administrator Console.

2. Select the User Roles node in the administration view and double-click the Administrator user role to open the User Role Properties For Administrator dialog.

3. Click the Members tab, click the Add button in the lower-right corner, and add the default action accounts you wrote down in the previous set of steps (Figure 3.26).

FIGURE 3.26
Adding members to the VMM Administrator role

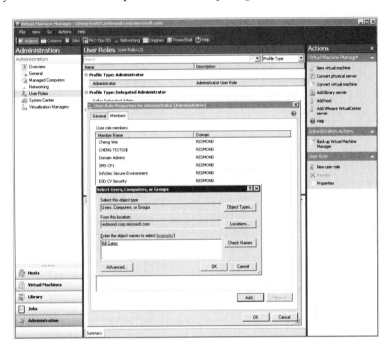

ENABLING POWERSHELL REMOTE EXECUTE ON ALL MANAGEMENT SERVERS AND THE VMM SERVER

For PRO to invoke scripts remotely on VMM or the Operations Manager management server, Windows PowerShell must be enabled for remote script execution in the Virtual Machine Manager PowerShell snap-in. This needs to be done on each management server and on the VMM server.

You can launch a VMM PowerShell session by either clicking the PowerShell button on the VMM Administrator Console or clicking the Windows PowerShell – Virtual Machine Manager program option on the Windows Programs menu. Then follow these steps:

1. Choose All Programs ➤ Microsoft System Center ➤ Virtual Machine Manager 2008 R2.

2. At the prompt, select Always to always trust remote signed scripts from this snap-in. If you don't see a prompt, the policy already allows PRO to run scripts.

CONFIGURING RMS IN THE VMM ADMINISTRATOR CONSOLE

This is the key part of integrating the VMM and Operations Manager products. To add or change the Operations Manager server in VMM, follow these steps:

1. Click the System Center node in administration view.

2. Open the Operations Manager Server dialog box.

3. In the Server Name field, enter the computer name, NETBIOS, or fully qualified domain name (FQDN) of the root management server for Operations Manager. In a disjointed namespace, you must enter the FQDN (Figure 3.27).

FIGURE 3.27
Adding Operations
Manager into VMM

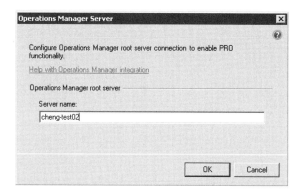

4. If you did not install the required management packs onto your OpsMgr management server or still have leftover older versions (versions before 2.0.4071.0) of the VMM management pack in the RMS, this operation will fail and the error message shown in Figure 3.28 will appear.

FIGURE 3.28
Failure to add
Operations Manager
RMS error message

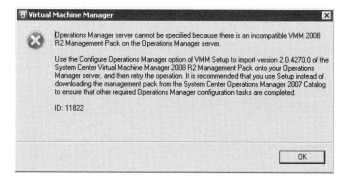

5. If you run into the error shown in Figure 3.28 stating that the Operations Manager server cannot be specified because there is an incompatible VMM 2008 R2 management pack on it, open your Operations Manager console and remove any VMM MP that has a smaller version number than 2.0.4071.0, as shown in Figure 3.29.

6. To evaluate a successful Operations Manager integration, check the diagram views in the Operations console to ensure that a view has been added for the VMM server, as shown in Figure 3.30.

FIGURE 3.29
Wrong MP versions in the management server

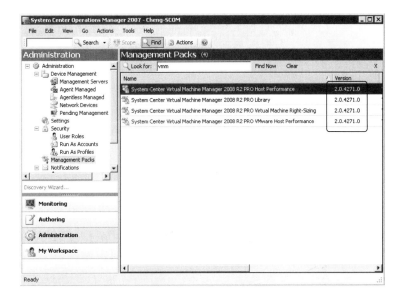

FIGURE 3.30
Integration verification on Operations Manager console

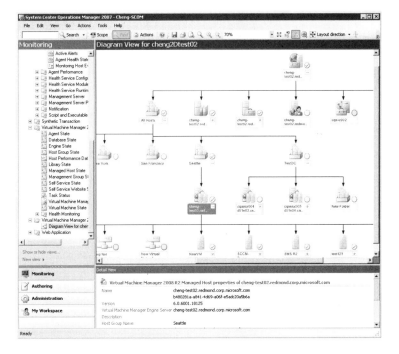

After you configure the Operations Manager server in VMM, the diagram view should begin populating immediately and should also be launchable from the VMM Administrator Console. For very large VMM virtualized environments, the initial discovery might take as long as an hour to complete.

KNOWN ISSUES WITH VMM AND OPERATIONS MANAGER INTEGRATION

Here are some of the commonly known causes that may lead to VMM and Operations Manager integration configuration failure:

◆ Operations Manager does not begin monitoring a host group until at least one host has been added. For this reason, the diagram shows the status of empty host groups as Not Monitored.

◆ If Operations Manager integration is not successful, a Discovery Failed error is added to the VM Manager event log on the VMM server.

◆ If VMM Administrator Console is not installed on a management server, the PRO tip remediation action may fail.

◆ If the default agent action account for a management server is not added to the VMM Administrator role, the PRO action will fail with Access Denied.

Configure Reporting for VMM

In VMM, reports are generated by Operations Manager, but they can be opened in reporting view in the VMM Administrator Console. Please note that the VMM Administrator Console shows the reporting view only after you have configured reporting in VMM.

Before you perform the VMM reporting configuration, make sure you set up your reporting server in Operations Manager 2007 SP1 or later. For instructions for deploying reporting in Operations Manager 2007 or Operations Manager 2007 R2, see "How to Deploy Reporting in Operations Manager 2007" (http://go.microsoft.com/fwlink/?LinkId=130663). You should also complete all Operations Manager integration steps before you enable reporting.

ENABLING REPORTING IN VMM

VMM leverages Operations Manager's reporting capability for customers to mine historical data. Perform the following steps to enable reporting in Virtual Machine Manager:

1. Through Operations Manager Administrator Console, add VMM administrators' accounts to the Report Operator role to enable them to view and use reports generated in Operations Manager.

2. Log on to VMM Administrator Console as a VMM administrator, navigate to the System Center node in the administration view, right-click Operations Manager Reporting URL, and select Modify.

3. Check the Enable Reporting check box. And specify the URL for the Operations Manager reporting server by using the following format:

   http[s]://<OpsMgrReportServer>[:<port>]/<ReportServer>

   ◆ <OpsMgrReportServer> is the fully qualified domain name (FQDN) of your reporting server.

   ◆ <ReportServer> is the name of the reporting server virtual directory (by default, ReportServer). The name of the reporting server cannot contain Unicode characters.

4. To find the URL for your reporting server, in the administration pane of the Operations console for Operations Manager, click Settings. In the results pane, right-click Reporting, and then click Properties. You will find the URL in the reporting server URL field.

5. Click OK. VMM will check for a valid reporting server and then save the settings.

VERIFYING REPORTING IN VMM

After you finish the reporting configuration process, you can verify that the reports are available in Virtual Machine Manager. To verify that reporting was successfully enabled in VMM, do the following:

1. In the VMM Administrator Console, make sure the Reporting button has been added to the navigation pane.

2. If you do not see a Reporting button, close and then reopen the VMM Administrator Console.

3. Click the Reporting button to display reporting view. If no report shows up in reporting view, you may not have been added to the Report Operator role in Operations Manager.

What More You Can Monitor in Your VMM Environment

The VMM server is now configured to integrate with OPSMGR. If you want to take full advantage of the Operations Manager integration, you should plan to do the following:

♦ Deploy Operations Manager agents on all your hosts and virtual machines. You must install an Operations Manager agent on each Hyper-V host and Virtual Server host and on the guest operating system of each virtual machine to collect data for PRO. You will also be able to monitor these servers using whichever management packs you have loaded into your OpsMgr environment.

♦ If you are using VMM to manage a VMware Infrastructure 3 environment, you don't need to install any Operations Manager agents for the vCenter server and ESX Server hosts; the Operations Manager agent on the VMM server monitors the VMware components.

♦ Enable PRO in VMM for individual host groups and host clusters and for VMM server-level actions.

♦ If VMM is managing a VMware Infrastructure 3 environment, you do not need to install any Operations Manager agents on the managed VMware ESX Server hosts. For the ESX Server hosts, the Operations Manager agent on the VMM server provides health and performance data to Operations Manager and to PRO. However, if you want to add guest monitoring of virtual machines, you must deploy an Operations Manager agent on the guest operating system of each VMware virtual machine.

Chapter 9 takes you on a "deep dive" tour to see what a PRO pack is composed of and how to author your own PRO pack.

Installing and Configuring VMM Self-Service Portal

Unlike the VMM Administrator Console, the VMM Self-Service Portal is an optional client component. It's designed to for self-service users to create and manage their own virtual machines within a controlled environment through a portable and accessible browser-based interface, thereby avoiding the need to install the VMM administrative client.

THINGS YOU SHOULD KNOW ABOUT SELF-SERVICE PORTAL

For better performance, it's recommended that VMM Self-Service Portal should be installed on a different computer than the computer on which the VMM server is installed. And the more self-service users you plan to have, the more Self-Service Portals you should deploy.

You can install more Self-Service Portals to scale out, but there is no native load balancing. Most web server environments already have a load balancing scheme in place for an IIS environment. And installing more SSP does not increase the total number of concurrent connections (50) supported per VMM installation.

Installing Self-Service Portal on a domain controller is not supported.

Installing Self-Service Portal

Here are the steps to install the Self-Service Portal:

1. First, select a server on which to install the Self-Service Portal, check for the prerequisites described in earlier in this chapter, and ensure that all prerequisites are met.

2. Open the media and select VMM Self-Service Portal on the Setup splash screen to launch the installation of the Self-Service Portal.

3. Read and accept the EULA and click Next.

4. If there are failures from prerequisite checks, you need to resolve the required dependencies before you can move on to the next page; if you pass prerequisite checks, click Next.

5. Select the program installation location and click Next.

6. Fill in the desired web portal settings in the Web Server Settings page (Figure 3.31) and click Next.

FIGURE 3.31
The Web Server Settings page of the VMM Self-Service Portal Setup Wizard

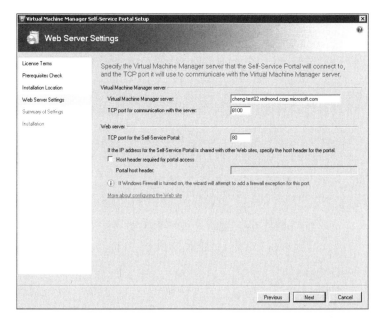

ABOUT WEB SERVER SETTINGS

When you want to change the web server settings for the Self-Service Portal, please be aware of the following facts:

◆ If the IIS web server is shared with other web-based applications and the default port (80) is already used, you must specify a different port or specify a host header for the portal. Please note that, depending on your IIS server's operating system version, you will need to follow an OS-specific approach to set up the host header.

◆ The Self-Service Portal Setup will attempt to add a firewall exception for the port you specify on the Web Server Settings page.

◆ By default, the portal is installed in a nonsecure mode. To enable Secure Sockets Layer (SSL) for your Self-Service Portal, follow the generic IIS SSL enablement process (roughly 4 steps):

   1. Obtain a certificate.

   2. Create an SSL binding.

   3. Test the configuration.

   4. Configure the SSL options.

7. On the summary page, review the settings for the Self-Service Portal and click Next (Figure 3.32).

FIGURE 3.32
The Summary of Settings page

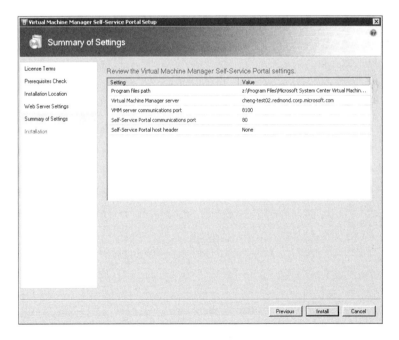

8. It's a fairly fast process to install the web components. Within a minute, the process should finish.

9. Once the portal installation completes successfully, you can open up the IIS Manager console to check out the new Self-Service Portal. Browse underneath the Sites node to find VMM R2 Self Service Portal. Figure 3.33 shows what your website is going to look like. And if you launch your browser and navigate to the website you just created, you should see the Self-Service Portal home page.

FIGURE 3.33
VMM Self-Service
Portal in IIS

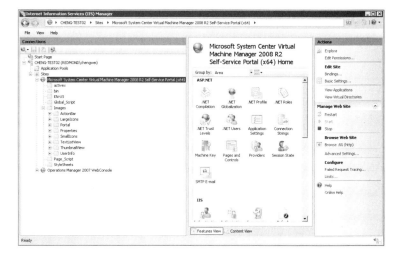

Setting Up Constrained Delegation for Self-Service Portal

When VMM Self-Service Portal and the VMM server are installed on different computers, constrained delegation for the VMM service account must be configured on the web server. Constrained delegation establishes a trust relationship under which an Active Directory account is granted permission to delegate credentials to another specific service.

In this case, since the IIS web server is not on the same computer as the VMM server, the web server will need to be granted permission to delegate the connecting client's credentials to the VMM server so the VMM server can properly authorize the self-service users based on their assigned rights. This allows administrators to grant authorization to specific Self-Service Portal features directly to end users and have the VMM server honor those settings directly.

To set up constrained delegation for the Self-Service Portal, you need to first enable the Integrated Windows authentication on the IIS server. If your web server is IIS 7.0, follow these steps to enable Integrated Windows authentication:

1. From Server Manager, open Internet Information Services (IIS) Manager.

2. Navigate to the IIS web server that hosts the VMM Self-Service Portal.

3. In the Features View pane, double-click Authentication.

4. On the Authentication page, ensure that Windows Authentication is enabled. If not, enable it. If Windows Authentication is not listed, install the Windows Authentication Role Service for the Web Server (IIS) role.

5. Disable all other authentication types.

Perform the following steps only if your web server is IIS 6.0:

1. In Administrative Tools, open Internet Information Services (IIS) Manager.

2. Navigate to the IIS web server that hosts the VMM Self-Service Portal.

3. Under Web Sites, right-click Microsoft System Center Virtual Machine Manager 2008 Self-Service Portal, and then click Properties.

4. In the Authentication access section, on the Directory Security tab, click Edit.

5. Select the Integrated Windows authentication check box.

6. Clear the Enable Anonymous Access check box.

To configure the VMM service account to be trusted for delegation by Kerberos, follow these steps:

1. Create a Kerberos service principal name (SPN) for the VMM server. Open a command prompt with proper AD privilege and type in **setspn -R <vmmserviceaccount>**.

   Note that <vmmserviceaccount> is either the machine account of the VMM server if VMM-Service is running as Local System or the domain user account under which VMM runs.

2. You should see output similar to the following:

   ```
   Registered ServicePrincipalNames for CN=Self Service
   Test,CN=Users,DC=contoso,DC=com:
           HOST/vmmserviceaccount
           HOST/vmmserviceaccount.contoso.com
   ```

3. In Administrative Tools, open Active Directory Users and Computers, locate the computer account for the self-service web server, and then open the Properties dialog of that computer account.

4. On the Delegation tab, click Trust This Computer For Delegation To Specified Services Only, and then click Use Kerberos Only.

5. Click Add, and then navigate to the SPN that you created earlier (say, HOST/<vmmservice-account>). Select the HOST service type for your VMM server, and then click OK.

6. On the IIS web server that hosts the Self-Service Portal, run regedit and create a Registry key:

   a. Locate the registry hive HKEY_LOCAL_MACHINE\SOFTWARE\Microsoft\Microsoft System Center Virtual Machine Manager Self-Service Portal\Settings\.

   b. Create a new Registry key with key name = VMMServerSPN and key value = the SPN you registered (for example HOST/vmmserviceaccount).

 **Real World Scenario**

CONFIGURING CONSTRAINED DELEGATION FOR MY LAB

It's actually quite often in a medium or large environment that you will set up your Self-Service Portal IIS server on a different computer from your VMM server. In fact, in one of our test labs, we had five computers joined to a test domain. To test various configurations, we had one computer (MyVMMServer05) running the VMM server and the library, one stand-alone Self-Service Portal IIS server (TestWeb05), and a three-node Hyper-V host cluster.

Since our Self-Service Portal and VMM server were installed on different OpsMgr computers, we had to configure the VMM service account to be trusted for delegation in Active Directory. Here's what we did:

1. Since the servers were all Windows Server 2008 R2, we enabled Integrated Windows authentication and disabled all other authentication types on for the VMM Self-Service Portal website by using Server Manager.

2. We then created a Kerberos SPN for the VMM server (MyVMMServer05) by running the following command:

   ```
   setspn -R HOST/MyVMMServer05
   ```

3. Then we used administrator tool to update TestWeb05 (the web server) delegation properties by adding the VMM Server's SPN (HOST/MyVMMServer05).

4. Finally, we updated the Registry key on the web server (TestWeb05) with the VMM server's SPN too.

Now the Self-Service Portal users can authenticate with the VMM server and have access to the resources to which they are designated.

Configuring Self-Service User Roles

Role-based security in the VMM 2008 release and later is implemented to allow users to define fine-grained control over who can perform what action on which VM or VM host objects.

UNDERSTANDING THE DELEGATED ADMINISTRATION MODEL

In VMM, there are three types of users:

◆ VMM administrators control access through policies that designate capabilities.

◆ Delegated administrators manage a scoped environment, and within that scope, they can control access through policies that further designate capabilities.

◆ Self-service users have access to only the web portal, can create or manage their own VMs (i.e., virtual machines for which they are listed as the owner in the properties of the virtual machine), typically have quota as to how many VMs they can create, and can script through PowerShell.

The user roles are defined in the same way as roles are defined in System Center Operations Manager (User Role = Membership + Profile + Scope). The following is a brief list of what each component of a user role means:

◆ Membership

  ◆ Determines which users are part of a particular user role.

  ◆ Members may be individual users or groups.

  ◆ Members may be in multiple user roles, including user roles based on different profiles.

- ◆ Profile
    - ◆ Determines which actions are permitted.
    - ◆ Determines which user interface is accessible.
    - ◆ Determines how the scope is defined.
- ◆ Scope
    - ◆ Determines the objects on which a user may take actions.

Figure 3.34 shows how a delegated administration can be modeled.

FIGURE 3.34
Delegated administration model

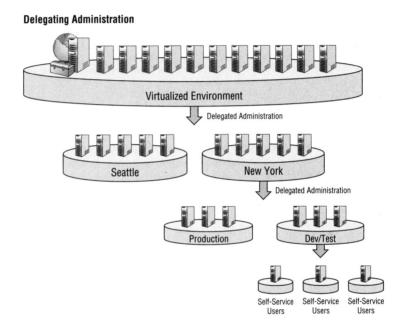

Delegating Administration

LIMITATIONS FOR SELF-SERVICE USERS

Here are some known limitations for the Self-Service User role:

- ◆ Only VMM administrators and delegated administrators can log on to the Administrator Console.
- ◆ VMM self-service users cannot log on to the Administrator Console.
- ◆ VMM self-service users can only use the Self-Service Portal as their interface to access the VM creation and management functionalities.

USER ROLE CREATION WORKFLOW

Now, let's walk through an example of creating a user role. The required information to create a user role corresponds to the definition of the user role: the membership of the user role, the profile of the user role, and the scope of the user role. Here are the steps:

1. To create a new user role, navigate to the administration view.

2. Click User Role in the tree view.

3. Click New User Role on the actions pane to bring up the Create User Role Wizard. These first three steps are illustrated in Figure 3.35.

FIGURE 3.35
Launching the Create User Role Wizard

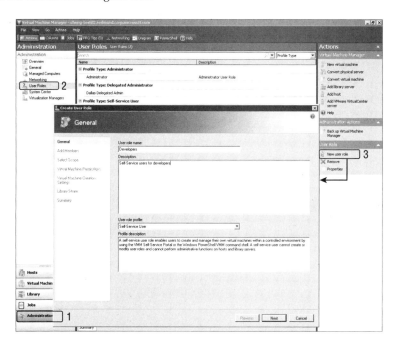

4. After providing a name and description for the new user role, click Next to add members to this user role. Click the Add button to bring up the user selection dialog, shown in Figure 3.36. Type in the user names, click Check Names, click OK, and then click Next to proceed to the next wizard page.

5. On the Select Scope page, check the host groups to which you want this new user role to have access, and then click Next.

6. On the Virtual Machine Permissions page, specify what action this new user role can take on the VMs in the scope, as shown in Figure 3.37, and click Next.

7. The next page is the Library Share page (Figure 3.38). This is where you allow users to store virtual machines in a library and the libraries to which this user role has access.

8. This is the last step before the user role creation job is submitted to the VMM server (Figure 3.39). After confirming that all the settings are correct, click Next to start the user role creation job.

FIGURE 3.36
Adding members
to the role

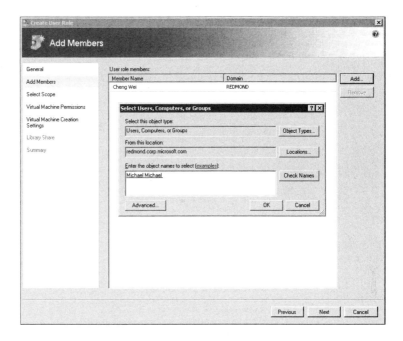

FIGURE 3.37
Defining what actions
are allowed for this
user role

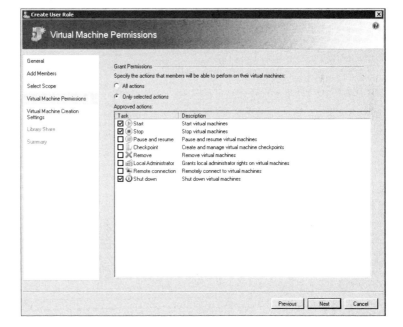

FIGURE 3.38
Define the libraries to
which this user role has
access

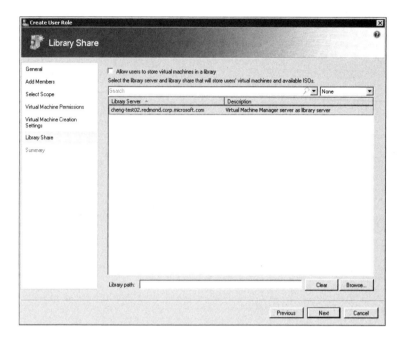

FIGURE 3.39
The Summary page of
the Create User Role
Wizard

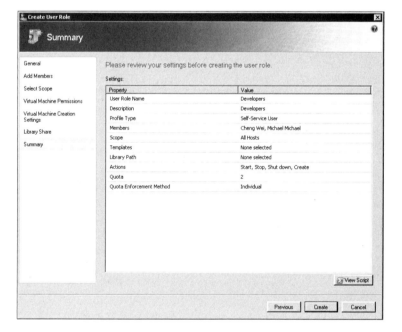

And there you have it. A new user role is created. The users specified in the user role will immediately have access to the host (for creating VMs if you grant VM creation rights to them) through the Self-Service Portal.

A Few Notes for Self-Service Users

Here are few more tips for self-service users that you should know when creating or managing them:

◆ When you assign a scope (host group) to a user role, it does not mean all the users in that user role automatically get access to all the hosts and VMs on those hosts.

◆ For a self-service user to get access to a VM, three things have to happen:

  ◆ The user must be member of a user role.

  ◆ This user role must have scope that covers the host where this VM is hosted.

  ◆ This user must be the owner of the VM.

◆ The user will not be able to see, access, or control this VM, if any one of preceding three things is not met.

◆ You can assign an AD group as the owner of a VM; you can also add an AD group as a member of a user role. AD group ownership is useful for VMs shared across a team of people. At the same time, be aware that this sharing model also means no exclusive access control and that all users in the same group have exactly the same set of privileges to the same VM.

◆ Last, unlike self-service users, users in the Delegated Administrator user role can see and take any action on all VMs and hosts within their scope regardless of the owner of those VMs. Delegated administrators are implicit owners of everything under their scope.

Configuring Self-Service Administrative Contact

The last optional Self-Service Portal setting is to set the self-service administrative contact. When the self-service users run into problems or failures and they need help troubleshooting or fixing issues, an email address can be offered to them. Unless your environment is small enough that every user knows who the VMM administrator is, this may be important for new users to get help when they are stuck. When this email address is configured, the Contact Administrator link on Self-Service Portal will be updated with it. Self-Service Portal users can click the link to send an email to the administrator.

In administration view, click the General node from the tree view, and then double-click Self-Service Administrative Contact in the list view. You should see something similar to Figure 3.40.

FIGURE 3.40
Configuring
the self-service
administrative contact

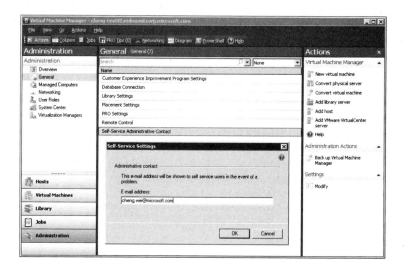

Installing and Configuring VMM Hosts and Libraries

Now that you have deployed VMM server components and client components, you've laid down the infrastructure and you are ready to open shop. But without any VM host, you have nothing to offer — your shop is a house with bare walls.

So what do you need? Two last steps:

◆ Deploy host computers on which you or your users can build virtual machines.

◆ Deploy one or more repositories to store the building blocks for virtual machines.

VM Host vs. Library

In VMM, from a hypervisor technology point of view, three types of VM hosts are supported: Hyper-V, Virtual Server, and VMware ESX Server. For Hyper-V and Virtual Server VM hosts, the VMM agent is installed onto the computers. After that, all management of the hosts are done through the agent. You manage VMware ESX Server through VMware vCenter Server, but there is no agent involved — you do not install an agent on either ESX Server or vCenter Server. All VMware management is done either through the VMware published standard Web Services API with vCenter Server or through the SSH/SFTP sessions directly with ESX hosts.

VMM libraries are essentially managed shares. The management model is very similar models to the model for managing virtual machine host computers:

◆ You install the same agent to libraries and to VM hosts. Hence the deployment methods are fundamentally the same for VM hosts and libraries.

◆ From a functionality point of view, they can both serve as the initiator as well as receiver for content transfers. So they share a same set of services too.

On the other hand, they are two distinct resource types. They are modeled internally with different object types. There are different commands, cmdlets, and UI actions for each type.

Adding VM Hosts

There are three ways that you can categorize ("bucketize") the types of virtual machine hosts VMM manages. Here they are:

◆ From hypervisor technology perspective, you can divide all VM hosts into three types: Hyper-V hosts, Virtual Server hosts, and VMware ESX hosts.

◆ From the host's network environment (hence different authentication methods), you may have domain-joined Windows Server–based hosts, and Windows Server–based hosts that are in a perimeter network (also known as a DMZ).

◆ From an agent deployment methods point of view, there are two equally valid host agent deployment methods: server remote push install and agent local install.

So, the VMM product's Add Hosts Wizard is designed to cater to how people naturally "bucketize" the virtual machine hosts and lead users down a different path for each type based on how they are put under management. Basically, based on the type, location, and trust level of the computer in relation to the VMM server, users will be guided through slightly different workflow.

ADDING DOMAIN-JOINED VM HOSTS

The workflow in this section describes the most typical use model for adding domain-joined Hyper-V or Virtual Server hosts, which is adding hosts from the VMM Administrator Console by remotely push-installing the agent. Please note that the agent local install is covered in Chapter 5, and if you need to deploy an agent to Windows hosts that are in a perimeter network (also known as DMZ), you must deploy the agent locally. Follow these steps to add VM hosts that are members of an Active Directory domain:

1. From the Administrator Console, click the Add Host action from the global actions menu.

2. The Add Hosts Wizard appears. On the first page, users can select the host location.

3. For this section, we assume that the hosts are joined to an AD domain, so the radio button should be left at Windows Server-Based Host On An Active Directory Domain, as shown in Figure 3.41.

4. Enter the credentials that have administrative privilege on the target host.

5. If there are no two-way trust relationships between the domain the VMM server is in and the domain the host is in, uncheck the option Host Is In A Trusted Domain.

6. After entering all required information, click Next.

7. At the Select Host Servers page, there are two ways you can add computers into the list of servers:

◆ Click the Search button to bring up the Computer Search dialog and type in the name or part of the name, and select if you want to filter the results with only Hyper-V or Virtual Server computers. Then click the Search button (Figure 3.42).

◆ You can also enter a host computer name directly into the Computer Name field to add the computer into the list of selected servers (Figure 3.43).

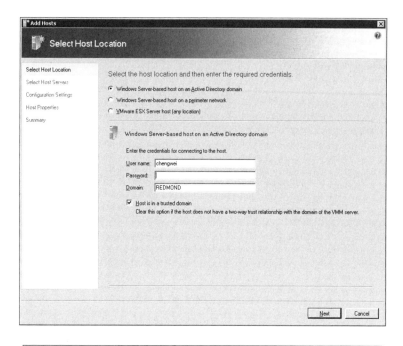

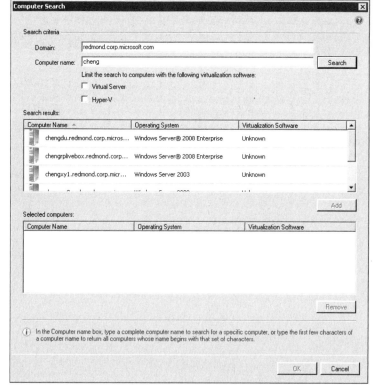

FIGURE 3.43
The Select Host
Servers page

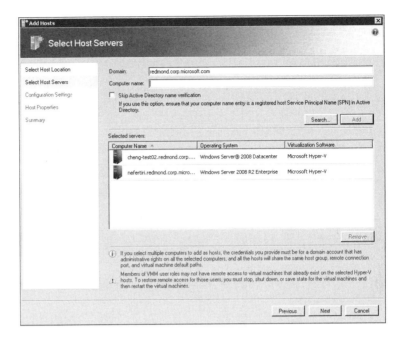

8. If the list of target host computers contains one or more Hyper-V hosts, when you click Next, a warning pop-up dialog appears (Figure 3.44). The warning is to remind you that the VMM Add Host job would automatically enable Hyper-V role as part of the Add Host process, which will result in reboots if the Hyper-V role is not already enabled.

FIGURE 3.44
Selected hosts warning
dialog

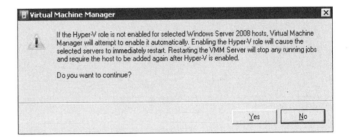

9. Next, in the Configuration Settings page, select the host group you want the new hosts to join, and specify whether you want to reaffirm ownership of the host even if the host is managed by another VMM server. Click Next to continue.

10. Now you are at the Host Properties page, where you can specify a set of paths on the host to be used for storing VMs or define the Hyper-V remote connection port. This is an optional step. Clicking Next will take you to the summary page.

11. On the Summary page, if you click the View Script button, you will be able to see the exact PowerShell script that is to be submitted for this job (Figure 3.45).

FIGURE 3.45
Viewing the script

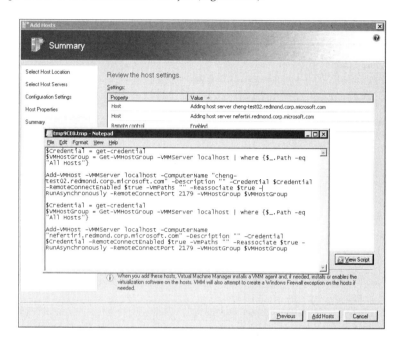

12. After the job is submitted, a Jobs dialog pops up showing the progress of the Add Hosts job (Figure 3.46).

FIGURE 3.46
Add Host Wizard – Jobs View

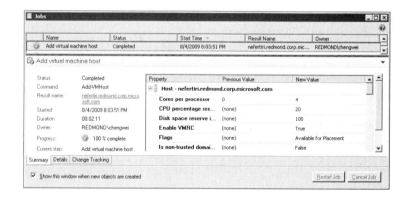

After the job is complete, the Administrator Console looks like Figure 3.47 after the hosts are added.

FIGURE 3.47
Hosts view after the Add
Hosts job completes

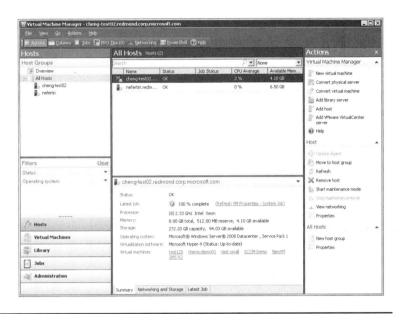

ADDING VMWARE VCENTER SERVER AND ESX HOSTS WORKFLOW

The workflow for managing VMware vCenter Server and ESX Server is covered in Chapter 4.

Adding a VMM Library

Typically, when you install a VMM server, you created a library share on the VMM server as your default library. As your environment grows to be more geographically distributed and the number of deployments increases, you should consider adding new library servers. And in many cases, for a larger environment, we recommend that our customers not put the library on their VMM server. This is simply because the VMM server is already busy with handling all the user-initiated job requests and schedule-based refresher work, so you can quickly exhaust CPU or I/O capacity on your VMM server.

When you plan to add a library, open the Administrator Console, and launch the Add Library Wizard by clicking the Add Library Server link on the global action section of the actions pane and then follow these steps:

1. Enter the credentials that have administrative privilege on the target library server and click Next, as seen in Figure 3.48.

2. On the Select Library Servers page, you can type in the computer name if you know it, or you can click the Search button to search the computer from AD. Then click Next.

3. The share should have been pre-created on the target library server. On the Add Library Shares page, you can select which shares (if there are more than one) you want to add as VMM library shares (Figure 3.49).

FIGURE 3.48
The Enter Credentials
page of the Add Library
Server Wizard

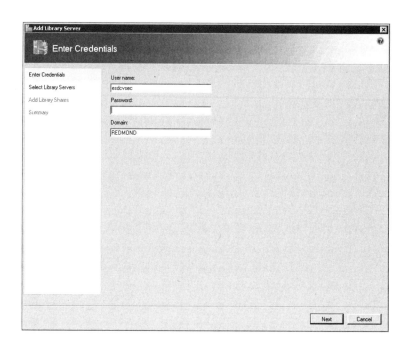

FIGURE 3.49
The Add Library
Shares page

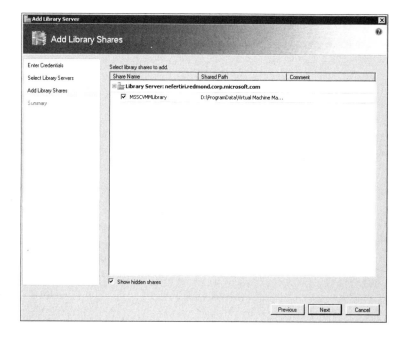

4. After reviewing all the configurations for the library, click Add Library Servers to start the
   job (Figure 3.50).

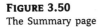

FIGURE 3.50
The Summary page

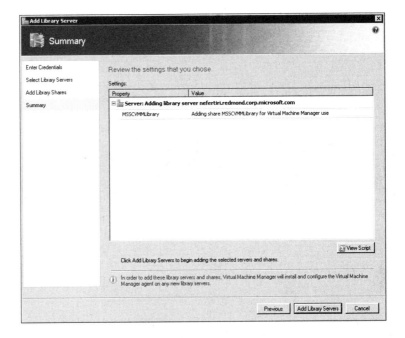

As soon as the wizard closes, the Jobs dialog should pop up and you can monitor the progress of the recently submitted jobs.

UNDER THE HOOD: LIBRARY AND DFSR

DFSR stands for Distributed File System Replication, or DFS Replication, which is built into Windows Server. It's a new state-based, multimaster replication engine that supports replication scheduling and bandwidth throttling. DFS Replication uses a new compression protocol called Remote Differential Compression (RDC), which can be used to efficiently update files over a limited-bandwidth network. RDC detects insertions, removals, and re-arrangements of data in files, thereby enabling DFS Replication to replicate only the changes when files are updated. Additionally, a function of RDC called cross-file RDC can help reduce the amount of bandwidth required to replicate new files.

DFS Namespaces (DFSN), formerly known as Distributed File System, allows administrators to group shared folders located on different servers and present them to users as a virtual tree of folders known as a namespace. A namespace provides numerous benefits, including increased availability of data, load sharing, and simplified data migration.

A VMM library does not natively support DFSR because VMM is not DFS aware; neither is it location aware. There is no special logic in the product for DFSR or DFSN. And VMM does not work with the global namespace in DFSN.

To VMM, each share is a separate entity, and each copy of the same file on each share is a separate entity. Hence, each copy of the same file on each share is given a unique GUID in the VMM database and is updated as a unique database object.

However, without going into too many VMM implementation details, just note that users can choose to take advantage of DFSR with the costs of the following known issues:

◆ To take advantage of DFSR, you will need to create and manage a separate virtual machine template on a local library share. The template references a VHD copy on the local library share so that virtual machine creation can be directed to use the local copy of the VHD on the local library.

◆ Changes to any of the DFSR shares will result in missing content on other shares:

  ◆ When you move files around folder structures on one DFSR share, the file paths on that share are updated in VMM. However, on the library shares that contain the replicated files, the moved files show up as new files in VMM, and the original files (in the original paths) show up as missing in VMM. You will need to manually clean up (remove) the missing files from other VMM library shares.

  ◆ When you deploy virtual machines out of one DFSR share in the VMM library, the virtual machine will appear as missing in VMM for other DFSR shares and will need to be manually removed from those library shares. Hence, it may not be a good idea to store VMs to DFS-R shares.

◆ Due to the following competing events, there will be minor network traffic every time the library refresher runs (by default, it runs every 60 minutes, although, this can be adjusted by turning down/off library refresher frequency from the library settings via the VMM Administrator Console):

  ◆ DFSR auto-replicates and keeps all file copies *and* their paths in sync.

  ◆ VMM tries to tag each copy of the same file with a unique library ID.

HIGHLY AVAILABLE LIBRARY

A VMM library hosts important "building blocks" for the virtual machines. It's also the repository for some saved VMs. It's recommended that you back up your library share regularly. For a highly available library, although VMM does not have built-in fault-tolerant library management, what you can do is to take advantage of functionality built into Windows and use a clustered file share for the VMM library. This way, the content on your library will be made highly available.

Please note that VMM 2008 and VMM 2008 R2 support only highly available library servers that are configured as a Windows Server 2008 failover cluster. Windows Server 2003 clusters are not supported for highly available libraries in VMM 2008. When you're adding a file server running on a Windows Server 2008 failover cluster into VMM by using the Add Library Server Wizard, VMM will discover all the nodes of the cluster and install VMM agents on all the nodes. The highly available file server will be added to the library view as a single library entity, and the individual nodes of the cluster will not be shown as libraries. If you need to manage or view all the nodes in the cluster, you can always view them in the Managed Computers node in the administration view of the Administrator Console.

The Bottom Line

Install and configure a VMM server.   Identify the prerequisites for a VMM server and various SQL database options.

> **Master It**   Which OS versions does a VMM server support?

> **Master It**   What limitation does it have when you use SQL Server Express Edition for a VMM database?

Install and configure Administrator Console.   Identify the prerequisites for Administrator Console and various client component dependencies.

> **Master It**   Can you install the VMM PowerShell layer without the Administrator Console?

> **Master It**   Why are you prompted to uninstall Administrator Console when you try to run the Configure Operations Manager option from Setup?

Install and configure the OpsMgr integration component.   Understand the prerequisites for OpsMgr integration configuration and know the steps involved to configure the integration.

> **Master It**   What MPs do you need to install before PRO can be installed?

> **Master It**   For the integration to work, what do you need to install on the VMM server and the OpsMgr management servers?

Install and configure Self-Service Portal.   Understand the prerequisites for Self-Service Portal, how user roles are created, and the steps involved to configure the portal.

> **Master It**   Can the Self-Service User role log in to the Administrator Console?

> **Master It**   Will Self-Service Portal installation automatically enable the IIS role?

Install and configure a local VMM agent.   Understand the prerequisites for agent configuration and know the steps involved to configure the agent.

> **Master It**   What port numbers should you use when installing an agent?

> **Master It**   Which name should you choose when installing an agent for a DMZ host?

Install and configure VM hosts.   Understand the prerequisites for host configuration and know the steps involved to configure the hosts.

> **Master It**   Does VMM automatically enable the Hyper-V role if it's not enabled already?

Master It What operations do you do to make the Add Hosts process Microsoft-cluster-aware?

Install and configure a VMM library. You should understand the prerequisites for VMM library configuration and know the steps involved to configure the library.

Master It Does VMM automatically replicate contents across libraries?

Master It Why would you see missing library objects in your library shares that are replicated by using DFS-R?

Chapter 4

Managing VMware ESX Using VMM

For machine virtualization, the most popular hypervisors on the market today include Citrix Xen, Microsoft Hyper-V and Virtual Server, Linux KVM (Kernel-based Virtual Machine), and VMware Server and ESX/ESXi. Companies new to virtualization typically start with one hypervisor, while companies familiar with virtualization may have more than one hypervisor deployed in their environment.

In some cases, a specific hypervisor is designated for a particular workload. That typically means that the hypervisor is best of breed to meet the performance, scale, or budget requirements set forward. In other cases, changes to organizational structure through mergers and acquisitions may bring two different IT groups together, each one deploying a different virtualization product. With multiple hypervisors on the market and changing business demands, managing a heterogeneous virtualization environment is more the norm than the exception.

For many IT groups, managing a heterogeneous environment is common. Server and client machines might be sourced from different OEMs, a networking backbone could be built using products from one vendor with edge devices provided by another, or islands of storage arrays and switches from different vendors may be in every datacenter. Common or not, the cost and complexity of managing a heterogeneous environment tends to increase as the portfolio of products to manage increases. The key to reducing cost and administrative overhead is to automate the most common day-to-day tasks and use cross-product management consoles for the remaining.

We begin this chapter with a brief overview detailing how VMM and vCenter interact. This information is important considering that an active connection to vCenter is required for the life of the VMM service. With the connection established, we continue on with the management of ESX hosts. With ESX hosts under management, you can take advantage of VMM's core building blocks, including templates, guest operating system profiles, and Intelligent Placement.

In the virtualization space, VMM offers a cross-product management console experience for Hyper-V, Virtual Server, and ESX.

In this chapter, you will learn to:

◆ Recognize the important features that are enabled by managing ESX hosts using VMM

◆ Set up a connection between VMM and vCenter and change an ESX host from OK (Limited) to the OK state

◆ Determine what monitoring is available for ESX hosts out-of-box using PRO

The Need to Support Multiple Hypervisors

Administrators deploying virtualization solutions typically do so with the intent of reducing costs and complexity in their environment. The reduction in cost comes from the consolidation of multiple workloads onto fewer computers by using virtual machines. However, to reduce complexity, an administrator also needs to aggregate virtual machine hosts, virtual machines, virtual machine clusters, library resources, and workload resources under one interface. The ability to aggregate these resources is an important step in standardizing procedures and policies across technology disciplines.

VMM's management model enables access to heterogeneous environments through a single interface serving as an abstraction layer that all hypervisor interfaces communicate with. From the console, users are presented with a standard set of commands across all hypervisors under management. Translating the commands to the actual hypervisor implementation is left up to VMM. Virtual Server exposes a COM interface to enable management of a single host. Hyper-V developed a set of WMI classes. VMware provides VI API as a set of web services that work on ESX and ESXi.

With VMM as the layer of abstraction between the user and underlying programmatic interfaces, supporting multiple hypervisors turns into a big value-add for customers. The user is never burdened with the heavy lifting of understanding individual commands, translating inputs and outputs, and orchestrating complex workflows. The standard set of commands in the console and PowerShell interface now make it possible to streamline common day-to-day tasks, training material, runbooks, and process guidelines for operations and support. If you currently have multiple hypervisors with multiple management tools and are looking to consolidate tools, or if you're trying to avoid the situation of multiple management tools in the first place, VMM can provide you with significant value in reduced learning curve, costs, and complexity.

Another great benefit is realized if you plan to migrate from one hypervisor to another. The underlying work to convert virtual machines from one hypervisor to another requires effort to coordinate downtime with application owners, but existing scripts used to automate common tasks do not require modification after migration.

Undertaking the effort to build a single console across three machine virtualization products — Hyper-V, Virtual Server, and ESX — is best left to a management company. The real value-add for the administrator is the ability to automate day-to-day tasks, streamline business logic, and build advanced features on top of VMM.

How VMM and VMware vCenter Interact

vCenter is the management product offered by VMware to manage ESX virtual machine hosts. The server side of vCenter is the main task execution, policy, and resource management engine. vCenter Server installs as a service on Windows or Linux operating systems. The client component is the user interface into vCenter Server. The vCenter client connects remotely to the server over HTTP/HTTPS to retrieve virtual machine, host, storage, network, policy, alert, and task information stored in the database used by vCenter Server. VMware also offers web services hosted by vCenter to enable programmatic access to this same information. Advanced users can leverage these web services based API to develop products that extend the functionality offered in-box.

Based on VMware's design of vCenter and ESX, full management capability of ESX is available only through the vCenter client interface (Figure 4.1) or the web services API hosted on vCenter. VMware offers VIX as a set of APIs for direct ESX host management, but the functionality is limited to the single host. This means features like VMotion are not supported. For a detailed list of each VMware management tool, see Table 4.1. To provide full and complete management of VMware environments, VMM uses the vCenter APIs as the integration point rather than directly talking to ESX hosts. This also means no agents need to be installed on the VMware platform and existing vCenter deployments do not need to be removed. You can think of VMM as a "manager of managers."

FIGURE 4.1
The vCenter console

TABLE 4.1:   VMware Management Tools

VMWARE TOOL	DESCRIPTION	LIMITED/FULL MANAGEMENT?
vCenter	Graphical user interface to connect to VMware server component	Full
VMware Remote CLI	Command-line interface using vCenter web services	Limited
VMware VIX	C/Perl	Limited

Setting Up the Connection between VMM and vCenter

Before you can manage VMware ESX hosts with VMM, a connection between vCenter Server and the VMM server component is required. VMM uses VMware's web services based APIs to control ESX host servers programmatically. The connection is established over HTTPS. Once a connection is established, it is kept open to allow for bidirectional data flow. VMM is designed to coexist with vCenter. What this means for your environment is that any changes you make in VMM will be reflected in vCenter. Likewise, changes you make in vCenter will be reflected in VMM. The settings and data VMM actually manages is a subset of what vCenter offers.

The main purpose of using VMM to manage ESX hosts through vCenter is to give you the power of managing a heterogeneous virtualization environment through one interface. While there are some relatively infrequent tasks administrators may need to accomplish through vCenter, the goal of VMM is to effectively allow administrators and operational personnel to accomplish the vast majority of day-to-day tasks through VMM. For this reason, the settings and data VMM actually manages is a subset of what vCenter offers.

To set up the connection between VMM and vCenter, follow these steps:

1. Open the VMM console.

2. Click the Administration wonder bar, shown in Figure 4.2.

FIGURE 4.2
The Administration
wonder bar

3. Click the Virtualization Managers node (Figure 4.3).

FIGURE 4.3
The Virtualization
Managers node

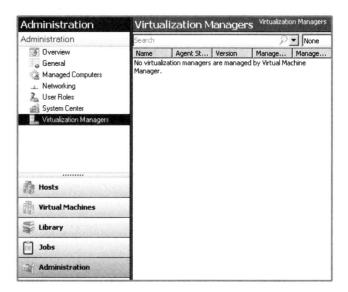

4. Click the Add VMware vCenter Server action in the right actions menu (Figure 4.4).

FIGURE 4.4
The Add VMware
vCenter Server action

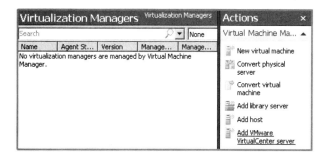

5. Type in the host name of the machine running vCenter Server. VMM supports machines joined to a domain or to a workgroup. The domain does not have to be the same as the one to which VMM is joined. At a minimum, the computer network name must resolve properly from the VMM server.

6. Provide the username of the account you want VMM to use to connect to vCenter. The account can be a domain account or local user account. Refer to Table 4.2 for supported account options.

TABLE 4.2: Supported account options

DOMAIN/ WORKGROUP	USER ACCOUNT TYPE	WINDOWS SECURITY LEVEL	VMWARE SECURITY LEVEL
Domain	Domain	Administrator	Administrator
Domain	Local	Administrator	Administrator
Workgroup	Local	Administrator	Administrator
Domain	Domain	User	Datacenter/Host Administrator
Domain	Local	User	Datacenter/Host Administrator
Workgroup	Local	User	Datacenter/Host Administrator

7. Provide the password for the user account specified. The password is masked for security reasons, so make sure you provide the correct one. If the password is not correct, adding vCenter to VMM will fail.

8. Provide the domain to which the machine hosting the vCenter server is connected. If the machine is domain-joined, provide the NETBIOS name of the domain. If the machine is joined to a workgroup, you need to provide the computer name.

9. You can choose to use the secure mode for communication channels between Windows VM hosts and ESX VM hosts. For better security, communication between Windows

and ESX hosts should be secured using encrypted channels. Communication channels between Windows and ESX hosts are required for transferring files using SFTP or HTTPS. VMM uses SFTP to transfer files to and from ESX. For ESXi, VMM depends on HTTPS for file transfers. Refer to Figure 4.5 for vCenter connection settings.

FIGURE 4.5
vCenter connection settings

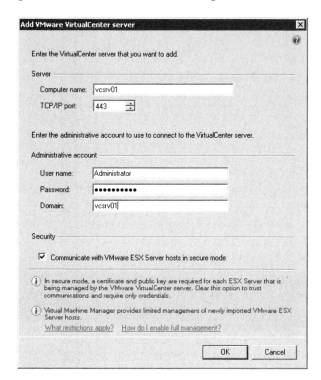

10. Click OK. At this point the dialog will close. You can click the Jobs wonder bar to check the status of the Add VirtualCenter Server job.

What to Expect When VMM and vCenter Interact?

To understand the interaction between VMM and vCenter, you must understand how various vCenter concepts map to VMM. The first interaction point after adding the vCenter Server to VMM is the virtual machine host tree view. This tree view is updated as part of importing vCenter information. After you add vCenter, the scalability maximums for VMM do not change. Any existing virtual machine hosts already managed by vCenter simply count the maximum limits. In the following sections, we'll also cover security, port groups, maintenance mode, library server, and out-of-scope operations.

IMPORTING THE TREE STRUCTURE

Once a connection between VMM and vCenter is established, VMM will start to import data. This new data is stored in the VMM database. The first set of data imported is your datacenter, folder, and cluster tree structure. The tree structure is translated and merged into VMM's host group structure. The full tree structure mapping is detailed in Table 4.3.

TABLE 4.3:   Tree structure mapping

VMWARE NODE TYPE	VMM NODE TYPE
Root	Host Group
Datacenter	Host Group
Folder	Host Group
Cluster	Cluster Host Group

Resource pools in VMware can exist either on a host or on a cluster. After importing VMware's tree structure, you will notice that resource pools are not displayed in the tree structure presented by VMM. Instead, resource pool information is stored under host or cluster properties.

Host groups in VMM are agnostic as to what hypervisors are contained within. A host group can contain Microsoft Hyper-V and VMware ESX hosts side by side. The flexibility in VMM host groups allows you to standardize the organization of your hosts across VMM and vCenter. VMM supports adding multiple vCenter servers to VMM, so overlapping tree structures will simply merge into a common tree structure. Depending on how your environment is structured, this is a very powerful feature that allows management of your environment from a single console. VMM does not limit how many vCenter servers you can add; however, the tested maximum is two.

SCALABILITY

Both VMM and vCenter publish scale limits for the number of hosts and virtual machines supported per instance of each server. VMM's published scale limit is 400 hosts and 8,000 virtual machines. vCenter's published scale limit is 200 hosts. The hosts managed by a vCenter instance counts against VMM's limits. Keep in mind that the vCenter server itself does not count as a host.

For every host managed by vCenter, VMM will open a new vCenter session to get host, VM, and performance data. This communication channel is necessary because VMM does not make direct connections to ESX. Each host session is kept alive for the entire time vCenter is connected to VMM. VMM limits the number of sessions to 35. If VMM or vCenter is rebooted or the services are shut down, upon restart the sessions are reestablished. VMM will make sure to end any open/idle sessions left around to avoid session starvation on vCenter. For this reason, you should use a dedicated service account when adding vCenter to VMM. Typically, service accounts are not used by users for interactive logons. Therefore, when VMM cleans up open/idle sessions, there is no risk that a user will be disconnected.

LIBRARY SERVERS

VMM centralizes resource building blocks for virtual machines in the VMM library. The following building blocks are stored in the library:

◆   Templates

◆   Hardware profiles

♦ Operating system profiles

♦ Virtual hard disks

♦ Virtual floppy disks

♦ ISO

♦ Virtual machines

VMM supports multiple library servers, depending on your network topology and deployment requirements. To optimize virtual machine creation and deployment from the library, at least one library server in every datacenter helps isolate network traffic. WAN links would still be used to propagate files between datacenters, but typically during off-peak hours. If you plan to scale out your virtualization environment in a datacenter, additional library servers might be required to further optimize creation and deployment times. Figure 4.6 shows two datacenters, each with a dedicated library server. With vCenter, VMware does not offer a library concept. Instead, users store templates and image files on shared VMFS storage or mounted NFS volumes.

FIGURE 4.6
Multiple datacenters and multiple library servers

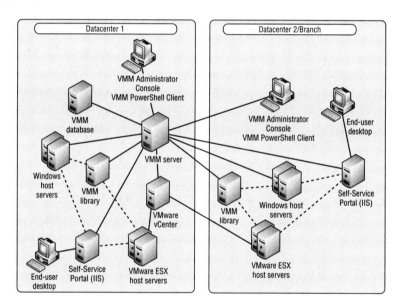

VMM's library depends on the network to transfer files to ESX hosts. Creating a new virtual machine from a template requires copying the VMDK files attached to the template along with any image files associated with the virtual machine. By default, these files are copied into a single folder location on the library server.

HOST MAINTENANCE MODE

When you plan to perform maintenance on an ESX host, you can set the host into maintenance mode through vCenter or VMM. When setting a host into maintenance mode through

VMM, you can use the UI or the CLI. In either case, you need to keep in mind that VMM will automatically evacuate all running virtual machines (VMs) from the host. Any VMs powered off or in saved state will remain on the host. VMM will not present you with a placement page to migrate each VM. The migration target will be calculated using Intelligent Placement. To enter maintenance mode, follow these steps:

1. Select the Hosts wonder bar, shown in Figure 4.7.

FIGURE 4.7
The Hosts wonder bar

2. Click the Start Maintenance Mode action in the menu on the right (Figure 4.8).

FIGURE 4.8
Start Maintenance
Mode action

3. Select the action that VMM should perform as part of starting maintenance mode (Figure 4.9). If VMware Distributed Resource Scheduler (DRS) is not enabled for the ESX host, you will need to take manual action before starting maintenance mode. You need to first power off all running virtual machines or migrate the running virtual machines to another host.

FIGURE 4.9
Start Maintenance Mode

FIGURE 4.9
Start Maintenance Mode

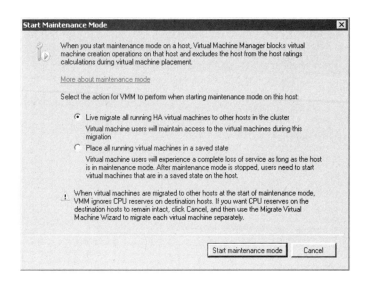

4. In the Hosts view, the host in maintenance mode will have an icon next to it (Figure 4.10).

FIGURE 4.10
The In Maintenance
Mode icon

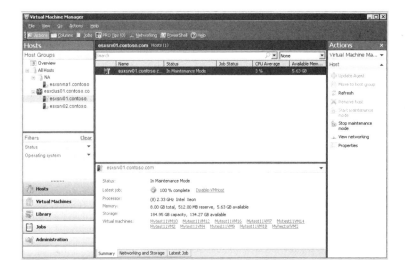

While a host is in maintenance mode, you are allowed to perform a very limited set of actions on it. While in this mode, the host no longer appears in host ratings to prevent you from selecting it during creation, deployment, or migration. However, if jobs are in progress, they are allowed to complete without disruption. When using maintenance mode, please keep in mind that you will need to wait for jobs in flight to complete before performing maintenance on the host. Refer to Table 4.4 for the list of actions allowed/disallowed while a host is in maintenance mode.

TABLE 4.4:   Maintenance mode–allowed operations

ACTION	ALLOWED?
Deploying a new virtual machine	ø
Placing virtual machine on host	ø
Migrating virtual machine to maintenance mode host	ø
Changing power state of virtual machine	✓
Removing host	✓
Changing host properties	✓

NETWORK PORT GROUPS

VMware uses network port groups to apply specific policies to groups of virtual network ports on the virtual switch. An ESX host can contain multiple virtual switches, each with one or more network port groups defined. By default, a VM Network port group is created for VM traffic. vCenter connects to an ESX host on the service console port group. The service console serves as an out-of-band management interface. This port group is separate from the one used by virtual machines. Ideally, the service console and virtual machine port groups are not in the same virtual switch. This mitigates potential downtime due to hardware failure. The service console and the virtual machine port group can share the virtual switch, but you must explicitly configure it through the vCenter client.

Table 4.5 lists the settings and policies you can modify using VMM.

TABLE 4.5:   Supported Port Group Settings and Policies

SETTINGS/POLICY	DESCRIPTION	SUPPORTED IN VMM
VLAN ID	The VLAN that the traffic on the port group will use	Yes
Security	Setting promiscuous mode, MAC address changes, and forged transmits policies	No
Traffic Shaping	ESX Server shapes traffic by controlling three outbound traffic characteristics: average bandwidth, burst size, and peak bandwidth.	No
NIC Teaming	Settings load balancing, network failover detection, notify switches, and failback policies	No

USER SECURITY MODEL

Both System Center Virtual Machine Manager and VMware vCenter offer a role-based administration model to support users with different job functions. VMM defines a profile as the set of operations a user can perform. vCenter calls this a role. Roles in vCenter represent a collection of privileges required to manage high-level objects, like virtual machines. With vCenter, you can secure resource pools, hosts, clusters, or datacenters using its role-based administrator model. VMM offers a similar model using user roles.

VMM user roles are composed of the following:

A scope   The objects to which the user role has access

A profile   The collection of actions associated with the user role

Members   The list of Active Directory users assigned to the user role

VMM supports three user roles:

Administrator   Administrators can perform all operations available in VMM. This user role cannot be scoped (have access to all objects).

Delegated Administrator   Delegated administrators are granted administrative-level operations on a specific scope of objects.

Self-Service User   Self-service users have a very limited set of approved operations. The scope of a self-service user is limited to templates, virtual machines, and library shares. The user role can deploy to a predefined set of hosts, but the user does not have access to the host itself, nor can he or she select which host to deploy to.

When a VMware environment is managed through VMM, any security settings already defined in vCenter will not be reflected in VMM. In addition, any user roles created to manage ESX hosts and virtual machines through VMM will not affect the security setting you have already defined in vCenter. VMM implements its own authorization system, and so you will need to model VMware-specific security requirements using VMM user roles. Table 4.6 compares the roles provided by each product.

TABLE 4.6:   Role comparison

ROLE	VMM	VCENTER EQUIVALENT
Administrator	Administrators have access to all objects and actions in VMM, including adding users to the Administrator user role.	Administrator
Delegated Administrator	Delegated administrators have access to all objects and settings within their assigned scope (host groups and libraries). They cannot modify the Administrator user role and have limited access to global settings.	Mix of Datacenter Administrator and Resource Pool Administrator
Self-Service User	Grants a user access to VMM's Self-Service Web Portal and PowerShell interface. Self-service users have access to a specific set of virtual machines of actions and the ability to deploy new virtual machines from a predefined list of templates assigned to the self-service user. These users do not have access to the VMM's Administrator Console.	Combination of Virtual Machine Power User and Virtual Machine User

MANAGEMENT OPERATIONS NOT IN SCOPE WITH VMM'S MANAGEMENT MODEL

VMM provides you with sufficient functionality parity with vCenter to help streamline day-to-day operational tasks. You can streamline redundant tasks using VMM's PowerShell interface, which gives you even more control and power compared to the user interface. For tasks that are in scope with VMM's management model, you can use still use vCenter. The following list details the vCenter actions that VMM does expose:

VM resource allocations (CPU, memory, disk, network)   No support for setting these properties through the console or PowerShell

Configure VM processor affinity policy   No support for setting this property through the console or PowerShell

Install or upgrade VMware Tools   VMM automates the installation of Virtual Server VM Additions and Hyper-V Integration Services. To fully automate the installation, VMM injects an agent into the guest OS by mounting the virtual disk. VMM does not ship with VMDK mount capabilities and so installation of VMware Tools is not supported through VMM.

VMware Tools power control settings   Power control settings are available in the VMM client and Self-Service Portal but not in the remote console session window

View the location of a VM's configuration file   You can view this information only through PowerShell

```
PS C:\> Get-VM | where {$_.Name -eq "<vmname>"} | ft Name, Path, Location
```

Configuration of HA, DRS, Backup, Update Manager   Although HA is not configurable via VMM, if you have HA in place, VMM Intelligent Placement will acknowledge this and honor availability requirements of VMs as they are migrated and created. VMM offers Performance and Resource Optimization, or PRO, as an alternative for DRS. As a result, DRS isn't directly managed. If you do enable DRS, be sure to disable PRO and vice versa.

Swap Configuration   Swap Configuration manages the swap file allocated to a virtual machine that enables it to use more memory than the server can physically allocate.

Modify user role settings   VMM does not use vCenter's roles.

Assign WWN to VM (NPIV support)   VMM supports only NPIV for Windows hosts.

Set VM or cluster-level (EVC) CPUID masks   VMM supports setting only the NX/XD CPUID mask.

Managing VMware ESX Hosts

Once VMM is connected to vCenter through the web services interface, you will see existing hosts and clusters imported into VMM, along with the associated tree structure. After this point, you can add or remove ESX hosts through either vCenter or VMM. If you choose to add or remove a host through vCenter, VMM will eventually refresh that information into the database. To manually refresh vCenter data in VMM, open a VMM PowerShell window and type in the following command:

```
PS C:\> $vc = Get-VirtualizationManager | where {$_.Name -eq vcsrv.contoso.com}
PS C:\> Refresh-VirtualizationManager -VirtualizationManager $vc
```

> **ADDING ESX CLUSTER**
>
> VMM does not support adding ESX clusters. Instead, use vCenter to add the cluster and then refresh the data into VMM.

Adding an ESX Host

Adding an ESX host in VMM is the same as adding a Virtual Server or Hyper-V host. To add an ESX host, follow these steps:

1. Select the host group where you want to place the new ESX host and click Add Host in the actions menu on the right, as shown in Figure 4.11.

2. Select VMware ESX Host from the radio button list.

FIGURE 4.11
The Add Host action

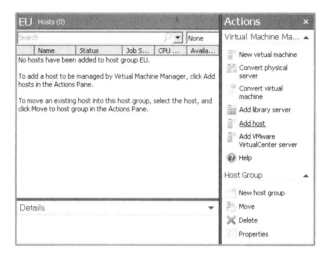

3. Provide the local host credentials — username and password (typically this is the root account) — and click Next (Figure 4.12).

4. Provide the FQDN or IP address of the ESX host (Figure 4.13).

5. Select the Virtual Center server to add the host to from the drop-down list.

6. Select the host group in which you want to place the ESX host (Figure 4.14).

7. If VMM is set up to communicate with vCenter and ESX hosts in secure mode, then you need to retrieve the certificate from the ESX. Click Retrieve to get the certificate thumbprint and public key fingerprint associated with the host, as shown in Figure 4.15.

8. Make sure to click Accept Both The Certificate And Public Key For This Host.

9. Click Add Host to include the host as a selected host, as shown in Figure 4.16.

FIGURE 4.12
ESX host credentials

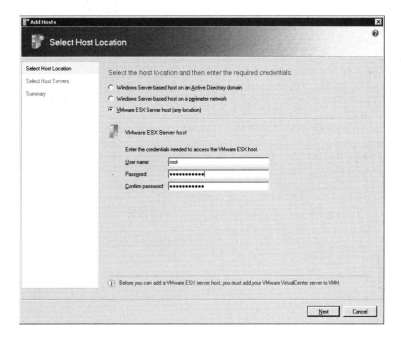

FIGURE 4.13
ESX host information

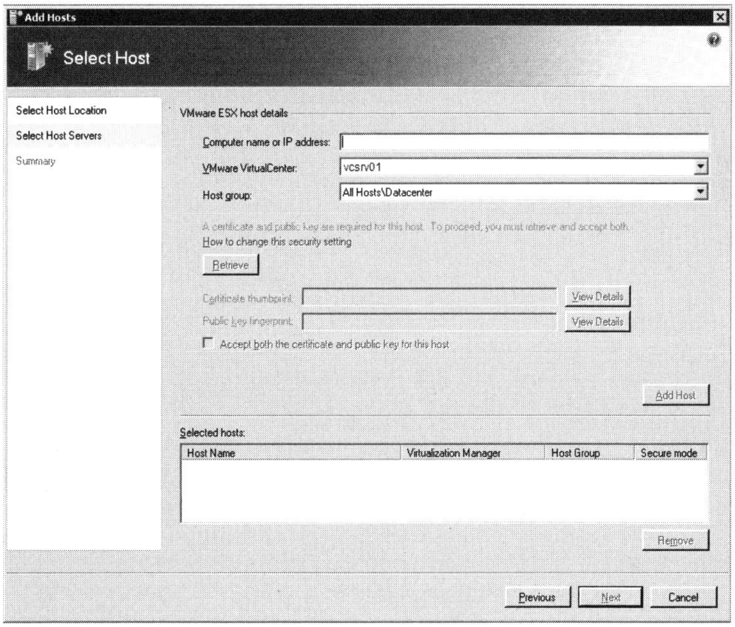

FIGURE 4.14
Select the host group

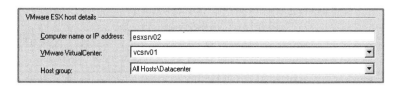

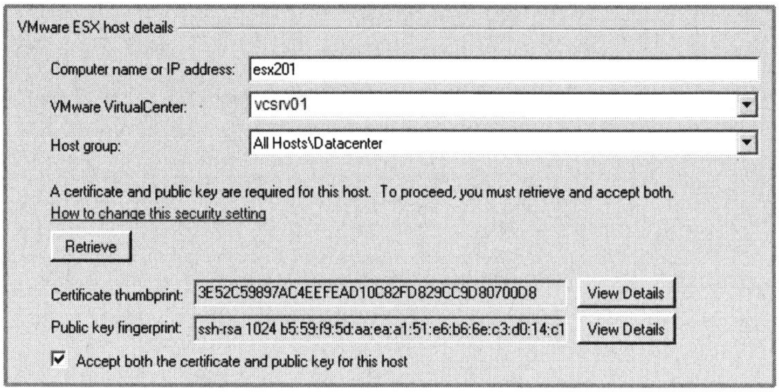

FIGURE 4.15
ESX host certificate
and public key

FIGURE 4.16
Add host to
selected hosts

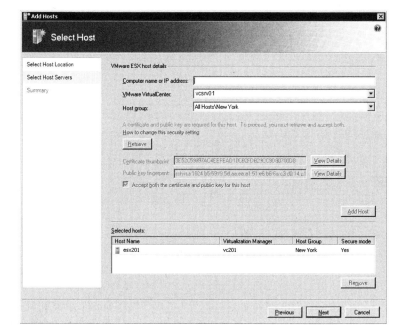

10. Repeat steps 4 through 9 for each host you would like to add. When complete, click the Next button to proceed.

11. Click the Add Hosts button at the bottom of the wizard (Figure 4.17) to complete the wizard.

FIGURE 4.17
Completing the wizard

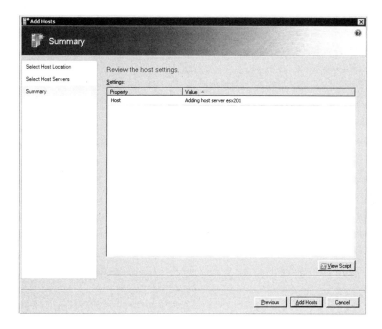

VM Host Properties

VMM refers to a physical machine with Virtual Server, ESX, or Hyper-V as a virtual machine host. For Windows-based hypervisors, VMM depends on a local agent installed on the machine. In the case of ESX, all management operations are processed through vCenter. VMM uses VM host objects as the point of interaction in either the Administrator Console or PowerShell. Each hypervisor may have different implementations under the covers, but you manage them using the same object. To access VM host properties and settings, right-click a VM host and select Properties (Figure 4.18).

FIGURE 4.18
Selecting host properties

The following list summarizes each tab in the host properties page and the information contained in each page. The details for each screen are VMware specific.

Summary: Identification   Includes the computer name used by vCenter to connect to the machine and the domain the host is joined to (which may not apply to your ESX host). Location is the name of the vCenter instance that manages the ESX host.

Summary: Identification: description   This is the field where you can add additional information to describe the virtual machine host. This data is VMM specific and stored in the database only.

Status: Overall status   The status here will reflect that the host is in the OK (Limited) state or the OK state.

Connection status, virtualization service status, and virtualization service version all reflect the health of the host. Agent status and version are not applicable to an ESX host.

Status: This host is available for placement   This reflects if the ESX host is not available for virtual machine placement because it is in maintenance mode. Exiting maintenance mode will enable this host for virtual machine placement.

VMs: Resources   This represents a tree diagram with virtual machines and resource pools. By default, ESX has a Resources resource pool where all virtual machines are placed. Any resource pools you create on a virtual machine host will be nested under the Resources resource pool. Through VMM, you can move a virtual machine in and out of a resource pool by dragging the node in the tree. Clicking a resource pool will also expose all its settings for processor and memory.

VMs: Register the following virtual machines   Use this feature to browse the local file system on the ESX host and find virtual machine configuration files that you want to register on the virtual machine host. vCenter refers to this as adding virtual machines to inventory.

Reserves: Reserved resources   Host reservations are used by VMM's Intelligent Placement engine when calculating star rating. You can specify CPU (in percentage), amount of memory (in MB), disk space (in MB), disk IO (in IOPS), and network capacity (in percentage). You can also specify these settings at the host group level. Changing these settings will not affect the virtual machine host configuration.

Hardware: CPU, memory, floppy drives, DVD/CD-ROM drives   These represent physical resources on the host. This information is read-only.

Hardware: Storage: volume details   This represents volumes exposed to the host. You have the option of excluding a volume from placement to avoid virtual machines getting deployed on it.

Hardware: Network adapters: adapter details   The physical network ports on the virtual machine host. Since VMM cannot discover network location automatically on an ESX host, you have the option of manually setting a location from a list of discovered locations.

Networking: Virtual network details   Each network port will represent a virtual switch on the virtual machine host. If the virtual switch already exists on the ESX host, then the name will be imported based on vCenter information. You can set the network tag and description for the switch as well. Network Tag represents a category you assign to the virtual switch VMM uses to automatically assign a virtual network to a virtual network adapter when creating a virtual machine. The tag information is user specific.

Networking: Network bindings   A virtual switch can be used for either private network communication between virtual machines on the same host or external communication between virtual machines on the same host and other machines on the physical network. Binding a virtual switch to a private network ensures that all communication is isolated on the host only. Binding to a physical network adapter will expose virtual machines to the physical network the adapter is connected to.

Placement: Specify default virtual machine paths to be used during virtual machine placement   This is the default path on the ESX host where you want to place all your virtual machines.

Remote   These are no ESX settings for remote console access.

Security   This is where you specify the local root account and password along with retrieving and storing certificates required for secure communication.

Custom: Assign custom properties to this host   A set of 10 properties you can set for a virtual machine host.

SUPPORTED VM HOST ACTIONS FOR ESX

For a given ESX host in the VMM Administrator Console, you can take one of several actions by clicking an action in the menu presented on the right side of the interface.
The following are VM host actions for ESX:

Move To Host Group   In VMM, you can place a VM host in any host group under All Hosts. In the case of ESX, however, you are restricted to moving a host within a vCenter instance. If you manage multiple vCenter instances with VMM, then you cannot change which vCenter instance manages the ESX host.

Refresh   This runs the Host Refresher on demand to reflect the most up-to-date configuration of the host. This is useful if you make changes to the ESX host in vCenter and you want to reflect the changes immediately in VMM.

Remove Host   This removes the ESX host from management under vCenter.

Start Maintenance Mode   Indicates to vCenter that the ESX host should be put into maintenance mode

Stop Maintenance Mode   Indicates to vCenter that an ESX host should be taken out of maintenance mode.

Configure Security   Opens the security tab of the ESX host properties where you can specify the root account password and certificates for secure communication.

View Networking   Displays a networking diagram of the ESX host with each virtual switch and associated virtual machines, including connection lines indicating port bindings between the virtual network adapter and the virtual switch.

Properties   Opens the properties page for the ESX host.

CONFIGURING A VIRTUAL NETWORK

For a Windows-based host, Network Location Awareness (NLA) determines the logical network to which an adapter is connected. VMM retrieves this information from the virtual machine host and stores the network location value for each physical network adapter that is bound to a virtual switch. For ESX hosts, however, this information is not available, so by default no network location is assigned to the virtual switch. You need to override the network location for the virtual switch manually. Once the virtual switch has a network location, you can specify network location for each virtual network adapter in a template. At deployment time, VMM will match the desired network location specified in the template to the network location for a virtual switch.

To override the default network location, follow these steps:

1. Click the Host wonder bar.

2. Click an ESX host.

3. Click the Properties action under Hosts in the actions menu to open the properties page of the ESX host, as shown in Figure 4.19.

FIGURE 4.19
The Properties action

4. Click the Hardware tab.

5. Click a network adapter in the Network Adapters sidebar (Figure 4.20).

6. Select Override Discovered Network Location.

7. Type in the DNS suffix of the network the ESX host is connected to.

8. You can also type in a description if necessary in the Connection Description area, as shown in Figure 4.21.

9. Click OK to accept the changes.

VMM also offers the option of decorating a virtual switch with user-specific information called a network tag. The tag is also used during the deployment of a virtual machine to help identify the correct virtual network to attach the virtual network adapter to. A tag is useful if you need to differentiate between multiple virtual switches connected to the same logical network.

FIGURE 4.20
The Network
Adaptors sidebar

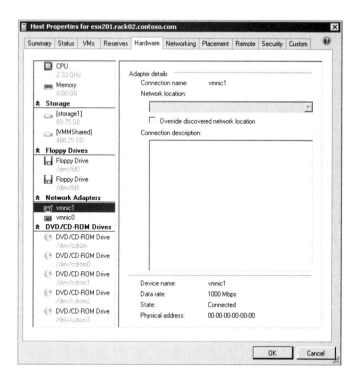

FIGURE 4.21
Adding a
network location

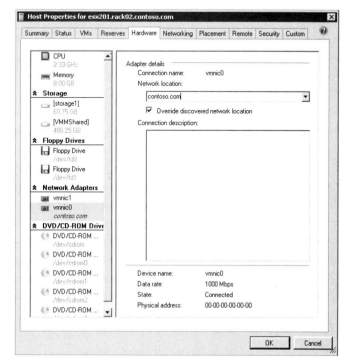

To set the network tag for a virtual network, follow these steps:

1. Click the Host wonder bar.

2. Click an ESX host.

3. Click the Properties action under Hosts in the actions menu to open the properties page of the ESX host.

4. Click the Networking tab.

5. Click the virtual switch in the Virtual Networking sidebar, as shown in Figure 4.22.

FIGURE 4.22
Choosing a
virtual switch

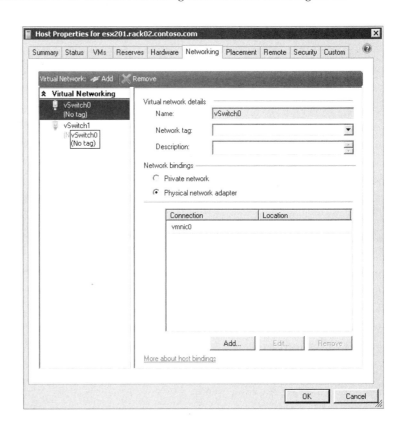

6. Type the name of the desired tag into the Network Tag field.

7. Optionally, add a description for the virtual network, as shown in Figure 4.23.

8. Click OK to accept the changes.

FIGURE 4.23
Adding a description for
the virtual network

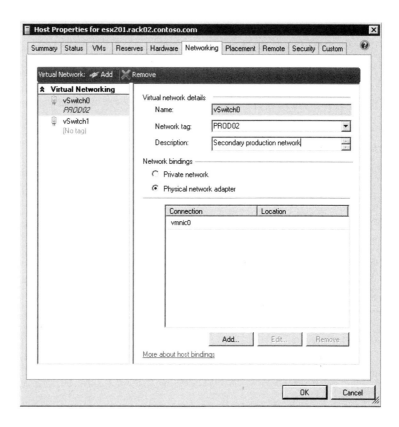

Enabling ESX Full Management

As VMM discovers hosts through vCenter (e.g., after connecting VMM and vCenter) or
new ESX hosts are added manually, you will notice that the overall status for all these
hosts is OK (Limited), as shown in Figure 4.24. This status signifies that the host is online
and communicating with vCenter but you cannot transfer files to or from ESX hosts. VMM
stores all virtual hard disk, virtual floppy disk, and ISO files on a library server. To create
a new VM from a template, VMM must transfer a set of files to the ESX host as part of the
deployment.

ESX 3.0.2 and ESX 3.5 both offer a console operating system (i.e., a service console) that
natively supports transferring files over SSH using Secure File Transfer Protocol (SFTP) on
network port 22. For ESXi (3.5), the console operating system is locked down and natively
supports HTTPS for file transfers on network port 443. VMM supports both protocols out of
the box. You do not need to install any additional software on your ESX hosts or on the VMM
server to enable file transfer.

FIGURE 4.24
Overall host status

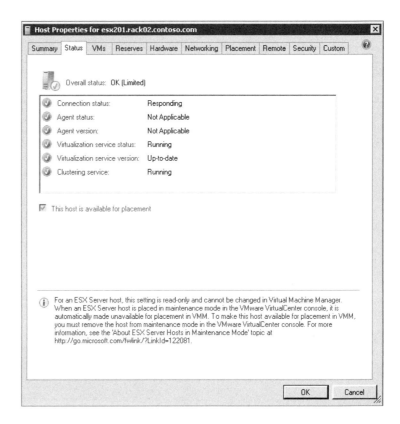

ENABLING FULL MANAGEMENT OF ESX HOSTS THROUGH VMM

To enable full management of ESX hosts through VMM, you need to provide VMM with local host credentials for each ESX host. Local host credentials are required to initiate file transfers directly between the host and the library server. To enable full management, follow these steps:

1. Click the Hosts wonder bar.

2. Select an ESX host that is in OK (Limited) state.

3. Click the Configure Security action.

4. Provide the local account name and password associated with the account. By default, you can provide the root account. This will require that you enable remote SSH access to the host. A Delegate User account can also be provided.

When you added vCenter to VMM as a virtualization manager, you were provided with an option to require secure connections between VMM and hosts. If you required secure mode, then all connections to an ESX host must be secured with a certificate and public key.

You now have the option to use Secure Mode Enabled or Secure Mode Disabled.

Secure Mode Enabled

To use Secure Mode Enabled, follow these steps:

1. Click the Retrieve button to retrieve the certificate and public key from the ESX host (Figure 4.25).

FIGURE 4.25
Choosing the Retrieve button on the Security tab

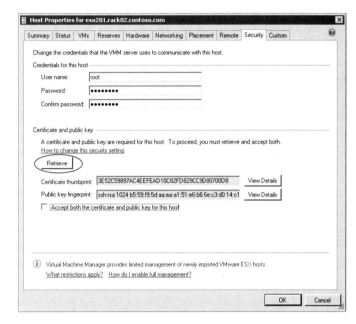

2. Optionally, you can click on View for the certificate to install manually. Please note that this action brings up the Certificate dialog box (Figure 4.26).

FIGURE 4.26
The Certificate dialog box

3. Clicking the View button for the public key will present its associated fingerprint, as shown in Figure 4.27.

FIGURE 4.27
Public key fingerprint

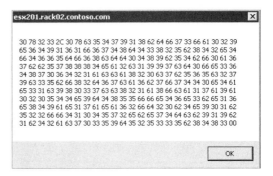

4. Select the Accept Both the Certificate and Public Key for This Host check box (Figure 4.28).

FIGURE 4.28
Accept both the
certificate and
public key

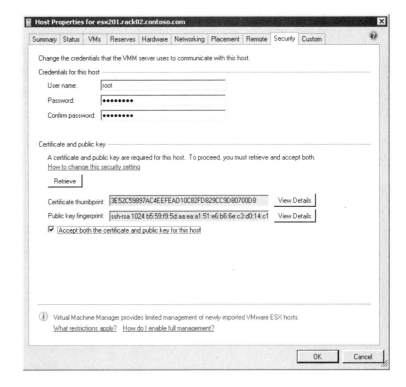

5. If the credentials provided are correct, the host status will change to OK (Figure 4.29).

FIGURE 4.29
Overall host status
after choosing Secure
Mode Enabled

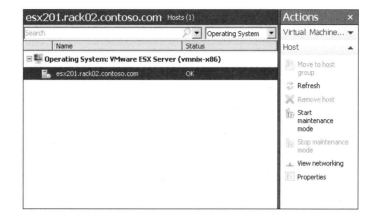

Secure Mode Disabled

In this mode, you do not need to provide any certificates or keys to secure the communication channel between the host and a library server. By default, the communication is considered "trusted."

To choose Secure Mode Disabled, provide the local host credentials and click OK (Figure 4.30). If the credentials provided are correct, the overall host status will change to OK.

FIGURE 4.30
ESX host credentials

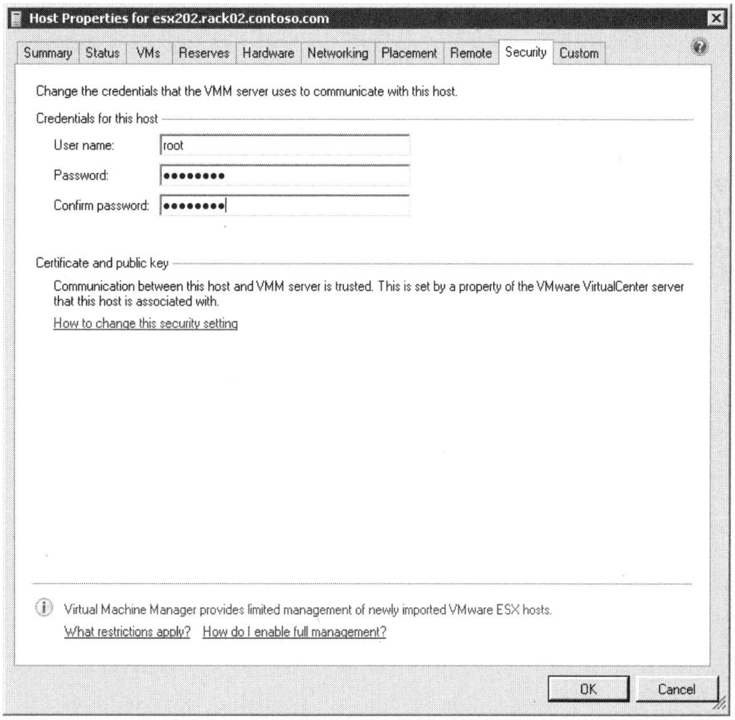

ENABLING REMOTE SSH ACCESS (ESX 3.0.2 AND 3.5 ONLY)

VMware disabled remote SSH access for the root account out of the box. This is a security measure, considering that the root account is well known. On an ESX host, the root account is equivalent to the Administrator account on a Windows host. To transfer files to and from ESX yourself, you do not need to use the root account. You can transfer with an account with less privilege.

ESX file-level security is based on Linux style user/group ownerships. All files on an ESX host are typically owned by the root account. For this reason, if you log into a host with a less-privileged account, you cannot modify files owned by root. This limitation is expected. To modify files owned by root, you need to elevate your privileges using SUDO or an equivalent method.

The root account owns all files because vCenter uses the root account under the covers to make modifications on the ESX host and transfer files between ESX hosts. For this reason, the account that VMM uses to transfer files to and from an ESX host must have ownership rights. To enable remote SSH access for root, follow these steps:

1. Open a remote console session to the ESX host, using PuTTy, for example (Figure 4.31).

FIGURE 4.31
Remote console session to an ESX host using PuTTy

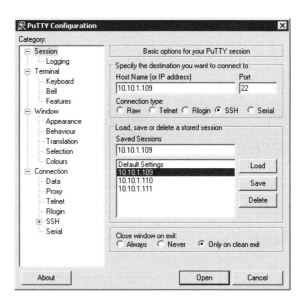

2. Log into the service console using a local account.

3. Elevate your privileges to root (Figure 4.32).

4. Open sshd_config using your favorite editor. In this example, we use nano (Figure 4.33).

5. For PermitRootLogin change no to yes, as shown in Figure 4.34.

6. Save the file and exit the program.

7. Open another remote console session to the host.

8. Log into the service console using the root account.

9. If you can successfully log in, remote SSH login is properly enabled for root.

FIGURE 4.32
Elevate privileges to root

FIGURE 4.33
Open the
sshd_config file

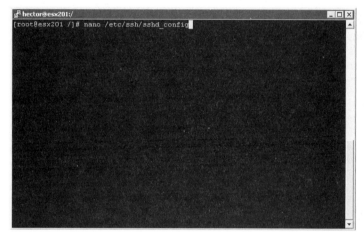

FIGURE 4.34
Permit root login
authentication
permission

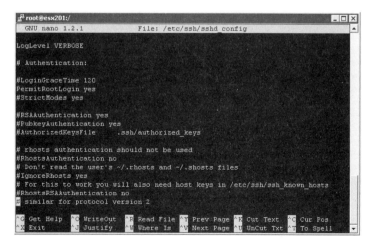

CREATING A DELEGATED USER

vCenter uses the root account for all file-level operations on ESX hosts. For environments using Fibre Channel and iSCSI storage, there are no management issues with this approach. However, for users who want to leverage NFS as a storage location, it is important to know if the root account is in use. The NAS device might consider the root account a very well-known account and by default will reject file requests under this account, a security measure known as "root squash." One option to work around this security limitation is to allow connections using root. Another option is to change the default account used by vCenter for all file-level operations on ESX hosts using a VMware experimental feature called Delegate User to work around root squash. VMware labels certain features as "experimental" for testing and experimenting purposes. These features are not expected to be deployed into a production.

Setting the Delegate User account through vCenter changes the ownership of all files modified/created by vCenter moving forward to the account you specify. If you cannot enable remote SSH access for root on your ESX hosts, you may want to consider leveraging the Delegate User account. It is important to note that if you plan to the use the Delegate User account, you need to set up the same account on all your ESX hosts to avoid enabling SSH root login. For more information on Delegate User, consult VMware's ESX Server Configuration Guide at www.vmware.com/pdf/vi3_35/esx_3/r35u2/vi3_35_25_u2_3_server_config.pdf.

DELEGATE USER EXPERIMENTAL FEATURE USAGE

The Delegate User account is still considered an experimental feature by VMware. Based on VMware support documentation, experimental features are not supported in production environments. If you plan to implement this feature outside of a test environment, please consult VMware guidance and understand what support VMware will provide.

Virtual Machine Building Blocks

VMM presents a common experience across hypervisors when creating virtual machines. The common experience is reflected in the graphical user interface and the CLI. By linking commonalities across the three hypervisors, you avoid the need to duplicate efforts when setting up virtual machines through VMM. The operational manuals you create do not require long subsections for each hypervisor for each piece of functionality. Instead, you can concentrate on the feature itself and present a common set of actions required regardless of the underlying hypervisor. In the same way, automation scripts you create do not require extensive branching using IF/ELSE statements or SWITCH blocks to cover feature functionality for each hypervisor.

At the most basic level, virtual machines in VMM are composed of virtual hardware and operating system settings. Hardware settings between hypervisors differ very little (e.g., CPU count and memory amount). Windows operating system settings are standard across all three hypervisors. You should keep in mind, however, that some hypervisors may not support specific operating systems due to limitations in the technology. For example, Virtual Server does not support 64-bit operating systems.

Hardware and guest operating system profiles serve as the building blocks to define a template. These profiles simplify the creation process by encapsulating many settings. Specifying these values manually every time is a time-consuming and error-prone process. Once a template is created, you can use it to create other templates or virtual machines. With templates, you streamline the creation process by reducing the amount of settings that you have to specify when deploying a new virtual machine. With a template, you get consistency and repeatability, which is very important as you scale out your virtualization environment.

Hardware and Guest Operating System Profiles

VMM hardware and operating system profiles are like a bag of settings that you apply to virtual machines and templates at creation time. Templates and profiles are used to supply default values for virtual machines but can freely be changed afterward without cascading impact. If you decide to change a hardware or operating system profile, any virtual machines or templates in which the profile was used are not affected. If you modify hardware or operating system properties on an existing virtual machine or template, the original profile used during creation is unaffected. Since hard links do not exist, VMM does not need to create a versioned copy of the profile with the new property.

HARDWARE PROFILE

Hardware profiles contain the most common settings users need to set on a virtual machine. An VMM hardware profile is not the superset of functionality across all three hypervisors. You can create a hardware profile independent of a virtual machine or template. Hardware profiles created in this manner can be used at any time during the creation of a virtual machine or template. If you make any modifications to the hardware settings, you can save the new configuration as a new hardware profile.

Hardware profiles include the following properties:

Name The name of this profile allows you to search for it in the UI and CLI. You can summarize the settings contained within by using the names if you plan to standardize on a few key configurations in your environment.

Description The description is for more detailed information about the profile. This can include specific information about the use for which the hardware profile is intended.

Owner An owner can be set on a profile if deemed necessary. However, this setting has no implications on security or visibility in the UI or CLI.

BIOS Setting BIOS options is supported only for Microsoft Hyper-V.

CPU: Number of CPUs The number of virtual CPUs can be set for VMware ESX 3.0, ESX 3.5, and ESXi 3.5, which all support one, two, and four virtual CPUs per virtual machine. Note that as we were writing this book, VMM did not support ESX 4.0, which offers up to eight virtual CPUs per virtual machine.

CPU: Type The type of CPU does not reflect a VMware setting. Instead, the model selected here is used by VMM's Intelligent Placement engine. The placement engine models new workloads on a VM host and gives you a star rating based on the expected utilization of the workload. So if you know from previous experience that the operating system and application combination you plan to deploy in the VM ran well on a single Pentium 4 processor physical machine, then you can select that processor model from the list. When you place that virtual machine workload, the star ratings calculated for each host will take into account the CPU type and factor that into the model used for placement. VMM uses models borrowed from another Microsoft product called Capacity Planner. (Note that to use VMM, you do not have to install Capacity Planner.)

CPU: Limit CPU Functionality This setting will mask specific CPU features at the hypervisor level so older operating systems like Windows NT 4 can boot properly. You need to enable this setting only if you plan to run operating systems that fail to boot properly in a VM due to specific CPU features that are incompatible with the guest OS.

CPU: Limit CPU For Migration For VMware, VMM will mask the No Execute/Execute Disable feature of a processor. This feature allows the operating system to mark memory in the virtual machine as code to prevent malicious attacks using buffer overrun exploits. Setting custom CPUID masks is not supported through VMM.

Memory Setting memory for a virtual machine depends on the version of ESX you plan to deploy a virtual machine to. For a new virtual machine, a new template, or a new hardware profile, you can set the minimum memory of 4 MB or the maximum of 65536. However, VMware supports the following:

ESX 3.0 Minimum: 4 MB
Maximum: 16384

ESX 3.5/ESXi 3.5 Minimum: 4 MB
Maximum: 65532 (64 GB, 4 MB)

Note that as we were writing this book, VMM did not support ESX 4.0, which supports up to 256 GB of RAM per virtual machine.

Floppy Drive VMware virtual machines support two virtual floppy drives. VMM manages only the first floppy drive. The second virtual floppy drive attached to the host floppy drive or with a virtual floppy already attached will not be changed by VMM.

Floppy Drive: No Media Captured This setting removes the virtual floppy disk attached to the virtual floppy drive or disconnects it from the host floppy drive. Removing a virtual floppy will delete the file from the ESX host.

Floppy Drive: Physical Floppy Drive Use this setting to attach the virtual floppy drive to the host floppy drive.

Floppy Drive: Existing Virtual Floppy Disk File Use this setting to attach the virtual floppy drive to a virtual floppy stored in the library.

COM VMware supports up to four COM ports per virtual machine. VMM manages the first two.

COM: None This setting removes the named pipe or text file associated with a COM port.

COM: Named Pipe This sets up a named pipe for COM serial port communication.

COM: Text File This setting associates the virtual COM port to a file on the local file system of the ESX host.

IDE Devices (Controller) VMware supports up to two IDE controllers per virtual machine. VMM exposes up to two IDE controllers per virtual machine.

SCSI Adapter (Controller) VMware supports up to four SCSI controllers per virtual machine. VMM exposes up to four SCSI controllers per virtual machine.

SCSI Adapter: Shared Controller   This sets the SCSI controller as a virtual shared controller useful for creating guest clusters on the same host.

Virtual DVD Drive   VMware supports up to four virtual IDE-based DVD drives per virtual machine. VMM exposes up to four virtual DVD drives per virtual machine.

Virtual DVD Drive: Channel   You can attach a DVD virtual drive to any available slot on the IDE controllers present in the hardware profile. Channel displays both the controller ID and location ID. ESX supports up to two DVD devices per IDE controller.

Virtual DVD Drive: No Media   This disconnects the physical CD/DVD or image file from the virtual DVD drive.

Virtual DVD Drive: Physical CD/DVD Drive   This attaches the virtual CD/DVD drive to a CD/DVD drive in the physical host.

Virtual DVD Drive: Existing Image File   This associates an image file to the virtual DVD drive. If the template or virtual machine is stored in the library, then the hardware profile will only link the objects together (no files are copied). However, if the virtual machine is already on an ESX host, the file is copied from the library over the network to the local file system of the host.

Virtual DVD Drive: Existing Image File: Share Image Instead Of Copying It   This is not supported for VMware ESX. Currently there is no way to share an ISO file from a network location. VMM will always copy the ISO file to the local host.

Virtual Disk   This is the common object used by VMM to represent a virtual hard disk across all hypervisors. Specifically for VMware, a virtual disk contains a virtual hard disk of type VMDK.

Virtual Disk: Channel   You can attach a virtual disk to any available slot on any SCSI controller present in the hardware profile. Channel displays both the controller ID and location ID. ESX supports up to 15 devices per SCSI controller. Keep in mind that ESX only supports booting guest operating systems from SCSI-based virtual disks. Even though VMM will not block you from creating a virtual machine or template where the VMDK file is attached to the IDE controller, during placement, VMM will inform you of the incorrect configuration.

Virtual Disk: Use An Existing Virtual Hard Disk   You can browse VMM's library for an existing virtual disk (VMDK file) to attach to the virtual machine or template. You cannot attach a virtual disk to a hardware profile by itself. If the template or virtual machine is stored in the library, then the hardware profile will only link the objects together (no files are copied). However, if the virtual machine is already on an ESX host, then the file is copied from the library over the network to the local file system of the host.

Virtual Disk: Create A New Virtual Hard Disk   If you need a blank disk created with the virtual machine, then use this option to dynamically generate a fixed VMDK file when deploying the virtual machine.

Virtual Disk: Pass Through To Physical Drive On Host   This setting attaches a Raw Device Mapping (RDM) device to the virtual machine at deployment time. RDM disks reside on the virtual machine host and cannot be stored in the library. When creating a virtual machine, you simply indicate you want to use an RDM disk. After placement, VMM will list all available RDM disks on the host. VMM does not support creating RDM disks. You need to open the vCenter console to perform this action. Once the RDM disk is created, it will show up in the list of available storage devices.

Virtual Disk: Type   You can select dynamic or fixed disks as the virtual disk type. ESX, however, supports creating only fixed disks. Linked clones are not supported as a disk type.

Virtual Disk: Size   The size of the virtual disk can vary from 1 GB to 2048 GB. VMware VMFS allows different maximum size VMDK files depending on the block size specified when formatting the VMFS volume. Refer to table 4.7 for maximum file sizes supported on VMFS-3.

Virtual Disk: File Name   By default, VMM will assign a name to the virtual disk. You can override the name when creating the virtual machine.

Network Adapter   ESX supports up to four virtual network adapters per virtual machine. VMM distinguishes between emulated and synthetic adapters. Hyper-V introduces the term *synthetic adapters*. However, ESX supports an equivalent technology using VMXNET-based adapters. VMM does not support creating VMXNET adapters on virtual machines. By default, adapters are created as VLANCE.

Network Adapter: Network Location   Network Location is used to dynamically associate a virtual network adapter to the most appropriate virtual switch on a host. VMM uses Network Location Awareness Service on Windows hosts to determine the associated domain servicing the IP and DNS information to the host.

Network Adapter: Network Tag   A network tag is a user-specified tag to decorate a virtual switch on a host with extra information that is specific to the deployment of the host. For example, a virtual machine host may be connected to three distinct physical networks — Primary Production, Secondary Production, and Backup. If you plan to deploy a virtual machine with multiple virtual network adapters, you can use a network tag to automatically associate them to the appropriate virtual switch. Simply decorate the virtual switch with the associated tag information in host properties.

Network Adapter: Port Group   A port group is the entity that virtual network adapters are bound to for network connectivity. ESX 3.0.2 and 3.5 hosts support three network port types on a virtual switch: VM network, service console, and VM kernel. For virtual machine network connectivity, the VM network port type is a collection of virtual ports on the virtual switch. The service console port is used for vCenter management access to the ESX host. The VM kernel port is used exclusively for VMotion and iSCSI network traffic.

Network Adapter: Enable Virtual LAN Identification   This enables setting a VLAND ID for an individual virtual network adapter.

Network Adapter: VLAN ID   You can associate one VLAN ID per virtual adapter.

Network Adapter: Ethernet (MAC) Address Dynamic   ESX hosts support generating MAC addresses for virtual network adapters during deployment. VMware ESX 3.0.2 and 3.5 generate MAC addresses within the following range: 00:50:56:40:00:00 to 00:50:56:FF:FF:FF.

Network Adapter: Static   ESX hosts support manually assigning a MAC address to a virtual network adapter. You can assign a static MAC to a virtual machine or template in the library or a virtual machine on a host. VMware ESX 3.0.2 and 3.5 support static MAC addresses within the following range: 00:50:56:00:00:00 to 00:50:56:3F:FF:FF. Setting a static MAC address outside of this range will result in an error when powering on the virtual machine.

Network Adapter: Generate   VMM supports generating a MAC address from a predefined MAC range managed by VMM. You have to set the start and end of the range in the Administration section of VMM. The setting is global and applies to ESX, Hyper-V, and Virtual Server virtual machines.

Network Adapter: Enable Spoofing Of MAC Addresses   Allowing MAC spoofing or MAC learning is important for NLB-like applications running in the virtual machine. This setting does not apply to virtual machines on ESX. ESX can only enable/disable MAC Learning at the port group level.

Priority   ESX hosts can assign a relative weight to a virtual machine using VMware "shares." With VMM, you can set Low, Normal, High, and Custom relative weights. For VMware, VMM will translate Low, Normal, and High to the relevant share quantity.

High Availability   VMM classifies virtual machines deployed on a cluster with VMware's HA feature enabled as highly available VMs. If a virtual machine or template has this setting enabled, then during placement, the placement engine will give a higher rating to ESX clusters with HA enabled.

Integration Services   These settings are not supported for ESX hosts.

VMDK FILE SIZE MAXIMUMS

The maximum size of a virtual disk file supported on VMware VMFS-based volumes depends on the block size used to format the volume. VMM supports creating VMDK files based on VMFS-3 maximums only. Table 4.7 lists all the supported VMDK maximums.

TABLE 4.7:   Maximum VMDK file size supported

VMFS VERSION	EXTENT SIZE	BLOCK SIZE	VOLUME SIZE	MAXIMUM FILE SIZE
VMFS-2	2 TB	1 MB	64 TB	456 GB
VMFS-2	2 TB	8 MB	64 TB	3.5 TB
VMFS-2	2 TB	64 MB	64 TB	28.5 TB
VMFS-2	2 TB	256 MB	64 TB	64 TB
VMFS-3	2 TB	1 MB	~50 TB	256 GB
VMFS-3	2 TB	2 MB	64 TB	512 GB
VMFS-3	2 TB	4 MB	64 TB	1 TB
VMFS-3	2 TB	8 MB	64 TB	2 TB

OPERATING SYSTEM PROFILE

An operating system profile, like a hardware profile, represents a collection of settings you can apply to a new template or a new virtual machine created from an existing template. VMM will use the settings in the operating system profile to generate an answer file consumed by a Windows mini-setup during the customization (or specialization) phase of Windows setup. During deployment, VMM will generate a virtual floppy file with an embedded answer file and attach the file to the virtual floppy drive of the virtual machine. During the customization phase of the virtual machine, Windows setup will look for the answer file in several locations, including the floppy drive. After customization is complete, the virtual floppy file is deleted. This sequence is often referred to as the "sysprep" process in reference to the underlying Windows tools used to create the template and to customize using the answer file.

For virtual machines deployed in ESX, you can use the operating system profile only for Windows guests. VMM does not support customization of non-Windows guests.

Virtual Machine Template

VMM templates encapsulate all the hardware and operating system settings required to create a new virtual machine. If you created hardware and guest operating system profiles in the library, then you can use them when creating a template. As part of creating a template, you can now add a virtual disk as part of hardware settings. If the virtual disk file exists in the library, the file is simply linked to the template. You can also specify the intention of using a pass-through disk (RDM). Keep in mind that you select the actual RDM when you deploy the virtual machine to an ESX host.

CREATING TEMPLATES

When creating a template, VMM does not give preference to one hypervisor over another. Instead, the user is expected to know the proper setup of the virtual machine for the intended hypervisor. Even though this approach requires more work up front when creating the templates, subsequent creations of virtual machines require less customization and so are less susceptible to human error. Because of the differences in hypervisor capabilities, it's not possible to have a single template that works by default across both hypervisors. If you try to go this route, you'll always have to make changes to the configuration at deployment time, depending upon the target hypervisor. It's typically easier to just create different templates for each hypervisor up front. To help further standardize the creation of templates, make sure to take advantage of hardware and operating system profiles.

CREATING TEMPLATES THAT REQUIRE NO CUSTOMIZATION

An important variation of the typical template is the Customization Not Required template. If the virtual disk associated with the template contains an operating system that VMM cannot generate an answer file for, the new virtual machine job will fail. For example, Linux is an operating system that VMM does not know how to customize.

To successfully deploy a new virtual machine from a template with a virtual hard disk that contains a Linux operating system, set the guest operating system in the template to Customization Not Required (Figure 4.35). Doing so will indicate to VMM that it should not wait for customization of the new virtual machine, which essentially leaves you with a clone of the template. However, if you need the resultant virtual machine to have a unique identity on the network, make sure to embed a customization script inside the virtual hard disk. When you deploy the virtual machine from a template, set the virtual machine to power on after deploying it to a host so it runs through its customization script.

FIGURE 4.35
Selecting Customization Not Required when creating a template

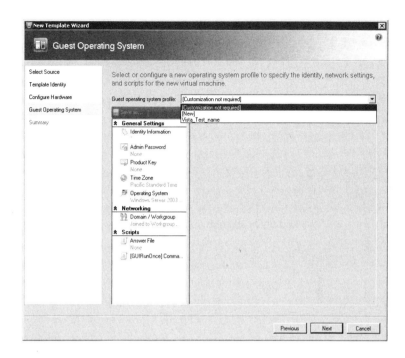

IMPORTING TEMPLATES FROM VCENTER

Templates that you created in vCenter can be imported into VMM's library. Importing the template means that you remove the template from the ESX host and store it in the library as an VMM template. Once the template is in the library, you can take advantage of applying hardware and operating system profiles.

To import a template, follow these steps:

1. Click the Administration wonder bar, as shown in Figure 4.36.

FIGURE 4.36
The Administration wonder bar

2. Click the Virtualization Managers node.

3. Select an instance of vCenter in the middle pane.

4. Click the Import Templates action in the menu on the right (Figure 4.37).

5. In the window, all templates that exist in your vCenter instance are displayed (Figure 4.38). You can select one or more templates by marking the check box next to it.

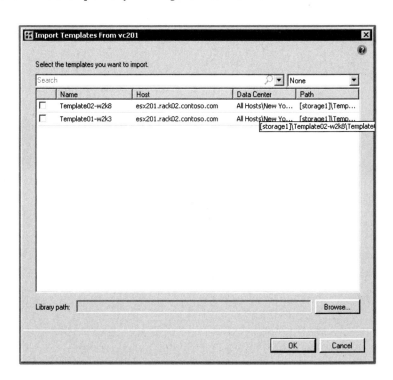

6. Select the VMM library share where you want to store the template, as shown in Figure 4.39. Keep in mind that you can only select one library location at a time.

FIGURE 4.39
Select a Library Share

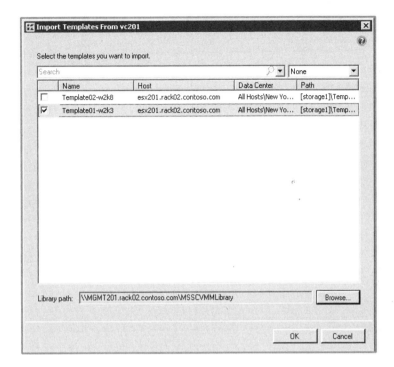

FIGURE 4.39
Select a Library Share

7. Click OK to start the file transfer of the template files.

IMPORTING VMWARE TEMPLATES INTO VMM

As part of importing VMware templates into the library, VMM will delete the source template stored on the ESX host after the import is complete. Before importing the template, VMM will ask you to confirm the import given that the source template will be deleted from the ESX host.

 **Real World Scenario**

CLONING AND IMPORTING VMWARE TEMPLATES USING VMM POWERSHELL

The Windows administrator at Acme Company uses VMM to manage her VMware and Microsoft virtualization environments. She uses a VMM library extensively to store all virtual machines and templates. She uses VMM's VMware template import feature to move a template residing on an ESX host to the library server. She is aware that the template will be deleted as part of the move. She decides to keep a copy of the template on the ESX host by cloning the template object. The template copy is what she imports into VMM. She uses the PowerShell interface to clone the template. Using the following script, she clones all Windows Server 2008 templates that exist on an ESX host.

```
PS C:\> $t = @ (Get-VM | where {$_.IsTemplate -eq $true})
PS C:\> $w2k8_t = @ ($t | where {$_.OperatingSystem -match `w2k8´})
PS C:\> $template_clones[$w2k8_templates.count-1]
PS C:\> $n = 0
PS C:\> foreach ($template in $w2k8_templates)
>> {
>>   $c [$n] = New-VM -VM $template -Name $template.Name+"_"+$n -IsTemplate $true
>>   $n++
>> }
>>
PS C:\> foreach ($template in $c)
>> {
>>   New-Template -Template $template -Name $template.Name+`Import´
>> }
>>
```

NEW TEMPLATE FROM A VIRTUAL MACHINE

If you already have a virtual machine deployed on ESX hosts or stored in the library, you can create a new template from it. The source virtual machine is stored in the library as an VMM template object. VMM will not sysprep the virtual machine before storing it into the library as it does with Hyper-V or Virtual Server templates. Keep in mind that the source virtual machine is removed from its current location. If you want to keep the virtual machine, make sure to clone it before creating a template from it.

Creation and Migration of Virtual Machines

Understanding the building blocks that VMM offers to help administrators define virtual machines and templates is an important prerequisite to discussing the creation and migration of virtual machines. VMM offers several avenues for creating a virtual machine and placing it on a virtual machine host. Once a virtual machine is placed on a virtual machine host, migration also plays an important part in its life cycle.

New Virtual Machine Variations

The previous section covered the template concept in VMM. Templates are great if you want to standardize on a few virtual machine models for your environment. In many cases, however, chargeback is associated with a specific configuration of a virtual machine. For example, a virtual machine expected to run low utilization workloads may require only one virtual CPU and 1024 GB of RAM. More demanding workloads require a virtual machine with four virtual CPUs and 3072 GB of RAM. Since workloads vary, the template is great for encapsulating specific variations into a package that is simple to understand and easy to deploy.

When creating a virtual machine, VMM supports three other experiences in the administrative console aside from the template:

- New virtual machine from blank disk

- New virtual machine from existing virtual hard disk

- New virtual machine from existing virtual machine

Once a virtual machine is created, VMM supports several virtual machine–specific actions that enable you to change configuration and power state and remove the virtual machine.

New Virtual Machine from Blank Disk

When you first deploy VMM, the product does not assume you have any existing virtual hard disks or virtual machines in the environment. If you are planning to deploy virtualization for the first time in your datacenter, then a template may hold little value for you until you actually have a few virtual machines deployed. You can, however, create a new virtual machine with a blank disk.

In this case, there is no virtual disk supplied at creation time. Instead, a new disk is generated on the ESX host and attached to the new virtual machine. When the virtual machine boots, it will fail to find an operating system, which is expected. At this point you can attach an ISO to the virtual DVD drive and allow the virtual machine to boot into Windows setup. If you use PXE to deploy operating systems to bare metal, then the same process can be used for a virtual machine. Over time, the expectation is that you will use this method less and less to deploy virtual machines, instead preferring to depend mostly on templates.

New Virtual Machine from Existing Virtual Hard Disk

When creating a new virtual machine, you can select an existing virtual hard disk from the library. During deployment, the VMDK file is copied from the library to the ESX host. Be sure that the virtual machine you are deploying has a properly configured operating system installed or use a template in order to run the customization.

New Virtual Machine from Existing Virtual Machine

If you need to deploy an exact copy of a virtual machine that is not stored as a template, you can select a virtual machine deployed on an ESX host or stored in the library as the source of a clone operation. As part of cloning, VMM will not sysprep and customize the clone, and so to avoid network conflicts, do not connect it to the same network as the source virtual machine.

Supported VM Host Actions for ESX

For virtual machines on an ESX host, VMM's administration console provides several actions in the actions menu presented on the right side of the interface (Figure 4.40).

FIGURE 4.40
VM actions

The menu includes the following virtual machine actions for ESX:

Start   Powers on a virtual machine in a powered-off state or saved memory state.

Stop   Stops a virtual machine by powering it off. This is the equivalent of unplugging a physical computer.

Pause   This action is not supported by ESX.

Save State   Referred to as Suspend in vCenter, this action will flush the current memory state of the virtual machine to disk. Resuming the virtual machine will reinstate its saved memory state from disk.

Discard Saved State   This action is not supported by ESX.

Shut Down   This action relies on sending a shutdown command to VMware Tools residing within the guest operating system; if the command is successful, the guest will gracefully shut down.

Connect To Virtual Machine   Opens the window that connects to the remote console of the virtual machine.

Migrate   Opens the migration wizard. From this wizard you can VMotion to a supported destination or over the network.

New Checkpoint   Takes a new snapshot.

Manage Checkpoints   Opens a window to manage existing snapshots.

Disable Undo Disks   This action is not applicable to ESX hosts.

Repair   If an action targeted at a virtual machine fails, you can repair the virtual machine by retrying or undoing the action.

Install Virtual Guest Services   This action is not applicable to ESX hosts.

New Template   Generates a new template out of a selected virtual machine. In the case of ESX, the virtual machine is unregistered from the ESX host and copied to the library

Clone   Clones the selected virtual machine. The wizard will guide you through Intelligent Placement, where you can choose to clone the virtual machine to the same host or a different host.

Store In Library   Stores the virtual machine in VMM's library. This will require a network copy.

Delete   Deletes the virtual machine and all its associated files. This action is not the same as Remove From Inventory.

View Networking   Displays a diagram with the network for that ESX host.

Properties   Opens the properties page for the virtual machine.

Intelligent Placement and the New Star Rating System

Creating a new virtual machine using VMM always starts with defining the characteristics of the workload, including hardware and operating system information, before selecting a host to which you will deploy the virtual machine. Fully defining the workload beforehand allows you to concentrate on the requirements of the application that will run in the virtual machine instead of trying to mold the workload to the limits of the host. The distinction is not subtle considering that capacity planning modeling is used to generate star ratings for hosts, taking into account host reserves, existing workloads, and the new theoretical load. This rating system will present you with the capabilities of the host at a certain point in time. Previous to this technology, you did not have a snapshot view of your hosts. Instead, you were expected to know or guess the suitability of a host with data that may not be recent or accurate.

VMM's administration console uses Intelligent Placement in the following cases:

Initial placement when you first place the virtual machine on a host

Migration anytime you migrate a virtual machine between hosts

Library deployment when you deploy a virtual machine stored in the library to a host

Clone when you create a clone of a virtual machine to a host

The purpose of Intelligent Placement is to present you with a star rating for each of the potential destination hosts. The higher the star rating, the more adequate the host is for that workload. Keep in mind that VMM is modeling the theoretical workload on each of the hosts. If a host receives a low star rating or no stars, then the Rating Explanation tab will probably explain why the host is not recommended.

VMM supports customization of the rating by changing the inputs into the modeling engine. By clicking on the Customize Rating button, you can modify placement goals; the relative importance of CPU, memory, disk, and network utilization; and the expected CPU, disk, and network utilization. The following list details the difference between resource maximization and load balancing:

Resource Maximization   Using this placement goal will rank hosts from most utilized to least utilized. The goal of this ranking is to maximize the host by utilizing as much of the resources possible before moving on to a new host.

Load Balancing   This placement goal will distribute virtual machines evenly across a set of hosts.

In addition to important rating explanations, Intelligent Placement lists the transfer type available per host. Following is a list of the VMM supported transfer types:

Network Migration   Involves the migration of files between one location and another over the network. This migration type is supported on ESX, Hyper-V, and Virtual Server.

Live Migration   Hypervisor proprietary migration technology that migrates memory state of a running virtual machine. As part of migration, the virtual machine instance is transferred over, incurring no perceivable downtime. This migration type is supported on ESX and Hyper-V.

Cluster Migration   Hyper-V–specific migration based on Microsoft's failover clustering technology. The unit of failover in this case is the storage volume. As part of the migration, the virtual machine state is saved to disk before the ownership of the virtual machine configuration changes from one node to another. VMM requires that the disk contain only one virtual machine.

SAN Transfer   Migration of the virtual machine involves moving the storage location from one host to another. This migration requires masking and unmasking storage LUNs, leveraging VDS hardware providers or N_Port Identification Virtualization (NPIV). This migration type is supported on Hyper-V and Virtual Server.

If you deploy a stored virtual machine from the library, the transfer type will be Network. A virtual machine migration between nodes in a cluster will most likely show Live as the transfer type. This indicates that VMware VMotion is supported between the nodes and so the migration will cause no perceivable downtime to the applications running in the virtual machines. VMM attempts to determine Live migration capabilities as quickly as possible across a potentially large list of hosts. To do this, it performs a light check that includes verifying that the hosts reside within the same vCenter datacenter and that both hosts can see the same storage that the virtual machine resides on. If both of these checks return true, Intelligent Placement will show Live as a supported transfer type. When you select a host from the list, however, VMM will initiate a deep check or "verification" using VMware vCenter's APIs. The deep check will verify that the migration is actually supported. If not, the rating explanation page will update with any errors returned by vCenter. An example of a deep check returning a different result is if you attempt to move a virtual machine between hosts with incompatible CPUs. The initial light check does not take into account CPU mismatch. The deep check however, will verify that the CPUs match and return any errors indicating that VMotion is not supported. In addition, if the VM's template or hardware profile indicates that the VM must be "highly available" (configured using the check box in the properties page), Intelligent Placement will ensure that only VMware hosts configured for VMware HA are considered for placement.

Storage Location

Until vCenter 2.5, file transfers out of and into an ESX host typically required using an FTP or secure FTP program. vCenter 2.5 introduced support for HTTPS-based file transfers natively. Since VMM supports ESX 3.0, ESX 3.5, and ESXi 3.5, there is a need to support multiple protocols to get files transferred into and out of an ESX host. Table 4.8 lists the supported file transfer protocols for various ESX versions.

TABLE 4.8:   Supported file transfer protocols

ESX VERSION	PROTOCOL
ESX 3.0	SFTP
ESX 3.5	SFTP
ESXi 3.5	HTTPS

The HTTPS protocol is natively supported by ESXi 3.5. However, out of the box, ESX supports only SSH. To avoid requiring the installation of a third-party FTP daemon on ESX hosts, VMM uses the SSH port to transfer files over SFTP. The section Enabling ESX Full Management earlier in this chapter discussed how to enable SFTP transfers on ESX 3.0.2 and 3.5 hosts in more detail.

During creation of a new virtual machine, VMM will suggest a storage location for the files on the host based on saved defaults. The storage path will typically map to a VMFS volume that one or more ESX hosts have read/write access to. You can choose to browse the host for an alternate path. To ensure that the virtual machine is VMotion capable, make sure to select a storage location that is visible by all hosts that share a common VMotion network.

If the virtual machine contains pass-through disks (RDM), then you are also presented with a binding section to assign available RDMs to the virtual machine pass-through disks. Once VMM maps the RDM in physical mode to a virtual machine, specific actions are no longer supported by ESX. Primarily, snapshots are not supported with RDM in physical compatibility mode. However, this mode does allow the guest operating system to access the underlying hardware directly, which is useful for guest agents that need to take hardware-based snapshots of storage or virtual machine–based Microsoft failover clusters.

Migration

After a virtual machine is deployed to an ESX host, its mobility is an important ongoing issue for any administrator. With virtual machines, however, migration from one location to another is actually very easy and ultimately reflects some amount of downtime to the workload running in the virtual machine. Before virtual machines, a physical machine migration meant physically moving it from one rack location to another. Depending on the size of the organization, this may require a coordinated effort with multiple internal and potentially external groups. Another option administrators have when migrating a physical machine is to instantiate a secondary host with the exact configuration as the primary and at some point reroute all new requests to the secondary host, draining the primary host of current connections until it is no longer servicing requests. This is another coordinated effort with a high chance of failure due to error.

Moving a virtual machine from one location to another requires moving a set of files that constitute the machine's configuration and virtual disks. Migration of a virtual machine also migrates the workload running in the guest operating system. Migrating a virtual machine is a simplified migration model compared to migrating physical computers from one location to another (for example, from one rack to another) or manually migrating workloads from one computer to another. With physical migrations, downtime is much more apparent to administrators and end users. With virtual machines, however, migration is simple and involves much less downtime. In fact, with specific hypervisor technologies, there is no perceived downtime with migration of virtual machines. Administrators can now move a virtual machine within business hours, enabling intraday load balancing of datacenter resources.

VMotion

To minimize downtime, vCenter supports moving a virtual machine from one host to another with no perceivable downtime by using VMotion technology. VMotion uses proprietary memory replication technology to map a virtual machine's memory state to another ESX host. ESX will continue to transfer memory deltas until a minimum threshold is met, which will trigger the final memory transfer and change ownership of the virtual machine to the destination host. VMotion requires that the source and target reside within the same vCenter datacenter and share the same storage location. A shared virtual machine network is recommended to ensure network connectivity at the destination. A dedicated VMotion network is also recommended to segregate VMotion-specific traffic from normal virtual machine network traffic. With an ESX cluster, you can enable Distributed Resource Scheduler (DRS), a feature that leverages VMotion within a cluster to automatically load balance virtual machines over time based on utilization. Table 4.9 lists VMotion maximums supported by ESX. You can also use VMM's PRO feature on your VMware environment. PRO has the advantage of being extensible and application-aware using integration with System Center Operations Manager (a monitoring product). More details about this later in this chapter and in Chapter 8, which details creating your own PRO-enabled management pack.

TABLE 4.9:   VMotion-related maximums

ITEM	MAXIMUM
Number of ESX hosts that share the same VMFS volume	32
Number of nodes supported in an ESX cluster	32
Number of VMFS volumes per ESX host	256

CPUID MASKING AND ENHANCED VMOTION COMPATIBILITY (EVC)

When you're migrating virtual machines between hosts using VMotion, the physical CPUs on the source and destination hosts must match. At a minimum, CPUs should be from the same manufacturer. This requirement is in place for any hypervisor that supports migrating running virtual machines. Using vCenter, you have the option of masking specific CPU features that may increase the mobility of a virtual machine. Keep in mind it is assumed that the application running in the guest operating system queries for the CPU features using CPUID standard calls at startup. CPUID can query processor features in privileged code or nonprivileged code. In privileged code, the CPUID will return CPU features presented by ESX, including any masking settings you specify. However, nonprivileged runs against the hardware will return the actual CPU features supported, irrespective of CPUID masking. For this reason, CPUID masking will only address mobility using VMotion in some cases. For VMware, VMM will mask the No Execute/Execute Disable feature of a processor. This feature allows the operating system to mark memory in the virtual machine as code to prevent malicious attacks using buffer overrun exploits. Since this is a feature queried by the operating system in privileged code, CPUID masking will return the final mask applied by ESX.

VMware vCenter supports more advanced masking of CPUID features using Enhanced VMotion Compatibility (EVC), specifically clusters. This feature depends on specific capabilities of the CPU that allow masking of CPUID features at the hardware level. Intel calls this technology VT-x Flex Migration and AMD refers to it as Enhanced Migration. vCenter allows you to set a CPUID mask that essentially makes all CPUs in the cluster look the same, effectively ensuring VMotion compatibility at the cluster level. A requirement of EVC is that all virtual machines must be powered off before the CPUID mask is set for the cluster.

Storage VMotion

Storage VMotion is a feature specifically introduced by VMware to support migration of VMDK files between storage devices with little to no perceived downtime. VMotion transfers virtual-machine memory between hosts on the same storage location. Storage VMotion transfers virtual-machine virtual disks between storage locations on the same host. VMM supports this feature in the Administrator Console and PowerShell interface.

To move virtual disks attached to a virtual machine between storage locations on ESX, follow these steps:

1. Select the virtual machine in the Administrator Console.

2. Right-click the virtual machine and select the Migrate Storage action from the menu (Figure 4.41).

FIGURE 4.41
The Migrate Storage action

3. In the migration wizard, you can specify an alternate storage location on the same ESX host for the VMDK file (Figure 4.42).

4. Click Finish to start Storage VMotion on the ESX host.

Network Migration of ESX Virtual Machine

In addition to VMotion and Storage VMotion, VMware supports moving virtual machines over the network. Using VMM, you can migrate a virtual machine over the network within a vCenter instance. Workload downtime is required, of course, if VMotion is not supported between the selected source and destination ESX hosts. VMM relies on vCenter to transfer mechanisms, in this case meaning that SFTP is not used between ESX hosts.

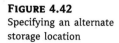

FIGURE 4.42
Specifying an alternate
storage location

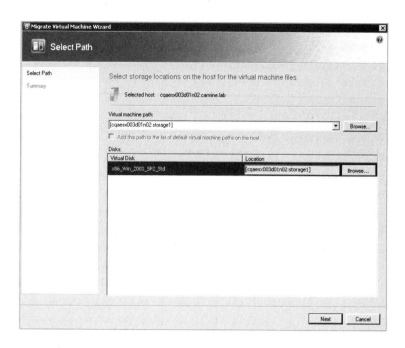

With VMM, you can store VMware virtual machines in the library as virtual machine objects. From the library, you can deploy stored virtual machines to an ESX host. The library also supports VMDK files. You can create a new virtual machine using a stored VMDK file. Moving virtual machines and virtual disks to and from an ESX host does require using a transfer mechanism that is not natively supported on ESX 3.0.2 and ESX 3.5. VMM implemented PuTTy to enable SFTP transfers to and from ESX hosts over SSH. For ESXi 3.5, VMM uses HTTPS-based transfers supported natively by the host. After associating vCenter with VMM, ESX hosts in OK (Limited) state indicate that additional security information is required to enable full transfer capabilities. After enabling full transfer capabilities, you can store and deploy to and from the library with no limitations.

With full transfer capabilities enabled, you can use the library as a storage location for virtual machines. You can store virtual machines from any vCenter instance associated with VMM. From VMM's perspective, there is no segregation of host groups based on vCenter instances. VMM treats different vCenters as peers in the host group hierarchy. Moving a virtual machine across vCenter instances directly is not supported. However, you can use the library as a temporary storage location to help you get around this restriction. First store the virtual machine managed by one vCenter instance into the library or clone it. Then deploy that stored or cloned virtual machine to an ESX host managed by another vCenter instance.

Monitoring Alerting Using PRO

VMM manages virtual machine and virtual machine hosts. You can couple it with System Center Operations Manager (OpsMgr) to enable robust monitoring, alerting, and reporting of all resources under management. In addition to managing the virtual machine host, OpsMgr uses management packs to enhance its understanding of the environment. Management packs exist for specific applications like Microsoft Exchange and hardware like Brocade Fibre Channel switches. The number of partners producing management packs continues to grow daily. A powerful addition to the management pack family is VMM Performance and Resource Optimization (PRO) Management Packs. PRO Management Packs build off of management pack framework to deliver workload-specific alerts, referred to as PRO tips, directly in VMM's Administrator Console. Upon receiving a PRO tip, you can choose to implement the remediation or recovery logic associated with the PRO tip or dismiss the alert. You can also script this in PowerShell.

How PRO Works for ESX

To enable PRO for VMware, you will need OpsMgr agents. Installing an agent in the guest operating system will provide monitoring, alerting, and reporting coverage for the workload running in the virtual machine. For ESX host-level monitoring, installing the OpsMgr agent on ESX is not an option. Instead, VMM relies on the OpsMgr agent installed in the VMM server to query vCenter's data to gather ESX host-level information. VMM leverages the health service of the agent for ESX monitoring.

For PRO, there is a specific flow for monitoring and performance information. The ESX host monitoring data flow is as follows:

- Agent on the VMM server starts to monitor each ESX host managed by vCenter for the host group or cluster host group that has PRO turned on.

- For the ESX host, the agent configures the monitor to collect data from vCenter associated with the VMM server.

- Based on predefined thresholds, OpsMgr determines whether or not to raise an alert.

- If OpsMgr raises an alert on a PRO target class, that alert is copied into VMM as a PRO tip.

- When the PRO tip is implemented, PRO executes the recovery that is associated with the monitor that generated the alert.

- Depending on the recovery action, if some change is required in vCenter or the ESX host, the recovery calls back into VMM and initiates a request through the vCenter's APIs on behalf of the end user.

The Bottom Line

Identify the important features that are enabled by managing ESX hosts using VMM. VMM enables very robust day-to-day management of Hyper-V– and ESX-based environments. With the exception of a few nontypical operations, administrators can use VMM as a single management interface across multiple hypervisors. VMM can also aggregate multiple vCenter instances in addition to multiple hypervisors. VMM is the best management product for users who want to standardize how virtual machines are created, deployed, and managed in their environment. A common console across hypervisors helps reduce the barrier to entry for users who want to standardize on a management product that supports multiple hypervisors. Standardization of procedures helps reduce the learning curve for new operations staff. Standard PowerShell-based scripts that work across hypervisors help make operations staff more productive.

Master It

1. Write out the how VMM maps Host & Clusters, Datacenter, Folder, and Cluster objects in vCenter to Host Group and Host Cluster objects.

2. List the three management tools VMware provides for managing ESX hosts and virtual machines.

3. Using PowerShell, create a sample script to get the percentage of hosts responding in your environment and the percentage of running virtual machines per host.

Set up a connection between VMM and vCenter and change an ESX host from OK (Limited) to OK. VMM uses vCenter's web service APIs to enable management of ESX hosts. Using vCenter is a requirement to support features like VMotion. The web service APIs, however, are not sufficient to enable full management of ESX in VMM. Transferring files to and from an ESX host requires additional software. VMM ships with SFTP support for ESX file transfers.

Master It

1. What information is missing from VMM if an ESX host is in OK (Limited) state?

2. Why does VMM open multiple sessions to vCenter?

3. How can you access resource pool information?

Determine what monitoring is available for ESX hosts out of box using PRO. VMM and OpsMgr make a powerful combination for monitoring, alerting, and reporting your entire datacenter, including physical and virtual resources. Monitoring is not limited to the virtual machine hosts. Instead, using OpsMgr Management Packs, you have access to in-depth application knowledge.

Master It

1. Where do you need to deploy OpsMgr agents to get the most out of PRO?

2. Instead of requiring the OpsMgr agent for each ESX host, how does VMM get ESX data?

Chapter 5

Managing Hyper-V Using VMM

Microsoft originally released Hyper-V in 2008, several months after releasing Windows Server 2008. Hyper-V is Microsoft's first software-based native (type 1) hypervisor. It is specifically designed to provide a higher level of isolation, stability, and scalability compared to previous virtualization offerings (i.e., Virtual Server 2005). This technology is similar to Citrix XenServer and VMware ESX/ESXi Server.

This chapter will focus on managing Hyper-V using VMM. We won't actually detail the differences between the various hypervisors as this would be out of scope for this chapter and book. If you intend to deploy Hyper-V in large quantities, VMM offers the best management experience. With native clustering support, Hyper-V can leverage Microsoft failover clusters to deliver highly available virtual machines. Coupled with OpsMgr, Performance and Resource Optimization (PRO) gives you the most comprehensive monitoring solution for your Hyper-V environment.

In this chapter, you will learn to:

- ◆ Understand Hyper-V requirements

- ◆ Understand deployment considerations

- ◆ Manage Hyper-V hosts and virtual machines

Understanding Hyper-V Requirements

Similar to the other hypervisors, Hyper-V consists of a software layer called the hypervisor that executes directly on hardware. The hypervisor software controls and arbitrates access to the underlying hardware. Before going into the details of how VMM manages Hyper-V, let us take some time to understand Hyper-V by covering the following topics:

- ◆ Hyper-V architecture

- ◆ Hyper-V security

- ◆ Host operating system requirements

- ◆ New features in Windows Server 2008 R2 Hyper-V

- ◆ Guest operating system requirements

Hyper-V Architecture

Similar to XenServer, but unlike ESX/ESXi, Hyper-V does not load the drivers for peripherals available to the computer in the hypervisor layer. Instead, it loads the hardware drivers on a privileged partition called the *parent partition*, which has direct access to underlying hardware. The Hyper-V approach is labeled as *microkernelized* hypervisor, which differs from ESX/ESXi's monolithic hypervisor implementation. These terms refer to operating system kernel design in which a microkernel defines a simple abstraction layer over the hardware that uses system calls to implement a minimal set of operating system services like memory management, task management, and interprocess communication. Other services are implemented in the user space. A monolithic kernel, however, runs all operating system services in the main kernel execution thread, providing robust hardware access. In Figure 5.1, the Hyper-V architecture is illustrated. The figure defines the following components of Hyper-V:

Windows hardware   Computer equipment compatible with the Windows Server operating system.

Hypervisor   A software layer that provides isolated environments, allowing a host computer to run multiple independent guest operating systems concurrently.

VMBus   In-memory channel-based communication mechanism used to enable communication between partitions.

Parent Partition   The privileged partition hosts kernel and user mode services. Kernel mode services include the Windows kernel, device drivers for the underlying hardware, virtual service providers (VSPs), and the VMBus. User mode services include the virtualization stack comprising the WMI provider, VM service, and VM worker process. This partition is required for all Hyper-V instances. This partition is not meant to run user workloads. Instead, this is a management partition that runs virtualization core services.

Virtual service providers (VSPs)   Since the parent partition is the only partition with access to the underlying hardware, all other partitions need a mechanism to access storage and network devices. Microsoft implemented VSPs in the parent partition to present physical devices to child partitions as synthetic devices over the VMBus. With this approach, there is no need for device vendors to develop and distribute proprietary device drivers for the Windows hypervisor. Instead, you can load existing drivers certified by Windows Hardware Quality Labs (WHQL) for the present devices. VSPs map to specific devices that need to be shared with child partitions. Not all devices will have a corresponding VSP.

Child partitions   The isolated partition runs a guest operating system. This partition hosts kernel and user mode services. Kernel mode services include the Windows kernel, Virtual Service Clients (VSC), and the VMBus. User mode services include all user specific workloads. Since this is not a privileged partition, it does not have direct access to hardware. To gain access to the hardware, the guest operating system uses the storage and network devices presented by VSCs to communicate with the VSPs in the parent partition. Hyper-V uses the VMBus to enable communication between parent and child partitions.

Virtual service clients (VSCs)   Virtual service clients in child partitions communicate with a corresponding VSP in the parent partition. The synthetic device drivers loaded in the guest operating system of the child partition use the VMBus to get storage and network I/O requests to the VSP in the parent partition.

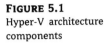

FIGURE 5.1
Hyper-V architecture
components

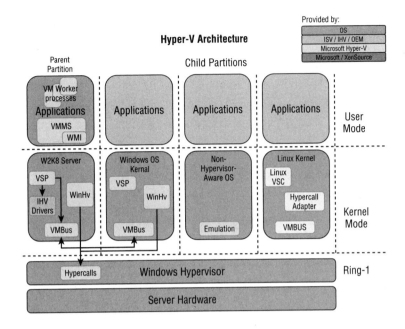

Hyper-V Security

The security model around Hyper-V focuses on protecting the integrity of the hypervisor and properly sandboxing virtual machines from each other and the hypervisor. The hypervisor leverages processor technology to ensure execution at the appropriate privilege levels, restricts access to hypervisor functions through a controlled interface, and uses an in-memory channel-based transport for any communication between partitions. VMM introduces a few additional security enhancements by integrating its role-based administration model with the Hyper-V Authorization Manager (AzMan) authorization store and support for hosts in perimeter networks and non-trusted Active Directory (AD) domains.

Hypervisor

Machine virtualization using software-based hypervisors introduces a layer of abstraction between the physical hardware and the operating system. It is imperative to protect the hypervisor from unauthorized access either from an external attack source or internally from a partition. Hyper-V requires support for hardware-assist virtualization available in modern Intel and AMD processors, referred to as Intel VT-x and AMD-V, respectively. These processors support the new virtual machine extensions (VMX) mode. VMX mode provides four new less-privileged levels (rings) in addition to the standard four IA-32 privilege levels (rings). VMX mode allows the processor to be in either VMX root operation or VMX non-root operation. The intention is for the Hyper-V hypervisor software to work in VMX root operation while the partitions work in VMX non-root operation.

The hypervisor behavior in VMX root operation is similar to how it would function with a processor that does not offer VMX mode. Partitions that work in VMX non-root operation have access to the four privileged levels (rings) and can expect similar behavior on a normal processor with some limitations. The limitation is with access to critical system resources. The expectation is that these resources remain under the control of the hypervisor in VMX root operation. The limitation also extends to VMX non-root operation in ring zero. This is how the parent partition on a Hyper-V host gains access to the underlying hardware. The hypervisor software does not manage hardware I/O devices. This is why you need to load drivers in the parent partition.

Microsoft protects the integrity of the hypervisor by doing the following:

♦ Specifying a controlled interface to access hypervisor functions. Hyper-V partitions do not have direct access to the hypervisor. Microsoft defined the Hyper-V hypercall API to give partitions the necessary controlled access to the hypervisor to execute specific operations. The hypercall API is fully documented by Microsoft: `http://www.microsoft.com/downloads/details.aspx?FamilyId=91E2E518-C62C-4FF2-8E50-3A37EA4100F5&displaylang=en`.

♦ Handling interpartition communication outside of the hypervisor by the VMBus. Hyper-V provides a channel-based transport mechanism for inter-partition communication called the VMBus. This transport exists between the parent and child partitions only and is not hosted by the hypervisor. Synthetic devices presented to the child partitions using a VSC communicate to the corresponding VSP in the parent partition over the VMBus.

♦ Not sharing memory space between the hypervisor and partitions.

♦ Not loading the hypervisor hardware I/O drivers or executing non-hypervisor-related software. By design, all drivers and software execute in the parent partition.

PARTITIONS

Hyper-V supports one parent partition and zero, one, or more child partitions. In addition to protecting the hypervisor, Hyper-V offers security measures to protect from an attacker attempting to gain unauthorized access to another partition. The parent partition is a privileged virtual machine with direct access to the underlying I/O hardware. It does not control the physical memory or processors of the system; this is handled exclusively by the hypervisor. To gain access to hardware devices, you need to load device-specific drivers provided by Microsoft or device manufacturers in the parent partition. Child partitions do not have access to the devices directly. Instead, Hyper-V ships with a set of virtualization service providers (VSPs) for network- and storage-related devices. VSPs execute in kernel mode in the parent partition and communicate with child partitions over the VMBus.

In the parent partition, Hyper-V exposes a WMI provider for programmatic access by users and management software. The interface is part of the Virtual Machine Management Service (VMMS), which controls the state of the virtual machines in child partitions and controls the tasks that can be performed on a virtual machine. For each virtual machine started by the VMMS, a Virtual Machine Worker Process (VMWP) is started. The process is responsible for the interaction between Windows Server 2008 in the parent partition and virtual machines in the child partitions. The VMWP is responsible for changing the state of the virtual machine.

Microsoft protects the partitions by doing several things:

♦ Creating a separate instance of the VMBus for each child partition

♦ Requiring that the Execute Disable/No Execute bit be enabled in the motherboard of the physical Hyper-V host

♦ Running VMWP in user mode

♦ Not sharing a virtual device between any two virtual machines

AUTHORIZATION MANAGER (AZMAN)

Hyper-V's hypervisor and partition safeguards protect against malicious attack against a particular component. To address the need for user-level authorization of tasks, Hyper-V uses the Authorization Manager (AzMan). AzMan defines the roles, operations, tasks, and policies necessary to properly authorize a user to a set of objects. When you manage a Hyper-V host using VMM, the same interface is used to store the user roles defined by VMM's authorization model. These are Administrator, Delegated Administrator, and Self-Service User. VMM will make the following changes to the Hyper-V authorization store as part of adding the host to VMM:

◆ A new authorization store is created with the intention of storing VMM-specific authorization data. The store is persisted in a file labeled `HyperVAuthStore.xml` and stored in `%ProgramData%\Microsoft Virtual Machine Manager`.

◆ VMM also imports any authorization data defined in the root scope of the default authorization store (`initialstore.xml`).

VMM refreshes the authorization store of a Hyper-V host every 30 minutes. Any changes to the scopes other than the root scope are overwritten. Changes to the root scope after VMM creates the new authorization store are preserved.

As part of removing a Hyper-V host, VMM will back up the existing authorization store before removing all user roles and scopes that were defined through VMM.

HOSTS IN PERIMETER NETWORKS AND NON-TRUSTED AD DOMAINS

Hyper-V's security features ensure the integrity of the hypervisor, partitions, and inter-partition communication. Depending on where you plan to deploy your Hyper-V hosts, there is also a need to ensure that VMM can properly manage the hosts in various trust levels:

Host in trusted Active Directory (AD) domain　VMM supports deploying virtual machines to a host in a trusted AD domain and migrating virtual machines to other trusted hosts and the VMM library.

Host in a perimeter network　VMM can manage a host that resides in a separate network and has no access to the network in which the VMM server resides. The separate network might be an Internet facing network with no access to protected internal network resources. Resources that reside on an Internet facing network typically cannot be trusted due to higher exposure to viruses and unauthorized access. For this reason, VMM can deploy only virtual machines to a host in a perimeter network. Migration between hosts and storing to the library are not supported for perimeter network hosts. In addition, VMM does not assume that an AD domain is available in a perimeter network and so the VMM agent runs under a local system account. With VMM 2008 R2, you can now migrate VMs between hosts in the DMZ, so you can be slightly more permissive but still do not allow customers to take data from the DMZ and bring it back inside, since once in the DMZ, it is no longer trusted.

Host in a non-trusted AD domain　VMM only supports adding standalone host in a non-trusted AD. A cluster must always be in an AD domain to add it to VMM.

Requirements for the Host Operating System

The host operating system requirements for Hyper-V is very simple since the hypervisor ships as a native role in Windows. Hyper-V is not available as a stand-alone installable package, so there are no configurations possible where you install a new release of Hyper-V on an older operating system (and vice versa). You are permitted two variations: enabling the Hyper-V role on a full installation or core installation of Windows Server 2008 R2. A core installation of Windows Server is a minimal installation of the operating system. It offers a console for limited command-line interaction and offers only a subset of roles. A core installation is not another version of the operating system, simply an installation option. Hyper-V is offered in three editions of Windows Server 2008 R2:

◆ 64-bit edition of Windows Server 2008 R2 Standard

◆ 64-bit edition of Windows Server 2008 R2 Enterprise

◆ 64-bit edition of Windows Server 2008 R2 Datacenter

Another option is to install Hyper-V Server 2008 R2. Hyper-V Server is a stand-alone hypervisor server that consists of the following elements:

◆ Windows Server 2008 R2 core installation

◆ Hyper-V role enabled by default

◆ Specialized command-line scripts to simplify management

USE CASES FOR HYPER-V SERVER

Hyper-V Server is meant only to be used as a hypervisor server and so no other Windows roles can be enabled. If you plan to cohost other roles with Hyper-V, you will need to use a full or core installation of Windows Server 2008 R2.

Table 5.1 summarizes the features available with Windows Server 2008 R2 Enterprise Edition (EE) and Datacenter Edition (DC) and Hyper-V Server 2008 R2.

TABLE 5.1: Host operating systems with Hyper-V

FEATURE	WINDOWS SERVER 2008 R2	HYPER-V SERVER 2008 R2
Host clustering	Yes	Yes
Live Migration	Yes	Yes
> 32GB host memory support	Yes	Yes
>4 host processor support	Yes	Yes

Windows Server 2008 R2 Hyper-V Features

With Windows Server 2008 R2, Microsoft delivers several important Hyper-V features and scalability enhancements:

Improved scalability   Hyper-V now supports 64 logical processors and up to 1 TB of RAM on the physical host. With these new physical resource limits, Hyper-V also increased the maximum number of virtual machines that you can have powered on concurrently on a single host.

Hyper-V supports a maximum of 384 powered-on virtual machines per host. The maximum number of virtual processors supported is 512. Table 5.2 lists the supported maximum number of virtual machines by processor count. Hyper-V supports any combination of virtual machine configurations as long as the maximums are not exceeded. It also supports up to 64 GB of RAM per virtual machine.

TABLE 5.2: Maximum supported virtual machines per Hyper-V host

VIRTUAL CPUs PER VIRTUAL MACHINES	MAXIMUM VIRTUAL MACHINES SUPPORTED	TOTAL VIRTUAL CPUs
Single processor	512	384
Dual processor	256	512
Quad processor	128	512

Live Migration Hyper-V supports the migration of running virtual machines between two nodes of a Hyper-V cluster with no perceived downtime. This technology differs from other migration types (e.g., network, SAN transfer) in that the memory state of the running virtual machine is transferred to another host. Since the virtual machine is still running on the host, the memory state will change during the migration. Hyper-V makes sure to sync up the modified memory pages. It will continue to do this until the delta is so small that the virtual machine can be paused for a brief amount of time while the virtual machine itself is migrated to another host and resumed.

To minimize any interruption to the guest operating system and running applications, Live Migration depends on a new technology developed by Microsoft called Cluster Shared Volumes (CSV). CSV functions as a distributed-access file system; you can store the associated virtual hard disks and configuration files of virtual machines in one storage location and access them from any node in a cluster. Since all nodes in the cluster can read and write to a CSV, during live migration there is no need to change ownership of the CSV from one node to another.

LIVE MIGRATION WITHOUT CSV

In a Microsoft failover cluster, you can live migrate a virtual machine between nodes without CSV. The main difference is with downtime. Live migrating without CSV incurs a 5- to 30-second interruption. In this configuration, you should also consider deploying one virtual machine per storage location.

Processor Compatibility Hyper-V introduces a new Processor Compatibility feature that improves the mobility of a virtual machine during migration with memory state. When you enable this feature before powering on a virtual machine, Hyper-V will take care of normalizing the features exposed to the virtual processor. Since this masking is performed in software, there is no requirement for advanced features from Intel and AMD, referred to as Flex Migration and Extended Migration, respectively.

This feature enables seamless migration of virtual machines with memory state between hosts with processors from the same manufacturer but different families. This still means you can migrate between AMD and AMD, Intel and Intel. The feature does not allow live migration between different processor manufacturers like AMD and Intel or vice versa.

Hot add and remove storage   Hyper-V supports adding and removing virtual disks while a virtual machine is running. It only supports adding or removing the virtual disk drives from the synthetic SCSI controller. The UDE controller does not support this feature.

MAC spoofing disabled by default   Hyper-V supports a new secure mode for legacy and synthetic virtual network adapters that disables MAC spoofing. With MAC spoofing disabled, the guest operating system cannot override its permanent MAC address (OID_802 _3_PERMANENT_ADDRESS). The permanent MAC address is seeded by the virtual network adapter using the current MAC address (OID_802_3_CURRENT_ADDRESS), which you can set in the Registry of the guest operating system. When MAC spoofing is disabled, switch learning is disabled for the port on the virtual switch. Only the configured MAC address is associated with the virtual switch port. In addition, the port with MAC spoofing disabled will not receive any flooded packets.

Jumbo Frame Support   Hyper-V supports Jumbo Frame Support for 1 Gb/E networks. This feature allows Hyper-V virtual machines to send packets in groups of 7,500 to 9,000 message transfer units (MTUs) instead of the usual 1,500 MTUs, improving network throughput.

Virtual Machine Queue and Chimney support   Hyper-V supports Chimney and Virtual Machine Queue (VMQ) for 10 Gb/E networks. These two technologies enable network offload to reduce the overhead on the CPU of processing network packets.

Requirements for the Guest

Hyper-V supports a large mix of operating systems, including uni- and multiprocessor configuration and 32-bit and 64-bit operating system architectures. Table 5.3 lists the supported operating systems and any processor limitations. Windows 7 and Windows Server 2008 R2 ship with Integration Services in the box. The services are automatically enabled if you install these operating systems in a virtual machine on Hyper-V. Any devices that Plug and Play (PnP) recognizes will also get automatically installed since the drivers are present (e.g., synthetic devices). Operating systems that ship with outdated integration services or none at all will require that you install them manually using either the Hyper-V MMC or the VMM Administrator Console.

TABLE 5.3:   Hyper-V–supported operating systems

OPERATING SYSTEM	PROCESSOR CONFIGURATION	INTEGRATION SERVICES AVAILABILITY
Windows Server 2000 Server and Advanced Server with SP4	1	Yes
Windows XP SP3 32-bit	1	Yes
Windows Vista SP1 32- and 64-bit	1	Yes

TABLE 5.3: Hyper-V–supported operating systems *(CONTINUED)*

OPERATING SYSTEM	PROCESSOR CONFIGURATION	INTEGRATION SERVICES AVAILABILITY
Windows 7 client 32- and 64-bit	1, 2	Yes
Windows Server 2003 SP2 32- and 64-bit	1, 2	Yes
Windows Server 2003 R2 SP2 32- and 64-bit	1	Yes
Windows Server 2003 R2 SP2 32- and 64-bit	1 ,2	Yes
Windows Server 2008 32- and 64-bit	1, 2, 4	Yes
Windows Server 2008 R2 64-bit	1, 2, 4	Yes
SUSE Linux Enterprise Server 10 (x86/x64)	1	Yes
SUSE Linux Enterprise Server 11 (x86/x64)	1	Yes
Red Hat Enterprise Linux (RHEL) 5.2 (x86/x64)	1	Yes
Red Hat Enterprise Linux (RHEL) 5.3 (x86/x64)	1	Yes

Understand Deployment Considerations

As part of deploying VMM in your environment, you need to consider the deployment requirements of Hyper-V. Windows Server 2008 R2 Hyper-V is a high-performance enterprise-ready virtualization platform that leverages several technologies to deliver on performance, reliability, and availability. To help you better understand this, we will now explore the following topics:

◆ Infrastructure requirements

◆ Installation type

◆ Failover clustering

Infrastructure Requirements

Hyper-V is the enabling technology that helps you realize virtualization in your environment. VMM is the management tool that gives you the necessary control to help you scale that environment. Under the covers, however, there are several technologies that need to come together to make all this a reality. The following sections explore these technologies.

PROCESSOR

Hyper-V ships with the 64-bit edition of Windows Server 2008 RTM and R2 as a standard Windows role. After installing Windows Server, you can enable Hyper-V by enabling the role. For the hypervisor to load, Hyper-V requires an x64-based processor, hardware-assisted virtualization, and hardware data execution protection (DEP). Hardware-assisted virtualization, specifically Intel VT or AMD V, must be enabled in the BIOS before you enable the Hyper-V role within Windows. Hardware DEP, specifically Intel XD bit (execution disable bit) or AMD NX bit (no execute bit), must be enabled in the BIOS before you enable the Hyper-V role within Windows. Enabling one feature but not the other will prevent the hypervisor from loading.

   To determine if your current processor supports hardware-assisted virtualization and DEP, you can optionally download SecurAble from www.grc.com/securable.htm to determine what features are supported. Figure 5.2 is an example of an Intel Pentium 4 CPU that offers DEP but does not offer hardware-assisted virtualization.

FIGURE 5.2
No hardware-assisted virtualization

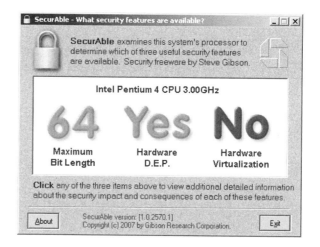

Figure 5.3 is an example of an Intel Core 2 CPU that offers DEP and hardware-assisted virtualization.

NETWORK

Network connectivity requirements depend on how you plan to use Hyper-V. If you deploy Hyper-V as a sandboxed environment under a user's desk, you may need only one network connection. If the intention is to use Hyper-V for a small team, to consolidate multiple computers onto one, then you should consider at least two network connections: one for management of Hyper-V, including backup, and the other for virtual machine network traffic. In larger deployments, you should consider at a minimum two network connections. Hardware permitting, you should segregate network traffic to avoid bandwidth bottlenecks. If you need fault tolerance for the network connections, network teaming will require at least two physical network ports for each connection. Deploying Hyper-V failover clusters will increase the number of network connections because you need to account for a dedicated private cluster network and a dedicated cluster shared volume network. Table 5.4 lists the maximum number of ports required for a Hyper-V host (including cluster requirements).

FIGURE 5.3
Example of Hyper-V–compatible processor

STORAGE

The storage infrastructure deployed for a Hyper-V environment is crucial to the overall success of the project. A poorly designed storage environment will not allow you to scale Hyper-V properly and may lead to unplanned downtime and data loss.

Performance

Proper design is especially important since storage tends to be the first external bottleneck of any virtualized environment. Due to the physical limitations of disks with spinning components, there is only so much performance you can get from the media. External storage array vendors mitigate this problem by offering larger systems with more disks, more cache, and more bandwidth, making it difficult to hit storage-related physical scale limits typically encountered with virtualization environments. One reason for this problem is typically due to poor planning. From a storage perspective, there is no prescriptive guidance on how to classify storage utilization and I/O patterns in the same way a database administrator can more precisely profile the I/O requirements of a database server. Since the applications that drive the I/O requests execute in the guest operating system of a virtual machine, there is no simple mechanism to segregate virtual machines by application type unless all virtual machines have the same application.

TABLE 5.4: Hyper-V network port requirements

NETWORK TYPE	RECOMMENDED/ MINIMUM	DESCRIPTION
Management network	2/1	Required for management of the Hyper-V instance. Two ports are recommended to allow for teaming of the network connections. However, one connection is sufficient with the understanding that if the connection goes down, you will lose management capabilities of the Hyper-V instance.
Virtual machine network	2/1	Used for child partition network traffic. Two ports are recommended to allow for teaming of the network connections. However, one connection is sufficient with the understanding that if the connection goes down, virtual machines will lose network connectivity.
Backup network	1/1	If you plan to back up the Hyper-V instance and the virtual machines that exist on the host, you should consider a dedicated connection specifically for backup traffic. One connection is sufficient with the understanding that if the connection goes down, you will lose the ability to back up the host and/or virtual machines. In addition, backup traffic (full backups in particular) can require significant bandwidth, which might end up competing with user traffic if not correctly scheduled.
Cluster Private Network	1/1	If you deploy Hyper-V in a cluster configuration, you should have a dedicated private network for cluster-specific traffic (cluster heartbeat). One connection is sufficient with the understanding that if the connection goes down, Microsoft failover clustering will use the public network (if configured to do so).
Cluster Shared Volume Network	1/1	If you plan to use Cluster Shared Volumes (CSV) with a Hyper-V cluster, you should have a dedicated network for CSV traffic. CSV generates traffic when it is put into redirected I/O mode. In this mode, the coordinator node (i.e., the node that owns the CSV LUN) is the only one with read/write access. All other nodes pass their I/O request to the coordinator using SMBv2. One connection is sufficient with the understanding that if the connection goes down, Microsoft failover clustering will use the cluster private network.
iSCSI Network	2/1	If you plan to use iSCSI storage to host your virtual machines, you should consider segregating iSCSI traffic from virtual machine traffic.

Backup and Restore

Performance aside, backing up and restoring data is very daunting in any virtualized environment. If you back up too much, you incur extremely high storage costs. However, if you do not back up enough, there is a high probability of data loss. Also, you have to consider where to back up the data. Depending on the level of importance of the data in your environment, you may need to back it up to a separate datacenter to mitigate data loss in the event of a catastrophic datacenter or site failure. Considerations for how to restore the data is as important as backing it up. Certain restore methods may take too long to complete and cause your company to incur fines or loss in productivity. An example of this type of recovery is bare-metal restore. In this case, the data recovered consists of the following elements:

◆ Operating system binaries

◆ Operating system configuration

◆ Application binaries

◆ Application configuration

◆ Application data

Other recovery methods require a high amount of preparation before data can be restored. An example of this type of recovery is referred to as an incremental-application-data-only restore. In this case, the backup consists of only changed operating system and application files. To restore, the administrator needs to first install and configure the operating system and application. Only after completing this can the administrator overlay the restored data. Each approach has its pros and cons, but in a virtualized environment, the backup and restore process requires additional consideration in order to get the full benefit of virtualization.

For virtualized environments, if you decide to back up the computer with the hypervisor, you need to capture the operating system and all the virtual disks files. This approach makes restoring very easy because all the virtual machines are captured without any additional work. However, the burden is now on the storage. A virtualized environment may have terabytes of data to back up. Many existing file backup products are unable to take incremental backups of virtual hard disks (VHDs). These products typically back up any file that has changed as part of incremental backups, and since the VHD is constantly changing, it always requires a full backup. More advanced backup methods that rely on incremental backups still require periodic full backups of the files. Another approach is to have a backup agent in every guest operating system. While this places less of a burden on the amount of storage required for a backup and allows for restoring individual files from within the VM, there is still a need to recover the virtual machine with the guest operating system and application first. If you have a small number of templates in your environment (a template in this context consists of a virtual machine configuration, and a virtual disk with an operating system and application), then you can minimize the administrative cost and overhead. Ideally, most customers want the ability to take consistent host/VHD-level backups incrementally but still get the benefits of individual file restore that is offered by in-guest backup.

Discussing the proper design for a storage environment is not in scope for this book; the following list summarizes common storage recommendations for any virtualized environment:

Fibre Channel (FC) SAN   FC SAN is ideal for large production environments. You will typically get the best performance from a FC configuration. Depending the actual SAN configuration, you may have sufficient room to scale your storage as you virtualize more of your environment. SAN is typically more expensive than DAS storage because of the investment in the FC fabric. FC environments typically require engineering and operations personnel, which also adds to the cost.

iSCSI SAN   iSCSI has the benefit that it can use standard IP networks as the transport for SCSI I/O traffic between a virtual machine host and storage. You might initially consider deploying iSCSI over FC. Keep in mind, however, that if you need to scale your environment, it is highly recommended that you segregate your application network from your data network. To do this, you will mostly likely have to deploy a second switched IP network specifically for iSCSI. Keep this in mind if cost avoidance is the reason you are considering iSCSI over FC.

Direct-Attached Storage (DAS)   Locally attached storage tends to be the cheapest storage but the most inflexible and unmanageable. Typically, you have a fixed amount of disks you can deploy under a DAS configuration, which limits your capacity to scale. In addition, DAS is not a shared resource across multiple hosts. So if you ever need to plan for more complicated deployment models, DAS will need to get replaced at some point. This storage type is great for legacy and small test/dev environments. You can consider DAS for branch office deployments as well.

WMI API

The Microsoft Management Console (MMC) snap-in and the server configuration command-line interface (CLI) are the in-box tools provided for administrators to configure Hyper-V after installing it. If you plan to deploy only a handful of servers, these tools may be sufficient to help you perform common management tasks. As you increase the number of Hyper-V servers deployed, the quantity of tasks will likely increase. At some point, management of your Hyper-V deployment through a console or command line will simply consume too much of your time.

To reduce the overhead of managing multiple systems, automation is very important. To automate common Hyper-V tasks, use the WMI API. Hyper-V's WMI Provider resides in the parent partition and is meant to provide access to the local hypervisor from a remote location. In fact, VMM uses the same WMI interface to manage with Hyper-V. VMM, however, does not expose Hyper-V's WMI interface as WMI. Instead, VMM offers a management abstraction layer over all the supported hypervisors using PowerShell. There are several advantages to using VMM's PowerShell for automation over Hyper-V's WMI API.

◆ The syntax is simplified.

◆ There is a common script for all hypervisors.

◆ VMM takes care of the basics and provides more advanced automation.

After the VMM agent is installed on the Hyper-V server, the agent issues WMI calls to configure and manage Hyper-V and virtual machines on the server. From an VMM perspective, there is no need to understand Hyper-V's WMI APIs to use the VMM PowerShell interface. For less-common tasks, however, if VMM does not provide the controls, you can still use Hyper-V's WMI API to automate the necessary changes.

REMOTE CONSOLE

Remote access to a Hyper-V server involves connecting to the parent partition or one of the virtual machines. Accessing the parent partition requires Remote Desktop Connection and gives you access to the Windows Server 2008 installation in the parent partition. The operating system must be available and accessible on the network. If the operating system is still booting up, you cannot connect remotely. You can use Remote Desktop Connection to access the guest operating system installed in one of the virtual machines on the Hyper-V host.

Similar to connecting to the parent partition, the guest operating system must be fully booted and accessible on the network. If you need access to the virtual machine before an operating system is installed or fully booted, then you need to connect to the remote console of the virtual machine hosted by the Hyper-V server using the Virtual Machine Connection utility. By default, the utility connects to the Hyper-V server using port 2179. Virtual Machine Connection displays the console of the virtual machine and supports interacting with the console if necessary. For example, if the virtual machine is configured with a legacy network adapter, the adapter will attempt to boot from the network by sending out a PXE request and will wait for a Windows Deployment Server (or similar service) to respond. At this point, you can interface with the virtual machine by responding to the screen prompt.

USING VMConnect.exe

The Hyper-V MMC connects to the console of the virtual machine using VMConnect.exe. You can access this file directly from C:\Windows\System32\Hyper-V. Make sure to run the utility as Administrator.

Installation Type

Windows Server 2008 and Windows Server 2008 R2 ship Hyper-V as a role of Windows. With in-box support for enabling the hypervisor, the installation experience is very simple. There are three ways of deploying Hyper-V in your environment. Deploying Windows Server 2008 R2, there are two installation types to choose from (similar to Windows Server 2008): full and core. Full installation is the typical installation of Windows Server that everyone is familiar with. Core is a minimal footprint installation of Windows Server that does not offer all the roles and features of a full installation. A third deployment option is Hyper-V Server. With Hyper-V Server, Windows Server Core is installed by default and Hyper-V is enabled by default.

Full installation   A full installation of Windows Server 2008 R2 by default offers the complete set of in-box roles and features available based on the edition of Windows Server installed. A full installation also offers the full graphical user experience at the console with a Start menu, Desktop, and so on. There is no limitation to which roles or features you can enable or what software you can install or run on a full installation of Windows Server (except of course for software that is not compatible with Windows Server 2008). You can manage a full installation of Windows Server from the local console or remotely using the MMC or other tools.

Core installation   Windows Server 2008 R2 offers Windows Server Core as an installation option in addition to full installation. Core is not a feature of Windows but simply an installation type that causes Window Server to run with a minimal footprint on disk and in memory. Even though this installation type is still Windows Server 2008 R2, there are some limitations to what applications you can install since Core does not offer a graphical interface and much of the operating system binaries. For this reason, before using it, make sure you understand the implication of managing this type of server and what applications can run on Windows Server Core. For example, software that you would install on Window Server for management and backup purposes may not function properly (if at all) on Windows Server Core.

Hyper-V Server Hyper-V Server is another option for deploying Hyper-V in your environment. Hyper-V Server is simply Windows Server 2008 R2 Core Server with Hyper-V enabled by default and a specialized command-line management interface. Hyper-V Server is a free license, so only the Hyper-V role is enabled. If you need more roles enabled, you should consider deploying a full or core installation of Windows Server 2008 R2.

 Real World Scenario

CONFIGURING HYPER-V SERVER 2008 R2

Al is interested in deploying Hyper-V to host virtual machines that are Internet facing. Since the potential for an external attack is guaranteed in this environment, he decides to deploy the smallest footprint installation of Hyper-V using Hyper-V Server 2008 R2. He knows this installation of Hyper-V installs the core of Windows Server and layers a simplified management interface to make setup easy.

1. To get started, Al locates the ISO with Hyper-V Server 2008 R2 and burns the image to a DVD.

2. Since he does not have direct access to the server, he decides to load the DVD remotely using the remote management board.

3. The bootable media prompts Al to confirm that he wants to boot into the DVD.

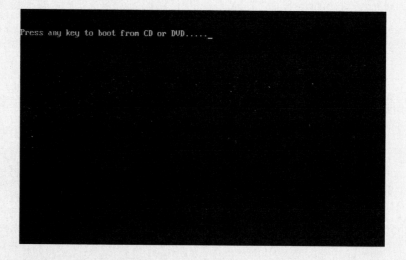

4. Windows loads from the bootable media to start Setup.

5. Al accepts the default English language selection for the operating system, the time and currency format, and the keyboard method.

6. He clicks Install Now to start the installation process.

7. Al accepts the language selection and the EULA.

8. He then selects the custom (advanced) installation type.

9. Al doesn't have a specific requirement to change the disk layout, so he just accepts the default.

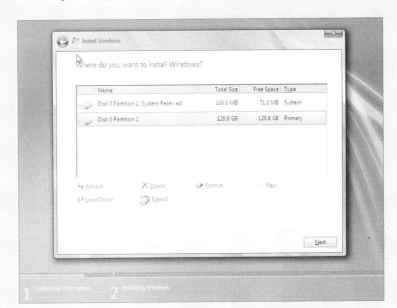

10. He waits for the operating system to complete the installation.

11. After setup completes and the server reboots, Windows prompts Al to change the password before logging in for the first time.

12. Al enters the password twice.

13. After Windows logs him in, the Server Configuration shell appears.

14. In Server Configuration, Al selects option 2 to change the computer name and then reboots the server.

15. In Server Configuration, Al selects option 1 and joins the server to a domain. He needs to join the computer to domain Contoso. He provides the domain name and the credentials necessary to add the computer account into the domain. After that step completes, he reboots the server.

```
Enter number to select an option: 1

Change Domain/Workgroup Membership
Join <D>omain or <W>orkgroup? <Blank=Cancel> D
Join Domain
Name of domain to join: contoso
Specify an authorized domain\user:  contoso\admin
```

16. In Server Configuration, Al selects option to add users to the local Administrators group. In this step Al can specify additional local users or domain users.

```
Enter number to select an option: 3

In a domain environment, specify domain\username.
In a workgroup environment, specify username.

Enter account to join local Administrators group <Blank=Cancel>: contoso\user01
```

17. In Server Configuration, Al selects option 4 to configure Remote Management.

18. In Server Configuration, Al selects option 5 to set Windows Update to automatically download and apply updates.

19. In Server Configuration, Al selects option 7 to enable Remote Desktop.

20. In Server Configuration, Al selects option 8 to configure the IP address, gateway, and subnet. Option 8 is also used for specifying primary and secondary DNS servers.

```
Administrator: C:\Windows\System32\cmd.exe - sconfig                _ □ X

NIC Index               0
Description             Intel 21140-Based PCI Fast Ethernet Adapter (Emulated)
IP Address             192.168.100.105
Subnet Mask            255.255.255.0
DHCP enabled           False
Default Gateway        192.168.0.1
Preferred DNS Server   192.168.10.10
Alternate DNS Server   172.100.10.5

1) Set Network Adapter IP Address
2) Set DNS Servers
3) Clear DNS Server Settings
4) Return to Main Menu

Select option: 1

Select <D>HCP, <S>tatic IP <Blank=Cancel>: s
Set Static IP
Enter static IP address: 192.168.100.110
Enter subnet mask <Blank = Default 255.255.255.0>: 255.255.255.0
Enter default gateway: 192.168.100.1
```

Failover Clustering

So far we have discussed enabling Hyper-V on a stand-alone installation of Windows Server 2008 R2. Depending on how you plan to use virtualization in your environment, multiple stand-alone hosts might be sufficient. With virtualization, since you are sharing one physical server with multiple operating systems running in virtual machines, there is a greater impact to your users when the server fails. If you plan to deploy critical applications into the guest operating system of virtual machines, you want to minimize any unplanned downtime incurred due to hardware failure or software issues. To increase the availability of a virtual machine, you need to consider deploying Hyper-V in a Microsoft failover cluster configuration. With a failover cluster, the virtual machine becomes the unit of failover. The application that resides in the virtual machine is unaware that it is participating in a failover cluster.

A typical Hyper-V cluster requires shared storage and a dedicated network. Windows Server 2008 R2 introduces a new technology called Clustered Shared Volume (CSV). With CSV, all nodes of a Hyper-V cluster have read and write access to a shared disk. Virtual machines that reside on the same CSV storage location can be started and run on any node of the cluster. Virtual machines can be migrated independent of the underlying storage. In the event of a host failure, the cluster would take care of starting up the virtual machines on any of the remaining nodes. In contrast to Windows Server 2008, without CSV, all virtual machines that resided on a storage location had to migrate together. There was no way of independently moving virtual machines without also moving the storage location. In the event of a node failure, all virtual machines have to be restarted on only one of the remaining cluster nodes.

SUPPORT FOR ALTERNATE CLUSTERED FILE SYSTEMS

In addition to CSV, Microsoft Hyper-V failover clustering and VMM support alternate clustered file systems. Sanbolic's Melio FS File System installs on Windows Server 2008 R2 with Hyper-V and serves as a replacement for CSV since the file system has no dependency on NTFS. With Melio FS, a shared disk is accessible from all nodes in a cluster. A Hyper-V cluster with Melio FS supports live migration of virtual machines between nodes in the cluster. La Scala is the volume management interface to Melio FS, used in place of the Windows native volume manager.

Managing Hyper-V Hosts and Virtual Machines

VMM is strictly focused on managing the virtualization aspects of a Hyper-V host. With VMM, for example, you cannot deploy Windows Server 2008 R2 to a physical computer with no operating system (commonly referred to as *bare-metal deployment*). However, enabling the Hyper-V role is a function of deploying the VMM host agent to a computer with Windows Server 2008 R2.

Adding a Hyper-V Host to VMM

Adding a computer to VMM involves first deploying an agent. For a Windows computer, an agent is required. Unlike for VMware which is agentless since VMM uses vCenter's web APIs to manage ESX hosts. To manage a stand-alone installation of Hyper-V or Hyper-V Server or to bring a Windows computer under management, follow these steps:

1. In the VMM Administrator Console, click the Add Host action (Figure 5.4).

2. In the Select Host Location dialog, select Windows Server-Based Host On An Active Directory Domain. Type in the credentials of a local administrator on the server (Figure 5.5).

3. In the Select Host Servers dialog, type the computer name of the Hyper-V server you want to add (Figure 5.6). Then click the Add button so the wizard can verify the computer in AD.

FIGURE 5.4
The Add Host action in
the VMM console

FIGURE 5.5
Adding the credentials
for the local admin-
istrator in the Select
Host Location dialog

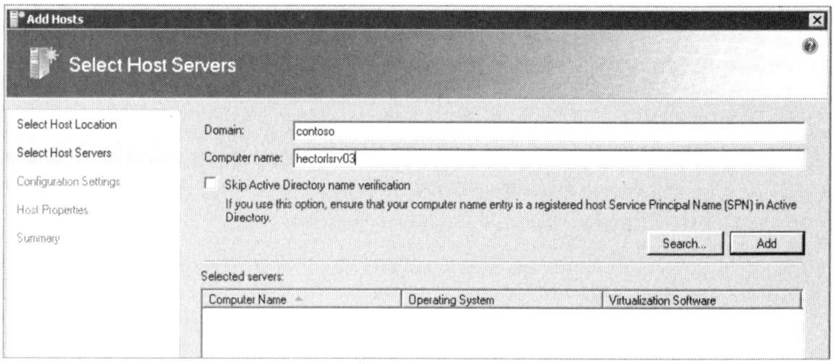

FIGURE 5.6
Providing the
computer name

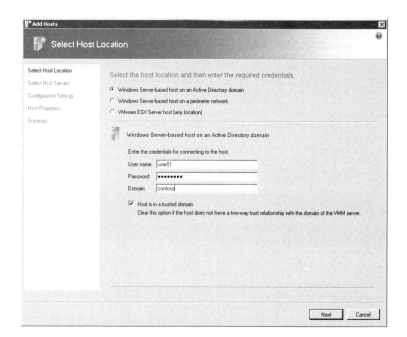

4. In the warning dialog, click Yes to continue (Figure 5.7).

FIGURE 5.7
The VMM Will Enable
Hyper-V warning dialog

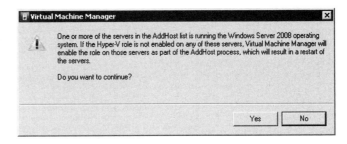

5. In the Configuration Settings dialog, select the host group to which you want to add the Hyper-V host.

6. In the Host Properties dialog, provide the default paths VMM should use when deploying virtual machines to this host and set the port user for remote connections to the virtual machines.

7. In the Summary dialog, confirm the Hyper-V server(s) you want to add.

CLUSTERED HOSTS

When you add a Hyper-V host that is part of a Windows Server 2008 failover cluster, the VMM Administrator Console will automatically detect that this target computer is part of a failover cluster and automatically pull in other nodes on the same cluster and group them under the same cluster object.

INSTALL VMM AGENT LOCALLY

VMM provides users with an easy remote agent deployment method. As long as users provide appropriate credentials with administrator privilege to the target computer and the computer is joined to an AD domain, they can "push-install" the agent from the VMM Administrator Console.

However, there is always the option of installing the VMM agent locally. This can be useful for perimeter network (sometimes also called as demilitarized zone, or DMZ) VM host computers or in a troubleshooting scenario in which you want to find out why a failure occurred during the agent deployment process.

You can either use the media or copy over the media to a share, or you simply copy the installer package from the media (\amd64\msi\Agent\vmmAgent.msi) to the target computer. The setup splash screen from the media simply calls the VMMAgent.msi package and all the user interfaces after that are from the MSI package.

Here are the steps to install the VMM agent on a local computer:

1. Select the Local Agent option from the setup splash screen.

2. Click Next on the welcome page from the agent MSI package and then on the usual EULA page.

3. Choose the destination folder and click Next.

4. Enter the ports that the VMM server uses to connect to the virtual machine host (Figure 5.8). The ports include the WinRM port used as the command channel as well as the port used by BITS for data transfer. The default settings are 80 for WinRM and 443 for BITS. If you changed the default settings when the VMM server was installed, you need to use the customized ports here.

FIGURE 5.8
The Configuration Settings page of the local agent wizard

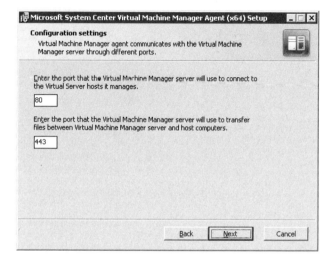

5. On the next page (Figure 5.9), you will need to decide if this computer is in a perimeter network. If this is not a perimeter network computer and it joins to an Active Directory domain, you should leave the This Host Is On A Perimeter Network option unchecked and click Next. This is the last page before launching the actual install process.

If this is a perimeter network host, continue with the next steps.

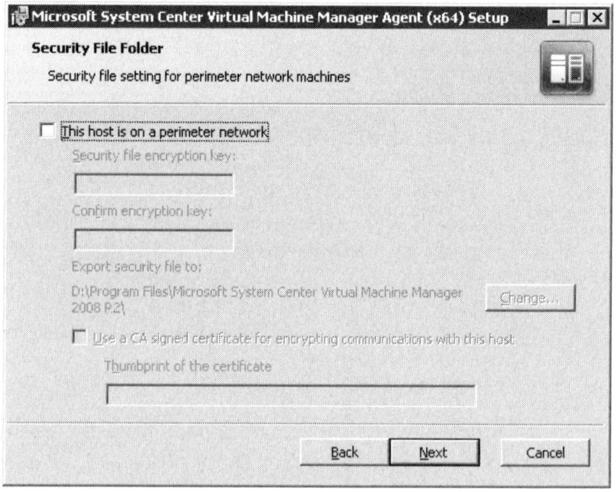

FIGURE 5.9
The Security File Folder page for a non-perimeter network computer

6. If this is indeed a virtual machine host that is on a perimeter network, you'd need to provide the following information (Figure 5.10):

   ◆ An encryption key (password) for the security file to be generated by the VMM agent setup

   ◆ The location (file path) to export the security file to

   ◆ Whether you want to use a CA-signed certificate (instead of using the self-signed certificate, by default)

   Since this is a perimeter network host, you should check the This Host Is On A Perimeter Network option. Review the encryption key, security file location, and CA-signed certificate thumbprint, and then click Next.

FIGURE 5.10
The Security File Folder page filled out for a perimeter network host

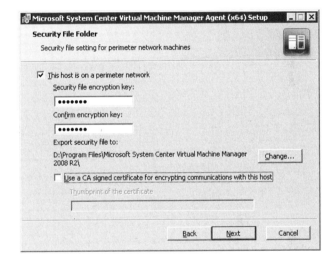

7. Next, select the name that the VMM server will need to use to connect to the host. The name can be either the local computer name (the NetBIOS name) or an IP address of the computer (Figure 5.11).

8. Complete the wizard by clicking Next to launch the actual install process.

WHICH NAME SHOULD I PICK?

If you are using a CA-signed certificate, the host name you choose when you install the VMM agent on a local computer must match up with the subject name in your CA signed cert. Check the cert or check with the person who obtained the cert to understand what name to be used here.

If you are not using a CA-signed certificate, it's not important which host name you choose to use. You can choose any host name as long as the host name (or IP address) is reachable by the VMM server.

◆ If the NetBIOS name can be reached from the VMM server, you can use that; otherwise, you might want to pick the IP address option.

◆ If the host has more than one network adaptor and they connect to different networks, make sure you pick the IP address that the VMM server can reach.

How is the host name used? Essentially, the host name is matched up with the host name the VMM server establishes a connection to for management purposes.

Either the name matches the subject name in the CA-signed certificate or it will be used as the subject in the certificate that the VMM agent setup generates. When users go to the VMM Administrator Console, add the host by using the perimeter network host option, and upload the security file generated from this local agent install process, the name must be used as the name of the host to be added. Otherwise, the Add Hosts job will fail.

FIGURE 5.11
Choose how VMM will
contact the host

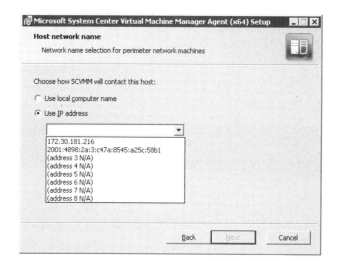

Configuration

Adding a Hyper-V host to VMM initially configures the remote console port and the service account to run the VMM service under. Once the Hyper-V host is under management, VMM creates a virtual machine host object that you can interact with in the Administrator Console. In addition to status information about the host and the agent installed, there are several more properties associated with the virtual machine host object that you can modify in the console and CLI. You can modify network and storage configuration, resource reservations, and custom properties and add virtual machines to management.

VM host object properties are accessible via the Administrator Console or PowerShell. To access VM host properties and settings, right-click a VM host and select Properties (Figure 5.12).

FIGURE 5.12
VM Host Properties

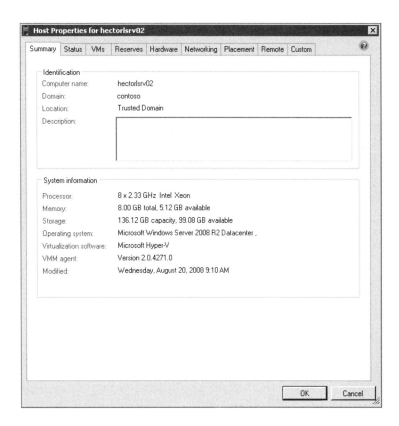

The following list includes descriptions of the properties for a Hyper-V virtual machine host:

Summary: Identification   This includes the computer name of the Hyper-V host and the domain to which the host is joined.

Summary: Identification: Description   This is the field where you can add additional information to describe the virtual machine host. The data is stored in the VMM database only.

Status: Overall Status   The status here will reflect whether the host is in the OK state. Connection status, virtualization service status, virtualization service version, agent status, and agent version all reflect the status of the individual components that contribute to the host's overall status.

Status: This host Is Available For Placement   This property reflects whether the Hyper-V host is available for virtual machine placement. If this check box is not selected, then the VMM placement engine will not include this host in the list of possible choices to deploy new virtual machines to. In addition, when the host is in maintenance mode, this setting is selected. This feature allows you to remove a host from any placement decision temporarily and ensures that VMM users do not inadvertently create or migrate virtual machines to the host.

VMs: Resources   This represents the flat list of virtual machines that reside on the host.

VMs: Register The Following Virtual Machines   Use this feature to browse the local file system on the Hyper-V host and find virtual machine configuration files that you want to register on the virtual machine host. Hyper-V refers to this as importing a virtual machine.

Reserves: Reserved Resources   Host reservations are used by VMM's Intelligent Placement engine when star ratings are calculated. You can specify CPU (in percentage), amount of memory (in MB), disk space (in MB), disk I/O (in IOPS), and network capacity (in percentage). You can also specify these settings at the host group level. Changing these settings will not affect the virtual machine host configuration.

Hardware: CPU, Memory, Floppy Drives, DVD/CD-ROM Drives   These represent physical resources on the host. This information is read-only.

Hardware: Storage: Volume Details   This represents volumes exposed to the host. You have the option of excluding a volume from placement to avoid virtual machines getting deployed on it.

Hardware: Network Adapters: Adapter Details   The physical network ports on the virtual machine host. VMM discovers the network location automatically for each port on a Hyper-V host and populates this list. You also have the option of manually setting a location from a list of discovered locations.

Networking: Virtual Network Details   Each network port will represent a virtual switch on the virtual machine host. If a virtual switch already exists on the Hyper-V host, it will be imported into VMM's database when the host is added to management. You can set the network tag and description for the switch as well. Network Tag represents a category you assign to the virtual switch VMM uses to automatically assign a virtual network to a virtual network adapter when creating a virtual machine. The tag information is user specific.

Networking: Network Bindings   A virtual switch can be used for either a private network (communication between virtual machines on the same host), an internal network (communication between virtual machines and the parent partition), or for external/physical network (communication between virtual machines on the same host and other machines on the physical network). Binding a virtual switch to a private or internal network ensures that all communication is isolated on the host only. Binding to a physical network adapter will expose virtual machines to the physical network to which the adapter is connected.

Networking: Host Access   Selecting this option indicates to Hyper-V that it can use this virtual switch for virtual machine network traffic and management traffic. For this connection, you can also specify the VLAN ID that the management traffic uses.

Networking: Switch Binding   For a particular host network adapter, you can enable VLANs in either access mode or trunk mode.

Placement: Specify Default Virtual Machine Paths To Be Used During Virtual Machine Placement   This is the default path on the Hyper-V host where you want to place all your virtual machines.

Remote   This sets the TCP port that VMM will use to connect to the remote console session of virtual machines that reside on the Hyper-V host. By default, this port is 2179.

Custom: Assign Custom Properties To This Host   This is a set of 10 properties you can set for a virtual machine host.

Using Maintenance Mode

As part of deploying a hypervisor like Hyper-V, it is necessary to mitigate the impact of both planned and unplanned downtime of the underlying host. This is especially true in production scenarios where each virtual machine is running a critical application. With Windows Server 2008 R2, Hyper-V now supports live migration of running virtual machines with no perceived downtime. Aside from the benefits of migrating virtual machines to balance resources across your hosts, live migration is also very important for minimizing the impact of planned downtime of a Hyper-V host.

VMM enhances this experience by supporting maintenance mode for clustered Hyper-V hosts. Maintenance mode is specifically designed to evacuate running virtual machines off a Hyper-V node to another node in the cluster using Live Migration. Maintenance mode takes care of placing the virtual machine on a node using Intelligent Placement. This experience is unique in the VMM Administrator Console since multi-selecting a group of virtual machines and migrating them is not supported. Once evacuated, the Hyper-V node is in maintenance mode and no new virtual machines can be deployed to it. It is important to note that Hyper-V currently supports only one live migration between two nodes at a time. To help avoid the overhead of live migrating virtual machines one at a time, VMM supports queuing live migrations when a node is put into maintenance mode.

Test development environments often do not require a high level of availability and so (planned or unplanned) downtime of virtual machines typically has very little impact to the users. However, this is also subject to the density of virtual machines that reside on each host. With Windows Server 2008 R2, Hyper-V now supports running up to 384 virtual machines concurrently per host. There is no simple solution for mitigating the impact of downtime in a dense test/dev environment except to either accept the inconvenience or deploy Hyper-V in a clustered configuration using iSCSI. With a cluster, you can quickly evacuate all the virtual machines using quick migration, for example. As stated previously, VMM maintenance mode will queue live migrations. In a test/dev environment, the minimal interruption incurred by quick migration might actually be acceptable. If so, consider quick migration of all the virtual machines using the VMM PowerShell console before placing a host into maintenance mode.

Importing and Exporting a Virtual Machine

Manually migrating a virtual machine between two storage locations on the same Hyper-V host or between two Hyper-V hosts is a two-step process. First you need to export the virtual machine you want to migrate. The exporting process generates a configuration file that has an `.exp` filename extension and contains the virtual machine configuration. The file itself is not meant to be modified by users. After migrating the virtual machine's exported configuration file and virtual disks to a new location, you need to import the virtual machine. As part of importing the virtual machine, Hyper-V reads the exported configuration file and creates the virtual machine on the new host.

VMM supports migration of a virtual machine between two storage locations or two hosts using the export and import mechanism. In one special case, VMM does not use the export and import mechanism as part of migrating a virtual machine. If you store a virtual machine that does not have snapshots to the VMM library, the migration will transfer only the virtual disk file to the library location. The virtual machine configuration is maintained only in the VMM database. When deploying the virtual machine back to a Hyper-V host, VMM will copy the virtual disk to the designated storage location on the host and then create a new virtual machine using the configuration stored in the database.

With this information in mind, remember that if you ever need to remove a library share or library server from VMM, the virtual machine configuration stored in the database will be deleted. If you add the server or share back to VMM, the library refresher will import only the virtual disk file. Since there is no configuration file, VMM cannot generate a virtual machine. This is an important detail to keep in mind if you decide to remove a library server or share from VMM.

Hardware and Guest Operating System Profiles for Hyper-V Virtual Machines

Hardware and guest operating system profiles contain the most common settings users need to set on a virtual machine. A VMM hardware profile is not the superset of settings for a Hyper-V–based virtual machine, however. Similar to a guest operating system profile, the settings account for only some of the more common customizations used during Windows mini-setup.

HARDWARE PROFILE PROPERTIES

A hardware profiles include the following properties:

Name   The name of a profile allows you to search for it in the UI and CLI. You can summarize the settings contained within by using the names if you plan to standardize on a few key configurations in your environment.

Description   The description is for more detailed information about the profile. This can include specific information about how you intend to use the hardware profile.

Owner   An owner can be set on a profile if deemed necessary. The user specified must be a valid AD user. However, this setting has no implications on security or visibility in the UI or CLI.

BIOS: Startup Order   Hyper-V supports configuring the startup order of devices in the virtual machine's BIOS. The startup order dictates only the order which the virtual machine will use for the four devices. Startup order does not exclude any of the devices. Supported startup devices are as follows:

CD   The virtual machine should search for bootable media in the virtual DVD/CD drive.

IDE Hard Drive   The virtual machine should search for bootable virtual hard disks present on either of the IDE controllers. This is not supported for virtual hard disks that reside on a virtual SCSI controller.

PXE Boot   The virtual machine should attempt to boot from the network using the PXE-enabled legacy network adapter. This option is not supported for the synthetic network adapter.

Floppy   The virtual machine should search for bootable media in the virtual floppy drive.

BIOS: Enable Num Lock   Indicates if the BIOS will enable Num Lock for the virtual machine at start up.

CPU: Number of CPUs   The quantity of virtual CPUs you can set for Hyper-V include one, two, and four per virtual machine. Note: At this writing, VMM does not support setting three virtual CPUs for a virtual machine.

CPU: Type   The type of CPU you specify does not reflect a Hyper-V setting. Instead, the type selected here is used by VMM's Intelligent Placement engine. The placement engine models new workloads on a VM host and gives you a star rating based on the expected utilization of the workload.

CPU: Limit CPU Functionality   This setting will mask specific CPU features at the hypervisor level so older operating systems like Windows NT 4 can boot properly. You need to enable this setting only if you plan to run operating systems that fail to boot properly in a VM due to specific CPU features that are incompatible with the guest OS.

CPU: Limit CPU For Migration   Hyper-V (Windows Server 2008 R2) supports the ability to mask CPU features from the guest operating system installed in a virtual machine. Masking CPU features increases the compatibility of a virtual machine when migrating it between hosts with processors from the same manufacturer (e.g., Intel) but different processor families.

Memory   Setting memory for a virtual machine depends on the version of Hyper-V to which you plan to deploy a virtual machine. For a new virtual machine, new template, or new hardware profile, you can set the minimum memory of 4 MB or the maximum of 65,536. Windows Server 2008 RTM Hyper-V supports up to 32GB per virtual machine. Windows Server 2008 R2 supports up to 65536 MB.

Note: It is highly recommended to set the memory value in increments of 2 MB. With Windows Server 2008 R2, this is a requirement.

Floppy Drive   Hyper-V supports one floppy drive per Hyper-V virtual machine.

Floppy Drive: No Media Captured   Removes the virtual floppy disk attached to the virtual floppy drive or disconnects it from the host floppy drive. Removing a virtual floppy will delete the file from the Hyper-V host.

Floppy Drive: Physical Floppy Drive   Attaches the virtual floppy drive to the host floppy drive.

Floppy Drive: Existing Virtual Floppy Disk File   Attaches the virtual floppy drive to a virtual floppy (VFD) stored in the library.

COM   VMM supports up the two Hyper-V COM ports per virtual machine.

COM: None   Removes the named pipe or text file associated with a COM port.

COM: Named Pipe   Sets up a named pipe for COM serial port communication.

COM: Text File   Associates the virtual COM port to a file on the local file system of the Hyper-V host.

IDE Devices (Controller)   VMM supports the two Hyper-V IDE controllers per virtual machine.

SCSI Adapter (Controller)   VMM supports Hyper-V's SCSI controller per virtual machine.

SCSI Adapter: Shared Controller   This setting is not supported for Hyper-V.

Virtual DVD Drive   VMM supports up to four Hyper-V virtual DVD drives per virtual machine.

Virtual DVD Drive: Channel   You can attach a DVD virtual drive to any available slot on the IDE controllers present in the hardware profile. Channel displays both the controller ID and location ID. Hyper-V supports up to two DVD devices per IDE controller.

Virtual DVD Drive: No Media   This disconnects the physical CD/DVD or image file from the virtual DVD drive.

Virtual DVD Drive: Physical CD/DVD Drive   Attaches the virtual CD/DVD drive to a CD/DVD drive in the physical host.

Virtual DVD Drive: Existing Image File   This associates an image file to the virtual DVD drive. If the template or virtual machine is stored in the library, then the hardware profile will only link the objects together (no files are copied). However, if the virtual machine is already on a Hyper-V host, the file is copied from the library over the network to the local file system of the host.

Virtual DVD Drive: Existing Image File: Share Image Instead Of Copying It   Avoids the over-the-network copy of the file to the host and instead associates the image directly from its current location. Typically this is used with image files hosted on network file shares. To support this, you need to enable constrained delegation between the VMM library and the Hyper-V host.

Virtual Disk   This is the common object used by VMM to represent a virtual hard disk across all hypervisors. Specifically for Hyper-V, Virtual Disk contains a virtual hard disk of type VHD.

Virtual Disk: Channel   You can attach a virtual disk to any available slot on any SCSI controller present in the hardware profile. Channel displays both the controller ID and location ID. Hyper-V supports up to 64 SCSI devices. Keep in mind that Hyper-V does not support booting guest operating systems from SCSI-based virtual disks. Even though VMM will not block you from creating a virtual machine or template where the VHD file is attached to the SCSI controller, during placement, VMM will inform you of the incorrect configuration.

Virtual Disk: Use An Existing Virtual Hard Disk   You can browse VMM's library for an existing virtual disk (VHD file) to attach to the virtual machine or template. You cannot attach a virtual disk to a hardware profile by itself. If the template or virtual machine is stored in the library, the hardware profile will only link the objects together (no files are copied). However, if the virtual machine is already on an Hyper-V host, then the file is copied from the library over the network to the local file system of the host.

Virtual Disk: Create A New Virtual Hard Disk   If you need a blank disk created with the virtual machine, then use this option to dynamically generate a fixed VHD file when deploying the virtual machine.

Virtual Disk: Pass Through To Physical Drive On Host   Attaches a pass-through device to the virtual machine at deployment time. When creating a virtual machine, you simply indicate that you want to use a pass-through disk. After placement, VMM will list all available pass-through disks on the host. Note: VMM does not manage pass-through disks on the host.

Virtual Disk: Type   You can select dynamic or fixed disks as the virtual disk type. Hyper-V supports creating both virtual disk types.

Virtual Disk: Size   The size of the virtual disk can vary from 1 GB to 2,040 GB.

Virtual Disk: File Name   By default, VMM will assign a name to the virtual disk. You can override the name when creating the virtual machine.

Network Adapter   Hyper-V supports up to four legacy virtual network adapters and eight synthetic virtual network adapters per virtual machine. VMM distinguishes between emulated and synthetic adapters. Hyper-V introduces the term *Synthetic* adapters.

Network Adapter: Network Location   Network Location is used to dynamically associate a virtual network adapter to the most appropriate virtual switch on a host. VMM uses Windows Network Location Service on Windows hosts to determine the associated domain servicing IP addresses and DNS on hosts to which the virtual switch is attached.

Network Adapter: Network Tag   A network tag is a user-specified setting to decorate a virtual switch on a host with extra information that is specific to the deployment of the host. For example, a virtual machine host may be connected to three distinct physical networks: Primary Production, Secondary Production, and Backup. If you plan to deploy a virtual machine with multiple virtual network adapters and can use network tag to automatically associate them to the appropriate virtual switch, simply decorate the virtual switch with the associated tag information in host properties.

Network Adapter: Enable Virtual LAN Identification   Enables a VLAN ID for an individual virtual network adapter.

Network Adapter: VLAN ID   You can associate a VLAN ID per virtual adapter.

Network Adapter: Ethernet (MAC) Address Dynamic   Hyper-V hosts support generating MAC addresses for virtual network adapters during deployment.

Network Adapter: Static   Hyper-V hosts support manually assigning a MAC address to a virtual network adapter. You can assign a static MAC to a virtual machine or template in the library or a virtual machine on a host.

Network Adapter: Generate   VMM supports generating a MAC address from a predefined MAC range managed by VMM. You have to set the start and end of the range in the Administration section of VMM. The setting is global and applies to ESX, Hyper-V, and Virtual Server virtual machines.

Network Adapter: Enable Spoofing Of MAC Addresses   Allowing MAC spoofing or MAC learning is important for an NLB-like application running in the virtual machine. This setting applies only to Windows Server 2008 R2 Hyper-V.

Priority   Hyper-V hosts can assign a relative weight to a virtual machine using priority. With VMM, you can set Low, Normal, High, or Custom relative weights.

   High   Relative weight value of 200

   Normal   Relative weight value of 100

Low   Relative weight value of 50

Custom   Relative weight value supported: 1–10,000

High Availability   VMM classifies virtual machines deployed on a Microsoft failover cluster as a highly available VM. If a virtual machine or template has this setting enabled, then during placement, the placement engine will give a higher rating to Hyper-V clusters.

Integration Services   Hyper-V supports enabling and disabling integration services that reside in the guest operating system:

- Operating system shutdown
- Time synchronization
- Data exchange
- Heartbeat
- Backup (volume snapshot)

OPERATING SYSTEM PROFILE

An operating system profile, like a hardware profile, represents a collection of settings you can apply to a new template or a new virtual machine created from an existing template. VMM will use the settings in the operating system profile to generate an answer file consumed by a Windows mini-setup during the customization (or specialization) phase of Windows setup. During deployment, VMM will generate a virtual floppy file with an embedded answer file and attach the file to the virtual floppy drive of the virtual machine. During the customization phase of the virtual machine, Windows Setup will look for the answer file in several locations, including the floppy drive. After customization is complete, the virtual floppy file is deleted. This sequence is often referred to as the `sysprep` process in reference to the underlying Windows tools used to create the template and customize using the answer file.

For virtual machines deployed on Hyper-V, you can use the operating system profile only for Windows guests. VMM does not support customization of non-Windows guests (e.g., Linux).

Supported Virtual Machine Actions

For virtual machines on an ESX host, VMM's Administrator Console provides a number of actions in the actions menu presented on the right side of the interface. The virtual machine actions for Hyper-V are as follows:

Start   Powers on a virtual machine in a powered off state or saved memory state.

Stop   Stops a virtual machine by powering it off. This is the equivalent of unplugging a physical computer.

Pause   This action is not supported by ESX.

Save State   Referred to as Suspend in vCenter, this action will flush the current memory state of the virtual machine to disk. Resuming the virtual machine will reinstate its saved memory state from disk.

Discard Saved State   This action is not supported by ESX.

Shutdown   This action relies on sending a shutdown command to Integration Services residing within the guest operating system; if it's successful, the guest will gracefully shutdown.

Connect To Virtual Machine   Opens the window that connects to the remote console of the virtual machine

Migrate   Opens the Migration Wizard. From this wizard, you can VMotion to a supported destination or over the network.

New Checkpoint   Takes a new snapshot.

Manage Checkpoints   Opens a window to manage existing snapshots.

Disable Undo Disks   This action is not applicable to ESX hosts.

Repair   If an action targeted at a virtual machine fails, you can repair the virtual machine by retrying or undoing the action.

Install Virtual Guest Services   This action is not applicable to ESX hosts.

New Template   Generates a new template out of a selected virtual machine. In the case of ESX, the virtual machine is unregistered from the ESX host and copied to the library.

Clone   Clones the selected virtual machine. The wizard will guide you through Intelligent Placement where you can choose to clone the virtual machine to the same host or a different host.

Store In Library   Stores the virtual machine in VMM's library. This will require a network copy.

Delete   Deletes the virtual machine and all its associated files. This action is not the same as Remove From Inventory.

View Networking   Displays a diagram with the network for the ESX host.

Properties   Opens the properties page for the virtual machine.

The Bottom Line

Understand Hyper-V requirements.   Hyper-V is a very different technology compared to Virtual Server. It is instead in a similar class of hypervisors as VMware ESX and Citrix XenServer. It is worth taking the time to understand the specific requirements Hyper-V has so you can plan your deployment accordingly.

> **Master It**   Explain the difference between a microkernelized hypervisor architecture versus a monolithic hypervisor architecture, and give at least one example of each.

> **Master It**   What behavior should you expect if you live migrate a virtual machine that does not reside on CSV?

> **Master It**   How does Hyper-V Server 2008 R2 differ from Hyper-V in Windows Server 2008 R2?

> **Master It**   Explain how Hyper-V uses Intel VT-x/AMD-V processor technology?

Understand deployment considerations. The underlying infrastructure that Hyper-V resides on is critical to a successful deployment. Your intended use cases and scalability goal drive the requirements for hardware components and the connectivity used to deploy Hyper-V. Some environments require very little infrastructure and redundancy while others demand the highest availability, performance, and scalability.

Master It List the various network types you need to consider in a Hyper-V deployment?

Master It Describe a characteristic of each storage option in a Hyper-V deployment?

Master It What advantages does a Server Core installation of Windows Server 2008 R2 have over a full installation?

Manage Hyper-V hosts and virtual machines As part of managing Hyper-V and the virtual machines that reside on Hyper-V, it is good to understand the subtle differences that are not obvious in the UI or CLI.

Master It What artifact does exporting a virtual machine using the Hyper-V MMC create in place of the configuration file?

Master It Explain one limitation with Hyper-V Live Migration and how does VMM help in this situation?

Chapter 6

Managing Virtual Server Using VMM

When Virtual Machine Manager 2007 was originally released, the only virtualization platform it supported was Microsoft Virtual Server 2005 R2. VMM has come a long way in a short period of time, however, now supporting both Hyper-V and VMware ESX. Yet, the basic principles and scenarios that VMM used for supporting Virtual Server have remained. Once a user gets familiar with VMM, the virtualization platform is abstracted in the easy-to-use wizards and he or she can deploy and manage a virtual machine on any virtualization platform.

Virtual Server became very popular in 2005 since it provided a low-cost virtualization solution (Virtual Server was later provided by Microsoft as a free download) that could run on commodity hardware. This is still the case today, making the product an ideal candidate for development and testing environments that have older hardware and for companies that want to evaluate virtualization before they invest in expensive hardware.

The main in-the-box management solution for Virtual Server is the Administration Website, which provides a single-server view of the system. The Administration Website can't manage more than one virtual server at any given time, however, which limits the scalability of a Virtual Server environment when VMM is not in place. In this chapter, we will show you how Virtual Machine Manager enables customers to deploy and manage many Virtual Server hosts, significantly increasing the virtualization environment with a low-management overhead.

In this chapter, you will learn to do the following:

◆ Determine the requirements for the host and guest operating systems for Virtual Server

◆ Manage Virtual Server host clusters with VMM

◆ Use the permissions model for virtual machines

◆ Migrate a virtual machine from Virtual Server to Hyper-V

Understanding Virtual Server and Its Requirements

Virtual Server 2005 was Microsoft's entry product in the virtualization space after it had acquired Connectix in 2003. Now a free download from Microsoft's website, Virtual Server is classified as a "type 2" hypervisor. A type 2 hypervisor is typically hosted in software on top of a traditional operating system. In the case of Virtual Server, it runs on top of the Windows Server operating system as a separate layer, providing the virtualization capabilities. Guest operating systems, or virtual machines, run on top of the Virtual Server layer.

DOWNLOADING VIRTUAL SERVER 2005

Virtual Server 2005 R2 SP1, the latest release of Virtual Server, can be downloaded from the Microsoft Download Center website. The Download Center website also includes the latest release of an update for Virtual Server 2005 R2 SP1. This update, KB article 948515, provides support for the Windows Server 2008, Windows Vista SP1, and Windows XP SP3 operating systems.

Outside VMM, the management tools available for Virtual Server today include the Administration Website and the public COM application programming interface (API). PowerShell can also be used to manage Virtual Server through its integration with COM.

Requirements for the Host Operating System

Virtual Server can run on top of either a 32-bit or a 64-bit hardware platform for a variety of server operating systems. VMM supports managing Virtual Server when it is installed on either the Windows Server 2003 or the Windows Server 2008 operating system families. Even though Virtual Server can be installed on Windows Vista, such a configuration is not a supported platform for production environments and VMM will not allow you to add it as a host under management.

Virtual Server will be the default virtualization software that VMM deploys on hosts that have 32-bit architectures and for hosts running Windows Server 2003.

MORE ABOUT VIRTUAL SERVER 2005 R2 SERVICE PACK 1

Virtual Server 2005 R2 SP1 was a minor release of Virtual Server, albeit a very important one. With SP1, a set of new features was released that made Virtual Server a more competitive product in the market. The following list includes some of these features:

◆ Support for hardware-assisted virtualization, as seen here:

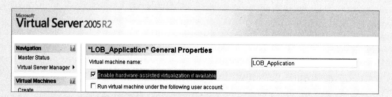

◆ VHD mount capabilities through an API and a command-line tool that allows more partners to get on board with the VHD format

◆ A Volume Shadow Copy Service (VSS) writer that facilitates integration with backup technologies, including System Center Data Protection Manager

♦ Host clustering capabilities through a script resource

♦ The ability for hosts to have up to 256 GB of memory when Physical Address Extension (PAE) is enabled

The following list includes the supported maximum limits for physical hardware for Virtual Server host machines.

Virtual Networks — 128

Physical memory addressable for virtualization — 256 GB

Number of hosts per cluster — 8

Physical NICs — 9,999

Requirements for the Guest Operating System

Virtual Server 2005 R2 SP1 also introduced a new set of operating systems that are supported to run as guests. Table 6.1 lists the supported operating systems that can be installed inside a virtual machine (VM) for Virtual Server. As you will notice, even though Virtual Server supports running on top of 64-bit hardware, it can run only 32-bit VMs. All VMs in Virtual Server are also limited to a single processor regardless of the number of processors that exist on the physical host server.

TABLE 6.1: Supported guest operating systems for virtual server

GUEST OPERATING SYSTEM	OPERATING SYSTEM CUSTOMIZATION POSSIBLE IN VMM THROUGH A TEMPLATE
Windows NT Server 4.0	✓
Windows 2000 Server	✓
Windows 2000 Advanced Server	✓
Windows XP Professional	✓
Windows Vista Ultimate Edition (32-bit)	✓
Windows Vista Business Edition (32-bit)	✓

TABLE 6.1:   Supported guest operating systems for virtual server *(CONTINUED)*

GUEST OPERATING SYSTEM	OPERATING SYSTEM CUSTOMIZATION POSSIBLE IN VMM THROUGH A TEMPLATE
Windows Vista Enterprise Edition (32-bit)	✓
Windows Server 2003 Web Edition	✓
Windows Server 2003 Standard Edition (32-bit)	✓
Windows Server 2003 Enterprise Edition (32-bit)	✓
Windows Server 2003 Datacenter Edition (32-bit)	✓
Windows Web Server 2008	✓
Windows Server 2008 Core Edition (32-bit)	✓
Windows Server 2008 Standard Edition (32-bit)	✓
Windows Server 2008 Enterprise Edition (32-bit)	✓
Windows Server 2008 Datacenter Edition (32-bit)	✓
Windows Server 2008 Small Business Server Edition (32-bit)	✓
SuSE Linux Enterprise Server 9.0	ø
SuSE Linux Enterprise Server 10.0 (32-bit)	ø
Red Hat Linux 9.0	ø
Red Hat Enterprise Linux 3.0 (32-bit)	ø
Red Hat Enterprise Linux 4.0 (32-bit)	ø
OS/2 4.5	ø
Other Linux (32-bit)	ø

Virtual machines residing on Virtual Server have distinct hardware capabilities that are surfaced in VMM through a hardware profile. Table 6.2 lists the maximum possible value for each of the hardware capabilities of such VMs.

TABLE 6.2:   Virtual machine virtual hardware supported limits

VIRTUAL HARDWARE	SUPPORTED LIMIT
Memory	3.6 GB
Processors	1
Processor architecture	32-bit only
SCSI controllers	4
Devices per SCSI controller	7
Size of SCSI Virtual Hard Disk (VHD)	2 TB
Maximum storage per VM	56 TB
COM ports	2
DVD drives	4 (IDE based)
Floppy drives	1
Network adapters	4 (emulated)
IDE devices	4

HOW TO TROUBLESHOOT THE STAR RATING FOR YOUR VIRTUAL MACHINE

When you're trying to create a virtual machine through VMM for placement on a Virtual Server host, the placement page could show a zero-star rating for this host. To troubleshoot the zero rating, click the Rating Explanation tab, shown in the following screen shot. That tab should contain information that explains why this host received a zero-star rating. In general, you might have received a zero-star rating because the VM requires multiple processors or perhaps a 64-bit processor. To create Virtual Machines with multiple processors or Virtual Machines with 64-bit processors, you must use either Windows Server 2008 Hyper-V hosts or VMware ESX hosts. Use the information in this section, along with Table 6.2, to ensure that the virtual machine meets the requirements for placement on a Virtual Server host. You can go back to the Configure Hardware page to change the properties of the VM to match the Virtual Server restrictions.

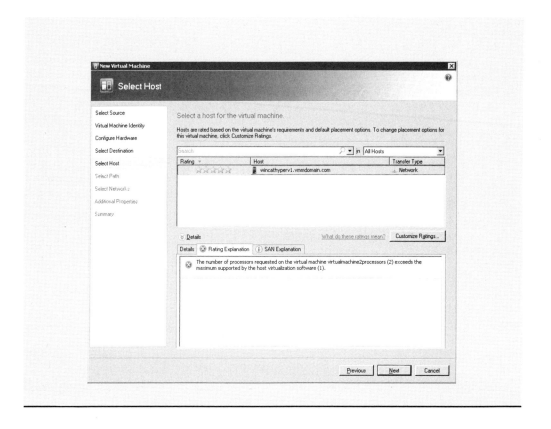

Deployment Considerations

Virtual Machine Manager can manage Virtual Server with few deployment considerations. We will go through the prerequisites for management as well as any clustering and high-availability requirements for Virtual Server.

There is only one prerequisite for managing Virtual Server, and that is applicable only for Windows Server 2003 host operating systems: WS-Management v1.1 (also known as WinRM) needs to be downloaded and installed on the host computer prior to adding it as a managed host in VMM. For Windows Server 2003, WinRM was released as an out-of-band (OOB) package that can be downloaded for free from the Microsoft Download Center website. This package applies to all editions of Windows Server 2003 and it replaces the WinRM version that shipped in Windows Server 2003 R2. Virtual Server hosts on the Windows Server 2008 operating system do not require this package because it is already part of the operating system.

Real World Scenario

HOW TO DEPLOY VIRTUAL SERVER ON A 64-BIT WINDOWS SERVER 2008 OS

When you're adding a host through the Add Host Wizard, VMM will automatically deploy Virtual Server if the operating system meets any of the following characteristics:

◆ It is a 32-bit operating system.

◆ It runs Windows Server 2003.

◆ It runs Windows Server 2008 without the hardware enhancements for virtualization. (For certain hardware, there is an option in the BIOS to enable the hardware enhancements for virtualization.)

However, there are cases where it would be useful to install Virtual Server on a 64-bit platform that is also capable of running Hyper-V. VMM by default does not give the user the option to choose the virtualization platform. It will automatically enable the Hyper-V role.

There is a workaround to allow Virtual Server to be deployed in such an environment, and that is to manually follow these steps:

1. Ensure that the Hyper-V role is removed from the system and reboot the computer. Running both Hyper-V and Virtual Server on the same computer is not supported and could lead to unexpected results.

2. Manually install Virtual Server in the system.

3. Launch the Add Host Wizard in VMM and select the computer. VMM will detect the fact that Virtual Server is installed and will choose that virtualization platform.

By first installing Virtual Server and then trying to add the host under management in VMM, you are telling the VMM engine that you would like to manage this machine as a Virtual Server host instead of enabling Hyper-V. If at any point in time you would like to make it a Hyper-V server, you would have to remove this host from VMM, uninstall Virtual Server, and then enable the Hyper-V role on the machine. You can then add this computer as a host in VMM.

Clustering and High Availability

VMM 2008 R2, VMM 2008, and VMM 2007 do not have a complete clustering and high-availability support with respect to Virtual Server. In effect, VMM is "cluster agnostic" when it comes to Virtual Server. You can manage clustered Virtual Server hosts, but the VMM Administrator Console will not provide any cluster-specific controls or policies as it does with

Hyper-V or VMware high-availability clusters. Part of the reason is the ongoing investments in Hyper-V and failover clustering for Windows Server 2008 and beyond. However, the current host clustering solution for Virtual Server is compelling, and it allows you to create highly available virtual machines that can fail over from one cluster node to another and to maintain your service-level agreement for computer availability.

CONFIGURATION

Virtual Server host clustering needs to be initially configured through the clustering management tools that ship with the Windows Server operating system. This means that cluster resources like storage, network, and script resources need to be configured using the Cluster Administrator snap-in in Microsoft Management Console for Windows Server 2003. Host clustering for Virtual Server is not supported for the Windows Server 2008 operating system. To help in the configuration of your cluster, you can refer to the white paper "Managing Virtual Server Host Clustering using System Center Virtual Machine Manager 2007" written by the VMM team.

WHERE TO FIND THE WHITE PAPER

The "Managing Virtual Server Host Clustering using System Center Virtual Machine Manager 2007" white paper is available at www.microsoft.com/downloads/details.aspx? FamilyID=75BD4642-B731-42A2-9770-FF8AEFF9EED9&displaylang=en.

This white paper is available on the Microsoft Download Center website and provides an introduction to the methods and concepts you can use to enable host clustering in Virtual Server and manage highly available virtual machines through VMM. In addition to step-by-step instructions for setting up the cluster resources, it includes an updated HAVM.vbs script resource. This script resource is a requirement for managing highly available VMs through VMM.

CREATING ONE LUN PER VIRTUAL MACHINE

For Virtual Machines to be migrated via SAN in VMM, they have to each reside on their own LUN. Bundling more than one Virtual Machine on the same LUN will force VMM to always perform a LAN migration when moving the virtual machine. This requirement also exists for highly available VMs, but that's not applicable to Virtual Server VMs.

When you're performing SAN migrations, the storage hardware subsystems change the ownership of LUNs between physical hosts. When you migrate a VM, underneath the covers, the storage system takes the physical host that currently owns the LUN on which the VM resides and changes the ownership to the new physical host to which you are trying to migrate. If multiple VMs were stored on that LUN, all of the VMs would be migrated together and the results would be unpredictable. Some of the VMs may not start correctly on their new host, introducing unnecessary downtime to the VMs and violating service-level agreements. As a result, VMM limits you to one VM per LUN in order to initiate a SAN-based migration. This approach does not come without a cost. The Storage Administrator would have to carve several smaller-sized LUNs, one for each VM residing on a SAN. Managing a large number of

LUNs is not a best practice in the storage world, from both a storage savings perspective and a management perspective. In a virtual desktop infrastructure (VDI), it is not uncommon to have thousands of computers, making the SAN option for migrating VMs a very expensive solution.

MANAGEMENT

Once host clustering is set up, you would need to add all the nodes of the cluster under management in VMM. Add each cluster node individually using its fully qualified domain name. Once all nodes are added under management, VMM will start discovering the virtual machines residing on them. Some of the VMs might be highly available and some might be regular VMs. VMM will not show any information as to whether a VM is highly available or not since it is clustering agnostic with respect to Virtual Server. The check box for high availability that exists in the VM properties, as shown Figure 6.1, is used only for VMs that reside on Hyper-V or ESX hosts. If you would like to distinguish highly available VMs from regular VMs, you can either use one of the Custom Properties to denote that or create a naming convention for each type of VM.

FIGURE 6.1
The Make This VM
Highly Available option

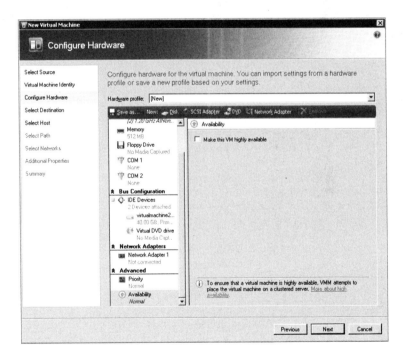

After managing the cluster, if there is a need to add a new cluster node, you can simply add that newly added cluster node as an individual host under management in VMM after it is deployed. VMM will automatically import any VMs that reside on that node.

Virtual machines can be created in two ways in a host clustering scenario:

◆ You can create them outside VMM through the Virtual Server Administration website and then use the white paper instructions to make them highly available.

◆ You can create them through VMM. VMM will create a regular VM and place it on the host of your choice. Ensure that when you are creating this VM, you place all its files under a disk that is owned by clustering. This will make the process of making the VM highly available much easier. Once the VM is created, follow the white paper instructions to make it highly available.

VMM does not offer the ability to move disk resources from one cluster node to another. Using the Cluster Administrator snap-in, you can modify disk resources. Any changes to a disk, however, are not immediately propagated into VMM. To ensure that VMM is up-to-date with the configuration of a virtual machine and its disks, you should execute the `refresh-vmhost` PowerShell cmdlet followed by `refresh-vm`. These cmdlets will update the disk hardware associations for a given host and update the entire configuration of a virtual machine to reflect the information in Virtual Server.

Once both VMM and clustering are enabled in the environment, it is possible for the administrator to manage both through Windows PowerShell. Since Windows Clustering offers a WMI interface and VMM offers a full PowerShell interface, it is possible to write a set of PowerShell scripts that check the health of the system and make any desired changes. For more information on Windows PowerShell, see Chapter 8.

WHAT HAPPENS DURING A FAILOVER

A failover is the process of moving a set of cluster resources from one cluster node to another. This usually happens during unplanned downtime for a server. The script resource `HAVM.vbs` will ensure that the virtual machine is started on the new node. The same script resource governs when a failover needs to happen through virtual machine heartbeats.

During a failover, a virtual machine will undergo *quick migration*, which is a new term introduced with host clustering for Virtual Server. It includes the process of saving the virtual machine state on the source host, moving the resource group (which includes the virtual machine and its resources) from one cluster node to another, and restoring the state of the virtual machine. The Running state is both the beginning and the end state of the virtual machine. The cluster resource group as well as the storage associated with the VM can move very fast from one server to another due to the shared storage model of Windows clustering. Most of the quick migration time is spent in saving and restoring the virtual machine state. Therefore, the amount of time it takes to perform a quick migration is directly proportional to the amount of memory assigned to the VM.

In the Virtual Machine Manager Administrator Console, when a virtual machine fails over from one host to another, it will change its owner field automatically. Even though no user action is needed for the change to be propagated in VMM, it could take up to 2 minutes to reflect the change in host ownership and refresh the VM. It is also possible that the VM goes from a healthy state to a missing state for that same period of time. The VM could be reported missing because it no longer exists on the source host machine. Once the VM is refreshed on the destination host, it will appear in a running and healthy state in VMM.

In the failover case, if VMM is not managing the destination host, the virtual machine will remain in a missing state in the console. An administrator can remove this virtual machine from management by deleting it, adding the destination host under management so that the VM can go into a healthy state, or using the Cluster Administrator snap-in to manually move the VM's resource group to a node that is managed by VMM.

Managing Virtual Server Hosts

VMM offers a very simple interface for adding hosts under management once all prerequisites are met. By clicking the Add Host action in the VMM Administrator Console, you can go through an easy-to-navigate wizard and add a host to VMM. Figure 6.2 through Figure 6.5 show the entries displayed in the wizard when you're trying to search for and add a Virtual Server host. Figure 6.2 shows the standard Select Host Servers wizard page of the Add Host action. Clicking on the Search button on this page will open the Computer Search dialog (Figure 6.3). This dialog allows a user to limit his or her search only to Virtual Server hosts. Once a host is found and selected for addition, as seen in Figure 6.4, VMM recognizes that the host has already deployed Virtual Server and it lists that under the Virtualization Software column.

FIGURE 6.2

Searching and selecting a Virtual Server host

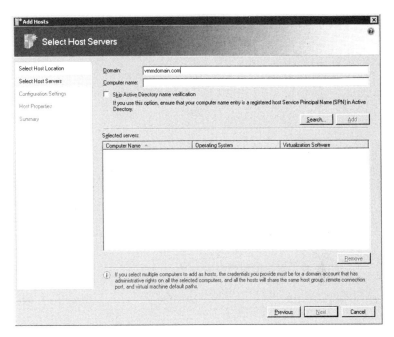

If VMM can't find any virtualization software for a host, Unknown is listed, as seen on Figure 6.5. When Unknown is listed in the wizard page, it does not mean anything more than the fact that VMM does not know if any virtualization software is already deployed on this host. VMM uses an Active Directory marker on the computer objected called Service Connection Point to detect any existing virtualization software. The name of the service connection point for Virtual Server is MS Virtual Server.

Once the wizard is complete, VMM will go ahead and deploy Microsoft Virtual Server on the host computer (if Virtual Server is already installed, VMM will skip this step). In addition to Virtual Server, VMM will deploy the Microsoft System Center Virtual Machine Manager Agent (VMM agent) on the host. Like Virtual Server, the VMM agent can be preinstalled on the host. If the agent has already been installed, VMM will also skip this step. The VMM agent is implemented as a Windows service with vmmagent as the service name.

The VMM agent implements a set of WMI classes that abstract the public COM application programming interface (API) defined by Virtual Server. These classes are defined under the

VMM interface with a full path of wmi/root/VMM. The WMI namespace for VMM is authenticated such that only host administrators and the VMM service account can invoke it. The high-level WMI classes defined in this namespace are itemized in Table 6.3. This is not a supported way to interact with VMM and this WMI interface is not public. It is listed here as a reference only to the WMI classes created on Virtual Server hosts for management.

FIGURE 6.3
Searching for all
Virtual Server hosts in
the domain

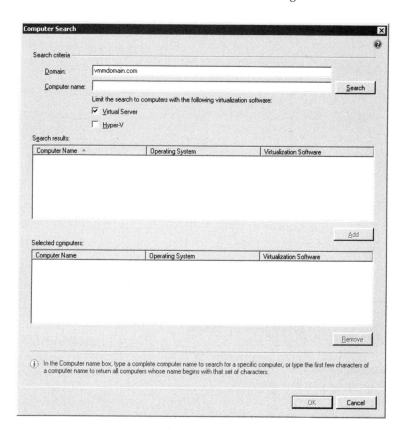

The rationale behind implementing this set of WMI providers for VMM rests on the fact that the only public API for Virtual Server is a COM API. Invoking COM APIs remotely (also known as Distributed COM, or DCOM) creates a set of problems when dealing with firewalls and opening the proper ports for COM calls to pass through. By creating a WMI interface for Virtual Server, VMM was able to abstract the COM API and be able to invoke the APIs through WinRM from the VMM server component. Since WinRM transfers data via the HTTP protocol, the only firewall port that needs to be opened is port 80. In addition to the flexibility in terms of HTTP, creating a WMI interface for Virtual Server allows VMM to create an API that closely resembles the WMI interface that Hyper-V has. Such an approach saves development time during the implementation of VMM.

When you choose to deploy Virtual Server through VMM, the Add Host job in VMM will not install the Virtual Server Administration Website. The website is considered an optional component and is not necessary since an administrator can manage Virtual Server through VMM. If you would like to install the website separately, you can launch Virtual Server setup independently of VMM and select the Virtual Server Web Application component under Custom Setup as shown in Figure 6.6.

FIGURE 6.4
Adding the Virtual Server host to VMM

FIGURE 6.5
Selecting a host with no virtualization software installed

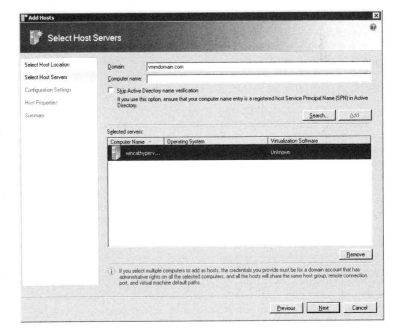

TABLE 6.3:   WMI classes for the VMM namespace

CLASS NAME
AgentManagement
AsyncTask
AzManUtility
CIM_ManagedSystemElement
DeploymentClientJob
DeploymentServerJob
ErrorInfo
FileInformation
HostPerformanceCounter
HttpPostDeploymentJob
IPartialObject
MountDisk
P2VServerJob
P2VSourceFixup
SFTPDeploymentJob
SftpFileInformation
V2VServerJob
VirtualizationSanUtility
VMAttachedMedia
VMTask
VssRequestor

Once Virtual Machine Manager starts managing a host, you can click the host properties and see its status, as shown in Figure 6.7. Table 6.4 explains what each status property means. VMM will mark the host in a Needs Attention status if any of the status items are not in a healthy (green check box) state.

FIGURE 6.6
Enabling the
Administration
Website component

FIGURE 6.6
Enabling the
Administration
Website component

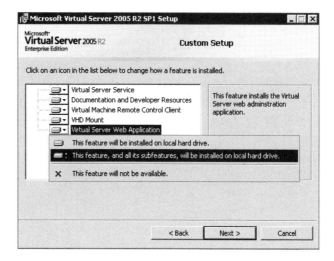

FIGURE 6.7
Host status page

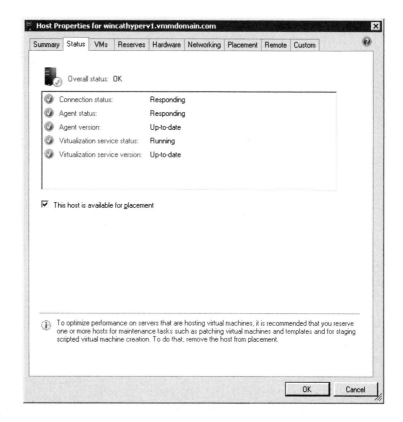

TABLE 6.4: Demystifying the host status page

STATUS	DESCRIPTION
Connection status	Details the overall status of the host in VMM. If the VMM server is not able to execute commands through WinRM on this host, the connection status will be in an unhealthy state.
Agent status	Checks whether the VMM agent Windows service on the host computer is healthy and responding.
Agent version	Indicates whether the VMM agent on the host is up to date. The released version of the agent for VMM 2008 is 2.0.3444.0. The agent can be updated from the Managed Computers section of the Administration page. Figure 6.8 shows the specific information about the managed computers and agents in VMM.
Virtualization service status	Checks whether the main service for the virtualization software is healthy and responding. For Virtual Server, the service is named Virtual Server.
Virtualization service version	Indicates whether the virtualization software on the host is up to date. Table 6.5 contains the version information for the supported releases of Virtual Server. Virtual Server can be updated through an action on the Host object in VMM.

FIGURE 6.8

Agent management page

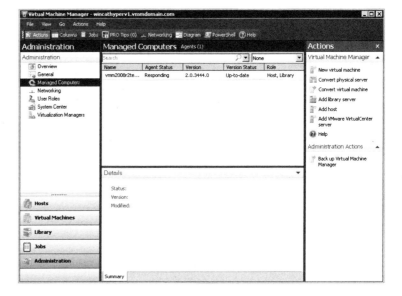

Table 6.5 lists the supported versions of Virtual Server for VMM. If the version of Virtual Server is anything different from the ones listed in the table, VMM will force the administrator to update Virtual Server before continuing to manage the host.

TABLE 6.5:   Supported versions of Virtual Server for VMM

VIRTUAL SERVER RELEASE	VERSION NUMBER	NOTES
Virtual Server 2005 R2 SP1	1.1.603.0	This is the minimum supported release of Virtual Server. If you have this release installed on a host computer, VMM will list the virtualization service version as Upgrade Available. The Update Virtual Server option is available for a host in this state.
Virtual Server 2005 R2 SP1 KB948515 Update to support Windows Vista and Windows Server 2008	1.1.629.0	This is the release of Virtual Server that VMM will install on a compatible host computer and is considered the up-to-date release. More information on KB948515 can be obtained from the Microsoft Help and Support website.

Remote Connections to Virtual Machines

When the VMM Server component is installed on your computer, it will install a set of files specific to Virtual Server that are used throughout the management of a Virtual Server host. In the bin folder of the VMM installation location for the VMM server and in the ActiveX folder of the Self-Service Portal, VMM will place the files necessary for the Virtual Machine Remote Control (VMRC) program. Table 6.6 has the complete list of Virtual Server components that get installed with VMM.

VMM uses VMRC to connect to a virtual machine through remote control. VMRC is used in the Administrator Console as well as in the Self-Service Portal website and can be enabled or disabled on a per-host basis. VMRC does not implement the Remote Desktop Protocol and is based on the VNC protocol. The default port for VMRC on the host computer is 5900, and it is configurable, as shown in Figure 6.9. If the Allow Multiple VMRC Connections option is enabled on the Remote tab of Host Properties, multiple users can view the same console session on the VM. Each user would not have any knowledge as to whether other users are viewing the same session. This feature introduces information disclosure risks, so we recommend that you disable this option. One scenario in which enabling multiple users to view the same console is acceptable is in training sessions or when demonstrating an application to a set of users.

If only one user is allowed to connect to a virtual machine at a time, any subsequent connections will fail once a user is connected. This behavior is a little bit different than the behavior of VMConnect in Hyper-V. VMConnect will terminate the session of previous users when a new user tries to connect to a virtual machine. Another difference between VMRC and VMConnect is that VMRC will automatically start a virtual machine if the VM was in a stopped state when you initiated the connection.

TABLE 6.6:   Virtual Server components present in the VMM directory structure

FILE	VMM COMPONENT	FILE VERSION	DESCRIPTION
VMRC EXE	VMM Administrator Console bin folder	1.1.603.0	VMRC.exe is launched by the VMM Administrator Console when a user clicks the Connect To Virtual Machine action for a Virtual Server VM.
VMRCActiveX Client DLL	VMM Administrator Console bin folder	1.1.603.0	This is the ActiveX control DLL for the VMRC connection that is established on the VMM Administrator Console.
VMRCActiveX Client CAB	VMM Self Service Portal ActiveX folder	1.1.603.0	This cabinet file contains the VMRC ActiveX control as well as the Keyboard Hook DLL for 32-bit and 64-bit clients of the Self-Service Portal.

FIGURE 6.9
Remote tab of Host
Properties

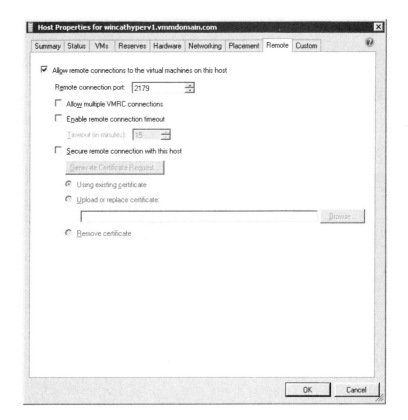

Since VMRC does not encrypt the data transmitted by default, it is highly recommended that you secure VMRC using Secure Sockets Layer (SSL). SSL will encrypt data communications over VMRC through the use of a certificate. Here are the steps involved to secure VMRC:

1. On a Windows Server 2008 computer, add the Active Directory Certificate Services role and the Certification Authority Role service.

2. From the Remote tab of the Host Properties dialog, click Generate Certificate Request and fill in the details (Figure 6.10 shows an example dialog). Save the generated file as <hostname>VMRCRequest.txt.

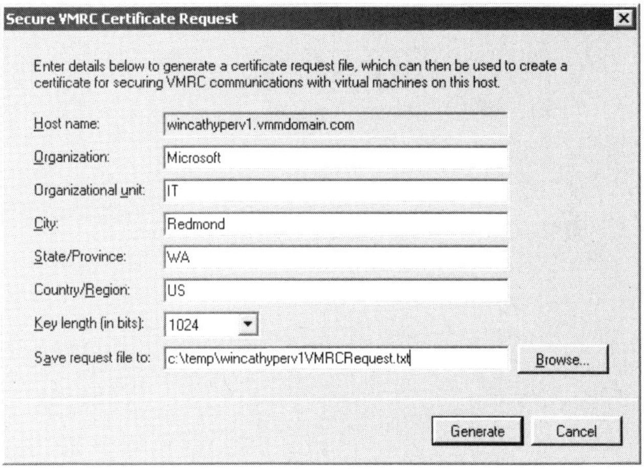

FIGURE 6.10
Generating a certificate request

3. Open the Certification Authority Administrative tool and submit a new request for a certificate using the text file created in the previous step.

4. The certificate will go into the pending state at this time (under the Pending Requests list).

5. Click the pending certificate and issue it. The certificate will move into the Issued Certificates list.

6. The certificate can now be exported as binary data to a file. Export the certificate locally on disk as <hostname>VMRCCert.tmp.

7. Return to the Remote tab of Host Properties in VMM to upload the exported certificate. VMM will now create a job that will track the progress of enabling encryption for VMRC.

Once the proper certificate is created for VMRC, open a new VMRC connection to a virtual machine and import the certificate on the client machine. The certificate should have all the details and information of the certificate authority and you can instruct your clients to install this once per client computer. A client computer in this case could be an Administrator Console computer or a customer running Internet Explorer and connecting to the Self-Service Portal.

CERTIFICATE AUTHORITY

It is not necessary to use the certificate authority built in to Windows Server 2008. If your environment uses a different certificate authority or you have a Public Key Infrastructure (PKI) in place, you can follow the same set of steps to secure the VMRC communication channel.

Host Properties

Virtual Machine Manager abstracts most of the host properties across all the virtualization platforms it supports. In previous sections, we talked about some of the specific Virtual Server properties, like VMRC. We will use this section to identify a few other Virtual Server–specific properties as they show up in the Host Properties dialog in the Administrator Console.

The Summary tab of the Host Properties dialog box, shown in Figure 6.11, lists the virtualization software installed on the host as well as the operating system and the VMM agent version.

FIGURE 6.11
Summary tab of Host Properties

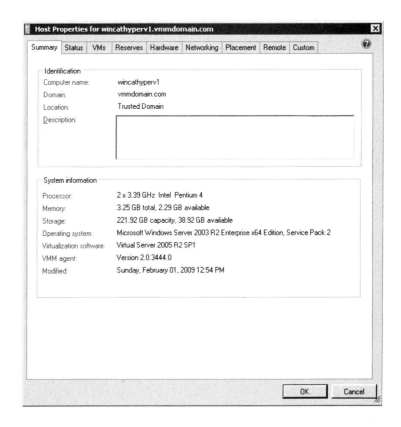

The VMs tab shows a list of all the currently registered VMs on the host. From that same dialog, you can remotely browse the Virtual Server computer and look for a VMC file (`.vmc` is the filename extension of the files that contain the virtual machine configuration for Virtual Server). Once you register a VM, VMM will add this preexisting VM to Virtual Server. Once

Virtual Server imports it successfully, VMM will pick up the newly added virtual machine through a system job called a refresher and import it into the VMM Administrator Console. This process can take up to 2 minutes to execute, and it is the same process that VMM uses to initially import any VMs that exist on a host when it is added under management.

The Networking tab, shown in Figure 6.12, lists all of the virtual networks available for virtual machines. Upon installation of Virtual Server, at least two virtual networks are created by default:

Internal Network   This network can be used as an internal networking connection between virtual machines. This network comes with the DHCP server enabled.

External Network (physical NIC name)   For each physical network adapter (NIC) that is installed on the server computer, an external network will be created in Virtual Server. The name of the virtual network will also include the name of the NIC for easy identification. The DHCP server is disabled by default on this virtual network.

FIGURE 6.12
Host Networking
Properties

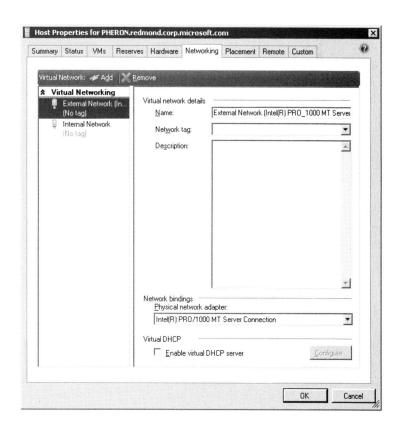

From the same tab, you can create, modify, or delete virtual networks. Once created, a virtual network is represented by a VNC file on disk. VNC files are created under this path:

```
%SystemDrive%\Documents and Settings\All Users\Documents\Shared Virtual Networks
```

The Placement tab has a list of default virtual machine paths that VMM can use during virtual machine placement. By default, VMM uses the default virtual machine configuration folder defined in Virtual Server. Virtual Server will create the path to this location during a fresh installation:

```
%SystemDrive%\Documents and Settings\All Users\Documents\Shared Virtual Machines
```

An administrator can define more paths for virtual machine creation.

Virtual Server and Virtual Machine Permissions

When VMM starts managing a Virtual Server host, the Active Directory account of the VMM Windows service (vmmservice.exe) becomes a member of the Local Administrators group on the Virtual Server computer. Since the Local Administrators group has a defined entry in the Virtual Server security properties with full permissions, the VMM server has full access to all APIs for Virtual Server. The VMM server's identity also has access to any local files and other APIs because it is a local administrator.

Virtual Machine permissions are managed based on the VMM user roles applicable for the virtual machine as well as the owner of the VM. A user role will be applicable to a VM if its scope contains the host that the VM resides on (VMM user role scopes are defined at the Host-Group level, with hosts belonging to a HostGroup hierarchy). Since Virtual Server does not have an explicit API for setting VM permissions, everything is controlled based on the security discretionary access control lists (DACLs) of the VMC file that defines the VM as well as the DACLs of the Virtual Server configuration file, Options.xml. The following list has the details on the privilege assignment for each VMM user role:

VMM administrators get read and execute permissions for the VMC file.

VMM delegated administrators get read and execute permissions for the VMC files of VMs that are part of the host groups the delegated administrator is managing.

VMM self-service users get read and execute permissions for the VMC file. There are two prerequisites for these permissions to be set: (1) The self-service user has to be listed as the owner of the virtual machine in VMM. You can set the owner of a virtual machine in the virtual machine properties dialog. The owner can be an individual user or an Active Directory security group. (2) The Self-Service User role should be managing the host group that contains this virtual machine and the user role should be granted the remote connection permission in the list of approved actions. None of the other permissions in that list have an impact on Virtual Server. The rest of the permissions are VMM-specific permissions that control the access to VMs through the VMM interfaces.

VMM administrators get read permissions for the Options.xml file.

VMM delegated administrators get read permissions for the Options.xml file of hosts that are part of the host groups the delegated administrator is managing.

VMM self-service users get read access to the Options.xml file for hosts when some prerequisites are met. The user has to be an owner of a VM on the host, he or she has to have the remote connection permission set in the Self-Service User role, and the user role should be managing the host group that contains this host.

Read and execute permissions on the VMC file allow a user to connect to the virtual machine's console through VMRC.exe (none of the permissions in the preceding list allow a user to connect to the Virtual Server Administration Website). Manually setting the DACLs in the VMC file so that other users can access the console of the VM will work only temporarily. VMM refreshes this information every 30 minutes and will ensure that the only DACLs in the VMC file correspond to VMM user roles. To give access to more users for a particular VM, you need to add them to a VMM Self-Service User role and give them the appropriate permissions for the set of VMs the user role is managing. Once the proper permissions are set for a self-service user, he or she can manage VMs through the VMM Self-Service Portal, through the Windows PowerShell cmdlets for VMM, or through the console using `VMRC.exe`.

VMM also has a feature for optionally specifying global VMRC access accounts. These accounts can connect to all virtual machines running on Virtual Server hosts managed by VMM and they get read and execute permissions on all virtual machine VMC files. To add access accounts, follow these steps:

1. Choose the Administration view of the VMM Administrator Console.

2. Click General.

3. Select Remote Control in the results pane and click the Modify action.

4. Click the Add button to add domain accounts that will have remote control access to all Virtual Server virtual machines.

What Is Missing from VMM?

Even though VMM has a comprehensive coverage of all features of Virtual Server, there is a small subset of not so commonly used features that are exposed only through the Virtual Server Administration Website. Some of these features are listed here:

◆ Support for Virtual Server scripts, as shown in Figure 6.13.

◆ Full support for CPU Resource Allocation settings. Only the relative weight (Figure 6.14) is exposed in VMM through the Priority Advanced setting on the Hardware Configuration tab of the Virtual Machine Properties dialog box (Figure 6.15). The rest of the CPU Resource Allocation properties are not exposed in VMM and are not factored into the Priority setting.

◆ Support for undo disks. (Virtual Server undo disks are not explicitly needed since VMM supports differencing disks using the checkpointing feature. Checkpoints provide a super-set of undo disk functionality. With that said, VMM will allow you to automatically collapse or discard undo disks for virtual machines that have already been configured to use them. The next section provides more details on undo disk support.)

◆ Support for LPT ports in a virtual machine.

VMM does not expose any features that utilize the VSS Writer for Virtual Server for creating virtual machine snapshots. This is intentional since the VSS interface is designed to be used by backup/recovery products such as System Center Data Protection Manager. Backup and recovery of Virtual Server hosts is covered in Chapter 10, "Planning for Backup and Recovery."

Undo Disk Support

The Virtual Machine Manager team made a decision to not support undo disks for Virtual Server. VMM exposes a new feature called checkpointing, which is built on top of differencing disks in Virtual Server. Undo disks are primarily used to capture the state of the system at a point in time and revert back to it later on. They are especially useful in dev/test and lab scenarios where a set of users needs to go through a series of tests many times, each time starting with a clean state. This same feature can be achieved through the creation of a checkpoint, running the scenarios, and then restoring the checkpoint to get back to the initial state.

FIGURE 6.13
Virtual server scripts

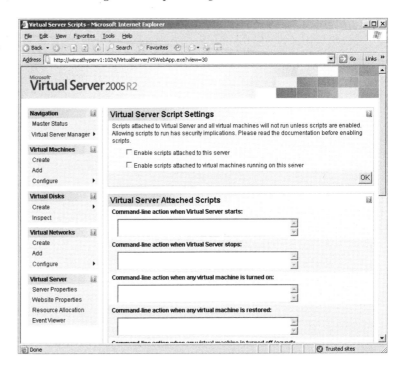

FIGURE 6.14
Relative Weight property of CPU Resource Allocation settings

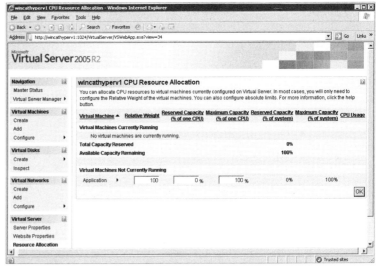

Once you add a Virtual Server host under management, any virtual machines with the undo disk feature enabled will show up in the Administrator Console with an unhealthy state called Unsupported Undo Disk. In such a case, the only two actions available for this VM are to disable the undo disks or to delete the VM. Choosing to disable the undo disks will allow you to either discard the undo disks without saving any of the changes in them or merge the undo disks into the VHDs attached to the VM, as shown in Figure 6.16. There is no option in VMM to convert an undo disk into a checkpoint.

FIGURE 6.15
Virtual machine priority

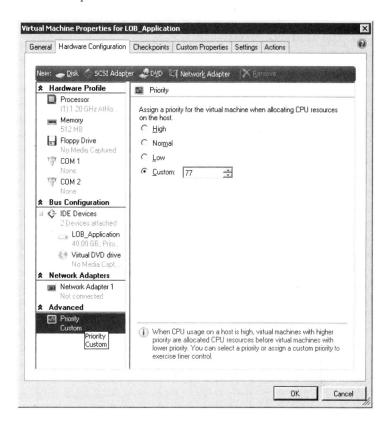

FIGURE 6.16
Disabling the undo disks

VHD Mount Utility

Virtual Server 2005 R2 SP1 is released with a new utility called VHD Mount. VHD Mount is an optional component of the Virtual Server setup, and it can even be installed on a system that does not have Virtual Server. This utility allows you to mount a VHD file into the host operating system as a virtual disk device. The process exposes the volumes and data contained inside the VHD at the host level. The VHD Mount utility has two public interfaces: a command-line tool called vhdmount.exe and a public API that is documented in the Virtual Server Programmer's Guide on the Microsoft TechNet website.

With the introduction of VHD Mount, third-party independent software vendors (ISVs) can now parse a VHD file and understand the data inside of it. This is especially useful for backup technologies when you want to back up a virtual machine and be able to do more granular recovery at the file level. Being able to expose the VHD to the local file system and traverse it like a local disk is a winning scenario for enhancing the ecosystem around Virtual Server.

Even though the VHD Mount utility has not been officially certified to work with Hyper-V VHDs, the VHD format has not changed between Virtual Server and Hyper-V, making it possible to mount VHDs from both virtualization platforms without any known issues. Hyper-V also has the officially supported WMI interface for mounting VHDs, but that interface requires the Hyper-V role to be enabled in the computer.

Migrating Virtual Machines from Virtual Server to Hyper-V

Virtual Machine Manager makes it very easy to migrate from an older virtualization platform like Virtual Server to Hyper-V. This process is also called V2V conversion, which stands for Virtual-to-Virtual conversion. VMM will only allow you to migrate a virtual machine residing on Virtual Server to the Hyper-V virtualization platform. The only prerequisite for the migration is that the latest additions are installed inside the VM (if any additions are installed at all). This means that the VM has to have Virtual Machine Additions version 13.813 or later installed. As shown in Figure 6.17, you can check your current Virtual Machine Additions version through the Administrator Console. If the VM Additions column is not present in the Virtual Machines view of the Administrator Console, you can add it manually by selecting the View and then the Columns menu options. If the Additions version is older than version 13.813, you should manually uninstall the additions from within the VM before performing the migration.

FIGURE 6.17
Displaying the Virtual Machine Additions version

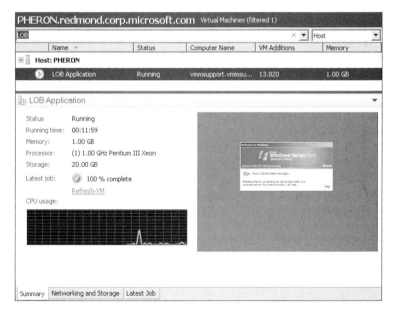

FIGURE 6.18
Error while trying to
V2V a saved virtual
machine

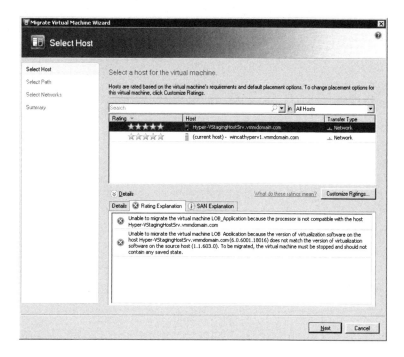

FIGURE 6.18
Error while trying to
V2V a saved virtual
machine

Once you have identified the set of systems that you would like to migrate to Hyper-V, you can select them in VMM and chose the Migrate action. Selecting a Hyper-V server as the destination host will trigger the V2V conversion. VMM will copy their data files (VHD files only), uninstall the Virtual Machine Additions from them, and then upgrade to Hyper-V. The upgrade contains two essential components:

- Upgrade of the Hardware Abstraction Layer (HAL) so that the VM can execute on the Hyper-V platform

- Install the Integration Services from Hyper-V. This feature is called Virtual Guest Services in VMM.

A V2V conversion of a Virtual Server VM to a Hyper-V VM does not require the Virtual Server VM to reside on a host computer. A Virtual Server VM can be in a stopped state in the VMM library and VMM would know how to deploy it properly to a Hyper-V host. VMM will then follow the same process outlined earlier when upgrading the HAL and installing the Integration Services for Hyper-V. However, trying to migrate a saved or running virtual machine from Virtual Server to Hyper-V would not work, as shown Figure 6.18. Since Virtual Server and Hyper-V have separate virtualization software, the memory state for the virtual machine would not be compatible.

V2V OF VIRTUAL MACHINES NOT SUPPORTED IN HYPER-V

The VMM team recommends that you don't migrate any virtual machines with operating systems that are not supported by the Hyper-V Integration Services.

SCSI DISK CONSIDERATIONS

Hyper-V does not support booting VMs from a SCSI disk. Make sure the boot VHD of your VM is attached on the IDE channel.

The Bottom Line

Determine the requirements for the host and guest operating systems for Virtual Server. Being able to identify the different requirements for host and guest operating systems makes it easier to provision hardware for your virtualization needs.

Master It   What are the new features of Virtual Server 2005 R2 SP1?

Master It   Which versions of Virtual Server does VMM support?

Master It   What is the architecture of the processor for virtual machines running inside a 64-bit host operating system?

Manage Virtual Server host clusters with VMM.   Clustering and high availability ensure that a virtual machine can continue to run through hardware downtime, maintaining the availability of a critical workload.

Master It   How can you identify a highly available virtual machine in the Administrator Console?

Master It   List the steps taken by the script resource during failover.

Master It   What are the conditions under which a virtual machine will be in a missing state in the Administrator Console?

Use the permissions model for virtual machines.   Understanding the different permissions and user role options offered in VMM allows administrators to properly configure access to their VMs.

Master It   List the types of virtual machine access that self-service users can be granted.

Master It   Why would VMM remove access to an account from a VMC file?

Master It   Which tools can self-service users utilize to connect to virtual machines outside VMM?

Migrate a virtual machine from Virtual Server to Hyper-V. Migrating virtual machines from one host to another allows the administrator to load balance the resource and possibly evacuate a host for maintenance. Moving virtual machines from a Virtual Server host to a Hyper-V host enables the administrator to retire the old hardware and still be able to gain access to the VMs that have moved to a Hyper-V host.

Master It   What is the minimum version of the Virtual Machine Additions that is necessary for V2V to work?

Master It   List the steps that are required to migrate a VM from Virtual Server to Hyper-V.

Master It   Why are migrations of VMs in a saved state not possible?

Chapter 7

Virtual Machine Management

Creating, migrating, and deleting virtual machines is relatively easy compared to performing the same actions with physical machines. The flexibility that virtualization enabled has many benefits for an IT group. Virtualization means better utilization of resources through consolidation, faster deployment time for virtual machines, and improved optimization in the datacenter by migrating virtual machines. There are, however, some potential disadvantages to virtualization that can be mitigated or completely avoided. The negative impact of virtualization is mostly centered on poor management of a virtual machine environment — oversubscription of hosts (placing too many virtual machines on a single physical machine) and virtual machine sprawl (creating too many virtual machines with no controls). VMM can help maximize the positive impact of virtualization while reducing the negative through improved management capabilities that center around the life cycle of a virtual machine.

In this chapter, you will learn to:

♦ Create and delete a virtual machine

♦ Convert a physical machine or non-Windows hypervisor virtual machine to a Windows hypervisor virtual machine

♦ Migrate a virtual machine between hosts

Creating a Virtual Machine

VMM enables you to create a virtual machine in several ways, depending on what you need to do. VMM subdivides creation of virtual machines into three areas:

Source   The location (virtual machine host or library) in which virtual machine and template building blocks reside (virtual disk, template, virtual machine)

Action   The explicit task you execute in the console or CLI to create the virtual machine from the source

Target   The location (virtual machine host or Library) in which the virtual machine or template will be placed.

The source of a virtual machine indicates the initial components that make up the configuration. You can start with a blank disk, an existing disk, a template, or an existing virtual machine.

The action indicates what workflow VMM will execute to create the virtual machine. For example, with a blank disk you can create a new virtual machine on a hypervisor host, with an existing disk you can create a new template, and you can create a new virtual machine from an existing virtual machine (this is also referred to as a virtual machine clone).

The target is the location where the resultant virtual machine or template will reside. The target location includes the VMM library or hypervisor host. In some cases, an action determines the target. For example, creating a new template using an existing virtual machine deployed on a host requires that you select the library as a target location to store the new template. In any case, VMM will always guide you through the appropriate sequence of steps.

To help you better understand virtual machine creation in VMM, the following sections will cover in detail the common building blocks used in creating a virtual machine and the various actions supported by VMM to create a virtual machine.

Virtual Machine Building Blocks

Virtual machine creation in VMM can be split into four common building blocks:

◆ Source disk

◆ Hardware profile

◆ Guest OS profile

◆ Template

Defining these building blocks is important because they can be reused in multiple locations, which encourages standardization of configurations and processes in your virtualization environment.

SOURCE DISK

The primary objective of using a template is to deploy a virtual machine with a guest operating system. For this reason, the source disk used to create the template is very important. You can use an existing virtual disk file stored in the library as the source disk for a template. For templates that use existing virtual disks, you will need to make sure the guest operating system is prepared using sysprep before adding the file to VMM's library. Sysprep instructs the guest operating system to run Mini-Setup on the next bootup. Windows uses Mini-Setup to assign a unique identity to the guest operating system, like a new computer SID and computer name. This process is required for VHDs, virtual disks that will be deploy to Virtual Server or Hyper-V. For VMDK files, preparing the operating system with Sysprep is not required.

HOW TO SYSPREP WINDOWS

Sysprep is a tool that prepares a Windows operating system for duplication. You need to execute Sysprep from the command line in the guest operating system. For example, to prepare Windows Vista, type in the following command: `%WINDIR%\System32\Sysprep\sysprep.exe /generalize /oobe /shutdown`. This command shuts down the guest operating system.

Another way to create a template is to use an existing virtual machine. The virtual machine needs to be hosted on ESX, Hyper-V, or Virtual Server. As part of creating the template, VMM orchestrates the execution of Sysprep in the operating system for you, stores the virtual disk to the library, and creates the template object in the library. The virtual machine used as the source for this template will get deleted from the host, so this is a destructive operation. If you intend to keep your source VM after the template process completes, be sure to clone it before creating the template from it. In the case of ESX, the existing virtual machine is stored to the library and marked as a template. VMM does not need to first execute Sysprep in the guest operating system.

HARDWARE PROFILE

The hardware profile contains a typical virtual machine virtual hardware configuration and settings that you can apply to a new template or virtual machine. The hardware profile by itself does not represent a virtual machine. VMM does not create links between hardware profiles and the templates or virtual machines that use the hardware profile. Without this hard link, you are free to make changes at any time to any hardware profile without affecting existing templates or virtual machines. It is simply a convenient way to specify defaults that can be modified at any time. Following is a description of each setting or property contained in a hardware profile:

Name   The name of the profile allows you to search for it in the UI and CLI.

Description   The description field is for more detailed information about the profile.

Owner   Active Directory account explicitly set as the owner of the profile.

BIOS   Allows you to set the virtual machine boot order as part of the configuration. Also allows setting the default NumLock state.

CPU: Number of CPUs   The number of virtual CPUs that will be assigned to the virtual machine.

CPU: Type   Represents a processor model used by VMM's Intelligent Placement engine to calculate the appropriate star rating for each potential destination virtual machine host based on the expected load of a virtual machine.

CPU: Limit CPU Functionality   This setting will mask specific CPU features at the hypervisor level so older operating systems like Windows NT 4.0 can boot properly.

CPU: Limit CPU For Migration   This setting will mask specific CPU features to make the virtual machine compatible across multiple virtual machine hosts independent of the processor family installed in the machine.

Memory   Specifies the amount of memory assigned to the virtual machine.

Floppy Drive   Represents the virtual floppy drive assigned to the virtual machine.

Floppy Drive: No Media Captured   Removes the virtual floppy disk attached to the virtual floppy drive or disconnects it from the host floppy drive. Removing a virtual floppy will delete the file from the virtual machine host.

Floppy Drive: Physical Floppy Drive   Attaches the virtual floppy drive to the host floppy drive.

Floppy Drive: Existing Virtual Floppy Disk File   Attaches the virtual floppy drive to a virtual floppy stored in the library.

COM   Represents the COM ports assigned to the virtual machine.

COM: None   Removes the named pipe or text file associated with a COM port.

COM: Named Pipe   Sets up a named pipe for COM serial port communication.

COM: Text File   Associates the virtual COM port to a file on the local file system of the virtual machine host.

IDE Devices (Controller)   Represents the IDE controller assigned to the virtual machine.

SCSI Adapter (Controller)   Represents the SCSI controller assigned to the virtual machine.

SCSI Adapter: Shared Controller   Sets the SCSI controller as a virtual shared controller useful for creating guest clusters on the same host.

Virtual DVD Drive   Represents the virtual DVD drive assigned to the virtual machine.

Virtual DVD Drive: Channel   You can attach a DVD virtual drive to any available slot on the IDE controllers present in the hardware profile. Channel displays both the controller ID and location ID.

Virtual DVD Drive: No Media   Disconnects the physical CD/DVD or image file from the virtual DVD drive.

Virtual DVD Drive: Physical CD/DVD Drive   Attaches the virtual CD/DVD drive to a CD/DVD drive in the physical host.

Virtual DVD Drive: Existing Image File   Associates an ISO image file stored in the library to the virtual DVD drive.

Virtual DVD Drive: Existing Image File: Share Image Instead of Copying It   Uses the ISO image file directory from the network location instead of copying to the virtual machine host.

Virtual Disk   Represents the virtual disk attached to the virtual machine.

Virtual Disk: Channel   You can attach a virtual disk to any available slot on any IDE controller available or to any SCSI controller present in the hardware profile.

Virtual Disk: Use an Existing Virtual Hard Disk   This selection allows you to browse VMM's library for an existing virtual disk.

Virtual Disk: Create a New Virtual Hard Disk   If you need a blank disk created with the virtual machine, use this option to dynamically generate a dynamic or fixed virtual disk file when deploying the virtual machine.

Virtual Disk: Pass through to Physical Drive on Host   Attaches a disk exposed to the virtual machine host to the virtual machine.

Virtual Disk: Type   When creating a new virtual disk, you can select the disk type — dynamic or fixed.

Virtual Disk: Size   Specifies the size of the new virtual disk.

Virtual Disk: File Name   Specifies the filename of the virtual disk.

Network Adapter   Represents a virtual network adapter assigned to the virtual machine.

Network Adapter: Virtual Network   Specifies the virtual network to which the virtual network adapter should connect.

Network Adapter: Network Location   Specifies the network location the virtual network adapter should default to when searching for a virtual network to connect to.

Network Adapter: Network Tag   Specifies the network tag the virtual network adapter should default to when searching for a virtual network to connect to.

Network Adapter: Port Group   Specifies the port group that the virtual network adapter should connect to (VMware specific).

Network Adapter: Enable Virtual LAN Identification   Enables setting a VLAND ID for an individual virtual network adapter.

Network Adapter: VLAN ID   Specifies the VLAN ID for the virtual network adapter.

Network Adapter: Ethernet (MAC) Address Dynamic   Indicates that the hypervisor should assign a MAC address to the virtual network adapter.

Network Adapter: Static   Allows you to specify a MAC address for the virtual network adapter.

Network Adapter: Generate   Generates a new MAC address from a predefined MAC range managed by VMM.

Network Adapter: Enable Spoofing of MAC Addresses   Enables MAC spoofing or MAC learning.

Priority   Assigns the CPU priority for the virtual machine.

High Availability   Specifies that the virtual machine must be deployed on a clustered system.

Integration Services   Enables/disables specific settings for services running within the virtual machine operating system.

To create a hardware profile, follow these steps:

1. Click the Library tab in the VMM console (Figure 7.1).

FIGURE 7.1
Library tab in Administrator Console

2. Click New Hardware Profile in the actions menu on the right side of the console, as shown in Figure 7.2.

FIGURE 7.2
The New Hardware Profile action

3. In the General tab, type a name and description for the hardware profile and assign an owner (a Windows user), as seen in Figure 7.3.

FIGURE 7.3
New Hardware Profile
General settings

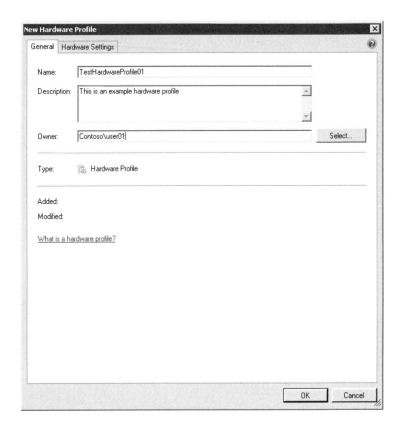

4. Click the Hardware Settings tab to specify hardware-specific settings.

5. Click the icons on the left on the Hardware Settings tab to access individual settings (which were covered earlier in this section), as shown in Figure 7.4.

6. Click Cancel to close out of the New Hardware Profile window without saving it to the database.

7. Click OK to save the profile to the database.

8. Click the Profiles node under a specific library server to access the list of profiles. Remember that hardware profiles reside only in the database (Figure 7.5).

FIGURE 7.4
New Hardware Profile
Hardware settings

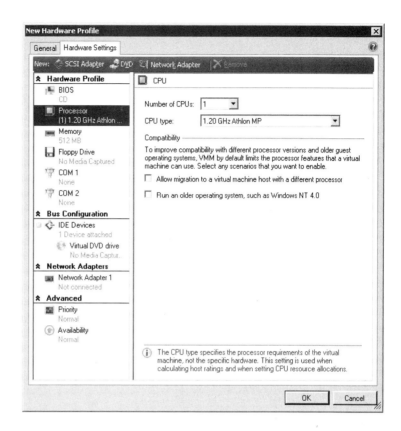

FIGURE 7.5
New Hardware Profile
stored in library

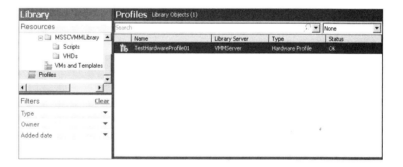

UNDERSTANDING NETWORK LOCATION AND TAGS

VMM can create a virtual machine or template directly into the VMM library. A virtual machine in the library is not actually running; it is simply stored there. A virtual machine host is never selected as part of creating a template. Instead, the settings stored with the template represent the desired configuration of a virtual machine. For most settings, you do not need to know where the virtual machine will eventually reside. These settings can be specified independent of a host selection. However, some settings are specific to a virtual machine host and so there would be no value in storing that information as part of a template.

For example, CPU and memory settings are common virtual machine settings irrespective of the hypervisor. On the other hand, a virtual network to which the virtual network adapter will bind for communication purposes is specific to the virtual machine host. To simplify the selection of a virtual network, VMM stores additional metadata for each virtual network adapter. These are the network location and network tags:

Network Location   This represents the logical network identity for an individual physical network adapter. The Network Location Awareness (NLA) service provider on the Windows-based virtual machine host is used to return this information for every active network connection. NLA will first identify the logical network by DNS domain name. If that fails, information stored in the Registry is used. If custom static information is not available, then the subnet address is used. VMM stores the identified logical network as part of the virtual machine host object. You can query the network adapter of the virtual machine host for this information. When deploying the virtual machine to a host, VMM will match the desired logical network with the actual logical network advertised by the host. You can also override the default logical network discovered using NLA and specify your own logical network string.

Network Tag   You can decorate a virtual network with additional metadata called Network Tag. This property is user specified and so is not automatically populated as Network Location is. Tagging a virtual network is important if you need to differentiate two networks that return the same logical network information.

OPERATING SYSTEM PROFILE

Similar to hardware profiles, the operating system profile contains typical operating system settings that you can apply to a template or new virtual machine created from a template. The settings in an operating system profile do not change the configuration of the virtual machine. Instead, these settings are used as part of the customization of the guest operating system contained in a virtual disk and deployed as part of a new virtual machine from a template. VMM stores the settings in the database but at virtual machine deployment time will generate an answer file. The answer file is used by Mini-Setup to automate the customization of the guest operating system, avoiding the need for you to provide the values when deploying the virtual machine. The following list outlines each setting or property contained in an operating system profile:

Name   The name of this profile allows you to search for it in the UI and CLI. You can summarize the settings contained within by using the names if you plan to standardize on a few key configurations in your environment.

Description   The description is for more detailed information about the profile. This can include specific information about how the operating system profile is intended for use.

Owner   An owner can be set on a profile if deemed necessary. However, this setting has no implications on security or visibility in the UI or CLI.

General Settings: Identity Information   Use Computer Name field to specify the new Windows computer name that should be applied as part of the Mini-Setup experience. For XP and Windows Server 2003 you can set Full Name and Organization Name.

General Settings: Admin Password   The local administrator password.

General Settings: Product Key   Specify the specific Windows SKU product key. This field is not required for Windows XP and Windows Server 2003, Windows 7, and Windows Server 2008 R2.

General Settings: Time Zone   Specify the time zone for the guest operating system.

General Settings: Operating System   Specify the operating system to which the profile applies.

Networking: Domain / Workgroup   You have the option of joining the guest operating system installed in the virtual machine to a workgroup or a domain. To join the guest operating system to a domain, you need to specify the domain name, the domain user with privileges to add computers to the domain, and the user password.

Scripts: Answer File   To specify the superset of answer properties as part of the guest operating system profile, specify an answer file. Based on the operating system selected, you will see INF files for Windows 2000, Windows XP, and Windows Server 2003 and XML files for Windows Vista, Windows Server 2008, Windows 7, and Windows Server 2008 R2.

Scripts: [GUIRunOnce] Commands   Specify one or more commands to run the first time an interactive account logs into the Windows operating system.

To create an operating system profile, follow these steps:

1. Click the Library tab in the VMM console.

2. Click New Guest OS Profile in the actions menu on the right side of the console (Figure 7.6).

FIGURE 7.6
The New Guest OS
Profile action

3. In the New Guest OS Profile dialog on the General tab, type a name and description for the operating system profile and assign an owner with a valid Windows user account, as shown in Figure 7.7.

4. In the New Guest OS Profile dialog, click the Settings tab to specify operating system settings.

5. Click the icons on the navigation menu on the left side of the Guest OS tab in the New Guest OS Profile window to access individual settings covered earlier in this section (Figure 7.8).

FIGURE 7.7
New Guest OS Profile
General settings

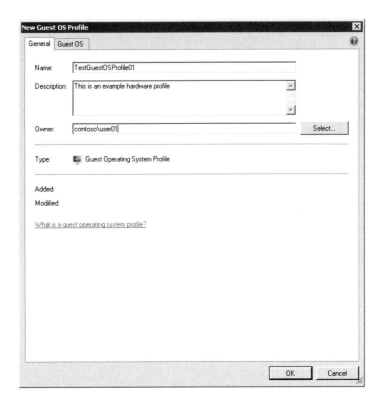

FIGURE 7.8
New Guest OS Profile
Guest OS settings

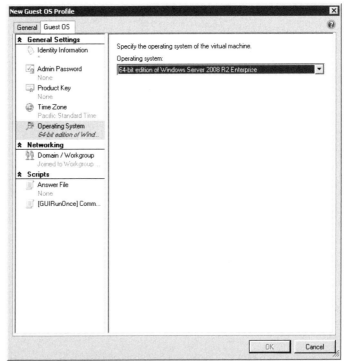

6. Click OK to save the profile to the database. VMM will save operating system profiles to the library selected when you clicked the New Guest OS Profile action.

7. Click the Profiles node under a specific library server to access the list of profiles. Remember that hardware profiles reside only in the database (Figure 7.9).

FIGURE 7.9
Guest OS profiles stored in library

MERGING EXISTING ANSWER FILES WITH A GUEST OS PROFILE

An VMM Guest OS profile is a simplified interface to the answer file that Windows Mini-Setup uses during customization. The answer file is required if you want to automate the customization of the guest operating system during deployment. The settings in the VMM Guest OS profile, however, are only a subset of all the settings supported for unattended customization. If specific settings are not exposed through VMM, you can append an answer file to the Guest OS profile in VMM. The actual answer file that VMM generates merges the settings in the Guest OS profile and the settings in the appended answer file. If a setting is specified in the Guest OS profile and the appended answer file, the setting in the Guest OS profile is used.

Administrators who already have a mechanism to generate answer files with all the settings necessary can use that answer file to populate the properties of a Guest OS profile. In this case, the administrator not only wants to append the answer file to the Guest OS profile, they also want to import the settings from the answer file into the Guest OS profile.

To merge an answer file with a Guest OS profile, follow these steps:

1. Copy and paste the following text to a file and name it unattend.xml. The following code is the XML used by Mini-Setup to automate the customization process. The answer file is what you will merge into a Guest OS profile later on.

```xml
<?xml version="1.0" encoding="utf-8"?>
<unattend xmlns="urn:schemas-microsoft-com:unattend">
    <settings pass="oobeSystem">
        <component name="Microsoft-Windows-Shell-Setup"
processorArchitecture="x86"
publicKeyToken="31bf3856ad364e35"
language="neutral"
versionScope="nonSxS"
xmlns:wcm="http://schemas.microsoft.com/WMIConfig/2002/State"
xmlns:xsi="http://www.w3.org/2001/XMLSchema-instance">
```

```
        <OOBE>
            <HideEULAPage>true</HideEULAPage>
            <ProtectYourPC>2</ProtectYourPC>
            <SkipUserOOBE>true</SkipUserOOBE>
            <NetworkLocation>Work</NetworkLocation>
        </OOBE>
        <UserAccounts>
            <LocalAccounts>
                <LocalAccount wcm:action="add">
                    <Password>
                        <Value>password</Value>
                        <PlainText>true</PlainText>
                    </Password>
                    <Group>administrators;users</Group>
                    <Name>TestUser</Name>
                    <DisplayName>Test</DisplayName>
                    <Description>Local Admin</Description>
                </LocalAccount>
            </LocalAccounts>
            <AdministratorPassword>
                <Value>password</Value>
                <PlainText>true</PlainText>
            </AdministratorPassword>
            </DomainAccounts>
        </UserAccounts>
        <AutoLogon>
            <Password>
                <Value>PASSWORD</Value>
                <PlainText>true</PlainText>
            </Password>
            <Domain></Domain>
            <Enabled>true</Enabled>
            <Username>administrator</Username>
            <LogonCount>1</LogonCount>
        </AutoLogon>
    </component>
</settings>
<settings pass="specialize">
    <component name="Microsoft-Windows-UnattendedJoin"
processorArchitecture="x86"
publicKeyToken="31bf3856ad364e35"
language="neutral"
versionScope="nonSxS"
xmlns:wcm="http://schemas.microsoft.com/WMIConfig/2002/State"
xmlns:xsi="http://www.w3.org/2001/XMLSchema-instance">
        <Identification>
            <Credentials>
```

```
                    <Domain>DOMAIN.com</Domain>
                    <Username>domain admin account</Username>
                    <Password>PASSWORD</Password>
               </Credentials>
               <JoinDomain>DOMAIN.com</JoinDomain>
               <MachineObjectOU>OU=computers,DC=domain,DC=com
               </MachineObjectOU>
               <JoinWorkgroup></JoinWorkgroup>
               <DebugJoin>false</DebugJoin>
               <MachinePassword/>
               <UnsecureJoin>false</UnsecureJoin>
          </Identification>
       </component>
       <component name="Microsoft-Windows-Shell-Setup"
processorArchitecture="x86"
publicKeyToken="31bf3856ad364e35"
language="neutral"
versionScope="nonSxS"
xmlns:wcm="http://schemas.microsoft.com/WMIConfig/2002/State"
xmlns:xsi="http://www.w3.org/2001/XMLSchema-instance">
            <ComputerName></ComputerName>
            <ProductKey>11111-11111-11111-11111-11111</ProductKey>
       </component>
   </settings>
   <settings pass="generalize">
       <component name="Microsoft-Windows-Security-Licensing-SLC"
processorArchitecture="x86"
publicKeyToken="31bf3856ad364e35"
language="neutral"
versionScope="nonSxS"
xmlns:wcm="http://schemas.microsoft.com/WMIConfig/2002/State"
xmlns:xsi="http://www.w3.org/2001/XMLSchema-instance">
            <SkipRearm>1</SkipRearm>
       </component>
   </settings>
   <cpi:offlineImage
   cpi:source="wim://PC/image/install.wim#Windows Vista ENTERPRISE"
   xmlns:cpi="urn:schemas-microsoft-com:cpi"/>
</unattend>
```

2. Copy the file to the VMM library. You can wait for the refresher to pick up the new file (refresher runs every 60 minutes) or manually force the refresh of the library.

3. Using PowerShell, create a new guest operating system profile and provide a product key. Type the following commands in the VMM CLI:

```
PS C:\> Get-VMMServer localhost
PS C:\> $pid = "22222-22222-22222-22222-22222"
```

```
                      PS C:\> New-OperatingSystemProfile -Name "Test"
                      -Description "" -ProductKey $pid
```

4. Confirm that the new operating system profile contains the product key specified. Type the following command in VMM CLI.

```
PS C:\>$os | ft name, productkey
Name                               ProductKey
----                               ----
Test                               22222-22222-22222-22222-22222
```

5. Using the operating system profile you just created, merge it with the unattend.xml file in the Library. Type the following commands in the VMM CLI.

```
PS C:\>Get-VMMServer localhost
PS C:\>$answerfile = Get-Script | where {$_.Name -eq "unattend.xml"
-AND $_.LibraryServer -eq "VMMLibrary.lab.local" -AND $_.LibraryShare
-eq "Scripts"}
PS C:\>Set-OperatingSystemProfile -OperatingSystem $os -AnswerFile
$answerfile -MergeAnswerFile
```

6. Confirm that the operating system profile contains the product key contained in the answer file. Type the following commands in the VMM CLI.

```
PS C:\>$os | ft name, productkey
Name                               ProductKey
----                               ----
Test                               11111-11111-11111-11111-11111
```

VIRTUAL MACHINE TEMPLATE

VMM templates encapsulate all the hardware and operating system settings required to create a new virtual machine. If you created profiles in the library, you can use them when creating a template. When creating a template, VMM does not preference one hypervisor over another. Instead, the user is expected to know the proper setup of the virtual machine for the intended hypervisor. Even though this approach requires more work upfront when creating the templates, subsequent creations of virtual machines require less customization and so are less susceptible to human error. To help further standardize the creation of templates, make sure you take advantage of hardware and operating system profiles.

Creating a Template from a Virtual Disk in the Library

The simplest and quickest way to create a template is to use an existing virtual hard disk file stored in the library. The template that VMM creates simply creates an association between the virtual hard disk and the template. You can also specify the intent of using a pass-through disk or raw device map (RDM) in the template, but at this point you do not actually select the disk. When you create a new virtual machine from the template and place it on a virtual machine host, VMM will give you the opportunity to select a pass-through/RDM disk available on the host.

Creating a template starts in the Administration Console in library view. To create a template, follow these steps:

1. Click New Template in the Library Actions menu on the right side of the console (Figure 7.10). The New Template Wizard opens.

FIGURE 7.10
The New
Template action

2. In the Select Source dialog, select Use an Existing Template or a Virtual Hard Disk Stored in the Library and then click Browse.

3. Locate a virtual hard disk from the list. In this example, the name of the virtual disk is os3.vhd. Click OK to accept the selection and return to the Select Source page of the wizard (Figure 7.11).

FIGURE 7.11
Virtual hard disk
selected

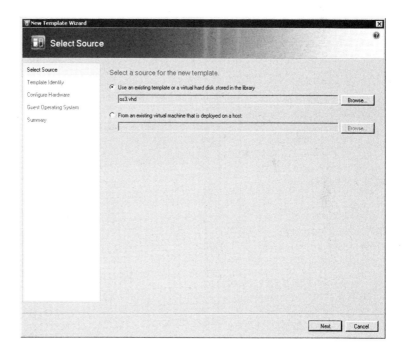

4. In the Template Identity dialog, specify the name of the template, an owner (Windows user account), and a description (Figure 7.12).

5. In the Configure Hardware dialog, select an existing hardware profile from the list or input hardware settings manually (Figure 7.13).

6. In the Guest Operating System dialog, select an existing operating system profile from the list or input operating system settings manually (Figure 7.14).

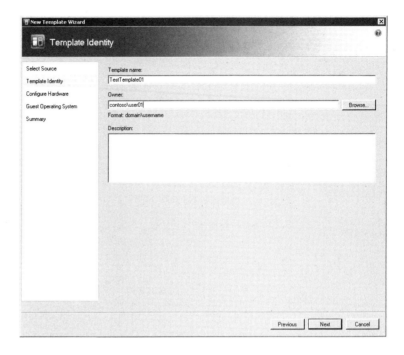

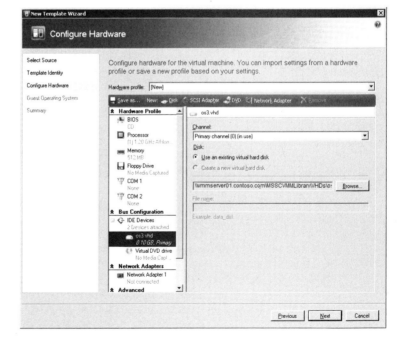

FIGURE 7.14
The Guest Operating
System page of the New
Template Wizard

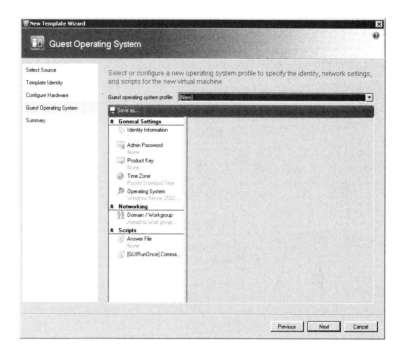

7. In the Summary dialog, review the template configuration and then complete the wizard by clicking the Create button (Figure 7.15).

After creating a template, you can open it and set a few additional properties:

◆ Cost center

◆ Tag

◆ Ten custom properties

◆ Aquota value

Setting a quota value is important if you plan to use quotas to limit the number of virtual machines a self-service user can deploy.

Creating a Template from an Existing Virtual Machine

With VMM, you can automate the creation of a template by avoiding the manual preparation of the virtual hard disk and using an existing virtual machine under management as the source of a template. If you have a virtual machine that is prepared with all the necessary applications and desired configuration settings, you can use VMM to create the template from the virtual machine simply by selecting it as a source object.

To create a template from a virtual machine, follow these steps:

1. Right-click a stopped virtual machine and select New Template (Figure 7.16).

FIGURE 7.15
The Summary page of the New Template Wizard

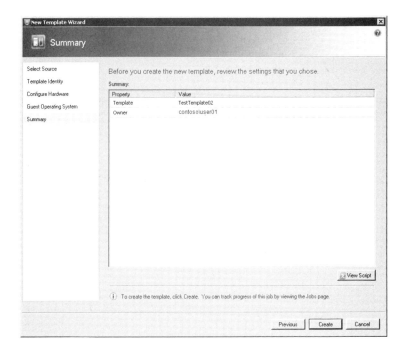

FIGURE 7.16
The New Template option

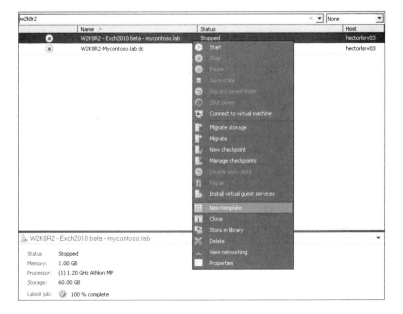

2. VMM will display a warning informing you that the virtual machine will be destroyed. To continue, click Yes (Figure 7.17).

FIGURE 7.17
Warning Message
before Creating a
New Template from a
Virtual Machine

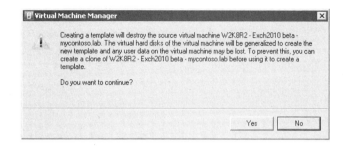

3. In the Template Identity dialog, specify the name, owner, and description for the template (Figure 7.18).

FIGURE 7.18
Specifying the identity
of the new template

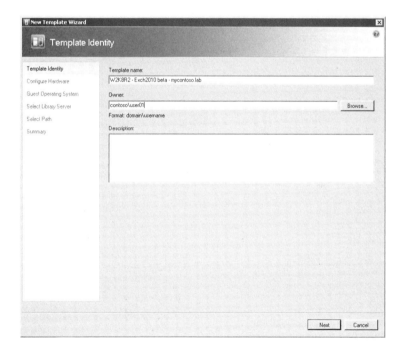

4. In the Configure Hardware dialog, all the settings will be disabled. If you need to make changes to the configuration of the virtual machine, you will need to cancel out of the wizard (Figure 7.19).

5. In the Guest Operating System dialog, select an existing guest OS profile or specify the settings manually (Figure 7.20).

FIGURE 7.19
The Configure
Hardware page of the
New Template Wizard

FIGURE 7.20
Selecting the guest
operating system

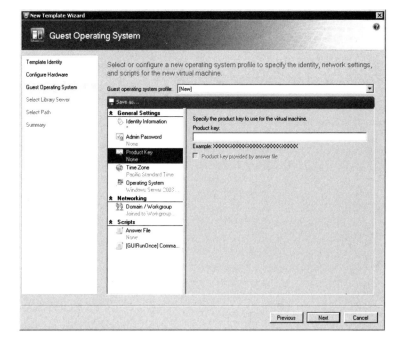

6. In the Select Library Server dialog, select the library server where you want to store the new template (Figure 7.21).

FIGURE 7.21
Selecting the library server

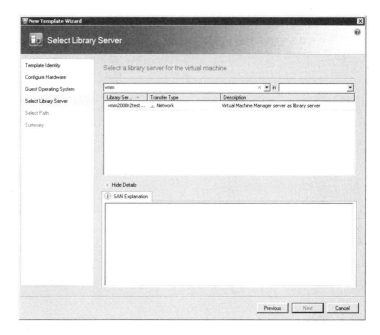

7. In the Select Path dialog, select the path on the library server where the new template will be stored (Figure 7.22).

FIGURE 7.22
Selecting the path for the new template

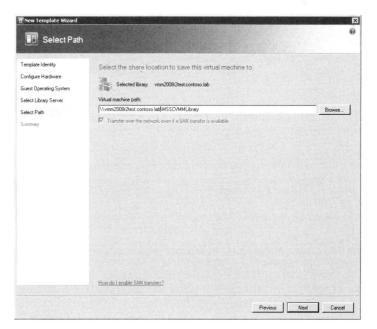

8. In the Summary dialog, review the template configuration and then complete the wizard by clicking on the Create button (Figure 7.23).

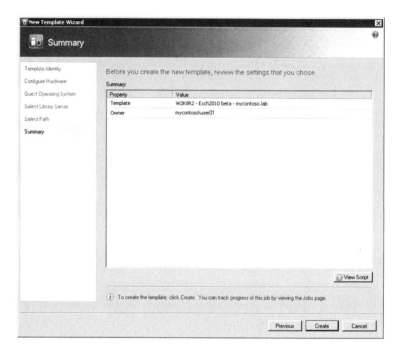

Creating a Template from an Existing Template

Once a template is created, the object is stored in the database. The file that represents the virtual hard disk attached to the template resides on the file system of the library server. In the VMM Administrator Console, you will notice that the template object resides in the VMs and Templates folder of the library server where the virtual hard disk file resides. If you need to alter a template, you can clone it. As part of that process, VMM simply stores a link to the virtual disk file and so the cloned template does not consume any additional space on the library server. No lineage is kept between the source and target template, so you can make changes to each independently.

To create a template from an existing template, follow these steps:

1. Right-click a template stored in the library and select New Template (Figure 7.24).

2. In the Template Identity dialog, specify the name, owner, and description for the template.

3. In the Configure Hardware dialog, all the settings will be disabled. If you need to make changes to the configuration of the template, you will need to cancel out of the wizard.

4. In the Guest Operating System dialog, select an existing guest OS profile or specify the settings manually.

5. In the Summary dialog, review the template configuration and then complete the wizard by clicking the Create button.

FIGURE 7.24
Selecting New Template

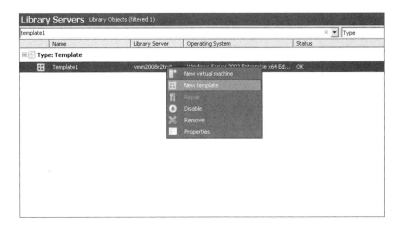

Understanding Customization Not Required Templates

An important variation of the typical template is the Customization Not Required template. If the virtual disk associated with the template contains an operating system for which VMM cannot generate an answer file, then the new virtual machine job will fail because VMM cannot guarantee that the guest operating system was customized during Mini-Setup. As an example, Linux is an operating system that VMM does not support for customization. To successfully deploy a new virtual machine from a template with a virtual hard disk that contains a Linux operating system, select Customization Not Required in the Guest Operating System profile page when creating the new template. Doing so will indicate to VMM that it should not wait for customization of the new virtual machine.

When the new virtual machine is powered on, if there is no embedded mechanism to generate a unique identity for the guest operating system, the guest operating system might collide with existing operating systems on the network with the same identity. Using a template that does not require customization is the same as cloning a virtual machine. However, if you need the resultant virtual machine to have a unique identity on the network, make sure to either make the guest operating system unique before storing the virtual hard disk in the Library or embed a customization script with the guest operating system in the virtual hard disk.

To create a Customization Not Required template, make sure to select Customization Not Required in the Guest Operating System dialog (see Figure 7.25).

CLONING A VIRTUAL MACHINE USING THE SELF-SERVICE PORTAL

VMM's Self-Service Portal allows you to assign templates to users and a quota of how many virtual machines they can deploy. Assigning a Customization Not Required template to Self-Service Portal users allows them to clone virtual machines and deploy new virtual machines with guest operating systems that VMM does not support for customization.

Creating a New Virtual Machine From a Disk

After installing VMM, the most common action that administrators do to simply "kick the tires" is the creation of a new virtual machine. For example, an administrator may decide to create a new virtual machine with a new virtual disk on a virtual machine host. This simple action exercises the following components:

◆ VMM's Administrator Console

◆ Back-end VMM server and database

◆ Communication between the VMM server and the virtual machine host

◆ Virtualization stack on the virtual machine host

Even after a more thorough verification of the VMM deployment, the first task is to create the virtual machines that you will use in your environment. VMM offers several options for creating a new virtual machine from a disk:

◆ New virtual machine with a blank disk

◆ New virtual machine from an existing disk

FIGURE 7.25
Customization Not Required in Guest OS Profile

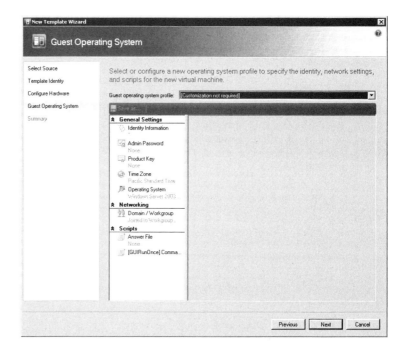

USING A NEW BLANK DISK

In the simplest case, you can create a new virtual machine and specify that the hypervisor create a new disk for you as part of the deployment. You can specify the size of the virtual hard disk and its type (dynamic or fixed). The disk will not contain any information at this point. If you want to install an operating system in the virtual machine, you have the option of booting into an ISO or from the network. Using an ISO will instruct VMM to copy an ISO stored in the library to the virtual machine host and attach it to the virtual CD/DVD drive. You can also link the ISO from the library to the new virtual machine over the network to avoid copying it over the network.

Following are the differences between the types of virtual hard disks:

Dynamic   A dynamic disk attaches to a virtual machine. The VHD file itself is less than 1 MB at creation time. However, it can represent any capacity you specify. The size of the file will grow dynamically as data is written to it, but it will grow in size only to the capacity you specified. If you delete files from the guest operating system running the virtual machine, the VHD file itself will not reduce in size. You can reduce the size of the virtual hard disk only by compacting it. A dynamically expanding virtual hard disk is very space efficient but may present performance degradation as the file expands because the physical blocks that make up the file are not contiguous on disk. For production scenarios, the recommendation is to use fixed virtual hard disks. VMware refers to this disk type as thin.

> **Supported in VMM**
>
> Virtual Server: Yes
>
> Hyper-V: Yes
>
> VMware: No

Fixed   A fixed disk attaches to a virtual machine. At creation time, the size of the VHD file itself is equal to the capacity you specified. The file will not grow or shrink. If you delete files from the guest operating system running the virtual machine, the VHD file itself will not change in size. You cannot reduce the size of the virtual hard disk by compacting it. A fixed virtual hard disk presents the best performance because the file uses contiguous blocks on physical disk. For production scenarios, this disk type is recommended. VMware refers to this disk type as thick.

> **Supported in VMM**
>
> Virtual Server: Yes
>
> Hyper-V: Yes
>
> VMware: Yes

Differencing   A differencing disk attaches to a virtual machine only if the file is linked to another virtual disk (e.g., a dynamic disk, fixed disk, or another differencing disk). The parent/child relationship between the virtual disks can be more than one level, creating a differencing disk chain. The VHD file itself is less than 1 MB at creation time and must be linked to an existing virtual hard disk. The differencing disk keeps track of all write operations that occur in the virtual machine without making changes to the original virtual hard disk. With one or more differencing disks, the only disk in a chain that can track write operations is the leaf disk — the last disk in a chain with no child disks attached to it.

A differencing disk still represents the maximum size of the base disk (the first virtual disk in the chain). The size of the file will grow dynamically as data is written to it. If you delete files from the guest operating system running the virtual machine, the differencing disk VHD file itself will not reduce in size. A differencing virtual hard disk is very space efficient but may present performance degradation as the file expands because the physical blocks that make up the file are not contiguous on disk. For production scenarios, the recommendation is to use fixed virtual hard disks.

Supported in VMM

Virtual Server: No

Hyper-V: No

VMware: No

LINKING LIBRARY FILES TO A HYPER-V VIRTUAL MACHINE

For Hyper-V, you will need to set up constrained delegation so the virtual machine host can access the necessary ISO remotely. Constrained delegation authorizes the proper impersonation required between the library server and the Hyper-V host.

Follow these steps to enable constrained delegation:

1. Verify that the VMM server service (`vmmservice.exe`) is running under a domain account and not the LocalSystem account.

2. Open Active Directory Users and Computers MMC.

3. Connect to a domain controller.

4. Locate the computer account of the server running Hyper-V.

5. Right-click the computer account and select Properties.

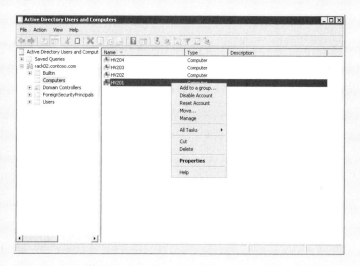

6. Select the Delegation tab.

7. Select Trust This Computer for Delegation to Specified Services Only.

8. Select Use Any Authentication Protocol.

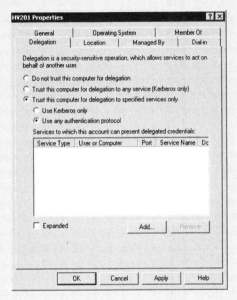

9. Click the Add button.

10. Click Users or Computers and search for the computer account of the server with the VMM library.

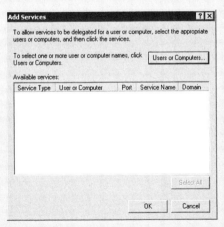

11. Select the `cifs` service type.

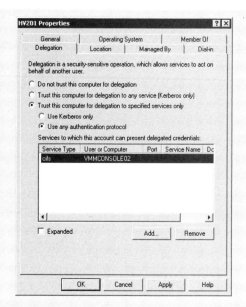

12. Accept the changes and close the Properties window for the computer account.

You will need to repeat these steps for every Hyper-V host that you want to link ISOs to the VMM library.

If you have an existing network-based build environment that uses Windows Deployment Services (WDS), for example, you can also boot the virtual machine from the network. You will need to make sure the new virtual machine has a virtual network adapter. For Hyper-V, you can specify the boot order of the virtual machines in a way that's similar to specifying the boot order of physical machines. Make sure to set the network as the first device in the boot order. This will ensure that the virtual machine will always attempt to boot from the network first before booting from the local virtual hard disk in case you decide to rebuild the virtual machine in the future. You can also install an operating system from ISO media that you attach to the virtual CD/DVD drive. Depending on the workload you plan to deploy in the virtual machine, you may want more than one virtual hard disk. From VMM, you can specify as many disks as you need, keeping in mind that each hypervisor has limits on how many disks can attach to a particular controller.

With VMM, you can deploy a virtual machine with a new blank disk to any of the supported hypervisor hosts or the library as a target. In the first case, a virtual machine host is the most common target. When configuring the new virtual machine, you need to keep in mind that each hypervisor has different requirements. For Hyper-V, the new blank disk you will use as the boot disk must be attached to the IDE controller. Hyper-V does not support booting from the SCSI controller. ESX, on the other hand, only supports booting a virtual machine from the SCSI controller. Virtual Server supports booting from IDE or SCSI. To speed up virtual machine creation, you can save hypervisor-specific settings in hardware profiles and templates.

VMM also supports creating a virtual machine directly to the library. In this case, the library server must also have a hypervisor installed. Since VMM supports installing the Library role only on Windows Server, Virtual Server or Hyper-V must be installed as well. A hypervisor is required because the VMM depends on specific APIs to create the disk on the target. Without these APIs, creation will fail. VMM can only create disks with the filename extension .vhd on the target library. Creating VMDK files directly in the library is not supported by VMM; only storing VMDK files is supported.

USING AN EXISTING DISK

VMM's library supports two virtual disk formats: VHD and VMDK. Typically, VHD files can be used with Virtual Server and Hyper-V. VMDK files are strictly for ESX.

To get a virtual disk into the library, follow these steps:

1. Copy the file(s) to a share managed by VMM. The library refresher indexes new files discovered and uploads relevant metadata to the database.

2. At this point, you will see the new file(s) appear in the Administrator Console in the library view or through PowerShell and can create a new virtual machine using that disk. VMM is not aware of the contents of the disk. The virtual disk may contain a valid operating system, user or application data, or nothing at all.

As part of creating the virtual machine, VMM will copy the virtual hard disk file(s) from the VMM library to the target virtual machine host. A virtual hard disk that contains a valid operating system can be specified when a new virtual machine is created. Deploying the virtual machine and powering it on will allow the operating system to boot up. Deploying multiple virtual machines using the same virtual hard disk will simply result in all virtual machines containing a copy of the same operating system. The identity embedded in the operating system will not change as part of the deployment. Keep this in mind when connecting the virtual machine to the network since identical operating system instances on the network may cause issues with connectivity and authentication. To modify the identity of the virtual machine after deployment, you'll need to use VMM templates that enable this functionality for a variety of Windows-based operating systems.

Creating a New Virtual Machine from an Existing Virtual Machine (Virtual Machine Cloning)

VMM can use an existing virtual machine as a source for future virtual machines. The source in this case can reside on a virtual machine host or on the library server. Creating a virtual machine from a virtual machine is referred to as cloning. The New VM wizard experience does not refer to cloning directly; it simply lists virtual machine as a source type. Cloning a virtual machine involves copying the virtual disks, any memory state, and associated configuration files to the host. The source is not deleted or modified. To clone a virtual machine, it must be in a powered-off or saved state if it is located on a virtualization host. Virtual machines in the library are in a valid state for cloning. Cloning is also supported for virtual machines with snapshots. Table 7.1 lists the cloning variations supported by VMM.

CLONING VIRTUAL MACHINE IDENTITY

A cloned virtual machine is an identical copy of the source, including Active Directory identity, SID, computer name, and MAC addresses statically assigned to the virtual network adapters. If both virtual machines are powered on and connected to the same network, you will have two identical computers potentially communicating on the same network.

TABLE 7.1: Cloning variations

SOURCE TYPE	SOURCE LOCATION	DESTINATION
Hyper-V virtual machine	Host	Hyper-V host, library
ESX virtual machine	Host	ESX host, library
Virtual Server machine	Host	Hyper-C host, Virtual Server host, library
Hyper-V virtual machine	Library	Library Hyper-V host
ESX virtual machine	Library	Library ESX host
Virtual Server machine	Library	Library Virtual Server host

Creating a New Virtual Machine from a Template

Creating virtual machines using a virtual disk involves a repetitive set of tasks to specify virtual hardware configuration and operating system customization settings. VMM exposes a large range of settings for a virtual machine across all supported hypervisors. With so many settings, typically administrators standardize on a few common configurations. The need to standardize is not a requirement, especially with virtualization because you no longer have the same restrictions compared to a purely physical environment. However, operational practices, business processes, and application license models typically drive some level of standardization.

To help administrators create virtual machines based on a standard configuration, use templates stored in the VMM library. Templates represent the desired virtual hardware configuration and operating system customization settings for a virtual machine. There are three main components of a template: source disk, hardware profile, and guest operating system profile.

To create a virtual machine from a template, follow these steps:

1. Click the New Virtual Machine action (Figure 7.26).

FIGURE 7.26
The New Virtual Machine action in the Administrator Console

2. In the Select Source dialog, select the Use an Existing Virtual Machine, Template, or Virtual Hard Disk radio button and click the Browse button (Figure 7.27).

3. In the Select Virtual Machine Source dialog, select the template you want to use for this new virtual machine.

FIGURE 7.27
The Select Source page
of the New Virtual
Machine Wizard

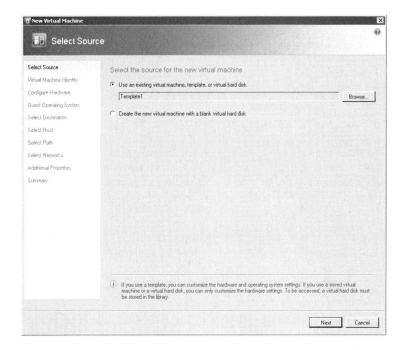

4. In the Virtual Machine Identity dialog, specify the name, owner, and description for the new virtual machine.

5. In the Configure Hardware, customize the hardware settings of the virtual machine. Since the source is a template, the virtual hard disk associated with the template cannot be removed. You can only add new virtual hard disks.

6. In the Guest Operating System dialog, you can modify the guest operating system profile settings.

7. In the Select Destination dialog, the option to place the virtual machine on a host is the only one available.

8. In the Select Host dialog, select the best-suited host for the workload rated by Intelligent Placement.

9. In the Select Path dialog, specify the location where VMM should place the virtual machine configuration files and virtual disks. You can click Browse to view the local volumes and folder structure for that host.

10. In the Select Networks dialog, select the virtual network that each virtual network adapter should be connected to. You can also specify Not Connected if you do not want network connectivity.

11. In the Additional Properties dialog, specify the startup option for the virtual machine in the event that the host reboots and an action when the host is shutdown.

12. In the Summary dialog, review the virtual machine configuration. By clicking View Script, you can view the set of PowerShell commands executed by VMM to create that virtual machine (Figure 7.28).

FIGURE 7.28

Viewing the PowerShell script

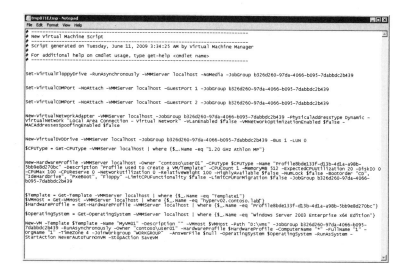

Importing a Virtual Machine

Virtual machines serve as great self-contained vehicles for an operating system and applications. They can be shared within a company or downloaded as a preconfigured appliances from the Web. An appliance includes a preconfigured operating system and an application preinstalled, so there is very little to configure after deployment. The appliance is meant to be used for a specific purpose and not as a general-purpose virtual machine. In some case, the operating system is customized for a specific application.

Virtual Server–based virtual machines typically consist of two files: a VHD file containing the operating system and application(s), and a VMC file containing configuration information.

If a library server encounters a new VMC file in a managed share, it will use the configuration information contained within the file to create a virtual machine object in the database and link it to the associated VHD file. The VMC and VHD should be contained in the same folder.

ESX-based virtual machines typically consist of three files: two VMDK files containing the operating system and application(s), and a VMX file containing configuration information.

A VMDK-based virtual hard disk is made up of two files: a metadata file (human readable) that points to another VMDK file with all the operating system, and application data (not human readable). The latter file is typically very large. VMM will read the metadata VMDK file to discover the associated VMDK file, and it will read the VMX file to generate a virtual machine object in the database and link it to the associated VMDK (metadata) file. For Virtual Server and ESX, you also have the option of adding the virtual machine to inventory directly from the host.

Hyper-V–based virtual machines typically consist of two files: a VHD file containing the operating system and application(s), and an XML file containing configuration information. Unlike with Virtual Server and ESX, if a library server encounters the configuration file of a Hyper-V virtual machine (in this case an XML) in a managed library share, it will not recognize it as a valid configuration. This is because Hyper-V requires that a virtual machine go through an export process.

Once you have a virtual machine in your possession, you will need to get it under management in VMM. VMM supports two ways of importing an existing virtual machine into the environment:

◆ Registering a virtual machine to a virtual machine host

◆ Importing a virtual machine to the VMM library

REGISTERING A VIRTUAL MACHINE TO A VIRTUAL MACHINE HOST

Registering a virtual machine to a virtual machine host involves copying the virtual hard disks and an associated configuration file to the host and then registering the virtual machine using VMM. Registration adds the virtual machine to the host inventory. Since the configuration file contains all the necessary information that constitutes a valid virtual machine instance, registration is a very fast process.

To add a virtual machine into inventory using VMM, follow these steps:

1. Copy all virtual machine files to the hypervisor host.

2. In the VMM Administrator Console, right-click the host you want the virtual machine registered to and choose Properties to open the properties page for the host.

3. In the Host Properties dialog for the host, click the VMs tab (Figure 7.29).

FIGURE 7.29
The VMs tab in the Host Properties dialog

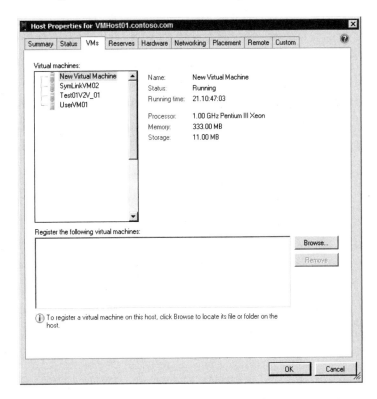

4. Click the Browse button.

5. In the Select Destination Folder dialog, browse the local file system of the host and locate the folder that contains the virtual machine files (Figure 7.30).

FIGURE 7.30
The Select Destination Folder dialog

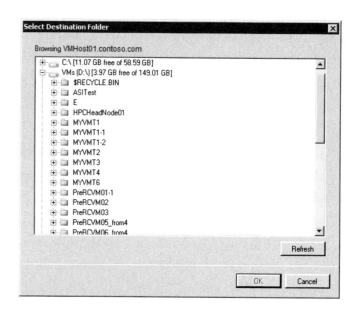

6. Click OK and the virtual machine will be added to inventory.

IMPORTING A VIRTUAL MACHINE TO THE VMM LIBRARY

Importing a virtual machine into the VMM library involves copying the virtual hard disks and an associated configuration file to a library share hosted on the library server. The library refresher will index the new files, read the configuration file, and generate a virtual machine object in the library. Once the virtual machine is imported into the library, you can clone or deploy it to a virtual machine host. If you plan to reuse the virtual machine or want to share it with other users, the library approach is the better option.

Exporting a Virtual Machine

Manually copying a virtual machine (virtual hard disks and configuration file) to a separate location is typically a simple operation. For Virtual Server and ESX, you can copy the associated virtual hard disks and configuration files with no modification. However, for Hyper-V, you need to properly export the virtual machine.

Exporting a virtual machine from a Hyper-V host generates an EXP file. The EXP file contains the virtual machine configuration in a format that Hyper-V understands when importing the virtual machine at a later point. The VHD file is not altered as part of the export process. A library server will recognize an EXP file as a virtual machine configuration and create the object in the database along with the necessary link to the VHD file. You can also add the exported virtual machine to inventory directly from the host.

Removing a Virtual Machine

Removing a virtual machine using VMM's Administrator Console will delete the virtual machine instance from inventory and all associated files from the file system. Since this is a destructive action, make sure you have a backup of the virtual machine files before removing it unless you truly want to completely eliminate the virtual machine from your environment. Using VMM, you can preserve a copy of the virtual machine by cloning it before deleting it, if necessary. You also have the option of going directly to the virtual machine host and removing the virtual machine from inventory. Here are a few ways you can do this:

◆ Virtual Server allows you to remove the virtual machine from its inventory (leaving behind the VMC and VHD files, which you have to delete manually).

◆ ESX allows you to remove a virtual machine from its inventory (leaving behind the VMX and VMDK files) or delete the virtual machine from the datastore entirely (removing it from inventory and deleting the files from the file system).

◆ Hyper-V allows you to remove a virtual machine, which will remove its configuration from inventory and delete the associated XML files. The VHDs files are left on the file system.

While all of these techniques let you delete a virtual machine from management without deleting the files, this can result in a cluttered environment filled with unmanaged files lying around on your hosts. If you think you might need the VM later but want to remove it from a host, store it in the library or ensure that you have a backup system in place.

If you have a virtual machine with snapshots (stored in AVHD files), then deleting the virtual machine will actually cause the AVHD files to be merged into the parent VHD. This behavior is by design, resulting in a VHD with all contents from associated AVHD files merged into it. So, for example, assume you started off with a virtual machine and a blank virtual disk and then installed an operating system. Take a snapshot at this point and then install the latest operating system updates. Take another snapshot and install an application. Take another snapshot. At this point, apply the latest snapshot. Deleting the virtual machine at this point will cause a merge of the snapshots into the original blank virtual disk. So at a later time, if you want to re-create the virtual machine using that existing virtual disk, you will have an operating system with the latest updates and the application you installed. If you do not care about preserving the data in the snapshots, then before deleting, simply apply the first snapshot and then delete the virtual machine.

Converting to a Virtual Machine

Based on the information covered so far, you can create a virtual machine from a blank virtual disk, a virtual disk, or a template. An alternate way of creating a virtual machine is to convert an existing physical machine to a virtual machine and an existing virtual machine from a different hypervisor to Hyper-V or Virtual Server virtual machine. Creating a new virtual machine by converting a physical machine is known as Physical to Virtual (P2V) conversion. Creating a new virtual on Hyper-V or Virtual Server from a virtual machine on ESX is known as Virtual to Virtual (V2V) conversion.

P2V first deploys and installs an agent on a machine running Windows. The agent inspects the Windows instance and returns data to the VMM server. This data is analyzed to figure out the CPU, memory, disk, and network configuration of the source. Using this information, VMM can create a virtual machine that is an exact clone of the source, including the Windows operating system configuration, Windows identity, machine credentials, static IP addresses (if any), and installed applications. Virtual network adapters attached to the virtual machine are also assigned the same MAC address of the physical network adapter on the source.

VMM offers the ability to perform an online or offline conversion. In the case of an online conversion, P2V can capture the source machine while it's powered on and responding to user requests. There is no interruption in service. Offline conversion, on the other hand, requires rebooting the source machine into WINPE. The VMM agent running in WINPE will capture the necessary information from the source machine and transfer that to the hypervisor host where the virtual machine will reside. After the source capture is complete, the source machine is rebooted back to the original Windows instance. Online conversion has the benefit of not requiring downtime, but in practice, you likely don't want users to be making changes or using the system while you are converting since those changes will not be applied to the new virtual machine. With that said, online works well for nondisruptive testing or for some types of servers where it's not required to maintain user state.

V2V is used to convert a virtual machine created on VMware ESX to a virtual machine that can run on Microsoft Virtual Server or Hyper-V. You can select an ESX virtual machine stored in the library or in a powered-off state residing on a host. The VMDK file that represents the virtual disk for the virtual machine is converted to a VHD file compatible with Virtual Server and Hyper-V as part of V2V. The virtual machine configuration stored in VMM is used to create the new virtual machine on the destination host, but the VMX configuration file itself is not converted into a VMC or XML file. If you have custom data stored in the VMX configuration file, that information will not be preserved as part of V2V.

Physical to Virtual (P2V) Conversion

Converting from an existing physical machine to a virtual machine is the fastest and most efficient way to preserve your operating system and application installation and make better utilization of your hardware investment by consolidating workloads.

To convert a physical machine to virtual, using VMM P2V, follow these steps:

1. In the VMM Administrator Console, click the Convert Physical Server action, as shown in Figure 7.31.

FIGURE 7.31
The Convert Physical Server action

2. In the Select Source dialog, type the computer name (NETBIOS or FQHN) or IP address of the source machine. You can browse for the computer in Active Directory by clicking the Browse button.

3. Provide credentials with local administrator access to the computer in the User Name field and the associated password and domain. You can provide an Active Directory user account or a local user account on the source computer itself (Figure 7.32).

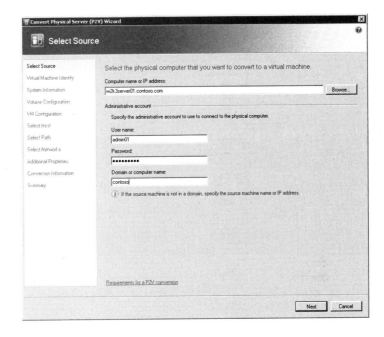

4. In the Virtual Machine Identity dialog box, specify the name of the virtual machine that P2V will create as part of the P2V process. Specify an owner (Active Directory account) and a description (optional), as shown in Figure 7.33.

FIGURE 7.33
Providing the identity of
the virtual machine

5. In the System Information dialog, click the Scan System button. VMM will submit a new job to install the P2V agent on the source machine. VMM supports a specific list of Windows operating systems for P2V. Refer to Table 7.2 for the list of supported operating systems. To successfully complete this task, make sure the source machine firewall allows incoming WMI connections.

TABLE 7.2: P2V-supported operating systems

OPERATING SYSTEM	ARCHITECTURE	CONVERSION MODES SUPPORTED
Windows 2000 Server SP4	32-bit	Offline Only
Windows XP SP2+	32-bit	Online/Offline
Windows XP SP2+	64-bit	Online/Offline
Windows Server 2003 SP2	32-bit/64-bit	Online/Offline
Windows Vista SP1	32-bit/64-bit	Online/Offline
Windows Server 2008	32-bit/64-bit	Online/Offline
Windows 7	32-bit/64-bit	Online/Offline
Windows Server 2008 R2	32-bit/64-bit	Online/Offline

6. Once the agent is successfully installed, it will retrieve information necessary for P2V and return it to the VMM server. The information is stored in the database as a MachineConfiguration object.

7. The wizard page will indicate that the scan is complete and will show processor, memory, network, and volume information retrieved from the source computer (Figure 7.34).

8. In the Volume Configuration dialog, select the volumes you want VMM to capture using P2V (Figure 7.35).

The Volume Configuration page lists all the volumes discovered by the P2V agent. You can select which volumes to capture as part of P2V. The system volume with the operating system installed is mandatory and so must be captured. For each volume captured, a VHD file will be created. Even if the source computer has only one physical disk installed, if it contains more than one volume, P2V will create a VHD per volume (not per physical disk). P2V relies on Volume Shadow Copy Service (VSS) to capture the source volumes. VSS supports creating snapshots of the volumes without requiring any downtime of the virtual machine. It creates a point-in-time snapshot of the volumes, so any changes to the data after P2V starts will not be captured. For each VHD file, you can specify the size, disk type, and channel, which are listed here:

File size: The size of the resultant VHD can be equal to or greater than the size of the source volume. VMM does not support reducing the size of the volume.

Disk type: The VHD created by P2V can be fixed or dynamic. Typically, creating a fixed type virtual disk is recommended for production deployments.

FIGURE 7.34
Gather System Information Complete

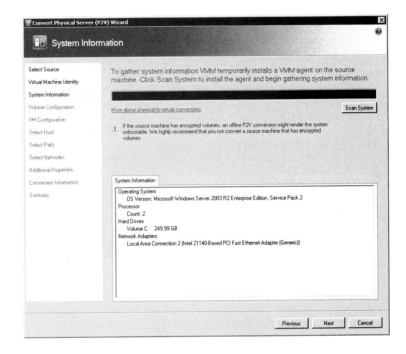

FIGURE 7.35
The Volume Configuration dialog

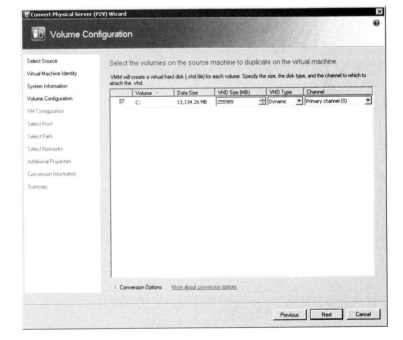

Channel: Each VHD created must be connected to either an IDE or a SCSI controller. On each controller, there are a number of available slots. For example, IDE 0:0 is the default channel selected for the system volume.

9. To change the conversion mode between online and offline, click the Conversion Options chevron icon to expand the options.

In some cases, P2V will need to use offline conversion. P2V will recommend or force offline conversion for the following reasons:

◆ VMM P2V does not support Windows 2000 Server with SP4 using online conversion. Windows 2000 Server does not support the technologies used by P2V for online conversion. The Volume Configuration page will reveal additional options related to the conversion mode (online or offline) and the power state of the source machine after conversion. In the case of Windows 2000 Server, the wizard blocks online conversion.

◆ If the source machine is an Active Directory domain controller, the P2V wizard will default to offline conversion. Offline conversion is the default mode recommended by the Active Directory product group. The P2V wizard however does not block using online conversion in this case.

◆ If the source machine has a Fat32 volume, then the P2V wizard will force offline conversion. You can uncheck the volume from the list and exclude it from being captured by P2V. In this case, the wizard will allow online and offline conversion.

For both online and offline conversion, you can choose to turn off the source computer after P2V completes (Figure 7.36). This is important if you plan to power on the virtual machine once it is created. Since the operating system in the virtual machine is an exact clone of the source computer, it is not recommended that you have both on the network at the same time.

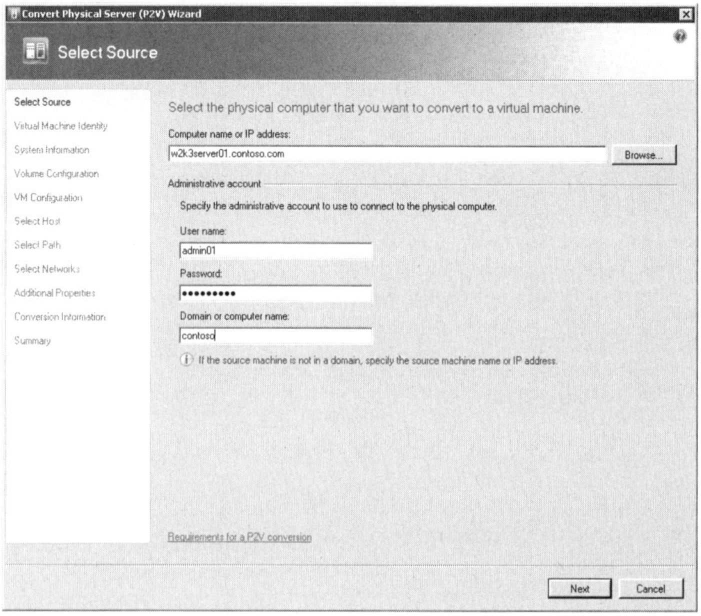

FIGURE 7.36
Expanded Volume
Configuration Dialog in
Convert Physical Server
Wizard

OFFLINE CONVERSION

If you're doing an offline conversion, in the Offline Conversion Options dialog in the wizard, you need to provide the IP information that the WINPE image will use to communicate on the network.

Offline conversion supports the following IP address options:

Obtain IP Address Automatically   If the network segment to which the source machine is connected supports DHCP, then select this option.

Use IPv4 Address   If you want WINPE to use a specific IPv4 address, select the corresponding option on the Offline Conversion Options page. You will need to provide the IP address, subnet, and gateway.

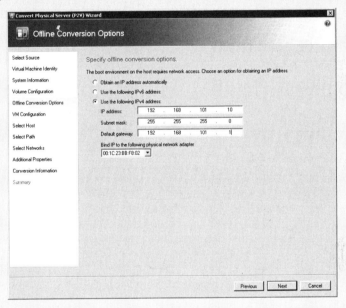

Use IPv6 Address   If you want WINPE to use a specific IPv6 address, select this option. You will need to provide the IP address, subnet prefix, and gateway.

Bind IP Address to this MAC   If the source computer has multiple network adapters, the drop-down list will specify the MAC address of each. You have the option at this point to specify which MAC WINPE you should bind the IP information to.

Default IP Address   If you chose IPv4 or IPv6 and the source machine has static IP addresses defined for the network adapter, VMM will automatically default IP-based information collected from the source computer.

10. In the Virtual Machine Configuration dialog, select the number of processors and amount of memory for the virtual machine (Figure 7.37).

The maximum amount of processors and memory allowed is imposed by the virtual machine host you will select later in the wizard.

FIGURE 7.37
The Virtual Machine
Configuration dialog

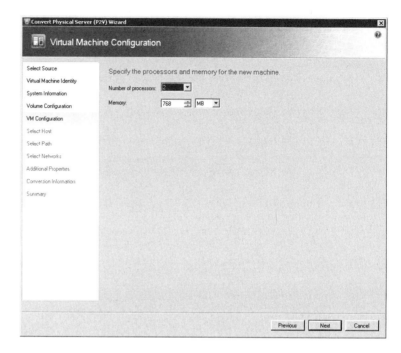

If the source computer is Windows 2000 Server, then you can only select one processor.

If you choose two virtual processors, you cannot select a Virtual Server host as a destination.

If you select four virtual processors, you cannot select a Hyper-V host with two physical processors.

Limitations on the amount of RAM you can specify are also imposed by the virtual machine host. Keep this in mind when specifying processor and memory settings because the P2V wizard will not enforce hypervisor-specific limitations.

11. In the Select Host dialog, select the most suitable host based on the star ratings returned by Intelligent Placement (Figure 7.38).

    If you know for a fact that the source computer is very processor intensive, you can change the priority Intelligent Placement uses when modeling the workload by clicking Customize Ratings. The Customize Ratings dialog box is shown in Figure 7.39. Make sure you review any warning messages displayed by Intelligent Placement. In some cases, there are error message that explain why the virtual machine host selected is not adequate. Once you select a viable host, you can proceed to the Select Path page by clicking the Next button.

FIGURE 7.38
The Intelligent Placement recommendation on the Select Host page

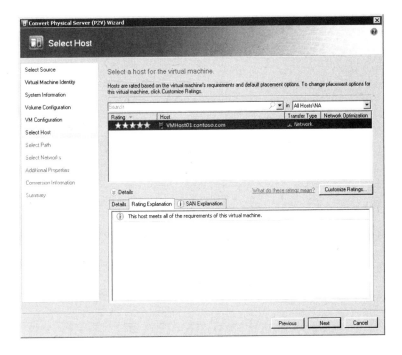

FIGURE 7.39
The Customize Ratings dialog box

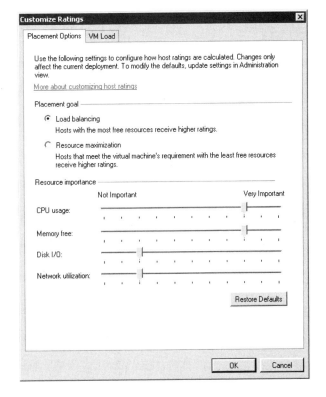

12. In the Select Path dialog (Figure 7.40), select the destination volume and folder for the virtual machine.

   By default, P2V will autoselect the default path stored for the virtual machine host. You can click the Browse button to select a different volume and/or folder.

   If this host selected is a node of a Microsoft failover cluster, you can select only cluster storage that is available for placement.

FIGURE 7.40
The Select Path
dialog box

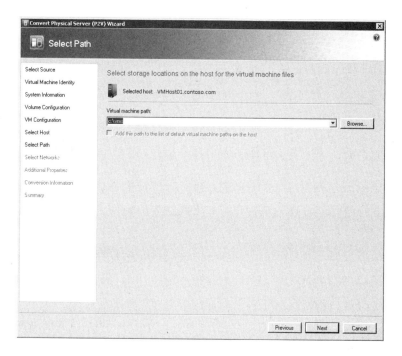

If the storage location is not a CSV, then it must not be in use by another virtual machine.

   For CSV, since the storage location is shared across all nodes in the cluster, you can select it as a storage location even if it already contains other virtual machines.

13. In the Select Networks dialog, select the virtual networks to which each virtual network adapter should be connected (Figure 7.41).

   By default, VMM creates a virtual network adapter for each network connection the source computer has.

   For each one in the list, you can select a virtual network present on the host.

   If you do not want the virtual machine to have network connectivity, you can set each virtual network adapter to Not Connected.

14. In the Additional Properties dialog, specify the automatic startup actions for the virtual machine when the host starts and stops (Figure 7.42).

FIGURE 7.41
The Select Networks dialog

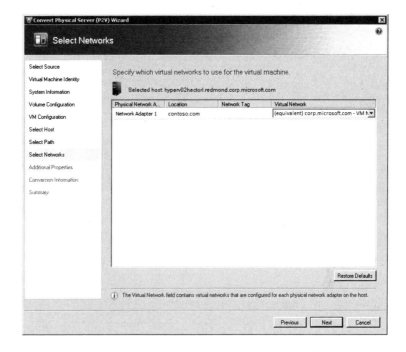

FIGURE 7.42
The Additional Properties dialog

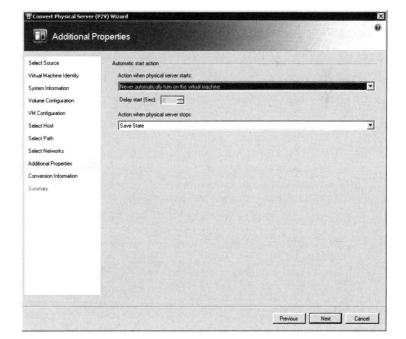

15. In the Conversion Information dialog, the wizard will present any issues encountered due to either lack of drivers or patch levels on the source computer (Figure 7.43).

FIGURE 7.43
The Conversion Information dialog

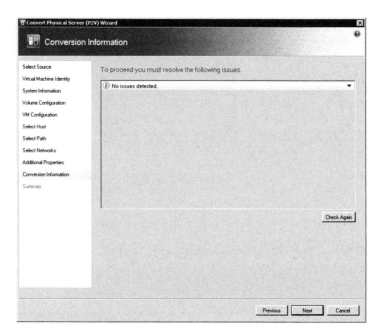

MISSING WINPE DRIVERS REQUIRED FOR OFFLINE CONVERSION

With offline conversion, the WINPE image used to boot the source computer must have the necessary network and storage drivers. The drivers in this case are specific to the source machine, but they must be drivers compatible with Windows Vista or above since the WINPE image used for P2V is based on Vista. WINPE already contains a set of drivers for common hardware components. For newer source computers or advanced network and storage devices, you will need to provide the drivers. The P2V wizard will present the list of missing drivers using the friendly name and the associated device ID, as seen in the following screen shot. The device ID is important so you can match the necessary driver with the component that needs it. Once you locate the requested drivers, place them in the Driver Import folder on the VMM server. To load the Vista 32-bit compatible drivers, place the driver files in the Driver Import folder on the VMM server (C:\Program Files\Microsoft System Center Virtual Machine Manager 2008 R2\Driver Import).

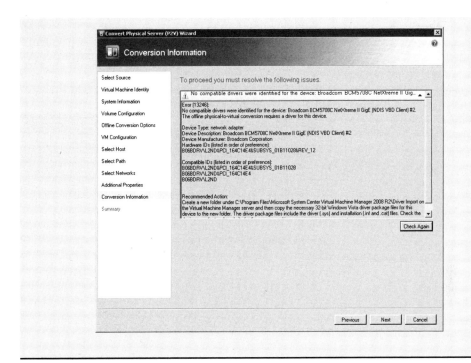

MISSING BINARIES REQUIRED FOR CONVERSION TO VIRTUAL SERVER

If the virtual machine host you selected on the Intelligent Placement page is Virtual Server, you will need to provide additional patches and drivers that P2V will automatically load into the resultant virtual machine as part of the fix-up process. The P2V wizard will specify the necessary patch files you need to place in the Patch Import folder on the VMM server (C:\Program Files\Microsoft System Center Virtual Machine manager\bin\Patch Import). To import the patches into VMM, click the Check Again button.

16. In the Summary dialog, the wizard summarizes the virtual machine configuration that will be created using P2V (Figure 7.44).

SELECTING A VIRTUAL MACHINE AS A P2V SOURCE

P2V does not make any distinction between physical or virtual source computers. P2V captures the Windows instance where the P2V agent is installed. So even if the Windows instance is a virtual machine, P2V treats it as a physical source machine. If, however, the physical computer you select as a P2V source is a Hyper-V virtual machine host, then even if P2V can capture the source, the result is an unusable workload because Hyper-V cannot load within a virtual machine. In all other cases, the fact that P2V does not block converting a virtual machine is useful since that allows you to P2V a VMware virtual machine in addition to using V2V. You can also use P2V with a virtual machine to clone it with no downtime.

FIGURE 7.44
The Summary dialog

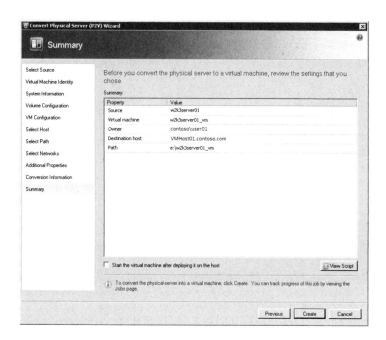

Virtual to Virtual (V2V) Conversion

Deploying and maintaining virtual machines is a big investment in capital, time, and effort, similar to the investment you have made in deploying and maintaining the physical machines in your environment. To help protect that investment while giving you the flexibility to migrate the virtual machine to another hypervisor, VMM offers virtual to virtual conversion (V2V). For V2V, the source must be an ESX virtual machine located in the library or residing on an ESX host (managed by VMM). In this case, since the source is the virtual machine container, there is no need to install an agent in the guest operating system running in the virtual machine. Instead, V2V will convert the virtual disk that contains the virtual machine data directly from VMDK format to VHD format. The conversion is done independent of volume and file system information contained within the VMDK file. For this reason, V2V can "convert" any x86-compatible operating systems — Windows, Linux, or Sun. However, as part of V2V, VMM fixes up the operating system in the resultant virtual machine to ensure that it is bootable. Fix-up requires that VMM can understand and manipulate files and folders on the file system. VMM only supports fix-up of operating systems installed on volumes formatted with NTFS or FAT32. Any other file systems are ignored as part of V2V.

V2V OF A VIRTUAL MACHINE THAT CONTAINS A NON-WINDOWS OPERATING SYSTEM

VMM offers no guarantee that a non-Windows operating system will boot after V2V. Any fix-up is left to the administrator to perform manually.

DISABLE SERVICE OR DRIVER USING P2V

On the VMM server, open the following location: `C:\Program Files\Microsoft System Center Virtual Machine Manager 2008 R2\VMMData`.

In this folder, locate `BlockList.xml`. In this file, you can list the services and drivers to disable in the virtual machine during P2V. The syntax of this file is simple and uses the short name for services and drivers. Keep in mind that editing this file is not supported by Microsoft:

```xml
<?xml version="1.0" encoding="utf-8" ?>
<BlockList>
    <!-- services to disable -->
    <Service>
     <Name> </Name>
    </Service>
    <!-- drivers to disable -->
    <Driver>
        <Name> </Name>
    </Driver>
    <!-- programs to disable -->
    <Program>
        <Name> </Name>
    </Program>
</BlockList>
```

To convert an ESX virtual machine using VMM V2V, follow these steps:

1. In the VMM Administrator Console, click the Convert Virtual Machine action (Figure 7.45).

2. In the Select Source dialog, click the Browse button to select an ESX virtual machine stored in the library or powered off on an ESX host.

   If you select a virtual machine from the library, V2V will leave the source on the library.

   If the virtual machine is on an ESX host, the virtual machine is removed from the host after V2V completes. In this case. if you need to preserve the virtual machine, make sure you clone it before converting the virtual machine using V2V.

3. In the Virtual Machine Identity dialog, specify the virtual machine name, an owner (Windows user account), and a description.

4. In the Virtual Machine Configuration page, you can select the number of processors and amount of memory for the virtual machine (Figure 7.46).

FIGURE 7.45
The Convert Virtual
Machine action

FIGURE 7.46
The Virtual Machine
Configuration dialog

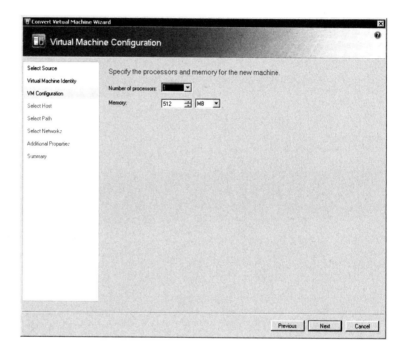

V2V does not gather system information as P2V does. For this reason, there is no need to install an agent in the guest operating system of the virtual machine. VMM uses the virtual machine configuration stored in its database to understand the disk layout, network connection, and any other information necessary for V2V. V2V does require that the VMDK files be in a specific supported format. Refer to Table 7.3 for specific VMDK formats supported by V2V.

5. In the Select Host dialog, select the most appropriate virtual machine host from the list.

6. In the Select Path dialog, select the destination volume and folder for the virtual machine.

7. In the Select Networks dialog, select a virtual network for each virtual network adapter that the virtual machine will have.

8. In the Summary dialog, review the configuration of the virtual machine. You can view the script VMM uses by clicking the View Script button.

TABLE 7.3: Supported VMDK formats

FORMAT	DESCRIPTION
monolithicflat	This is a preallocated virtual disk represented as one file.
monolithicsparse	This is a dynamically growing virtual disk represented as one file.
Vmfs	This is similar to the monolithicflat format but used specifically on ESX.
twoGbMaxExtentSparse	This is a dynamically growing virtual disk represented as a set of 2 GB files.
twoGbMaxExtentFlat	This is a preallocated virtual disk represented as a set of 2 GB files.

CONVERTING VMWARE WORKSTATION AND VMWARE SERVER VIRTUAL MACHINES USING VMM

VMM natively supports converting VMware virtual machines created on ESX 3.0 and 3.5. To convert virtual machines created by VMware 2.5 (or earlier), VMware Workstation or VMware Server, first use VMware's Converter product to convert the virtual machine to ESX format. After converting the virtual machine, copy the files to VMM's library or to an ESX host and register it. After the virtual machine is imported into VMM, you can use the V2V wizard.

UNSUPPORTED CONVERSIONS TYPES

VMM does not support converting a virtual machine that resides on Hyper-V or Virtual Server to ESX. Third-party products on the market provide this functionality.

VMM does not convert virtual machines to physical machines, typically referred to as V2P. Third-party products on the market provide this functionality. If you need to convert a Windows 7 client or Windows Server 2008 R2 from a virtual machine to a physical, you can explore the option of using the VHD to boot the computer directly from the VHD. This feature in Windows 7 and Windows Server 2008 R2 is referred to as boot from VHD and is natively supported in the operating system.

Migrating a Virtual Machine

Creation of a virtual machine involves selecting a virtual machine host or library and placing the configuration file and the virtual disks in a storage location associated with the host. This action is obviously performed only once for the life of the virtual machine. Migration of the virtual machine, on the other hand, is an action that may occur more than once throughout the existence of the virtual machine. For the purpose of this discussion, the existence of a virtual machine is defined by the GUID VMM assigns to a virtual machine record in the database when it is created or imported. The assigned GUID remains with the virtual machine until it is deleted.

VMM offers multiple ways to migrate a virtual machine. In some cases, it depends on what you want to accomplish as part of the migration. Table 7.4 lists all the migration types supported by VMM. The migration type supported depends on the underlying technologies available on the virtual machine host. The most common migration VMM can perform is a network-based migration from one host to another. You can set up VMM to take advantage of advanced technologies like VDS and NPIV to migrate the storage logical unit in its entirety from one host to another without requiring the migration of the files over the network.

TABLE 7.4: VM migration technologies supported in VMM's portfolio

VM MIGRATION TYPE	PLATFORMS AVAILABLE ON	TECHNOLOGY USED FOR TRANSFER	EXPECTED DOWNTIME FOR VM
Network-based migration	Virtual Server, Hyper-V, ESX	BITS for Virtual Server and Hyper-V, sFTP for ESX 3.0 and 3.5, HTTPS for ESXi 3.5	Minutes to hours (W2K8, W2K3 hosts) VM needs to be stopped or in a saved state for the entire duration of transfer. Under 1 minute in most cases (W2K8R2). VM can remain running for almost the entire duration of the transfer of its virtual disks from one location to another, VM is put into save-state for a brief interval to migrate its memory state and automatic differencing disks.
Quick Migration	Hyper-V	Windows Server 2008 Failover Cluster, Hyper-V	Under 1 minute in most cases. VM is put into save state while it is moved from one cluster node to another using the cluster failover mechanism.
SAN Migration	Virtual Server, Hyper-V	Windows Server 2008 Hyper-V and Virtual Disk Service (VDS) Hardware Providers, N-Port Identification Virtualization (NPIV) on Emulex and QLogic Fibre Channel HBAs, iSCSI on EMC, HP, Hitachi, NetApp, EqualLogic arrays	Under 1 minute in most cases. VM is put into save state while it is moved from one virtual machine host to another using unmasking and masking operations at the SAN level.

More advanced migrations offered in Hyper-V and ESX allow you to move a virtual machine from one host to another with minimal or no perceived downtime. In this case, there is no need to move files over the network. Instead, this migration relies on features provided by the hypervisor and the underlying operating system.

If you need the flexibility of migrating between two Windows Server 2008 R2 hosts over the network with independent storage locations (i.e., storage not exposed to all hosts) and minimal downtime, use VMM's Quick Storage Migration feature. This feature allows you to move the virtual disks of a running virtual machine from one storage location to another on the same host with minimal downtime.

You can also move a running virtual machine with its virtual disks from one host to another with minimal downtime. VMware refers to this feature as Storage VMotion, a feature of ESX that VMM supports as well. The key difference between Quick Storage Migration and Live or Quick Migration is that the virtual machine does not need to be highly available on a Microsoft failover cluster. Migration of a virtual machine using Quick Storage Migration is available independent of underlying storage array type, storage protocol, shared storage, or clustering technology. Table 7.5 lists the two storage-based migrations supported by VMM.

TABLE 7.5:   Storage migration technologies supported in VMM's portfolio

STORAGE MIGRATION TYPE	PLATFORMS AVAILABLE ON	TECHNOLOGY USED FOR TRANSFER	EXPECTED DOWNTIME
Storage VMotion	ESX 3.5	Storage VMotion	None. No perceived service interruption while the virtual disks associated with a virtual machine are moved from one storage location to another.
Quick Storage Migration	Hyper-V R2	BITS, Hyper-V	Under 1 minute in most cases (W2K8R2). VM can remain running for almost the entire duration of the transfer of its virtual disks from one storage location to another; VM is put into save state for a brief interval to migrate its memory state and automatic differencing disks.

Network-Based Migration

Network-based migration is the basic transfer type supported in VMM involving only the network. This type of migration is allowed between any two hosts managed by VMM or a host and a library server. With network-based migration, VMM will first copy the virtual machine configuration and associated virtual hard disks to a specific location on either a host or library server. VMM relies on Background Intelligent Transfer Service (BITS) to transfer files between Windows computers. For transfers that involve ESX, VMM uses Secure File Transfer Protocol (SFTP) or HTTP to transfer the files. This migration type does not depend on advanced SAN or cluster features and so is very flexible with regard to the source and target hosts. At a minimum, the source and target hosts should be the same operating system and have the same hypervisor version. In this case, VMM simply copies the files from one location to another, so no other work is required to make the virtual machine bootable on the target host.

You can also move virtual machines to and from a library server. The library server simply stores the virtual machine object and associated files. You do not have the option of powering on the virtual machine when it is stored in the library. Network migration is the only migration type supported to and from the library unless VMM detects that a SAN transfer is available.

Migrating from Virtual Server to Hyper-V

VMM can manage a Virtual Server and Hyper-V host side by side. A virtual machine currently running on Virtual Server is for the most part compatible with Hyper-V. However, the VMC file that contains the configuration of the virtual machine used by Virtual Server is not natively supported by Hyper-V. Instead of re-creating the virtual machine manually, you can use VMM to create the virtual machine on the Hyper-V host. The VHD file associated with the virtual machine on Virtual Server does not require any changes after the migration to Hyper-V. In fact, you can take the VHD of a Virtual Server virtual machine and copy it manually to a Hyper-V host. You can then create a new virtual machine using the transferred virtual disk on the Hyper-V host. The only cleanup steps involve uninstalling the Virtual Server VM Additions and installing Hyper-V Integration Services (IS). Uninstalling the VM Additions and installing IS requires several reboots — one to process the VM Additions uninstall, a second one to allow the IC installer to replace the HAL (from non-ACP to ACPI), and a third to complete the installation of IC.

VMM supports the migration of a virtual machine residing on Virtual Server to Hyper-V. As part of the migration, VMM will uninstall the VM Additions and install IS. Since the VHD format is fully compatible between hypervisors, there is no need to convert the file. This is the reason you *migrate* the virtual machine from Virtual Server to Hyper-V as opposed to *converting* the virtual machine.

Migration of a virtual machine from Virtual Server to Hyper-V using the migration wizard can be accomplished by following these steps:

1. Right-click a powered-off virtual machine that resides on a Virtual Server host and select Migrate (Figure 7.47).

2. In the Select Host dialog, select the best-suited Hyper-V host (Figure 7.48).

3. In the Select Path dialog, specify the default location where the virtual machine configuration and virtual disks will be placed.

4. In the Select Networks dialog, specify which virtual networks each virtual network adapter should connect to, if any.

5. In the Summary dialog, review the source and destination information for this migration.

After you submit the migration job, VMM creates a placeholder virtual machine on the destination host and starts to copy the VHD files associated with the virtual machine from the source host to the destination host. After the VHD files are copied, they are mounted serially on the Hyper-V host to locate the boot volume. Once the boot volume is located, VMM injects an agent into the guest operating system. The VHD is unmounted. The virtual machine on the Hyper-V host is powered on and the Windows operating system is allowed to boot. The agent in the operating system starts to uninstall VM Additions. After the VM Additions uninstall completes, the virtual machine is rebooted. The agent then starts to install Hyper-V Integration Services. The Integration Services installer first upgrades the HAL from non-ACPI to ACPI. The virtual machine is rebooted so the HAL can be replaced. The agent continues installing Integration Services. When the installer completes, the agent marks itself for deletion and then reboots the virtual machine one last time. At this point, the virtual disk is mounted and the Integration Services installation logs are copied to the virtual machine folder on the host for diagnostic purposes (if necessary). The migration job is marked completed.

FIGURE 7.47
The Migrate action for a stopped VM

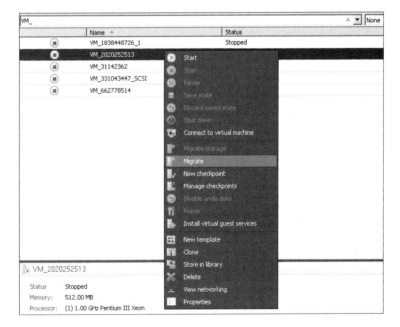

FIGURE 7.48
The Select Host dialog
of the Migrate Virtual
Machine Wizard

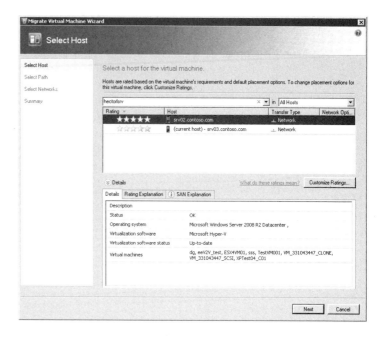

Cluster-Based Migration

Cluster-based migrations in VMM include Windows Server 2008 Quick Migration, Windows
Server 2008 R2 Live Migration, and ESX 3.0/3.5 VMotion. These migration types require a cluster and/or shared storage and a common network. For Windows Server 2008, Quick Migration
builds on Microsoft failover clustering.

ENABLING QUICK MIGRATION

To enable Quick Migration, you must configure a virtual machine in a cluster resource group.
In a cluster environment, the virtual machine must meet specific cluster requirements to ensure
that it is highly available in the event of a host failure. High availability for a virtual machine
means that the storage it resides on must be available to all nodes in a cluster. Cluster software takes care of moving the cluster resource (this includes changing the ownership of the
storage location) from one node in a cluster to another in the event of a failure. Starting the
virtual machine cluster resource on another node after a host failure is not Quick Migration.
Quick Migration takes advantage of the cluster configuration to move the virtual machine from
one node to another, independent of any failures.

Quick Migration of a virtual machine can be accomplished as follows:

1. Right-click a running virtual machine that resides on a Windows Server 2008 failover cluster and select Migrate.

2. In the migrate wizard, Intelligent Placement will rate the hosts.

3. The hosts in the list that reside within the cluster support Cluster as the migration type.

4. Select a cluster node from the list (other than the current host) and click Finish to complete the wizard.

5. At this point VMM will save the state of the virtual machine.

6. Once the state of the virtual machine is saved to disk, clustering will change the ownership of the storage location to the target node selected.

7. After ownership of the storage location changes, the virtual machine is started on the target node.

To ensure minimal downtime of any virtual machine cluster resource during Quick Migration or in the event of a node failure, only one virtual machine (configuration and virtual disks) should reside on a clustered storage location. In a Windows Server 2008 cluster, a storage location cannot be accessed by multiple nodes concurrently. For this reason, Quick Migration requires moving the ownership of the storage location from one node to another, which requires saving the state of the virtual machine as part of the migration. If you run multiple virtual machines on the same storage location concurrently, then Quick Migration of any one of the virtual machines will cause all of them to move as well. VMM only supports one virtual machine on a cluster storage location.

MULTIPLE QUICK MIGRATIONS

The VMM Administrator Console does not support selecting multiple virtual machines using the migration wizard. The wizard uses Intelligent Placement to find a suitable host for one virtual machine at a time.

ENABLING LIVE MIGRATION

With VMM and Windows Server 2008 R2, you can move a virtual machine from one host to another using Live Migration. Live Migration still relies on Microsoft failover clustering and cluster storage but introduces new technology to minimize the downtime of the virtual machine. Live Migration relies on transferring memory state between hosts in real-time as part of the migration, compared to Quick Migration, which requires saving the memory state to storage before the migration occurs. While transferring the memory and disk state of the virtual machine in real-time, the virtual machine can remain in a running state while the migration is in progress. Once memory state is transferred, any state that changed since the last transfer is then copied over. Copying of memory state continues until a small enough delta remains, at which point the virtual machine is paused, migrated to the other node in the cluster, and resumed. The migration itself is very fast, and so depending on the storage type used, the perceived downtime is very small.

To minimize the downtime with Live Migration, you have the choice of using a typical storage location (like the one used by Quick Migration) or a new storage type introduced by Windows Server 2008 R2 called Cluster Shared Volumes (CSV). With Cluster Shared Volume storage, all nodes can access the storage location concurrently, so ownership of the storage location does not need to transfer as part of Live Migration. Without the need to transfer ownership, the actual downtime is less than the typical TCP/IP time-out window. Cluster Shared Volume is not a clustered file system implementation. A volume in this configuration is still owned by only one node of the cluster, but read and write access is allowed by all nodes. Any file metadata operations to the file system (file open, delete, extend) are done only by the node that owns the volume. Any raw data writes can be performed by any node in the cluster. Operations that need to be performed by the owning node of a CSV are automatically directed over the cluster network (which is typically a dedicated network) to the owning node. The user does not need to worry about which node owns what volume. VMM is optimized to always perform any metadata operations through the node that owns the volume.

To simplify access to the shared storage, cluster shared volumes exist under a common namespace: `C:\clusterstorage\`. This directory path exists on all nodes in a cluster. A new location is created under `C:\clusterstorage\` for every new volume that is added to the cluster: `Volume1`, `Volume2`, and so on. Depending on the number of virtual disks you need to store on the CSV, you will need to properly plan the size and performance characteristics of the storage location. This configuration is optimized for the fastest Live Migration with no perceived downtime with only a few storage volumes per cluster. With multiple machines on a single volume, keep in mind that storage performance might be an issue during times of peak load.

On the other hand, if you need to maintain isolation of virtual machines at the storage level and enable Live Migration, then you will need to deploy one virtual machine per storage location. This configuration allows you to use advanced SAN features for backup and recovery while guaranteeing the best storage performance. Since the virtual machine is still on a cluster shared volume, there is no perceived downtime during Live Migration, but you will need to provision many volumes to a cluster.

USING VMOTION

VMware ESX offers migration with no perceived downtime of the virtual machine with VMotion. The technology is similar to Live Migration; the memory state of the virtual machine is copied from host to host in real-time. The basic requirements for VMotion are shared storage and a common network. Advanced features like Dynamic Resource Scheduling (DRS), available only on ESX clusters, use VMotion to migrate virtual machines with no downtime. DRS uses VMotion to migrate virtual machine, balancing resources across cluster nodes with no user intervention or application downtime. Alternatively, you can enable VMM's PRO feature to provide application-aware load balancing, which also leverages VMotion technology on VMware or Live Migration on Hyper-V. VMware also offers high availability using its clustering technology. Once the feature is enabled at the cluster level, VMware will guarantee that virtual machines are started on other nodes of a cluster in the event of a node failure. It's similar to how Microsoft failover clustering for Hyper-V works.

For shared storage, VMware offers Virtual Machine File System (VMFS), which allows read and write access from any computer that is configured to use the volume. This file system is available on any ESX host and does not require an ESX cluster. Volumes formatted with VMFS3 support up to 32 nodes accessing the storage location.

VIRTUAL MACHINE MOBILITY AND DIFFERENT PROCESSOR FAMILIES

The hypervisor needs to ensure that the guest operating system in the virtual machine and applications continue to execute after migration from one host to another. Compatibility is typically an issue if the source and destination hosts have different processors. With different processors, the features exposed to the operating system and applications are not the same, so after a migration, an expected processor feature may no longer be available, resulting in a failure. Hyper-V R2 ensures that a virtual machine cannot be moved between hosts with incompatible processors by comparing processors before the migration. If the destination host processor has the same features as the source, then migration is allowed. Table 7.6 lists various migration cases and their results.

To increase the mobility of the virtual machine across hosts with different processor versions (within the same processor family), Windows Server 2008 R2 Hyper-V introduces *processor compatibility mode*. This feature masks processor feature differences between a source and destination host with processors from different families. With this enabled, you can migrate a virtual machine from a host with Pentium 4 processors to a host with Nehalem processors and back with no compatibility issues. Table 7.7 lists the CPU features that Windows Server 2008 R2 Hyper-V masks.

Please note that VM's cache line flush size is set to 8 bytes when in processor compatibility mode.

Windows Server 2008 R2 Hyper-V implements this feature with no requirement for advanced processor features like Intel VT Flex Migration or AMD-V Extended Migration. Hyper-V performs the CPU feature masking at the software level. The means that privileged and nonprivileged code running in the guest operating system enumerate the same features when using CPUID. Applications that enumerate processor features using CPUID are considered well behaved.

TABLE 7.6:   Processor feature check in Hyper-V R2

HOST A PROCESSOR FEATURES	HOST B PROCESSOR FEATURES	MIGRATION PATH	MIGRATION RESULT
A, B, C	A, B, C	Host A to Host B	Success
		Host B to Host A	Success
A, B, C	A, B	Host A to Host B	Fail
		Host B to Host A	Success
A, B	A, B, C	Host A to Host B	Success
		Host B to Host A	Fail
A, B	B, C	Host A to Host B	Fail
		Host B to Host A	Fail

TABLE 7.7:   Processor features masked by processor compatibility mode

PROCESSOR MANUFACTURER	FEATURES MASKED
Intel	SSSE3, SSE4.1, SSE4.2, POPCNT, Misaligned SSE, XSAVE, AVX
AMD	SSSE3, SSE4.1, SSE4.A, SSE5, POPCNT, LZCNT, Misaligned SSE, AMD 3DNow!, Extended AMD 3DNow!

VMware ESX can also mask CPU features, but only privileged code executing CPUID will see the remaining unmasked features. Nonprivileged code executing CPUID will run directly on hardware, essentially ignoring any masks overridden for the guest. VMware introduced a cluster-level setting called Enhanced VMotion Compatibility (EVC) that leverages Intel and AMD hardware to ensure CPU compatibility cluster wide (for privileged and nonprivileged code) without requiring manual manipulation of override masks. EVC still uses masking, but with the assistance of the underlying physical processors.

Table 7.8 summarizes the various processor limits supported by VMM for each hypervisor.

To enable processor compatibility mode for a virtual machine, follow these steps:

1. Power off the virtual machine.

2. Open the virtual machine properties.

3. Click the Hardware tab.

4. Click the Processor section in the left navigation menu (Figure 7.49).

5. Check the setting labeled Allow migration to a virtual machine host with a different processor version.

6. Click OK to accept the changes and close the properties window.

7. Power on the virtual machine.

TABLE 7.8:   Processor feature limits by hypervisor supported in VMM

HYPERVISOR	PROCESSOR FEATURE LIMITS SUPPORTED
Windows Server 2008 R2 Hyper-V	Limit processor features to increase mobility Limit processor features specific to NT4.0 compatibility
Windows Server 2008 Hyper-V	Limit processor features specific to NT4.0 compatibility
Virtual Server 2005 R2 SP1+	None
ESX 3.0, 3.5	Limit processor features specific to NT4.0 compatibility. Note: VMware offers CPUID masking to help increase the mobility of a virtual machine across different processor families. VMM, however, does not manage these settings.

PLANNED VS. UNPLANNED DOWNTIME

Application downtime (unavailability) is generally referred to as an *outage*. The impact of application unavailability depends on whether or not the event was planned. During planned downtime, administrators will typically schedule work during a predefined maintenance window. The window of time allotted to planned downtime is typically minimal, so administrators need to complete the work quickly and precisely so that the application can be put back into service. If for some reason an application remains unavailable after the planned downtime, it is considered unplanned downtime.

FIGURE 7.49
Virtual machine processor configuration

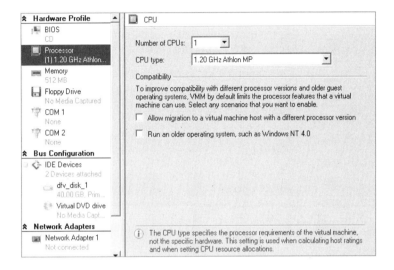

Another example of unplanned downtime is the unexpected failure of an application or physical machine. In this case, to minimize downtime, technologies like Microsoft failover clustering are important to ensure that workloads are available on other nodes in the cluster in the event of a node failure.

With virtual machines, clustering treats the virtual machine container as a single cluster resource group. If a node in the cluster fails to boot up or crashes, all virtual machine resources can quickly and easily recover on another node in the cluster. There is no need for the application running in the virtual machine to be cluster aware. With that said, to avoid downtime of the application altogether, application-specific clustering within the guest OS is required.

SAN Transfer

SAN-based transfers involve the migration of a storage location from one host to another. This migration type relies on Virtual Disk Service (VDS) or N_Port Identification Virtualization (NPIV). VDS is an extensible framework for which SAN vendors can develop providers to enable heterogeneous SAN management through Windows. VMM uses the VDS hardware providers created by SAN vendors to migrate the storage location of a virtual machine (including the virtual machine configuration) with minimal downtime. Unlike with Live Migration and Quick Migration, a Microsoft failover cluster is not required. Using VDS, you can transfer a volume from host to host, host to library, library to host, and even cluster to cluster with no network copy.

NPIV leverages technology available with specific host-based adapters (HBAs) that allows the creation of virtual ports on a single physical fibre channel host bus adapter (HBA) port. Each virtual port can be assigned a unique World Wide Name (WWN) to distinguish it from other ports. With a WWN assigned, the virtual port can be used to assign SAN-based storage from an array to a host or library server.

To set up SAN transfer using VDS hardware providers, follow these steps:

1. For VDS 1.1 and above, install VDS 1.1 on every machine connected to the FC SAN. On Windows Server 2003 R2, open Control Panel, navigate to Add/Remove Windows Components, and select Management And Monitoring Tools. Select Storage Manager For SANs. Restart the machine after the install is complete. If the host being used is Windows Server 2008, then VDS 2.1 is available in-box, so there is no need to install anything.

2. For an MPIO Installation, install the MPIO software as provided by the SAN storage vendor on the host/library.

3. Install the VDS hardware provider developed by the storage array vendor.

4. Create the logical unit on the SAN array and mount it on the virtual machine host. Once mounted, you can create a new virtual machine on the storage location.

5. Once the LUNs have been provisioned to the hosts, create a volume on them. Create VMs on this volume. Try to migrate the VMs. They should do a SAN migration. The placement page should have a green check mark for the transfer type and the job should mention that it's doing a SAN transfer.

To set up SAN transfer using NPIV, follow these steps:

1. Enable NPIV for the HBA installed on the hosts and libraries. (As this is being written, VMM supports NPIV-Enabled HBAs from Emulex, Brocade, and QLogic.)

2. For VDS 1.1 and above, install VDS 1.1 on every machine connected to the FC SAN. On Windows Server 2003 R2, open Control Panel, navigate to Add/Remove Windows Components, and select Management and Monitoring Tools. Select Storage Manager for SANs. Restart the machine after the install is complete. If the host being used is Windows Server 2008, then VDS 2.1 is available in-box, so there is no need to install anything.

3. For MPIO Installation, install the MPIO software as provided by the SAN storage vendor on the host/library.

4. For Provision LUNs, once the basic configurations steps have been done, the LUNs are assigned to the virtual hosts. Now, you need to create the virtual ports on these machines to enable NPIV transfers. Use the vendor-specific utility to create the virtual ports for host and library machines.

5. Once the LUNs have been provisioned to the hosts, create a volume on them. Create VMs on this volume. Try to migrate thee VMs. They should do a SAN migration. The placement page should have a green check mark for the transfer type and the job should mention that it's doing a SAN transfer.

6. Verify that LUNs and vports are created. To verify that the virtual ports have been created, you can run wbemtest from the command line. Using this tool, you can query the root\wmi namespace.

7. Install the VMM agent on the machine, open a WMI query, and type **select * from msfc_fibreportnpivattributes**. Check the property for the number of vports returned by this query to verify. Also open the virtual port properties to see if it's the same world wide port name (WWPN).

To set up SAN transfer using VDS hardware providers, follow these steps:

1. For VDS 1.1 and above, install VDS 1.1 on every machine connected to the FC SAN. On Windows Server 2003 R2, open Control Panel, navigate to Add/Remove Windows Components, and select Management and Monitoring Tools. Select Storage Manager for SANs. Restart the machine after the install is complete. If the host being used is Windows Server 2008, then VDS 2.1 is available in-box, so there is no need to install anything.

2. Select a machine as your Microsoft iSCSI target machine. This is the machine that will host the iSCSI disks.

3. Install the latest Microsoft iSCSI Initiator for Windows 2003.

   If you are using Windows 2008, open Administrative Tools and enable the iSCSI Initiator. Open the Initiator and note its IQN (iSCSI Qualified Name). Log in to the machine that you want to allow to connect to this target. Open Control Panel and select iSCSI Initiator. Switch to the General tab. The Initiator Node Name field contains the name of this particular iSCSI Initiator.

4. For VDS hardware provider installation, the Microsoft VDS hardware provider needs to be installed only on the VMM server box.

5. Create the target and assign a disk to it:

   a. Log in to the machine on which you installed the Microsoft iSCSI software target.
   b. Navigate to Programs, select Administrative Tools, and click Microsoft iSCSI Software Target.
   c. Right-click the iSCSI Targets node and select Create ISCSI Target.
   d. Select a name for the target.
   e. Identify the hosts that will be allowed to connect to this target. For this you will need the IQN (iSCSI qualified name) of the host.
   f. Cut and paste this initiator name in the Create Target Wizard. If you want to use VMM iSCSI migration between two machines, you will need to add the initiators of both the machines to the list.
   g. Right-click the target you just added and select Create Virtual Disk For ISCSI Target.
   h. Follow the wizard and create a disk of the size you want. This is the disk that will be visible to host machines.

6. Log on from Initiator by following these steps:

   a. On the machine on which the initiator is installed, navigate to Control Panel and double-click iSCSI Initiator.
   b. Switch to the Discovery tab.
   c. Select Add and add the FQDN of the machine hosting the Microsoft ISCSI software target.
   d. Click Refresh.
   e. Switch to the Targets tab.
   f. Click Refresh. You should now see the iSCSI targets exposed.
   g. Select the target you just created and click Log On.

7. To test the SAN transfer using VMM, follow these steps:

   a. Open diskmgmt.msc and identify the iSCSI disk.
   b. Add a drive letter or mount point to the disk.

  c. Create a virtual machine on this disk.

  d. Perform a SAN transfer, and to verify, check to see if the placement page marks it as SAN transfer and whether the job mentions SAN transfer.

SAN transfer is not available under the following circumstances:

◆ if any other VM exists on the same LUN

◆ if it shares any files with an existing VM

◆ if the volume on SAN disk is dynamic

Storage Migration

System Center Virtual Machine Manager 2008 R2 introduces a new feature called Quick Storage Migration (QSM) that enables the migration of a running virtual machine from one storage location to another, either on the same host or as part of a host to host migration. QSM relies on Windows Server 2008 R2 Hyper-V and Background Intelligent Transfer Service (BITS).

QSM can move the virtual disks of a running virtual machine from one location to another, independent of storage protocols (iSCSI, FC) or storage type (local, DAS, SAN) with minimal downtime. In situations where Live or Quick Migration is not available, QSM can move a running virtual machine with its associated virtual disks from one virtual machine host to another while performing a storage migration.

QSM uses native Windows platforms and Hyper-V technologies. With the minimal list of requirements, the source and destination possibilities for QSM are significant. There are two types of QSM-based migration: intra-host or across hosts.

You can initiate storage migration from the Administrator Console as follows:

  1. Right-click a running virtual machine in the Administrator Console and select Migrate Storage (Figure 7.50).

FIGURE 7.50
The Migrate Storage option

2. In the Select Path dialog, specify the path where the virtual machine configuration file should be stored.

If you decide to change the path for any of the virtual disks attached to the virtual machine, you must specify a new path for the virtual machine configuration. This is required, so you need to specify a new path for the virtual machine configuration files. If you plan to consolidate all virtual disks into the folder that holds the virtual machine configuration file, make sure the virtual disks file path is the same as the virtual machine configuration path.

VMM takes a Hyper-V snapshot of the running virtual machine. This will create a differencing disk for each VHD connected to the VM. All disk write operations from that point forward go into the differencing disk. The original base VHD is no longer changing since it is in a read-only state. With the base VHD in a read-only state, VMM starts to transfer the file from the source location to the target location using BITS. This represents the bulk of the data that needs to be transferred, and the VM remains running during this transfer. In addition, QSM does not depend on storage types, and the user is free to select any storage destination that is accessible to the Hyper-V host. Once the base virtual disk is transferred, the virtual machine is put into saved state. In saved state, VMM can transfer the differencing disk created by the snapshot and memory associated with the saved state to the destination location for the VM. Once all the files are transferred, VMM exports and then reimports the virtual machine on the same Hyper-V host with any necessary modifications to the configuration. The snapshot created is merged back into the base VHDs and the virtual machine is restarted from saved state. Table 7.9 compares QSM to Storage VMotion.

TABLE 7.9: Comparing QSM to VMware Storage VMotion

	VMM 2008 R2 + WINDOWS SERVER 2008 R2 AND HYPER-V	**VMWARE (VCENTER 2.5 + ESX 3.5)**
Migration of virtual machines across two hosts with independent storage	Supported	Not supported
Migration of virtual machines with snapshots	Supported	Not supported
Migration of virtual machines with virtual disks	Supported	Supported (persistent mode)
Migration of virtual machines with pass-through disks (RDM)	Not supported (Hyper-V does not support snapshots of pass-through disks.)	Supported
Sufficient resources to support two instances of the virtual machines running concurrently	Not required	Required
Additional license required	None	VMotion License

TABLE 7.9: Comparing QSM to VMware Storage VMotion *(Continued)*

	VMM 2008 R2 + WINDOWS SERVER 2008 R2 AND HYPER-V	VMWARE (VCENTER 2.5 + ESX 3.5)
Minimum requirements for access to source and target storage locations	Storage migration; visibility to both source and target storage locations required for host	Minimum requirements for access to source and target storage locations
Number of concurrent storage migrations allowed	10	4
Storage migrations supported in the Administrator Console	Yes (QSM and Storage VMotion)	No
Storage migrations supported in the CLI	Yes (QSM and Storage VMotion)	Yes
Protocol agnostic	Yes	Yes
Support for migrations of VMs and storage between hosts with different processor versions (same manufacturer)	Yes (no requirement for Intel VT Flex Migration or AMD-V Extended Migration)	Not applicable

Placement of a Virtual Machine

VMM simplifies the creation of virtual machines and performs all the heavy lifting when moving them between hosts. Intelligent Placement is the technology that recommends which host to place the virtual machine on. With other products, placement typically centers on simply choosing a host before creating a new virtual machine or migrating an existing one. This approach gives you no visibility into the actual capabilities of the host you selected and the effect of deploying the virtual machine to that host. For example, suppose you select a host with two processors and 2 GB of available RAM. You then attempt to create a virtual machine with 4 GB of RAM. Some hypervisors would allow this oversubscription of RAM while others won't. In either case, if the application that will run in the virtual machine needs the full 4 GB of RAM, then the host selection is not adequate. With VMM, before selecting the destination host, you model your virtual machine configuration with the exact specifications you need based on the intended workload (for example, SQL). Intelligent Placement takes that model along with the existing load of the host and any host-level resource reserves and calculates a star rating for each available host. The more stars a host has, the more adequate it is for hosting the new virtual machine. The maximum stars for a host is four.

The star rating is simply a suggestion produced by the Capacity Planner algorithms that VMM provides. You do not have to select the host with the most stars even though that's what VMM deems to be the best match. The decision on which host to select is left up to you. In fact, you can select any host from the list. The only time you cannot select a host is if Intelligent Placement knows for a fact that the virtual machine is not compatible with the host. For example, you cannot place a virtual machine that need four processors on a host with only two processors. Other times, Intelligent Placement will show no stars for a host but still allow you to select it. This is considered a soft block. VMM provides reasons why a host is not suitable.

Intelligent Placement is used in the following scenarios:

◆ New virtual machine (from template, from disk, from virtual machine)

◆ New P2V

◆ New V2V

◆ Migrate virtual machine (Quick Migration, Live Migration, storage migration, network-based migration)

◆ Deploy virtual machine from library

Virtual Machine Configuration

The configuration of a virtual machine is a big factor in how Intelligent Placement rates a host. Some virtual machine configurations are hypervisor specific, so there is no reason to give star ratings for incompatible hypervisors. For example, ESX requires that you place the bootable virtual disk on a SCSI controller. If you configure a virtual machine with no SCSI controllers, Intelligent Placement will inform you that the configuration is not supported on the hypervisor, and as a result, hosts running that hypervisor will be given zero starts. In the configuration, you can also specify a level of service for the virtual machine. Making a virtual machine highly available requires that you deploy it to a cluster. Table 7.10 lists the virtual machine settings and properties with the most impact on Intelligent Placement.

TABLE 7.10:   Virtual machine settings and properties that impact Intelligent Placement

SETTING/PROPERTY	IMPACT
Processor Count	Hosts with less processors receive zero stars.
Memory Amount	Hosts with less available memory receive zero stars.
Virtual Disks On IDE Controller	ESX hosts do not support virtual disks in the IDE controller.
Virtual Disks On SCSI Controller	Hyper-V does not support virtual disks, *only* on the SCSI controller. At least one virtual disk is required on the IDE controller.
High Availability	Hosts that are not part of a cluster receive zero stars.
Virtual Disk Size	Hosts with less space available than the size of the virtual disk(s) attached to the virtual machine receive zero stars.

Host Reservation

VMM can reserve host resources, which Intelligent Placement takes into account when calculating a star rating for a host. The reservation is not done at the hypervisor level. This means that the reservations you set in VMM will not change the configuration of the hypervisor. Instead, Intelligent Placement will simply discount the reserves from free resources. Host reserves can be set at the host and host group level. Reserves are useful if you want to ensure that you keep enough spare capacity around to handle spikes in demand or to handle failover scenarios. If you have a cluster, VMM supports the cluster reserve property for a host cluster that specifies the number of node failures a cluster must be able to sustain and continue to support all the running virtual machines deployed on the host cluster. Placement will ensure that the cluster does not become overcommitted in order to honor the cluster reserve. In effect, VMM manages the failover reservations for you. Table 7.11 lists all the host reserve settings available and their default values.

TABLE 7.11:   Host reserves and default values

HOST RESERVE	DEFAULT VALUE
CPU percentage	20
Memory (in MB)	1,024
Disk space (in MB)	100
Maximum disk I/O per second (IOPS)	10,000
Network capacity percentage	10

To change host reserves settings, follow these steps:

1. Right-click either a host or a host group.

2. Click Properties and then Reserves for a host or Host Reserves for a host group.

3. After modifying the settings for the host properties (Figure 7.51), click OK to save and close the window.

Modeled Load and Existing Load

Another factor that contributes to host star rating results is the load on the host. As part of Intelligent Placement, VMM considers the existing load on the host generated by the virtual machines already running on it and overhead from management agents. Intelligent Placement will use the Capacity Planner algorithms to model the effect of deploying the virtual machine to that host. Taking into account the existing load plus the new modeled load, hosts with fewer resources available due to higher workload receive fewer stars when rated against other hosts with the same configuration but more available resources. Depending on what resource is least available, Intelligent Placement may hard-block the deployment of the virtual machine (for example, no memory available, no disk available) or simply warn you that a resource is not available (for example, network locations available on the host do not match virtual machine configuration). The performance data required to calculate star ratings is collected by VMM, so there is no need to deploy another product to get this information. VMM will retain up to seven days' worth of performance data for this purpose.

FIGURE 7.51
Host properties

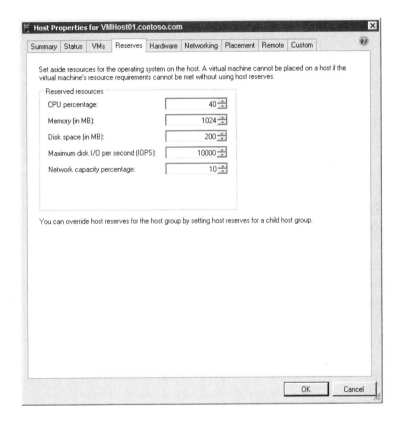

Customizing Ratings

Based on the workload that will execute in the virtual machine, you may need to customize the workload that is modeled for Intelligent Placement. If a particular application is very CPU intensive, you'll want to make sure Intelligent Placement takes that into account when calculating star ratings. This way, when star ratings are calculated, you know with a high level of confidence that the host you select is the most appropriate for the workload. VMM provides three dimensions for customizing the rating results. The first is by specifying whether VMM should preference hosts with the most resources available or hosts that meet the virtual machine's requirements with the least free resources available. The former is referred to as *load balancing*. Over a large deployment of virtual machines, VMM will spread virtual machines to as many hosts as possible to avoid overloading any one host. The latter is referred to as *resource maximization*. In this case, VMM will deploy virtual machines to the fewest hosts possible. This approach maximizes the utilization of each host and minimizes the number of hosts required to run the same number of virtual machines.

The second way to customize ratings is to assign an importance or weight to the main resources measured by VMM: CPU, memory, disk I/O, network utilization. For resource importance, Intelligent Placement will simply place more or less importance on a particular resource. The final way you can customize ratings is to specify an expected load generated by the CPU. This differs from resource importance because here you specify an actual amount of resources that will be consumed by the virtual machine, not just how important the resource is compared to others. For VM load, you specify an amount based on different units for each resource.

Table 7.12 summarizes the different ways to customize Intelligent Placement star ratings.

TABLE 7.12:   Customize Intelligent Placement

CUSTOMIZATION	SETTING
Placement Goal	Load Balancing: Preference hosts with the most resources available Resource Maximization: Preference hosts that meet the virtual machine's requirements with the least free resources available
Resource Important (rated from Not Important to Most Important)	CPU Memory Free Disk I/O Network Utilization
VM Load	CPU: Expected Utilization (in %) Disk: Required physical disk space (in GB), expected disk I/O per second (IOPS) Network: Expected network utilization (megabits per second)

An excellent example of how to utilize star rating customization involves performing a P2V of an existing machine. You know the performance characteristics of the workload when it is running on a physical machine, so you can fine-tune Intelligent Placement to give you the most suitable host based on performance characteristics that you already know about the machine. So if you plan to convert a SQL workload that is CPU intensive, you can customize Intelligent Placement as follows:

1. In the New P2V Wizard, select an existing machine.

2. Progress through the wizard until you get to the Select Host page. The initial star ratings presented are using the default settings.

3. Click the Customize Ratings button to open the Customize Ratings dialog box.

4. For Placement Goal, leave the default setting.

5. For Resource Importance, set the slider to the far right for CPU Usage (see Figure 7.52).

6. Click the VM Load tab.

7. Based on historic performance data collected beforehand, set Expected Utilization to 100% (see Figure 7.53).

FIGURE 7.52
Customizing rating
settings for P2V
host rating

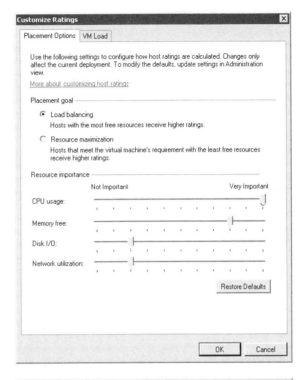

FIGURE 7.53
VM load settings for
P2V host rating

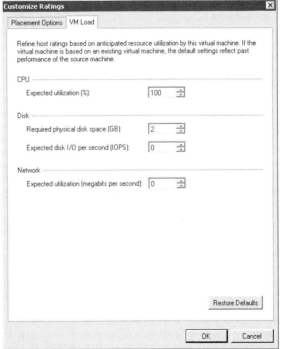

8. Click OK to accept the changes and close the Customize Ratings dialog box. Star ratings are now recalculated and hosts are re-ordered accordingly.

The Bottom Line

Create and delete a virtual machine.   VMM provides several ways to create new virtual machines using different sources: template, VHD, or virtual machine.

Master It

1. Explain the three virtual disk types supported by Hyper-V.

2. What is the difference between Network Location and Network Tag?

3. What is the purpose of a template that does not require customization?

4. Why does VMM delete the virtual machine configuration and virtual hard disk files?

Convert a physical machine or non-Windows hypervisor virtual machine to a Windows hypervisor virtual machine.   P2V can capture the operating system, application stack, and configuration from an existing machine and create a virtual machine. V2V converts existing virtual machines running on ESX to Virtual Server or Hyper-V.

Master It

1. Explain how VMM uses `BlockList.xml` during P2V.

2. List the VMDK file types supported by V2V.

3. Can you select a virtual machine as a P2V source? If so, why would you ever do this?

Migrate a virtual machine between hosts.   With VMM, migration of a virtual machine between hosts is possible using various in-box technologies.

Master It

1. Explain the difference between Quick Storage Migration and Live Migration.

2. In Windows Server 2008 R2, explain the advantage of using a CSV storage location for Live Migration.

3. List all the transfer types in VMM's portfolio.

Chapter 8

Automation Using PowerShell

Virtual Machine Manager is one of the first Microsoft software products to fully adopt Windows PowerShell and offer its users a complete management interface tailored for scripting. From the first release of VMM 2007, the Virtual Machine Manager Administrator Console was written on top of Windows PowerShell, utilizing the many cmdlets that VMM offers. This approach made VMM very extensible and partner friendly and allows customers to accomplish anything that VMM offers in the Administrator Console via scripts and automation. Windows PowerShell is also the only public application programming interface (API) that VMM offers, giving both developers and administrators a single point of reference for managing VMM. Writing scripts that interface with VMM, Hyper-V, or Virtual Server can be made very easy using Windows PowerShell's support for WMI, .NET, and COM.

In this chapter, you will learn to:

◆ Describe the main benefits that PowerShell offers for VMM

◆ Use the VMM PowerShell cmdlets

◆ Create scheduled PowerShell scripts

VMM and Windows PowerShell

System Center Virtual Machine Manager (VMM) 2007, the first release of VMM, was one of the first products to develop its entire graphical user interface (the VMM Administrator Console) on top of Windows PowerShell (previously known as Monad). This approach proved very advantageous for customers that wanted all of the VMM functionality to be available through some form of an API. The VMM team made early bets on Windows PowerShell as its public management interface, and they have not been disappointed with the results. With its consistent grammar, the great integration with .NET, and the abundance of cmdlets, PowerShell is quickly becoming the management interface of choice for enterprise applications.

Unlike other traditional public APIs that focus on developers, VMM's PowerShell interface is designed for the administrator. With the extensive help contents and the well-documented System Center Virtual Machine Manager Scripting Guide that is available from the Microsoft Download Center, the VMM team positioned its cmdlets to be the premier way of scripting in your virtualization environment. In addition to the VMM cmdlets, your scripts can be enhanced by the built-in support that Windows PowerShell has for a variety of data stores, like the filesystem, the Registry, and WMI.

Installing the VMM PowerShell Cmdlets

Even though the VMM PowerShell interface does not have its own installer, it is always installed as part of the VMM Administrator Console setup. VMM Setup will install the 32-bit version of the Administrator Console on 32-bit systems and the 64-bit version of the Administrator Console on 64-bit systems. Due to the nature of the VMM cmdlets, some utilize both native and .NET binaries in their implementation. This approach prohibits the VMM PowerShell cmdlets from being architecture independent, which means that only 32-bit PowerShell cmdlets will work on a 32-bit system. The 64-bit PowerShell cmdlets have the same issue and will work on only a 64-bit system. Any process that attempts to load the PowerShell runspace and invoke the VMM cmdlets needs to be aware of this restriction and factor this limitation in the design.

VMM 2008 is certified to work with both Windows PowerShell version 1.0 and version 2.0. Windows PowerShell is already included as part of Windows Server 2008 and Windows Server 2008 R2, and it can be downloaded for free from the Microsoft website at the following location:

http://www.microsoft.com/windowsserver2003/technologies/management/powershell/download.mspx

Windows PowerShell 1.0 officially supports Windows XP Service Pack 2, Windows Server 2003, Windows Vista, and Windows Server 2008. Windows PowerShell 2.0 was released with the Windows 7 and Windows Server 2008 R2 operating systems. PowerShell 2.0 will be eventually pack-ported to other operating systems as well.

When you first launch Windows PowerShell in your system and import the VMM PowerShell snap-in, you will be prompted to add Microsoft Corporation to the list of trusted publishers, as per Figure 8.1. Enter **A** in this case for Always Run.

FIGURE 8.1
Adding Microsoft Corporation to the list of trusted publishers for Windows PowerShell scripts

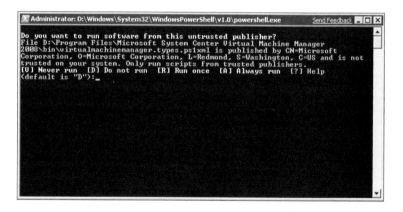

It is possible Windows PowerShell will still prevent you from running scripts in your system, so you need to set the proper execution policy for scripts before any Windows PowerShell scripts are allowed to run on your computer. This can be achieved using the Set-ExecutionPolicy cmdlet. Figure 8.2 shows the help contents of this cmdlet. Type in **get-help Set-ExecutionPolicy -detailed | more** for more information on the policy options. To invoke the Set-ExecutionPolicy cmdlet, you need to run Windows PowerShell as Administrator.

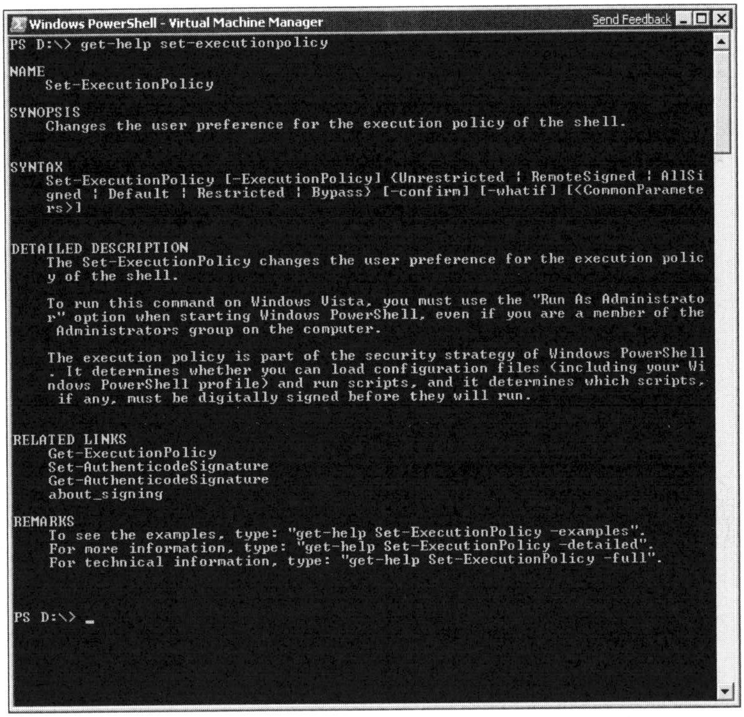

FIGURE 8.2

Setting the execution policy for Windows PowerShell

Exposing the VMM Cmdlets

To get started with VMM and Windows PowerShell, open a console window that has the VMM PowerShell snap-in loaded. There are a few ways to accomplish this, as shown here:

1. Click Start ➤ All Programs ➤ Microsoft System Center ➤ Virtual Machine Manager 2008 R2 and launch Windows PowerShell - Virtual Machine Manager. This command will automatically launch Windows PowerShell version 1.0 and pass as input the VMM PowerShell Console file located at

   ```
   %SystemDrive%\Program Files\Microsoft System Center Virtual
     Machine Manager 2008 R2\bin\cli.psc1
   ```

2. Open a regular Windows PowerShell console window and add the VMM snap-in using the following command. Once the VMM snap-in is added, you can use all the VMM cmdlets.

   ```
   Add-PSSnapin "Microsoft.SystemCenter.VirtualMachineManager"
   ```

3. Windows PowerShell can also be launched from the Administrator Console by clicking the PowerShell button in the toolbar of the main view.

Once the VMM PowerShell snap-in is added, you can get a list of all VMM cmdlets using the get-command cmdlet.

```
# This cmdlet will get all cmdlets that can be executed by the currently
# loaded PowerShell snapins
Get-command

# This cmdlet will list only the cmdlets exposed by the VMM Windows
# PowerShell snapin
get-command -module "Microsoft.SystemCenter.VirtualMachineManager"
```

Getting Help on VMM Cmdlets

If you have the name of a VMM cmdlet, you can get more information on it, including a list of examples. The following code shows how to get the definition of the Refresh-VM cmdlet:

```
PS D:\> get-command refresh-vm


CommandType     Name                           Definition
-----------     ----                           ----------
Cmdlet          Refresh-VM                     Refresh-VM [-VM] <VM> [-RunA...
```

The following code shows how to get the detailed view of the parameters that can be passed to the Refresh-VM cmdlet:

```
PS D:\> get-command refresh-vm | format-list

Name             : Refresh-VM
CommandType      : Cmdlet
Definition       : Refresh-VM [-VM] <VM> [-RunAsynchronously] [-JobVariable <St
                   ring>] [-PROTipID <Nullable`1>] [-Verbose] [-Debug] [-ErrorA
                   ction <ActionPreference>] [-WarningAction <ActionPreference>
                   ] [-ErrorVariable <String>] [-WarningVariable <String>] [-Ou
                   tVariable <String>] [-OutBuffer <Int32>]

Path             :
AssemblyInfo     :
DLL              : D:\Program Files\Microsoft System Center Virtual Machine Man
                   ager 2008 R2\bin\Microsoft.SystemCenter.VirtualMachineManager.d
                   ll
HelpFile         : Microsoft.SystemCenter.VirtualMachineManager.dll-Help.xml
ParameterSets    : {[-VM] <VM> [-RunAsynchronously] [-JobVariable <String>] [-P
                   ROTipID <Nullable`1>] [-Verbose] [-Debug] [-ErrorAction <Act
                   ionPreference>] [-WarningAction <ActionPreference>] [-ErrorV
                   ariable <String>] [-WarningVariable <String>] [-OutVariable
                   <String>] [-OutBuffer <Int32>]}
ImplementingType : Microsoft.SystemCenter.VirtualMachineManager.Cmdlets.Refresh
                   VmCmdlet
```

```
Verb            : Refresh
Noun            : VM
```

The following code shows how to get the help for the Refresh-VM cmdlet:

```
PS D:\> get-help refresh-vm

NAME
    Refresh-VM

SYNOPSIS
    Refreshes the properties of a virtual machine so that the Virtual Machine M
    anager Administrator Console displays updated information about the virtual
    machine.

SYNTAX
    Refresh-VM [-VM] [<String VM>] [-JobVariable <String>] [-PROTipID <Guid>] [
    -RunAsynchronously] [<CommonParameters>]

DETAILED DESCRIPTION
    Refreshes the properties of a virtual machine so that the Virtual Machine M
    anager Administrator Console displays updated information about the virtual
     machine. The updated properties include Name, Location, Status, OperatingS
    ystem, and other properties.

RELATED LINKS
    Get-VM
    Refresh-LibraryShare
    Refresh-VMHost

REMARKS
    To see the examples, type: "get-help Refresh-VM -examples".
    For more information, type: "get-help Refresh-VM -detailed".
    For technical information, type: "get-help Refresh-VM -full".
```

The next code shows the different parameters that can be passed to the get-help cmdlet:

```
# To show detailed information on the refresh-vm cmdlet, use the
# -detailed parameter
PS D:\> get-help Refresh-VM -detailed

# This command will show examples on using the cmdlet refresh-vm
PS D:\> get-help Refresh-VM -examples

# This command will show the full information on using the refresh-vm cmdlet
PS D:\> get-help Refresh-VM -full
```

Some VMM cmdlets offer different parameters sets. In Figure 8.3 and Figure 8.4, you can see the different parameter sets for the Get-VM cmdlet. For example, you can get a list of virtual machines (VMs) by a matching name, by using the ID of the VM object, or by executing the cmdlet against a specific host. Any parameter that is included in square brackets is optional. If a required parameter is not specified, PowerShell will prompt for it as Figure 8.5 shows.

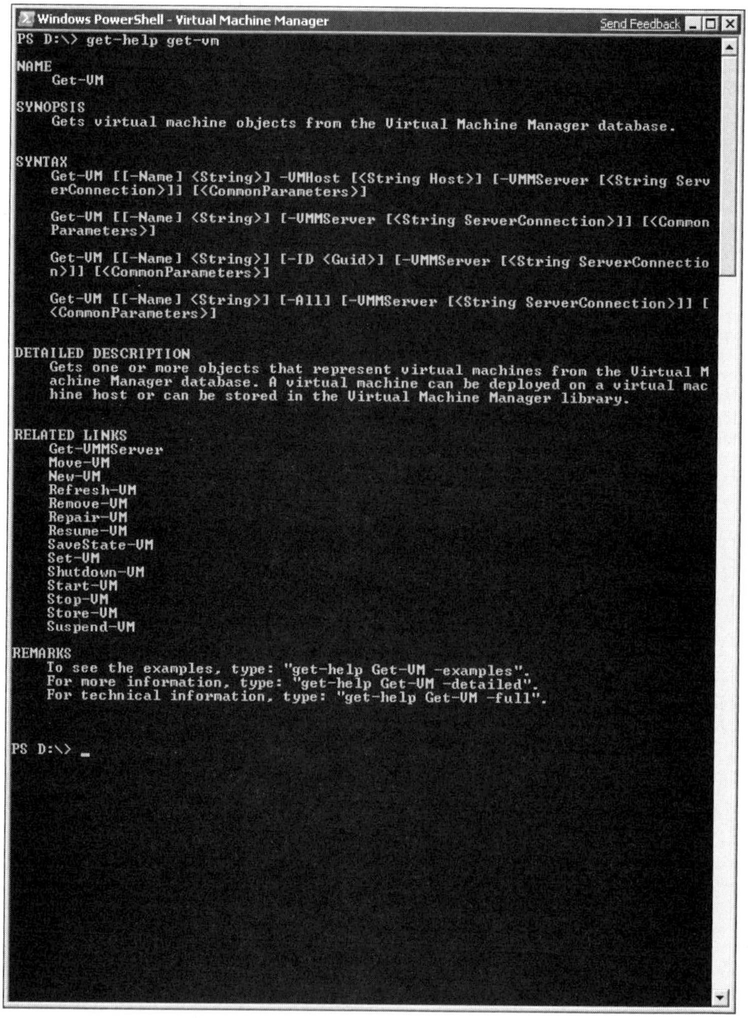

FIGURE 8.3
Get-VM's different parameter sets

```
Windows PowerShell - Virtual Machine Manager                    Send Feedback  _ □ ×
PS D:\> get-help get-vm

NAME
    Get-VM

SYNOPSIS
    Gets virtual machine objects from the Virtual Machine Manager database.

SYNTAX
    Get-VM [[-Name] <String>] -VMHost [<String Host>] [-VMMServer [<String Serv
    erConnection>]] [<CommonParameters>]

    Get-VM [[-Name] <String>] [-VMMServer [<String ServerConnection>]] [<Common
    Parameters>]

    Get-VM [[-Name] <String>] [-ID <Guid>] [-VMMServer [<String ServerConnectio
    n>]] [<CommonParameters>]

    Get-VM [[-Name] <String>] [-All] [-VMMServer [<String ServerConnection>]] [
    <CommonParameters>]

DETAILED DESCRIPTION
    Gets one or more objects that represent virtual machines from the Virtual M
    achine Manager database. A virtual machine can be deployed on a virtual mac
    hine host or can be stored in the Virtual Machine Manager library.

RELATED LINKS
    Get-VMMServer
    Move-VM
    New-VM
    Refresh-VM
    Remove-VM
    Repair-VM
    Resume-VM
    SaveState-VM
    Set-VM
    Shutdown-VM
    Start-VM
    Stop-VM
    Store-VM
    Suspend-VM

REMARKS
    To see the examples, type: "get-help Get-VM -examples".
    For more information, type: "get-help Get-VM -detailed".
    For technical information, type: "get-help Get-VM -full".


PS D:\> _
```

Using the VMM Cmdlets

By now you know how to get a list of all VMM cmdlets and their descriptions. To get more information about each cmdlet, including details on each parameter and examples on how to invoke them, you can use the get-help cmdlet with the -full, -examples, or -detailed parameter.

FIGURE 8.4
Get-VM's required
parameters

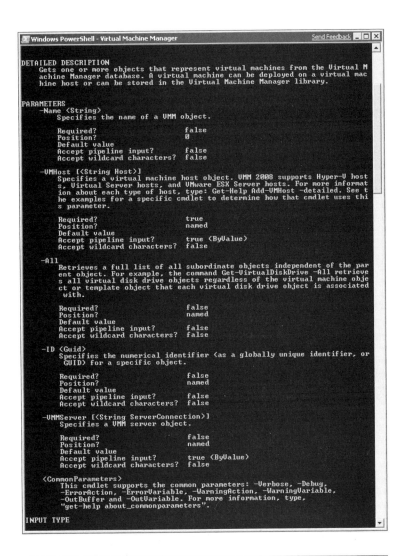

FIGURE 8.4
Get-VM's required
parameters

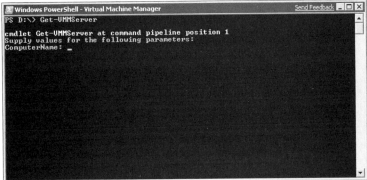

FIGURE 8.5
Windows PowerShell
will prompt for required
parameters.

The Virtual Machine Manager Scripting Guide is also a great reference for learning how to use Windows PowerShell with VMM. VMM published a scripting guide with both VMM 2007 and VMM 2008. You can find the scripting guides at `http://www.microsoft.com/downloads/details.aspx?familyid=3DA5BA7E-AD72-4D2C-B573-1B74894D1DDF&displaylang=en` and at `http://technet.microsoft.com/en-us/library/cc764259.aspx`. A scripting guide update for VMM 2008 R2 should be available on the System Center Virtual Machine Manager TechCenter shortly.

Appendix B, "VMM Windows PowerShell Object Properties and VMM Cmdlet Descriptions," contains a reference list of Virtual Machine Manager cmdlets and a short description of their functionality.

Noun Properties

Windows PowerShell uses a verb-noun format for the names of the cmdlets. The verb identifies the action to be performed, such as *get*, *add*, *set*, *remove*, or *new*. The Windows PowerShell team has a published list of common verbs for cmdlet developers to adhere to.

The noun identifies the type of object on which the cmdlet will operate. Example nouns include VM (virtual machine), VMHost (virtualization host), VMHostCluster (Failover Cluster), and VirtualNetwork (virtual network). In this section, we will look at three of the most frequently used nouns in VMM and explain their property values.

VMM cmdlets will in most cases return back to the pipeline the noun of the cmdlet. This allows you to use the pipeline and combine multiple VMM cmdlets for more complicated scripts. For Get-* cmdlets, like Get-VM for example, it is possible for the value that is returned to the pipeline to be a collection instead of a single object. You can check the type of the return value using the code snippet in the next paragraph.

POWERSHELL PIPELINE

The PowerShell pipeline is similar in concept to the "pipeline" seen in Unix shell scripting environments. The pipeline allows you to create a multitude of single-purpose and easy-to-understand cmdlets and then combine them to achieve a bigger task (just like building blocks).

The following code shows how to invoke the Get-VM cmdlet and check the result:

```
# Execute Get-VM on a VM that does not exist. In this case $vm should be null
$vm = Get-VM "VMDoesNotExist"
$vm -eq $null


# Execute Get-VM as a targeted get for a single VM. In this case
# the result should not be an array
$vm = Get-VM "virtualmachine1"
$vm -is [Array]


# Execute Get-VM to get all VMs in the system. In this case the
# result may be an array
$vm = Get-VM
$vm -is [Array]
```

VMMSERVER OBJECT

VMMServer represents the object that contains the connection to the Virtual Machine Manager. This object also contains some of the global settings of the VMM server installation and environment. Once a connection to the VMM server is established, the connection is cached and future cmdlets that need a connection object will automatically use the existing cached connection.

To see the VMMServer noun and a list of its properties with an explanation for each property, see Appendix B.

VM OBJECT

VM represents the object that contains a virtual machine instance in Virtual Machine Manager.

To see the virtual machine noun and its properties, see Appendix B. Each property also contains a definition for its value or values.

VMHOST OBJECT

VMHost represents the object that contains a physical computer that is a virtual machine host. A virtual machine host could be a Virtual Server host, a Hyper-V host, or a VMware ESX host. The following code shows you how to get a list of all the properties of a host and inspect their values:

```
PS D:\> $vmhost = Get-VMHost "hostname"
PS D:\> $vmhost

Windows PowerShell will output all the properties and values for the
 supplied host.
```

To see the VMHost noun and its properties, see Appendix B. Each property also contains a definition for its value or values.

Leveraging the Public PowerShell API

Virtual Machine Manager uses the Windows PowerShell cmdlets for VMM as the single point of entry for VMM. Developers can integrate with VMM programmatically by leveraging the publicly available VMM PowerShell cmdlets. Calling cmdlets programmatically is not much different than invoking them in a Windows PowerShell command window. In this section, we will look at programmatically invoking the cmdlets and give you example code to achieve this type of integration with VMM.

PROGRAMMATICALLY CALLING THE VMM CMDLETS

The set of Windows PowerShell cmdlets for VMM is the only supported API for integrating with VMM. To programmatically call the cmdlets and manage VMM, you would need to create a PowerShell runspace and invoke the cmdlets in the same way you would if you were using the Windows PowerShell command window.

To start, you need to know the path to the VMM assemblies that are needed to resolve the VMM objects and cmdlets. You can find the installation path for the Virtual Machine Manager Administrator Console under the Registry key HKLM\Software\Microsoft\Microsoft System Center Virtual Machine Manager Administrator Console\Setup. The InstallPath value of this Registry key contains the root of the installation path for VMM. The four assemblies that are needed for the programmatic usage of VMM cmdlets are located in the bin folder of the installation directory. These binaries are listed here:

- `Microsoft.SystemCenter.VirtualMachineManager.dll`
- `Remoting.dll`
- `Utils.dll`
- `Errors.dll`

Because none of these VMM assemblies are listed in the Global Assembly Cache (GAC), if you want your application to be able to resolve them without copying the binaries, you need to use an assembly resolve handler. The following code shows you how to add such a handler and how to properly load the correct assembly. The `InstallPath` value from the Registry is needed for this purpose:

```
// Add the code for the assembly resolver before any of the VMM binaries
are invoked.
Thread.GetDomain().AssemblyResolve += new
 ResolveEventHandler(VMMResolveEventHandler);

// In this example, we automatically resolve everything to
the VirtualMachineManager DLL. A smart resolver would look
at the args.Name and match the assembly to be resolved with
its proper full path.
static Assembly VMMResolveEventHandler(object sender, ResolveEventArgs args)
{
    return Assembly.LoadFrom("D:\Program Files\Microsoft System
 Center Virtual Machine Manager 2008 R2\bin\
 Microsoft.SystemCenter.VirtualMachineManager.dll");
}
```

In addition to the required binaries, the WCF port number of the VMM server is needed to establish a successful connection. You can find the TCP port number for WCF under the VMM server Registry key `HKLM\Software\Microsoft\Microsoft System Center Virtual Machine Manager Server\Settings`. The `IndigoTcpPort` value contains the port number that all VMM clients need to use to connect.

Now we have all the data we need to connect to VMM and execute some PowerShell cmdlets. It is recommended to use a utility to create a wrapper on top of the VMM PowerShell snap-in. Such a wrapper would produce a familiar .NET interface for developers and provide type safety for all PowerShell cmdlets. There are a few publicly available tools to create such wrappers. In the following example, I am using the native PowerShell implementation, directly invoking cmdlets using their string names. You can see that any mistakes in this code will not be caught by the compiler.

Listing 8.1 is a complete program that creates a PowerShell runspace, adds the VMM Power-Shell snap-in to it, creates a connection to the VMM server on default port 8100, and gets a list of all VMs that the current user is authorized to see. The list of VMs returned is written on the console window as in Figure 8.6.

FIGURE 8.6
Output from the
programmatic
invocation
of Get-VM

LISTING 8.1:   Invoking the VMM cmdlets programmatically

```
// Add the proper namespaces
using System;
using System.Management.Automation;
using Microsoft.VirtualManager.Utils;
using Microsoft.SystemCenter.VirtualMachineManager;
using Microsoft.SystemCenter.VirtualMachineManager.Cmdlets;
using Microsoft.SystemCenter.VirtualMachineManager.Remoting;
using Microsoft.VirtualManager.Remoting;
using System.Management.Automation.Runspaces;
using System.Collections.ObjectModel;

namespace ConsoleApplication
{
    class Program
    {
        static void Main(string[] args)
        {
            // Create a default RunspaceConfiguration
            RunspaceConfiguration config = RunspaceConfiguration.Create();

            // Add the VMM PowerShell snapin
            PSSnapInException warning = null;
            config.AddPSSnapIn("Microsoft.SystemCenter.VirtualMachineManager",
out warning);
            if (warning != null)
            {
                Console.WriteLine(warning.Message);
                return;
            }
```

```
            // Create the Runspace using this configuration
            Runspace runspace = RunspaceFactory.CreateRunspace(config);
            try
            {
                runspace.Open();
                Command psCommand = null;
                ServerConnection serverConnection = null;
                VM vmObject = null;

                // Create a Pipeline
                using (Pipeline pipeline = runspace.CreatePipeline())
                {
                    // Call the get-vmmserver cmdlet to get a connection to VMM
                    // If you plan to use VMM as a platform and develop
                    // a separate GUI on top of VMM, you might also want to
                    // set the RetainDeletedObjects and RetainObjectCache
                    // properties of the Get-VMMServer cmdlet. For more
                    // information on these properties, look at the help
                    // for the cmdlet.
                    psCommand = new Command("Get-VMMServer");
                    psCommand.Parameters.Add("ComputerName", "localhost");
                    psCommand.Parameters.Add("TCPPort", "8100");
                    pipeline.Commands.Add(psCommand);

                    // Invoke the cmdlet
                    Collection<PSObject> psObjList = pipeline.Invoke();
                    serverConnection =
(ServerConnection)(psObjList[0].BaseObject);
                }

                // Create a Pipeline
                using (Pipeline pipeline = runspace.CreatePipeline())
                {
                    // Call the get-vm cmdlet to get all VMs in the system
                    psCommand = new Command("Get-VM");
                    pipeline.Commands.Add(psCommand);

                    // Invoke the cmdlet
                    Collection<PSObject> psObjList = pipeline.Invoke();

                    // Enumerate the results of the cmdlet
                    foreach (PSObject obj in psObjList)
                    {
                        vmObject = (VM)obj.BaseObject;
                        Console.WriteLine("VM Name: {0},
ID: {1}", vmObject.Name, vmObject.ID);
```

```
                }
            }
        }
        finally
        {
            // Close the runspace if it is already open
            if (runspace.RunspaceStateInfo.State == RunspaceState.Opened)
            {
                runspace.Close();
            }
        }
    }
}
```

When trying to programmatically code against VMM, it is useful to understand and know all the different values and properties for the various VMM classes and enumerations. To get familiar with the nouns and their properties, you can load the Microsoft.SystemCenter.VirtualMachineManager.dll into the Object Browser of Visual Studio and start looking into the classes defined in this assembly.

The following code snippet shows the Status property of a virtual machine object as defined by the VM class. Figure 8.7 shows the list of possible values for the VMComputerSystemState enumeration.

```
public class VM
{
    public VMComputerSystemState Status { get; }
}
```

The Host class has multiple state objects. In the following code snippet, along with Figure 8.8 and Figure 8.9, we show you how to get the CommunicationState and the ComputerState of a host object and the possible values for the two enumerations.

```
public class Host
{
    public CommunicationState CommunicationState { get; }
    public ComputerState ComputerState { get; }
}
```

CREATING POWERSHELL SCRIPTS

PowerShell scripts are simple text files that you can author in Notepad and save with the file-name extension .ps1. You can also choose to download a PowerShell interactive development environment (IDE). Such an IDE will accelerate development through rich syntax coloring, IntelliSense, tabbing, and rich debugging.

FIGURE 8.7

Getting the state enumeration for a VM

```
Microsoft.VirtualManager.Utils.VMComputerSystemState
using System;
using System.ComponentModel;

namespace Microsoft.VirtualManager.Utils
{
    [TypeConverter(typeof(VMStateHelper))]
    public enum VMComputerSystemState
    {
        Running = 0,
        PowerOff = 1,
        PoweringOff = 2,
        Saved = 3,
        Saving = 4,
        Restoring = 5,
        Paused = 6,
        DiscardSavedState = 10,
        Starting = 11,
        MergingDrives = 12,
        Deleting = 13,
        DiscardingDrives = 80,
        Pausing = 81,
        UnderCreation = 100,
        CreationFailed = 101,
        Stored = 102,
        UnderTemplateCreation = 103,
        TemplateCreationFailed = 104,
        CustomizationFailed = 105,
        UnderUpdate = 106,
        UpdateFailed = 107,
        UnderMigration = 200,
        MigrationFailed = 201,
        CreatingCheckpoint = 210,
        DeletingCheckpoint = 211,
        RecoveringCheckpoint = 212,
        CheckpointFailed = 213,
        InitializingCheckpointOperation = 214,
        FinishingCheckpointOperation = 215,
        Missing = 220,
        HostNotResponding = 221,
        Unsupported = 222,
        IncompleteVMConfig = 223,
        UnsupportedSharedFiles = 224,
        UnsupportedCluster = 225,
        P2VCreationFailed = 240,
        V2VCreationFailed = 250,
    }
}
```

FIGURE 8.8

Getting the communication state enumeration for a Host

```
Microsoft.VirtualManager.Remoting.CommunicationState
using System;
using System.ComponentModel;

namespace Microsoft.VirtualManager.Remoting
{
    [TypeConverter(typeof(CommunicationStateEnumHelper))]
    public enum CommunicationState
    {
        Responding = 0,
        NotResponding = 1,
        AccessDenied = 2,
        Connecting = 3,
        Disconnecting = 4,
        Resetting = 5,
        NoConnection = 6,
    }
}
```

FIGURE 8.9

Getting the computer state enumeration for a Host

```
Microsoft.VirtualManager.Remoting.ComputerState

using System;
using System.ComponentModel;

namespace Microsoft.VirtualManager.Remoting
{
    [TypeConverter(typeof(ComputerStateEnumHelper))]
    public enum ComputerState
    {
        Adding = 0,
        Removing = 1,
        Responding = 2,
        NotResponding = 3,
        AccessDenied = 4,
        Updating = 5,
        Reassociating = 6,
        Pending = 7,
        MaintenanceMode = 8,
    }
}
```

To create a PowerShell script file, follow these instructions:

1. Open Notepad.exe or your favorite editor.

2. Add the PowerShell cmdlets you want the script to execute. For example, Get-VM | Refresh-VM.

3. Save the file as RefreshVirtualMachines.ps1.

Once you have created your PowerShell script file, you can invoke it by using the full path to the file in PowerShell. If the following code snippet fails due to the PowerShell execution policy, refer to Figure 8.2 for more information:

```
PS D:\> .\demo.ps1
This is a demo script
```

Passing parameters to a PowerShell script is similar to passing them in other scripting languages. Inside the script, you can use the $args variable to get the parameters passed to the script:

```
PS D:\> .\demo.ps1 3 parameters passed
This is a demo script
Parameter # 1 : 3
Parameter # 2 : parameters
Parameter # 3 : passed
```

Even though creating PowerShell scripts is easy, debugging scripts is harder than debugging individual cmdlets. It is recommended to try your sequence of cmdlets in the interactive Windows PowerShell window and make sure they work before putting everything in a script file.

WINDOWS POWERSHELL AND THE ADMINISTRATOR CONSOLE

In addition to the documentation on the VMM cmdlets, the Virtual Machine Manager Administrator Console provides a few other ways to get familiar with PowerShell and VMM. The additional features for enhancing your PowerShell knowledge are in the following list:

Viewing the PowerShell script that VMM will execute   All VMM wizards in the Administrator Console have a View Script button in the last wizard page. Clicking it opens up Notepad and shows you the Windows PowerShell cmdlets that VMM will invoke to execute the actions the user chose in the wizard. Figure 8.10 has an example script that was generated during the migration of a VM from one host to another. This is a great way to start learning more about PowerShell and automating some of the actions that VMM provides in the wizard pages.

FIGURE 8.10
The View Script button at the end of the migration wizard and an example script

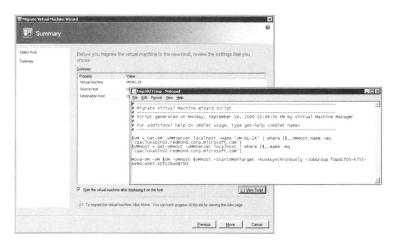

Viewing the PowerShell cmdlet equivalent for a VMM job   The Administrator Console's jobs view has a column that lists the VMM cmdlet used for each VMM job that changes data (for example, the Get-* cmdlets will not have an entry in this view since a VMM job is not created for such cmdlets). Each job has a friendly name that indicates the action performed, and you can get more information on the specific cmdlet invoked through the Get-Help cmdlet. Figure 8.11 shows you a list of VMM jobs and their associated cmdlet names. The result type that is listed indicates the type of object on which this operation was performed. This is usually the noun of the cmdlet.

VMM library support for Windows PowerShell scripts   The VMM library has built-in support for PowerShell scripts. You can place all your files with the .ps1 filename extension in the library shares and VMM will automatically import them into the library view. From the library, you can view and edit the scripts (editing the PowerShell Scripts requires that the user of the Administrator Console has write permissions on the library share and the associated Power-Shell script file), or you can execute the scripts as per Figure 8.12. Through the Run PowerShell Script action of the VMM library, VMM will launch a new Windows PowerShell process and invoke this PowerShell script. Because VMM executes your script after it obtains a connection to the VMM server, you don't need to execute Get-VMMServer at the beginning of your script. VMM will also keep the PowerShell window open for inspecting the results.

FIGURE 8.11
The Command column
in the jobs view of the
Administrator Console

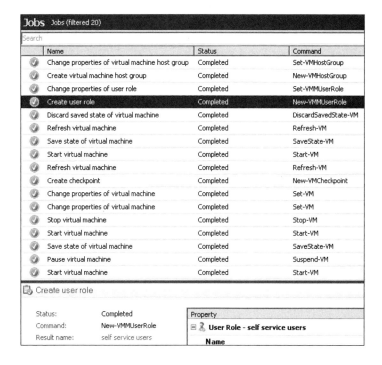

FIGURE 8.12
PowerShell scripts in
the VMM library

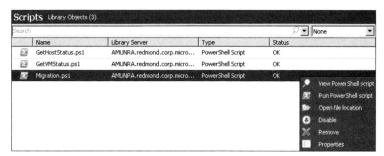

Interfacing with Hyper-V and Virtual Server

Hyper-V has a well-documented WMI API that can be accessed from the Microsoft Developer Network's website. It is listed under the Virtualization WMI Provider documentation, and the namespace for the WMI is root\virtualization. The WMI provider is hosted by the Hyper-V Virtual Machine Management Windows Service. The following code shows how to get all virtual Machines from a Hyper-V server using Windows PowerShell and the WMI API for Hyper-V:

```
# Get list of Virtual Machine and host machine from Hyper-V WMI API
$computerlist = get-wmiobject Msvm_ComputerSystem -namespace root\virtualization
```

```
# Show in tabular format the list of VMs and Host
# (Host is identified in the caption as "Hosting Computer System")
# The Name for Virtual Machines contains the unique GUID that identifies a VM
# ElementName contains the user-friendly name of the VM
$computerlist | select Name, ElementName, Caption
```

A simple way to test WMI queries before executing them in Windows PowerShell is through the wbemtest utility. This utility is installed in the %SystemDrive%\Windows\System32\wbem\ Windows folder. To execute a WMI query using this utility, follow these steps:

1. Launch wbemtest.exe.

2. Click Connect and type **root\virtualization** in the Namespace field.

3. Click Query and type a WMI query, such as

   ```
   select Name, ElementName, Caption from Msvm_ComputerSystem
   ```

4. The results will include the same list as the preceding PowerShell example. Click on each individual result to see the Name, ElementName, and Caption values.

Virtual Server's COM interface is documented on the Microsoft Developer Network under the title of Microsoft Virtual Server Reference. To be able to invoke this API using PowerShell, you need to meet the security prerequisites.

By default, PowerShell does not have the necessary COM security level to invoke the Virtual Server COM API. To accomplish that, follow these steps:

1. Create a new library DLL that allows you to set the COM security level to Impersonate for any COM object. To accomplish this, add a new API to the library DLL called SetVSSecurity. In this API, you need to invoke CoSetProxyBlanket with the RPC_C_IMP_LEVEL_IMPERSONATE parameter for the COM object that is passed as a parameter.

2. Once you create this DLL, you can use the System.Reflection.Assembly.LoadFrom() .NET API and pass the DLL's full path as a parameter.

3. Once you have a Virtual Server object in PowerShell, you need to invoke the API from this DLL to set the COM security to Impersonate so that the object can be used. The API SetVSSecurity should take a PowerShell object as a parameter.

4. You might need to set other objects' COM security as well, as you start working with Virtual Server and PowerShell. For example, the VM object will need to have its COM security elevated to Impersonate before it can be used. The following code shows how to get the Virtual Server root object using PowerShell.

   ```
   # Create a new Virtual Server COM instance
   $VirtualServer = new-object -com VirtualServer.Application -Strict

   # Now set the COM security of the $VirtualServer object to "Impersonate"
   # and then you can use this object to manage Virtual Server
   [Full namespace path for the DLL created in step 1 above]::SetVSSecurity
     ($VirtualServer)
   ```

```
# After setting the property of $VirtualServer to "Impersonate", you can
# get a list of Virtual Machines and use the full COM API of
# Virtual Server
```

Automating Common Tasks Using the Windows Scheduler

IT personnel today spend a lot of time on repetitive tasks to accomplish various jobs. PowerShell provides a powerful language that can be used to write and execute scripts. These scripts can eliminate repetitive tasks and add the necessary logic to complete complex jobs. Since VMM is built entirely on top of PowerShell, anything an administrator can do in the Administrator Console can also be accomplished via PowerShell cmdlets. If you combine that with the ability to integrate with .NET and other data stores that are PowerShell ready, an administrator should be able to translate a lot of manual work into PowerShell scripts. The ability to schedule PowerShell scripts at specified intervals allows an administrator to do passive management of their system and let PowerShell do some of the heavy lifting during nonworking hours.

Once you have a PowerShell script ready, you may want to execute it at regular intervals and capture its results in a log file. If the cmdlets change data in VMM, you can also view the results in the Administrator Console's jobs view. There are a couple of ways to create a scheduled task in Windows Server. In this section, we will show you how to do this from the Task Scheduler user interface. Optionally, you can use the `schtasks.exe` utility to create a scheduled task.

To schedule a task from the Task Scheduler, follow these steps:

1. Open the Task Scheduler MMC snap-in. Task Scheduler is located in either `Control Panel\System and Security\Administrative Tools\Task Scheduler` or `Control Panel\Administrative Tools\Task Scheduler`, depending on the version of Windows installed.

2. Select Create Task.

3. Enter a Task Name like **Windows PowerShell automated script**.

4. Select Run Whether User Is Logged On Or Not and chose to store the password.

5. Select Change User Or Group to enter a user that has the proper VMM privileges to execute this PowerShell script.

6. In the Triggers tab, enter the schedule you would like to create for this scheduled task. For example, you can chose to run this script daily at 8 p.m.

7. In the Actions tab, as shown in Figure 8.13, add a new action and select Start A Program. In the program path, enter **D:\Windows\System32\WindowsPowerShell\v1.0\powershell.exe**.
   This is the full path to Windows PowerShell 1.0.
   For arguments, enter the following:

   ```
   -PSConsoleFile "D:\Program Files\Microsoft System Center Virtual Machine
   Manager 2008 R2\bin\cli.psc1" -Command " & '\\hypervhost1.vmmdomain.com\
   MSSCVMMLibrary\Scripts\GetVMStatus.ps1'"
   -NoProfile -Noninteractive
   ```

If you were to execute this command from a regular command window, it would look like this:

```
D:\Windows\System32\WindowsPowerShell\v1.0\powershell.exe
 -PSConsoleFile "D:\Program Files\Microsoft System Center Virtual
 Machine Manager 2008 R2\bin\cli.psc1" -Command " &
 '\\hypervhost1.vmmdomain.com\MSSCVMMLibrary\Scripts\GetVMStatus.ps1'"
 -NoProfile -Noninteractive
```

8. Click OK and enter the password for the account that will execute the scheduled task.

9. From the Task Scheduler MMC, you can view all your scheduled tasks, check for their last run time, and see if there were any errors in execution based on the last run result.

FIGURE 8.13
Adding the scheduled task action

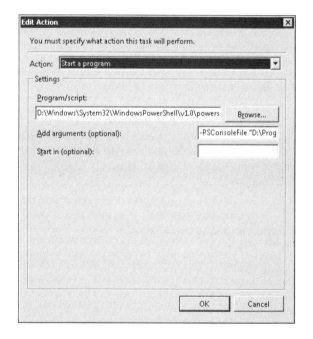

Sometimes, it is easier to check if a scheduled task is executing by looking at a log file. The following sample PowerShell script shows you how to log that information to a file:

```
Write-Output "Script executing at " (date)

# Get a connection to the local VMM server
$c = get-vmmserver localhost

# Make a sample query to get some data from VMM
$results = get-vm | select name, status, vmid, ID, hostname
```

```
# Create a log file in the temp directory
$filepath = "$env:temp\PSscriptOutput.log"

# Append to the log file the current time and the data retrieved from VMM
Add-Content (date) -Path $filepath
Add-Content $results -Path $filepath
Add-Content "-------------" -Path $filepath
```

Because scheduled PowerShell scripts don't offer the same degree of debugging, you need to ensure that the proper execution policies are in place for PowerShell scripts. It is recommended that all scripts you execute using the Task Scheduler are signed using a code signing certificate issued by a certificate authority. This will enable you to set the PowerShell execution policy to a more secure level like the AllSigned option. After you sign a script using the Set-AuthenticodeSignature cmdlet, you will need to add the publisher of the script to your trusted publishers. PowerShell will prompt you to do that on the first execution of the script.

In Chapter 9, "Writing a PRO Pack," we will cover the PRO feature of VMM. PRO allows an administrator to execute a PowerShell script or perform a VMM action based on a set of alerts detected by System Center Operations Manager (OpsMgr). OpsMgr is a comprehensive datacenter monitoring tool. In this case, a PowerShell script is executed in response to a dynamic event.

Windows PowerShell Examples

In the following sections, we will list a few different Windows PowerShell scripts that leverage the VMM cmdlets to accomplish important tasks in VMM, make it easier for an administrator to execute repetitive actions, and allow an administrator to get quick status on the health of VMM objects.

Creating Virtual Machines

There are many ways to create a virtual machine in VMM. In this section, we will take a look at an example of how to create a highly available (HA) VM and find the best suitable host on which to place it. The best suitable host is found by the Intelligent Placement feature of VMM based on the properties of the VM and the available hosts. Listing 8.2 contains the code for creating the HA virtual machine.

LISTING 8.2:   Creating a new highly available virtual machine

```
# Get a connection to the VMM server
$c = Get-VMMServer "localhost"

# Create the Job Group ID. This is the Guid that pairs all the cmdlets
# necessary to ensure that the new Virtual Machine creation is
# Successful. Every cmdlet that specifies the same Job Group ID will
# be part of a set and will be executed in order after the final command
# that includes the same Job Group ID runs. In this case, the final
```

```
# command is the New-VM cmdlet.
$JobGroupID = [System.Guid]::NewGuid().ToString()

# Enter the VM Name
$VMName = "virtualmachine1"

# Create a virtual NIC
New-VirtualNetworkAdapter -JobGroup $JobGroupID -PhysicalAddressType
Dynamic -VLANEnabled $false

# Create a virtual DVD
New-VirtualDVDDrive -JobGroup $JobGroupID -Bus 1 -LUN 0

# Check if another HW profile has the same name and delete it if there is
$HardwareProfile = Get-HardwareProfile | where {$_.Name -eq "HWProfile"}
if ($HardwareProfile -ne $null)
{
   Write-Warning "Deleting the existing hardware profile with the same name"
   Remove-HardwareProfile $HardwareProfile
}

# Create a new hardware profile with the user preferences
# The -HighlyAvailable property of this cmdlet is the one indicating
# that this Virtual Machine should be a Highly Available one
$HardwareProfile = New-HardwareProfile -Owner "vmmdomain\administrator"
 -Name "HWProfile" -CPUCount 1 -MemoryMB 2048 -HighlyAvailable $true
-NumLock $false -BootOrder "CD", "IdeHardDrive", "PxeBoot",
"Floppy" -LimitCPUFunctionality $false -JobGroup $VMGuid

# Create a new VHD for the VM
$DiskDrive = New-VirtualDiskDrive -IDE -Bus 0 -LUN 0 -JobGroup
$JobGroupID -Size 10240 -Dynamic -Filename "virtualmachine1.vhd"

# Get all the hosts and their ratings for this VM's HW profile
$AllHosts = Get-VMHost
$hostrating = Get-VMHostRating -VMHost $AllHosts
 -HardwareProfile $HardwareProfile -DiskSpaceGB 10 -VMName $VMName

# Order the host ratings and check if we have at least one
# positive star rating for this VM
$orderedrating = $hostrating | sort-object rating -descending
Write-Output $orderedrating

# If the rating is 0, exit and don't call new-vm
if ($orderedrating -is [Array])
{
   # we have multiple results, so pick the top one
   $targethost = $orderedrating[0].VMhost
```

```
    if ($orderedrating[0].Rating -eq 0)
    {
        Write-Warning "There is no suitable host for this VM's profile"
        Write-Warning $orderedrating[0].ZeroRatingReasonList[0]
        break
    }
}
else
{
    $targethost = $orderedrating.VMhost
    if ($orderedrating.Rating -eq 0)
    {
        Write-Warning "There is no suitable host for this VM's profile"
        Write-Warning $orderedrating.ZeroRatingReasonList[0]
        break
    }
}

Write-Output "We will be creating a new VM on host $targethost"

# Get the operating system from a list of predefined OS Names in VMM
$OperatingSystem = Get-OperatingSystem | where {$_.Name -eq
"64-bit edition of Windows Server 2008 Enterprise"}

# Find the path for the LUN/Disk to host the files for the new HA VM
# Make sure this volume is not in use, is a cluster volume
# (with cluster resources already created), and is available
# for placement

$targetpath = get-vmhostvolume -VMHost $targethost
 | where-object -filterscript {$_.IsClustered -eq $true}
 | where-object -filterscript {$_.InUse -eq $false}
 | where-object -filterscript {$_.IsAvailableForPlacement
 -eq $true}
if ($targetpath -eq $null)
{
    Write-Warning "There is no suitable cluster disk to place this VM on"
    Break
}

if ($targetpath -is [Array])
{
    # Pick the first available disk to place this VM on
    $targetpath = $targetpath[0].Name
}
else
{
    $targetpath = $targetpath.Name
}
```

```
# Create the new-vm in an asynchronous way
New-VM -VMMServer $c -Name $VMName -Description
 "new HA VM to learn more about PowerShell"
 -Owner "vmmdomain\administrator" -VMHost
 $targethost -Path $targetpath -HardwareProfile $HardwareProfile
 -JobGroup $JobGroupID -RunAsynchronously -OperatingSystem
 $OperatingSystem -RunAsSystem -StartAction NeverAutoTurnOnVM
 -StopAction SaveVM
```

P2V Conversion

VMM makes consolidating old servers a breeze with a simple wizard for converting physical servers (also known as Physical to Virtual (P2V) conversion). In this section, we will show you a couple of examples of creating a virtual machine from a given computer system. Listing 8.3 has the PowerShell code for an online P2V.

LISTING 8.3:   Converting a physical server to a virtual machine without any downtime

```
# Get the connection to the VMM server
Get-VMMServer -ComputerName "localhost"

# Get the administrative credentials for accessing the source
# machine (this has to be domain credentials)
$PSCredential = Get-Credential

# Get the target host for this Virtual Machine
$VMHost = Get-VMHost -ComputerName "localhost"

# Initiate the asynchronous P2V operation
New-P2V -SourceComputerName "localhost" -VMHost $VMHost -Name
 "resultVMName" -Path $VMHost.VMPaths[0] -MemoryMB 1024 -Credential
$PSCredential -RunAsynchronously
```

To initiate an offline conversion of a Windows Server 2000 computer, or to force the offline conversion of a Windows Server 2008 computer, you need to use the -Offline flag of the New-P2V cmdlet. Listing 8.4 has the PowerShell code for an offline P2V.

LISTING 8.4:   Offline conversion of a physical server to a virtual machine

```
# Get the connection to the VMM server
Get-VMMServer -ComputerName "localhost"

# Get the administrative credentials for accessing the
# source machine (this has to be domain credentials)
$PSCredential = Get-Credential
```

```
# Get the target host for this Virtual Machine
$VMHost = Get-VMHost -ComputerName "localhost"

# Create a new machine configuration for the physical source
# computer. This triggers the hardware scout to retrieve the data
# from the source computer.
New-MachineConfig -SourceComputerName "sourcemachine.vmmdomain.com"
-Credential $PSCredential
$MachineConfig = Get-MachineConfig | where {$_.Name
-eq "sourcemachine.vmmdomain.com"}

# Initiate the asynchronous offline P2V operation, using a static
# IP Address for the conversion
# If a patch file or driver is missing, download the required
# patches or driver files to the Patch Import directory on the
# VMM server (the default path is <SystemDrive>:\Program Files
# \Microsoft System Center Virtual Machine Manager 2008\
# Patch Import), and extract the files by using the
# Add-Patch cmdlet.

New-P2V -Credential $PSCredential -VMHost $VMHost -Path
 $VMHost.VMPaths[0] -Owner "vmmdomain\administrator" -Trigger
 -Name "resultVMName"
-MachineConfig $MachineConfig -Offline -Shutdown
-OfflineIPAddress "192.168.100.23" -OfflineNICMacAddress
"00:11:22:33:44:55" -OfflineDefaultGateway "192.168.100.1"
-OfflineSubnetMask "255.255.255.0" -CPUCount 1 -MemoryMB 1024
-RunAsSystem -StartAction NeverAutoTurnOnVM
 -UseHardwareAssistedVirtualization $false -StopAction SaveVM
-StartVM -RunAsynchronously
```

Virtual Machine Migrations

When you're migrating a virtual machine through Virtual Machine Manager, the transfer type (or speed) for the migration is determined during Intelligent Placement and it is based upon the properties and capabilities of the source virtual machine and the destination host along with the connectivity between them. In Listing 8.5, we attempt to migrate a virtual machine while enforcing a requirement that only SAN or cluster migrations are eligible. This puts a requirement on the script to not only check for good host ratings but also to ensure that the transfer can be accomplished quickly using a SAN or a failover cluster.

LISTING 8.5:   Migrating a virtual machine using cluster or SAN and tracking the migration progress

```
# Get a connection to the VMM server
$c = Get-VMMServer "localhost"
```

```
# Get the VM to migrate
$VM = Get-VM "virtualmachine1"

# Get all the hosts
$AllHosts = Get-VMHost

# The IsMigration flag allows the current host of the VM
# to be considered as the migration target
$hostrating = Get-VMHostRating -VMHost $AllHosts -VM $VM -IsMigration

# Order the host ratings
$orderedrating = $hostrating | sort-object rating -descending
Write-Output $orderedrating

# Now search for the top rated host that can do a Cluster or a SAN migration
# All other migration options are not considered here
$targethost = $null
foreach ($rating in $orderedrating)
{
  if ($rating.Rating -gt 0)
  {
   switch ($rating.TransferType)
   {
       # These options are listed in order of decreasing transfer speed
       "Live"
          {
             Write-Output "$rating.Name has a transfer type of Live"
             $targethost = $rating.Name
             break
          }
       "Cluster"
          {
             Write-Output "$rating.Name has a transfer type of Cluster"
             $targethost = $rating.Name
             break
          }
       "San"
          {
             Write-Output "$rating.Name has a transfer type of SAN"
             $targethost = $rating.Name
             break
          }
       "Network"
          {
             Write-Output "$rating.Name has a transfer type of Network"
          }
       default
```

```
        {
            Write-Output "$rating.Name has an invalid TransferType"
        }
    }
  }

}

if ($targethost -eq $null)
{
    Write-Warning "We were not able to find a suitable destination
host for this VM with a fast transfer (SAN or Cluster)"
    break
}

# Migrate the VM to the target host
$VMHost = Get-VMHost -ComputerName $targethost
$resultvm = Move-VM -VM $VM -vmhost $VMHost -Path $VMHost.VMPaths[0]
-RunAsynchronously

# Get the VMM Job that was launched for this migration
$job = $resultvm.MostRecentTask

# Iterate the loop until the Job is finished while reporting progress
while ($job.Status -eq "Running")
{
    $progress = $job.Progress
    Write-Progress $VM Progress -PercentComplete $job.ProgressValue -ID 1
    Start-Sleep 3
}

# The VMM job is now finished (either with a failed or a completed status)
$status = $job.Status
Write-Warning "Migration of $VM to host $VMHost finished
with a status of: $status"
$error = $job.ErrorInfo | select DisplayableErrorCode,
Problem, RecommendedActionCLI
Write-Warning $error
```

In some cases, it is beneficial to force a LAN migration even when a faster migration option is available. The only change from the code in Listing 8.5 would be a small change in the Move-VM cmdlet to add the UseLAN option as indicated here.

```
# Use the -UseLAN option to force a Network transfer of the Virtual Machine
$resultvm = Move-VM -VM $VM -vmhost $VMHost -Path $VMHost.VMPaths[0]
-RunAsynchronously -UseLAN
```

Provisioning Multiple Virtual Machines

Virtual machines are usually provisioned on demand based on customer requirements. However, there are cases where having many virtual machines available for immediate use is a requirement. Such scenarios might include hosted desktops allocating virtual machines from a pool of VMs or allocating VMs to an enterprise application based on load. In the PowerShell script in Listing 8.6, we read the input from a text file and create virtual machines in blocks of five at a time (the throttling rate is customizable). This allows us to customize and repeat the automated provisioning process by updating a text file rather than having to adjust a PowerShell script.

LISTING 8.6:   PowerShell script for creating multiple VMs based on an input file

```
# get the command line arguments passed to this script
$length = $args.length
$expectedArgsLength = 2

# The script takes as input the customization filepath and the VMM server name
$usage = "Usage: ScriptName.ps1 <customizationfile.txt> <vmm-server-name>"
if ($length -ne $expectedArgsLength)
{
   write-warning $usage;
   break
}

# The ArrayList to use for tracking new-vm creations
$arraylist = New-Object System.Collections.ArrayList
$arraylist.Clear()

# The max number of concurrent VM creations (throttling rate)
$MaxCreations = 5

# Get a connection to the VMM server
$servername = $args[1]
get-vmmserver -ComputerName $servername

# now open the customization file to read its input
$customFile = $args[0]
$content = get-content $customFile
foreach ($values in $content)
{
   # $values contains one line of input. Each line represents a VM
   # now split the CSV input line
   $newvalues = $values |% {$_.split(",")}

   # Perform a test to ensure the proper number of parameters exist
   if ($newvalues.length -ne 14)
```

```
    {
        write-warning "The proper number of parameters does not exist for $values";
        break
    }

    # get the input variables from the file and into the specific variables
    $vmname = $newvalues[0]              # The virtual machine name
    $computername = $newvalues[1]        # The guest OS computer name
    $memory = $newvalues[2]              # The amount of RAM to allocate to the VM
    $OSSKU = $newvalues[3]               # The OS name (VMM has these
already defined)
    $ProductID = $newvalues[4]           # The Windows Product ID
    $description = $newvalues[5]         # A description for the VM
    $vmpath = $newvalues[6]              # The path where to create this VM
    $vnetworkname = $newvalues[7]        # The Virtual Network Name
    $hostname = $newvalues[8]            # The name of the host to place this VM on
    $cpuvalue = $newvalues[9]            # The CPU Name (VMM has these
already defined)
    $cpucount = $newvalues[10]           # The number of CPUs
    $owner = $newvalues[11]              # The owner of the VM
    $adminpwd = $newvalues[12]           # The guest OS administrator password
    $templatename = $newvalues[13]       # The template name from
which to create this VM

    # Create the Job Group ID and the hardware profile name
    $jobguid = [guid]::NewGuid().ToString()
    $profilename = "Profile" + $jobguid

    # create the VM based on the settings in the file - this will
happen asynchronously
    Set-VirtualFloppyDrive -RunAsynchronously -VMMServer $servername
-NoMedia -JobGroup $jobguid
    New-VirtualNetworkAdapter -VMMServer $servername -JobGroup
 $jobguid  -PhysicalAddressType Dynamic -VirtualNetwork $vnetworkname
-VLanEnabled $false
    New-VirtualDVDDrive -VMMServer $servername -JobGroup $jobguid  -Bus 1 -LUN 0
    $CPUType = Get-CPUType -VMMServer $servername | where {$_.Name -eq $cpuvalue}
    New-HardwareProfile -VMMServer $servername -Owner $owner
-CPUType $CPUType -Name $profilename -Description "Profile used to
create a VM/Template" -CPUCount $cpucount -MemoryMB
$memory -ExpectedCPUUtilization 20 -DiskIO 0 -NetworkUtilization
10 -RelativeWeight 100 -HighlyAvailable $false -NumLock $false
-BootOrder "CD", "IdeHardDrive", "PxeBoot", "Floppy"
-LimitCPUFunctionality $false -JobGroup $jobguid
    $Template = Get-Template -VMMServer $servername | where
{$_.Name -eq $templatename}
    $VMHost = Get-VMHost -VMMServer $servername | where {$_.Name -eq $hostname}
    $HardwareProfile = Get-HardwareProfile -VMMServer localhost |
```

```
    where {$_.Name -eq $profilename}
        $OperatingSystem = Get-OperatingSystem -VMMServer localhost |
    where {$_.Name -eq $OSSKU}

      # Before we start the new-vm creation we need to check
      # if we reached the maximum number of concurrent creations
      while ($arraylist.Count -eq $MaxCreations)
      {
          $toremove = $null
          foreach ($jobid in $arraylist)
          {
              # get the current status of the job
              $tempjobid = [string]::join("", $jobid.Keys)
              $tempjob = Get-Job -ID $tempjobid;
              if ($tempjob.Status -ne "Running")
              {
                  # This job completed, so remove it from the tracking list
    so that new VMs can be created
                  Write-Output "Job $tempjobid finished running"
                  $toremove = $jobid
                  break
              }
          }

          if ($toremove -ne $null)
          {
              $arraylist.Remove($jobid)
          }

          Start-Sleep 2
      }

      # if we reached here, it is safe to create the new VM
      $resultvm = New-VM -Template $Template -Name $vmname
    -Description $description -VMHost $VMHost -Path $vmpath -JobGroup
    $jobguid -Owner $owner -HardwareProfile $HardwareProfile
    -ComputerName $computername -FullName "" -OrgName "" -ProductKey
    $ProductID -TimeZone 4 -JoinWorkgroup "WORKGROUP" -OperatingSystem
    $OperatingSystem -RunAsSystem -StartAction
    NeverAutoTurnOnVM -UseHardwareAssistedVirtualization $false
    -StopAction SaveVM -RunAsynchronously

      # Now start tracking this new-vm instance
      if ($resultvm -ne $null)
      {
          # Get the VMM Job that was launched for this migration
```

```
        $job = $resultvm.MostRecentTask
        $arraylist.Add(@{$job.ID = $job})
    }
}

write-output "Done creating All VMs!"
```

The following code contains a sample line from an input text file that can be used in the script in Listing 8.6. This line contains the values for the different virtual machine properties that are needed by the PowerShell script. These values need to be specified in order, and their descriptions are as follows:

1. The virtual machine name

2. The guest OS computer name

3. The amount of RAM or memory to allocate to the VM

4. The OS name (VMM has these already defined)

5. The Windows product ID

6. A description for the VM

7. The path describing where to create this VM

8. The virtual network name

9. The name of the host on which to place this VM

10. The CPU name (VMM has these already defined.)

11. The number of CPUs

12. The owner of the VM

13. The guest OS administrator password

14. The name of the template from which to create this VM

```
vmname1,vmname1ComputerName,1024,64-bit edition of Windows Server 2008
  Enterprise,55555-55555-55555-55555-55555,scripted VM,D:\ProgramData\Microsoft
\Windows\Hyper-V,Broadcom NetXtreme 57xx Gigabit Controller - Virtual
  Network,hypervhost1.vmmdomain.com,2.40 GHz Xeon,1,vmmdomain\administrator,
password,MyTemplate
```

Automating the Addition of Managed Hosts

Adding a virtual machine host to VMM requires administrative credentials for the physical computer. The requirement of credentials makes it hard to automate any tasks that need to run unattended without sacrificing the security of your credentials. Since the credentials are required parameters to the VMM cmdlets in the script and storing them in clear text might compromise security, you can save your credentials to a file for later use. See the following PowerShell cmdlets for an example:

```
# First, call Get-Credential to store your credentials to a PowerShell variable
$PSCredential = Get-Credential

# Now construct the file path of the file that will store the credentials
$SecureFilePath = $PSCredential.UserName + ".cred"
$SecureFilePath = $SecureFilePath.Replace("\", "_")

# Store the credentials to this file
$PSCredential.Password | ConvertFrom-SecureString | Set-Content $SecureFilePath
```

When it is time to execute the automated task, you can retrieve this file from the same location and add a host to VMM. In the following code snippet, we are looking to add all Hyper-V hosts in the environment:

```
# Get the password from the file that we used earlier to store it in
$Password = Get-Content $SecureFilePath | ConvertTo-SecureString

# Create a new PsCredential object for our administrator
# using the stored password
$PSCredential_Out = New-Object
System.Management.Automation.PsCredential("vmmdomain\administrator",
$Password)

# Now discover all the Hyper-V hosts in the domain whose name starts with HyperV
$Computers = Discover-Computer -ComputerNameFilter "HyperV" -Domain
"vmmdomain.com" -FindHyperVHosts -ExcludeVMMHost | select Name

# The output of the discover-computer cmdlet can now be used to
# add these hosts to VMM
foreach ($computer in $Computers)
{
    # Instead of prompting for credentials, $PSCredential_Out contains the values
    # required by VMM to add a new host
    Add-VMHost -Credential $PSCredential_Out -ComputerName $computer
}
```

Working with MAC Addresses

Virtual Machine Manager manages a static range of MAC addresses that can be used when attaching a virtual network device to a Virtual Machine. MAC addresses that are consumed from this static range can never be reused, in the same way the MAC addresses on physical machines are all unique. To configure the MAC address range, click on the administration view of the VMM Administrator Console and select the Networking option. Figure 8.14 shows a sample MAC address range for a VMM deployment.

FIGURE 8.14
Global Static MAC
Address Range
dialog box

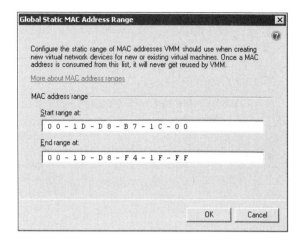

Listing 8.7 shows how to get the next available MAC address from this range and how to commit the selection. Once the MAC address is committed, it will never be used again by VMM.

LISTING 8.7:   PowerShell script to retrieve the next available MAC address

```
# First, invoke the New-PhysicalAddress cmdlet to view the next
# available MAC address in the range
# Output will be something like this: 00:1D:D8:B7:1C:00
New-PhysicalAddress

# if you execute the New-PhysicalAddress multiple times, the
# output will not change from 00:1D:D8:B7:1C:00
New-PhysicalAddress

# Now, let's save this MAC address and commit the change in VMM
$MacAddress = New-PhysicalAddress -Commit

# Print the MAC address we just committed (should be 00:1D:D8:B7:1C:00)
$MacAddress

# Show that the next invocation of New-PhysicalAddress will
# return a new MAC Address from the range. (00:1D:D8:B7:1C:01)
New-PhysicalAddress

# Once you have a MAC address, you can invoke the Set-VirtualNetworkAdapter
# cmdlet to set the MAC Address
# First, let's get the virtual network adapter for our Virtual Machine1
$vnic = get-virtualnetworkadapter -vm "<insert Virtual Machine name>"
```

```
# Now set the properties of the adapter to include this static MAC Address
$vnic | Set-virtualnetworkadapter -Physicaladdresstype Static
-PhysicalAddress $MacAddress
```

Evacuating a Host for Maintenance

It is sometimes necessary to service the physical computer running the virtualization software, resulting in several hours of downtime. We will show you a script that you can use to evacuate a host from all of its virtual machines instead of the virtual machines being inactive as well. Make sure you monitor the progress of the VMM jobs to ensure that all virtual machines have successfully migrated to a different host. Listing 8.8 contains the code for asynchronously moving all the VMs from a host.

VMM 2008 R2 also introduced a new feature called maintenance mode. A host managed by VMM can be placed into maintenance mode if you want to perform maintenance tasks on the physical host (e.g., replace hardware or install security updates that might require a server reboot). Once a host is in maintenance mode, VMM will no longer allow that host to be the target host for a new virtual machine. In addition, a host that is in maintenance mode is excluded from host ratings calculations during virtual machine placement.

When maintenance mode is initiated on a host, all running virtual machines are put into a saved state. If the host is part of a cluster, then the user is presented with the option to either live migrate all its virtual machines to another host or to save the state of all virtual machines on that host. Live migration is an option only if the host cluster is capable of live migration. This behavior is a little bit different for VMware hosts. Once a VMware ESX host is put into maintenance mode in VMM, VMM will send an "Enter maintenance mode" request to VMware Virtual Center. The behavior of the VMs on that host is determined based on the configuration of the maintenance mode feature in Virtual Center.

When maintenance mode is stopped on a host, VMM will allow that host to be the target host of migrations and that host will start receiving a star rating in placement calculations. However, no VMs are restarted on that host, and the VMs that were migrated away from that host are not placed back automatically.

When you're using the maintenance mode feature of VMM 2008 R2, the `Disable-VMHost` cmdlet places a virtual machine host into maintenance mode while `Enable-VMHost` removes a host from maintenance mode.

LISTING 8.8:   PowerShell script to asynchronously move all the VMs from a given host

```
# get the command line arguments passed to this script
$argslength = $args.length
$expectedArgsLength = 2

# The script takes as input the VMM server name and
# the FQDN of the host to evacuate
$usage = "Usage: ScriptName.ps1 <vmm-server-name> <Host FQDN>"
if ($argslength -ne $expectedArgsLength)
{
    write-warning $usage; break
}
```

```powershell
# helper function to move a VM to the host with the highest star rating
# This function could be easily modified to only move VMs within a
SAN or a cluster
function MoveVM($vmobj, $hostobj)
{
    $hostrating = get-vmhostrating -vmhost $hostobj -vm $vmobj
    $orderedrating = $hostrating | sort-object rating -descending
    Write-Output $orderedrating

    $targethost = $null
    if ($orderedrating -is [Array])
    {
        if ($orderedrating[0].Rating -ne 0)
        {
            $targethost = $orderedrating[0].VMhost
        }
    }
    else
    {
        if ($orderedrating.Rating -ne 0)
        {
            $targethost = $orderedrating.VMHost
        }
    }

    if ($targethost -ne $null)
    {
        write-warning "Moving VM $vmobj to host $targethost"
        $resultvm = move-vm -VM $vmobj -vmhost $targethost
-Path $targethost.VMPaths[0] -RunAsynchronously
    }
    else
    {
        Write-Warning "There is no suitable host for this VM $vmobj
and it will not be migrated!"
    }
}

# get a connection to the VMM server
$vmmserver = $args[0]
$c = get-vmmserver -ComputerName $vmmserver

# Now call Get-VM to cache all the VMs in Powershell
$vms = Get-VM

# Get the host computer and all hosts
$hostname = $args[1]
$VMHost = Get-VMHost -ComputerName $hostname
$AllHosts = Get-VMHost
```

```
# Now set this host to maintenance mode to prevent VMs from
# being deployed here
$VMHost | Set-VMHost -MaintenanceHost $true

# Enumerate all VMs on this host and move them asynchronously
foreach ($VM in $VMHost.VMs)
{
    MoveVM $VM $AllHosts
}
```

Utilizing Rapid Provisioning

VMM 2008 R2 introduced a new feature called Rapid Provisioning. This feature was implemented in response to customer demand to improve the time required to create virtual machines. In VMM 2008, the only way to create and deploy a new virtual machine was by utilizing a template, another virtual machine, or a VHD from the VMM library. During the new virtual machine creation process, VMM copied all the required VHDs over the network using the BITS protocol. Depending on the size of VHD and the available bandwidth, this operation could take several minutes to complete.

Several customers have sophisticated SAN technologies that enable them to clone a LUN that contains the VHD and present it to the host. However, customers still want to leverage the VMM template capabilities with operating system (OS) customization. Rapid Provisioning allows you to take advantage of your fast SAN infrastructure to move (or copy) the actual VHD files to the host but tie that back to VMM's rich template customization process. With Rapid Provisioning, you can now create a template that includes the OS configuration and references a "dummy" blank VHD. The blank VHD will not be used and will be replaced through the `Move-VirtualHardDisk` cmdlet. This cmdlet will let VMM know that it should not be using the VHD that is referenced in the template. Instead, VMM should use a VHD that resides locally on the host computer. To indicate to VMM that Rapid Provisioning needs to be used, the `New-VM` cmdlet takes a new switch called `UseLocalVirtualHardDisk`. Rapid Provisioning is only available through Windows PowerShell cmdlets.

Listing 8.9 shows an example creation of a virtual machine by utilizing Rapid Provisioning. In this example, `C:\Win2k8_Base_OS_Sysprep.vhd` has to locally exist on the host computer before the `New-VM` cmdlet is invoked.

LISTING 8.9:   Creating a new virtual machine using Rapid Provisioning

```
# Start by specifying the file location for the VHD that will
# be used by the Virtual Machine
$VHDName = "c:\Win2k8_Base_OS_Sysprep.vhd"

# Specify other variables for new-vm cmdlet
$vmname = "vm1"
$hostname = "host.contoso.com"
```

```
# Get an instance of the host that will be the target
# for the Virtual Machine
$vmhost = get-vmhost $hostname

# Create the jobgroup ID for new-vm from template
$JobGuid = [System.Guid]::NewGuid().ToString()

# Specify the local location for the VHD
# That will replace the "dummy" VHD that exists in the template
# VMM expects that $VHDName already exists on the host computer
# when the new-vm cmdlet is called.
Move-VirtualHardDisk -Bus 0 -LUN 0 -IDE -Path $VHDName -JobGroup $JobGuid

# Get the instance of the template that will be used for OS Configuration
$template = Get-Template | where {$_.Name -eq "VMMTemplate"}

# Get the current username to be passed as the Virtual Machine owner
$callerUsername = whoami

# Create the new-vm from template and specify the Rapid
# Provisioning flag (-uselocalvirtualharddisks)
New-VM -Template $template -Name $vmname -Description
"a Virtual Machine created with RP" -Owner $callerUsername
-VMHost $vmhost -UseLocalVirtualHardDisks -Path $vmhost.VMPaths[0]
-RunAsynchronously -JobGroup $JobGuid | Out-Null
```

Even though Virtual Machine Manager does not provide UI support for creating a virtual machine using differencing VHD disks, this can be accomplished using Rapid Provisioning. Using the public Hyper-V WMI interface, you can create a differencing disk for the c:\Win2k8_Base_OS_Sysprep.vhd VHD file used in Listing 8.9. Then, when the Move-VirtualHardDisk cmdlet is executed, you can pass the full path to the child VHD. The differencing disk will then be used as the target VHD for the new virtual machine creation. Such a process would make it easy for customers to copy a single base disk with the operating system on a host and then use the Rapid Provisioning feature to create multiple virtual machines using differencing disks off that same parent VHD. The following code snippet shows you a partial script that creates a differencing disk from the base VHD. Then it supplies the new VHD file path to VMM for Rapid Provisioning. The following code can be used within Listing 8.9 to create a new virtual machine using differencing disks and Rapid Provisioning:

```
# Get the Image Management Service WMI instance for the host computer
$VHDService = get-wmiobject -class "Msvm_ImageManagementService"
-namespace "root\virtualization" -computername $hostname

# Create a differencing disk from the base disk
$DiffVHDName = "c:\Win2k8_Base_OS_Sysprep_child.vhd"
$Result = $VHDService.CreateDifferencingVirtualHardDisk($DiffVHDName, $VHDName)
```

```
# Wait until the Hyper-V differencing disk creation is complete
# and then pass DiffVHDName to the Move-VirtualHardDisk cmdlet
# This will notify VMM to use the differencing disk for New-VM
# instead of the base disk $VHDName
Move-VirtualHardDisk -Bus 0 -LUN 0 -IDE -Path $DiffVHDName
-JobGroup $JobGuid
```

In addition to the new UseLocalVirtualHardDisks, VMM 2008 R2 has added one more new switch for New-VM called SkipInstallVirtualizationGuestServices. This switch notifies VMM to skip the installation of the Integration Components (ICs) (also known as Virtual Guest Services) as part of the New-VM cmdlets, decreasing the amount of time required for New-VM to complete. This switch should be used only if you are already certain that your template either contains the ICs or contains an operating system that has built-in integration components. It is important that you ensure that all your VMs have the integration components correctly installed to take full advantage of virtualization and virtualization management. The SkipInstallVirtualizationGuestServices will take effect only in the following three New-VM scenarios:

◆ New virtual machine from VHD

◆ New virtual machine utilizing an existing virtual machine

◆ New virtual machine from a template that does not have an OS configuration specified

The following code shows an example invocation of the New-VM cmdlet that utilizes this new switch. This new switch can also be used along with the UseLocalVirtualHardDisks switch to further speed up the New-VM process. Here's the code:

```
# Specify variables needed for the new-vm cmdlet
$vmname = "vm2"
$hostname = "host.contoso.com"

# Get an instance of the host that will be the target
# for the Virtual Machine
$vmhost = get-vmhost $hostname

# Create the jobgroup ID for new-vm from template
$JobGuid = [System.Guid]::NewGuid().ToString()

# Get the instance of the template that will be used for OS Configuration
$template = Get-Template | where {$_.Name -eq "VMMTemplate"}

# Get the current username to be passed as the Virtual Machine owner
$callerUsername = whoami

# Create the new-vm from template and specify the
# SkipInstallVirtualizationGuestServices switch to skip
# the Install VM components step of the New-VM cmdlet
New-VM -Template $template -Name $vmname -Description
"a Virtual Machine created with RP" -Owner $callerUsername
```

```
-VMHost $vmhost -SkipInstallVirtualizationGuestServices
-Path $vmhost.VMPaths[0] -RunAsynchronously
-JobGroup $JobGuid | Out-Null
```

Specifying CPU Settings

The Virtual Machine Manager Administrator Console only exposes the Virtual Machine Priority setting as part of the virtual machine properties. The priority of a VM, which decides how to allocate CPU resources on the host for this VM, can be specified in the Hardware Configuration tab, as shown in Figure 8.15. VMM exposes two more CPU properties for a virtual machine through Windows PowerShell only and the Set-VM cmdlet:

CPUMax   Specifies the highest percentage of the total resources of a single CPU on the host that can be used by a specific virtual machine at any given time.

CPUReserve   Specifies the minimum percentage of the resources of a single CPU on the host to allocate to a virtual machine. The percentage of CPU capacity that is available to the virtual machine is never less than this percentage.

A third PowerShell property, called RelativeWeight, is the same as the VM Priority property seen in Figure 8.15. Use this command to create a new hardware profile with the three CPU properties set at different levels.

FIGURE 8.15
CPU priority for a virtual machine

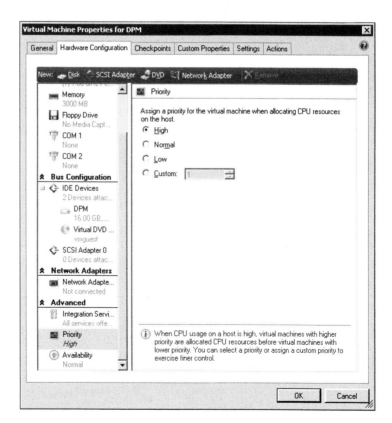

The following code shows an example creation of a virtual machine with the CPU properties:

```
# Get the instance of a host
$vmhost = get-vmhost "host.contoso.com"

# Get the instance of a VHD that will be used during New-VM
$vhd = (Get-VirtualHardDisk)[0]

# Create a new hardware profile with the CPU settings set
$hwProfile = New-HardwareProfile -Name "cpuHWProfile" -description ""
 -CPUMax 70 -CPUReserve 50 -RelativeWeight 80

# Create the new Virtual Machine with the hardware profile specified
New-VM -Name "cpuVM" -VirtualHardDisk $vhd -VMHost $vmhost -HardwareProfile
 $hwProfile -Path $vmhost.VMPaths[0]

# Show that the new Virtual Machine created has the specified CPU settings
Get-VM -Name "cpuVM" | Select Name, Hostname, CPUMax, CPUReserve,
 RelativeWeight
```

Clustering Cmdlet Switches

VMM 2008 R2 provides support for the new Windows Server 2008 R2 Hyper-V features, including Live Migration in a failover cluster environment. From the VMM Administrator Console, if Live Migration is available for a virtual machine, then that is the only option offered to an administrator for migrating the virtual machine to another node in the cluster. If you want to force the transfer type of the virtual machine to be Quick Migration (Quick Migration saves the state of a virtual machine prior to changing its ownership to another node in the cluster) even if Hyper-V Live Migration is available, use the UseCluster switch with this command:

```
Move-VM -VM $myVM -vmhost $VMHost -Path $VMHost.VMPaths[0] -UseCluster
```

Hyper-V Live Migration allows only one cluster node to participate in a live migration at any point in time. VMM implemented a queue to track active live migrations and ensure that all user-executed live migrations complete in order. If you would like the Move-VM cmdlet to fail if a Hyper-V live migration is in progress and your live migration cannot start immediately, use the BlockLMIfHostBusy switch with this command (this switch will not utilize the VMM Live Migration queue):

```
Move-VM -VM $myVM -vmhost $VMHost -Path $VMHost.VMPaths[0] -BlockLMIfHostBusy
```

Monitoring and Reporting

Creating automated tasks that checks the health of your system and emails the administrator on critical errors can be accomplished very easily with a few cmdlets. In this section, we will show you a few cmdlets that can prove useful in assessing the overall health of your system. If you would like to bundle these scripts into an automated task and enable email notification, you can look into the SMTP emailing properties of the class System.Net.Mail.MailMessage.

Use this command to get the overall status of the virtual machines' health:

```
Get-VM | Select Name, ID, Status | sort-object Status
```

Use this command to get a list of all virtual machines and their host names:

```
# VMID is the unique identifier of the VM on the virtualization platform
(i.e. Hyper-V)
# ID is the unique identifier of the VM in Virtual Machine Manager
Get-VM | Select Name, ID, HostName, VMID
```

Use this command to get a list of the last job run on each virtual machine:

```
Get-VM | Select Name, ID, MostRecentTask
```

Use this command to get the health information of the hosts:

```
Get-VMHost | select Name, OverallState, CommunicationState,
VirtualServerState, VirtualServerVersionState
```

Use this command to get the health information of the managed physical computers:

```
Get-VMMManagedComputer | select Name, State, VersionState, UpdatedDate
```

Use this command to create a report of two custom properties of a virtual machine:

```
# You can use the Customer Properties of a VM to add any data you would like to
# associate with a VM. In this example, we chose CostCenter and
# LastUpdated for the first two custom properties
Get-VM |select Name, Status,
 @{Name='CostCenter';Expression={$_.CustomProperties[0]}},
 @{Name='LastUpdated';Expression={$_.CustomProperties[1]}}
```

Use this command to get the list of virtualization platforms in VMM:

```
Get-VMHost | select Name, VirtualizationPlatformDetail | sort-object
 VirtualizationPlatformDetail -descending
```

Use this command to get the last 10 jobs that were run in VMM, their owners, and the affected objects:

```
$jobs = get-job | sort-object StartTime -Descending | select Name,
ResultName, ResultObjectType, Status, Owner
$jobs[0..10]
```

When invoking Windows PowerShell cmdlets, it is useful to be able to identify if an error occurred. Use the following command to clear any existing errors in the error pipeline and then use the same object to check for errors:

```
# Clear any existing errors from the error pipeline
$Error.Clear()
```

```
# Invoke a cmdlet. As an example, I used get-vmmserver
$c = get-vmmserver -ComputerName "localhost"

# Check if any errors occurred
if ($Error.Count -ne 0)
{
    # An error occurred here. Do something about it and terminate
    # the script
}
```

The Bottom Line

Describe the main benefits that PowerShell offers for VMM.   Windows PowerShell is a relatively new technology that was developed by Microsoft Corporation. Virtual Machine Manager utilized this technology as the scripting public API for VMM and as the backbone of the Administrator Console.

Master It   What version of Windows PowerShell does VMM support?
Which are the VMM assemblies needed for programmatically integrating with VMM's cmdlets?
List the benefits that Windows PowerShell cmdlets offer as a public API.

Create scheduled PowerShell scripts.   Scheduling PowerShell scripts allows an administrator to perform operations during nonwork hours and get reports on the progress and the results of those operations.

Master It   How can you create a scheduled task in Windows?
List an example PowerShell script that checks if any host is in an unhealthy state and needs an administrator to take a look at it.

Use the VMM PowerShell cmdlets.   Understanding the usage, scope, and association of the different VMM cmdlets and PowerShell objects allows an administrator to effectively manage VMM through Windows PowerShell.

Master It   How can you identify the proper parameters and syntax for the Add-VMHost cmdlet?
How can you add the VMM PowerShell snap-in programmatically to a PowerShell script?
How does the Windows PowerShell pipeline work?

Chapter 9

Writing a PRO Pack

System Center Virtual Machine Manager (VMM), Performance and Resource Optimization (PRO), and System Center Operations Manager (OpsMgr) team together to provide administrators with the dynamic infrastructure to ensure that their virtualization environment is functioning at an optimal performance. Health issues can be automatically resolved through PRO tips, which help maintain a balanced environment without user intervention and provide the highly coveted end-to-end services management. Due to its dynamic nature, PRO is a key feature in reducing IT costs and minimizing downtime while improving the reliability and health of virtualized workloads.

In this chapter, you will learn to:

◆ Integrate VMM with OpsMgr for end-to-end service management

◆ Use the PRO infrastructure to create a new PRO pack

VMM and Operations Manager

Integrating System Center Operations Manager (OpsMgr) with VMM is critical in expanding the VMM management functionality to include end-to-end services management. OpsMgr provides real-time health monitoring for datacenters and is extensible using pluggable management packs. VMM helps you manage and optimize your virtualized infrastructure. The integration between these two products enables you to use OpsMgr to find opportunities to optimize by monitoring applications and servers and to have VMM automatically remediate the issue and execute on the optimization opportunity.

Through the integration with OpsMgr, VMM also delivers the Performance and Resource Optimization (PRO) feature. PRO allows you to extend the management services and augment the available knowledge in the management packs (MPs) to make recommendations or take actions that take advantage of the additional capabilities available when workloads are running in a virtualized environment. PRO leverages the collection of health, performance, and configuration data that OpsMgr collects from managed computers to provide intelligent recommendations to administrators that respond to environmental changes.

In addition to monitoring, PRO leverages the alerting and remediation capabilities of OpsMgr. PRO supports all virtualization platforms that VMM supports, including Hyper-V, ESX, and Virtual Server. OpsMgr alerts are surfaced as PRO tips in the VMM infrastructure. PRO tips make recommendations to the VMM administrator with remedial actions to return VMs and hosts to a healthy state. By taking advantage of the OpsMgr infrastructure, PRO tips can alert an administrator about issues ranging from the health and performance of workloads inside a virtual machine to hardware issues on the physical servers and accelerate time to resolution. Administrators can chose to manually implement the PRO tips, triggering the recovery tasks of the alerts, or they can have VMM auto-implement the tips based on severity levels and minimize potential downtime. Figure 9.1 illustrates a high-level overview of PRO in action.

FIGURE 9.1

High-level overview of
PRO in action

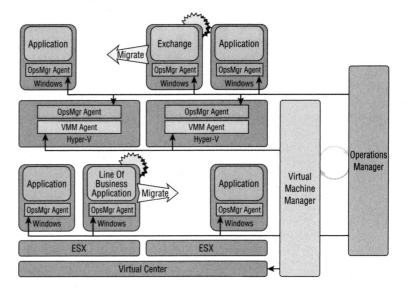

PRO tips are implemented in OpsMgr management packs that target the PRO public classes. These special management packs are also known as PRO packs or PRO-enabled management packs. The PRO public classes and the PRO functionality are included in the VMM management packs that we will import and configure in the next section.

Setup and Configuration

Setting up the integration between VMM and OpsMgr requires VMM to be functioning and operational first. Once you have set up your VMM environment, you are ready to integrate with OpsMgr. In this section, we will look at the steps required to configure the integration of VMM with OpsMgr and enable the PRO functionality of VMM. An OpsMgr management group can integrate with multiple VMM environments (i.e., multiple VMM servers); however, a single VMM server can integrate with only one OpsMgr management group. It is important to note that even though an OpsMgr management group can integrate with multiple VMM servers, all VMM servers have to be of the same version. If an OpsMgr environment is integrating with VMM 2008 R2, it can integrate only with other VMM servers that are also running VMM 2008 R2.

There are a few criteria to enabling this integration:

◆ You need to install System Center Operations Manager 2007 SP1 or System Center Operations Manager 2007 R2.

◆ For full management to be enabled and to take advantage of all the features and functionality of PRO, you need to deploy an OpsMgr agent to all Windows-based computers in the VMM environment. That means that Windows-based hosts and library servers as well as Windows-based virtual machines should be managed by OpsMgr.

- ◆ The VMM server, the database server, and the Self-Service Portal web server should also be managed by OpsMgr.

- ◆ For non-Windows-based hosts and non-Windows-based virtual machines, you should check the OpsMgr documentation for management pack support.

- ◆ From a VMM perspective, ESX hosts and Virtual Center servers are monitored through the health service of the OpsMgr agent on the VMM server (the VMM server acts as a monitoring proxy). You do not need to install any additional software within your VMware environment, either the Virtual Center Server or the ESX hosts.

IMPORTING THE VMM MANAGEMENT PACK

Now that OpsMgr is configured and all agents are deployed, let's go ahead and import the VMM management pack. You can get the VMM management packs and their dependencies from a few different places:

- ◆ You can find them in the System Center Operations Manager 2007 catalog (referenced at `http://technet.microsoft.com/en-us/opsmgr/cc539535.aspx`).

- ◆ You can use the DVD that you used to install VMM. (The VMM management packs are included in the `amd64\VirtualizationMP` folder.)

- ◆ You can download them from within the OpsMgr console.

For the VMM management packs to be imported, the following prerequisite management packs need to be already imported in OpsMgr (if you have older versions of these management packs imported into OpsMgr, remove them first). Failure to import the prerequisite management packs prior to running VMM Setup on the OpsMgr server will result in the error seen in Figure 9.2.

Microsoft Windows Server Internet Information Services (IIS) management packs You can download the IIS management packs from the Microsoft Download Center under the name "Windows Server Internet Information Services for System Center Operations Manager 2007." VMM requires the following IIS management packs:

- ◆ Windows Server Internet Information Services 2003

- ◆ Windows Server 2008 Internet Information Services 7.0

- ◆ Windows Server Internet Information Services Library

Microsoft SQL Server management pack You can download the SQL Server management pack from the Microsoft Download Center under the name "Microsoft SQL Server Management Pack for Operations Manager 2007." VMM requires the SQL Server Core library management pack to be imported.

The VMM management packs reference the management packs in the preceding list using the following version information and public key tokens:

```
<ReferenceAlias="IISServer2003">
  <ID>Microsoft.Windows.InternetInformationServices.2003</ID>
  <Version>6.0.5000.0</Version>
  <PublicKeyToken>31bf3856ad364e35</PublicKeyToken>
</Reference>
```

```
<ReferenceAlias="IISServer2008">
  <ID>Microsoft.Windows.InternetInformationServices.2008</ID>
  <Version>6.0.6278.0</Version>
  <PublicKeyToken>31bf3856ad364e35</PublicKeyToken>
</Reference>
<ReferenceAlias="IISCommon">
  <ID>Microsoft.Windows.InternetInformationServices.CommonLibrary</ID>
  <Version>6.0.5000.0</Version>
  <PublicKeyToken>31bf3856ad364e35</PublicKeyToken>
</Reference>
<ReferenceAlias="SQLCommon">
  <ID>Microsoft.SQLServer.Library</ID>
  <Version>6.0.5000.0</Version>
  <PublicKeyToken>31bf3856ad364e35</PublicKeyToken>
</Reference>
<ReferenceAlias="InstanceGroupLibrary">
  <ID>Microsoft.SystemCenter.InstanceGroup.Library</ID>
  <Version>6.0.5000.0</Version>
  <PublicKeyToken>31bf3856ad364e35</PublicKeyToken>
</Reference>
```

FIGURE 9.2
VMM Setup fails if prerequisite management packs are missing.

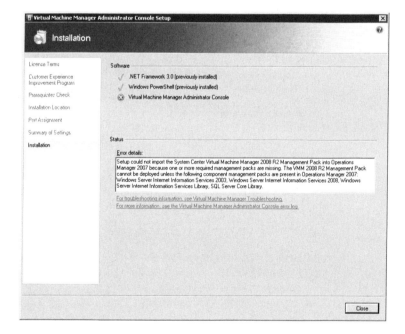

INSTALLING THE VMM MANAGEMENT PACK

Before installing any of the VMM management packs, make sure the OpsMgr environment does not have any previous versions of the VMM management packs installed. If any exist in the Management Packs folder of the Administration view of the Operations console, click on them and select Delete. To install the VMM management packs in OpsMgr, you have a couple of different options. Either you can manually import the management packs from the OpsMgr console or VMM Setup can do this for you. To manually import a management pack, follow these steps:

1. Open the OpsMgr Operations console.

2. Click the Administration view.

3. Select the Management Packs folder.

4. From the actions menu, select Import Management Packs.

5. Add the management pack either from disk or from the OpsMgr catalog.

The easier approach is to launch VMM Setup on the Operations Manager Root Management Server and let VMM do the entire required configuration. To do this, follow these steps:

1. From Setup, select the Configure Operations Manager option as seen in Figure 9.3.

FIGURE 9.3
VMM Setup option for configuring OpsMgr

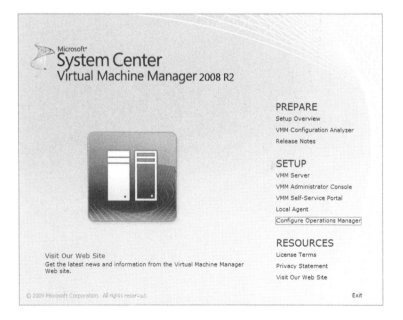

2. In the wizard's Port Assignment page, enter the VMM server name and VMM server port, as seen in Figure 9.4.

3. Setup will then install the VMM management and reporting packs as well as the VMM Administrator Console on that server. In addition, this wizard will grant the log on account of the VMM Windows Service the necessary access to the OpsMgr server.

4. Once this step is completed, go ahead and install the VMM Administrator Console on the rest of the OpsMgr management servers in your environment. The VMM Administrator Console is required on all management servers because it will also install the VMM Power-Shell cmdlets that are used by PRO packs during recovery actions.

5. A PRO recovery task will execute on the management server that currently owns the agent where the monitor was running when it became unhealthy. This means that the VMM PowerShell cmdlets need to be present on that management server for the recovery task to be successful.

FIGURE 9.4
Administrator Console
Setup requires the name
of the VMM server

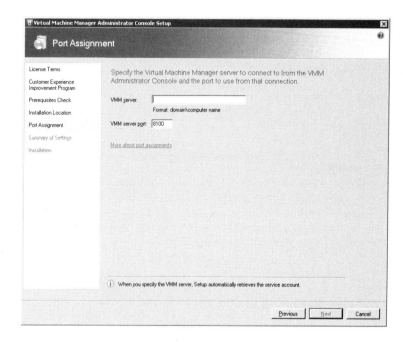

The VMM management packs include the following:

◆ System Center Virtual Machine Manager 2008

◆ Microsoft.SystemCenter.VirtualMachineManager.Pro.2008.HyperV.HostPerformance

◆ Microsoft.SystemCenter.VirtualMachineManager.Pro.2008.VMRightSize

◆ Microsoft.SystemCenter.VirtualMachineManager.Pro.2008.VMWare.HostPerformance

◆ System Center Virtual Machine Manager 2008 PRO Library

◆ System Center Virtualization Reports 2008

Please note that each management pack will have the same exact version as the version of the installation of VMM that provided the management packs.

Once the VMM management packs are installed on the OpsMgr root management server (RMS), follow these steps:

1. Launch the VMM Administrator Console and go to the Administration tab.

2. Click the System Center tree view entry and select Operations Manager Server.

3. When you enter the OpsMgr RMS server name and click OK, VMM will configure a connection to OpsMgr to enable the PRO functionality (the same action can also be

accomplished from PowerShell using the `Set-VMMServer -OpsMgrServer <RMS server name>` cmdlet).

In order for this action to be completed successfully, the OpsMgr Operations console needs to be installed on the VMM server computer. VMM uses components that get installed with the Operations console to communicate and interface with OpsMgr. Failure to install the Operations console will result in error 11808 with the following message:

```
Unable to set the Operations Manager root server in VMM because the
Operations Console for Operations Manager is not installed on the Virtual
Machine Manager server. Install the Operations Console for System Center
Operations Manager 2007 on the Virtual Machine Manager server and then
try the operation again.
ID: 11808
```

The execution of the `Set-VMMServer` cmdlet with the `-OpsMgrServer` option will also trigger the discovery process of the VMM components in OpsMgr. By default, snapshot discovery (which discovers everything) will run every 6 hours, but this cmdlet forces VMM to execute the discovery process immediately. Discoveries for the VMM management packs are executed by the VMM server through the OpsMgr SDK. VMM uses the Operations Manager SDK Connector interface to provide OpsMgr with information regarding the virtualization environment managed by VMM. VMM also provides OpsMgr with incremental discovery data. This can happen, for example, when a host is added or removed from management.

However, please note that virtual machine creations are updated only with snapshot discoveries.

The OpsMgr Connector is also used to retrieve alerts for the monitors that target PRO classes. The process occurs every 60 seconds. These alerts turn into PRO tips in the Administrator Console. When a PRO tip is implemented from the PRO Tips window, VMM will use the connector to initiate the recovery task for the monitor (OpsMgr will in turn run the recovery task). OpsMgr sets aside some buffers and cached data for each connector that is opened. To deal with its maximum supported scale of 400 hosts and 8,000 VMs, VMM opens 32 connectors to provide discovery information and load balance the requests without overloading a single connector.

Security Configuration

For the integration between VMM and OpsMgr to function correctly, there is a need for cross-trust to be established. The way to accomplish this functionality is through the following required steps:

1. Find the default action account that OpsMgr is configured to use for each management server and make that account a member of the Administrator user role in VMM. Visit the Administration view of the VMM Administrator Console and select User Roles to add a new VMM administrator. This option ensures that any actions performed by the OpsMgr health service are fully authorized in VMM. Such actions will most likely include the usage of VMM PowerShell cmdlets. If the action account for each management server is listed as a local system or network service account, as in Figure 9.5, add the machine account of the individual management servers instead (the format for the machine account is `<domainname\computername$>`).

2. Find the account that is used for running the VMM server Virtual Machine Manager Windows Service (VMMService is the service name) and make that account a local administrator on all OpsMgr management servers. Also make sure it is a member of the OpsMgr Operations Manager Administrators user role. To do so, follow these steps:

   a. In the Administration view of the Operations console, click Security ➢ User Roles.

   b. View the properties of the Operations Manager Administrator user role. This level of access is required so that the VMM server can connect to the OpsMgr through the SDK.

   c. If the service's log on as account is local system or network service, add the machine account instead.

   d. Once the proper accounts are added to OpsMgr, restart the OpsMgr SDK Service in order for Operations Manager to recognize the group membership changes.

FIGURE 9.5
Default action accounts
for OpsMgr

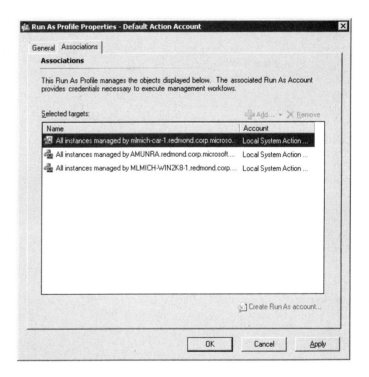

The OpsMgr default action account will execute VMM cmdlets in response to alert recovery tasks. This requires the execution policy for Windows PowerShell to be set correctly on all management servers and the VMM server.

To configure Windows PowerShell on each management server, follow these steps:

1. Open the VMM Administrator Console and from the toolbar and select PowerShell. This opens Windows PowerShell with the VMM snap-in loaded.

2. If prompted, select to always trust remote signed scripts from this snap-in. This can also be achieved using the Set-ExecutionPolicy cmdlet.

3. To ensure that Windows PowerShell cmdlets will execute correctly using the OpsMgr default action account, open a window under the credentials of the default action account.

You can use the `RunAs` command to open a window under a separate set of credentials than the logged-on user account.

4. Launch PowerShell with the VMM snap-in loaded in the window using the following command:

```
C:\Windows\System32\WindowsPowerShell\v1.0\powershell.exe -PSConsoleFile
"C:\Program Files\Microsoft System Center Virtual Machine Manager
2008 R2\bin\cli.psc1" -NoExit
```

To configure Windows PowerShell on the VMM server, follow these steps:

1. Open the VMM Administrator Console and from the toolbar and select PowerShell. This will open Windows PowerShell with the VMM snap-in loaded.

2. If prompted, select to always trust remote signed scripts from this snap-in.

Operations Manager and VMM are now configured to work together to provide monitoring and alerting within your virtualized environment. To verify that the integration has worked and data has started populating, follow these steps:

1. Open the OpsMgr Operations console and click the Monitoring tab. Two folders called Virtual Machine Manager 2008 R2 and Virtual Machine Manager 2008 R2 Views should exist.

2. In the Views folder, click the Diagram view for <VMM Server Name> to view a diagram of the health of your entire virtualized infrastructure for that VMM server.

The hierarchical diagram starts from the VMM server and extends to the hosts and virtual machines and all the way to the health of individual applications that are monitored inside the guest operating system of a virtual machine. Figure 9.6 has an example diagram of a virtualized environment.

FIGURE 9.6
Diagram view for a VMM server environment

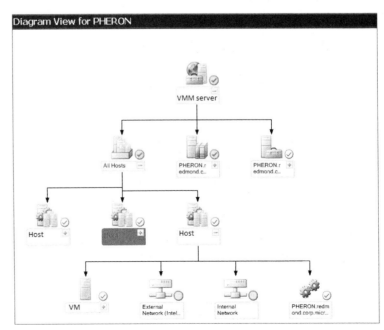

Leveraging Performance and Resource Optimization

Now that the VMM management packs are imported in OpsMgr, the environment is ready for PRO. PRO has two main settings:

◆ Monitoring level

◆ Automation level

The monitoring level controls which OpsMgr monitors to enable for PRO in order to publish PRO tips on the VMM console, while the automation level controls which monitors' recovery tasks should be configured to auto-implement their respective remediation.

PRO packs can define three high-level types of tips:

PRO tips that target hosts   These tips can access the health of the host and its hardware and recommend migrating virtual machines to improve performance or to vacate a host from its virtual machines.

PRO tips that target virtual machines   These tips can access the health of the virtual machine and its applications and recommend actions and modifications to improve that health.

PRO tips that target the VMM server   These tips can access the overall systemwide health of the virtualization environment and suggest actions that span multiple hosts and virtual machines. For example, a PRO tip that targets the VMM server can do dynamic load balancing across all the nodes of a cluster.

Enabling PRO

There are a couple of different ways to enable PRO, depending on the types of tips that need to be enabled:

◆ At the cluster level for both VMware and Hyper-V through the cluster properties in the Administrator Console

◆ At the Host Group level for All Hosts or an individual Host Group hierarchy

◆ At the VMM server level for PRO tips targeted for the VMM server

To enable PRO on a Host Group, the following steps are required (enabling PRO at the Host Group level enables PRO for all hosts and all virtual machines that are part of that host group):

1. From either the hosts or the virtual machines view of the VMM Administrator Console, find your host group and open its properties.

2. On the PRO tab, as seen in Figure 9.7, select the Enable PRO On This Host Group check box (you can also chose to inherit the PRO settings from the parent host group).

3. When PRO is enabled, the default monitoring level is set to Warning and Critical, which means that PRO will enable all monitors and display all PRO tips that have a warning or critical severity. To restrict the PRO tips to Critical alerts only, select the Critical Only option.

4. Through VMM, you can enable the automatic implementation of tips based on the severity of alerts. Select the Automatically Implement PRO Tips On This Host Group check box. By default, the automation level is set to Critical Only, which means that only PRO tips

with a critical severity level are automatically implemented. For all tips to be automatically implemented, select the Warning and Critical option.

5. Click OK to save your settings. PRO configuration changes do not take effect immediately. It takes a few minutes for VMM to update the memberships of the OpsMgr groups and then forward the settings to managed computers.

FIGURE 9.7
Enabling PRO for a host group

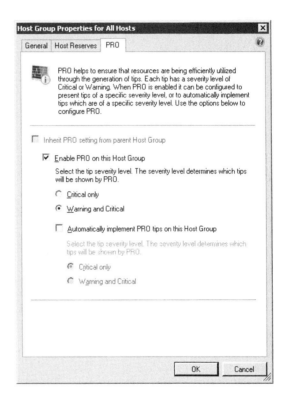

To enable PRO tips targeted at the VMM server component, the following steps are required (the example PRO pack in this chapter has PRO tips targeted at the VMM server):

1. In the Administration view of the VMM Administrator Console, click General.

2. Select (right click) the PRO Settings option and choose modify.

3. Select the Enabled PRO Tips check box, as seen in Figure 9.8.

4. When PRO is enabled, the default monitoring level is set to Warning and Critical, which means that PRO will enable all monitors and display all PRO tips that have a warning or critical severity. To restrict the PRO tips to critical alerts only, select the Critical Only option.

5. Through VMM, you can enable the automatic implementation of tips based on the severity of alerts. Select the Automatically Implement PRO Tips check box. By default, the automation level is set to Critical Only, which means that only PRO tips with a critical severity level are automatically implemented. For all tips to be automatically implemented, select the Warning and Critical option.

6. Click OK to save your settings.

FIGURE 9.8
Enabling PRO for the
VMM server

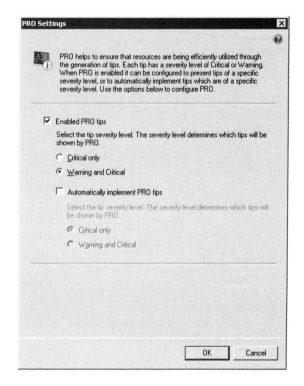

In general, PRO should be enabled for a while without auto-implementation so you can familiarize yourself with the types of PRO tips that are generated and make decisions on what should be auto-implemented and the scope to which the tips should be applied. As familiarity and trust with PRO increases, automatic implementation can be enabled for either critical or both critical and warning alerts. Because some administrators might chose to auto-implement PRO tips based on severity, it is very important for management pack authors to differentiate their alerts appropriately. For example, a customer might chose to auto-remediate only critical alerts. Due to the dynamic nature of virtualized environments, it is also possible that PRO tips may show up and disappear on their own without the need for implementation because the workload has returned to a healthy state on its own.

Once PRO is set up in VMM, PRO tips can be viewed through the PRO Tips window. The toolbar of the VMM Administrator Console contains a PRO Tips button, which opens the PRO Tips window as a new dialog. By default, the PRO Tips window automatically activates when new PRO tips are created (there is a check box at the bottom of the window to disable this option). Once open, the window shows all active PRO tips that the current Administrator Console user has access to. The top half of the screen lists the tips, and the bottom half shows details for the tip that is currently selected. The fields on the left side of the details pane are automatically generated based on the context of the Tip. The content on the right side is product knowledge for the alert, which is developed by the management pack author (in this case, the PRO pack author). The product knowledge for each alert can contain four sections:

◆ Description

◆ Recommended Action

◆ Causes

◆ Summary

Following is a listing of the PRO tip properties that show up in the PRO Tips window.

Name   The name of the PRO tip comes from the alert name as defined on the OpsMgr monitor.

Description   The description of the PRO tip comes from the alert description as defined on the OpsMgr monitor.

Summary   Provides an optional summary description of the implementation for this PRO tip. Can be set using this cmdlet:

```
Set-PROTip -PROTipId $ProtipId -ActionSummary "<enter summary>";
```

ActionDetail   Provides an optional detailed description of the implementation of this PRO tip. Can be set using this cmdlet:

```
Set-PROTip -PROTipId $ProtipId -ActionDetails "<enter details>";
```

ActionScript   Provides the optional script that will be run when the recovery task of this PRO tip executes. Can be set using this cmdlet:

```
Set-PROTip -PROTipId $ProtipId -ActionScript "<enter script>";
```

Figure 9.9 shows the PRO Tips window and its field descriptions within the context of an active tip. Figure 9.10 shows the alert in the OpsMgr Operations console that generated the PRO tip in VMM. For more information about the properties of a PRO tip, run the following Windows PowerShell cmdlets:

```
PS C:\> Get-Help Set-PROTip -Full
PS C:\> Get-Help Get-PROTip -Full
```

If a selected tip has an associated action and is still active, users can click the Implement button to initiate the associated recovery task for the alert that generated the PRO tip. Alternatively, if the administrator chooses to not implement a tip, it can be dismissed and removed from the view.

HOW PRO CHANGES THE OPSMGR MONITOR HEALTH

When a PRO tip is successfully implemented, VMM will reset the health of the OpsMgr monitor that generated the PRO tip or alert.

If a PRO tip is dismissed, no changes are made to the source monitor that generated it. However, VMM will close the alert associated with the PRO tip. This means that the monitor will remain in an unhealthy state but will not generate any new PRO tips because the user just chose to ignore those PRO tips.

When a PRO tip fails to be implemented, it will stay active and it can be implemented again. The monitor is not reset in this case.

When a monitor is in auto-implementation mode and a PRO tip fails to be implemented, VMM will reset the health of the monitor.

VMM will automatically reset monitors that are unhealthy and stale every 1 hour. However, this happens only for monitors that are set to auto-implement their recovery tasks.

Operations Manager might reset a monitor if an agent gets an update, if you manually reset the monitor, or if a computer returns from maintenance mode.

Once a PRO tip is implemented, VMM job(s) are created to track the progress of the actions initiated by the PRO tip. The Jobs view of the Administrator Console will show the currently active jobs in the system, including the jobs initiated by tips. To view the PRO tip associated with a job, select the PRO Tip tab of the details pane for a specific job. This allows you to distinguish which jobs were initiated by users and which were implemented through PRO tips for auditing and tracking purposes.

FIGURE 9.9
VMM PRO Tips window showing a tip from the Maintenance Mode PRO pack

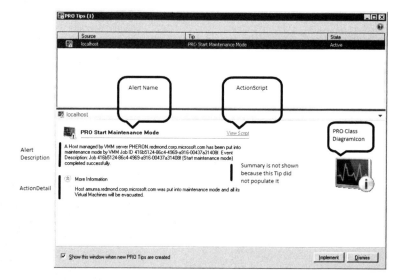

PRO Packs Released with VMM

The VMM management packs already include the PRO functionality as well as a couple of PRO packs to get you started:

Host Performance PRO pack   This PRO pack monitors the host CPU and memory performance and creates tips when the CPU exceeds 75 percent of capacity or when the memory consumed exceeds 90 percent of capacity. VMware, Virtual Server, and Hyper-V hosts are all monitored by this PRO pack. Once a tip is generated, it includes the cause of the tip and other relevant data. Implementing this tip will migrate the virtual machine that has the highest resource usage on the host. This virtual machine will be migrated within its host group to the host of the same virtualization platform with the highest star rating. The migration leverages the Intelligent Placement feature of VMM.

VM Right-Size PRO pack   This PRO pack monitors the virtual machine performance and offers tips on configuration changes if the virtual machine uses more than 90 percent of the CPU or memory that is allocated to it. The tips included in this PRO pack are not designed for auto-implementation.

FIGURE 9.10

OpsMgr Operations console showing an alert that generated a PRO tip

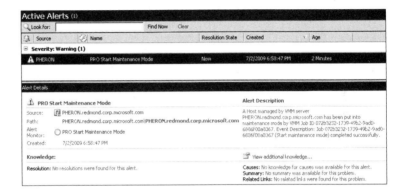

To test the provided PRO packs and see how PRO tips are surfaced and implemented in your environment, run a CPU stress utility both inside a virtual machine and on the host computer and wait for a few minutes. A PRO tip will be created and the user will have the option to either dismiss it or implement it. If auto-implementation is enabled, the PRO tip will automatically be implemented without showing up in the PRO Tips window. Figure 9.11 shows a couple of tips created as a result of performance alerts. Make sure to stop the CPU stress utility at the end of your test to return the host under normal operating conditions.

Since a PRO pack is really a management pack, OpsMgr provides the capability to customize a PRO pack using overrides. For example, you might want to change a threshold for host utilization to 90 percent for CPU rather than the default 75 percent. The rules and monitors defined in the VMM packs can be customized to meet the environment needs or to comply with enterprise policies. To learn how to customize PRO through OpsMgr overrides, refer to "Customizing PRO" Microsoft TechNet. This is available at `http://technet.microsoft.com/en-us/library/cc956018.aspx`.

In addition to the PRO packs published by the VMM team, several VMM and System Center partners are developing PRO packs for use with VMM. The PRO packs can be found on the System Center Operations Manager 2007 catalog at `http://technet.microsoft.com/en-us/opsmgr/cc539535.aspx`.

Creating Your Own PRO Pack

Now that you have set up the integration between VMM and OpsMgr, it's time to learn how to create your own PRO pack. In between the steps for creating an example PRO pack, PRO's specific functionality will be outlined and different options will be discussed.

FIGURE 9.11
Built-in PRO tips
indicating performance
issues

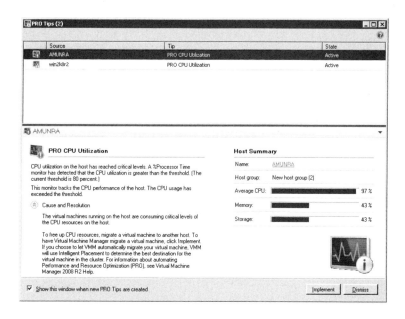

Building a PRO pack is very similar to building a management pack, and it involves the usage of the same tools. A PRO pack is, after all, a management pack that leverages the VMM PRO classes and targets the VMM virtualized environment. PRO packs, just like management packs, offer the ability to collect health and performance data from an application, gain knowledge about its workload, and offer recommendations to improve its health. To build a PRO pack, it is expected that you have good understanding of how to build a regular management pack and that you also have a thorough understanding of OpsMgr. In addition to following the steps for creating a PRO pack in this chapter, you can reference the System Center Operations Manager 2007 Management Pack Authoring Guide at `http://download.microsoft.com /download/7/4/d/74deff5e-449f-4a6b-91dd-ffbc117869a2/OM2007_AuthGuide.doc`. Building a PRO pack also requires a good understanding of VBScript, Windows PowerShell, and XML.

When you design a PRO pack, it is good to have a set of high-level goals in mind before you start development:

◆ Use the knowledge gathered from OpsMgr to provide meaningful and actionable PRO tips that can be either manually implemented or automatically implemented.

◆ Ensure that your OpsMgr monitors are dynamic in nature and can auto-heal if the issue resolves itself.

◆ Monitor the effects of host health and performance on virtual machines and provide meaningful actions.

◆ Monitor the health and performance of virtual machines and ensure that the virtualized environment is balanced and healthy.

Maintenance Mode PRO Pack Functionality

The PRO pack we will be building, called VMM.2008.R2. Pro.MaintenanceMode, will enhance and extend the functionality of the maintenance mode feature in VMM. The full source code of the maintenance mode PRO-enabled management pack will be available for download at this book's website at www.sybex.com/masteringvmm2008r2. Maintenance mode is one of the new features of VMM 2008 R2. A user can now put a managed host into maintenance mode. Once a host is in maintenance mode, VMM will no longer allow that host to be the target host for a new virtual machine. In addition, a host that is in maintenance mode is excluded from host ratings calculations during virtual machine placement.

When maintenance mode is initiated on a host, all running virtual machines are put into a saved state. If the host is part of a cluster, then the user is presented with the option to either live migrate all its virtual machines to another host or save the state of all virtual machines on that host. Live migration is an option only if the host cluster is capable of live migration. This behavior is a little bit different for VMware hosts. Once a VMware ESX host is put into maintenance mode in VMM, VMM will send an "Enter maintenance mode" request to VMware Virtual Center. The behavior of the VMs on that host is determined based on the configuration of the maintenance mode feature in Virtual Center.

When maintenance mode is stopped on a host, VMM will allow that host to be the target host of migrations and that host will start receiving a star rating in placement calculations. However, no VMs are restarted on that host, and the VMs that were migrated away from that host are not placed back automatically

This management pack will enhance the maintenance mode functionality in the following ways:

◆ When a host is put into maintenance mode, the management pack will trigger a PRO tip that notifies the administrator which host is in maintenance mode. If the PRO tip is implemented, it will go into OpsMgr and put that host into maintenance mode as well as migrate all VMs to other hosts. All VMs that are migrated are tagged using the Custom Properties feature of a VM so that they can be easily identified.

◆ When a host returns back from maintenance mode, the management pack will trigger a PRO tip that notifies the administrator which host is coming back from maintenance mode. If the PRO tip is implemented, it will go into OpsMgr and remove that host from maintenance mode. In addition, it will go and find all VMs that were originally on that host and return them back. If this PRO tip is not auto-implemented or manually implemented within 6 hours, the PRO tip will automatically be resolved and no VMs will be migrated.

 Real World Scenario

EVACUATING A HOST DURING MAINTENANCE MODE

We work with a lot of customers that have deployed a pretty big virtualization infrastructure. One of the challenges they face is how to minimize the downtime to virtual machines while a host is under maintenance. VMM makes this a lot better for hosts that are part of a cluster where live migration is enabled since it live migrates the VMs to other nodes of the cluster. However, the majority of the deployed hosts in the industry are not part of a cluster. Evacuating a host is a critical part of maintaining virtual machine availability and meeting customer service-level agreements. Because some hosts could undergo maintenance for extended periods of time, we developed this management pack that leverages PRO to evacuate any host when it undergoes maintenance mode.

Creating the Maintenance Mode PRO Pack

Let's start creating the management pack for maintenance mode. To get started authoring a management pack, you need to have the System Center Operations Manager 2007 R2 Authoring Console installed on a computer. Using the authoring console is the best way to create and edit classes and relationships for a management pack (direct XML editing would also work, but that option is more tedious and error prone). Through the use of the authoring console, you can define your management pack's health model and monitoring logic against the PRO public classes by following these steps:

1. Once you open the authoring console, click File ➤ New to create a new empty management pack. We are creating an empty management pack instead of a Windows application management pack because the VMM management pack has already discovered the VMM application and provided existing classes that this management pack can target.

2. Name the new management pack VMM.2008.R2.Pro.MaintenanceMode and click Next. The name you choose here will also become the filename of the management pack XML file.

3. Enter **VMM 2008 R2 Maintenance Mode PRO pack** in the Display Name field, enter an optional description, and click Create. A new management pack is created that defines no classes, no monitors, and no discoveries.

4. Once it's created, you need to save the management pack. Click File ➤ Save and save the unsealed management pack on the local disk.

If you wanted to also add discovery to the management pack, an easy way to discover the existence of VMM is to look for certain Registry attributes on the VMM server. You could configure a Registry probe that looks for the HKLM\SOFTWARE\Microsoft\Microsoft System Center Virtual Machine Manager Server\Setup Registry key. The value ProductVersion in that Registry key will contain the version information for an installation of VMM. An example product version is 2.0.4263.0.

Now that we have created the initial management pack that will form the basis for our PRO pack, let's continue with the creation of the PRO pack:

1. First, let's edit some of the properties of the management pack we just created. Click File ➤ Management Pack Properties.

2. In the Version field, for easy reference I will enter the same version number as the version of the VMM server that this PRO pack will target. In this case, it is **2.0.4263.0**. Any version number can be used here as long as it adheres to the versioning standards for your management packs.

3. In the References tab, some management pack references have already been preselected. To make this management pack a PRO pack, we need to reference a set of classes defined in the System Center Virtual Machine Manager 2008 PRO library management pack, Microsoft.SystemCenter.VirtualMachineManager.PRO.2008.Library.mp. This management pack should be part of the list of management packs you obtained for VMM 2008 R2. Find the location where this management pack exists on disk and add a reference to it. The VMM team recommends that you reference the PRO library management pack

with version 2.0.3451.0. Any PRO library management pack that has a version number greater than 2.0.3451.0 will not break backward compatibility, so it is okay to build your management pack with this reference.

4. Click OK and save the management pack.

CREATING A UNIT MONITOR

We have now set up the management pack. Because of the reference to the VMM 2008 PRO library management pack, we can leverage the VMM management packs and their discovery of VMM and its components. To start adding logic to our management pack, we need to create a unit monitor. A unit monitor will allow us to execute actions based on events that happen on the VMM server. In this PRO pack, we want to execute actions that are associated with the maintenance mode feature of VMM.

There are three types of monitors in OpsMgr:

♦ Aggregate monitor

♦ Unit monitor

♦ Dependency monitor

For PRO, it is required that you create either a unit monitor or an aggregate monitor. Using one of those two types of monitors is the only way to leverage the PRO infrastructure and generate PRO tips. Dependency monitors cannot be used with PRO. To create the monitor we will use for this PRO pack, follow these steps:

1. Click the health model view of the management pack and select the Monitors category.

2. In the results pane, right-click and select New ➤ Windows Events ➤ Simple ➤ Event Reset.

This type of monitor will be controlled by two events: one event that will put the monitor in an unhealthy state and one event that will put the monitor in a healthy state. It is important to understand the various types of unit monitors available in OpsMgr to achieve the desired implementation. Notice that the PRO feature of VMM will reset a PRO tip source monitor's health and state back to healthy when the PRO tip is successfully implemented (successful implementation for a PRO tip means that the recovery for that monitor is successfully implemented). When a PRO tip is dismissed, VMM makes no changes to the monitor or its health.

3. Enter **VMM.2008.R2.Pro.MaintenanceMode.StartMaintenanceUnitMonitor** as the element ID and **PRO Start Maintenance Mode** as the display name. The target for this monitor should be the VMM server itself. The public PRO class for the VMM server is Microsoft.SystemCenter.VirtualMachineManager.Pro.2008.Server.

By targeting the monitor against the VMM server, there can only be one instance of the PRO tip created at any point in time. This suits this feature because, in general, customers would be putting hosts in maintenance mode one at a time to minimize downtime to VMs. If we wanted to create a PRO tip for each host that enters maintenance mode and still target the monitor against the VMM server, the best way to achieve that is to define a new class in the management pack called HostOnVMMServer. The HostOnVMMServer should inherit from the Microsoft.SystemCenter.VirtualMachineManager.Pro.2008.Public class that the VMM PRO infrastructure defines. We will explain the PRO public class in more detail later on. Once that class is defined, we can discover an instance of it for each host that is managed by a VMM server and target the PRO monitor on those instances. That way, an individual PRO tip would be surfaced for each host that goes into maintenance mode.

ENABLING PRO WITHIN A MANAGEMENT PACK

To enable PRO within a management pack, you need to leverage the public classes that are defined in the PRO library management pack that we referenced earlier. VMM uses the target class of a monitor to determine if an alert created by that monitor is a PRO tip. Only the public classes defined in PRO or inherited from the PRO public class are eligible as targets for PRO tips. A monitor that targets a PRO class — for example, the ManagedHost.HyperV class — will run on each and every Hyper-V host that is managed by the current VMM server. These classes, which are defined in the following list, are available only for virtual machines and hosts that are being monitored by PRO:

Microsoft.SystemCenter.VirtualMachineManager.Pro.2008.VirtualMachine This class represents a virtual machine. VMM automatically discovers an instance of this class for each VM that it is managing. Monitors that target this class will run inside the virtual machine's guest operating system.

Microsoft.SystemCenter.VirtualMachineManager.Pro.2008.ManagedHost.HyperV This class represents a Windows Hyper-V host. VMM automatically discovers an instance of this class for each Hyper-V host managed by VMM. This class should be targeted by monitors that will watch the configuration and performance of Hyper-V hosts. Monitors that target this class will run in the parent partition of the Hyper-V hosts.

Microsoft.SystemCenter.VirtualMachineManager.Pro.2008.ManagedHost.ESXServer This class represents a VMware ESX host. VMM automatically discovers an instance of this class for each VMware ESX host managed by VMM (VMM manages VMware ESX hosts indirectly through VMware Virtual Center). Like the Hyper-V class above, this class should be targeted by monitors who will watch the configuration and performance of all ESX hosts. Monitors that target this class will run on the VMM server and remotely monitor ESX hosts.

Microsoft.SystemCenter.VirtualMachineManager.Pro.2008.ManagedHost.VirtualServer This class represents a Microsoft Virtual Server host. VMM automatically discovers an instance of this class for each Virtual Server host managed by VMM. This class should be targeted by monitors who will watch the configuration and performance of Virtual Server hosts. Monitors that target this class will run in the host operating system.

Microsoft.SystemCenter.VirtualMachineManager.PRO.2008.Server This class represents the VMM server component of the virtualized environment. A single instance of this class will be discovered for each VMM server being managed by an OpsMgr management group. Monitors that target this class will run on the VMM server. Consider using this class for monitors that want to span multiple hosts or virtual machines or make changes to the entire virtualized infrastructure.

In addition to the public classes defined in the preceding list, the PRO library management pack contains the Microsoft.SystemCenter.VirtualMachineManager.Pro.2008.Public class. This class is considered a valid PRO target, and management pack authors can inherit their own custom classes from this class. Figure 9.12 shows the inheritance hierarchy for the PRO classes. Custom classes inherited from this class will also be considered valid PRO targets for monitors. Hardware or software components on hosts and virtual machines can define their own PRO custom classes. This is often necessary when a particular set of hardware is present on only a subset of Hyper-V hosts.

FIGURE 9.12
Inheritance hierarchy for
PRO public classes

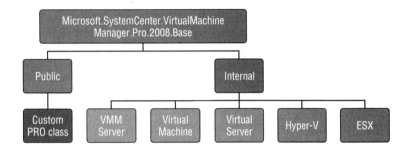

When defining your own class, there are a few additional considerations to be aware of:

◆ During discovery of the new inherited class, the Name property of the Microsoft.SystemCenter .VirtualMachineManager.Pro.2008.Base class needs to be set to the fully qualified domain name (FQDN) of the object you wish the PRO tips to target. For example, this could be the FQDN of the virtual machine, the FQDN of the host, or the FQDN of the VMM server.

◆ The inherited class can have as many properties as necessary.

◆ The inherited class must define a key property.

◆ Discovery for the PRO pack should run no less than every 4 hours.

Once the custom discoveries have run (you can use the OpsMgr MOMScriptAPI.Create-DiscoveryData, referenced at `http://msdn.microsoft.com/en-us/library/bb437588.aspx` to populate the discovery data) and created the required number of instances of the inherited custom PRO class, VMM will populate those instances with the VMM-specific information that the Base class properties define. Such information includes the VMM server name and PRO monitoring and automation levels. This process of populating the properties runs during discovery and is scheduled every 6 hours.

To manually trigger discovery, the `Set-VMMServer` cmdlet can be used as mentioned earlier in the chapter. Be aware that prior to discovery running and the properties of the base class being populated, any alerts that are generated and target your inherited custom class will not be considered PRO tips; however, only newly created instances of the custom class need to wait for discovery to execute before surfacing alerts as PRO tips. To investigate if your class and the Base class are properly getting populated, follow these steps:

1. Open the OpsMgr Operations console.

2. Click Monitoring View.

3. Click Discovered Inventory.

4. Click the Change Target Type action and select your custom class that inherits from the PRO public class.

5. In the results pane, you should view all the discovered instances of your class.

6. Right-click on a discovered instance to view its properties. All the VMM-specific properties should be populated if discovery has already run.

Let's get back to creating our unit monitor that was started in the previous section.

1. Select System.Health.EntityState as the parent monitor and Custom for the category and click Next.

2. The name of the event log to read events from should be VM Manager. This event log exists on the VMM server only, and it should contain all the events necessary to create intelligent management packs that respond to VMM actions. To figure out the exact details of an event, execute the desired action in VMM and observe the events that get created.

3. For the event that puts the monitor in an unhealthy state, enter **1705** as the event ID and **Virtual Machine Manager** as the event source.

4. Because the event ID 1705 is not unique to maintenance mode, we want to match one of the event parameters to the VMM job name for starting the maintenance mode on a host. Click Insert to add a new expression.

5. In the new expression, select the Specify Event Specific Parameter To Use option with the number 3 as the event parameter number. This will generate Parameter 3 as the parameter name.

6. Set this new expression to be equal to Start maintenance mode and click Next. Figure 9.13 shows the actual event in the VM Manager event log. The XML representation of such an event is listed here (as you can see, the third parameter in EventData is Start Maintenance Mode):

```
<Event xmlns="http://schemas.microsoft.com/win/2004/08/events/event">
    <System>
        <Provider Name="Virtual Machine Manager" />
        <EventID Qualifiers="0">1705</EventID>
        <Level>4</Level>
        <Task>0</Task>
        <Keywords>0x80000000000000</Keywords>
        <TimeCreated SystemTime="2009-06-30T14:29:26.000Z" />
        <EventRecordID>22828</EventRecordID>
        <Channel>VM Manager</Channel>
        <Computer><VMM Server computer name></Computer>
        <Security />
    </System>
    <EventData>
        <Data>Job 3b47f30a-2d4a-4851-89fe-4ad842113a90
 (Start maintenance mode) completed successfully.</Data>
        <Data>3b47f30a-2d4a-4851-89fe-4ad842113a90</Data>
        <Data>Start maintenance mode</Data>
        <Data>TaskSucceeded</Data>
    </EventData>
</Event>
```

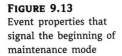

FIGURE 9.13
Event properties that
signal the beginning of
maintenance mode

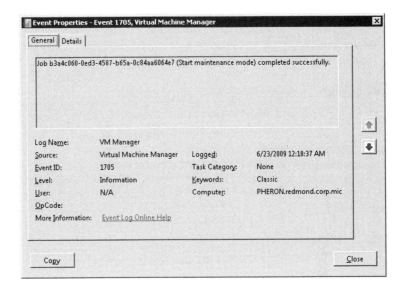

7. Select the VM Manager event log again for the healthy event.

8. For the event that puts the monitor in a healthy state, enter **1705** as the event ID and **Virtual Machine Manager** as the event source.

9. Click Insert to add a new expression. In the new expression, select the Specify Event Specific Parameter To Use option with the number 3 as the event parameter number. This will generate Parameter 3 as the parameter name. Set this new expression to be equal to `Stop maintenance mode` and click Finish. It is important to ensure that the monitors will return to a healthy state when a health problem is fixed. In this case, the problem would be fixed if the host returns back from maintenance mode.

10. Open the properties of the monitor we just created (i.e., VMM.2008.R2.Pro.MaintenanceMode .StartMaintenanceUnitMonitor) by finding the monitor in the Health Model ➢ Monitors view under the tree view created for the VMM Server PRO class.

11. By default, this monitor will not generate any alerts. To add alerts to a monitor, click the Alerting tab.

12. Select the Generate Alerts For This Monitor option and choose to generate an alert when the monitor is in a warning health state (the events raised that we configured earlier will put this monitor to a warning state). Make sure the alert will auto-resolve when the monitor returns to a healthy state.

13. In the alert properties, enter **PRO Start Maintenance Mode** for the alert name and the following code for the alert description. These values will be shown in the PRO Tips window in VMM. OpsMgr will substitute the $ quoted strings below to the proper values based on the alert data:

```
A Host managed by VMM server $Target/Property[Type="Microsoft
SystemCenterVirtualMachineManagerPro2008Library!Microsoft.SystemCenter.
```

```
VirtualMachineManager.Pro.2008.Base"]/VMMServer$ has been put
into maintenance mode by VMM Job ID $Data/Context/Params/Param[2]$.
Event Description: $Data/Context/EventDescription$
```

14. Leave the alert priority at medium and make the severity match the monitor's health. We are now complete in defining the alert settings for this monitor.

CREATING A DIAGNOSTIC TASK

We now need to add an optional diagnostic task. This diagnostic task will be used for populating the PRO tip with runtime data that will show up in the PRO Tips window in VMM. In certain cases, the data provided by the alert might not be enough for an administrator to make a decision. PRO can leverage diagnostic tasks to improve the knowledge included in the alert by populating the tip with additional data. For this PRO pack, these additional data will include the name of the host that just went into maintenance mode. Diagnostic tasks also provide a way for authors to present to the administrator the PowerShell script that will be used if the tip is implemented. Let's go ahead and create the diagnostic task:

1. Click the Diagnostic and Recovery tab.

2. Click Add Diagnostic For Warning Health State and use VMM.2008.R2.Pro.Maintenance-Mode.StartMMUpdatePROTip as the identifier. Use Update PRO Tip as the name and ensure that the target is the PRO VMM server class.

3. Keep the defaults for most of the diagnostic properties and click the Modules tab.

4. Create a new action and select System.CommandExecuterProbe as the module type. Enter **UpdateTipAction** as the module ID.

WINDOWS POWERSHELL MODULE FOR OPSMGR

With System Center Operations Manager 2007 R2, new module types were introduced that provide the ability to run Windows PowerShell scripts from within a management pack. Because the new modules use hosted Windows PowerShell runspaces, they are more efficient than the CommandExecuterProbe module and use significantly less resources. In this case, we could have used Microsoft.Windows.PowerShellProbe instead of CommandExecuterProbe. The only requirement of these modules is that if your management pack uses them, then the management pack can be imported only in an OpsMgr 2007 R2 environment because they are not backward compatible.

---

5. Now edit the newly created action and enter **%SystemRoot%\system32\windowspowershell\v1.0\powershell.exe** in the ApplicationName field, set the working directory to Empty, enter **"& '$file/DiagnosticActionScript.ps1$' '$Data/StateChange/DataItem/EventOriginId$' '$Target/Property[Type="MicrosoftSystemCenterVirtualMachineManagerPro2008Library!Microsoft.SystemCenter.VirtualMachineManager.Pro.2008.Base"]/VMMServer$' '$Data/StateChange/DataItem/Context/DataItem/Params/Param[2]$'"** in the CommandLine field, and enter **300** in the TimeoutSeconds field.

6. Click Edit for the UpdateTipAction and `Notepad.exe` will open with the following XML data shown. The DiagnosticActionScript file has not been defined yet, but it takes three parameters:

   ◆ `$Data/StateChange/DataItem/EventOriginId$` contains the PRO tip ID as it would be represented in the VMM infrastructure

   ◆ `$Target/Property[Type="MicrosoftSystemCenterVirtualMachineManagerPro 2008Library!Microsoft.SystemCenter.VirtualMachineManager.Pro.2008 .Base"]/VMMServer$` contains the FQDN of the VMM server computer

   ◆ `$Data/StateChange/DataItem/Context/DataItem/Params/Param[2]$` contains the second parameter of the EventData XML. The second parameter corresponds to the VMM job ID that created the event log entry that triggered the alert for this diagnostic action. The syntax for this parameter is based on the XML representation of the MonitorTaskDataType. This data type is used as input for a recovery task.

   ```
   <Configuration p1:noNamespaceSchemaLocation="D:\Users\mlmich\AppData\
   Local\Temp\2\UpdateTipAction - System.CommandExecuterProbe.xsd"
    xmlns:p1="http://www.w3.org/2001/XMLSchema-instance">
     <ApplicationName>%SystemRoot%\system32\windowspowershell\v1.0\
   powershell.exe</ApplicationName>
     <WorkingDirectory></WorkingDirectory>
     <CommandLine>"&amp; '$file/DiagnosticActionScript.ps1$'
    '$Data/StateChange/DataItem/EventOriginId$'
    '$Target/Property[Type="MicrosoftSystemCenterVirtualMachineManagerPro
   2008Library!Microsoft.SystemCenter.VirtualMachineManager.Pro.2008.Base"]
   /VMMServer$' '$Data/StateChange/DataItem/Context/DataItem/
   Params/Param[2]$'"</CommandLine>
     <TimeoutSeconds>300</TimeoutSeconds>
     <RequireOutput>true</RequireOutput>
   </Configuration>
   ```

7. Now edit this XML and configure it to the XML that defines the PowerShell script `DiagnosticActionScript.ps1`. This XML data is shown in Listing 9.1.

8. Once the XML is replaced, save the file and close `Notepad.exe`. As you can see, in the definition of the PowerShell script we use the input parameters to update the PRO tip in VMM with the proper ActionScript and ActionDetails. The ActionScript is what enables the View Script link to be shown for a tip in the details pane of the PRO Tips window.

LISTING 9.1:   Diagnostic task XML data for entering maintenance mode

```
<Configuration p1:noNamespaceSchemaLocation="D:\Users\mlmich\AppData\Local
\Temp\2\UpdateTipAction - System.CommandExecuterProbe.xsd"
 xmlns:p1="http://www.w3.org/2001/XMLSchema-instance">
  <ApplicationName>%SystemRoot%\system32\windowspowershell\v1.0\
```

```
powershell.exe</ApplicationName>
  <WorkingDirectory></WorkingDirectory>
  <CommandLine>"&amp; '$file/DiagnosticActionScript.ps1$'
  '$Data/StateChange/DataItem/EventOriginId$'
  '$Target/Property[Type="MicrosoftSystemCenterVirtualMachineManager
Pro2008Library!Microsoft.SystemCenter.VirtualMachineManager.Pro.
2008.Base"]/VMMServer$'
  '$Data/StateChange/DataItem/Context/DataItem/Params/Param[2]$'"
</CommandLine>
  <TimeoutSeconds>300</TimeoutSeconds>
  <RequireOutput>true</RequireOutput>
  <Files>
    <File>
      <Name>DiagnosticActionScript.ps1</Name>
      <Contents>

Param($ProtipId, $VMMServerName, $vmmjobid);

$debugMessage = 'Starting PRO Tip Diagnostic. Parameters passed:
VMM server Name: ' + $VMMServerName + ', Tip Id : ' + $ProtipId +
', VMM job id: ' + $vmmjobid;
eventcreate /T Information /ID 88 /L APPLICATION /SO
 VMM.2008.R2.Pro.MaintenanceMode /D $debugMessage;

# add the VMM snapin
$Error.Clear();
add-pssnapin -name Microsoft.SystemCenter.VirtualMachineManager;
if ($Error.Count -ne 0)
{
   eventcreate /T Information /ID 88 /L APPLICATION /SO
 VMM.2008.R2.Pro.MaintenanceMode /D "Failed to add the
VMM server snapin";
     return;
}

# helper function that returns a string corresponding to the
View Script that is displayed on the PRO Tip window
function GetProScript
{
  return '$hostName = '''+ $hostName +
  '''; $serverName = '''+ $VMMServerName +
  '''; $ProtipId = '''+ $ProtipId +
  '''; $VMMJobId = '''+ $vmmjobid +
  ''';

  function Main
  {
    # Here, you can enter the exact details of the implementation
```

```
    of the PRO Tip
        # Anything that in included in this entire GetProScript function
    will show up
        # when the View Script button is pressed in the PRO Tips window
        # This functionality is useful to administrators so that
    they can see the exact
        # script that will be executed for a PRO Tip
        # For this particular PRO Pack, we could have included
     the full contents of
        # ImplementActionScript.ps1 here
      }
      Main;
        '

    }


# helper function for creating an event log entry with a message
function CreateEventLogGenericError
{
    $message = $args[0]
    $message2 = "Creating event log entry: " + $message
    Write-Warning $message2
    eventcreate /T Error /ID 88 /L APPLICATION /SO
 VMM.2008.R2.Pro.MaintenanceMode /D $message
}

function Main
{
    # create a connection to the VMM server
    $Error.Clear();
    $serverObj = get-vmmserver -computerName $VMMServerName;
    if ($Error.Count -ne 0)
    {
        CreateEventLogGenericError  "Failed to get a connection
to the VMM server host: " + $Error[0]
        return;
    }

    # get the host name from the VMM Job
    $vmmjob = get-job -id $vmmjobid
    $hostid = $vmmjob.ResultObjectID.ToString()
    $vmhost = get-vmhost -id $hostid
    $hostname = $vmhost.FQDN
    $ActionDetails = 'Host ' + $hostname + ' was put into
maintenance mode and all its Virtual Machines will be evacuated.';
    $ScriptBody = GetProScript;

    # now set the PRO tip details so that they can show up in the
 Tips Window in VMM
```

```
        Set-PROTip -PROTipId $ProtipId -ActionScript $ScriptBody
     -ActionDetails $ActionDetails;
   }
   Main;

   </Contents>
      </File>
    </Files>
 </Configuration>
```

9. Click OK and move to the Options tab. Select Public Accessibility and ensure that Enabled is set to true. Click OK again.

CREATING A RECOVERY TASK

Now we are ready to create a recovery task for the monitor. Recovery tasks are scripts or actions that can be executed when a monitor enters an unhealthy state. PRO tip implementations execute these recovery tasks. If you have a monitor that does not have an appropriate remediation, or the remediation requires a set of manual steps by the administrator, you should not create a recovery task for the monitor. PRO tips that do not have a recovery task cannot be implemented from the PRO Tips window in VMM, so it is much more important for the tip to have the appropriate knowledge for the administrator to correct the issue. In such a case, the Implement button will be disabled in the PRO Tips window. In general and as a best practice, all PRO tips should have recoveries so that they are actionable by administrators. To create a recovery task, follow these steps:

1. Click the Diagnostic And Recovery tab.

2. Click Add A Recovery For Warning Health State. Enter **VMM.2008.R2.Pro .MaintenanceMode.StartMMImplementPROTip** as the identifier.

3. Use **Implement PRO Tip** as the name and ensure that the target is the PRO VMM server class.

4. Keep the defaults for most of the recovery properties and click the Configuration tab. Change the time-out to 1 Day (to ensure that there is sufficient time to evacuate the host from its VMs).

5. In the Modules tab, create a new action and select System.CommandExecuter as the module type. Enter **ImplementTipAction** as the Module ID.

6. Now edit the newly created action and enter **%SystemRoot%\system32 \windowspowershell\v1.0\powershell.exe** in the ApplicationName field, set the working directory to Empty, enter "**& '$file/ImplementActionScript.ps1$' '$Data/StateChange/DataItem/EventOriginId$' '$Target/Property[Type= "MicrosoftSystemCenterVirtualMachineManagerPro2008Library!Microsoft .SystemCenter.VirtualMachineManager.Pro.2008.Base"]/VMMServer$' '$Data/StateChange/DataItem/Context/DataItem/Params/Param[2]$'** " in the CommandLine field, and enter **86400** in the TimeoutSeconds field.

7. Click Edit for the ImplementTipAction and Notepad.exe will open with the following XML data. The ImplementActionScript file has not been defined yet, but it takes the same three parameters as the Diagnostic action that we defined earlier.

```
<Configuration p1:noNamespaceSchemaLocation="D:\Users\mlmich\AppData\
Local\Temp\2\ImplementTipAction - System.CommandExecuter.xsd"
xmlns:p1="http://www.w3.org/2001/XMLSchema-instance">
  <ApplicationName>%SystemRoot%\system32\windowspowershell\v1.0\powershell.exe
</ApplicationName>
  <WorkingDirectory></WorkingDirectory>
  <CommandLine>"&amp; '$file/ImplementActionScript.ps1$'
 '$Data/StateChange/DataItem/EventOriginId$'
 '$Target/Property[Type="MicrosoftSystemCenterVirtualMachineManagerPro2008
Library!Microsoft.SystemCenter.VirtualMachineManager.Pro.2008.Base"]/
VMMServer$'
 '$Data/StateChange/DataItem/Context/DataItem/Params/Param[2]$'"</CommandLine>
  <TimeoutSeconds>86400</TimeoutSeconds>
  <RequireOutput>true</RequireOutput>
</Configuration>
```

8. Now edit this XML and configure it to the following XML data that defines the Power-Shell script ImplementActionScript.ps1. This XML is shown in Listing 9.2.

9. Once the XML is replaced, save the file and close Notepad.exe.

As you can see, in the definition of the PowerShell script we use the input parameters to update the PRO tip in VMM to Running and later on to Resolved. In addition, this Pow-erShell script finds all the VMs on the host that entered maintenance mode and migrates them to other hosts within the same host group while leveraging the Intelligent Placement feature of VMM.

This PowerShell script also puts the OpsMgr computer object that corresponds to the VMM host computer in maintenance mode. It is advised not to make the OpsMgr man-agement server and the VMM server roles a host or to run them as virtual machines on hosts that are not live-migration capable and are being put into maintenance mode. If these two roles also function as a host that is put into maintenance mode or they are vir-tual machines on hosts not capable of live migration and are ever put into maintenance mode, the health service will stop generating alerts for the computers, causing your PRO tips not to show up in VMM. Listing 9.2 shows the full code of the recovery task.

LISTING 9.2:   Recovery task XML data for entering maintenance mode

```
<Configuration p1:noNamespaceSchemaLocation="D:\Users\mlmich\AppData\Local
\Temp\2\ImplementTipAction - System.CommandExecuter.xsd"
 xmlns:p1="http://www.w3.org/2001/XMLSchema-instance">
  <ApplicationName>%SystemRoot%\system32\windowspowershell\v1.0\powershell.exe
</ApplicationName>
```

```
<WorkingDirectory></WorkingDirectory>
<CommandLine>"&amp; '$file/ImplementActionScript.ps1$'
'$Data/StateChange/DataItem/EventOriginId$'
'$Target/Property[Type="MicrosoftSystemCenterVirtualMachineManager
Pro2008Library!Microsoft.SystemCenter.VirtualMachineManager.Pro.2008.Base"]
/VMMServer$' '$Data/StateChange/DataItem/Context/DataItem/Params/Param[2]$'"
</CommandLine>
<TimeoutSeconds>600</TimeoutSeconds>
<RequireOutput>true</RequireOutput>
<Files>
  <File>
    <Name>ImplementActionScript.ps1</Name>
    <Contents>

# this PowerShell Script is expecting the following 3 parameters
Param($ProtipId, $VMMServerName, $vmmjobid);
$message = 'Starting PRO Tip Implementation. Parameters passed:
VMM server Name: ' + $VMMServerName + ', PRO Tip Id : ' + $ProtipId +
', VMM Job Id: ' + $vmmjobid;
eventcreate /T Information /ID 77 /L APPLICATION /SO
 VMM.2008.R2.Pro.MaintenanceMode /D $message;


# helper function to move a VM to the host with the highest star rating
function MoveVM($vmobj, $hostobj, $ProtipId)
{
    $hostrating = get-vmhostrating -vmhost $hostobj -vm $vmobj
    $orderedrating = $hostrating | sort-object rating -descending
    Write-Output $orderedrating | select Name, Rating, Description,
 TransferType, ZeroRatingReasonList, SANErrorDescriptionList

    $targethost = $null
    if ($orderedrating -is [Array])
    {
        if ($orderedrating[0].Rating -ne 0)
        {
            $targethost = $orderedrating[0].VMhost
        }
    }
    else
    {
        if ($orderedrating.Rating -ne 0)
        {
            $targethost = $orderedrating.VMHost
        }
    }

    if ($targethost -ne $null)
```

```
    {
        # set the custom field #4 of the VM to the host it used to
belong before the evacuation
        $sourcehostname = $vmobj.HostName
        $resultvm = Set-VM -VM $vmobj -Custom4
$sourcehostname -PROTipID $ProtipId

        write-warning "Moving VM $vmobj to host $targethost synchronously"
        $Error.Clear()
        $resultvm = Move-VM -VM $vmobj -vmhost $targethost
-Path $targethost.VMPaths[0] -PROTipID $ProtipId

        # check if the VM was moved successfully
        if ($Error.Count -ne 0)
        {
            $message = "Failed to move VM $vmobj to host $targethost
because of error: " + $Error[0]
            CreateEventLogGenericError $message
            FailPROTipGenericError $ProtipId $message

            # after we fail the PRO tip, continue to move the rest of the
VMs and also
            # set the OpsMgr computer to maintenance mode
        }
    }
    else
    {
        $message = "There is no suitable host for this VM $vmobj and it
will not be migrated!"
        CreateEventLogGenericError $message
        FailPROTipGenericError $ProtipId $message
    }
}

# helper function for updating VMM with the PRO Tip status and
 update the error details
function FailPROTipGenericError
{
    $tip = Set-PROTip -PROTipId $args[0] -LastError $args[1]
 -TipStatus Failed;
}


# helper function for creating an event log entry with a message
function CreateEventLogGenericError
{
    $message = $args[0]
    $message2 = "Creating event log entry: " + $message
    Write-Warning $message2
```

```
        eventcreate /T Error /ID 77 /L APPLICATION /SO
    VMM.2008.R2.Pro.MaintenanceMode /D $message
}


# add the VMM snapin
add-pssnapin Microsoft.SystemCenter.VirtualMachineManager

# add the OpsMgr snapin
Add-PSSnapin Microsoft.EnterpriseManagement.OperationsManager.Client

function Main()
{
    # clear all errors
    $Error.Clear()

    # get a connection to the VMM server
    $c = get-vmmserver -ComputerName $VMMServerName
    if ($Error.Count -ne 0)
    {
        CreateEventLogGenericError  "Failed to get a connection to the
VMM server host: " + $Error[0]
        return;
    }

    $tip = Set-PROTip -PROTipId $ProtipId -TipStatus Running;

    # Now call Get-VM to cache all the VMs in Powershell
    $vms = Get-VM

    # Get the host's name from the VMM Job
    $vmmjob = get-job -id $vmmjobid
    $hostid = $vmmjob.ResultObjectID.ToString()

    # Get the host computer and all hosts that are part of the same hostgroup
    $VMHost = Get-VMHost -Id $hostid
    Write-Warning "$VMHost is the host that was put into maintenance mode in VMM"
    $AllHosts = Get-VMHost -VMHostGroup $VMHost.VMHostGroup

    # Ensure host is in maintenance mode
    if ($VMHost.MaintenanceHost -eq $false)
    {
        CreateEventLogGenericError  "Host $VMHost is not currently
in maintenance mode but we will exit with success"
        $tip = Set-PROTip -PROTipId $ProtipId -TipStatus Resolved
        return;
    }
```

```
    # Enumerate all VMs on this host and move them asynchronously
    foreach ($VM in $VMHost.VMs)
    {
        if ($VM.ExcludeFromPRO -eq $false)
        {
            MoveVM $VM $AllHosts $ProtipId
        }
        else
        {
            $vmid = $VM.ID
            CreateEventLogGenericError  "VM $VM with ID $vmid will not
be moved from this host because it has to be excluded from PRO
host-level actions"
        }
    }

    # Get the OpsMgr Server Name
    $OpsMgrServer = $c.OpsMgrServer
    Write-Warning "$OpsMgrServer is the OpsMgr server for this VMM environment"

    # open the OpsMgr console
    $sd = Get-Childitem env:systemdrive
    $path = $sd.Value + "\Program Files\System Center Operations
Manager 2007\Microsoft.EnterpriseManagement.OperationsManager.
ClientShell.Functions.ps1"
    $path
    &amp; $path

    # start the OpsMgr client shell to execute cmdlets against
this OpsMgr server
    Start-OperationsManagerClientShell -ManagementServerName:
$OpsMgrServer -PersistConnection: $true -Interactive: $false;

    # Get the OpsMgr computer object corresponding to the host
that went into maintenance mode
    $ComputerClass = Get-MonitoringClass -Name 'System.Computer'
    $ComputerObject = Get-MonitoringObject -MonitoringClass
$ComputerClass -Path "\" | Where {$_.DisplayName -eq $VMHost.Name}

    # print the computer object to the console
    $ComputerObject

    # check if the computer object is valid
    if ($ComputerObject -eq $null)
    {
        $message = "Failed to get the OpsMgr computer object for host "
+ $VMHost.Name + " for PROTip " + $ProtipId
        CreateEventLogGenericError  $message
```

```
                FailPROTipGenericError $ProtipId $message
                return;
        }


        # Put the OpsMgr computer into Maintenance Mode
        $time = [DateTime]::Now
        New-MaintenanceWindow -MonitoringObject $ComputerObject -Comment
"PRO sets host into maintenance mode for one year timeframe"
-StartTime $time -EndTime $time.AddYears(1)

        # refresh the state and values of the host computer object in OpsMgr
        $ComputerObject = Get-MonitoringObject -MonitoringClass $ComputerClass
-Path "\" | Where {$_.DisplayName -eq $VMHost.Name}

        # print the computer object to the console
        $ComputerObject

        $message = "Host $VMHost is now in maintenance mode and evacuated
from its Virtual Machines as part of PRO Tip " +
 $ProtipId
        eventcreate /T Information /ID 77 /L APPLICATION
/SO VMM.2008.R2.Pro.MaintenanceMode /D $message

        $tip = Set-PROTip -PROTipId $ProtipId -TipStatus Resolved
}

# call the main entry point for this script
Main;
</Contents>
    </File>
  </Files>
</Configuration>
```

10. Click the Options tab and ensure the accessibility is set to Public and the action is in an Enabled="False" state. We want the action to be disabled so that we can control it using the automation overrides. Overrides will be covered later. Click OK to return back to the Monitor properties.

11. Click the Options tab and ensure that the accessibility is set to Public and the monitor is in an Enabled="False" state. We want the monitor to be disabled by default so that we can control it using the monitoring overrides. Overrides will be covered later in this chapter. Click OK to close the Monitor properties.

CREATING A SECOND MONITOR

The monitor we just created will ensure that when a host goes into maintenance mode, we execute the appropriate actions. However, for this scenario to be complete, we need an additional monitor that covers the scenario in which a host exits maintenance mode in VMM. This section will outline the high-level details of creating this monitor. These details can be combined with the detailed explanation of creating a monitor illustrated previously to create this second monitor. The full XML of the PRO pack will contain this monitor as well. The steps to create the second monitor are as follows:

1. To get started, click the monitors view of the authoring console.

2. Create a new monitor of type Windows Events ➢ Simple ➢ Timer Reset.

3. Enter **VMM.2008.R2.Pro.MaintenanceMode.StopMaintenanceUnitMonitor** as the element ID and **PRO Exit Maintenance Mode** as the display name.

4. The target for this monitor should be the VMM server itself. The public PRO class for the VMM server is Microsoft.SystemCenter.VirtualMachineManager.Pro.2008.Server.

5. Select System.Health.EntityState as the parent monitor and Custom for the category and click Next.

6. The event log name to read events from should be **VM Manager**.

7. For the event that puts the monitor in an unhealthy state, enter **1705** as the event ID and **Virtual Machine Manager** as the event source.

8. Because the event ID 1705 is not unique to maintenance mode, we want to match one of the event parameters to the VMM job name for ending the maintenance mode on a host. Click Insert to add a new expression. In the new expression, select the Specify Event Specific Parameter To Use option with the number 3 as the event parameter number. This will generate Parameter 3 as the parameter name. Set this new expression to be equal to Stop maintenance mode and click Next.

9. Specify the wait time before the monitor is auto-reset as 6 hours and click Finish.

10. Use the exact same steps you followed to create the StartMaintenanceUnitMonitor monitor to enable the alerts on this monitor, create a diagnostic task, create a recovery task, and set the monitor as public and disabled by default.

11. Set the alert description to the following text:

```
A Host managed by VMM server
 $Target/Property[Type="MicrosoftSystemCenterVirtualMachine
ManagerPro2008Library!Microsoft.SystemCenter.VirtualMachineManager
.Pro.2008.Base"]/
VMMServer$ has exited maintenance mode by VMM Job ID
 $Data/Context/Params/Param[2]$.
 Event Description: $Data/Context/EventDescription$
```

12. The diagnostic task should have the script configuration shown in Listing 9.3.

LISTING 9.3:   Diagnostic task XML data for exiting maintenance mode

```
<Configuration p1:noNamespaceSchemaLocation="D:\Users\mlmich\AppData\Local\
Temp\2\UpdateTipAction - System.CommandExecuterProbe.xsd" xmlns:p1="http://
www.w3.org/2001/XMLSchema-instance">
```

```
<ApplicationName>%SystemRoot%\system32\windowspowershell\v1.0\powershell.exe
</ApplicationName>
  <WorkingDirectory></WorkingDirectory>
  <CommandLine>"&amp; '$file/DiagnosticActionScript2.ps1$'
 '$Data/StateChange/DataItem/EventOriginId$'
 '$Target/Property[Type="MicrosoftSystemCenterVirtualMachineManagerPro
2008Library!Microsoft.SystemCenter.VirtualMachineManager.Pro.2008.Base"]
/VMMServer$' '$Data/StateChange/DataItem/Context/DataItem/
Params/Param[2]$'"</CommandLine>
  <TimeoutSeconds>300</TimeoutSeconds>
  <RequireOutput>true</RequireOutput>
  <Files>
    <File>
      <Name>DiagnosticActionScript2.ps1</Name>
      <Contents>

Param($ProtipId, $VMMServerName, $vmmjobid);

$debugMessage = 'Starting PRO Tip Diagnostic. Parameters passed: VMM
 server Name: ' + $VMMServerName + ', Tip Id : ' + $ProtipId + ', VMM
 job id: ' + $vmmjobid;
eventcreate /T Information /ID 88 /L APPLICATION /SO
VMM.2008.R2.Pro.MaintenanceMode /D $debugMessage;

# add the VMM snapin
$Error.Clear();
add-pssnapin -name Microsoft.SystemCenter.VirtualMachineManager;
if ($Error.Count -ne 0)
{
    eventcreate /T Information /ID 88 /L APPLICATION /SO VMM.2008.
R2.Pro.MaintenanceMode /D "Failed to add the VMM server snapin";
    return;
}

# helper function that returns a string corresponding to the View Script
 that is displayed on the PRO Tip window
function GetProScript
{
  return '$hostName = '''+ $hostName +
  '''; $serverName = '''+ $VMMServerName +
  '''; $ProtipId = '''+ $ProtipId +
  '''; $VMMJobId = '''+ $vmmjobid +
  ''';

  function Main
  {
    # Here, you can enter the exact details of the implementation of the PRO Tip
    # Anything that in included in this entire GetProScript function will show up
```

```
    # when the View Script button is pressed in the PRO Tips window
    # This functionality is useful to administrators so that they can see
the exact
    # script that will be executed for a PRO Tip
    # For this particular PRO Pack, we could have included the full contents of
    # ImplementActionScript2.ps1 here
  }
  Main;
    '

}


# helper function for creating an event log entry with a message
function CreateEventLogGenericError
{
    $message = $args[0]
    $message2 = "Creating event log entry: " + $message
    Write-Warning $message2
    eventcreate /T Error /ID 88 /L APPLICATION /SO VMM.2008.R2
.Pro.MaintenanceMode /D $message
}

function Main
{
    # create a connection to the VMM server
    $Error.Clear();
    $serverObj = get-vmmserver -computerName $VMMServerName;
    if ($Error.Count -ne 0)
    {
        CreateEventLogGenericError  "Failed to get a connection to the VMM
 server host: " + $Error[0]
        return;
    }

    # get the host name from the VMM Job
    $vmmjob = get-job -id $vmmjobid
    $hostid = $vmmjob.ResultObjectID.ToString()
    $vmhost = get-vmhost -id $hostid
    $hostname = $vmhost.FQDN
    $ActionDetails = 'Host ' + $hostname + ' has exited maintenance mode
and all its Virtual Machines will be returned back.';
    $ScriptBody = GetProScript;

    # now set the PRO tip details so that they can show up in the Tips
Window in VMM
    Set-PROTip -PROTipId $ProtipId -ActionScript $ScriptBody
 -ActionDetails $ActionDetails;
}
Main;
```

```
            </Contents>
          </File>
        </Files>
      </Configuration>
```

13. Make sure the recovery is public and disabled by default. The configuration script for the recovery should have the same contents as Listing 9.4.

LISTING 9.4:   Recovery task XML data for exiting maintenance mode

```
<Configuration p1:noNamespaceSchemaLocation="D:\Users\mlmich\AppData\Local\
Temp\2\ImplementTipAction - System.CommandExecuter.xsd"
 xmlns:p1="http://www.w3.org/2001/XMLSchema-instance">
  <ApplicationName>%SystemRoot%\system32\windowspowershell\v1.0\
powershell.exe</ApplicationName>
  <WorkingDirectory></WorkingDirectory>
  <CommandLine>"&amp; '$file/ImplementActionScript2.ps1$'
 '$Data/StateChange/DataItem/EventOriginId$'
 '$Target/Property[Type="MicrosoftSystemCenterVirtualMachine
ManagerPro2008Library!Microsoft.SystemCenter.VirtualMachineManager
.Pro.2008.Base"]/VMMServer$'
 '$Data/StateChange/DataItem/Context/DataItem/Params/Param[2]$'"
</CommandLine>
  <TimeoutSeconds>600</TimeoutSeconds>
  <RequireOutput>true</RequireOutput>
  <Files>
    <File>
      <Name>ImplementActionScript2.ps1</Name>
      <Contents>

# this PowerShell Script is expecting the following 3 parameters
Param($ProtipId, $VMMServerName, $vmmjobid);
$message = 'Starting PRO Tip Implementation. Parameters passed:
 VMM server Name: ' + $VMMServerName + ', PRO Tip Id : ' +
 $ProtipId + ', VMM Job Id: ' + $vmmjobid;
eventcreate /T Information /ID 77 /L APPLICATION
 /SO VMM.2008.R2.Pro.MaintenanceMode /D $message;


# helper function to move a VM to a specific host
function MoveVM($vmobj, $sourcehostobj, $targethost, $ProtipId)
{
    # set the custom field #4 of the VM to empty
    $resultvm = Set-VM -VM $vmobj -Custom4 "" -PROTipID $ProtipId

    write-warning "Moving VM $vmobj from host $sourcehostobj
```

```
to host $targethost synchronously"
    $Error.Clear()
    $resultvm = Move-VM -VM $vmobj -vmhost $targethost
-Path $targethost.VMPaths[0] -PROTipID $ProtipId

    # check if the VM was moved successfully
    if ($Error.Count -ne 0)
    {
        $message = "Failed to move VM $vmobj to host $targethost
because of error: " + $Error[0]
        CreateEventLogGenericError $message
        FailPROTipGenericError $ProtipId $message

        # after we fail the PRO tip, continue to move the rest
of the VMs and also
        # set the OpsMgr computer to maintenance mode
    }
}

# helper function for updating VMM with the PRO Tip status
 and update the error details
function FailPROTipGenericError
{
    $tip = Set-PROTip -PROTipId $args[0] -LastError
 $args[1] -TipStatus Failed;
}



# helper function for creating an event log entry with
 a message
function CreateEventLogGenericError
{
    $message = $args[0]
    $message2 = "Creating event log entry: " + $message
    Write-Warning $message2
    eventcreate /T Error /ID 77 /L APPLICATION
 /SO VMM.2008.R2.Pro.MaintenanceMode /D $message
}


# add the VMM snapin
add-pssnapin Microsoft.SystemCenter.VirtualMachineManager

# add the OpsMgr snapin
Add-PSSnapin Microsoft.EnterpriseManagement.OperationsManager.Client

function Main()
{
```

```
# clear all errors
$Error.Clear()

# get a connection to the VMM server
$c = get-vmmserver -ComputerName $VMMServerName
if ($Error.Count -ne 0)
{
    CreateEventLogGenericError  "Failed to get a connection
to the VMM server host: " + $Error[0]
    return;
}

$tip = Set-PROTip -PROTipId $ProtipId -TipStatus Running;

# Now call Get-VM to cache all the VMs in Powershell
$vms = Get-VM

# Get the host's name from the VMM Job
$vmmjob = get-job -id $vmmjobid
$hostid = $vmmjob.ResultObjectID.ToString()

# Get the host computer
$VMHost = Get-VMHost -Id $hostid
Write-Warning "$VMHost is the host that just exited maintenance
mode in VMM"

# Ensure host is not in maintenance mode
if ($VMHost.MaintenanceHost -eq $true)
{
    CreateEventLogGenericError  "Host $VMHost is currently
in maintenance mode but we will exit with success"
    $tip = Set-PROTip -PROTipId $ProtipId -TipStatus Resolved
    return;
}

# Enumerate all the VMs in the VMM environment which have
as custom field 4 the name of this host
# We need to move all those VMs back to this host
$vmswithcustom = Get-VM |select Name, ID,
@{Name='Custom4';Expression={$_.CustomProperties[3]}}
$vmswithcustom = $vmswithcustom | where {$_.Custom4
-eq $VMHost.Name}
foreach ($vmtemp in $vmswithcustom)
{
    # retrieve the VM from VMM based on its ID
    $VM = Get-VM -ID $vmtemp.ID.ToString()
    if ($VM.ExcludeFromPRO -eq $false)
    {
```

```
            MoveVM $VM $VM.HostName $VMHost $ProtipId
        }
        else
        {
            $vmid = $VM.ID
            CreateEventLogGenericError  "VM $VM with ID $vmid
will not be moved from its current host because it has to be
excluded from PRO host-level actions"
        }
    }

    # Get the OpsMgr Server Name
    $OpsMgrServer = $c.OpsMgrServer
    Write-Warning "$OpsMgrServer is the OpsMgr server
for this VMM environment"

    # open the OpsMgr console
    $sd = Get-Childitem env:systemdrive
    $path = $sd.Value + "\Program Files\System Center
Operations Manager 2007\Microsoft.EnterpriseManagement.
OperationsManager.ClientShell.Functions.ps1"
    $path
    &amp; $path

    # start the OpsMgr client shell to execute cmdlets against
this OpsMgr server
    Start-OperationsManagerClientShell -ManagementServerName:
$OpsMgrServer -PersistConnection: $true -Interactive: $false;

    # Get the OpsMgr computer object corresponding to the host
that just exited maintenance mode
    $ComputerClass = Get-MonitoringClass -Name 'System.Computer'
    $ComputerObject = Get-MonitoringObject -MonitoringClass
$ComputerClass -Path "\" | Where {$_.DisplayName -eq $VMHost.Name}

    # print the computer object to the console
    $ComputerObject

    # check if the computer object is valid
    if ($ComputerObject -eq $null)
    {
        $message = "Failed to get the OpsMgr computer object
for host " + $VMHost.Name + " for PROTip " + $ProtipId
        CreateEventLogGenericError  $message
        FailPROTipGenericError $ProtipId $message
        return;
    }
```

```
        # Put the OpsMgr computer out of Maintenance Mode
    effective immediately
        $time = [DateTime]::Now
        Set-MaintenanceWindow -MonitoringObject $ComputerObject
    -Comment "PRO sets host back to healthy" -EndTime $time.AddMinutes(2)

        # refresh the state and values of the host computer object in OpsMgr
        $ComputerObject = Get-MonitoringObject -MonitoringClass
    $ComputerClass -Path "\" | Where {$_.DisplayName -eq $VMHost.Name}

        # print the computer object to the console
        $ComputerObject

        $message = "Host $VMHost has now exited maintenance mode
    and its old Virtual Machines are moved back as part of PRO Tip " + $ProtipId
        eventcreate /T Information /ID 77 /L APPLICATION
    /SO VMM.2008.R2.Pro.MaintenanceMode /D $message

        $tip = Set-PROTip -PROTipId $ProtipId -TipStatus Resolved
    }

# call the main entry point for this script
Main;
</Contents>
    </File>
  </Files>
</Configuration>
```

SCRIPTING CONSIDERATIONS

While writing Windows PowerShell scripts using the VMM PowerShell cmdlets, it is important to utilize and honor two properties that are specific to PRO:

PROTipID Every cmdlet in VMM that has the capacity to make changes to the VMM environment has an optional parameter called PROTipID. By passing the GUID of the PRO tip to cmdlets executed from a recovery task, VMM knows that this specific PRO tip triggered this action for auditing purposes. In addition, as Figure 9.14 shows, VMM will populate a new tab called PRO Tip in the job details pane of the jobs view. In this figure, you can see that a start virtual machine cmdlet was executed from the recovery task of PRO tip PRO Start Maintenance Mode.

ExcludeFROMPRO Every virtual machine object in PowerShell has a property called ExcludeFromPRO. This property allows an administrator to specify that this VM should not participate in any host-level PRO actions. This is especially useful for mission-critical workloads that can't afford any downtime regardless of the health or performance of the host. PRO pack authors should check for the existence of this property on a VM before introducing any downtime to the VM. In general, VMs with this property set should be left intact. Figure 9.15 shows how to set this property from the Virtual Machine properties window.

FIGURE 9.14
VMM jobs associated with PRO tips

FIGURE 9.15
A virtual machine that is excluded from host-level PRO actions

PRO TIP STATES

PRO tips go through a number of states in the VMM infrastructure from the moment they are created to when they are resolved. Table 9.1 shows the different states that a PRO tip can enter and some examples on how to set them in the recovery task through Windows PowerShell cmdlets.

TABLE 9.1: PRO tip states

STATUS	DESCRIPTION	POWERSHELL EXAMPLE FOR RECOVERY TASKS
Active	A tip in this state is active and visible in the Tips window in VMM, and it is waiting to be implemented or dismissed.	Not applicable
Initialized	When a tip is implemented, it will first enter the initialized state until the OpsMgr recovery task on the monitor is executed and puts the tip in a running state.	Not applicable
Running	When a recovery task is invoked, one of the first things it needs to do is to put the tip status to a running state. If a tip is initialized and its status is not updated within 5 minutes to a running state, VMM will put the tip in a failed state.	`Set-PROTip -PROTipId $ProtipId -TipStatus Running;`
Resolved	Once a recovery task is complete and successful in the remediation of the tip, it should put the tip status to resolved.	`Set-PROTip -PROTipId $ProtipId -TipStatus Resolved;`
Closed	A PRO tip enters the closed state when the alert that generated the PRO tip is closed by OpsMgr. A PRO tip can now be reactivated.	Not applicable
Failed	Once a recovery task encounters an error in implementing the remediation of the tip, it should put the tip status to failed.	`Set-PROTip -PROTipId $ProtipId -TipStatus Failed;`
Dismissed	If an administrator dismisses the PRO tip from the PRO Tips window, the tip will automatically enter a dismissed state.	Not applicable

OVERRIDES

Now that we have created the monitors for this management pack, we need to create some overrides for them. As you might have already noticed, both the monitors and the recovery tasks are disabled by default. This is by design so that an administrator can control the enable/disable state of PRO tips via the VMM Administrator Console without ever having to open the OpsMgr Operations console. Earlier in this chapter we talked about how the administrator can enable and disable both the monitoring and the automation level of PRO tips for either critical or warning and critical tips. Using overrides is how this functionality is accomplished in the management pack.

For example, when an administrator enables PRO for a host group, VMM will update all the instances of the PRO target class that represent the objects in the host group. The update will ensure that all instances' PRO settings match those that were selected (in OpsMgr terms, they were overridden) by the administrator. The update in turn will cause those objects to be populated into or out of the PRO groups. VMM in essence is managing the membership of these groups and controls which monitors and recoveries need to be enabled. The groups defined by the VMM PRO library management pack are as follows:

Microsoft.SystemCenter.VirtualMachineManager.Pro.2008.EnableWC.Group Members of this group will have their warning- and critical-level monitors enabled. Warning- and critical-level PRO tips will show up in VMM for members of this group.

Microsoft.SystemCenter.VirtualMachineManager.Pro.2008.EnableC.Group Members of this group will have their critical-level monitors enabled. Only critical-level PRO tips will show up in VMM for members of this group.

Microsoft.SystemCenter.VirtualMachineManager.Pro.2008.RecoveryWC.Group Members of this group will have their warning- and critical-level recoveries enabled. Warning- and critical-level PRO tips will show up in VMM for members of this group, and those PRO tips will be automatically implemented by VMM.

Microsoft.SystemCenter.VirtualMachineManager.Pro.2008.RecoveryC.Group Members of this group will have their critical-level recoveries enabled. Only critical-level PRO tips will show up in VMM for members of this group, and those PRO tips will be automatically implemented by VMM.

Let's go ahead and create the overrides for this PRO pack. Because this PRO pack defines only warning alerts, we only need to create the overrides corresponding to the Warning and Critical monitors. For completeness, let's define the overrides for critical monitors as well. Here's how to create the overrides:

1. In the Health Model view of the authoring console, click the overrides tree view entry.

2. Right-click in the Details Pane and select New ➢ New Monitor Property Override.

3. Enter **VMM.2008.R2.Pro.MaintenanceMode.StartMaintenanceUnitMonitorEnableWC** as the identifier.

4. For the name of the override, enter **StartMaintenanceUnitMonitorEnableWC**.

5. Click the Configuration tab and select the VMM.2008.R2.Pro.MaintenanceMode .StartMaintenanceUnitMonitor Monitor. Leave property set to Enabled and enter **true** as the value. In the Context field, select Microsoft.SystemCenter.VirtualMachineManager .Pro.2008.EnableWC.Group to enable this monitor for warning and critical alerts. Click OK.

6. Right-click in the details pane and select New ➢ New Monitor Property Override.

7. Enter **VMM.2008.R2.Pro.MaintenanceMode.StartMaintenanceUnitMonitorEnableC** as the identifier.

8. For the name of the override, enter **StartMaintenanceUnitMonitorEnableC**.

9. Click the Configuration tab and select the VMM.2008.R2.Pro.MaintenanceMode
.StartMaintenanceUnitMonitor Monitor. Leave property set to Enabled and enter **true** as
the value. In the Context field, select Microsoft.SystemCenter.VirtualMachineManager
.Pro.2008.EnableC.Group to enable this monitor for critical alerts only. Click OK.

10. Right-click in the details pane and select New ➤ New Recovery Property Override.

11. Enter **VMM.2008.R2.Pro.MaintenanceMode.StartMMImplementPROTipRecoveryWC**
as the identifier.

12. For the name of the override, enter **StartMMImplementPROTipRecoveryWC**.

13. Click the Configuration tab and select the VMM.2008.R2.Pro.MaintenanceMode
.StartMMImplementPROTip Recovery. Leave property set to Enabled and enter **true** as
the value. In the Context field, select Microsoft.SystemCenter.VirtualMachineManager
.Pro.2008.RecoveryWC.Group to enable this monitor for automatic recovery of warning
and critical alerts. Click OK.

14. Right-click in the details pane and select New ➤ New Recovery Property Override.

15. Enter **VMM.2008.R2.Pro.MaintenanceMode.StartMMImplementPROTipRecoveryC** as
the identifier.

16. For the name of the override, enter **StartMMImplementPROTipRecoveryWC**.

17. Click the Configuration tab and select the VMM.2008.R2.Pro.MaintenanceMode
.StartMMImplementPROTip Recovery. Leave property set to Enabled and enter **true** as
the value. In the Context field, select Microsoft.SystemCenter.VirtualMachineManager
.Pro.2008.RecoveryC.Group to enable this monitor for automatic recovery of critical alerts
only. Click OK.

18. Using the same process, create the two monitor property overrides and the two recov-
ery property overrides for the VMM.2008.R2.Pro.MaintenanceMode.StopMaintenance
UnitMonitor monitor and the VMM.2008.R2.Pro.MaintenanceMode.ExitMMImplement
PROTip recovery.

Using Events to Redirect Task Execution

OpsMgr introduces a dilemma for management pack authors because of the restriction that
diagnostic and recovery tasks can execute only on the same computer that triggered the monitor. The multi-computer nature of a VMM environment ensures that both virtual machines and
hosts will be targets for OpsMgr monitors. Because diagnostic and recovery tasks require the
existence of PowerShell and the VMM PowerShell cmdlets, administrators would have to install
the VMM Administrator Console on every host and every virtual machine. To avoid this additional requirement of installing the console everywhere, it is possible to redirect the execution
of such tasks to the OpsMgr management server. That is why you were required to install the
VMM Administrator Console and associated PowerShell interface on all the OpsMgr management servers.

Redirecting the execution of tasks can be accomplished by changing the recovery task of
the monitor to write an event to the event log (this would be the local event log on the host
or virtual machine since recovery tasks execute on the same computer as the monitor) instead
of executing the real remediation of the monitor. This event should contain the exact same

data that the real recovery task needs to execute when it runs on the management server. The management pack author can then define a rule that monitors the event log for that event ID and invokes a PowerShell script on the OpsMgr management server. The PowerShell script that is invoked on the OpsMgr server would have the actual script contents of the remediation for the monitor that triggered the original PRO tip as well as the parameters it needs to execute. The parameters it needs to execute can be parsed from the event that was collected by the rule. Figure 9.16 shows the overall process work flow for task execution redirection.

FIGURE 9.16
Task execution redirection process
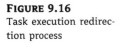
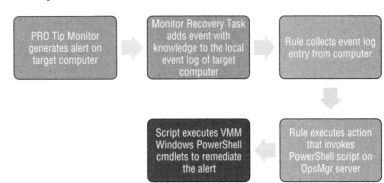

This specific PRO pack does not need to utilize events for redirecting recovery tasks because it targets the VMM server. However, let's walk through an example implementation of this concept. The final XML file of the PRO pack in this section will not contain the recovery task portion of this example. This is because PRO supports only one recovery task per monitor. In this example, from the recovery task of the same monitor we used earlier, we will put in the event log the PRO tip ID, the VMM server name, the name of the computer that is the target of this monitor, and the VMM job ID in this exact order separated by semicolons. These are the necessary parameters that `ImplementActionScript.ps1` needs in order to implement the remediation for this monitor. To create the recovery task for the task execution redirection, follow these steps:

1. In the Health Model view, select the Monitors tree view option. Click on the monitor VMM.2008.R2.Pro.MaintenanceMode.StartMaintenanceUnitMonitor and select Properties.

2. In the Diagnostic And Recovery tab, click Add A Recovery For Warning Health State. Enter **VMM.2008.R2.Pro.MaintenanceMode.WriteRecoveryEvent** as the identifier.

3. Enter **Write Recovery Task Event Log Entry** as the name and ensure that the target is the PRO VMM server class.

4. Keep the defaults for most of the recovery properties and click the Modules tab.

5. Create a new action and select Microsoft.Windows.ScriptWriteAction as the module type. Enter **WriteRecoveryEvent** as the module ID.

6. Now edit the newly created action and enter **WriteRecoveryEvent.vbs** in the ScriptName field, enter **$Data/StateChange/DataItem/EventOriginId$ $Target/Property[Type= "MicrosoftSystemCenterVirtualMachineManagerPro2008Library!Microsoft .SystemCenter.VirtualMachineManager.Pro.2008.Base"]/VMMServer$ $Target/ Property[Type="MicrosoftSystemCenterVirtualMachineManagerPro2008Library! Microsoft.SystemCenter.VirtualMachineManager.Pro.2008.Base"]/Name$**

$Data/StateChange/DataItem/Context/DataItem/Params/Param[2]$ in the Arguments field, enter **60** seconds in the TimeoutSeconds field, and click Edit. `Notepad.exe` will open with the following XML data:

```
<Configuration p1:noNamespaceSchemaLocation=
"D:\Users\mlmich\AppData\Local\Temp\2\
WriteRecoveryEvent - Microsoft.Windows.ScriptWriteAction.xsd"
 xmlns:p1="http://www.w3.org/2001/XMLSchema-instance">
  <ScriptName>WriteRecoveryEvent.vbs</ScriptName>
  <Arguments>$Data/StateChange/DataItem/EventOriginId$
 $Target/Property[Type="MicrosoftSystemCenterVirtualMachineManagerPro2008
Library!Microsoft.SystemCenter.VirtualMachineManager.Pro.2008.Base"]
/VMMServer$ $Target/Property[Type="MicrosoftSystemCenterVirtualMachine
ManagerPro2008Library!Microsoft.SystemCenter.VirtualMachineManager.
Pro.2008.Base"]/Name$ $Data/StateChange/DataItem
/Context/DataItem/Params/Param[2]$
</Arguments>
  <ScriptBody>ScriptBody</ScriptBody>
  <TimeoutSeconds>60</TimeoutSeconds>
</Configuration>
```

7. Now edit this XML as follows and configure it to define the ScriptBody. Once the XML is replaced, save the file and close `Notepad.exe`. Click OK.

```
<Configuration p1:noNamespaceSchemaLocation=
"D:\Users\mlmich\AppData\Local\Temp\2\
WriteRecoveryEvent - Microsoft.Windows.ScriptWriteAction.xsd"
 xmlns:p1="http://www.w3.org/2001/XMLSchema-instance">
  <ScriptName>WriteRecoveryEvent.vbs</ScriptName>
  <Arguments>$Data/StateChange/DataItem/EventOriginId$
 $Target/Property[Type="MicrosoftSystemCenterVirtualMachineManager
Pro2008Library!Microsoft.SystemCenter.VirtualMachineManager.Pro.2008.Base"]
/VMMServer$ $Target/Property[Type="MicrosoftSystemCenterVirtualMachine
ManagerPro2008Library!Microsoft.SystemCenter.VirtualMachineManager.
Pro.2008.Base"]/Name$ $Data/StateChange/DataItem
/Context/DataItem/Params/Param[2]$
</Arguments>
  <ScriptBody>     ' Create an event log entry based on the parameters
passed to this script
                Dim count
                Dim arguments
                Dim eventdescription
                Dim command

                Set arguments = WScript.Arguments

                count = arguments.Count
```

```
                   ' If no arguments were passed, exit
                   If count = 0 Then
                       WScript.Quit 1
                   End If

                   ' Append all the input parameters separated by a semicolon
                   eventdescription = arguments.Item(0)

                   For i = 1 to count - 1
                       eventdescription = eventdescription &amp; ":" &amp;
        arguments.Item(i)
                   Next

                   Set WshShell = WScript.CreateObject("WScript.Shell")
                   command = "EventCreate /T Information /ID 23 /L Application
        /SO VMMProRedirect /D " &amp; Chr(34) &amp; eventdescription &amp; Chr(34)
                   WshShell.Run command , 0</ScriptBody>
          <TimeoutSeconds>60</TimeoutSeconds>
        </Configuration>
```

8. Click the Options tab and ensure that the accessibility is Public and the action is in an `Enabled="False"` state. We want the action to be disabled so that we can control it using the automation overrides. Click OK to return to the monitor properties. Click OK to save the monitor. The data for the event log entry on the target computer can now be populated.

9. Now it is time to create overrides for the recovery task we just created. In the Health Model view of the authoring console, click the Overrides tree view entry.

10. Right-click in the details pane and select New ➤ New Recovery Property Override.

11. Enter **VMM.2008.R2.Pro.MaintenanceMode.WriteRecoveryEventRecoveryWC** as the identifier.

12. For the name of the override, enter **WriteRecoveryEventRecoveryWC**.

13. Click the Configuration tab and select VMM.2008.R2.Pro.MaintenanceMode .WriteRecoveryEvent Recovery. Leave the property set to Enabled and enter **true** as the value. In the Context field, select Microsoft.SystemCenter.VirtualMachineManager.Pro .2008.RecoveryWC.Group to enable this monitor for automatic recovery of warning and critical alerts. Click OK.

14. Click the rules view so that we can create a new rule that would read this event log entry that the recovery task created and perform the necessary work.

15. Right-click and select New ➤ Collection ➤ Event Based ➤ Windows Event Collection.

16. Set the element ID to **VMM.2008.R2.Pro.MaintenanceMode.CollectRecoveryEvent** and enter **Collect Recovery Event and Implement Remediation** as the display name.

17. Set the target to be Microsoft.SystemCenter.VirtualMachineManager.Pro.2008.Server and click Next.

18. Now we have to read the event log entry we created in the ScriptBody earlier. Select **Application** as the Log name and click Next. Set the event ID to **23** and the event source to **VMM-ProRedirect**. Click Finish.

19. Right-Click on the rule we just created and select Properties.

20. Click the Modules tab and then click Create A New Action. Choose System .CommandExecuter as the module type and set the module ID to ImplementCollectedEventRule. Click ImplementCollectedEventRule Module and select Edit.

21. Enter **%SystemRoot%\system32\windowspowershell\v1.0\powershell.exe** in the ApplicationName field, clear the WorkingDirectory field, set the TimeoutSeconds field to 86400, and enter "**& '$file/ImplementRuleActionScript.ps1$' '$Data/EventDescription$**" in the CommandLine field. Click Edit. Notepad.exe will open with the XML data shown here:

```
<Configuration p1:noNamespaceSchemaLocation=
"D:\Users\mlmich\AppData\Local\Temp\2\
ImplementCollectedEventRule - System.CommandExecuter.xsd"
 xmlns:p1="http://www.w3.org/2001/XMLSchema-instance">
   <ApplicationName>%SystemRoot%\system32\windowspowershell\
v1.0\powershell.exe</ApplicationName>
   <WorkingDirectory></WorkingDirectory>
   <CommandLine>"&amp; '$file/ImplementRuleActionScript.ps1'
 '$Data/EventDescription$'"</CommandLine>
   <TimeoutSeconds>86400</TimeoutSeconds>
   <RequireOutput>true</RequireOutput>
</Configuration>
```

22. Now edit this XML as follows so that it defines the ImplementRuleActionScript.ps1 PowerShell script. Once the XML is replaced, save the file and close Notepad.exe. Click OK. Now Close the Rule.

```
<Configuration p1:noNamespaceSchemaLocation=
"D:\Users\mlmich\AppData\Local\Temp\2\
ImplementCollectedEventRule - System.CommandExecuter.xsd"
 xmlns:p1="http://www.w3.org/2001/XMLSchema-instance">
   <ApplicationName>%SystemRoot%\system32\windowspowershell\v1.0\powershell.exe
</ApplicationName>
   <WorkingDirectory></WorkingDirectory>
   <CommandLine>"&amp; '$file/ImplementRuleActionScript.ps1'
 '$Data/EventDescription$'"</CommandLine>
   <TimeoutSeconds>86400</TimeoutSeconds>
   <RequireOutput>true</RequireOutput>
   <Files>
     <File>
       <Name>ImplementRuleActionScript.ps1</Name>
       <Contents>
```

```
    Param($EventData);
    $debugMessage = 'Executing PRO Rule on OpsMgr management server.
Rule picked up the following event data: ' + $EventData;
    EventCreate /T Information /ID 24 /L Application
 /SO VMMProRedirect /D $debugMessage;


        </Contents>
      </File>
    </Files>
  </Configuration>
```

If you noticed, inside `ImplementRuleActionScript.ps1`, we just created a new event that adds the event data collected into a new event log entry on the OpsMgr management server (basically we are collecting event data from the target of the monitor and publishing a new event log entry on the OpsMgr management server). In a real implementation where task redirection is needed, `ImplementActionScript.ps1` would not be defined in the recovery task of the monitor. Instead, it would be defined in the rule's action and its contents would be part of `ImplementRuleActionScript.ps1`. The first step would be to parse the `$EventData` parameter and use its contents to execute the desired remediation task for that monitor.

When we defined the rule and ImplementCollectedEventRule, we didn't specify where we want that action to be executed. The rule is targeted to execute on all VMM servers, which is where the monitor would place the initial event log entry. However, ImplementCollectedEventRule needs to run on the OpsMgr management server. To accomplish that, we need to manually edit the XML representation of the management pack, as shown in these steps:

1. Click File ➢ Save and then File ➢ Exit to close the authoring console.

2. Find the location on disk where you stored the PRO pack XML file (`VMM.2008.R2.Pro.MaintenanceMode.xml`) and open it with an editor like `Notepad.exe`.

3. Search for the single occurrence of the following line of XML:

```
<WriteAction ID="ImplementCollectedEventRule"
 TypeID="System!System.CommandExecuter">
```

4. Now replace that line with the following line of XML. Notice that we now added a target server type for the `WriteAction ImplementCollectedEventRule`. This means that the action will execute on the OpsMgr management server:

```
<WriteAction ID="ImplementCollectedEventRule"
 TypeID="System!System.CommandExecuter"
 Target="SC!Microsoft.SystemCenter.ManagementServer">
```

5. Save the XML file and close `Notepad.exe`. Open the XML file again with the OpsMgr authoring console and ensure that the rule definition remained as it was defined earlier.

Figure 9.17 shows the event properties for the event created on the same computer that is the target of the monitor. The event details contain all the relevant information from the alert. Figure 9.18 shows the event properties for the event created on the OpsMgr management server to show the capabilities of a potential remediation executing on the OpsMgr server.

FIGURE 9.17
Event properties written by the monitor to the local event log

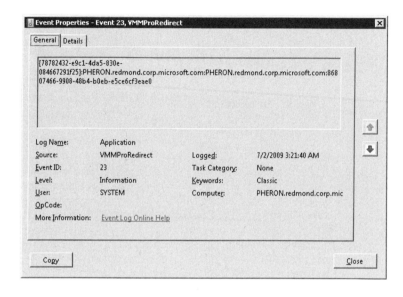

FIGURE 9.18
Event properties written by the rule on the OpsMgr management server

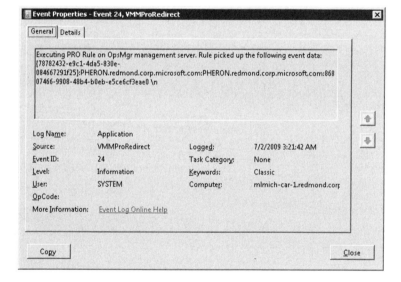

IMAGES

If you created a custom class in the PRO pack that is the target of a monitor, it is possible to add your own image that references that class. The image will show up in the VMM PRO Tips window when a PRO tip is created from a monitor that targets your custom PRO class. The image has to be 250 × 80 pixels. Follow these steps to add an image:

1. Click the presentation view of the authoring console.

2. Select images from the tree view.

3. In the results pane, right-click and select Add Image.

4. Name your image `custom-class-name.LargeImage`, browse to select the image, and select DiagramIcon as the image category.

5. Manually edit the PRO pack XML to add the reference of the image to your class:

```
<Presentation>
    <ImageReferences>
        <ImageReference ElementID="<custom-class-name>"
  ImageID="<custom-class-name>.LargeImage" />
    </ImageReferences>
</Presentation>
```

COMPLETING THE PRO PACK

The management pack is now complete and ready for testing. Click File ➤ Save and then upload the management pack to your OpsMgr RMS. Click Tools ➤ Export MP To Management Group, enter the OpsMgr RMS server name, and select Connect. The management pack is now uploaded in OpsMgr. To test it, assuming the integration between VMM and OpsMgr already exists, enable PRO monitoring (Enable PRO Tips) at the VMM server level from the Administration view. Wait for a few minutes for the group memberships to be updated in OpsMgr and put a host in maintenance mode. Follow these steps to put a host into maintenance mode and get the PRO Tip:

1. To put a host in maintenance mode, go to the hosts view in VMM and select a host in the list view. Right-click on that host and select the option to start the maintenance mode. Figure 9.19 shows you the warning VMM will display for stand-alone hosts when maintenance mode is starting. If you click the Start Maintenance Mode button, VMM will initiate the maintenance mode of the host and save the state of all its VMs or live migrate them to other nodes of the cluster.

2. A few seconds after the maintenance mode VMM Job completes, the PRO Tip window will pop up, indicating an active PRO tip. The administrator can then decide whether to dismiss or implement the PRO tip.

FIGURE 9.19
Starting maintenance mode forces all virtual machines to be saved.

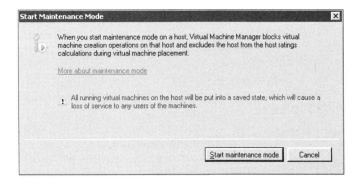

Once the management pack is tested and ready for distribution, the `MPSeal.exe` utility can be used to seal the XML definition of the management pack and convert it to a binary format.

For this example PRO pack, we did not define any product knowledge. However, any real production management needs to have product knowledge at the management pack level, at the monitor level, and at the rule level.

PRO PACK XML DEFINITION

You can save this XML file and import it in the authoring console to see how everything we talked about in this chapter was implemented. The version numbers of the referenced management packs might be different in your environment depending on your installation of VMM and OpsMgr. To alleviate that and allow the PRO pack to load in the console, manually edit the XML to include the proper version numbers and `PublicKeyToken` for the all referenced management packs.

DOWNLOADING THE CODE

The full XML definition of this PRO pack is available for download at the book's website at www.sybex.com/masteringvmm2008r2.

Troubleshooting

This section will outline some useful information in diagnosing and troubleshooting issues in the integration of VMM with OpsMgr and PRO.

Getting error 11804 when integrating VMM with OpsMgr: When the `Set-VMMServer -OpsMgrServer <RMS server name>` cmdlet is executed, it is possible that you'll get error 11804 with the content "VMM service does not have the necessary privileges to access the Operations Manager SDK service on <servername>." To correct this error, follow these recommended steps:

1. You need to check if the OpsMgr SDK service is running under domain credentials. If that is the case, you need to register service principal names (SPNs) for the following two accounts: `MSOMSdkSvc/<RMS FQDN>` and `MSOMSdkSvc/<RMS NETBIOSNAME>`. You can use the `SetSpn.exe` utility for this. To create an SPN, you will need domain administrator credentials. Also make sure that you provide the OprMgr RMS server's values in those commands. If this does not solve the issue, you can restart the OpsMgr SDK service (`net stop omsdk` and `net start omsdk`) and as a last resort reboot the OpsMgr RMS and the VMM server. That has been known to fix any lingering permissions issues that were not propagated properly.

2. The error might be a result of a permissions issue with OpsMgr. One way to troubleshoot this is to launch the OpsMgr Operations console using the same account that the VMM service uses from the VMM server computer. If, for example, the VMM service runs as local system, launch the OpsMgr console as system on the VMM server computer. If the proper permissions are set, the following command should work and the Operations console will open. You can obtain `PsExec.exe` from the Microsoft TechNet website.

```
PsExec.exe -e -i -s -x "C:\Program Files\System Center
Operations Manager 2007\Microsoft.MOM.UI.Console.exe"
```

PRO tips failing to start: If the VMM Administrator Console is not installed on the OpsMgr RMS server and on all the OpsMgr management servers, PRO tips will fail to start and present the following error message. Install the Administrator Console on all OpsMgr management servers including the RMS computer for PRO tips to function correctly.

```
Error (11825)
PRO tip implementation failed to start.


Recommended Action
Ensure that the VMM Administrative Console is installed on the
Operations Manager root management server and that the action
account that Operations Manager uses has access to Virtual
Machine Manager.
```

It is also possible that a PRO tip fails to start because OpsMgr was not able to launch the Windows PowerShell script that executes the recovery task. Check the Windows PowerShell execution policy for the OpsMgr action account on all computers where PowerShell scripts will be executed as a result of OpsMgr tasks.

Host group not monitored in OpsMgr: If a host group shows up as Not Monitored in the OpsMgr diagram view, it is because it has no hosts. Add a host to start monitoring this host group.

OpsMgr not recognizing your management pack updates during development: In certain situations while developing a PRO pack, OpsMgr might not be recognizing the changes made to the management pack. This could happen because many versions of the same management pack are being exported to the management group. To alleviate this situation, increase the version number of the management pack by one and export it to OpsMgr again.

Ensuring that the VMM server's OpsMgr health service received an updated management pack: When exporting a management pack using the authoring console, it is good to check and ensure that an event with event ID 1201 is created on the VMM server followed by the event with ID 1210. These events will be created in the Operations Manager event log on the VMM server, and they indicate that the management pack was received by the health service on that server and that its monitors are properly set up and active. Here is an example description of the details in these events:

```
Event ID 1201: New Management Pack with id:"VMM.2008.R2.Pro.MaintenanceMode",
 version:"2.0.4263.0" received.
Event ID 1210: New configuration became active. Management group "VMM",
configuration id:"70 06 58 A4 AF 3D AA DD 5B 7A 5F
2C 2E 75 4B A7 A5 BE 9F 1B ".
```

Issues with PRO tips: If the PRO pack monitors are not creating PRO tips or they are not auto-implementing tips as expected, you need to troubleshoot the monitor from the OpsMgr Operations console. To list the discovered instances of the VMM server PRO class, follow these steps:

1. Click the monitoring view and select Discovered Inventory in the tree view.
2. From the actions menu, select the Change Target Type option, and in the window that opens, find the target for your monitor that you want to troubleshoot. In the PRO pack we created in this chapter, we used a VMM server target, so let's select PRO VMM Server Target.

In this case, the Discovered Inventory list will show all instances of that target that are discovered by OpsMgr. You can play around with all the different PRO classes and see their discovered instances. This is a good way to troubleshoot if your instance was populated in OpsMgr. When you select the VMM server target, the list will show all VMM servers monitored by PRO.

You can right-click on an instance and see its properties, as seen in Figure 9.20. Make sure all properties are correctly populated for that class. In the list view, you will notice two columns: PRO Recovery Level and PRO Monitoring Level. Table 9.2 lists their possible values and what they represent. These values should be in sync with the administrator-specified PRO monitoring and recovery levels in the VMM Administrator Console for this computer.

FIGURE 9.20
VMM server PRO
object properties

TABLE 9.2:   PRO monitoring level and recovery level values

RECOVERY LEVELS	MONITORING LEVELS
0 = No auto-implementation is enabled.	0 = PRO tips are not enabled.
1 = Auto-implementation is enabled only for critical PRO tips.	1 = Only critical PRO tips are enabled.
2 = Auto-implementation is enabled for warning and critical PRO tips.	2 = Warning and critical PRO tips are enabled.

After checking the properties of the instance, select one of the VMM servers from the list to view its health properties. Right-click and select Open ➢ Health Explorer. In this window, you can see the monitors that target this computer, check their overall state, and view the properties of the monitor. Figure 9.21 shows the Health Explorer for one of the monitors we developed in this chapter.

FIGURE 9.21

Health Explorer for a monitor

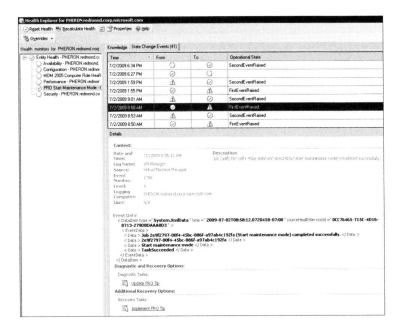

To view the monitor properties, right-click and select Monitor Properties. In the General tab, the monitor should be disabled. In the Overrides tab, click View Summary "For the monitor" and you should be able to see a parity between the overrides created in the authoring console for the monitor with what is listed in the dialog.

Other monitor properties can also be examined in this properties dialog. From the Health Explorer, a monitor can also be manually reset to aid in testing scenarios. The Health Explorer also provides a State Change Events tab for a selected monitor. In this tab, you can view a history of the events that were raised on this monitor and the state changes of the monitor. Event log data that triggered the alert is also listed as well as output from any diagnostic and recovery tasks run. This includes the output of messages from PowerShell scripts that were run, making this a great way to debug your monitors and ensure that the tasks are behaving as designed.

The Bottom Line

Integrate VMM with OpsMgr for end-to-end service management. Virtual Machine Manager is great for provisioning and managing virtual workloads. Through the integration of VMM with OpsMgr, health monitoring and end-to-end workload management are added to an already strong solution.

Master It Why are OpsMgr agents required on all Windows-based computers?

Explain why the Administrator Console needs to be installed on all OpsMgr management servers.

How can you initiate snapshot discovery and refresh the VMM environment into OpsMgr?

Use the PRO infrastructure to create a new PRO pack. PRO pack authors can leverage PRO to dynamically respond to environmental conditions that affect the health of the virtualized environment via actions based on OpsMgr monitors. PRO can monitor the performance of systems and allow customers to manage their infrastructure in a proactive and automated way.

Master It What is the relationship between an alert and a PRO tip?

Why does PRO require authors to create overrides?

What are the steps required for creating PRO tips against a specific hardware controller?

Chapter 10

Planning for Backup and Recovery

Planning for backup and recovery is one of the core elements of virtualization architecture, which is why every deployment of Virtual Machine Manager needs to include a comprehensive plan on how to back up the virtualization environment. You should also know the necessary steps to recover lost data and bring the environment to a healthy state. Planning ahead eliminates surprises, minimizes downtime, and keeps valuable data from being lost.

Protecting the virtualization environment mainly includes the backup and recovery of the Virtual Machine Manager database and the protection of the virtual machines that reside on virtualization hosts. A comprehensive backup plan should assign the highest priority to these components because they are the most critical to a VMM deployment.

The service-level agreement of your organization for service availability should determine how often and what you should protect within the virtualized environment. A good practice to follow is to frequently back up data that changes often, such as data on virtual machines. It is imperative to use backup software that is certified to work with the component you are protecting and meets the requirements of your organization around backup and recovery.

In this chapter, you will learn to:

- ◆ Protect the VMM server, including the VMM database
- ◆ Back up Hyper-V hosts using the Hyper-V VSS Writer

Backup and Recovery of the VMM Server

Almost the entire state of Virtual Machine Manager resides in the SQL database that is configured for VMM. A few configuration options are defined in the Registry, but either those options can be reentered at any point or VMM server setup will correct them. Such Registry configuration options include the ports used by VMM components and are defined under the `HKEY_LOCAL_MACHINE\SOFTWARE\Microsoft\Microsoft System Center Virtual Machine Manager Server\Settings` Registry key.

In the following sections, we will go through the different processes and procedures for backing up Virtual Machine Manager and the VMM database. Your virtualization protection plan should include the VMM server, virtualization hosts, library servers, the database server, and the Self-Service Portal. Backup and recovery of those components is discussed later in the chapter.

Database Backup

Since the main store for VMM information is the database, we will focus on the three different ways for backing up the VMM database:

◆ Using the VMM backup cmdlets

◆ Backing up using the VMM VSS writer

◆ Using SQL Server backup technologies

To find out the location of the database configured for VMM, inspect the following Registry value entries on the VMM server computer under the key [HKEY_LOCAL_MACHINE\SOFTWARE\ Microsoft\Microsoft System Center Virtual Machine Manager Server\Settings\Sql]:

DatabasePath   The full path to the location on disk where the VMM database files reside

ConnectionString   The SQL connection string that an application can use to connect to the VMM database

DatabaseName   The name of the SQL database used by VMM

InstanceName   The name of the SQL server instance that houses the VMM database

OnRemoteServer   An integer value that indicates whether the VMM database resides on the same server as the VMM server component (value: 0) or on a remote database server (value: 1)

MachineName and MachineFQDN   Two values that indicate the computer name of the remote SQL server in NETBIOS format and as a fully qualified domain name

After a backup, it is possible to restore the VMM database to a different database server as long as the Registry entries specified previously are updated accordingly to reflect the new database information. For the new Registry entries to be updated in VMM, follow these steps:

1. Make sure to stop the Virtual Machine Manager Windows Service on the VMM server computer.

2. After the update of the Registry entries is complete, start the VMM service and it will start using the new database information.

To recover the database for a different VMM server, see the section "Recovery on a New VMM Server" later in this chapter.

If you back up and restore only the VMM database, it is very important to use the exact same version of the VMM server component on the computer where the database will be restored.

USING THE VMM BACKUP CMDLETS

Virtual Machine Manager provides built-in support for backing up and restoring the VMM database. The backup of the database can be achieved either through the Administrator Console or by using the Backup-VMMServer Windows PowerShell cmdlet. To back up the VMM database from the Administrator Console, follow these steps.

1. Choose the Administration view in the Administrator Console.

2. Select the General view option.

3. Click the Back Up Virtual Machine Manager Administration action. Figure 10.1 shows the dialog that will prompt for the path on which to place the database backup file.

FIGURE 10.1
Virtual Machine
Manager Backup dialog

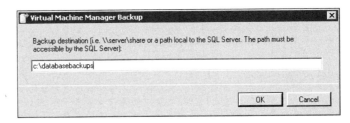

You can specify a local path on the SQL Server computer as long as it is not a root directory, or you can specify a file server share on another computer. Regardless of the backup location entered in this dialog, the logon account of the SQL Server Windows Service that is hosting the VMM database needs to have write access. If the backup location does not have the required security permissions for SQL Server, error 2208 will be returned by VMM, as shown in Figure 10.2.

FIGURE 10.2
Incorrect backup
location permissions
warning

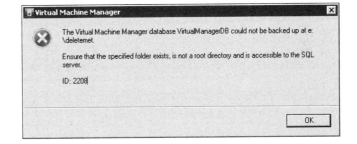

The backup operation can be tracked in the jobs view of the Administrator Console. Once the job is complete, a file with a filename extension of `.bak` will be placed in the backup destination. The filename will contain the name of the VMM database and the time of the backup in Greenwich mean time (GMT) format. For example, a typical filename will be `VirtualManagerDB-08122009-015956.bak`.

VMM also offers a Windows PowerShell cmdlet that implements the exact same backup operation as the one using the Administrator Console. In fact, that Administrator Console action will invoke the `Backup-VMMServer` cmdlet to do the work. Here is one example invocation of the cmdlet:

```
PS C:\> Backup-VMMServer -Path "E:\DBBackupLocations"
```

In the execution of the cmdlet, VMM uses Transact-SQL syntax and the `Backup` object to back up the full database and transaction log to disk. This is often referred to as a full backup. This type of database backup requires that the entire backup is restored during a recovery operation.

To restore the VMM database backed up by the `Backup-VMMServer` cmdlet, use the `VMMRecovery.exe` utility on the computer running SQL Server. This utility is available in the `Bin` folder of the installation path for the VMM server component (`C:\Program Files\Microsoft System Center Virtual Machine Manager 2008 R2\bin`) and needs to run with elevated privileges (open a command prompt window logged in as Administrator). The utility is not based on Windows PowerShell because it can't use the VMM infrastructure to facilitate the recovery. Since the utility is updating the VMM database, it also requires stopping the VMM service, which eliminates the possibility of executing this job as a VMM cmdlet and using the VMM job infrastructure. Before recovering a previous backup of the VMM database, it is highly advised to take a backup of the current database. This will ensure that you have the latest database backup in storage in case you need to recover to it.

As a first step to recover the database, the utility will stop and disable the Virtual Machine Manager Windows Service. To restore the full database from the database backup, VMMRecovery stops all active connections to the database and utilizes the Transact-SQL Restore object. The VMMRecovery utility takes only two inputs as parameters, the path to the database backup file and a confirmation flag. The following code snippet shows you an example usage of the utility, including the success error returned by VMM upon completion of the recovery operation. The utility also utilizes return (exit) codes, which can be checked by a script to ensure that the recovery was successful. Exit code 0 is returned on success, while a non-zero exit code indicates a failure and will most likely be accompanied with an error string.

```
C:\> "C:\Program Files\Microsoft System Center Virtual Machine Manager
 2008 R2\bin\VMMRecover.exe" -Path e:\DBBackupLocations\
 VirtualManagerDB-08112009-145340.bak -Confirm
VMMRecover 2.0 - Virtual Machine Manager database recovery command-line tool.
Copyright (c) 2008 Microsoft Corporation. All rights reserved.

Virtual Machine Manager database recovery completed.
```

Once the recovery procedure is complete, the utility will enable the VMM service and start it. Ensure that the Virtual Machine Manager Windows Service is in a started state and then open the Administrator Console to inspect the VMM environment.

BACKING UP USING THE VMM VSS WRITER

The Volume Shadow Copy Service (also known as VSS) is an infrastructure service for enabling online backups of computers and their applications. VSS has a multicomponent architecture with three main pieces:

The requester A requester manages shadow copies (also known as snapshots) for one or more volumes as part of backup software that facilitates backup and restore operations for a computer.

The writer Applications that want to participate in the backup and recovery operations to ensure that their data is in a consistent state inside a shadow copy implement a writer. A writer also surfaces to the requester the writer metadata that allows a requester to discover an application's data stores and requirements for backup and restore.

The provider Hardware and software providers manage the I/O infrastructure and the creation of volume shadow copies in the file system. A shadow copy is a point-in-time copy of the contents of a file system volume that can be uniquely identified in the system via a GUID. Windows Server releases with an inbox VSS software provider called Microsoft Software Shadow Copy provider 1.0.

Data protection applications like Data Protection Manager (DPM) act as requesters and utilize the VSS infrastructure to create shadow copies of volumes without introducing any downtime to an application. DPM, like other backup applications, relies on application VSS writers to ensure that the application data is consistent on disk at the time of a snapshot. Data from the snapshots can then be copied to a secondary backup location or transferred to tape for long-term archival. Once a snapshot is taken, applications and the file system continue to write data to disk while the backup application is copying the data from the snapshot. Because data is copied from the snapshot and not from the file system, there are no open files that could obstruct the copy operations.

To read more about Windows backup concepts and the Volume Shadow Copy Service, refer to the information at http://msdn.microsoft.com/en-us/library/dd851907.aspx.

Starting with the released version of VMM 2008 R2 installed on a computer with a released version of Windows Server 2008 R2, VMM introduces a new way to enable backup. VMM has developed a VSS Express writer that facilitates integration of Virtual Machine Manager with backup technologies. The VSS infrastructure is not intended for use directly by administrators. In general, the following documentation is intended for backup software vendors looking to include VMM backup capabilities as a feature of their product.

VOLUME SHADOW COPY EXPRESS WRITERS

VSS Express writers and their API is transparent to requesters. A backup application that is a VSS requester would not be able to differentiate between a regular VSS writer and a VSS Express writer. Applications like VMM might decide to implement a VSS Express writer because of the lower cost of development. Express writers, because of their lower development costs, make it simpler and easier to participate in the VSS infrastructure and make an application VSS aware.

Discovering the VMM Writer

When the VMM server component is installed on a Windows Server 2008 R2 computer, the inbox vssadmin.exe utility can be used to query and discover the VMM writer. Invoking the following command will return all the registered VSS writers for that computer:

```
D:\>vssadmin list writers
```

Figure 10.3 shows the listing for the VMM Express writer. The unique identifier for the VMM writer is {7aaa9b7b-e652-4f37-9057-a9627141b420}.

FIGURE 10.3
VSSAdmin listing of the VMM Express writer

To look at the VSS components exposed by the VMM writer, you can use the inbox DiskShadow.exe utility that is a VSS requester. DiskShadow.exe and its syntax are documented in the Microsoft TechNet article at http://technet.microsoft.com/en-us/library/cc772172(WS.10).aspx. DiskShadow is very similar to DiskPart, and it offers an interactive command interpreter as well as a scriptable mode.

Let's look at an example on how to get the metadata for the VMM writer:

1. Open a Notepad file and save it as `script.txt`.

2. Inside this script, enter the following data:

```
List writers
```

3. Save the file and invoke DiskShadow from an elevated command prompt using the following syntax:

```
DiskShadow.exe -s script.txt
```

The VMM writer will return the writer metadata, which is telling the requester that the VMM writer has only one component. The VMM writer is a referential writer. This means that it references a dependency to the SQL Server writer, which is where VMM houses the information that needs to be backed up. The VMM writer does not do any work during a snapshot as a regular writer would. It instead notifies a requester that to back up VMM, you need to select the VSS component `\<computer name>\MICROSOFT$VMM$\VirtualManagerDB` from the SQL Server VSS writer. The VSS component for the VMM database in the SQL Server VSS writer will also tell a requester the location of the database files to back up. The SQL Server writer is named `SqlServerWriter` and has a unique ID of `{a65faa63-5ea8-4ebc-9dbd-a0c4db26912a}`.

Here is an example output of the VMM writer metadata:

```
* WRITER "VMM Express Writer"
        - Writer ID    = {7aaa9b7b-e652-4f37-9057-a9627141b420}
        - Writer instance ID = {044b2648-e898-497e-adc0-86c8c7532e6e}
        - Supports restore events = FALSE
        - Writer restore conditions = VSS_WRE_NEVER
        - Restore method = VSS_RME_RESTORE_IF_CAN_REPLACE
        - Requires reboot after restore = FALSE
        - Excluded files:
        + Component "VMM Express Writer:\VMM Backup Component"
                - Name: VMM Backup Component
                - Logical path:
                - Full path: \VMM Backup Component
                - Caption: VMM Backup Component
                - Type: VSS_CT_DATABASE [1]
                - Is selectable: FALSE
                - Is top level: TRUE
                - Notify on backup complete: FALSE
                - Paths affected by this component:
                - Volumes affected by this component:
                - Component Dependencies:
                        - Dependency to "{a65faa63-5ea8-4ebc-9dbd-a0c4db
26912a}:\<computer name>\MICROSOFT$VMM$\VirtualManagerDB"
```

If you are an application developer and would like to test the capabilities of the VMM VSS writer, the VSS SDK offers a utility called `BETest.exe`. BETest is a VSS requester that can test advanced backup and restore operations. The Microsoft Developer

Network website has a more in-depth explanation of BETest's features and functionality at http://msdn.microsoft.com/en-us/library/bb530721(VS.85).aspx.

Using the VMM Writer

Now that you have learned how to discover the VMM writer, you can use DiskShadow to create a snapshot that utilizes the VMM writer and the SQL writer to produce a consistent copy of the database files on disk during the snapshot:

1. First, create a file called `script.txt`.

2. In the `script.txt` file, enter the following data:

   ```
   # DiskShadow script file to back up VMM
   set context persistent

   # make sure the path already exists for the VSS metadata
   set metadata d:\backupmetadata.cab
   set verbose on

   begin backup

   # Add to the backup the volume that contains the VMM database files
   add volume d: alias SystemAndDataVolumeShadowCopy

   # verify the "VMM Express Writer" writer will be included in the snapshot
   # by adding its unique identity
   writer verify {7aaa9b7b-e652-4f37-9057-a9627141b420}
   create

   end backup

   # expose the shadow copy as a drive letter W:\
   expose %SystemAndDataVolumeShadowCopy% W:
   ```

3. Save the file and invoke DiskShadow from an elevated command prompt using the following syntax:

   ```
   DiskShadow.exe -s script.txt
   ```

Once you execute the script, DiskShadow will create a persistent writer-aware and application-consistent snapshot that also contains the VMM database. The backup will be a full backup. The following DiskShadow output is shown in a shortened version to illustrate only the relevant parts. As you can see, all the components for the VMM writer and the SQL writer are selected to participate in the backup and the resulting shadow copy is exposed as a read-only volume with drive letter `W:\` (other writers might also participate in the writer-involved backup if they have components on the `D:\` volume selected for backup). Data can now be copied from the `W:\` folder structure and backed up to a safe location. The relevant SQL files for the VMM database would be `VirtualManagerDB.mdf` and `VirtualManagerDB_log.ldf`. Figure 10.4 shows that the `D:\` and the `W:\` hard disk drives are identical in total capacity, with W:\ being a point-in-time snapshot of the D:\ drive. Here's the DiskShadow output:

```
D:\>diskshadow.exe -s script.txt
Microsoft DiskShadow version 1.0
Copyright (C) 2007 Microsoft Corporation
On computer:  NEFERTIRI,  8/13/2009 12:11:54 AM


-> # DiskShadow script file to backup VMM
-> set context persistent
->
-> # make sure the path already exists
-> set metadata d:\backupmetadata.cab
The existing file will be overwritten.
-> set verbose on
->
-> begin backup
->
-> # Add to the backup the volume that contains the VMM database files
-> add volume d: alias SystemAndDataVolumeShadowCopy
->
-> # verify the "VMM Express Writer" writer will be included in the snapshot
-> # by adding its unique identity
-> writer verify {7aaa9b7b-e652-4f37-9057-a9627141b420}
-> create

All components from writer "{7aaa9b7b-e652-4f37-9057-a9627141b420}" are selected
.


* Including writer "VMM Express Writer":
        + Adding component: \VMM Backup Component

* Including writer "SqlServerWriter":
        + Adding component: \NEFERTIRI\MICROSOFT$VMM$\VirtualManagerDB

Alias SystemAndDataVolumeShadowCopy for shadow ID {40a16fe9-a132-4947-acc0-17443
02d6730} set as environment variable.
Alias VSS_SHADOW_SET for shadow set ID {4e6ec39a-d0a2-4737-bbb9-953b7552b07b}se
t as environment variable.
Inserted file Manifest.xml into .cab file backupmetadata.cab
Inserted file BCDocument.xml into .cab file backupmetadata.cab

Querying all shadow copies with the shadow copy set ID {4e6ec39a-d0a2-4737-bbb9-
953b7552b07b}

        * Shadow copy ID = {40a16fe9-a132-4947-acc0-1744302d6730}
%SystemAndDataVolumeShadowCopy%
                - Shadow copy set: {4e6ec39a-d0a2-4737-bbb9-953b7552b07b}
```

```
%VSS_SHADOW_SET%
                - Original count of shadow copies = 1
                - Original volume name: \\?\Volume{0242efe3-4eea-120b-b24f-806e6
f6e6963}\ [D:\]
                - Creation time: 8/13/2009 12:12:34 AM
                - Shadow copy device name: \\?\GLOBALROOT\Device\HarddiskVolumeS
hadowCopy2
                - Originating machine: NEFERTIRI.redmond.corp.microsoft.com
                - Service machine: NEFERTIRI.redmond.corp.microsoft.com
                - Not exposed
                - Provider ID: {b5946137-7b9f-4925-af80-51abd60b20d5}
                - Attributes:  No_Auto_Release Persistent Differential

Number of shadow copies listed: 1
->
-> end backup
->
-> # expose the shadow copy as a drive letter W:\
-> expose %SystemAndDataVolumeShadowCopy% W:
-> %SystemAndDataVolumeShadowCopy% = {40a16fe9-a132-4947-acc0-1744302d6730}
The shadow copy was successfully exposed as W:\.
->
```

FIGURE 10.4
Shadow copy exposed as
a hard disk drive

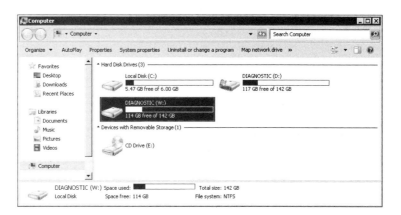

The DiskShadow application is great for backing up the database files and creating easy-to-use scriptable and scheduled backups. However, if you want to restore the database files backed up using the preceding DiskShadow scripts, there are additional considerations. The VSS infrastructure requires that a requester marks each VSS component with the attribute backupSucceeded when the component is successfully backed up. DiskShadow does not set this attribute, which means that during the restore operation, the VSS writer for SQL Server will not be invoked. The following DiskShadow script facilitates a restore of the database files for VMM that we backed up earlier. If you notice, there is an extra action during the restore operation that will invoke the executecopydatabase.cmd script. This script will ensure that the VMM and SQL services are stopped before the database and the log files are copied back to disk from the snapshot drive W:\. Because this script will stop the VMM service and the SQL service, any other applications depending on the same instance of SQL Server will experience a temporary loss of service.

```
# DiskShadow script file to restore the VMM database

# get the VSS metadata that was created during backup
load metadata d:\backupmetadata.cab


begin restore

# verify the "VMM Express Writer" writer will be included in the restore
# by adding its unique identity
writer verify {7aaa9b7b-e652-4f37-9057-a9627141b420}
writer verify {a65faa63-5ea8-4ebc-9dbd-a0c4db26912a}


# Execute a script that will copy the VMM database from a backup location
# to the location on disk that SQL server uses
exec executecopydatabase.cmd

end restore
```

The contents of the `executecopydatabase.cmd` referenced previously are as follows:

```
net stop vmmservice
net stop MSSQL$MICROSOFT$VMM$
xcopy "w:\Program Files (x86)\Microsoft SQL Server\MSSQL.1\MSSQL\
DATA\VirtualManagerDB.mdf" "d:\Program Files (x86)\Microsoft SQL
  Server\MSSQL.1\MSSQL\DATA\VirtualManagerDB.mdf" /y
xcopy "w:\Program Files (x86)\Microsoft SQL Server\MSSQL.1\MSSQL\
DATA\VirtualManagerDB_log.LDF" "d:\Program Files (x86)\Microsoft SQL
  Server\MSSQL.1\MSSQL\DATA\VirtualManagerDB_log.LDF" /y
```

Once the restore operation is complete, start the VMM and the SQL Server services and open the VMM Administrator Console to monitor the health of the restored environment.

BACKUP AND RESTORE SOFTWARE

There are a lot of utilities that allow you to back up and restore SQL Server databases. Even though DiskShadow offers a quick and easy way to back up the VMM database, the support it offers for restore is not optimal. Use Windows Server Backup and the procedures explained later in this chapter for a complete backup and recovery experience.

In general, backup software that is certified to work with the VMM VSS writer will offer the best and easiest backup and recovery of VMM. System Center Data Protection Manager (DPM) 2007 Service Pack 1, the latest release of DPM at the time of this book's authoring, cannot be used to back up VMM. It is expected that a future release of DPM will offer this support.

USING SQL SERVER BACKUP TECHNOLOGIES

SQL Server has been around for many years and backing up and restoring a database is a well-known entity. SQL Server provides several methodologies to help protect critical data that is stored in a database:

◆ SQL Server Management Studio can be used to back up and restore a database.

◆ Transact-SQL can be used to back up and restore a database using a script or programmatically.

◆ The SQL Server VSS writer can be used through backup software to back up and restore a database.

To learn more about the SQL Server backup and restore procedures, visit the Administration: How-to Topics page in the SQL Server Developer Center at http://msdn.microsoft.com/en-us/library/bb522544.aspx.

In addition to Transact-SQL and SQL Server Management Studio, SQL Server has a VSS writer that can be used to participate in snapshots initiated by the VSS infrastructure. The details of the SQL Server VSS writer were mentioned in the previous section.

Since the VMM server database is a SQL Server database, backing it up using the SQL Server backup technology of your choice will be enough to safeguard the critical VMM data. To successfully restore the VMM database, it is necessary that the Virtual Machine Manager Windows Service is stopped and disabled prior to the restore operation. This is a manual step that an administrator has to perform if the backup software does not do it automatically. Typically, backup software that is not certified to back up and restore Virtual Machine Manager will not stop the VMM service prior to a restore operation. The service needs to be manually enabled and started after the database is restored.

Full VMM Server Backup

Creating a full server backup of the VMM server is the best way to prepare for a possible disaster recovery. In this section, we will walk through the steps necessary to create a full server backup of the VMM server using the Windows Server Backup functionality in Windows Server 2008 R2. Windows Server Backup provides a complete solution for everyday backup and recovery operations.

For more details on Windows Server Backup, see these resources:

Backup and Recovery

http://technet.microsoft.com/en-us/library/cc754097(WS.10).aspx

Backup and Recovery Overview for Windows Server 2008

http://technet.microsoft.com/en-us/library/cc770593(WS.10).aspx

Windows Server Backup Step-by-Step Guide for Windows Server 2008

http://technet.microsoft.com/en-us/library/cc770266(WS.10).aspx

Windows Server Backup is not installed on a server by default. To install it, follow these steps:

1. Open the Server Manager Microsoft Management Console (MMC).

2. Click Features.

3. Add Windows Server Backup Features.

4. Once it's installed, launch the Windows Server Backup GUI from the Administrative Tools link in the Start menu.

Windows Server Backup will now automatically back up and restore data for any application that implements a VSS writer. However, the application has to first register with Windows Server Backup. Registration of an application and the Windows Server Backup API Registry keys are explained in the Microsoft Developer Network website at `http://msdn.microsoft.com/en-us/library/cc307260(VS.85).aspx`. To register the VMM and the SQL Server VSS writers with Windows Server Backup, copy the following contents into a newly created file called `RegisterVssWriters.reg` and double-click on the filename to merge it with the Windows Registry. Notice that the unique identifiers for the VMM and SQL Server writers are specified to Windows Server Backup:

```
Windows Registry Editor Version 5.00

[HKEY_LOCAL_MACHINE\SOFTWARE\Microsoft\Windows NT\CurrentVersion
\WindowsServerBackup]

[HKEY_LOCAL_MACHINE\SOFTWARE\Microsoft\Windows NT\CurrentVersion
\WindowsServerBackup\Application Support]

[HKEY_LOCAL_MACHINE\SOFTWARE\Microsoft\Windows NT\CurrentVersion
\WindowsServerBackup\Application Support\{7aaa9b7b-e652-4f37-9057-a9627141b420}]
"Application Identifier"="VMM VSS Writer"

[HKEY_LOCAL_MACHINE\SOFTWARE\Microsoft\Windows NT\CurrentVersion
\WindowsServerBackup\Application Support\{a65faa63-5ea8-4ebc-9dbd-a0c4db26912a}]
"Application Identifier"="SQL Server VSS Writer"
```

Now let's walk through the steps to back up the VMM server:

1. From the Windows Server Backup GUI, click the Backup Once action.

2. Select Different options to customize the backup.

3. In the Backup Configuration page, a full server backup can be requested. This type of configuration will back up all the server data, applications, and system state. If you want a full server backup that can be used to completely restore a server, you should select the full server backup option. In this step, choose Custom to see the different options presented by Windows Server Backup.

4. In the next wizard screen, click Add Items to select the backup items, as shown in Figure 10.5. Select the Bare Metal Recovery and System State options as well as the volumes that contain the VMM database files.

5. Click Advanced Settings to configure the VSS settings for this backup. Windows Server Backup is a generic VSS requester, and it will invoke and select all the VSS writers in the computer during the backup. Any writers that have components in the volumes selected for backup will participate in the backup of those VSS components. Since in this example we selected the volumes that contain the VMM database files, the VMM and the SQL Server writers will participate in the backup process.

FIGURE 10.5
Selecting items to
include in the backup

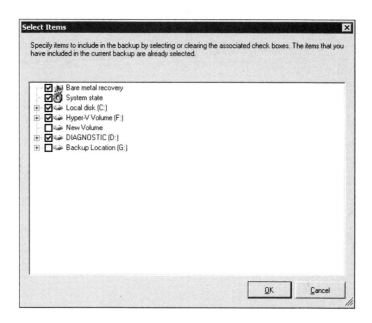

6. In the VSS Settings tab, shown in Figure 10.6, select the VSS Copy Backup option. This will
prevent Windows Server Backup from clearing any application log files that are needed by
another backup product.

FIGURE 10.6
VSS settings of Windows
Server Backup

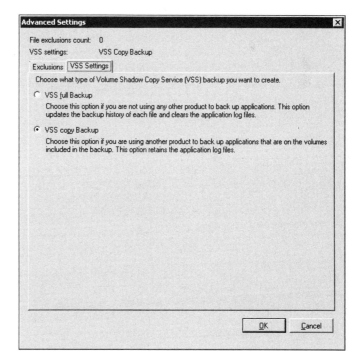

7. Next, select a local drive or a remote file server share as the backup destination and click the Backup button. The backup process will start and display its progress until it is complete. The status messages on the top of the Backup Progress page show the different steps that Windows Server Backup follows during the backup.

Now that the data on this server has been backed up, it can be copied to another server or to tape for long-term archival. If the VMM database becomes corrupt or is lost, Windows Server Backup can be used to recover the data. To do this, follow these steps:

1. From the Windows Server Backup GUI, select the Recover action.

2. Select the option to find a backup stored on another location.

3. Select the location where the backup files reside and select the name of the server whose data you would like to recover.

4. If multiple backups are available, select the date and time of the backup you want to use for the VMM database recovery.

5. Windows Server Backup provides you with a lot of options for recovery, from being able to recover the system state to being able to recover an individual file or a folder. Since VMM and SQL Server each has a VSS writer that is already registered with Windows Server Backup, they are considered applications. Select Applications to be able to recover only the VMM database.

6. Windows Server Backup will list all the applications that have registered their VSS writers and have available data in the backup set. Since the VMM database was in a volume selected for backup, the VMM VSS writer entry is included in the list of applications. Figure 10.7 shows the applications available for recovery, and Figure 10.8 shows the details of the VMM VSS writer showing the database dependency to the SQL Server VSS writer. Figure 10.9 shows the details of the SQL Server VSS writer, indicating that the VMM database VirtualManagerDB is available for restore.

FIGURE 10.7
Selecting the VMM
application for recovery

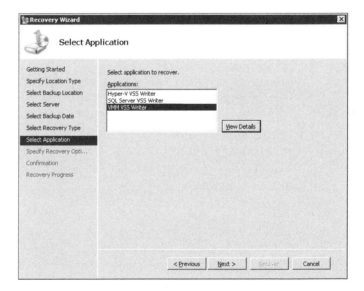

FIGURE 10.8
VMM VSS writer
components for recovery

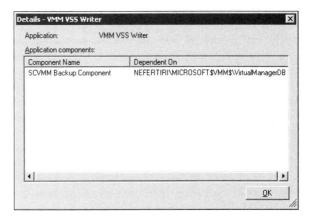

FIGURE 10.9
SQL Server VSS writer
components for recovery

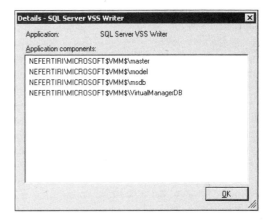

7. Stop the Virtual Machine Manager Windows Service before proceeding. This will terminate all VMM operations in anticipation of the recovery.

8. Select the VMM VSS writer application and choose to recover it to its original location. This option will ensure that the VMM and SQL Server VSS writers are involved in the recovery of the application. Once the recovery is complete, the VMM database would have been replaced with the database at the time of backup.

9. Start the VMM service and open the Administrator Console to inspect the restored VMM environment.

Recovery Considerations

After a VMM database is recovered and the Virtual Machine Manager Windows Service is started, VMM will start overwriting and updating the knowledge it has about the virtualization environment in the database with what exists on the host and library computers. While the synchronization is going on, you will see many jobs refreshing data into VMM. You may also notice that any jobs that were executing at the time of backup are listed as failed with error 1700, as Figure 10.10 shows.

FIGURE 10.10
Running jobs during a
backup will fail with
error 1700.

Once the Administrator Console is open, ensure that the environment reflects the state of the environment as it was taken during backup. The VMM refresher jobs will automatically start synchronizing the state of the hosts and virtual machines in VMM with the state of the hosts and virtual machines in the virtualization hosts. In general, any changes that you have made to your environment configuration (aside from newly deployed virtual machines) since the restored backup need to be reapplied. For this reason, relatively frequent backups are recommended (daily backups at a minimum). Here are some things to consider about this synchronization:

◆ Virtualization hosts that were added as managed hosts in VMM after the backup was taken need to be added again.

◆ Virtualization hosts that were removed from management after the backup need to be removed again. These hosts will have a Needs Attention status in the Administrator Console.

◆ Any virtual machines that were added to a managed host since the last backup will be discovered automatically by the refreshers. If you had entered any VMM-specific information about these VMs in the virtual machine properties, you will need to enter that information again. For example, any custom properties will need to be specified again for the VM.

◆ Any virtual machines that were deleted since the last backup will have a Missing status in the Administrator Console and need to be deleted again.

◆ Library servers or VMware VirtualCenter servers that were added or removed from VMM after the backup was taken need to be added or removed again.

◆ Templates that were created in VMM after the backup also need to be created again after the Library Refresher discovers the VHD files that are needed for the template.

Recovery on a New VMM Server

If the VMM server was lost (due to a hardware failure, for example) and the restore operation needs to restore the database on a new installation of the VMM server, there are additional steps to follow to ensure that the environment is healthy. Here are the steps to follow when recovering the database on a new installation of the VMM server:

1. In the VMM Administrator Console, choose the Administration view and select the Managed Computers view option.

2. Select all the managed computers that are in an Access Denied state and click the Reassociate action.

Please note that managed computers will be in an Access Denied state if the system identification number (also known as the computer security identifier, or SID) for the VMM server computer has changed and the VMM service is running with the Local System credentials. Changing the computer name of the VMM server computer would also lead to Access Denied issues. The VMM server is authorized on the managed computers (virtualization hosts and VMM library servers) using the Log On account of the VMM service. If the VMM service is using the Local System account, that account's security identifier as presented to other computers will be different if the computer SID has changed. Hosts will not know how to authorize the new SID and will be in an Access Denied state. This is by design and ensures that your hosts are not compromised by an unauthorized VMM server. If the VMM service was running under the same domain credentials before the failure and after the reinstallation, the hosts will not need to be reassociated unless they were restored as well.

3. Enter credentials for a domain account with administrator rights on all the managed computers. VMM will now launch jobs that will update the managed computers and reassociate them with this VMM server.

4. For templates in the VMM library that contain a guest operating system profile, do the following:

   a. Open the template properties and navigate to the OS Configuration tab.
   b. Clear the Admin Password field and reenter the information.

5. For guest OS profiles in the VMM library, do the following:

   a. Open the Guest OS profile properties and navigate to the Guest OS tab.
   b. Clear the Admin Password and reenter the information.

6. Perimeter network virtualization hosts — virtualization hosts that reside in a domain with no trust with the domain of the VMM server — and VMware VirtualCenter servers need to be removed from management and added again.

7. For virtual machines that reside on a Virtual Server host and are configured to automatically start after a reboot of the virtualization host, do the following:

   a. Open the virtual machine properties and navigate to the Actions tab.
   b. Clear the username and password fields and reenter the information.

If you have restored the encryption keys of the previous VMM server on the new installation of the VMM server computer, it is possible that the VMM will be able to decrypt some the sensitive data from the VMM database using the Data Protection application programming interface (DPAPI). However, to be absolutely sure that the VMM environment is functional, it is best to follow the recommendations stated earlier.

Bare Metal Recovery

Bare metal recovery procedures are required in situations in which you have to restore a server from a full backup without any requirements for a preexisting operating system or software. Bare metal recovery can recover the operating system, the system state, file system volumes and file system data, and applications, along with the application data. It can be used on the same hardware that the server had during the backup or on an entirely new set of hardware that has an identical configuration to the hardware of the computer that was backed up.

The Windows Recovery Environment (also known as Windows RE) can be used to perform a complete system recovery from "bare metal" using a full server backup that was taken using Windows Server Backup and the procedures outlined earlier in this chapter. A full backup includes system state backup, which, when restored, will also restore the computer SID that uniquely identifies the computer to the network.

Windows RE is an extensible recovery platform that is based on the Windows Preinstallation Environment (also known as Windows PE). When a computer fails to boot properly, an administrator is given the option to start the system recovery (Windows RE can also be launched by pressing the F8 key during the initial boot of a computer to open the Advanced Boot Options window, shown in Figure 10.11). The recovery console can also be started from the operating system installation DVD.

FIGURE 10.11
Windows Server advanced boot options

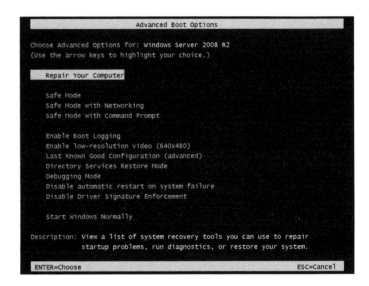

RECOVERING THE SYSTEM IMAGE

To recover the computer to a full backup, follow these steps:

1. From the menu, select the Recovery Environment option or the Repair Your Computer option.

2. After you enter your local administrator credentials, the System Recovery Options dialog opens.

3. Select the System Image Recovery option to recover the computer to a previous full backup.

4. Select the backup that you want to use for the recovery by picking an image from the list, or use the latest available system image, as in Figure 10.12. If the full backup is stored on removable media or on the network, follow these steps to select it:

   a. Click Select A System Image and select the Advanced option. Choose to search for a system image on the network and provide a file server share that contains the full backups for this computer.

   b. If the computer can't connect to the server, ensure that you have an IP address by opening a command prompt from the System Recovery Options dialog. To eliminate any DNS issues, use the IP address of the server when specifying the location of the backups.

5. In the next wizard page, select the option to format and repartition disks in order for the disks to match the layout of the backup.

FIGURE 10.12
Selecting a full backup
image for restore

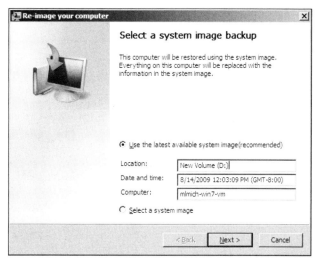

6. If you have any drivers for the disks you are restoring, the next wizard page will have an option to install those drivers from installation media.

7. You are now ready to initiate the restore operation of your computer from a full backup. Accept the warning that a system restore will erase all data on the drives and the restore process will begin. The computer will automatically reboot after the recovery procedures are completed. Doing a bare metal recovery or a system state recovery requires a reboot to complete the entire recovery operation.

Windows Server Backup also has a command-line interface, wbadmin.exe, which can be used to back up or restore a server. The following examples show you how to get the versions of a backup, to open the backup to see what components and applications were backed up, and to initiate a full system restore from a network share that contains the backups:

```
D:\>wbadmin get versions -backuptarget:\\<computer name>\<share name>
wbadmin 1.0 - Backup command-line tool
(C) Copyright 2004 Microsoft Corp.

Backup time: 8/14/2009 1:23 AM
Backup target: Fixed Disk labeled G:
Version identifier: 08/14/2009-08:23
Can recover: Volume(s), File(s), Application(s), Bare Metal Recovery,
 System State
Snapshot ID: {b038d27c-f6e3-4ece-87fd-40466951eae0}

D:\>wbadmin get items -version:08/14/2009-08:23
wbadmin 1.0 - Backup command-line tool
(C) Copyright 2004 Microsoft Corp.

Volume ID = {0242efe2-4eea-120b-b24f-806e6f6e6963}
Volume '<Unlabeled Volume>', mounted at C:
Volume size = 6.00 GB
Can recover = Full volume
```

```
Volume ID = {0242efe3-4eea-120b-b24f-806e6f6e6963}
Volume 'DIAGNOSTIC', mounted at D:
Volume size = 142.49 GB
Can recover = Full volume

Volume ID = {8ba60d38-189b-11dc-83f0-001aa0ad957e}
Volume 'Hyper-V Volume', mounted at F:
Volume size = 2.92 GB
Can recover = Full volume

Application = sqlserver
Component = master (NEFERTIRI\MICROSOFT$VMM$\master)

Component = model (NEFERTIRI\MICROSOFT$VMM$\model)

Component = msdb (NEFERTIRI\MICROSOFT$VMM$\msdb)

Component = VirtualManagerDB (NEFERTIRI\MICROSOFT$VMM$\VirtualManagerDB)

Application = VMM
Component = VMM Backup Component (\VMM Backup Component)

Application = Hyper-V
Component = 64C31DF6-FCEA-4808-9883-7F808CF7CA28 (\64C31DF6-FCEA-4808-9883-7F808
CF7CA28)

Component = 9F1987E9-FAD8-40C7-8527-0AF4EA8086E2 (\9F1987E9-FAD8-40C7-8527-0AF4E
A8086E2)

Component = A01EBA54-F720-45D7-A24B-AE2959D27A4E (\A01EBA54-F720-45D7-A24B-AE295
9D27A4E)

Component = B2A2FC02-6CD0-418D-9CB2-393D41AA4983 (\B2A2FC02-6CD0-418D-9CB2-393D4
1AA4983)

Component = Initial Store (\Initial Store)

D:\>wbadmin start sysrecovery -backuptarget:\\<computer name>\<share name>
 -version:08/14/2009-08:23 -recreatedisks -restoreallvolumes
 -machine:<server name to restore>
```

To learn more about the Windows Recovery Environment, visit the Microsoft TechNet website at http://technet.microsoft.com/en-us/library/cc766048(WS.10).aspx.

RECOVERING THE VMM SERVER

In a typical environment, after a new physical server is deployed, the administrator will take a full system backup before any applications are installed. This backup is the one that can be used in a bare metal recovery. Because the VMM server component is not installed on the system after a recovery is completed, follow these steps to get VMM up and running:

1. Install the SQL Server database if you are using a full SQL instance. If you want to use SQL Express, skip to step 2.

2. Install the VMM server component will all its prerequisites.

3. Install the VMM Administrator Console with all its prerequisites.

4. Now you are ready to recover the VMM database. This chapter has outlined a lot of different ways to back up and restore the VMM database. Depending on the method you used for backup, the recovery procedures may vary. Since we are talking about Windows Server Backup in this section, the recovery procedures are outlined in the section "Full VMM Server Backup" earlier in this chapter.

5. If your virtualization hosts or the library servers also need to be restored from "bare metal," follow the same procedure to restore from a full backup. For virtualization hosts, you would also need to install or enable the virtualization platform and restore the virtual machines from a backup. For library servers, you would need to recreate the file server shares that VMM was managing (if they are not part of the backup) and restore the physical files that were part of the library.

6. Once the database, virtualization hosts, and library servers are recovered, you can open the Administrator Console to inspect the environment. To ensure that the environment is healthy, follow the procedures and recommendations outlined earlier in this chapter in the sections "Recovery Considerations" and "Recovery on a New VMM Server," if applicable. New VMM agents will probably need to be deployed on virtualization hosts and library servers that were recovered from "bare metal."

7. Your VMM server should now be fully functional and ready to manage your virtualization environment.

Sysprep Considerations

Sysprep, the Windows System Preparation tool, is a utility that generalizes a computer into an image in preparation for deployment to multiple computers. When executed, sysprep will remove the system identity of the computer, allowing it to get a new identity when the image is deployed to a new computer and Windows Setup is run. Original equipment manufacturers (OEMs) use sysprep to prepare a golden image of a computer and then deploy that image on multiple computers that have identical hardware. In this section, we will not go through the details of sysprep, assuming that the reader is familiar with sysprep and creating factory images of servers. The Microsoft TechNet website has a lot of good information on the usage of sysprep. Visit `http://technet.microsoft.com/en-us/default.aspx` and search for "sysprep."

To prepare VMM for factory installation, follow these steps:

1. Start from a fresh installation of Windows Server 2008.

2. Join the computer to the domain and make sure that Windows Update is enabled to bring the server up to date.

3. You are now ready to deploy VMM. In the installation media that you have for VMM, look for the file `VMServer.ini` in the folder `\amd64\setup`. Copy this file to `C:\VMServer.ini`.

4. Modify the contents of the file to look like the following. You will have to replace the ProductKey value with your own legal product key. Other settings can also be modified to meet your preferences for a factory image. Parameters that start with the # sign are ignored by VMM Setup because they are classified as comments.

```
[OPTIONS]
ProductKey=xxxxx-xxxxx-xxxxx-xxxxx-xxxxx
# UserName=Administrator
# CompanyName=Microsoft Corporation
# ProgramFiles=C:\Program Files\Microsoft System Center Virtual
  Machine Manager 2008 R2
# DatabaseFiles=C:\Program Files\Microsoft System Center Virtual
  Machine Manager 2008 R2\DB
CreateNewSqlDatabase=1
CreateNewSqlInstance=1
SqlInstanceName= MICROSOFT$VMM$
SqlDatabaseName=VirtualManagerDB
# OnRemoteServer=0
# RemoteDatabaseImpersonation=0
# SqlMachineName=<sqlmachinename>
# IndigoTcpPort=8100
# WSManTcpPort=80
# BitsTcpPort=443
CreateNewLibraryShare=1
LibraryShareName=MSVMMLibrary
LibrarySharePath=C:\ProgramData\Virtual Machine Manager Library Files
# LibraryShareDescription=Virtual Machine Manager Library Files
# SQMOptIn = 0
# MUOptIn = 0
# VmmServiceLocalAccount = 0
```

5. From the VMM installation media, run setup.exe as shown below. The /prep flag that is passed to Setup.exe will perform an OEM installation of the VMM server component using the specified VMServer.ini file. VMM might take a few minutes to install, with no progress information shown to the user. If there are any errors, a Virtual Machine Manager Setup window will pop up with the error. Otherwise, the setup operation will complete and the VMM server component will have an entry in the Programs and Features dialog.

```
Setup.exe /server /prep /i /f C:\VMServer.ini
```

6. Next, you will need to generalize this computer and apply the generalization and cleanup techniques that your organization follows. The following list includes some of the things that can be deleted to help strip the computer from its identity and reduce its contents:

    a. Delete unnecessary temporary files from the computer.

    b. Clear the contents of the c:\ProgramData\VMMLogs folder.

    c. Clear the Windows logs from the Event Viewer.

    d. Empty the Recycle Bin.

    e. Remove any unnecessary accounts from the local Administrators security group.

    f. Delete the page file `pagefile.sys` (this will require booting into an alternate environment).

7. Make any necessary DNS changes to the system so that it can function correctly when deployed to another computer.

8. Execute `sysprep.exe`. `Sysprep.exe` ships with the operating system and is available at `%windir%\System32\Sysprep\Sysprep.exe`. From the System Preparation Tool dialog, select the Enter System Out-Of-Box Experience (OOBE) option and check the Generalize option, as shown in Figure 10.13. Select Shutdown from the Shutdown Options menu and click OK. The system will now undergo the sysprep operations and is stripped of its identity (generalized). Factory setup is now complete.

FIGURE 10.13
System Preparation
Tool dialog

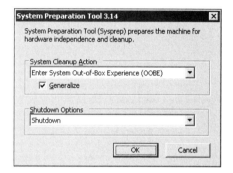

When a factory image is deployed to a new computer, you will notice a shortcut on the desktop of the VMM server computer called VMM Server Configuration. Running this file as an administrator will have it go through the rest of the steps to finalize the installation of VMM and specialize it for this computer.

Something to consider before you sysprep the VMM server is that not all software is sysprep-capable. Before you install any software on the VMM server, consult the software manufacturer to ensure that the software would continue to work after a sysprep option. SQL Server, a key component of VMM, is not certified to work with sysprep and does not have a sysprep provider. However, since VMM installs SQL Server Express as part of VMM Setup with a minimal configuration, it is possible to sysprep the computer. Once a new instance of the image is deployed, inspect the SQL Server settings and permissions to ensure that they meet your organization's standards.

High Availability

In the following sections, we will briefly cover the high availability options of the different components in a virtualized environment managed by VMM. Highly available (HA) components will reduce downtime and maintain your service-level agreement for Virtual Machine Manager, hosts, and virtual machine availability.

HIGHLY AVAILABLE VMM SERVER

The VMM server component does not have a cluster resource and thus does not natively support clustering. However, you can make the VMM server highly available by running VMM inside a Hyper-V virtual machine that is highly available through failover clustering. Running the VMM server inside a virtual machine is a fully supported configuration. In addition to enabling high availability, running VMM inside of a virtual machine allows you to take virtual machine snapshots to quickly recover to a previous point in time. Snapshots are not a substitute for a comprehensive backup plan as described earlier in this chapter, but they are an excellent way to augment such a scheme. In addition to enabling high availability, running VMM inside of a virtual machine allows you to take virtual machine snapshots to quickly recover to a previous point in time. Snapshots are not a substitute for comprehensive backup plans as described in this chapter but are an excellent way to augment such a scheme.

When the virtual machine that hosts the VMM server fails over to another host, the VMM server fails over automatically as well and can survive a hardware failure on the source host. Even though this is a supported configuration for a highly available VMM server, there are some additional considerations:

◆ If you are using failover clustering in Windows Server 2008, make sure you don't migrate the virtual machine hosting VMM from within the VMM Administrator Console. Such an operation will introduce downtime to the virtual machine and fail the migration task and any other running tasks.

◆ If you are using failover clustering in Windows Server 2008 R2, the virtual machine hosting VMM can be live migrated to another cluster node without any user-perceivable downtime to the VMM operations. Administrator Consoles installed on a separate client computer will not lose the connection to the VMM server during the live migration.

By keeping the VMM server component inside a highly available virtual machine, a failover will not impact the VMM server's name and identity. Users can still connect to it through the Administrator Console installed on other computers, and the virtualization hosts will authenticate with the same server.

A best practice is to have a highly available database residing on a different server. However, if you would like to run the SQL Server database also inside a virtual machine, consult the SQL Server technical article "Running SQL Server 2008 in a Hyper-V Environment: Best Practices and Performance Considerations" located at `http://download.microsoft.com/download/d/9/4/d948f981-926e-40fa-a026-5bfcf076d9b9/SQL2008inHyperV2008.docx`.

HIGHLY AVAILABLE VIRTUALIZATION HOSTS

Clustering and highly available virtualization hosts are deployed in environments where the virtual machines and the applications running inside the virtual machines need high availability. Virtual machines that reside on a cluster node are automatically migrated to redundant nodes when system components fail to achieve high availability of services. In Chapter 3, we had an in-depth discussion on how to set up and configure highly available (HA) virtualization hosts. HA Hyper-V hosts are configured through Windows Server 2008 failover clustering, which supports up to 16 cluster nodes in the same cluster. To achieve HA, virtual machines will fail over to another host in case their current cluster node fails.

Virtual Server host clustering is described in detail in Chapter 6. Chapter 4 describes in detail how to manage host clusters created in a VMware VirtualCenter environment.

HIGHLY AVAILABLE LIBRARY SERVERS

Highly available library servers ensure that all the physical files that are part of a library server in VMM are always available and can withstand system component failures. Chapter 3 included an in-depth discussion on how to set up highly available library servers. VMM supports highly available file servers that reside on a failover cluster created in Windows Server 2008 or Windows Server 2008 R2.

HIGHLY AVAILABLE SELF-SERVICE PORTALS

VMM does not support network load balancing, which provides high availability, scalability, and reliability to web servers. To achieve highly available Self-Service Portals (SSPs), VMM recommends that you deploy multiple SSPs in your organization and connect them to the same VMM server. If one SSP fails, self-service users can still connect to one of the other SSPs without encountering any downtime.

HIGHLY AVAILABLE DATABASE SERVER

SQL Server failover clustering procedures can be used to make the VMM database highly available. Deploying the SQL Server instance of the VMM database on a failover cluster will increase the availability of the database and directly increase the availability of the VMM server component. In an HA SQL Server environment, it is important to tune the SQL Server settings in the VMM component of the Windows Registry. To increase the likelihood of a successful database failover, make the following modifications to the Windows Registry of the VMM server component and restart the Virtual Machine Manager Windows Service:

1. Create a new value of type DWORD in the key [HKEY_LOCAL_MACHINE\SOFTWARE\ Microsoft\Microsoft System Center Virtual Machine Manager Server\Settings\Sql] with the name DBRetryInterval and put **2** in the value data field. This will ensure that VMM waits for two seconds before each retry attempt.

2. Create a new value of type DWORD in the key [HKEY_LOCAL_MACHINE\SOFTWARE\ Microsoft\Microsoft System Center Virtual Machine Manager Server\Settings\Sql] with the name DBRetryCount and put **5** in the value data field. This will ensure that VMM retries five times before it gives up on executing an operation with SQL Server.

To learn more about SQL Server 2008 failover clustering, visit the SQL Server Developer Center website at http://msdn.microsoft.com/en-us/library/ms189134.aspx. Chapter 3 also describes in detail how to make the VMM database highly available.

Backing Up the Virtualization Hosts

Hyper-V and Virtual Server 2005 R2 SP1 have built-in support for VSS by implementing a VSS writer. In this section, we will concentrate on Hyper-V backup operations. For VMware ESX host backup, VMware has published a Knowledge Base article at http://kb.vmware.com/kb/ 1355. This article contains information on backup technologies and compatible commercial tools for backing up ESX Server virtual machines. To back up Virtual Server, you can use backup software that supports the Virtual Server VSS writer in the same way that you would back up the Hyper-V VSS writer as outlined in this section.

The VSS writer in Hyper-V orchestrates the backup of a virtual machine at the host operating system level as well as at the guest operating system. What this means is that if a virtual machine is selected for backup using the Hyper-V VSS writer, Hyper-V will synchronize the backup of applications running inside the virtual machine's guest operating system to produce a consistent and application-aware snapshot of the virtual machine. VSS-aware applications like SQL Server and Exchange running inside the virtual machine will get to participate in the snapshot and ensure that their data is consistent inside the virtual machine VHD files. Because of the existence of the VHD files, host-level backups using the VSS writer are great because all you are backing up for an entire virtual machine is a handful of VHD and configuration files instead of the thousand or so files that need to be backed up if in-guest backup was used.

Host-level backups of virtual machines do not mean you should abandon your organization's in-guest backup policies. Devise a backup plan that will protect your data using the preferred method in your organization at the interval that your company is comfortable with. You can still use a combination of host-level and in-guest-level backups to protect your virtual machines. In addition, regularly capture bare metal recovery backups (or full server backups) of the virtualization hosts that can be used in a disaster recovery situation.

REQUIREMENTS FOR BACKING UP VIRTUAL MACHINES

The Hyper-V VSS writer can back up a virtual machine live with no downtime to the virtual machines and its applications if the virtual machine meets the following requirements:

◆ The virtual machine is in a running state and the Hyper-V Integration Services are installed and functioning.

◆ The Backup (volume snapshot) integration service is enabled on the virtual machine as shown in the following screen shot.

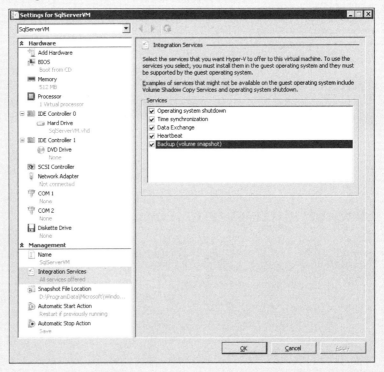

◆ The virtual machine does not contain dynamic disks in the guest operating system.

◆ The virtual machine does not contain FAT or FAT32 file systems in the guest operating system.

◆ The virtual machine's guest operating system is an operating system that supports the Volume Shadow Copy Services. This means that only Windows operating systems running Windows

Server 2003 or later are supported. Virtual machines running Windows 2000 and Windows XP operating systems need to be backed up offline.

◆ If the virtual machine resides on a highly available Hyper-V host, the cluster resource group for the virtual machine needs to be in an online state.

◆ The VSS Shadow Copy Storage volume assignments for the file system volumes inside the guest operating system of the virtual machine need to be on the same volume that is associated with them. To view the Shadow Copy Storage associations, run the following command inside the Virtual Machine: `vssadmin.exe List ShadowStorage`.

If a virtual machine cannot be backed up live, it can be backed up using offline backup. Offline backup puts a running or paused virtual machine to a saved state for a very brief period of time, executes the snapshot, and then returns the virtual machine to its previous state.

The Hyper-V VSS writer does not support backup for virtual machines that do not have storage on the host computer. The following configurations are not supported:

◆ Virtual machines that have pass-through disks attached to them. Pass-through disks are physical hard disks that are directly attached to a virtual machine. Because there is no VHD associated with these disks, a backup application would not know how to copy the files from a snapshot.

◆ Virtual machines that are using networked storage at the host level to store the VHDs on a separate computer.

◆ Virtual machines that use iSCSI storage inside the guest operating system of the VM. Because the virtual machine's entire storage and configuration is not contained within the VHD files, there is no way for the VSS writer to guarantee the consistency of the backup.

For virtual machines that cannot be backed up live, or for virtual machines that cannot be backed up by VSS at all, an alternative is to use backup software inside the guest operating system. In this configuration, you would be treating the virtual machine just like any other physical server in your environment and backing it up using an in-guest agent.

Only full backups are supported by the Hyper-V VSS writer. To prevent failures in backup and restore operations of virtual machines, install the following updates on all your Windows Server 2008–based Hyper-V hosts. The content of the individual updates, and the issues they fix, is documented in the Microsoft Help and Support website:

◆ Update 959962 at `http://support.microsoft.com/kb/959962`

◆ Update 960038 at `http://support.microsoft.com/kb/960038`

◆ Update 951308 at `http://support.microsoft.com/kb/951308`

◆ Update 958184 at `http://support.microsoft.com/kb/958184`

◆ Update 956697 at `http://support.microsoft.com/kb/956697`

First, let's register the Hyper-V VSS writer with Windows Server Backup. Copy the following contents into a newly created file called `RegisterVssWriters.reg` and double-click on the file to merge it with the Windows Registry. Notice the unique identifier for the Hyper-V writer, `{66841cd4-6ded-4f4b-8f17-fd23f8ddc3de}`, is specified to Windows Server Backup. The actual name of the Hyper-V VSS writer is Microsoft Hyper-V VSS Writer.

```
Windows Registry Editor Version 5.00

[HKEY_LOCAL_MACHINE\SOFTWARE\Microsoft\Windows NT\CurrentVersion\
WindowsServerBackup]

[HKEY_LOCAL_MACHINE\SOFTWARE\Microsoft\Windows NT\CurrentVersion\
WindowsServerBackup\Application Support]

[HKEY_LOCAL_MACHINE\SOFTWARE\Microsoft\Windows NT\CurrentVersion\
WindowsServerBackup\Application Support\{66841cd4-6ded-4f4b-8f17-fd23f8ddc3de}]
"Application Identifier"="Hyper-V VSS Writer"
```

The Hyper-V VSS writer exposes a set of VSS components to a requester. Each virtual machine is exposed as a separate component, allowing it to be backed up and restored individually by backup software. An additional component is exposed for the backup of the Initial Store, which is the Authorization Manager XML configuration that controls access to Hyper-V and the virtual machines. Figure 10.14 shows an example of the Hyper-V writer metadata indicating the separate components for the virtual machines and the Initial Store.

FIGURE 10.14
Hyper-V VSS writer metadata

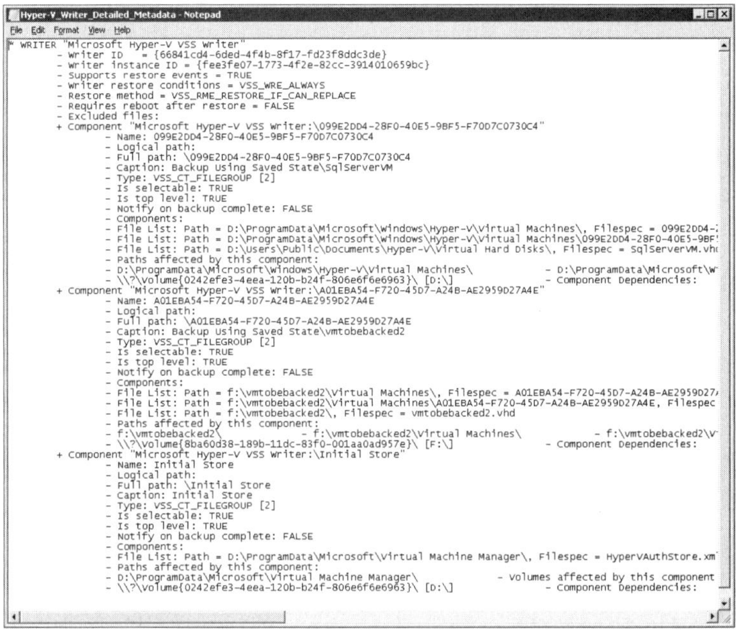

Backing Up a Hyper-V Server

Let's walk through the steps to back up a Hyper-V server:

1. From the Windows Server Backup GUI, click the Backup Once action.

2. Select Different Options to customize the backup.

3. In the Backup Configuration page, select Custom.

4. In the next wizard screen, click Add Items to select the backup items. Select the Bare Metal Recovery and System State options as well as the volumes that contain the Hyper-V virtual machines. Make sure to include all the volumes that contain VHDs as well as the volumes containing the virtual machine configuration files.

5. Click Advanced Settings to configure the VSS settings for this backup. Since in this example we selected the volumes that contain the virtual machine data, the Hyper-V VSS writer will participate in the backup process. In the VSS Settings tab, select the VSS Copy Backup.

6. Next, select a local drive or a remote file server share as the backup destination and click the Backup button. The backup process will start and display its progress until it is complete. The status messages on the top of the Backup Progress page show the different steps that Windows Server Backup follows during the backup.

Now that the data on this Hyper-V server has been backed up, it can be copied to another server or to tape for long-term archival.

Real World Scenario

RESTORING A SINGLE FILE FROM A VIRTUAL MACHINE BACKUP

We had a pretty substantial virtual machine environment, with virtual machines running different Windows Server workloads. All our virtual machines were being backed up to a file server share at a scheduled interval. One day, a file was accidentally deleted from our web server, which was running inside a virtual machine. Because we had regular backups of our virtual machines, we had two options at that point:

◆ Do a full virtual machine restore using either Windows Server Backup or another backup technology.

◆ Use the built-in support for mounting VHDs that is available in Windows Server 2008 R2.

It was much easier and faster to just restore the file we needed without having to roll back the web server to the previous night's backup. We followed these steps to get the file from the VHD:

1. We went through the backups and identified the VHD that would contain the file we needed. If your backup software does not expose the VHDs directly in the file system, you can recover the VM to a specific alternate location and grab the VHD from there.

2. We opened the Computer Management administrative tool and selected Disk Management.

3. Without having anything selected in the results pane, we clicked the Actions menu and selected the Attach VHD option.

4. As shown in the following image, we then browsed to the VHD file identified in Step 1 and attached it as a read-only disk.

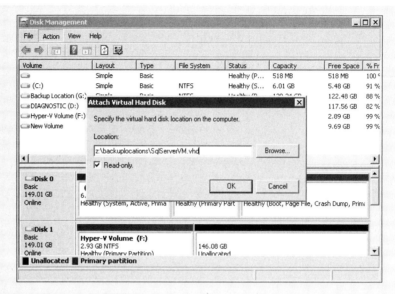

5. Once the VHD was mounted in the file system, it showed up in Disk Management with a drive letter for the volume contained inside the VHD. As seen here, the VHD was mounted and drive letter H:\ was exposed.

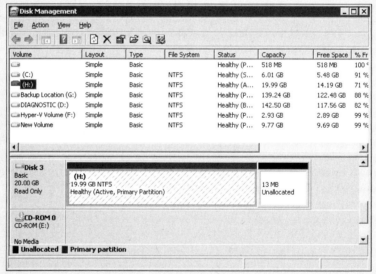

6. To recover the file that had been accidentally deleted inside the virtual machine, we opened the H:\ volume and navigated to the location of the file inside the backup. We copied the file and restored it inside the virtual machine. In a few easy steps, we were able to recover a file that had been deleted from a virtual machine backup.

7. Once the recovery operation was complete, we selected the disk that corresponded to the VHD in Disk Management and right-clicked to select the Detach VHD option.

Restoring Hyper-V Server Components

If an entire virtual machine needs to be recovered or the Hyper-V server needs to be rebuilt, you can use Windows Server Backup:

1. From the Windows Server Backup GUI, select the Recover action.

2. Select the option to find a backup stored on another location.

3. Select the location where the backup files reside and select the name of the server whose data you would like to recover.

4. If multiple backups are available, select the date and time of the backup you want to use for the virtual machine recovery.

5. Windows Server Backup provides you with a lot of options for recovery, from being able to recover the system state to being able to recover an individual file or a folder. Since Hyper-V has a VSS writer that is already registered with Windows Server Backup, it is considered an application. Select Applications to be able to recover only VSS components from Hyper-V. Selecting Application Restore will ensure that the VSS writer for Hyper-V will handle the restore operations.

6. Windows Server Backup will list all the applications that have registered their VSS writers and have available data in the backup set. Since Hyper-V has components that were in a volume that had been selected for backup, the Hyper-V VSS writer entry is included in the list of applications. Figure 10.15 shows the details of the Hyper-V VSS writer, indicating that multiple virtual machines are available for recovery. The GUIDs listed in the dialog are the unique identifiers of the virtual machines in Hyper-V. Even though the VSS infrastructure supports individual VSS components (i.e., virtual machines) to be restored, Windows Server Backup does not support that. If you choose to recover an application, all the virtual machines that were part of the volumes backed up will be recovered together.

FIGURE 10.15
Hyper-V VSS writer
components for recovery

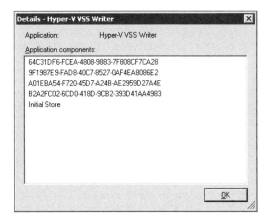

7. Select the Hyper-V VSS writer application and choose to recover it to its original location. This option will ensure that the Hyper-V VSS writer is involved in the recovery of the

virtual machines. Once the recovery is complete, Windows Server Backup will itemize the virtual machines and their recovery status, as shown in Figure 10.16.

FIGURE 10.16
Hyper-V virtual machine recovery status

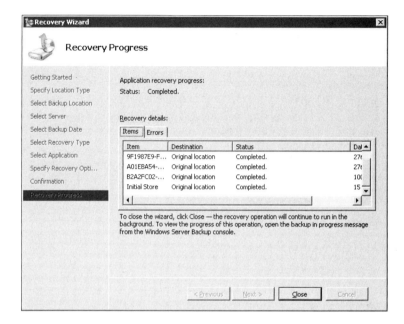

8. Open the Hyper-V Manager MMC GUI to inspect the restored virtual machines and their configuration.

WHAT HAPPENS DURING A RESTORE OPERATION?

During a restore operation, the Hyper-V VSS writer will perform the following operations:

◆ During the pre-restore operations, any virtual machine that is being restored will be turned off and deleted by Hyper-V.

◆ After data is copied by the backup application and the post-restore VSS sequence is called, Hyper-V will register the restored virtual machine.

Turning off the virtual machine as part of the restore process allows the Hyper-V writer to replace files for a running virtual machine.

Using System Center Data Protection Manager

DPM, with its DPM 2007 Service Pack 1 release (released as Update 959605), offers one of the most comprehensive and complete solutions for protecting Hyper-V virtualization hosts

(DPM can also protect Virtual Server 2005 R2 Sp1 hosts). In this section, we will go through the high-level protection features that DPM offers for Hyper-V.

With SP1, DPM now offers protection support for virtual machines residing on a Hyper-V host (the DPM agent is installed on the Hyper-V host) in addition to the existing support of protecting the individual guest operating systems (the DPM agent is installed inside the guest operating system, protecting it as it would a physical computer). Hyper-V hosts that are part of a failover cluster can also be protected by DPM. When a virtual machine fails over to another cluster node, DPM will continue protection. DPM supports the following host-based protection scenarios:

Live   Also known as online, this offers backup with no downtime to the virtual machine. This is the default protection mode for virtual machines.

Offline backup   Virtual machines that do not support live backup will be backed up using offline backup.

DPM will also not support the few configurations of virtual machines that are not supported for backup by the Hyper-V VSS writer. These configuration options were outlined earlier in this chapter.

The reader should be familiar with Data Protection Manager and its architecture. Follow these steps to protect and recover a Hyper-V virtual machine:

1. Create a new protection group for Microsoft Hyper-V and select all available subcomponents (Figure 10.17).

FIGURE 10.17
Creating a new protection group

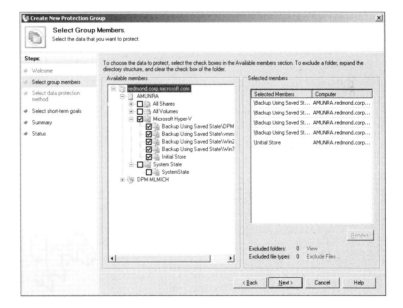

2. Select the short-term protection option using disk-to-disk backup (Figure 10.18).

FIGURE 10.18
Selecting the data
protection method

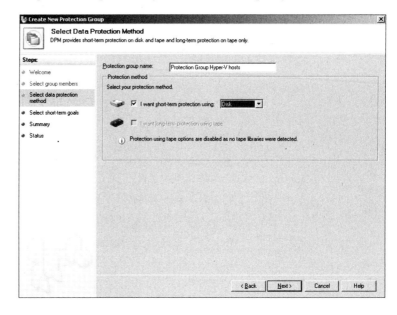

3. Select the retention range and recovery points (Figure 10.19).

FIGURE 10.19
Specifying the
short-term recovery
goals

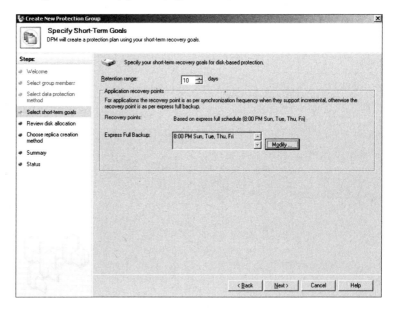

4. Select how DPM will create the initial replica of your VMs (Figure 10.20).

FIGURE 10.20
Choosing the replica
creation method

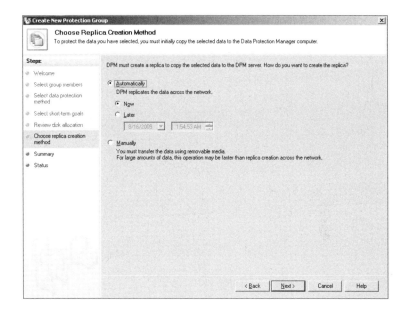

5. Ensure that the protection status of the Hyper-V server and its virtual machines is in a healthy state (Figure 10.21).

FIGURE 10.21
Hyper-V VM protected
by DPM

6. Initiate the recovery of a virtual machine (Figure 10.22).

7. View and confirm the recovery settings before recovery is initiated (Figure 10.23).

FIGURE 10.22
Recovering a virtual machine

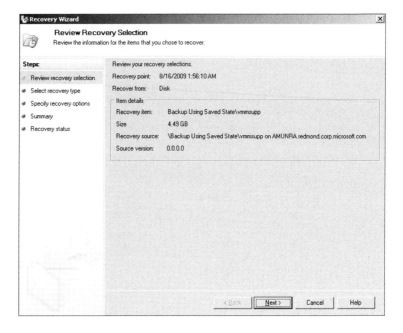

FIGURE 10.23
Confirming the virtual machine recovery settings

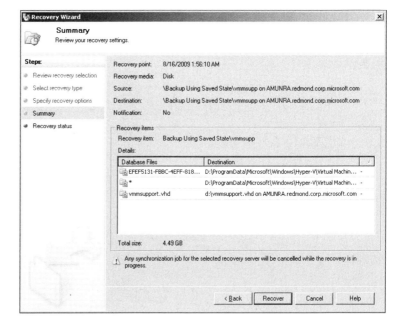

To read more about DPM 2007 SP1 and its support for Hyper-V, use the following links:

◆ System Center Data Protection Manager (DPM) 2007 Service Pack 1 website on Microsoft TechNet at `http://technet.microsoft.com/en-us/dpm/dd296757.aspx`

◆ What's New in Microsoft System Center Data Protection Manager 2007 Service Pack 1? on Microsoft TechNet at `http://technet.microsoft.com/en-us/library/dd347836.aspx`

◆ Protecting Hyper-V on System Center Data Protection Manager TechCenter on Microsoft TechNet at `http://technet.microsoft.com/en-us/library/dd347838.aspx`

Backing Up the Library Servers

VMM library servers are regular file servers that host file shares with the building blocks for creating virtual machines in VMM. Library server shares will include VHD, VMDK, ISO, PS1, INF, VFD, FLP, and XML files in addition to stored virtual machines. To back up and recovery a library server, use the same techniques your organization has adopted for backup and recovery of Windows file servers. In addition, regularly capture bare metal recovery backups (or full server backups) of the library servers that can be used in a disaster recovery situation. Figure 10.24 shows the creation of a new protection group in DPM for complete bare metal recovery protection of the library file server.

FIGURE 10.24
Creating a new protection group for complete protection of the library server

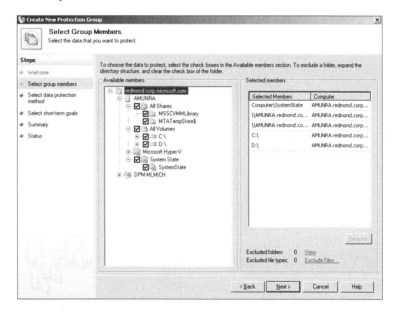

In the event of a recovery, adjust the Library Refresher interval to enable VMM to refresh the content of the file server share into VMM. To change the Library Refresher interval, do the following:

1. Choose the administration view in the Administrator Console.

2. Select the General view option.

3. Click the Library Settings option in the results pane. Change the library refresh interval as shown in Figure 10.25.

FIGURE 10.25
Setting the Library
Refresher interval

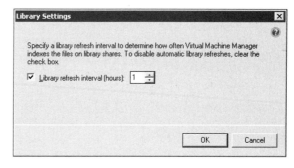

To manually trigger the Library Refresher, do the following:

1. Choose the library view in the Administrator Console.

2. Select the library server that you just recovered.

3. Right-click the server name and select the Refresh action. The library server selected will be refreshed. To track the progress of the jobs invoked, visit the jobs view of the Administrator Console.

The Bottom Line

Protect the VMM server, including the VMM database. The Virtual Machine Manager server is the centerpiece of VMM and controls the management of the virtualization environment. It is important to have a comprehensive plan in place on how to back up and recover the VMM server and the VMM database.

Master It How can you make the VMM server highly available?

Explain the importance of system state backup.

What is the best way to fully back up the VMM server?

Solution VMM server is not a certified cluster application, so the only way to make the VMM server highly available is to place the VMM server component inside a virtual machine. The virtual machine can then be promoted to a highly available virtual machine residing on a virtualization host that is part of a failover cluster. This configuration will ensure that the VMM server component is highly available and can fail over to other cluster hosts.

System state backup is very important to the recovery operations of a computer. Critical operating system components are included in system state backup, including the system SID that is used to authenticate the VMM server to virtualization hosts. If you are rebuilding the VMM server, it is important to restore the system state to ensure that the new system has the same system SID.

Windows Server Backup is currently among the best backup software for backing up and recovering the VMM server. It offers a comprehensive backup solution, including backing up for bare metal recovery. To back up the VMM server, use only software that is certified to work with VMM.

Back up Hyper-V hosts using the Hyper-V VSS writer.   Backup and recovery of Hyper-V hosts is one of the most important pieces of a protection strategy in a virtualization environment. Virtual machines can run a wide range of workloads, from easily replaceable web servers to highly sensitive and important database servers. These virtual machines are typically owned by end users, making it all the more important for administrators to have a plan in place to minimize downtime in case of a disaster recovery and to meet the SLAs.

Master It   What is the best way to fully back up a Hyper-V server?

Explain how to find the Hyper-V VSS writer.

What are the options to back up a virtual machine with pass-through disks?

Solution   Windows Server Backup and Data Protection Manager are currently some of the best backup software for backing up and recovering the VMM server. DPM offers the more comprehensive protection solution, including backing up for bare metal recovery. To back up the Hyper-V servers, use only software that is certified to work with the Hyper-V VSS writer.

The simplest way to find and identify the Hyper-V VSS writer is to invoke the `vssadmin.exe` command-line utility. The proper syntax to list all the VSS writers in the system and find the Hyper-V VSS Writer is `vssadmin.exe list writers`.

Virtual machines with storage that is not local to the Hyper-V host are not supported by the Hyper-V VSS writer. Even though pass-through disks are physical hard disks that are directly attached to the virtual machine, they are still not supported. Pass-through disks are presented as offline to the host's operating system, making it impossible to back them up. To back up a virtual machine with pass-through disks, use a backup agent inside the guest operating system of the virtual machine. This method will protect the virtual machine as if it was a physical computer.

Chapter 11

Troubleshooting

This book has walked you through each component of VMM, including architecture, installation, deployment, and management of a virtual environment. As you've seen, with full lifecycle management as the ultimate goal, there is plenty that VMM helps automate and simplify for administrators. Same goes for VMM's hypervisor abstraction layer, where you need to train with only one user interface and write one set of command-line scripts. VMM will automatically translate your scripts into the appropriate hypervisor-specific commands. And virtual machine resources like virtual disks and ISO files that would have been scattered across your environment now reside in a central location, the VMM library. With System Center Operations Manager and VMM PRO, you have deep visibility into the health of your environment and access to rich automation to remediate the issues you encounter.

With so many components in VMM focused on making your day-to-day routine more efficient and making you more productive, it is critical to understand how to troubleshoot this environment and minimize any downtime incurred. We will therefore cover what you need to understand about troubleshooting, common tools used for troubleshooting VMM, and issues you may encounter in your VMM environment. It is important to know how to distinguish between issues that are related to product or hypervisor limitations and informational warnings and errors that VMM surfaces to you in job logs. Having this knowledge will help you maintain VMM with a high level of availability.

In this chapter, you will learn to:

- ◆ Understand VMM from a troubleshooting perspective
- ◆ Use common troubleshooting tools
- ◆ Understand issues with VMM components

Understanding VMM from a Troubleshooting Perspective

With any management products, there are many interdependencies that need to function properly. In most cases, VMM can handle the irregularities and failures encountered in the infrastructure, allowing you to continue making forward progress in your activities. However, there are issues that are beyond VMM's control. In those cases, you might experience some instability in the product. For this reason, this chapter also addresses how to capture product traces to help the product support team troubleshoot the issue and come up with a solution. The ability to tolerate issues within VMM's control must remain balanced with the use of the rich error information VMM provides when necessary to avoid masking potentially severe issues. The information VMM provides through errors and warnings fall into three categories:

Support boundaries   Some errors and warnings are meant to inform you of a particular configuration that is not supported by VMM. For example, if a virtual machine exists on a Microsoft failover cluster that does not reside on shared storage (a local disk that is not shared with all the nodes in the cluster), the virtual machine is marked as "Unsupported Cluster Configuration." Once the virtual machine is in this state, you cannot take any actions on it. You must reconfigure the virtual machine using the Microsoft Failover Cluster Manager. Another example involves the VMM library and what file types it supports. The library supports only files with a specific filename extension. Some filename extensions indicate to the library that the contents of the file need to be parsed to create an object in the VMM database. A VMC file (that is, a file with the .vmc filename extension) represents a VMware virtual machine. The library will parse the VMC file and create a virtual machine object that you can use to deploy to a virtual machine host. The library ignores unsupported files. If the contents of a supported file cannot be parsed, the library will report an error.

Informational   Some errors and warnings are specifically meant to inform the user about a condition that occurred. Some require no user action, while others require a simple retry of the operation. Intelligent Placement will inform the user of changes in configuration that VMM will take automatically. You will encounter jobs in VMM that fail to initiate or complete due to a time-out. You can simply retry the operation at this point. Note that if a retry does not work, a more thorough investigation might be required.

Critical   Certain circumstances are outside the control of VMM and so the product needs to gracefully deal with these situations to ensure minimal impact to your productivity. If the VMM Administrator Console disconnects from the VMM server, it will report error 1612 to you. In this case, either the VMM server service restarted or the console itself dropped the connection to the server. If the VMM server service did in fact restart, then all in-progress jobs will be marked as "Failed" and need to be restarted by you. The VMM Administrator Console may itself crash, requiring a restart of the interface with no impact to the VMM server service.

The critical category is one that typically requires some investigation to identify a root cause. With that information, you take the necessary steps to remediate the issue and minimize interruption of service. As with any issue that does not have a clear reason at the beginning, the investigation process is critical to learning about how a product works, training your staff, and incorporating recovery plans into your operations manuals. As your environment grows in size and complexity, it is important to keep an ongoing record of its configuration and issues encountered along the way. This way, deep product knowledge is spread among multiple administrators, allowing your IT department to respond faster to service interruptions.

The underlying infrastructure in a VMM environment can span multiple computers, multiple communication types, multiple protocols, and multiple user personas. Table 11.1 sums up the number of computers required in a sample production virtualized environment managed by VMM.

TABLE 11.1:   Number of computers in a sample production deployment

COMPONENT	QUANTITY
Hyper-V (two-node cluster)	2
ESX (two-node cluster)	2
Stand-alone Virtual Server 2005	1
VMM database (two-node cluster)	2
VMM server (with cold standby)	2
VMM Self-Service Portal	1
VMM library (two-node cluster)	2
Total	12

VMM reports status information and job information for all of the components involved in common day-to-day tasks. Depending on the size of your environment and the complexity of your VMM deployment, it is necessary to have a clear understanding of the following:

♦ How the environment is configured

♦ The communication requirements between components that may be specific to your environment

♦ The engineering and operations groups that need to be involved when troubleshooting an issue

♦ Any service-level agreements that might be impacted by an issue with your virtualization environment

For example, end users might call the server operations team complaining of random performance issues with their virtual machines. If the virtual machines are deployed in a datacenter in a production environment on SAN storage, then you know immediately that you need to look for abnormalities with the virtual machine host, the network, or the storage. The worst case may involve all three or a combination of two. If your deployment team is having issues creating multiple virtual machines concurrently, you need to look at the network, the library server and its backend storage, or the virtual machine host and its storage. Which VMM components you need to troubleshoot and which groups you may need to involve really depends on your environment.

Make sure to always have an up-to-date diagram of the deployment and contact names in your VMM deployment plan. At this point, before going into the specific troubleshooting tools and techniques, it's probably a good idea to review the previous chapters in the context of how the various components interact with each other and what you may need to troubleshoot. Depending on the issue, it is difficult to anticipate the amount of time required to troubleshoot. The information in these chapters will provide the guidance and understanding for deploying, managing, and troubleshooting your VMM environment.

Use Common Troubleshooting Tools

All administrators have a set of tools and scripts in their toolbox that are useful for troubleshooting. Although troubleshooting is not a typical day-to-day task, it does require developing a set of critical skills (and some specialized skills, depending on the product supported). The skills you develop and the tools you use to troubleshoot complement each other very well and improve your productivity. The following sections detail the tools you will find useful when troubleshooting VMM issues.

Troubleshooting VMM Installation Issues

When troubleshooting, ruling out the obvious only gets easier with experience. To help identify common issues with VMM, you can use the Virtual Machine Manager Configuration Analyzer (VMMCA). This tool will identify an issue with your environment and save you the trouble of formally troubleshooting the issue or calling Microsoft support. The VMMCA tool will analyze the VMM server, Windows-based hypervisor host, VMware vCenter Server, VMM Operations Manager server, and Windows-based source computers used as part of Physical to Virtual (P2V) migration.

DOWNLOADING VMMCA

A prerequisite for using VMMCA is to install Microsoft Baseline Configuration Analyzer (MBCA). Since VMM only installs on 64-bit editions of Windows Server 2008, make sure to download the 64-bit version of the MBCA.

Download the MBCA from `http://go.microsoft.com/fwlink/?LinkID=97952`.

If you deployed R2 of VMM 2008, download the associated R2 version of the VMMCA from `http://www.microsoft.com/downloads/details.aspx?FamilyID=02d83950-c03d-454e-803b-96d1c1d5be24&displaylang=en`.

If you are still using VMM 2008 RTM, you can download the VMMCA tool from `http://www.microsoft.com/downloads/details.aspx?FamilyID=02d83950-c03d-454e-803b-96d1c1d5be24&displaylang=en`.

Troubleshooting VM Deployment Issues

To troubleshoot a virtual machine deployment, there are two potential culprits that you should investigate. Depending on the quality of the network connection between the library and the virtual machine host, you may experience deployments that take a long time because of insufficient bandwidth on the network. If the connection is not reliable due to physical port issues or the network operation is set to half-duplex when it should be full, deployments may fail randomly. To isolate potential network issues, Network Monitor is a good tool to use on the source and destination computers.

The second culprit is with the customization phase of the guest operating system. During customization, Windows Mini-Setup goes through the process of setting up the identity of the guest operating system, setting the product key, and joining the machine to an Active Directory domain. If you decide to include a custom sysprep answer file, then you need to make sure that it is valid to avoid errors during customization.

NETWORK MONITOR

If you suspect that an issue could be network related, Network Monitor is an important tool that helps you analyze network traffic between a source and destination resource on an IP network. This could involve agent-based traffic from hypervisor hosts, control traffic from VMM and/or vCenter servers, or storage traffic from an iSCSI-based SAN or a network file server serving as the VMM library server.

When using traffic analysis tools like Network Monitor, capturing traffic from either source or destination is not enough to provide a complete picture of a potential issue. You might get lucky and identify an issue by analyzing network traffic from only one computer. However, for most operations in VMM, there is a source computer and a target computer, and analyzing network traffic from both helps provide the necessary context to better understand the issue.

Analyzing source and target traffic is especially important when dealing with hardware-based firewalls that may sit in the path between the source and target computer. In a simple case, VMM may fail to connect to a Windows-based computer as part of P2V. Even if all necessary firewall exceptions are granted on each computer (software firewall), it is not until the traffic is analyzed that you realize that information is getting sent out by a source computer but never received by the destination computer.

WINDOWS AUTOMATED INSTALLATION KIT IMAGE MANAGER

If you plan to create your own answer files for unattended customization of Windows Vista and above, it is always important to validate the syntax of the file before using it with VMM. As part of the base installation of the VMM server, the Windows Automated Installation Kit (WAIK) Image Manager tool is installed. This tool can validate an answer file. You can also choose to use the Image Manager application to generate the answer file. If you need to automate the production of configuration files, look into the Component Platform Interface (CPI API) provided as part of WAIK.

To validate an answer file using the Image Manager, follow these steps:

1. On the VMM server, click the Start button and find Microsoft Windows AIK under All Programs.

2. In the Microsoft Windows AIK program folder, choose Windows System Image Manager. Figure 11.1 shows the Image Manager interface.

3. In the middle pane, right-click Create Or Open An Answer File and select Open Answer File, as shown in Figure 11.2.

4. Navigate to the folder location with the unattend.xml file (Figure 11.3).

5. Double-click on the unattend.xml file to load it into Image Manager.

FIGURE 11.1
Image Manager user
interface

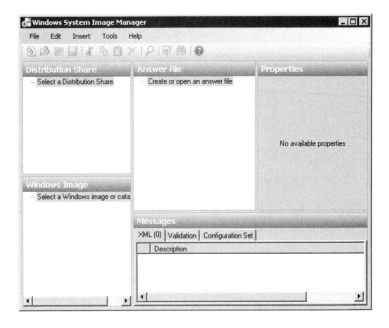

FIGURE 11.2
Opening an existing
answer file

6. Image Manager will parse the file and present any errors to the user. As shown in Figure 11.4, in this case, the file is missing the `<settings>` element.

7. Once you correct the issue, reattempt the import. If the import is successful, Image Manager will populate the various stages in the `unattend.xml` file in the middle pane (Figure 11.5).

FIGURE 11.3
Selecting an answer file

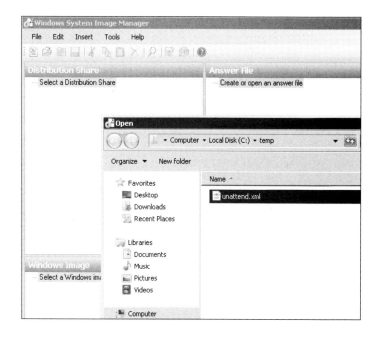

FIGURE 11.4
Validation error

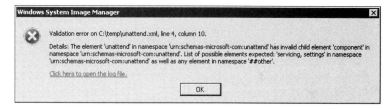

FIGURE 11.5
Successfully loaded
answer file

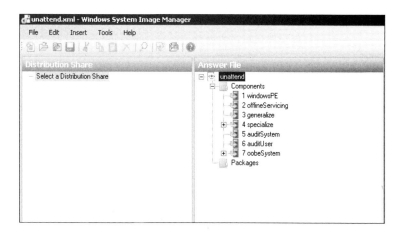

Troubleshooting Virtual Hard Disk Problems

Windows Server 2008 R2 offers native virtual hard disk (VHD) support. With this feature, you can natively mount VHD files using Disk Management without requiring Hyper-V. This capability is important if you need to mount a VHD on a library server for troubleshooting purposes or to retrieve files.

To mount a VHD, follow these steps:

1. Open the Computer Management MMC.

2. Right-click the Disk Management node and select Attach VHD, as shown in Figure 11.6.

FIGURE 11.6
Disk Management user interface

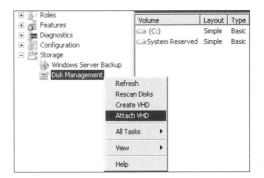

3. Specify the path to the VHD you want to mount (Figure 11.7).

FIGURE 11.7
Browsing for the VHD file

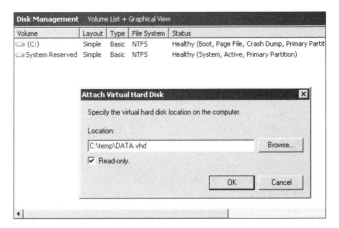

4. Make sure you select Read-Only unless you plan to modify the contents of the file.

5. Click OK and Disk Management will add the VHD to the list of logical disks.

6. If the VHD does not contain a file system, then the disk will be presented as uninitialized and offline (Figure 11.8). If you need to, initialize the disk and format the volume. This will assign a drive letter to it. At this point, you can manipulate the contents of the virtual disk.

7. If the VHD already contains a file system, all you have to do after attaching it is assign a drive letter.

FIGURE 11.8
Uninitialized disk

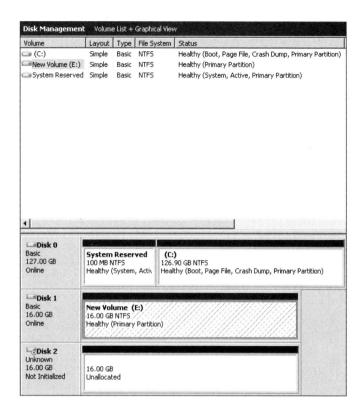

Troubleshooting Database Issues

As part of troubleshooting VMM issues, it may be necessary to attach to the VMM database using SQL Management Studio. In a production environment, it is not always the case that you can even attach to the live database, but if you can, make sure to do so with great caution. See the article "Troubleshooting Performance Problems in SQL 2005" (http://technet.microsoft.com/en-us/library/cc966540.aspx) for tips on how to identify potential bottlenecks in CPU, memory, and I/O. In addition to SQL Management Studio, you can use SQL Server Profiler to view all events generated by the database server. This information is useful to help identify performance issues due to poorly executing queries and stored procedures. If you attempt to connect to a SQL Express instance hosting the VMM database, you will get an error dialog like the one in Figure 11.9. To manage a SQL Express database instance remotely, you have to allow remote connections.

To enable remote SQL Express access, follow these steps:

1. Open the SQL Server Surface Area Configuration by choosing Start ➤ All Programs ➤ Microsoft SQL Server 2005 ➤ Configuration Tools ➤ SQL Server Surface Area Configuration.

2. Open the MICROSOFTVMM instance and select Database Engine and then Service.

FIGURE 11.9
Remote access to SQL
Express error

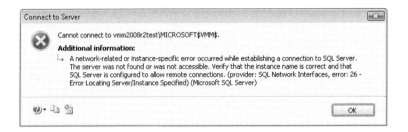

3. Stop the SQL service by clicking the Stop button (Figure 11.10).

FIGURE 11.10
Stopping the SQL service

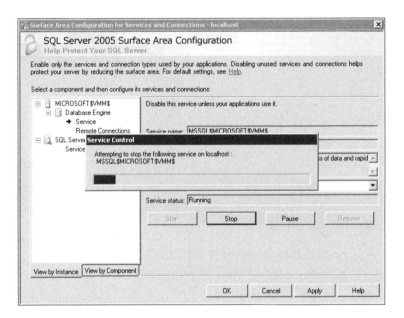

4. Click Remote Connections and select the Local and Remote Connections and then the Using TCP/IP Only option (Figure 11.11). Click OK to commit the changes. Before the Surface Area Configuration for Services and Connection window closes, an information dialog will appear informing you that the changes will not take effect until the next time the Database Engine service is restarted. Click OK to close the informational dialog.

5. Click on the Service node under Database Engine, and the Start button to start the to SQL service (Figure 11.12).

6. Open the SQL Service Browser and choose Service. Click the Start button to start the service.

7. You can optionally change the startup type to Automatic.

FIGURE 11.11
Using TCP/IP only
setting

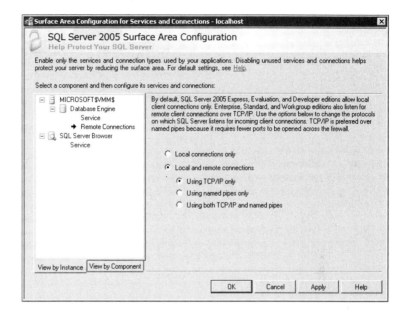

FIGURE 11.12
Starting the SQL service

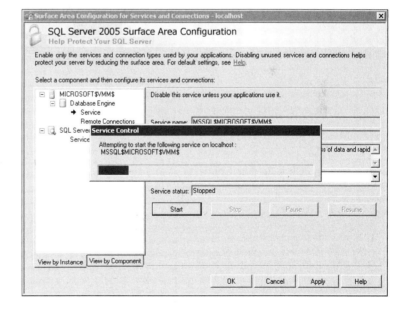

STARTING THE VMM SERVICE

After restarting the SQL service, make sure to restart the VMM service. From an elevated command prompt window, execute the following command:

```
C:\Windows\system32>net start vmmservice
The Virtual Machine Manager service is starting.
The Virtual Machine Manager service was started successfully.
C:\Windows\system32>
```

Troubleshooting Performance Issues

Performance Monitor is also known as Perfmon. This tool ships with Windows and is very effective at helping gather important system counters. You can capture live data by opening Performance Monitor and adding the desired counters for the local computer or a remote computer. Capturing performance information live is great if you need a small sample of data with a few counters. If you need to capture performance information over an extended period of time and/or with many counters, Performance Monitor can run in the background and automatically save data into a file using a data collector set. With a data collector set, you can set up when to start and stop gathering data, and it does not require you to be interactively logged into the machine.

To capture performance counter information live, follow these steps:

1. Open the Performance Monitor MMC by choosing Start ➤ Administrative Tools ➤ Performance Monitor.

2. Click Performance Monitor under Monitoring Tools to view the live capture view

3. Click the green + icon to add counters to the view.

4. Make sure <Local computer> is selected.

5. Find the Physical Disk object.

6. Select the instance of the object (in this case, select the instance with the system partition - C:) (Figure 11.13).

7. Expand the object to see all the associated counters.

8. Select Avg. Disk Queue Length and click Add (Figure 11.14).

9. Click OK to return to the live capture window (Figure 11.15).

To create a data collector set, follow these steps:

1. In Performance Monitor, select Data Collector Sets and then User Defined.

2. Right-click User Defined and select New and then Data Collector Set.

3. Name the data collector set and select Create From a Template (Figure 11.16). Click Next to proceed.

4. Select System Diagnostics. Click Finish to accept the remaining default values.

FIGURE 11.13
Selecting instances

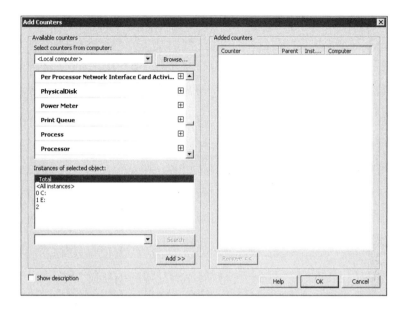

FIGURE 11.14
Adding counters

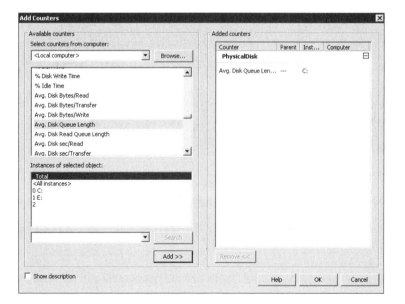

FIGURE 11.15
Live capture view
with counter

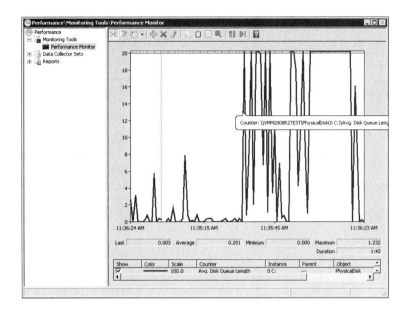

FIGURE 11.16
The Create New Data
Collector Set Wizard

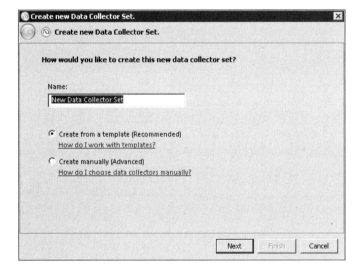

5. Right-click on the New Data Collector Set and select Start.

6. Let the collector run for some time.

7. Select the Data Collector Set and select Stop.

8. Choose Reports ➢ User Defined ➢ New Data Collector Set and select the report generated by the collector set.

9. Refer to Figure 11.17 and review the information in each category. In the example below, the system is low on memory and is paging heavily.

FIGURE 11.17
Data collector set report

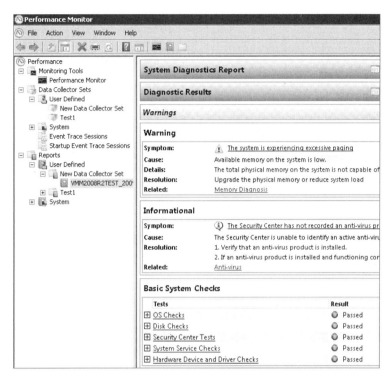

Troubleshooting Issues Using Debug Output and Tracing

If all other troubleshooting efforts fail to identify a root cause, you may need to capture debug output and traces for deeper analysis. This information comes from messages generated by the product that monitors its execution. Trace logs are not available out of the box. Instead, a user needs to enable tracing on the computers where trace information is required. As with Network Monitor, you should capture trace information on the source and target computers to help complete the picture when analyzing an issue. Table 11.2 details the three sources of trace information and where to collect them. The table also includes SQL tracing for completeness.

TABLE 11.2: Trace sources

TRACE INFORMATION SOURCE	SOURCE SYSTEMS	NECESSARY TOOLS
WinRM/WMI	Hyper-V virtual machine host agent Virtual Server virtual machine host agent	Windows SDK toolkit (tracelog)
VMM Debug Output	VMM server VMM library VMM Self-Service Portal Hyper-V virtual machine host agent Virtual Server virtual machine host agent	DebugView
SQL	VMM Database server	SQL Server Profiler

VMM DEBUG OUTPUT

Before capturing VMM debug output, you need to gather all the necessary files and tools and then populate your virtual machine hosts with the necessary files. With these steps complete, you can start capturing traces before reproducing a problem. Once the problem has been reproduced, you have sufficient information captured, so you can turn off tracing.

To prepare files, follow these steps:

1. Create a folder on the local file system of the VMM server (for example, C:\VMM_debug_trace).

2. Download DebugView for Windows. The latest version is located at http://technet. microsoft.com/en-us/sysinternals/bb896647.aspx. Save the EXE file to C:\VMM_debug_trace.

3. Copy and paste the following script into a new file named ODSFLAGS.CMD. Save file to C:\VMM_debug_trace.

```
@echo off
echo ODS control flags - only trace with set flags will go to ODS

if (%1)==() goto :HELP
if (%1)==(-?) goto :HELP
if (%1)==(/?) goto :HELP

echo Setting flag to %1...
reg ADD "HKLM\SOFTWARE\Microsoft\Windows
NT\CurrentVersion\Tracing\Microsoft\Carmine" /v ODSFLAGS /t REG_DWORD /d %1 /f
echo Done.
goto :EXIT

:HELP
echo Usage: odsflags [flag], where flag is
echo TRACE_ERROR = 0x2,
echo TRACE_DBG_NORMAL = 0x4,
echo TRACE_DBG_VERBOSE = 0x8,
echo TRACE_PERF = 0x10,
echo TRACE_TEST_INFO = 0x20,
echo TRACE_TEST_WARNING = 0x40,
echo TRACE_TEST_ERROR = 0x80,

:EXIT
```

4. Copy and paste the following script into a new file named ODSON.REG. Save file to C:\VMM_debug_trace.

```
Windows Registry Editor Version 5.00
 [HKEY_LOCAL_MACHINE\SOFTWARE\Microsoft\
Windows NT\CurrentVersion\Tracing\Microsoft\Carmine]
"ODS"=dword:00000001
```

5. Copy and paste the following script into a new file named ODSOFF.REG. Save file to
    C:\VMM_debug_trace.

    ```
    Windows Registry Editor Version 5.00


    [HKEY_LOCAL_MACHINE\SOFTWARE\Microsoft\
    Windows NT\CurrentVersion\Tracing\Microsoft\Carmine]
    "ODS"=dword:00000000
    ```

6. Copy the C:\VMM_debug_trace folder (including contents) to all the virtual machine hosts,
    library servers, and Self-Service Portal servers.

7. An optional step is to include this folder in your standard build for virtual machine hosts
    so all new deployments have these files.

To capture debug output, follow these steps:

1. In a command window on the machine where you plan to collect VMM debug output, run
    ODSON.REG and ODSFLAGS.CMD 255.

2. Before attempting to reproduce an issue, enable tracing by running ODSON.REG and
    ODSFLAGS.CMD 255 on the systems from which you need debug information.

3. Open DebugView with elevated privileges.

4. Make sure you select both Capture Win32 and Capture Global Win32 options in the
    Capture menu.

5. Open DebugView on all the systems where you need to capture trace information.

6. Restart the VMM service and agent on the VMM server. On all other systems, restart the
    VMM agent. On the Self-Service Portal server, reset IIS.

7. Attempt to reproduce the issue.

8. Once the issue has been successfully reproduced, turn off tracing by running the following
    command ODSOFF.REG.

9. Save the contents of DebugView for further analysis on a separate machine.

WINRM/WMI TRACING

Similar to capturing VMM debug output, there are specific files and tools you need before
capturing WinRM/WMI traces.

ANALYZING WINRM/WMI TRACE LOGS

The information contained in the trace log file is not readable by humans. This file needs to be
sent to Microsoft support for further analysis.

To prepare files, follow these steps:

1. Create a folder on the local file system of the VMM server (for example, `C:\VMM_WINRM_WMI_TRACES`).

2. Download the Windows SDK toolkit:

   Download W2K8 from `http://www.microsoft.com/downloads/details.aspx?FamilyId=E6E1C3DF-A74F-4207-8586-711EBE331CDC&displaylang=en`.

   Download W2K3, XP/Vista from `http://go.microsoft.com/fwlink?LinkID=55774`.

3. Install the Windows SDK toolkit on each system where you need to collect traces.

4. After installing the toolkit, locate `Tracelog.exe`.

5. Copy and paste the following script into a new file named `.STARTTRACING.CMD`. Save file to a folder that contains `Tracelog.exe`.

```
@echo off
@echo on

REM Usage:
REM     this.cmd  - turns all tracing on
REM     this.cmd 0xHHHH - turns tracing w/ for specific bits
REM         see bits in WPP_DEFINE_CONTROL_GUID for more details
REM         bits a counted from first entry (0th bit) to last entry (Nth bit)
REM
REM     E.g.: this.cmd 0x1C00 will turn on tracing for automation component
REM

@echo off
set FLAGS=0x1
if NOT {%1}=={} (
    set FLAGS=%1
)
@echo FLAGS=%FLAGS%
@echo ----------------------------------------------------------------
@echo attempting to stop and re-start Wmxlog logger for logging
@echo ----------------------------------------------------------------
tracelog.exe -stop Wmxlog
tracelog.exe -start Wmxlog -f wmxlog.etl -guid tctl.txt -ft 1 -flag %FLAGS%
@echo ----------------------------------------------------------------
@echo run your application now and then use displaytrace.cmd to
see the traces logged
@echo ----------------------------------------------------------------
goto End

:CtlNotExist
@echo tctl.txt is missing
```

```
goto End

:NtTreeNotDefined
@echo variable _NTTREE is not defined
goto End

:TraceFormatDirNotExist
@echo directory %_NTTREE%\Symbols.pri\TraceFormat (_NTTREE\Symbols.pri\
TraceFormat) does not exist
goto End

:End
```

6. Copy and paste the following script into a new file named STOPTRACING.CMD. Save file to a folder that contains `Tracelog.exe`.

```
@echo off
@echo -----------------------------------------------------------------
@echo stop Wmxlog logger
@echo -----------------------------------------------------------------
tracelog.exe -stop Wmxlog
```

7. Copy and paste the following text into a new file named TCTL.txt. Save file to a folder that contains `Tracelog.exe`.

```
04c6e16d-b99f-4a3a-9b3e-b8325bbc781e  WinRM
0a36be8-a515-4cfa-b2b6-2676366efff7   WinrsMgr
f1cab2c0-8beb-4fa2-90e1-8f17e0acdd5d  WinrsExe
03992646-3dfe-4477-80e3-85936ace7abb  WinrsCmd
```

To capture WinRM/WMI traces, follow these steps:

1. Before attempting to reproduce an issue, enable tracing by running the STARTTRACING.CMD on the systems from which you need debug information.

2. Attempt to reproduce the issue.

3. Once the issue has been successfully reproduced, turn off tracing by running the following comment STOPTRACING.CMD.

4. Locate the Event Trace Log file (ETL) with the trace data and send that to VMM product support for analysis.

Operating System Troubleshooting

Windows Sysinternals offers an excellent collection of tools that are useful for troubleshooting and diagnosing Windows-based systems and applications. We recommend that you download the suite of tools and make sure they are readily available over the network or locally on a computer. You can download the Windows Sysinternals Suite from `http://technet.microsoft.com/en-us/sysinternals/bb842062.aspx`.

Understanding Issues with VMM Components

With the thorough understanding of the VMM components covered in previous chapters coupled with the troubleshooting tools covered in the previous sections, you have what is necessary to tackle any problem you run into with a virtualized environment managed by VMM. Troubleshooting is ideally not a day-to-day task for any given product, but having the necessary troubleshooting information and tools will make you effective when the time comes. As you scale up the number of virtual machines per host and the number of virtual machine hosts in your environment, troubleshooting is a critical skill that will help you minimize downtime and keep your end users satisfied. The remainder of this chapter addresses some known issues with individual VMM components and offers information on causes and potential fixes.

Required Updates

With all installations of VMM and its components, make sure you always check online for the latest patches to ensure that your system is up-to-date from the beginning. Keep in mind, however, that the VMM installer accounts for only VMM-related patches; other fixes might be required for Microsoft failover clustering, Hyper-V, and so on. Table 11.3 contains a list of patches necessary in a VMM environment as this book was being written.

TABLE 11.3:   Relevant patches for a VMM environment

PATCH	ARTICLE TITLE	APPLICABLE COMPONENT
956589	Description of the Hyper-V update for issues that may occur when you manage the Hyper-V role on the 64-bit editions of Windows Server 2008 by using VMM (http://support.microsoft.com/kb/956589/).	Hyper-V server
956774	A Background Intelligent Transfer Service (BITS) client cannot handle files that have paths that contain the volume GUID in Windows Server 2008 or in Windows Vista (http://support.microsoft.com/kb/956774/).	Hyper-V server
950050	Description of the update for the release version of the Hyper-V technology for Windows Server 2008 (http://support.microsoft.com/default.aspx?scid=kb;EN-US;950050/).	Hyper-V server
958124	A wmiprvse.exe process may leak memory when a WMI notification query is used heavily on a Windows Server 2008–based or Windows Vista–based computer (http://support.microsoft.com/kb/958124/).	VMM server
954563	Memory corruption may occur with the Windows Management Instrumentation (WMI) service on a computer that is running Windows Server 2008 or Windows Vista Service Pack 1 (http://support.microsoft.com/kb/954563/).	VMM server

TABLE 11.3:   Relevant patches for a VMM environment (*CONTINUED*)

PATCH	ARTICLE TITLE	APPLICABLE COMPONENT
955805	Certain applications become very slow on a Windows Server 2008–based or Windows Vista S955805–based computer when a certificate with SIA extension is installed (http://support.microsoft.com/kb/955805/).	VMM Server
961983	Description of the hotfix rollup package for System Center Virtual Machine Manager 2008: April 14th, 2009 (http://support.microsoft.com/kb/961983/).	VMM server
957967	Stop error message on a Windows Server 2008–based computer that has the Hyper-V role installed: STOP 0x0000001A (http://support.microsoft.com/kb/957967/).	Hyper-V server
958124	A wmiprvse.exe process may leak memory when a WMI notification query is used heavily on a Windows Server 2008–based or Windows Vista–based computer (http://support.microsoft.com/kb/958124/).	Hyper-V server
954563	Memory corruption may occur with the Windows Management Instrumentation (WMI) service on a computer that is running Windows Server 2008 or Windows Vista Service Pack 1 (http://support.microsoft.com/kb/954563/).	Hyper-V server
955805	Certain applications become very slow on a Windows Server 2008–based or Windows Vista S955805–based computer when a certificate with SIA extension is installed (http://support.microsoft.com/kb/955805/).	Hyper-V server
957311	Recommended hotfixes for Windows Server 2008–based server clusters (http://support.microsoft.com/kb/957311/).	Hyper-V failover cluster

Troubleshooting VMM Installation

After receiving the VMM media, if you do not already have VMM in your environment, then you will most probably install the VMM server on a test or lab machine. In the simplest case, you allow the installer to set up SQL Express on the same computer and specify a local user account with administrative privileges as the VMM service account. In a production deployment, however, you will likely choose an existing SQL installation hosted on a different computer or cluster for the VMM database. You have the option of also specifying an Active Directory domain user account for the service. At this point, the most important external dependency is Active Directory. Same would go for the library server and Self-Service Portal.

For performance reasons, you may choose to use SAN storage for the database and library files and resources.

With a VMM deployment spanning multiple computers, you should work closely with your network and storage administrators to identify potential bottlenecks in the environment. Storage contention is typically a cause of reduced transaction throughput of the VMM database and slower file transfers to/from the VMM library. Ideally, VMM should have dedicated storage with multiple disks for the database and library files. If a dedicated location is not possible, at a minimum make sure the storage location has multiple disks to ensure a higher rate of operations supported. With shared storage, you should know what other applications are using the storage. Knowing the usage patterns of an application comes in handy when troubleshooting performance issues. Even if the storage location is dedicated, there is a good chance that the storage enclosure/array is shared with other computers and applications. Considering the expense of SAN, sharing is unavoidable. For these reasons, make sure to have the proper monitoring tools in place to raise alerts when specific performance conditions are not being satisfied.

Similar to storage, the network is always a shared resource across the datacenter. For networking, focus on the connections (uplinks) each VMM computer is given. Connections are always shared with multiple applications and services executing on the computer. However, segregating network traffic is highly recommended. Traffic generated by a backup agent should be on its own connection. If VMM uses iSCSI SAN storage, separate connections should be used for that traffic. For all other traffic, make sure the connections used by VMM have sufficient throughout to meet the needs of your environment. Make sure you have the proper monitoring tools in place to raise alerts when specific performance conditions are not being satisfied. Remember, your transfer of files either between hosts or between a host and the library will only be as fast and reliable as the network link between those endpoints (for LAN transfers) or as fast and reliable as the storage fabric connecting those endpoints (for SAN transfers).

Table 11.4 lists installation issues.

TABLE 11.4:   Installation issues

ISSUE	CAUSE	FIX
VMM experiences failures creating databases on remote MS SQL servers.	The database account does not have sufficient privileges.	At a minimum, the SQL account needs to have the following roles: dbcreator, securityadmin, and processadmin.
The VMM server installation fails if the computer has a name with more than 15 characters.	VMM fails to resolve the computer name.	The Computer must have a name with no more than 15 characters.
Installing a VMM server on a remote clustered MS SQL instance fails.	MS SQL is running under a local system account and/or the necessary SPNs are not created in Active Directory.	Refer to the following article to configure a remote instance of SQL: Configuring a Remote Instance of SQL Server http://technet.microsoft.com/en-us/library/bb740749.aspx

TABLE 11.4:   Installation issues (*CONTINUED*)

ISSUE	CAUSE	FIX
VMM Operations Manager Configuration fails to retrieve service account.	After the VMM Server is installed, specific information is added to Active Directory. This information might take some time to replicate.	Wait a few minutes before trying to run Configure Operations Manager using VMM.
VMM Configure Operations Manager fails if installed on a non-root management server	The computer that you are executing the VMM installer on is not an RMS server.	Run installer on the RMS server.

Troubleshooting Host Management

From a VMM perspective, management of Hyper-V or Virtual Server involves basic network connectivity, access to Active Directory, properly working protocols like WS-MAN and BITS, working services like VDS, and functional hypervisor services. Sharing of network and storage resources is also typical with managed hypervisors. With multiple virtual machine instances for every physical computer, resources are limited and so an underperforming infrastructure impacts multiple applications. From a VMM perspective, a computer with limited resources will experience time-out issues with various operations since resources are contending with each other. Time-outs that result in failed jobs due to resource constraints are usually indistinguishable from jobs that time out due to other other issues (e.g. network issues). For this reason, you need to make sure proper monitoring is in place by using a tool such as System Center Operations Manager, for example, for the Hyper-V or Virtual Server computer, so applications in virtual machines execute without interruption and the physical computer has sufficient resources to service requests from management applications like VMM.

VMM manages ESX differently than it manages Hyper-V and Virtual Server. The biggest difference is the lack of an agent. Instead of deploying an agent to each ESX host, VMM communicates indirectly with the ESX hosts with vCenter Server using VMware's Web Services API. VMM maintains this connection for the life of the VMM service and does not require a local agent on the vCenter computer. To enable file transfers between the VMM library and an ESX host, VMM uses SFTP or HTTPS. In addition to understanding the errors with communication and connectivity between a VMM server and vCenter, you will need to distinguish between errors returned by VMM and those returned by vCenter (which are displayed in VMM's job log). When troubleshooting, the distinction here is that a VMM-only error means that the issue may not reproduce in vCenter. On the other hand, an error returned by vCenter means that the issue will reproduce in both VMM and vCenter.

Table 11.5 lists host management issues.

Troubleshooting Libraries

Troubleshooting library issues is typically done in the context of a failed virtual machine creation or an issue with a file that the Library Refresher indexes to keep track of in the VMM database. The library server requires basic network connectivity, access to Active Directory, and properly working protocols like BITS. Since the VMM library is basically a file server, typical bottlenecks involve disk contention when deploying multiple virtual machines from the library.

TABLE 11.5: Host management issues

ISSUE	CAUSE	FIX
Adding a Hyper-V host to VMM fails at 75%.	If the Hyper-V role was not enabled before adding the host to VMM, then the Hyper-V role gets enabled and rebooted automatically as part of adding it to VMM. That process may fail due to an unknown state on the host after rebooting.	Attempt to add the Hyper-V host again using the Add Host Wizard. Enable the Hyper-V role manually before adding it to VMM.
Removing multiple Hyper-V hosts concurrently can cause the process to fail.	Removing multiple hosts concurrently may result in some internal locking of objects that VMM puts in place to properly process job.	Retry the virtual machine host removal.
Adding virtual machine hosts to VMM that are under load may take more than 5 minutes.	Some operations may time out on the host if it is under load.	Reduce the current load on the virtual machine host.
Certain operations fail on a virtual machine host through VMM because the computer does not properly support the Hyper-V role.	VMM does not probe the configuration of the system BIOS to ensure that Hyper-V is supported.	Check CPUID features at http://msdn.microsoft.com/en-us/library/bb969687.aspx. Ensure that virtualization technology is enabled in the BIOS of the computer. Ensure that No-Execute is enabled in BIOS.
Cannot register a VMware VM through the Administrator Console.	This feature is currently not supported in VMM.	No fix available.
Recently added Hyper-V host is in "Needs Attention" state.	VMM encountered some issue with the configuration of the virtual machine host.	Ensure that Image Management Service is started on the host. If the virtualization service status is listed as Upgrade Available, then make sure to upgrade to the latest related QFEs.

TABLE 11.5: Host management issues (*CONTINUED*)

ISSUE	CAUSE	FIX
Adding vCenter instance to VMM fails.	User might specify FQDN for domain.	Ensure that the DOMAIN field uses the NetBIOS name of the domain or computer.
Putting a Hyper-V host into maintenance mode fails if a P2V job is in progress.	Certain operations must complete before you can put the host into maintenance mode.	Wait until P2V completes, and then try again.
Unable to multi-select hosts in Administrator UI.	Feature currently not supported in VMM.	No fix available.
Virtual Network properties do not display Network Optimizations as being enabled (even if physical host and adapters support VMQ and Chimney).	By default, VMQ and Chimney are disabled on a Windows Server 2008 R2 host.	Enable Chimney and VMQ.
Network Location is not populated by VMM for a network.	VMM needs to be able to query the domain. In some cases, this might not be possible due to fenced networks. Host has statically bound IPs.	You will need to provide the Network Location information manually. Location might not get discovered with statically bound IPs. Set the Network Location manually.

Table 11.6 lists library issues.

TABLE 11.6: Library issues

ISSUE	CAUSE	FIX
Storing a virtual machine with a differencing disk causes certain tasks to fail (e.g., deploying a virtual machine from the library).	The config.xml stored with the virtual machine in the Library only accounts for the differencing VHD.	Open the config.xml file and specify the location of the base VHD file (the VHD file that the differencing disk points to).
Importing a VMware virtual machine to the library fails.	The library imposes certain requirements when importing objects.	One of the VMDK files referenced in the VMX file might be missing.

TABLE 11.6:   Library issues (*CONTINUED*)

ISSUE	CAUSE	FIX
The exported Hyper-V virtual machine where base and differencing disks resided on different directories is not being properly imported in the library.	The library imposes certain requirements when importing objects.	Make sure the virtual hard disks reside in the same folder before exporting.
Deploying a virtual machine with snapshots fails on the Hyper-V host with relatively low disk space.	Placement does not take into account the size of BIN/VSV files when calculating disk space requirements before placing the virtual machine.	Free up space on host and retry job. Undo failed job and try a different host.
A virtual machine residing on a VMM library server is cloned into a subfolder of the current location of the source virtual machine. The new virtual machine shows up in the VMs and Templates view but the folder does not appear in the Library Server folder list.	VMM uses the VM and Templates folders to organize all VMs and templates indexed by the that library.	The current behavior of VMM will only show the virtual machine object and not the nested folders.
Disabling encryption for file transfers does not improve performance of file transfers.	Encryption is controlled on both the source and target host.	Make sure to disable encryption for both the source and target.
Disabling encryption is *not* supported for ESX hosts.	Feature currently not supported in VMM.	No fix available.
Removing a library share from VMM and adding it back will refresh all the contained files as new objects. In some cases, virtual machines saved to the library no longer show up. Instead, just the virtual disk used by the virtual machine shows up.	VMM does not use Hyper-V Export for virtual machine without snapshots. In this case, only the VHD is transferred and the virtual machine configuration is maintained in the library. Once the library share is deleted, all the virtual machine configuration information is lost.	No fix available.

Troubleshooting Virtual Machine Creation

Troubleshooting problems that arise when you're creating virtual machines and templates involves understanding tools like sysprep, used to generalize a guest OS; WAIK, used to generate unattended answer files for OS customization; and BITS and SFTP/HTTPS, used to transfer files to and from virtual machine hosts. When creating a new template from an existing virtual machine, VMM does not control the sysprep process. It assumes that generalization successfully completed once the guest OS shuts down after initiating sysprep. If the guest OS was not properly generalized (sysprep failed to complete successfully), VMM will detect the invalid state only at the point of deployment of a new virtual machine from that template. VMM also does not control OS installations performed within the virtual machine using PXE boot over the network or installing from an ISO.

Similar to management of a hypervisor computer, deploying a virtual machine requires local resources to accomplish the task. If the computer is overloaded, the task may not complete. Disk space available to the hypervisor host is also very important. Intelligent Placement will evaluate which virtual machine host has the most available space, but over time, as more virtual machines resides on the same storage location, capacity may not be available as readily. If not monitored, a storage location with many dynamic disks can run out of disk space very fast.

Table 11.7 lists virtual machine creation issues.

TABLE 11.7:   Virtual machine creation issues

ISSUE	CAUSE	FIX
When using a rapid provisioning script, New-VM cmdlets fails with parameterbindingexception	This is caused by a missing parameter.	In this case, New-VM requires the -VMMServer parameter.
VMM fails if you try to create a new VM with a virtual DVD attached to a disabled optical drive.	If the physical optical drive was recently disabled, then the host refresher has not run in order to reflect that information.	Refresh host. Reenable optical drive.
Creating two virtual machine in parallel using a VHD with a GUID Partition Table (GPT) formatted volume will cause VMM to fail.	GPT is not supported for the file system that resides in the VHD.	Do not use VHDs with GPT volumes
Cannot cancel the creation of a virtual machine with a fixed size VHD	This is currently not supported by VMM.	No fix available.
If a virtual machine is configured with a virtual CPU count other than one, two, or four , the VMM Administrator Console will fail.	Virtual CPU counter other than one, two, or four currently not supported by VMM.	Configure the virtual machine with one, two, four virtual CPUs.
When you're creating two clones of one source virtual machine concurrently, one job will fail.	This is due to how VMM handles the export folder.	Introduce a delay between clone jobs.
Many jobs fail when creating 100 virtual machines concurrently to a single host.	There are some known limits with BITS.	Break up the creation of virtual machines into sets of 10 or fewer at one time.

TABLE 11.7: Virtual machine creation issues (*CONTINUED*)

ISSUE	CAUSE	FIX
While creating a new template from an existing Highly Available (HA) virtual machine, the virtual machine resource fails from one node of the cluster to another and the job fails.	After failover, the connection is lost and so transfer does not continue, causing the job to fail. Retrying the job will also fail because the state information for the BITS file transfer is maintained on the node on which the transfer started.	Using Microsoft Failover Cluster console, fail/move the virtual machine resource to the original node and retry the operation.
After a leaf snapshot of a Hyper-V virtual machine is deleted, certain operations fail, stating that a specific file that has a name ending with .avhd could not be located.	Hyper-V initiates a merge of the AVHD file to its parent file. This operation may take some time and only happens if the virtual machine is not powered on.	Allow the merge to complete. You can check progress in the Hyper-V UI. Once the file merge is complete, refresh the virtual machine.
Cloning a virtual machine with a Raw Device Mapping (RDM) fails.	This is currently not supported by VMM.	No fix available.
Creating a new virtual machine with an operating system that is not supported by ESX is allowed in the console but the job ultimately fails.	Currently VMM does not block the ability to create a virtual machine based on a guest OS that is not supported by the underlying hypervisor.	Refer to VMware documentation for the list of supported operating systems.
Converting a passthrough disk to VHD does not free up clustered disk resource.	The cluster might not have released the resource.	Go to Microsoft Failover Cluster console and remove the disk resource.
A virtual machine created through VMM Self-Service Portal defaults the local administrator account of the guest OS to AdminUser.	Self-Service Portal does not provide an input field to specify the administrator user account name. The default for Vista and above is AdminUser.	Use the PowerShell CLI to customize the creation of the virtual machine.

Troubleshooting Virtual Machine Migration

As with virtual machine creation, migration involves a source and a destination virtual machine host, with the important distinction that the virtual machine instance is the same before and after migration. Virtual machine creation from the library, on the other hand, creates a new independent instance. There are several migration types in VMM portfolio:

Network migration   Network migration performs a transfer of virtual disk and configuration files over the network. It applies to all managed hypervisors. Quick Storage Migration, supported on Hyper-V R2, relies on network migration.

Quick Migration   Specific to Hyper-V, Quick Migration relies on Microsoft failover cluster-ing to enable migration of the clustered resource (i.e., the virtual machine) from one node to another. In this case, instead of moving virtual disks, only the virtual machine configuration is moved between nodes. Minimum requirements for this type of migration include shared storage and shared network.

Live Migration/VMotion   Specific to Hyper-V and ESX, this one relies on hypervisor tech-nology to map memory between hosts and allow for a migration of the virtual machine with no perceived downtime. Similar to Quick Migration, the virtual disks do not move as part of the migration. The memory transfer is accomplished through a dedicated network to ensure the fastest throughout. Additional minimum requirements for this type of migration include shared storage.

SAN migration   Leveraging SAN-based technology allows VMM to mask and unmask stor-age between virtual machine hosts using Virtual Disk Service (VDS) HW providers or N_Port ID Virtualization (NPIV). With SAN-based migration, only the LUN mapping is moving between hosts. Minimum requirements for this type of migration include shared storage.

Table 11.8 lists virtual machine migration issues.

TABLE 11.8:   Virtual machine migration issues

ISSUE	CAUSE	FIX
Moving a virtual machine with a saved state from one ESX host to another and changing storage locations will cause lose of the saved state.	This behavior is consistent in the vCenter console.	Instead of saved state, put the virtual machine into powered-off state before attending.
Migration of a virtual machine using difference disks from Hyper-V R2 to Hyper-V RTM will fail.	Differencing disk created on Windows Server 2008 R2 are not compatible with Windows Server 2008 RTM.	Do not migrate to Hyper-V RTM. Merge the differencing disks into the parent disks.
Migration of a virtual machine residing on a dedicated CSV cannot be SAN trans-ferred to another cluster as part of a migration operation.	This is currently not supported by VMM.	No fix available.
If a Quick Storage Migration job failed and the virtual machine is subsequently deleted, the associated cluster resources are not deleted.	The cluster does not free up resources.	Using Microsoft Failover Cluster console, delete the cluster resources for the virtual machine manually.
SAN transferring a LUN between hosts on separate FC switches is not allowed.	Limitation in Brocade switches.	Check with Brocade for the latest updates, which may address this.
Migrating multiple virtual machines configured with differencing VHD that all share the same base VHD will result in a locking error and fail the job.	VMM uses object-level locks to ensure that jobs complete successfully.	In this case, migration operations should be performed in serial.

Troubleshooting VMM Security and Self-Service Portal

VMM's delegation model depends on two external components:

◆ Active Directory

◆ AzMan

VMM uses Active Directory to resolve the members of a user role that must be valid user accounts. It stores user role information in the local AzMan store of every Hyper-V host. A commonly used user role available in VMM is the Self Service User role. Members of this user role access virtual machines through the VMM Self-Service Portal. The portal depends on IIS and VMM itself to grant users access only to the virtual machines and templates in the user role scope. Basic network connectivity is required between the IIS instance hosting the portal, the VMM server, and access to the virtual machine hosts. If you plan on placing a firewall in between the Self-Service Portal and the virtual machine hosts, you need to open the necessary ports to allow remote access to the virtual machines.

Table 11.9 lists security and Self-Service Portal issues.

TABLE 11.9:   Security and Self-Service Portal issues

ISSUE	CAUSE	FIX
In a Windows 2003 Active Directory environment, the user will fail to log into the VMM Administrator Console using the account originally created under Windows 2000 Active Directory.	Special Active Directory permissions are not guaranteed to be present after domain upgrade. However, new accounts get the necessary permissions.	User a different user account for VMM.
If an administrator or delegated administrator creates a new virtual machine on a Hyper-V host and assigns it an owner that is a member of the Self-Service User role during creation, the user will have to wait up to 30 minutes before being able to access the virtual machine through the Self-Service Portal.	Since the owner of the virtual machine was set during creation, the local Hyper-V authorization store does not yet have an instance of a virtual machine to assign permissions to. The permissions are then set during the next scheduled refresh, which every 30 minutes.	Create the virtual machine with some other owner (for example, some default administrator account). After the virtual machine is created, change the owner to the appropriate one. This will force a refresh of the Hyper-V authorization store.
After restoring a checkpoint of a virtual machine on a Hyper-V host, the user can no longer access the virtual machine through the Self-Service Portal.	As part of restoring a checkpoint, the owner information is not refreshed into the Hyper-V authorization store.	After restoring the checkpoint of a virtual machine, change the owner to some other owner (for example, some default administrator account). Then change the owner back to the appropriate one. This will force a refresh of the Hyper-V authorization store.

TABLE 11.9:   Security and Self-Service Portal issues (*CONTINUED*)

ISSUE	CAUSE	FIX
Creating a virtual machine through the Self-Service Portal with an invalid computer name results in an "operation successful" message displayed to the user but a failed job only the administrator can see in the Administrator Console.	The Self-Service Portal does not return the job state of the new virtual machine. The computer name cannot contain certain characters, which the Self-Service Portal does not block the user from entering.	Avoid using characters that are not supported by Windows Setup (' ~ ! @ # $ % ^ & ( ) = + [ ] { } \ ; : ' " , < > / ? .).
Administrator Console does not reflect permissions set though MM PowerShell CLI for a Self-Service User role.	Settings are reflected in the Administrator Console only if set through the console.	To view the set permissions, use the VMM PowerShell CLI.

VMM allows administrators to customize what permissions are assigned to a Self-Service User role. The members of the user role that access the portal will be limited to those permissions. You can set these permissions in the VMM Administrator Console and through the VMM PowerShell interface. If you plan to use the CLI, the permissions must be provided in integer form. The following scenarios show the associated set of permissions required and the associated integer value for each. The sum of values for the permissions is what you would pass in to the Set-VMMUserRole cmdlet.

```
PS C:\> $ur = Get-VMMUserRole | where {$_.Name -eq "test1"}
PS C:\> Set-VMMUserRole -UserRole $ur -VMPermission 511
PS C:\> $ur.VMPermission Create, PauseAndResume, Start, Stop, AllowLocalAdmin,
RemoteConnect, Remove, Shutdown, Checkpoint
```

SCENARIO 1: ALL PERMISSIONS GRANTED

To grant a user role all permissions, you need to pass 511 to the Set-VMMUserRole cmdlet. Table 11.10 lists the permissions and associated values.

SCENARIO 2: REMOTE CONSOLE ACCESS ONLY

To grant a user role remote console access to a virtual machine, pass 32 to the Set-VMMUserRole cmdlet. In this case, users can connect to the console session of the guest operating system but cannot change the power state of the virtual machine. They can, however, shut down the guest operating system that would change the power state of the virtual machine. Table 11.11 lists the permission and associated value.

SCENARIO 3: CHANGE THE POWER STATE OF THE VIRTUAL MACHINE

To grant a user role the right to change the power state of a virtual machine, pass 140 to the Set-VMMUserRole cmdlet. In this case, users can change the power state of the virtual machine by starting or stopping it. However, you may not want to give them the right to pause a virtual machine because that will still consume memory on the virtual machine host. Table 11.12 lists the permissions and associated values.

TABLE 11.10:   Scenario 1 – All permissions granted

PERMISSION	VALUE
Create	1
Pause and Resume	2
Start	4
Stop	8
Local Administrator	16
Remote Connection	32
Remove	64
Shutdown	128
Checkpoint	256

TABLE 11.11:   Scenario 2 – Only the ability to connect remotely

PERMISSION	VALUE
Remote Connection	32

TABLE 11.12:   Scenario 3 – Power state permissions

PERMISSION	VALUE
Start	4
Stop	8
Shutdown	128

SCENARIO 4: READY FOR BUSINESS OPERATOR PERMISSIONS

To grant a user role the right to power on and resume a virtual machine, pass 6 to the Set-VMMUserRole cmdlet. In this case, you specifically want the operator to power on and resume virtual machines in preparation for business on Monday morning. Table 11.13 lists the permissions and associated values.

SCENARIO 5: CREATE AND MANAGE VIRTUAL MACHINE BUT CANNOT DELETE

To grant a user role the right to create and manage a virtual machine but not the right to remove it, pass 447 to the Set-VMMUserRole cmdlet. In this case, you want the user to create as many virtual machines as allowed, but you want to maintain control of when the virtual machine is removed. Table 11.14 lists the permissions and associated values.

TABLE 11.13:   Scenario 4 – Power state permissions

PERMISSION	VALUE
Pause and Resume	2
Start	4

TABLE 11.14:   Scenario 5 – Power state permissions

PERMISSION	VALUE
Create	1
Pause and Resume	2
Start	4
Stop	8
Local Administrator	16
Remote Connection	32
Shutdown	128
Checkpoint	256

SCENARIO 6: REMOVE VIRTUAL MACHINES

To grant a user role the right to remove a virtual machine, pass 232 to the `Set-VMMUserRole` cmdlet. In this case, you want the user to have sufficient permissions to remove a virtual machine from the environment, including remote access. Table 11.15 lists the permissions and associated values.

TABLE 11.15:   Scenario 6 – Remove Virtual Machine Permissions

PERMISSION	VALUE
Stop	8
Remote Connection	32
Remove	64
Shutdown	128

Troubleshooting PRO

With PRO, you will also need to know troubleshooting techniques for Operations Manager. If you do not manage the monitoring environment, then make sure to set up an open dialog with the team that does to ensure that they can respond to issues in your environment. The VMM and Operations Manager connection through the Operations Manager SDK must be monitored to alert you to issues might affect the connection. Any performance issues on the Operations Manager side will affect PRO's responsiveness. Before assuming that PRO is experiencing

performance issues, check Operations Manager to make sure it is performing optimally. In fact, Operations Manager can be used to monitor itself!

Table 11.16 lists PRO issues.

TABLE 11.16:   PRO issues

ISSUE	CAUSE	FIX
When multiple PRO tips are executed concurrently, some may fail with error 11825: "PRO tip implementation failed to start when run concurrently."	By default, the maximum number of asynchronous responses handled is five.	Modify the following Registry key to increase the limit: HKLM\SOFTWARE\Microsoft\ Microsoft Operations Manager\3.0\Modules\Global\ Command Executer, AsyncProcessLimit:DWORD Maximum is 100.
If an Extension Management Pack (MP) is bound to the engine object, any PRO tips generated against that object are not visible by a delegated administrator, only administrators.	Delegated administrators can only be scoped by the host group and virtual machines. The engine object falls outside the allowed scope.	If you want delegated administrators to see relevant PRO tips, make sure to associate PRO tips with host and virtual machine objects.
PRO tip Implementation will fail if a virtual machine host is not found while in automatic mode.	This will occur for the following states: migration in progress, entering maintenance mode, o stars.	No fix available if the virtual machine is in the states listed.
PRO tip Implementation that attempts to migrate a non-HA virtual machine will fail.	The virtual machine resides on a cluster but is not set up as an HA virtual machine.	Move the virtual machine to a stand-alone host or promote the non-HA virtual machine to an HA virtual machine.
PRO does not start to monitor virtual machines immediately.	Virtual machine objects are not created in Operations Manager until the next full discovery.	Wait for 6 hours (from the first time you enabled PRO for a host group). For an update, use Set-VMM Server -opsmgrserver <youropsmgrserver>.

TABLE 11.16: PRO issues (*CONTINUED*)

ISSUE	CAUSE	FIX
Changing a threshold for a PRO tip in the Operations Manager console is not reflected in the VMM Administrator Console.	Changes in Operations Manager are not updated in VMM.	Make threshold changes in the VMM Administrator Console.
If your VMM instance is running in a virtual machine and the host group the virtual machine host resides in is PRO enabled, a PRO implementation may try to migrate the virtual machine that contains the VMM instance.	PRO does not have any special logic to treat a virtual machine with the VMM instance any differently from another virtual machine.	No fix available.

Troubleshooting Performance and Scale

Troubleshooting performance issues is very difficult because the experience will differ for every implementation. Depending on your network topology, Active Directory environment, storage performance, server performance, Operations Manager (OpsMgr) performance, and several other factors, it is difficult to anticipate the issues you may encounter as your virtual environment grows. A common bottleneck that affects the VMM database, hypervisor hosts, and library servers, is storage. This is especially true as you increase the number of concurrent virtual machines you deploy in your environment. It is highly recommended to keep a journal or, if you have OpsMgr deployed, generate a report of VMM performance as your scale up. This is good reference when troubleshooting an issue because it helps answer the expected performance at scale. For example, as you scaled from 1,000 virtual machines to 4,000 in a few months, what was the average time required to complete an operation at 1,000 virtual machines, 1,500 virtual machines, 2,000 virtual machines, and so on?

Table 11.17 lists performance and scale issues.

TABLE 11.17: Virtual machine migration issues

ISSUE	REASON
You notice delays in deploying a virtual machine.	VMM performs several tasks as part of deploying a virtual machine, including mounting and unmounting the virtual machine VHD. If you deploy multiple virtual machines in parallel, these actions are serialized. This introduces a delay in deployment.
With 400 hosts and 7,000 virtual machines managed by VMM, the console may take up to 4 minutes to open.	This is expected. At larger scales, the VMM Administrator Console retrieves more data from the database.

The Bottom Line

Understand VMM from a troubleshooting perspective. It is important to understand that VMM offers several levels of error reporting to help you understand different failure situations. Only in the case that a problem does not have a good error or any error at all do you need to troubleshoot VMM.

Master It Name the three categories of errors and warnings in VMM.

Master It Why is it important to perform a root cause analysis for critical issues?

Master It List the components in a VMM deployment.

Master It Based on Table 11.1, what are the associated quantities for each VMM component in a production environment?

Use common troubleshooting tools. Over time you will collect an extensive number of tools to help you troubleshoot a wide array issues. Mastering these tools will help reduce the impact (downtime) of a critical issue in your virtualized environment.

Master It List some examples of how you would use Performance Monitor to troubleshoot an issue with VMM.

Master It If you plan to manage SQL Express remotely using SQL Management Studio, what tool do you need to use to enable remote access?

Master It If a virtual machine fails to customize during deployment and the error presented by Mini-Setup in the guest operating system hints at an issue with the answer file, what tool would you use to validate the answer file?

Understand issues with VMM components. Troubleshooting is not a required day-to-day task but involves an important set of skills that should be developed.

Master It What two external components does the VMM delegation model depend on?

Master It Name the four migration types in a VMM portfolio.

Master It When troubleshooting ESX host management issues, what additional piece of infrastructure do you need to account for?

Appendix A

The Bottom Line

Each of The Bottom Line sections in the chapters suggest exercises to deepen skills and understanding. Sometimes there is only one possible solution, but often you are encouraged to use your skills and creativity to create something that builds on what you know and lets you explore one of many possible solutions.

Chapter 1: Introduction to System Center Virtual Machine Manager 2008 R2

Identify and explain the components in the VMM architecture. Virtual Machine Manager has a distributed system architecture that administrators need to understand well before deploying VMM in their virtualized environment. Knowing the architecture of VMM gives you the opportunity to make educated choices during deployment of the various VMM components.

Master It Name the different components of Virtual Machine Manager.

Which VMM components can reside on a separate computer from the VMM server?

Name four new features of VMM 2008 R2.

Solution Virtual Machine Manager has the following components:

- VMM server
- VMM database
- VMM Windows PowerShell cmdlet interface
- VMM Administrator Console
- VMM Self-Service Portal
- VMM library
- Managed virtualization hosts (VMM agents are installed on these virtualization hosts.)
- Managed virtualization managers (i.e., Managed VMware VirtualCenter servers)
- OpsMgr management packs for monitoring, reporting, and PRO

The VMM components that can reside on a computer that is not the VMM server are the VMM database, the Self-Service Portal, and the Administrator Console. In addition, both library servers and virtualization hosts can reside on remote computers.

Four new features of VMM 2008 R2 are rapid provisioning, Quick Storage Migration, maintenance mode, and support for Live Migration and CSV.

Determine the ports and protocols required for communication between the various VMM components. Being able to identify the different ports and communication protocols used by VMM makes it easier to talk to the network administrator and plan for a secure network.

Master It Name the differences between regular RDP and the RDP Single Port Listener for Hyper-V.

What is the protocol that VMM uses for transferring virtual machine images from one server to another?

Describe the differences between the console access for Hyper-V and the console access for Virtual Server.

Solution Regular RDP can connect to any computer that is in a running state with the operating system loaded. However, in order for regular RDP to connect, you must know the computer name, and there has to be a firewall-free path to the port 3389 that RDP utilizes. The Single Port Listener for Hyper-V allows a user to connect to a virtual machine even while the virtual machine is booting. More importantly, the virtual machine does not have to be on the network or even have an operating system installed. The Single Port Listener requires the knowledge of the Hyper-V host computer name, the unique identifier for the virtual machine in Hyper-V, and a firewall-free path for port 2179 to the Hyper-V server.

VMM uses the Background Intelligent Transfer Service (BITS) protocol for transferring virtual machines from one server to another using Network migration.

Hyper-V will allow only one connection at a time to a virtual machine. If a second connection is attempted, the first connection will be terminated. Virtual Server behaves a little bit differently, giving the administrator the option to enable or disable multiple concurrent VMRC connections to a virtual machine.

Determine the various roles and privileges of VMM. VMM allows an administrator to define a variety of roles and privileges for delegated administrators and end users. Choosing the correct user roles and delegating access to these users will ease the burden on the administrator and allow users to be self-sufficient.

Master It Name the different user roles that VMM allows you to create.

What are the differences between a delegated administrator and a regular VMM administrator?

Can end users get console access to a virtual machine?

What are the interfaces that end users can utilize to access VMM?

Solution VMM allows you to create or add users in three user roles:

◆ Administrator

◆ Delegated Administrator

◆ Self-Service User

The only difference between the delegated administrator (DA) and an administrator is that a DA is scoped to a set of host groups and library servers while the administrator has access throughout the VMM environment.

End users, or self-service users, can get console access to a virtual machine if the following prerequisites are met:

◆ They are the owner of a virtual machine.

◆ They are a member of a Self-Service User role that includes this virtual machine.

◆ The Self-Service User role has the Remote Connection permission enabled.

End users can access VMM either through the Self-Service Web Portal or through the Windows PowerShell cmdlet interface for VMM.

Explain the differences of the migration options offered in VMM. Understanding the different migration options offered in VMM allows an administrator to properly configure his or her environment (from a hardware and software perspective). Such a configuration will take advantage of faster migration methods and minimize downtime of a VM.

Master It What are the different transfer types that VMM utilizes?

Which is the fastest transfer type?

If you receive a zero-star rating for a host, how would you find out what is causing this result?

Solution VMM offers four main transfer types for virtual machines:

◆ Live Migration and VMware vMotion

◆ Quick Migration for failover clusters

◆ SAN migration

◆ Network migration

The fastest transfer type in terms of the least downtime experienced by a virtual machine is Live Migration. During a live migration, there is little or no user-perceivable downtime.

The Rating Explanation tab will contain the details on why you received a zero-star rating for a host during a migration attempt.

Describe the authentication methods between VMM and hosts. Virtual machines are running the same type of critical workloads as physical machines. The need to secure the data in these VMs is even more important because everything is contained in a collection of a couple of files. When virtual machines move from one host to another, it is important to understand the authentication methods used to secure your data.

Master It What encryption method does VMM use when transferring data across hosts in a trusted domain?

Are transfers of data from a trusted domain to a perimeter network host secure?

Under what circumstances is constrained delegation required for the Self-Service Portal?

Solution When VMM transfers files across hosts during a Network migration, it utilizes the BITS protocol. BITS transfers are encrypted by default since we transfer files via the HTTP protocol over SSL.

Yes, they are secure. BITS transfers in such an environment are secured through a certificate that VMM creates and adds in the trusted root of the VMM server and the managed perimeter network host.

Kerberos Constrained Delegation is required for the Self-Service Portal if the Self-Service Portal server resides on a computer that is different from the VMM server computer.

Chapter 2: Planning a VMM Deployment

Identify the different components in VMM. VMM breaks down into three areas of interest with one or more components in each. The first step in deploying VMM is to understand each component.

Master It For one instance of VMM, what is the supported maximum number of hosts and virtual machines?

Solution 400 hosts and 8,000 virtual machines

Master It Name at least three functions performed by the VMM server.

Solution Permissions store; job execution engine; creation, deployment, and management of virtualization objects; workflow engine; job audit logging; integration point with Operations Manager

Master It What component links VMM to System Center Operations Manager to enable PRO functionality?

Solution System Center Operations Manager Management Pack framework

Learn about optimizing VMM. VMM can scale to meet the demands of your virtualized environment, but you need to make sure each component is optimized to perform well. Peak performing components minimize bottlenecks in the system.

Master It Name three refreshers VMM uses to collect information from your virtualized environment.

Solution (Light) Virtual machine refresher, (Heavy) Virtual machine refresher, Host refresher, Cluster refresher, Library refresher, performance refresher, security refresher, Virtual Center refresher

Master It Compared to the all-in-one configuration, what components have you placed onto a separate server in the I/O-optimized configuration?

Solution Database server, library server

Master It Using VMM's delegation model, how would you model your host group structure to ensure that your New York administrators do not have access to Boston resources?

Solution VMM allows delegating control of a host group. So you can easily group all your New York Hyper-V hosts in one host group and grant a Delegated Administrator access to New York only. Then do the same for Boston Hyper-V hosts.

Understand important design considerations required for VMM. VMM architecture breaks down into three categories: VMM server, VMM infrastructure, and VMM client. Each category accounts for multiple components that should be taken into account as part of your VMM deployment plan.

Master It Aside from serving as a container for virtual machine hosts and clusters, what other uses do host groups have?

Solution With delegated administration, the Administrator user can scope a Delegated Administrator user role to a specific subhost group to limit access. Intelligent placement can calculate star ratings for all hosts contained within a host group. Host-level reserves can be defaulted for all new virtual machine hosts by setting the properties at the host group level. PRO can be enabled or disabled at the host group level.

Master It Name the three major categories of components for VMM.

Solution VMM server, VMM infrastructure, VMM clients

Master It Explain the difference between administrative autonomy and isolation.

Solution Administrative autonomy — Role-based administration in VMM guarantees that an administrator has complete control over a portion of the environment based on the host group structure. There is always an administrator with more privileges than a delegated administrator.

Administrative isolation — The administrator is guaranteed exclusive control over the environment. VMM does not support this model.

Chapter 3: Installation and Configuration

Install and configure a VMM server. Identify the prerequisites for a VMM server and various SQL database options.

Master It Which OS versions does a VMM server support?

Solution A VMM server supports 64-bit Windows Server 2008 and Windows Server 2008 R2.

Master It What limitation does it have when you use SQL Server Express Edition for a VMM database?

Solution SQL Server Express has the following limitations:

◆ SQL Server Express Edition supports a database up to 4 GB in size. If you intend to use VMM in a large environment (more than 150 hosts), a full version of SQL Server is recommended.

◆ SQL Server Express Edition does not support the reporting functionalities in VMM. If you need reporting features in VMM, a full version of SQL Server is required.

Install and configure Administrator Console. Identify the prerequisites for Administrator Console and various client component dependencies.

Master It Can you install the VMM PowerShell layer without the Administrator Console?

Solution No. The way to get the VMM PowerShell snap-in is to install the VMM Administrator Console.

Master It Why are you prompted to uninstall Administrator Console when you try to run the Configure Operations Manager option from Setup?

Solution Because Configure Operations Manager contains the installation and configuration of the VMM Administrator Console. If you installed the console before launching Operations Manager configuration, you'd need to uninstall the console and rerun the Configure Operations Manager option.

Install and configure the OPSMGR integration component. Understand the prerequisites for OPSMGR integration configuration and know the steps involved to configure the integration.

Master It What MPs do you need to install before PRO can be installed?

Solution Three MPs: Windows Server MP, IIS MP, SQL Server MP

Master It For the integration to work, what do you need to install on the VMM server and the OPSMGR management servers?

Solution You need to install the VMM Administrator Console on the OPSMGR management server and the OPSMGR Administrator Console on the VMM server.

Install and configure Self-Service Portal. Understand the prerequisites for Self-Service Portal, how user roles are created, and the steps involved to configure the portal.

Master It Can the Self-Service User role log in to the Administrator Console?

Solution No. Self-service users can access the VMs only through the Self-Service Portal.

Master It Will Self-Service Portal installation automatically enable the IIS role?

Solution No. The IIS role must be preinstalled by users before installing the Self-Service Web Portal.

Install and configure a local VMM agent. Understand the prerequisites for agent configuration and know the steps involved to configure the agent.

Master It What port numbers should you use when installing an agent?

Solution You should specify the ports defined during VMM server setup in this agent local install process.

Master It Which name should you choose when installing an agent for a DMZ host?

Solution For a perimeter network host, you should pick a name that the VMM server can use to connect to this host.

Install and configure VM hosts. Understand the prerequisites for host configuration and know the steps involved to configure the hosts.

Master It Does VMM automatically enable the Hyper-V role if it's not enabled already?

Solution Yes. For Windows Server 2008 or later, the VMM server will attempt to enable the Hyper-V role on target hosts as part of the Add Hosts process.

Master It What operations do you do to make the Add Hosts process Microsoft cluster aware?

Solution The VMM Add Hosts Wizard detects the existence of the cluster and automatically pulls in all cluster nodes when one of the nodes of a cluster is being added.

Install and configure a VMM library. You should understand the prerequisites for VMM library configuration and know the steps involved to configure the library.

Master It Does VMM automatically replicate contents across libraries?

Solution No. Users need to manage content distribution outside of VMM.

Master It Why would you see missing library objects in your library shares that are replicated by using DFS-R?

Solution When you move files around folder structures on one DFS-R share, the file paths on that share are updated in VMM. However, on the library shares that contain the replicated files, the moved files show up as new files in VMM, and the original files (in the original paths) show up as missing in VMM. You will need to manually clean up (remove) the missing files from other VMM library shares.

Chapter 4: Managing VMware ESX Using VMM

Identify the important features that are enabled by managing ESX hosts using VMM.
VMM enables very robust day-to-day management of Hyper-V– and ESX-based

environments. With the exception of a few nontypical operations, administrators can use VMM as a single management interface across multiple hypervisors. VMM can also aggregate multiple vCenter instances in addition to multiple hypervisors. VMM is the best management product for users who want to standardize how virtual machines are created, deployed, and managed in their environment. A common console across hypervisors helps reduce the barrier to entry for users who want to standardize on a management product that supports multiple hypervisors. Standardization of procedures helps reduce the learning curve for new operations staff. Standard PowerShell-based scripts that work across hypervisors help make operations staff more productive.

Master It

1. Write out the how VMM maps Host & Clusters, Datacenter, Folder, and Cluster objects in vCenter to Host Group and Host Cluster objects.

2. List the three management tools VMware provides for managing ESX hosts and virtual machines.

3. Using PowerShell, create a sample script to get the percentage of hosts responding in your environment and the percentage of running virtual machines per host.

Solution

1. Hosts & Clusters is mapped to All Hosts as the root node; Datacenter maps to Host Groups; Folder maps to Host Groups; Cluster maps to Host Clusters.

2. vCenter, VMware Remote CLI, VMware VIX

3. Run the following PowerShell script:

```
$respond = $hosts | where {$_.StatusString -eq "Responding"}
$percenthostsrespond = [Math]::round(($respond.count/$hosts.count)*100)
foreach ($_host in $respond)
{
    $on = $_host.VMs  | where {$_.Status -eq "Running"}
    $percenton = [Math]::round(($on.count/$_host.VMs.count)*100)
}
```

Set up a connection between VMM and vCenter and change an ESX host from OK (Limited) to OK. VMM uses vCenter's web services APIs to enable management of ESX hosts. Using vCenter is a requirement to support features like VMotion. The web service APIs, however, are not sufficient to enable full management of ESX in VMM. Transferring files to and from an ESX host requires additional software. VMM ships with SFTP support for ESX file transfers.

Master It

1. What information is missing from VMM if an ESX host is in OK (Limited) state?

2. Why does VMM open multiple sessions to vCenter?

3. How can you access resource pool information?

Solution

1. Account with owner privileges on virtual machine files, certificate, and public key.

2. VMM will open a new vCenter session to get host, VM, and performance data. This communication channel is necessary since VMM does not make direct connections to ESX.

3. Resource pools are not displayed in VMM's tree view in the Administrator Console. Instead, view host or cluster host group properties to view resources pools and associated virtual machines.

Determine what monitoring is available for ESX hosts out of box using PRO.   VMM and OPSMGR make a powerful combination for monitoring, alerting, and reporting your entire datacenter, including physical and virtual resources. Monitoring is not limited to the virtual machine hosts. Instead, using OPSMGR Management Packs, you have access to in-depth application knowledge.

Master It

1. Where do you need to deploy OpsMgr agents to get the most out of PRO?

2. Instead of requiring the OpsMgr agent for each ESX host, how does VMM get ESX data?

Solution

1. VMM Server, Hyper-V hosts, Windows operating systems hosted in virtual machines.

2. An agent on the VMM server connects to vCenter remotely using its web service APIs to get the relevant performance data.

Chapter 5: Managing Hyper-V Using VMM

Understand Hyper-V requirements.   Hyper-V is a very different technology compared to Virtual Server. It is instead in a similar class of hypervisors as VMware ESX and Citrix XenServer. It is worth taking the time to understand the specific requirements Hyper-V has so you can plan your deployment accordingly.

Master It   Explain the difference between a microkernelized hypervisor architecture versus a monolithic hypervisor architecture, and give at least one example of each.

Solution   These terms refer to an operating system kernel design in which a microkernel defines a simple abstraction layer over the hardware that uses system calls to implement a minimal set of operating system services like memory management, task management, and interprocess communication. Other services are implemented in the user space. Examples of this in hypervisor architecture are Microsoft Hyper-V and Citrix XenServer. A monolithic kernel, however, runs all operating system services in the main kernel execution thread, providing robust hardware access. Examples of this in hypervisor architecture are VMware ESX and ESXi.

Master It   What behavior should you expect if you live migrate a virtual machine that does not reside on CSV?

Solution   In a Microsoft failover cluster, you can live migrate a virtual machine between nodes without CSV. The main difference is with downtime. Live migrating without CSV incurs a 5- to 30-second interruption.

Master It   How does Hyper-V Server 2008 R2 differ from Hyper-V in Windows Server 2008 R2?

Solution   Hyper-V Server 2008 R2 is a prepackaged solution that consists of a Windows Server 2008 R2, Server Core installation, the Hyper-V role enabled by default, and specialized command-line scripts to simplify management.

Master It   Explain how Hyper-V uses Intel VT-x/AMD-V processor technology?

Solution   These processors support the new virtual machine extensions (VMX) mode. VMX mode provides four new less-privileged levels (rings) in addition to the standard four IA-32 privilege levels (rings). VMX mode allows the processor to be in either VMX root operation or VMX non-root operation. The intention is for the Hyper-V hypervisor software to work in VMX root operation while the partitions work in VMX non-root operation. The hypervisor behavior in VMX root operation is similar to how it would function with a processor that does not offer VMX mode. Partitions that work in VMX non-root operation have access to the four privileged levels (rings) and can expect similar behavior on a normal processor with some limitations. One limitation is with access to critical system resources. The expectation is that these resources remain under the control of the hypervisor in VMX root operation. The limitations also extend to VMX non-root operation in ring 0. This is how the parent partition on a Hyper-V host gains access to the underlying hardware. The hypervisor software does not manage hardware I/O devices. This is why you need to load drivers in the parent partition.

Understand deployment considerations.   The underlying infrastructure that Hyper-V resides on is critical to a successful deployment. Your intended use cases and scalability goal drive the requirements for hardware components and the connectivity used to deploy Hyper-V. Some environments require very little infrastructure and redundancy while others demand the highest availability, performance, and scalability.

Master It   List the various network types you need to consider in a Hyper-V deployment.

Solution   Management network, virtual machine network, backup network, cluster private network, cluster shared volume network, iSCSI network.

Master It   Describe a characteristic of each storage option in a Hyper-V deployment.

Solution   Fibre Channel (FC) SAN: best performance, best scalability, but an expensive solution if you need to deploy a FC fabric.

iSCSI SAN: iSCSI traffic can share the same data network. The scale of your virtualization environment might require a separate network just for iSCSI traffic.

Direct Attach Storage (DAS): Cheapest storage solution but the least flexible in terms of expandability and not very well managed. DAS is not easily shared, so if you need to scale your environment, you might have to consider iSCSI or FC SAN.

Master It   What advantages does a Server Core installation of Windows Server 2008 R2 have over a full installation?

Solution   Core is not a feature of Windows but simply an installation type that causes Window Server to run with minimal footprint on disk and in memory. Core does not offer a graphical interface.

Manage Hyper-V hosts and virtual machines.   As part of managing Hyper-V and the virtual machines that reside on Hyper-V, it is good to understand the subtle differences that are not obvious in the UI or CLI.

Master It   What artifact does exporting a virtual machine using the Hyper-V MMC create in place of the configuration file?

Solution   The exporting process generates a configuration file that has an `.exp` filename extension and contains the virtual machine configuration. The file itself is not meant to be modified by users.

Master It   Explain one limitation with Hyper-V Live Migration and how does VMM help in this situation?

Solution   Hyper-V currently supports only one live migration between two nodes at a time. To help avoid the overhead of live migrating virtual machines one at a time, VMM supports queuing live migrations when a node is put into maintenance mode.

Chapter 6: Managing Virtual Server Using VMM

Determine the requirements for the host and guest operating systems for Virtual Server.
Being able to identify the different requirements for host and guest operating systems makes it easier to provision hardware for your virtualization needs.

Master It   What are the new features of Virtual Server 2005 R2 SP1?

Solution   The new features of Virtual Server 2005 R2 SP1 include support for hardware-assisted virtualization, a VHD mount utility, support for virtual machine backups through a VSS writer, host clustering capabilities, and new maximum limits for Virtual Server hosts.

Master It   Which versions of Virtual Server does VMM support?

Solution VMM supports Virtual Server 2005 R2 SP1 as well as Virtual Server 2005 R2 SP1 with update KB948515.

Master It What is the architecture of the processor for virtual machines running inside a 64-bit host operating system?

Solution Virtual machines running inside Virtual Server always have a 32-bit processor regardless of the architecture of the processor on the host operating system.

Manage Virtual Server host clusters with VMM. Clustering and high availability ensure that a virtual machine can continue to run through hardware downtime, maintaining the availability of a critical workload.

Master It How can you identify a highly available virtual machine in the Administrator Console?

Solution Virtual machines running in Virtual Server don't have a property that identifies them as highly available virtual machines. The administrator can use a specific tag as part of the name of the virtual machine to indicate high availability. In addition, one of the virtual machine custom fields can be used for this purpose.

Master It List the steps taken by the script resource during failover.

Solution A planned failover is a failover that happens when an administrator initiates a move of a cluster resource group to a new node. During this type of failover, the script resource will (1) save the state of the virtual machine on the source host, (2) move the resource group that contains the VM and its disk and network resources to the destination host, and (3) restore the state of the virtual machine so that it is in a running state again.

Master It What are the conditions under which a virtual machine will be in a missing state in the Administrator Console?

Solution A virtual machine could go missing in the Administrator Console if VMM can't find the VM on the host that it thinks it belongs to. VMM periodically queries a host for the list of virtual machines on it. If a virtual machine is not found on the host, then it goes to a missing state. During a failover between Virtual Server hosts, a VM could go missing for a small period of time until VMM discovers the VM on the destination host and updates its state. If the VM failed over to a destination Virtual Server host that is not under management by VMM, the VM will remain in a missing state indefinitely.

Use the permissions model for virtual machines. Understanding the different permissions and user role options offered in VMM allows administrators to properly configure access to their VMs.

Master It List the types of virtual machine access that self-service users can be granted.

Solution VMM self-service users can get access to virtual machines either through the Self-Service Portal or the Windows PowerShell interface for VMM. Through the use of

VMM user roles, an administrator can restrict the access to a set of VMs and enable privileges like remote connection, start VM, stop VM, save VM, and so on. Remote connection is the only privilege that a self-service user can use through tools other than VMM. A user can use VMRC to connect to the console connection of a virtual machine.

Master It   Why would VMM remove access to an account from a VMC file?

Solution   VMM will remove access to any accounts from the VMC file if they are not VMM administrators, delegated administrators scoped to the virtual machine's host, or self-service users with privileges to that virtual machine. VMM will perform this step on a periodic basis as part of a refresher.

Master It   Which tools can self-service users utilize to connect to virtual machines outside VMM?

Solution   Self-service users can use VMRC.exe to connect to the console session of a virtual machine.

Migrate a virtual machine from Virtual Server to Hyper-V.   Migrating virtual machines from one host to another allows the administrator to load balance the resource and possibly evacuate a host for maintenance. Moving virtual machines from a Virtual Server host to a Hyper-V host enables the administrator to retire the old hardware and still be able to gain access to the VMs that have moved to a Hyper-V host.

Master It   What is the minimum version of the Virtual Machine Additions that is necessary for V2V to work?

Solution   The minimum version of Virtual Machine Additions that is necessary for V2V is 13.813. Any version below that would require the Virtual Machine Additions to be manually uninstalled before the conversion takes place.

Master It   List the steps that are required to migrate a VM from Virtual Server to Hyper-V.

Solution   VMM makes it very easy to migrate a virtual machine from Virtual Server to Hyper-V. As long as the VM has no Virtual Machine Additions installed, or it has an up-to-date version of the Additions, VMM can take care of the rest of the process. The administrator can select a virtual machine to convert and chose the Migrate action in VMM. Selecting a Hyper-V host will trigger the V2V process and will convert a VM so that it can run on Hyper-V. The virtual machine at the end of the process will be placed on the destination Hyper-V host.

Master It   Why are migrations of VMs in a saved state not possible?

Solution   Saved state migrations are not possible because the memory state that is contained in the saved state file is not compatible between different types of virtualization software. Since Hyper-V can't understand the saved state file of a Virtual Server VM, VMM will prevent such a migration and will instruct the user to place a VM in a stopped state before initiating the process. This measure prevents the data loss that would occur if the saved state file was discarded during the process.

Chapter 7: Virtual Machine Management

Create and delete a virtual machine. VMM provides several ways to create new virtual machines using different sources: template, VHD, or virtual machine.

Master It

1. Explain the three virtual disk types supported by Hyper-V.

2. What is the difference between Network Location and Network Tag?

3. What is the purpose of a template that does not require customization?

4. Why does VMM delete the virtual machine configuration and virtual hard disk files?

Solution

1. Dynamic disks are virtual disks represented by a file that grows dynamically as the data stored in the file increases. Fixed disks are virtual disks represented by a file that is predefined in size. The file does not decrease or increase in size over time. Differencing disks are virtual disks represented by two files; one file is the parent disk, which contains all the data, and the other file is the child disk, which captures all write operations.

2. Network Location represents the location discovered by the Network Location Awareness (NLA) provider. Network Tag is a property manually configured by the user.

3. Templates that do not require customization do not need a guest OS profile because VMM is not expected to pass an answer file for customization during Mini-Setup.

4. Not deleting the virtual disk and configuration files of a virtual machine that gets deleted, results in a cluttered environment filled with unmanaged files residing on hosts.

Convert a physical machine or non-Windows hypervisor virtual machine to a Windows hypervisor virtual machine. P2V can capture the operating system, application stack, and configuration from an existing machine and create a virtual machine. V2V converts existing virtual machines running on ESX to Virtual Server or Hyper-V.

Master It

1. Explain how VMM uses `BlockList.xml` during P2V.

2. List the VMDK file types supported by V2V.

3. Can you select a virtual machine as a P2V source? If so, why would you ever do this?

Solution

1. `Blocklist.xml` contains a list of services and drivers that P2Vwill disable in the virtual machine offline (before it is ever powered on).

2. V2V supports the following file types: `monolithicflat`, `monolithicsparse`, `Vmfs`, `twoGbMaxExtentSparse`, `twoGbMaxExtentFlat`.

3. Yes, you can select a virtual machine as a P2V source. You would do so if V2V does not work or to clone the virtual machine without requiring any downtime.

Migrate a virtual machine between hosts.   With VMM, migration of a virtual machine between hosts is possible using various in-box technologies.

Master It

1. Explain the difference between Quick Storage Migration and Live Migration.

2. In Windows Server 2008 R2, explain the advantage of using a CSV storage location for Live Migration.

3. List all the transfer types in VMM's portfolio.

Solution

1. Quick Storage Migration uses Hyper-V snapshot and Windows BITS technology to move a running virtual machine with minimal downtime between two hosts or on the same host. With Quick Storage Migration, memory state is preserved but does not rely on Live Migration. Live Migration relies on memory mapping technology in Hyper-V to transfer the state of a running virtual machine between two hosts. With Live Migration, no storage is moved.

2. CSV can be shared in read/write mode across all nodes in a cluster. So when a virtual machine is migrated, the CSV location does not need to migrate as well, which reduces the time to move the virtual machine and restart it.

3. Network, SAN, cluster, storage.

Chapter 8: Automation Using PowerShell

Describe the main benefits that PowerShell offers for VMM.   Windows PowerShell is a relatively new technology that was developed by Microsoft Corporation. Virtual Machine Manager utilized this technology as the scripting public API for VMM and as the backbone of the Administrator Console.

Master It   What version of Windows PowerShell does VMM support?

Which are the VMM assemblies needed for programmatically integrating with VMM's cmdlets?

List the benefits that Windows PowerShell cmdlets offer as a public API.

Solution   Virtual Machine Manager is certified to work with Windows PowerShell versions 1.0 and 2.0. When you open a VMM PowerShell, VMM automatically knows to use the correct release of PowerShell.

To programmatically integrate with VMM and be able to invoke the Windows PowerShell cmdlets that are part of the VMM PowerShell console, you need to reference the following four assemblies:

◆ `Microsoft.SystemCenter.VirtualMachineManager.dll`

◆ `Remoting.dll`

- `Utils.dll`

- `Errors.dll`

Windows PowerShell offers the following benefits to VMM as its public API:

- VMM offers only one public API interface that is delivered through Windows Power-Shell cmdlets.

- The PowerShell interface focuses on administrators instead of developers, is fully extensible and well documented, and can be integrated with other System Center products.

- PowerShell provides the ability to control the entire VMM product's functionality through the use of cmdlets. (The VMM Administrator Console uses cmdlets to drive VMM's functionality as well.)

Create scheduled PowerShell scripts.   Scheduling PowerShell scripts allows an administrator to perform operations during nonwork hours and get reports on the progress and the results of those operations.

Master It   How can you create a scheduled task in Windows?

List an example PowerShell script that checks if any host is in an unhealthy state and needs an administrator to take a look at it.

Solution   You can create a scheduled task in Windows using the Task Scheduler MMC snap-in. To execute a PowerShell script as part of the scheduled task, you need to construct a command line with the proper arguments. First, you need to invoke `PowerShell.exe` followed by the PowerShell console file and the PowerShell script as shown here:

```
D:\Windows\System32\WindowsPowerShell\v1.0\powershell.exe -PSConsoleFile
 "D:\Program Files\Microsoft System Center Virtual Machine Manager
 2008 R2\bin\cli.psc1" -Command " &
 '\\hypervhost1.vmmdomain.com\MSVMMLibrary\Scripts\GetVMStatus.ps1'"
 -NoProfile -Noninteractive
```

PowerShell script that checks for host health has to check a few different properties on a host to identify and pinpoint a health issue. The first cmdlet below gives an aggregate view of all hosts in VMM and their respective states. To specifically check for agent status, you can use the second cmdlet. To check for hosts that have only an unhealthy overall state, the third cmdlet can be used.

```
PS D:\> Get-VMHost | select Name, OverallState, CommunicationState,
VirtualServerState, VirtualServerVersionState, ComputerState

PS D:\> Get-VMMManagedComputer | select Name, State, VersionStateString

PS D:\> Get-VMHost | select Name, OverallState, CommunicationState,
VirtualServerState, VirtualServerVersionState, ComputerState | Where-Object
-FilterScript {$_.OverallState -ne "OK"}
```

```
# In the last cmdlet above, only Hosts that don't have a healthy overall state
will be returned
# In this case we see that the following host is in a NeedsAttention state
because the
# communication state with the VMM Agent on the host is lost.
Name                       : host.vmmdomain.com
OverallState               : NeedsAttention
CommunicationState         : NotResponding
VirtualServerState         : Running
VirtualServerVersionState  : UpToDate
ComputerState              : NotResponding
```

Use the VMM PowerShell cmdlets.   Understanding the usage, scope, and association of the different VMM cmdlets and PowerShell objects allows an administrator to effectively manage VMM through Windows PowerShell.

Master It   How can you identify the proper parameters and syntax for the Add-VMHost cmdlet?

How can you add the VMM PowerShell snap-in programmatically to a PowerShell script?

How does the Windows PowerShell pipeline work?

Solution   The proper way to identify the syntax of a cmdlet and get the parameter sets is by invoking the Get-Help cmdlet. The Full parameter will ensure that all content about this cmdlet is retrieved from the help file.

```
PS D:\> Get-Help Add-VMHost -Full
```

The Add-PSSnapin cmdlet will add a Windows PowerShell snap-in to the current console. The name of the VMM snap-in is Microsoft.SystemCenter.VirtualMachineManager.

```
PS D:\> Add-PSSnapin "Microsoft.SystemCenter.VirtualMachineManager"
```

The Windows PowerShell pipeline can be thought of as an assembly line of cmdlets. Each cmdlet has an individual purpose that is well defined and at the end gets to publish its results. The pipeline takes these results from the finished cmdlet and passes them to the next cmdlet in the pipeline so that it can perform its work. All together, the set of cmdlets are serially combined together to achieve a bigger task.

Chapter 9: Writing a PRO Pack

Integrate VMM with OpsMgr for end-to-end service management.   Virtual Machine Manager is great for provisioning and managing virtual workloads. Through the integration of VMM with OpsMgr, health monitoring and end-to-end workload management are added to an already strong solution.

Master It   Why are OpsMgr agents required on all Windows-based computers?

Explain why the Administrator Console needs to be installed on all OpsMgr management servers.

How can you initiate snapshot discovery and refresh the VMM environment into OpsMgr ?

Solution   OpsMgr agents are required for all Windows-based computers in the VMM environment so that OpsMgr can provide comprehensive monitoring of the entire virtual infrastructure. This monitoring would start from the VMM server and extend to the applications running inside virtual machines. In addition, PRO packs could target any computer in the virtual infrastructure, and OpsMgr has to have an agent on these computers for the entire feature set of PRO to be leveraged.

The VMM Administrator Console needs to be installed on all management servers because it also installs the VMM PowerShell interface that is used as part of PRO recovery tasks. It is far more efficient to install the Administrator Console on the management servers instead of on every host and virtual machine that needs to be the target of a recovery task.

The `Set-VMMServer -OpsMgrServer <RMS server name>` cmdlet can manually and immediately initiate snapshot discovery and refresh the VMM environment into OpsMgr.

Use the PRO infrastructure to create a new PRO pack.   PRO pack authors can leverage PRO to dynamically respond to environmental conditions that affect the health of the virtualized environment via actions based on OpsMgr monitors. PRO can monitor the performance of systems and allow customers to manage their infrastructure in a proactive and automated way.

Master It   What is the relationship between an alert and a PRO tip?

Why does PRO require authors to create overrides?

What are the steps required for creating PRO tips against a specific hardware controller?

Solution   OpsMgr alerts that target one of the PRO public classes are surfaced in VMM as PRO tips when PRO tips are enabled for the target computer of the alert.

PRO requires PRO pack authors to create overrides so that VMM administrators can control the enable and disable switch of the PRO tips from the VMM Administrator Console.

If a PRO pack author would like to create a PRO tip against a specific hardware controller, then a new custom class needs to be defined. This class has to derive from the PRO public class and it has to have its own discovery. As part of discovery, every host or virtual machine that has this specific hardware controller needs to be discovered and create an instance of this custom class. PRO tips can then be targeted against this custom class and surfaced in VMM. The steps for creating a diagnostic task and a recovery task are the same as the ones followed in this chapter while creating a maintenance mode PRO pack.

Chapter 10: Planning for Backup and Recovery

Protect the VMM server, including the VMM database.   The Virtual Machine Manager server is the centerpiece of VMM and controls the management of the virtualization environment. It is important to have a comprehensive plan in place on how to back up and recover the VMM server and the VMM database.

Master It   How can you make the VMM server highly available?

Explain the importance of system state backup.

What is the best way to fully back up the VMM server?

Solution   VMM server is not a certified cluster application, so the only way to make the VMM server highly available is to place the VMM server component inside a virtual machine. The virtual machine can then be promoted to a highly available virtual machine residing on a virtualization host that is part of a failover cluster. This configuration will ensure that the VMM server component is highly available and can fail over to other cluster hosts.

System state backup is very important to the recovery operations of a computer. Critical operating system components are included in system state backup, including the system SID that is used to authenticate the VMM server to virtualization hosts. If you are rebuilding the VMM server, it is important to restore the system state to ensure that the new system has the same system SID.

Windows Server Backup is currently among the best backup software for backing up and recovering the VMM server. It offers a comprehensive backup solution, including backing up for bare metal recovery. To back up the VMM server, use only software that is certified to work with VMM.

Back up Hyper-V hosts using the Hyper-V VSS writer.   Backup and recovery of Hyper-V hosts is one of the most important pieces of a protection strategy in a virtualization environment. Virtual machines can run a wide range of workloads, from easily replaceable web servers to highly sensitive and important database servers. These virtual machines are typically owned by end users, making it all the more important for administrators to have a plan in place to minimize downtime in case of a disaster recovery and to meet the SLAs.

Master It   What is the best way to fully back up a Hyper-V server?

Explain how to find the Hyper-V VSS writer.

What are the options to back up a virtual machine with pass-through disks?

Solution   Windows Server Backup and Data Protection Manager are currently some of the best backup software for backing up and recovering the Hyper-V server. DPM offers the more comprehensive protection solution, including backing up for bare metal recovery. To back up the Hyper-V servers, use only software that is certified to work with the Hyper-V VSS writer.

The simplest way to find and identify the Hyper-V VSS writer is to invoke the vssadmin.exe command-line utility. The proper syntax to list all the VSS writers in the system and find the Hyper-V VSS Writer is vssadmin.exe list writers.

Virtual machines with storage that is not local to the Hyper-V host are not supported by the Hyper-V VSS writer. Even though pass-through disks are physical hard disks that are directly attached to the virtual machine, they are still not supported. Pass-through disks are presented as offline to the host's operating system, making it impossible to back them up. To back up a virtual machine with pass-through disks, use a backup agent inside the guest operating system of the virtual machine. This method will protect the virtual machine as if it were a physical computer.

Chapter 11: Troubleshooting

Understand VMM from a troubleshooting perspective.   It is important to understand that VMM offers several levels of error reporting to help you understand different failure situations. Only in the case that a problem does not have a good error or any error at all do you need to troubleshoot VMM.

Master It   Name the three categories of errors and warnings in VMM.

Solution   Support boundaries, information, critical.

Master It   Why is it important to perform a root cause analysis for critical issues?

Solution   As with any issue that does not have a clear reason, the investigation process in critical to learning about how a product works, training your staff, and incorporating recovery plans into your operations manuals. As your environment grows in size and complexity, it is important to keep an ongoing record of the configuration of your environment and issues encountered along the way.

Master It   List the components in a VMM deployment.

Solution   Hyper-V, ESX, stand-alone Virtual Server 2005, VMM database, VMM server, VMM Self-Service Portal, VMM library.

Master It   Based on Table 11.1, what are the associated quantities for each VMM component in a production environment?

Solution   Hyper-V (two-node cluster), ESX (two-node cluster), stand-alone Virtual Server 2005 (one server), VMM database (two-node cluster), VMM server (one server with a cold standby), VMM Self-Service Portal (one server), VMM library (two-node cluster).

Use common troubleshooting tools.   Over time you will collect an extensive number of tools to help you troubleshoot a wide array issues. Mastering these tools will help reduce the impact (downtime) of a critical issue in your virtualized environment.

Master It   List some examples of how you would use Performance Monitor to troubleshoot an issue with VMM.

Solution   Gather disk performance information from the server with the VMM database to identify potential contention. Gather memory and CPU performance information from the VMM server and Operations Manager server to pinpoint potential resource starvation issues.

Master It   If you plan to manage SQL Express remotely using SQL Management Studio, what tool do you need to use to enable remote access?

Solution   SQL Server Surface Area Configuration.

Master It   If a virtual machine fails to customize during deployment and the error presented by Mini-Setup in the guest operating system hints at an issue with the answer file, what tool would you use to validate the answer file?

Solution   Windows Automated Installation Kit.

Understand issues with VMM components.   Troubleshooting is not a required day-to-day task but involves an important set of skills that should be developed.

Master It   What two external components does the VMM delegation model depend on?

Solution   VMM's delegation model depends on two external components: Active Directory and AzMan (specifically for Hyper-V hosts).

Master It   Name the four migration types in a VMM portfolio?

Solution   Network migration, quick migration, Live/VMotion migration, and SAN migration.

Master It   When troubleshooting ESX host management issues, what additional piece of infrastructure do you need to account for?

Solution   VMware vCenter.

Appendix B

VMM Windows PowerShell Object Properties and VMM Cmdlet Descriptions

This appendix includes material that is directly related to the content in Chapter 8 and includes Virtual Machine Manager Windows PowerShell cmdlet descriptions. Table B.1 includes the properties of the VMMServer object, Table B.2 lists the properties of the VM object, and Table B.3 lists the properties of the VMHost object.

TABLE B.1:   The properties of the VMMServer Windows PowerShell object

NOUN PROPERTY	DESCRIPTION
Name	VMM server name.
IsConnected	Status of the connection to the VMM server.
ServerInterfaceVersion	The version of the server interface.
Profile	Current connected user's VMM user role profile.
FullyQualifiedDomainName	FQDN name for the VMM server.
FQDN	FQDN name for the VMM server.
ObjectCache	Object cache for faster retrieval of VMM objects in queries. The cache is updated automatically using WCF callback events. This is used internally by VMM.
MOMReportingEnabled	Flag to indicate if OpsMgr reporting is enabled.
OpsMgrReportingEnabled	Flag to indicate if OpsMgr reporting is enabled.
MOMReportingServerURL	OpsMgr reporting server URL.
OpsMgrReportingServerURL	OpsMgr reporting server URL.
OpsMgrServer	OpsMgr server name.

TABLE B.1: The properties of the VMMServer Windows PowerShell object *(CONTINUED)*

NOUN PROPERTY	DESCRIPTION
SelfServiceContactEmail	Contact email for the administrator of the Self-Service Portal.
PlacementGoal	The placement goal of either Consolidate or LoadBalance.
MemoryPriority	Memory priority placement setting.
DiskIOPriority	Disk IO priority placement setting.
CPUPriority	Processor priority placement setting.
NetworkPriority	Network priority placement setting.
CEIPOptIn	Flag to indicate the Customer Experience Improvement Program option.
VMRCAccessAccount	Domain accounts that can connect to all virtual machines running on Virtual Server through the VMRC protocol.
VMRCDefaultPort	Default port for VMRC remote control.
VMConnectDefaultPort	Default port for connecting to Hyper-V virtual machines.
MinimumSupportedAgentVersion	The minimum supported agent version.
LibraryRefresherEnabled	Flag to indicate whether the Library Refresher is enabled.
LibraryRefresherFrequency	The frequency in hours of the Library Refresher.
PROMonitoringLevel	The PRO monitoring level.
PROAutomationLevel	The PRO automation level.
PhysicalAddressRangeStart	The Global Static MAC Address range starting address.
PhysicalAddressRangeEnd	The Global Static MAC Address range ending address.
DatabaseServerName	The SQL Server name.
DatabaseInstanceName	The instance name for the SQL Server database.
DatabaseName	The name of the database containing the VMM data.
UserName	The VMM administrator's username. VMM is licensed to this user.
CompanyName	The VMM administrator's company name.

TABLE B.1: The properties of the VMMServer Windows PowerShell object *(CONTINUED)*

NOUN PROPERTY	DESCRIPTION
ProductVersion	The detailed product version for this instance of VMM.
ProductID	The product ID for VMM.
IsEvaluationVersion	Flag to indicate if this is an evaluation or beta installation.
IsWorkgroupEdition	Flag to indicate if this is the Workgroup Edition of VMM.
EvaluationDaysLeft	Number of evaluation days remaining before VMM expires.

TABLE B.2: The properties of the VM Windows PowerShell object

NOUN PROPERTY	DESCRIPTION
VMCPath	The path to the configuration file for this virtual machine.
MarkedAsTemplate	A flag to indicate if this is a template.
VMId	The unique ID of this virtual machine on the virtualization platform.
VMResourceGroup	The resource group for a highly available VM.
VMConfigResource	The configuration resource for a highly available VM.
VMResource	The resource for a highly available VM.
UnsupportedReason	The reason for the unsupported VM status.
HostGroupPath	The full host group path to this VM.
TotalSize	The total size that all the VHDs of the VM are occupying on disk in bytes.
HasPassthroughDisk	Flag to indicate if the VM has pass-through disks attached.
Status	The current status of the VM as an enumeration value.
StatusString	The current status of the VM as a string that is localized.
StartAction	The start action for the VM when the host server starts
StopAction	The stop action for the VM when the host server stops.
RunGuestAccount	The account to use for executing the VM.

TABLE B.2:   The properties of the VM Windows PowerShell object *(CONTINUED)*

NOUN PROPERTY	DESCRIPTION
DelayStart	The delay in seconds to start the virtual machine (can be used to achieve staging of VMs coming online).
CPUUtilization	The average CPU utilization of the VM.
PerfCPUUtilization	Performance numbers internal to VMM and used for placement of VMs on hosts.
PerfDiskBytesRead	Performance numbers internal to VMM and used for placement of VMs on hosts.
PerfDiskBytesWrite	Performance numbers internal to VMM and used for placement of VMs on hosts.
PerfNetworkBytesRead	Performance numbers internal to VMM and used for placement of VMs on hosts.
PerfNetworkBytesWrite	Performance numbers internal to VMM and used for placement of VMs on hosts.
VirtualizationPlatform	The virtualization platform for this VM.
ComputerNameString	The name of the guest operating system computer.
CreationSource	The name of the object that created this VM, such as, for example, the VMM template name.
SourceObjectType	The source that created this VM, such as, for example, Template.
OperatingSystemShutdownEnabled	Flag to indicate if this property of the Integration Services is enabled.
TimeSynchronizationEnabled	Flag to indicate if this property of Integration Services is enabled.
DataExchangeEnabled	Flag to indicate if this property of Integration Services is enabled.
HeartbeatEnabled	Flag to indicate if this property of Integration Services is enabled.
BackupEnabled	Flag to indicate if this property of Integration Services is enabled.
ExcludeFromPRO	Flag to indicate if this VM should not participate in host-level PRO tip implementations.

TABLE B.2:   The properties of the VM Windows PowerShell object *(CONTINUED)*

NOUN PROPERTY	DESCRIPTION
FailedJobID	An ID indicating the VMM job that put the VM in a failed state. This entry is used internally by VMM for the Repair-VM cmdlet.
CheckpointLocation	The location where checkpoints for this VM are stored.
SelfServiceUserRole	The name of the Self-Service User role that this VM is a part of.
PassThroughDisks	A list of pass-through disks for the VM.
LastRestoredVMCheckpoint	The name of the last VMM checkpoint this VM is operating on. If you have just checkpointed your VM, the name of that checkpoint will be listed here.
Location	The folder location that contains the VM's files.
CreationTime	The creation time (or the discovered time) for this VM.
OperatingSystem	The operating system inside the virtual machine.
HasVMAdditions	Flag to indicate if the VM has Virtual Guest Services enabled.
VMAddition	The version number for Virtual Guest Services if the virtualization platform has such a version. Otherwise, this field will be Detected.
NumLockEnabled	Flag to indicate that the Num Lock BIOS option is enabled.
CPUCount	The number of virtual processors assigned to the VM.
IsHighlyAvailable	Flag to indicate that the VM is a highly available VM deployed in a cluster.
LimitCPUFunctionality	Flag to indicate that CPU functionality is limited.
Memory	The amount of RAM assigned to the VM.
BootOrder	The BIOS boot order for the VM.
ComputerName	The computer name of the guest operating system.
UseHardwareAssistedVirtualization	Flag to indicate that the VM should use the hardware extensions for virtualization (used in Virtual Server).
SANStatus	Indicates if this VM is capable of SAN migration.

TABLE B.2:   The properties of the VM Windows PowerShell object *(CONTINUED)*

NOUN PROPERTY	DESCRIPTION
CostCenter	The cost center for this VM.
QuotaPoint	The number of quota points this VM is allocated for.
UserRoleID	The VMM GUID for the user role this VM is a part of.
IsTagEmpty	Flag to indicate whether the VM tag is defined.
Tag	A user-facing string that can be used as a logical grouping mechanism for VMs in the Administrator Console.
CustomProperties	The list of 10 custom properties for the VM.
UndoDisksEnabled	Flag to indicate that undo disks are enabled
CPUType	The CPU type for this VM. This variable is used only for placement decisions.
ExpectedCPUUtilization	The expected CPU utilization for this VM. This entry is used in placement decisions.
DiskIO	The disk IO of this VM.
NetworkUtilization	The network utilization of this VM.
RelativeWeight	The priority of the VM when allocating CPU resources on the host.
CPUReserve	The percentage of CPU reserved for this VM.
CPUMax	The maximum CPU that can be consumed by this VM.
VirtualDVDDrives	The virtual DVD drives attached to the VM.
VirtualHardDisks	The virtual hard disks attached to the VM.
VirtualDiskDrives	The virtual disk drives attached to the VM.
ShareSCSIBus	Flag to indicate if a shared SCSI bus exists.
VirtualNetworkAdapters	The virtual NICs attached to the VM.
VirtualFloppyDrive	The virtual floppy drive attached to the VM.
VirtualCOMPorts	The virtual COM ports attached to the VM.
VirtualSCSIAdapters	The virtual SCSI adapters attached to the VM.

TABLE B.2: The properties of the VM Windows PowerShell object *(CONTINUED)*

NOUN PROPERTY	DESCRIPTION
VMCheckpoints	The VMM checkpoints associated with this VM.
TieredPerfData	The GUID for the tiering data used internally by VMM for placement.
HostId	The VMM GUID for the host of this VM.
HostType	The type of host for this VM (either a host server or a library server).
HostName	The name of the host for this VM.
VMHost	The name of the host for this VM.
LibraryServer	If the VM is stored in the library, the name of the library server is set here.
LibraryGroup	The library group for this VM.
Owner	The VM owner's name.
OwnerSid	The VM owner's security identifier in the domain.
ObjectType	The type of object. In this case it would be VM.
Accessibility	This value is always public.
Name	The name of the VM.
Description	The description of the VM.
AddedTime	The creation time (or the discovered time) for this VM.
ModifiedTime	The last time this VM was modified in VMM.
Enabled	If this VM is enabled. It is set to True.
MostRecentTask	The most recent VMM job that was run against this VM.
ServerConnection	The VMM server connection object.
ID	The GUID for this VM. This is the unique identifier of this VM in VMM.
MarkedForDeletion	Flag to indicate that the VM is marked for deletion. This is always False.
IsFullyCached	Flag to indicate that the VM is fully cached in Windows PowerShell.

TABLE B.3:   The properties of the VMHost Windows PowerShell object

NOUN PROPERTY	DESCRIPTION
OverallStateString	The overall state of the host (localizable string).
OverallState	The overall state of the host.
CommunicationStateString	The communication status for the agent on the host (localizable string).
CommunicationState	The communication status for the agent on the host.
Name	The host name.
FullyQualifiedDomainName	The host's FQDN.
FQDN	The host's FQDN.
ComputerName	The NetBIOS name of the host.
DomainName	The Active Directory domain for this host.
Description	The description for this host object.
RemoteUserName	The name of the account VMM uses to manage a perimeter network host.
CPUPercentageReserve	The CPU percentage set aside for the host as a percentage of the overall resource. This is used for placement decisions for new VMs.
NetworkPercentageReserve	The network capacity percentage set aside for the host as a percentage of the overall resource. This is used for placement decisions for new VMs.
DiskSpaceReserveMB	The disk space in megabytes set aside for this host. This is used for placement decisions for new VMs.
MaxDiskIOReservation	The maximum number of disk I/O operations per second set aside for the host. This is used for placement decisions for new VMs.
MemoryReserveMB	The host memory in megabytes set aside for the host as a reserve. This is used for placement decisions for new VMs.
VMPaths	The path(s) that placement uses to create new VMs.
PROEnabled	Flag to indicate if PRO is enabled.
MaintenanceHost	Flag to indicate if this is a maintenance host.

TABLE B.3:   The properties of the VMHost Windows PowerShell object *(CONTINUED)*

NOUN PROPERTY	DESCRIPTION
AvailableForPlacement	Flag to indicate if this host can accept new VMs during placement.
IsEmbedded	Flag to indicate if this host has SSH capabilities.
CredentialsNeeded	Flag to indicate if the credentials of an administrator account are needed on the host.
LogicalProcessorCount	The logical processor count.
LogicalCPUCount	The logical CPU count for the server.
PhysicalCPUCount	The physical CPU count for the server.
CoresPerCPU	The cores per CPU.
L2CacheSize	The L2 cache size for the server.
L3CacheSize	The L3 cache size for the server.
BusSpeed	The bus speed.
ProcessorSpeed	The processor speed for the server.
CPUSpeed	The processor speed for the server.
ProcessorModel	The processor model for the server.
CPUModel	The processor model for the server.
ProcessorManufacturer	The processor manufacturer.
CPUManufacturer	The processor manufacturer.
ProcessorArchitecture	The processor architecture.
CPUArchitecture	The processor architecture.
ProcessorFamily	The processor family.
CPUFamily	The processor family.
CpuUtilization	The average CPU utilization on the host.
TotalMemory	The total memory allocated to the host in bytes.
AvailableMemory	The available memory in megabytes.
OperatingSystem	The operating system edition running on the host server.

TABLE B.3:   The properties of the VMHost Windows PowerShell object *(CONTINUED)*

NOUN PROPERTY	DESCRIPTION
OperatingSystemVersion	The OS version for the host.
DVDDrives	The DVD drives on the host.
DVDDriveList	The DVD drives on the host.
VirtualizationPlatformString	The virtualization platform running on this host (localizable string).
VirtualizationPlatform	The virtualization platform running on this host. This string can be used for comparison purposes.
VirtualizationPlatformDetail	The virtualization platform running on this host in a detailed string. The virtualization platform could also be unknown.
IsViridianHost	Flag to indicate if this host is running Hyper-V.
SupportsLiveMigration	Flag to indicate if this host supports Live Migration.
FloppyDrives	The list of floppy drives for this host.
FloppyDriveList	The list of floppy drives for this host.
VMHostGroup	The parent HostGroup object for this host.
HostCluster	The host cluster if this host is part of a cluster.
VMRCEnabled	Flag to indicate if remote console connections are enabled.
RemoteConnectEnabled	Flag to indicate if remote console connections are enabled.
VMRCPort	The port used for remote console connections.
RemoteConnectPort	The port used for remote console connections.
VMRCTimeoutEnabled	Flag to indicate if VMRC time-out is enabled for Virtual Server hosts.
RemoteConnectTimeoutEnabled	Flag to indicate if VMRC time-out is enabled for Virtual Server hosts.
VMRCTimeoutMinutes	VMRC time-out in minutes.
RemoteConnectTimeoutMinutes	VMRC time-out in minutes.

TABLE B.3:   The properties of the VMHost Windows PowerShell object *(CONTINUED)*

NOUN PROPERTY	DESCRIPTION
VMRCMultipleConnectionsEnabled	Flag to indicate if multiple VMRC connections are enabled for Virtual Server hosts.
RemoteConnectMultipleConnectionsEnabled	Flag to indicate if multiple VMRC connections are enabled for Virtual Server hosts.
SecureVMRCEnabled	Flag to indicate if SSL is enabled on the VMRC channel.
SecureRemoteConnectEnabled	Flag to indicate if SSL is enabled on the VMRC channel.
VMRCCertificateAvailable	Flag to indicate if a VMRC SSL certificate if available.
RemoteConnectCertificateAvailable	Flag to indicate if a VMRC SSL certificate if available.
SslTcpPort	The SSL TCP port.
SslCertificateHash	The SSL certificate hash.
SshTcpPort	The SSH TCP port.
SshPublicKeyHash	The SSH public key hash.
SshPublicKey	The SSH public key.
ClusterNodeStatus	The state of the cluster node if this host is part of a cluster.
VirtualServerState	The state of the virtualization platform service.
VirtualServerStateString	The state of the virtualization platform service (localizable string).
VirtualServerVersion	The version of the virtualization platform.
VirtualServerVersionState	The state of the virtualization platform and whether it is supported or needs an upgrade.
PerimeterNetworkHost	Flag to indicate if this is a perimeter network host.

TABLE B.3:   The properties of the VMHost Windows PowerShell object *(CONTINUED)*

NOUN PROPERTY	DESCRIPTION
NonTrustedDomainHost	Flag to indicate if this host is a member of a non-trusted Active Directory domain.
MaximumMemoryPerVM	The maximum memory per VM for this virtualization platform.
MinimumMemoryPerVM	The minimum memory per VM for this virtualization platform.
SuggestedMaximumMemoryPerVM	The suggested memory per VM for this virtualization platform.
ModifiedTime	The last time this VM was modified in VMM.
Agent	The FQDN of the VMM agent on this host.
VMs	List of VMs residing on this host. This property is populated only after all the VMs for this host are cached using the Get-VM cmdlet.
Disks	Physical disks attached on this host.
DiskVolumes	List of volumes visible to the host operating system.
VMwareResourcePool	The VMware resource pool for this host.
MostRecentTask	The most recent VMM job that ran against this host.
Custom1 through Custom10	The custom properties 1 through 10 of the host.
FibreChannelSANStatus	The Fibre Channel SAN status for this host and a flag to indicate if this host is FC SAN capable.
ISCSISANStatus	The iSCSI status for this host and a flag to indicate if this host is iSCSI capable.
NPIVFibreChannelSANStatus	The NPIV status for this host and a flag to indicate if this host is NPIV capable.
CertificateRequest	The certificate request for this host.
ComputerState	The computer state of the operating system running on this host.

TABLE B.3:   The properties of the VMHost Windows PowerShell object *(CONTINUED)*

NOUN PROPERTY	DESCRIPTION
VirtualizationManager	The virtualization manager managing this host (VMware specific).
ServerConnection	The VMM server connection object.
ID	The GUID for this host. This is the unique identifier of this host in VMM.
MarkedForDeletion	Flag that indicates that the host is marked for deletion. This is always False.
IsFullyCached	Flag that indicates that the host is fully cached in Windows PowerShell.

TABLE B.4:   Virtual Machine Manager Cmdlet descriptions from the VMM help file

VMM CMDLET NAME	CMDLET DESCRIPTION
Add-LibraryServer	Adds a computer as a library server to Virtual Machine Manager.
Add-LibraryShare	Adds Windows shares on the file system of a library server as library shares to the Virtual Machine Manager library.
Add-Patch	Adds information about patches and binaries to the Virtual Machine Manager patch cache. The patch cache is primarily used by P2V operations.
Add-VirtualizationManager	Adds a VMware VirtualCenter Management Server, also called a VirtualCenter Server, to your Virtual Machine Manager environment so that Virtual Machine Manager can connect to the VirtualCenter Server and import its data. After you add the VirtualCenter Server to Virtual Machine Manager, Virtual Machine Manager can manage VMware ESX hosts associated with the VirtualCenter Server and the virtual machines deployed on those hosts.
Add-VMHost	Adds one or more computers as virtual machine hosts to the Virtual Machine Manager database. A virtual machine host (also called a "host") is a physical computer managed by Virtual Machine Manager whose role is to host one or more virtual machines.

TABLE B.4: Virtual Machine Manager Cmdlet descriptions from the VMM help file (*CONTINUED*)

VMM CMDLET NAME	CMDLET DESCRIPTION
Add-VMHostCluster	Adds an existing Windows Server 2008 failover host cluster to the Virtual Machine Manager database so that Virtual Machine Manager can start managing the host cluster. You need to create the failover host cluster before executing this cmdlet.
Add-VMHostNetworkAdapter	Adds a physical network adapter (also called a network interface card, or NIC) on a host managed by Virtual Machine Manager to a virtual network. Each virtual machine on that host can also connect (through a virtual network adapter) to that virtual network.
Associate-VMHost	Associates a VMware ESX Server with Virtual Machine Manager as a virtual machine host and specifies the credentials to use with this ESX host when it is managed by Virtual Machine Manager.
Backup-VMMServer	Backs up the Virtual Machine Manager database.
Compress-VirtualDiskDrive	Compresses a dynamically expanding virtual hard disk attached to a virtual disk drive object on a stopped virtual machine on a Windows-based host managed by Virtual Machine Manager to reduce the size of the virtual hard disk.
Convert-VirtualDiskDrive	Converts an existing virtual hard disk attached to a virtual disk drive object from dynamic to fixed or from fixed to dynamic; or converts a pass-through disk attached to a virtual disk drive object to a virtual hard disk.
Copy-HardDisk	Copies a volume of a physical hard disk on a source computer to a Windows-based virtual hard disk file (a.vhd file) on the specified Virtual Machine Manager host.
Copy-VMDK	Copies a VMware virtual hard disk file (a .vmdk file) to a Microsoft-compatible virtual hard disk file (a .vhd file) and converts the virtual hard disk for use in a Virtual Machine Manager environment.
DisableUndoDisk-VM	Merges or discards undo disks associated with a virtual machine on a Virtual Server host managed by Virtual Machine Manager. Virtual Machine Manager does not support Undo Disks on Virtual Server.
DiscardSavedState-VM	Discards the saved state of virtual machines managed by Virtual Machine Manager.

TABLE B.4:   Virtual Machine Manager Cmdlet descriptions from the VMM help file (*CONTINUED*)

VMM CMDLET NAME	CMDLET DESCRIPTION
Discover-Cluster	Discovers the specified failover cluster in a Virtual Machine Manager environment.
Discover-Computer	Discovers computer(s) by querying Active Directory, and returns the computer objects.
Discover-LibraryShare	Discovers all of the shares on the specified computer or library server managed by Virtual Machine Manager on which it is possible to add a library share.
Dismiss-PROTip	Dismisses a PRO tip object that is no longer needed in Virtual Machine Manager
Expand-VirtualDiskDrive	Expands a virtual hard disk attached to a virtual disk drive object on a stopped virtual machine deployed on a host managed by Virtual Machine Manager.
Get-Certificate	Gets a security certificate object from a VMware VirtualCenter server or from an ESX Server.
Get-CPUType	Gets objects that represent CPU types for use in virtual machines, or for use in templates or hardware profiles used to create virtual machines, in a Virtual Machine Manager environment. Virtual Machine Manager has a set of predefined CPU types in the database.
Get-DependentLibraryObject	Identifies dependencies between Virtual Machine Manager objects in the Library.
Get-DirectoryChildItem	Gets all files and subdirectories in the specified directory on a virtual machine host or on a library server managed by Virtual Machine Manager.
Get-GuestOSProfile	Gets guest operating system profile objects from the Virtual Machine Manager library.
Get-HardwareProfile	Gets hardware profile objects from the Virtual Machine Manager library.
Get-ISO	Gets ISO objects from the Virtual Machine Manager library.
Get-Job	Gets Virtual Machine Manager job objects on the Virtual Machine Manager server.

TABLE B.4: Virtual Machine Manager Cmdlet descriptions from the VMM help file (*CONTINUED*)

VMM CMDLET NAME	CMDLET DESCRIPTION
Get-LibraryRating	Calculates the placement rating of virtual machine libraries managed by Virtual Machine Manager to determine whether a SAN transfer can be used to transfer a virtual machine from a host to the library.
Get-LibraryServer	Gets Virtual Machine Manager library server objects from the Virtual Machine Manager database.
Get-LibraryShare	Gets Virtual Machine Manager library share objects from the Virtual Machine Manager library.
Get-MachineConfig	Gets physical machine configuration objects from the Virtual Machine Manager database.
Get-NetworkLocation	Gets the list of network locations that the specified Virtual Machine Manager server can access.
Get-OperatingSystem	Gets valid operating system objects from the Virtual Machine Manager database.
Get-PROTip	Gets Performance and Resource Optimization tip (PRO tip) objects from the Virtual Machine Manager database.
Get-Script	Gets script objects from the Virtual Machine Manager library. With appropriate permissions, you can also use Get-Script to view or edit any script, or to view, edit, or run a Windows PowerShell script.
Get-SshPublicKey	Gets the public key object from a VMware ESX Server that you want Virtual Machine Manager to manage.
Get-Step	Gets the steps for the specified job on a Virtual Machine Manager server.
Get-Template	Gets virtual machine template objects from the Virtual Machine Manager library.
Get-VirtualCOMPort	Gets Virtual Machine Manager virtual communication (COM) port objects from a virtual machine, template, or hardware profile.
Get-VirtualDiskDrive	Gets virtual disk drive objects on templates or on virtual machines managed by Virtual Machine Manager.

TABLE B.4: Virtual Machine Manager Cmdlet descriptions from the VMM help file
(*CONTINUED*)

VMM CMDLET NAME	CMDLET DESCRIPTION
Get-VirtualDVDDrive	Gets Virtual Machine Manager virtual DVD drive objects from a virtual machine, template, or hardware profile.
Get-VirtualFloppyDisk	Gets virtual floppy disk objects from the Virtual Machine Manager library.
Get-VirtualFloppyDrive	Gets Virtual Machine Manager virtual floppy drive objects from a virtual machine, template, or hardware profile.
Get-VirtualHardDisk	Gets virtual hard disk objects from a virtual machine, from a template, or as a standalone file stored in the Virtual Machine Manager library.
Get-VirtualizationManager	Gets objects that represent VMware VirtualCenter Servers managed by Virtual Machine Manager from the Virtual Machine Manager database.
Get-VirtualNetwork	Gets virtual network objects configured on a host managed by Virtual Machine Manager.
Get-VirtualNetworkAdapter	Gets Virtual Machine Manager virtual network adapter objects from a virtual machine, template, or hardware profile.
Get-VirtualSCSIAdapter	Gets Virtual Machine Manager virtual SCSI adapter objects from a virtual machine, template, or hardware profile.
Get-VM	Gets virtual machine objects from the Virtual Machine Manager database.
Get-VMCheckpoint	Gets virtual machine checkpoint objects from the Virtual Machine Manager database.
Get-VMHost	Gets virtual machine host objects from the Virtual Machine Manager database.
Get-VMHostCluster	Gets a host cluster object, or an array of host cluster objects, from the Virtual Machine Manager database.
Get-VMHostDisk	Gets a hard disk drive object for the specified host from the Virtual Machine Manager database.
Get-VMHostGroup	Gets a host group object from the Virtual Machine Manager database.

TABLE B.4: Virtual Machine Manager Cmdlet descriptions from the VMM help file (*CONTINUED*)

VMM CMDLET NAME	CMDLET DESCRIPTION
Get-VMHostNetworkAdapter	Gets physical network adapter objects on a host managed by Virtual Machine Manager.
Get-VMHostRating	Calculates the placement rating for one or more virtual machine hosts managed by Virtual Machine Manager on which you might want to deploy a specific virtual machine.
Get-VMHostVolume	Gets drive volume objects from a host managed by Virtual Machine Manager.
Get-VMMManagedComputer	Gets one or more objects that represent physical computers managed by Virtual Machine Manager. A Managed Computer is a system that has the Virtual Machine Manager Agent installed.
Get-VMMServer	Connects to a Virtual Machine Manager server (if a connection does not already exist) and retrieves the object that represents this server from the Virtual Machine Manager database.
Get-VMMUserRole	Gets an object that represents a Virtual Machine Manager user role.
Get-VMPerformance	Gets performance data for a specific virtual machine deployed on a host managed by Virtual Machine Manager. The performance data represent a point in time snapshot of the 60 seconds of CPU utilization history for the VM and the running time of the VM.
Get-VMwareResourcePool	Gets VMware resource pool objects from the Virtual Machine Manager database.
Get-VMXMachineConfig	Gets VMX machine configuration objects (from the Virtual Machine Manager database) that are associated with one or more VMware-based virtual machines.
Invoke-PROTip	Performs the action recommended by a PRO tip. You can use this cmdlet to manually invoke the action recommended by a PRO tip that is not set to be implemented automatically.
Merge-VMCheckpoint	Removes a virtual machine checkpoint object from the Virtual Machine Manager database.

TABLE B.4: Virtual Machine Manager Cmdlet descriptions from the VMM help file (*CONTINUED*)

VMM CMDLET NAME	CMDLET DESCRIPTION
Move-VirtualHardDisk	Moves a Windows-based virtual hard disk file (a .vhd file) from one location to another on the same host.
Move-VM	Moves a virtual machine currently stored in the Virtual Machine Manager library or deployed on a host server to a new location on a host server.
Move-VMHost	Moves a virtual machine host object managed by Virtual Machine Manager from one host group to another.
Move-VMHostCluster	Moves a Windows Server 2008 host cluster object managed by Virtual Machine Manager from one host group to another.
Move-VMHostGroup	Moves a host group object managed by Virtual Machine Manager from the current location to a new location under a different host group parent.
New-GuestOSProfile	Creates a guest operating system profile for use in Virtual Machine Manager.
New-HardwareProfile	Creates a hardware profile for use in Virtual Machine Manager.
New-MachineConfig	Creates a machine configuration object by gathering machine configuration information from a physical source machine that you plan to convert to a virtual machine managed by Virtual Machine Manager.
New-P2V	Converts a physical machine to a virtual machine on a Windows-based host (Hyper-V or Virtual Server) managed by Virtual Machine Manager.
New-PhysicalAddress	Returns the next available physical address (MAC address) if a range of MAC addresses has been configured for your Virtual Machine Manager environment.
New-Template	Creates a virtual machine template used to create virtual machines managed by Virtual Machine Manager.
New-V2V	Converts a virtual machine created on a VMware ESX Server host to a virtual machine deployed on a Windows-based host (Hyper-V or Virtual Server) managed by Virtual Machine Manager.

TABLE B.4: Virtual Machine Manager Cmdlet descriptions from the VMM help file (*CONTINUED*)

VMM CMDLET NAME	CMDLET DESCRIPTION
New-VirtualDiskDrive	Creates a virtual disk drive object on a virtual machine deployed on a host managed by Virtual Machine Manager, or on a template in the Virtual Machine Manager library.
New-VirtualDVDDrive	Creates a virtual DVD drive on a virtual machine, template, or hardware profile used in Virtual Machine Manager.
New-VirtualNetwork	Creates a virtual network object on a host managed by Virtual Machine Manager that enables virtual machines on that host to communicate over that virtual network.
New-VirtualNetworkAdapter	Creates a virtual network adapter on a virtual machine, template, or hardware profile used in Virtual Machine Manager.
New-VirtualSCSIAdapter	Creates a virtual SCSI adapter on a virtual machine, template, or hardware profile used in Virtual Machine Manager.
New-VM	Creates a virtual machine to be managed by Virtual Machine Manager.
New-VMCheckpoint	Creates a virtual machine checkpoint object for a virtual machine deployed on a host managed by Virtual Machine Manager.
New-VMHostGroup	Creates a Virtual Machine Manager host group object that can contain virtual machine host servers, other host groups, or host clusters.
New-VMMUserRole	Creates a Self Service User role or a Delegated Administrator user role for a group of Virtual Machine Manager users.
New-VMRCCertificateRequest	Generates a request for a signed certificate that Virtual Machine Manager can use to secure Virtual Machine Remote Control (VMRC) communications by encrypting information exchanged between a user and a virtual machine on a Virtual Server host.
New-VMXMachineConfig	Creates a VMX machine configuration object by gathering virtual machine configuration information from a virtual machine created in VMware that you plan to convert to a virtual machine deployed on a Windows-based host managed by Virtual Machine Manager.

TABLE B.4: Virtual Machine Manager Cmdlet descriptions from the VMM help file (*CONTINUED*)

VMM CMDLET NAME	CMDLET DESCRIPTION
Reassociate-VMMManagedComputer	Re-associates a managed computer on which Virtual Machine Manager agent software is installed (that is, a Windows-based host or library server) with a different Virtual Machine Manager server. You can also re-associate the managed computer with the current Virtual Machine Manager server if someone has removed the permissions needed by the VMM Agent to function properly
Refresh-LibraryShare	Refreshes the state and metadata of Virtual Machine Manager library objects stored in a library share.
Refresh-VirtualizationManager	Refreshes the properties of a VMware VirtualCenter Server so that the Virtual Machine Manager Administrator Console displays updated information about entities in VirtualCenter Server.
Refresh-VM	Refreshes the properties of a virtual machine so that the Virtual Machine Manager Administrator Console displays updated information about the virtual machine.
Refresh-VMHost	Refreshes virtual machine host properties in the Virtual Machine Manager Administrator Console.
Refresh-VMHostCluster	Refreshes host cluster properties in the Virtual Machine Manager Administrator Console.
Register-VM	Registers an existing virtual machine with Virtual Machine Manager that, currently, is not registered with the virtualization platform (Virtual Server, Hyper-V, or VMware) of any host managed by Virtual Machine Manager and is not stored in the Virtual Machine Manager library.
Remove-GuestOSProfile	Removes a guest operating system profile object from Virtual Machine Manager.
Remove-HardwareProfile	Removes a hardware profile object from Virtual Machine Manager.
Remove-ISO	Removes an ISO object from the library in Virtual Machine Manager.
Remove-LibraryServer	Removes a library server object from Virtual Machine Manager.

TABLE B.4:   Virtual Machine Manager Cmdlet descriptions from the VMM help file (*CONTINUED*)

VMM CMDLET NAME	CMDLET DESCRIPTION
Remove-LibraryShare	Removes a library share object from Virtual Machine Manager but does not delete the share from the Windows file system.
Remove-MachineConfig	Removes a machine configuration object from Virtual Machine Manager.
Remove-Script	Removes a script object from Virtual Machine Manager.
Remove-Template	Removes a template object from Virtual Machine Manager and deletes all files associated with this template.
Remove-VirtualDiskDrive	Removes a virtual disk drive object from a virtual machine or from a template in a Virtual Machine Manager environment.
Remove-VirtualDVDDrive	Removes a virtual DVD drive object from Virtual Machine Manager.
Remove-VirtualFloppyDisk	Removes a virtual floppy disk object from Virtual Machine Manager.
Remove-VirtualHardDisk	Removes a virtual hard disk object from a virtual machine or template or from the Virtual Machine Manager library.
Remove-VirtualizationManager	Removes a VMware VirtualCenter Server from Virtual Machine Manager.
Remove-VirtualNetwork	Removes a virtual network object from a host managed by Virtual Machine Manager.
Remove-VirtualNetworkAdapter	Removes a virtual network adapter object from Virtual Machine Manager.
Remove-VirtualSCSIAdapter	Removes a virtual SCSI adapter object from Virtual Machine Manager.
Remove-VM	Removes a virtual machine object from Virtual Machine Manager.
Remove-VMCheckpoint	Removes a virtual machine checkpoint object from the Virtual Machine Manager database.
Remove-VMHost	Removes a virtual machine host object from Virtual Machine Manager.

TABLE B.4: Virtual Machine Manager Cmdlet descriptions from the VMM help file (*CONTINUED*)

VMM CMDLET NAME	CMDLET DESCRIPTION
Remove-VMHostCluster	Removes a host cluster object from Virtual Machine Manager.
Remove-VMHostGroup	Removes a host group object from Virtual Machine Manager.
Remove-VMHostNetworkAdapter	Removes a physical host network adapter object from a virtual network that is configured on a host managed by Virtual Machine Manager.
Remove-VMMUserRole	Removes an existing Self Service User or Delegated Administrator user role from Virtual Machine Manager.
Remove-VMXMachineConfig	Removes a VMX machine configuration object from Virtual Machine Manager.
Repair-VM	Repairs a virtual machine on a host managed by Virtual Machine Manager if the virtual machine is in a failed state.
Restart-Job	Restarts a failed or canceled Virtual Machine Manager job.
Restore-VMCheckpoint	Restores a virtual machine on a host managed by Virtual Machine Manager to the specified checkpoint.
Resume-VM	Resumes paused virtual machines managed by Virtual Machine Manager.
SaveState-VM	Saves the state of virtual machines managed by Virtual Machine Manager.
Set-GuestOSProfile	Changes the properties of a guest operating system profile used in Virtual Machine Manager.
Set-HardwareProfile	Changes the properties of a hardware profile used in Virtual Machine Manager.
Set-ISO	Changes properties of an ISO object used in Virtual Machine Manager.
Set-LibraryServer	Changes specific properties of a Virtual Machine Manager library server object.
Set-LibraryShare	Changes the Description property of a Virtual Machine Manager library share object
Set-PROTip	Sets the status of a PRO tip object.

TABLE B.4: Virtual Machine Manager Cmdlet descriptions from the VMM help file (*CONTINUED*)

VMM CMDLET NAME	CMDLET DESCRIPTION
Set-Script	Changes properties of a script stored in the Virtual Machine Manager library
Set-Template	Changes properties of a template used in Virtual Machine Manager.
Set-VirtualCOMPort	Changes properties of a virtual COM port associated with a virtual machine, template, or hardware profile used in Virtual Machine Manager.
Set-VirtualDiskDrive	Modifies settings on a virtual disk drive object on a virtual machine or on a template in a Virtual Machine Manager environment.
Set-VirtualDVDDrive	Changes properties of a virtual DVD drive associated with a virtual machine, template, or hardware profile used in Virtual Machine Manager.
Set-VirtualFloppyDisk	Changes properties of a virtual floppy disk used in Virtual Machine Manager.
Set-VirtualFloppyDrive	Changes properties of a virtual floppy drive associated with a virtual machine, template, or hardware profile used in Virtual Machine Manager.
Set-VirtualHardDisk	Changes properties of a virtual hard disk object used in Virtual Machine Manager.
Set-VirtualizationManager	Changes properties of a VMware VirtualCenter Server that is managed by Virtual Machine Manager.
Set-VirtualNetwork	Changes properties of a virtual network on a virtual machine host managed by Virtual Machine Manager.
Set-VirtualNetworkAdapter	Changes properties of a virtual network adapter associated with a virtual machine, or with a template or hardware profile used to create virtual machines in Virtual Machine Manager.
Set-VirtualSCSIAdapter	Changes properties of a virtual SCSI adapter used in Virtual Machine Manager.
Set-VM	Changes properties of a virtual machine managed by Virtual Machine Manager.
Set-VMCheckpoint	Changes the Description property of a virtual machine checkpoint object in Virtual Machine Manager.

TABLE B.4: Virtual Machine Manager Cmdlet descriptions from the VMM help file (*CONTINUED*)

VMM CMDLET NAME	CMDLET DESCRIPTION
Set-VMHost	Changes properties of a virtual machine host managed by Virtual Machine Manager.
Set-VMHostCluster	Modifies the properties of a virtual machine host cluster managed by Virtual Machine Manager.
Set-VMHostGroup	Changes properties of a host group in Virtual Machine Manager.
Set-VMHostNetworkAdapter	Changes network-related properties of the specified physical network adapter on a host managed by Virtual Machine Manager.
Set-VMHostVolume	Modifies the setting for a volume on a host server that enables Virtual Machine Manager to evaluate that volume as available storage during the virtual machine placement process.
Set-VMMServer	Changes properties of the Virtual Machine Manager server.
Set-VMMUserRole	Modifies the settings for an existing Virtual Machine Manager user role.
Shutdown-VM	Shuts down a running virtual machine managed by Virtual Machine Manager.
Start-VM	Starts virtual machines managed by Virtual Machine Manager.
Stop-Job	Stops running jobs in Virtual Machine Manager.
Stop-VM	Stops virtual machines on hosts managed by Virtual Machine Manager.
Store-VM	Stores a virtual machine currently deployed on a virtual machine host by migrating it from the host to the Virtual Machine Manager library.
Suspend-VM	Suspends, or pauses, execution on virtual machines managed by Virtual Machine Manager.
Update-VMHost	Updates Virtual Server 2005 R2 software installed on a virtual machine host to the latest version of Virtual Server supported by Virtual Machine Manager.
Update-VMMManagedComputer	Updates Virtual Machine Manager agent software installed on a Windows-based managed computer.

Index

Note to the Reader: Throughout this index **boldfaced** page numbers indicate primary discussions of a topic. *Italicized* page numbers indicate illustrations.